The Methuen
Anthology of Modern

Also available from Bloomsbury Methuen Drama:
Modern Asian Theatre and Performance 1900–2000
Siyuan Liu, Kevin J. Wetmore, Jr. and Erin B. Mee

Play anthologies from Bloomsbury Methuen Drama:
The Methuen Drama Anthology of Irish Plays
The Methuen Drama Book of Naturalist Plays
The Methuen Drama Book of New American Plays
The Methuen Drama Book of Plays by Black British Writers
The Methuen Drama Book of Plays from the Sixties
The Methuen Drama Book of Post-Black Plays
The Methuen Drama Book of Royal Court Plays 2000–2010
The Methuen Drama Book of Twenty-First Century British Plays
Modern Drama: Plays of the '80s and '90s
National Theatre Connections 2011: Plays for Young People
National Theatre Connections 2012: Plays for Young People
National Theatre Connections 2013: Plays for Young People
Not Black and White
Producers' Choice: Six Plays for Young Performers
Six Ensemble Plays for Young Actors
Theatre in Pieces: Politics, Poetics and Interdisciplinary
Collaboration

The Methuen Drama Anthology of Modern Asian Plays

Father Returns

Hot Pepper, Air Conditioner
and the Farewell Speech

Sunrise

I Love XXX

Bicycle

The Post Office

Hayavadana

The Struggle of the Naga Tribe

Trương Ba's Soul in the Butcher's Skin

Edited by

SIYUAN LIU AND KEVIN J. WETMORE, JR.

B L O O M S B U R Y

LONDON · NEW DELHI · NEW YORK · SYDNEY

Bloomsbury Methuen Drama

An imprint of Bloomsbury Publishing Plc

50 Bedford Square
London
WC1B 3DP
UK

1385 Broadway
New York
NY 10018
USA

www.bloomsbury.com

Bloomsbury is a registered trade mark of Bloomsbury Publishing Plc

First published 2013

Introduction © Methuen Drama 2014

British Library Cataloguing-in-Publication Data
A catalogue record for this book is available from the British Library.

ISBN: HB: 978-1-4081-7648-1
PB: 978-1-4081-7647-4
ePDF: 978-1-4081-7650-4
ePub: 978-1-4081-7649-8

Library of Congress Cataloging-in-Publication Data
A catalog record for the book is available from the Library of Congress.

Typeset by Deanta Global Publishing Services, Chennai, India
Printed and bound in Great Britain

Contents

Permissions

Acknowledgements

Gratitude is due to Mark Dudgeon, Emily Hockley and the editorial and production staff at Bloomsbury Methuen Drama.

We also wish to thank Erin B. Mee, Girish Karnad, Khai Thu Nguyen, David Mason, Aya Ogawa, M. Cody Poulton, John Swain, Yoshiko Fukushima and Cobina Gillett for their advice, input and introductions. This book would also not have been possible without the aid of Okada Toshiki, Wan Fang, Huan Linnan, Li Ruru, Meng Jinghui, Claire Conceison, Amy Dooling, Beijing Foreign Language Press, Ah-jeong Kim, R. B. Graves, Max Lane, Sagaree Sengupta, Patricia Nguyen, Kim Nguyen Tran, Tam Van Tran, Nhung Walsh, Nausheen Abidi Raza, Ananya Deb, Blanca Pauliukevicius and Charisse D. Smith.

Thanks to Brianna Berlen, who transcribed several of the plays.

Thanks to the William H. Hannon Library and its staff of wonderful librarians.

For areas of Asian drama with which the editors are less familiar, we have relied upon the scholarship of others. We would like to thank the members of the Association for Asian Performance. We are truly standing on the shoulders of giants.

This project would have been impossible without the generous support of the Henry Luce Foundation, which gave a grant to support the work of the translators and the playwrights. Thanks are due to Michael Gilligan, Helena Kolenda and Li Ling of the Henry Luce Foundation for their backing of this project. Gratitude is also due to LMU President David W. Burcham, whose sponsorship, along with the tireless work of Cathy Grove, was instrumental in obtaining such support. The editors are truly grateful.

Dedicated to our wives for their support and inspiration: Lacy Wetmore and Guoping Ma.

Introduction

Asia has a long and rich theatrical tradition that utilises combinations of speech, singing, dance, acrobatics, puppets and masks to tell fascinating stories. Its modern Western-style theatre, which relies predominantly on speech, started in the late nineteenth and early twentieth centuries as either part of the colonial experience or an important factor in the modernisation movement in countries that were not colonised, such as Japan and China. As a companion to *Modern Asian Theatre and Performance 1900–2000*, this anthology includes nine spoken theatre plays written between 1912 and 2009 in Japan, China, Korea, India, Indonesia and Vietnam.

Several themes link these plays together; one of them being Asia's tumultuous history in the past century, from colonialism of South and Southeast Asia, to Japan's occupation of Korea and, for eight years, China, to civil wars in many countries, to postcolonial turmoil on political, ideological and economic fronts, to globalisation in recent decades. The earliest play in the anthology is *The Post Office* (1912), an allegorical gem about a bedridden boy's desire for spiritual freedom. Its author is the Nobel Laureate Rabindranath Tagore of Bengal, the site of the first British colony in the subcontinent and its earliest modern theatre. In contrast to the boy's physical weakness, W. S. Rendra's *The Struggle of the Naga Tribe* (1975) depicts the fighting spirit of indigenous people in postcolonial Indonesia against a corrupt government under the influence of multinational companies and international powers. National political and ideological history is also part of the background these plays address. O Tae-sŏk's *Bicycle* (1983), for example, deals with the brutal burning of 127 suspected anti-communists in a South Korean village by retreating soldiers of North Korean People's Liberation Army in 1950. Meng Jinghui's *I Love XXX* (1996), staged in a politically sensitive environment several years after the Tiananmen Incident of 1989, makes numerous allusions to the Chinese ideological and political experience in the 1970s and 1980s, while Lưu Quang Vũ's *Trương Ba's Soul in the Butcher's Skin* (1988) ostensibly uses a folk story to question the choice between body and soul as a result of market-oriented reform policies of the Vietnamese government.

Another way to read the plays is to follow a chronological order, which shows a rough pattern of modern Asian theatre's complicated relations with Western theatre on the one hand and indigenous performance on the other. The first phase was one of hybrid forms when Western and indigenous theatrical and cultural elements were mixed even as the plays were predominantly speech-based, as is the case of *The Post Office*. Gradually, hybridity was replaced by realistic plays based on Ibsen's social critical realism and Stanislavski's realistic production principles, a period that was roughly between late 1910s and late 1950s–1970s (depending on the country) and represented in the anthology by *The Father Returns* (1917, Japan) by Kikuchi Kan and *Sunrise* (1936, China) by Cao Yu, prime examples of realistic drama. By the 1960s, the rise of nationalism and postwar European theatre, especially theatre of the absurd, led to a re-examination of strict realism. In one way or another, the plays from the 1970s and 1980s in this anthology – Girish Karnad's *Hayavadana* (1971, India), Rendra's *The Struggle of the Naga Tribe*, O's *Bicycle* and Luu's *Truong Ba's Soul in the Butcher's Skin* – all incorporate indigenous cultural and/or theatrical elements as part of the presentation, either in Rendra's use of the dramatic structure of the shadow puppet *wayang kulit* and Karnad and Luu's appropriation of folk stories, or in O's reliance on a ghost to bridge the present and past. In the past two decades, this rediscovery of indigenous identity by Asian spoken theatre merged with contemporary theatrical globalisation that are often intercultural, postdramatic and kinetic. Two good examples are Meng's *I Love XXX*, often called an 'anti-play' because of its lack of plot and characters and a structure that starts every line with 'I love . . .', and Okada Toshiki's *Hot Pepper, Air Conditioner and the Farewell Speech* (2009), which depicts the insecurity of office workers in the latest financial crisis through colloquial, fragmented and hyper-realistic language. Extensive choreography and movement accompanied both productions, which in a way marks the full circle modern Asian theatre has travelled in its relations with native theatre.

No single volume can hope to encompass the giant panoply that is modern Asian drama, encompassing as it does dozens of nations for over a century, developed and performed by thousands of dramatists, actors and other theatre artists. We hope, however, that these exemplary texts give an idea of that panoply and open the doors to further reading, research and experience, not just of modern Asian drama, but also of the cultures and contexts that produce and are reflected by these plays.

Father Returns

Kikuchi Kan
Translated by John D. Swain

Kikuchi Kan (1888–1948), novelist, essayist, journal and magazine editor, and playwright, was part of a vanguard of writers in the early twentieth century who sought to use literary drama to modernise society. He attended college in Tokyo, studying modern English and Irish drama, reading and being inspired by Sir Arthur Pinero, Sir J. M. Barrie, John Galsworthy, Oscar Wilde, W. B. Yeats, Lady Gregory, J. M. Synge and especially George Bernard Shaw.[1] He wrote a number of plays in the second decade of the twentieth century that received little notice when they were first published, but are now considered major early works of shingeki (new drama). *Umi no yūnsha* (Heroes of the Sea, 1916) was inspired by Synge's *Riders to the Sea*, and *Okujō no kyōjin* (Madman on the Roof, 1916) and *Tōjūrō no koi* (Tōjūrō's Love, 1919) followed, the latter concerning a kabuki actor and thus was also performed in kabuki theatres.[2]

Chichi Kaeru (Father Returns, 1917) was adapted from the 1905 British drama *The Return of the Prodigal* by St John Emile Clavering Hankin. Like Shaw, Hankin was a proponent of Edwardian 'New Drama' and inspired Kikuchi to use his play to advocate liberal values in Japan. The play initially did not make much of an impression when published, but Ichikawa Ennosuke I's staging of the play in Tokyo in 1920 was a huge hit. Ichikawa (1855–1922) was an innovative kabuki actor who also became involved in the staging of modern drama. *Father Returns* is regarded as a model one-act play because of its dramatic structure and realistic dialogue and as a model modern drama because of its depiction of a clearly identifiable conflict between traditional values and modern humanism.

Until the Meiji Restoration in 1868, Tokugawa Japan (named after the ruling Shogunate family) had stood for almost two and a half centuries with Confucian and samurai values enshrined in both the law and the culture. One of the primary concepts of Confucian Japan was *chū-kō* (loyalty and filial piety). Social order was maintained on the micro and macro level based on this principle. The cardinal relationships are rooted in this principle: ruler/subject, father/son and older brother/younger brother. The superior person is to be benevolent to and set an example for the inferior. The inferior position in these relationships was to be respectful and obedient to the superior. In the wake of the Meiji Restoration, a number of cultural movements occurred aimed at modernising Japanese culture and transforming Confucian virtues into Western-based liberal humanist virtues. Kikuchi's play is a primary example of this urge.

The play begins with a domestic scene, in which children and their mother naturalistically discuss their days and their plans, and are then interrupted by the return of the father who abandoned the family years before. The abandonment caused the family to suffer privations and pain and they have worked long and hard to succeed in the absence of a father in the household. Under Confucian precepts, the father's return is also a return to his status as the superior member of the household. His children and wife owe him respect, deference and obedience regardless of his behaviour towards them. Kikuchi instead shows a modern-educated elder son rejecting his father and rejecting the Confucian value system. The father, by leaving and abandoning the family, has abandoned his patriarchal authority and any right to obedience or even a place in the family, according to his son.

But Kikuchi has not written a simple didactic play in that sense. His characters are more complex and readers can find multiple themes and psychological complexity in the elder son. His cry at the end of the play is not of a young man, rejecting the older generation's values but of a child abandoned by his daddy. One might also read a Japanese longing for an imaginary cohesion with the past, impossible in the early Taishō era (1912–26). One can also do a class-based reading, seeing in the conversations that begin the play, the dreams and plans of an upwardly mobile family seeking money and respectability in a new capitalist system. Alternately, one can also read the play in the context of theatre history: a reaction against kabuki and its depictions of bushido.

Kikuchi argues that the gift of European literature to Japan is realism and 'the ideal of the brotherhood of man – humanistic idealism', and for Kikuchi, the two are linked.[3] Realism and naturalism, still young in the West as well in 1917 when this play was written, serve to provide a model for both a modern Japanese drama and a modern Japan. Kikuchi remained active in the shingeki world, remaining critical of Osanai Kaoru's announcement in 1924 that no Japanese-written drama would be performed at the Tsukiji Shōgeki-jō (Tsukiji Little Theatre) in Tokyo, writing essays on drama for journals and magazines, and advocating for modern theatre.

Father Returns

[*Chichi Kaeru,* 1917]

Characters:

Kuroda Ken'ichirō – Twenty-eight years old
His brother, Shinjirō – Twenty-three years old
His sister, Otane – Twenty years old
Their mother, Otaka – Fifty-one years old
Their father, Sōtarō – Fifty-seven years old

Time: 1907

Place: A town on the shores of the Inland Sea.[4]

Setting: (*A six-tatami[5] room in a modest middle-class home. Upstage center is a wardrobe, on top of which is an alarm clock. In front of it is an oblong charcoal brazier. Steam rises from the kettle there. There is a low general-purpose table.* **Ken'ichirō**, *home from work at the Town Hall, has just changed into his informal kimono and is leisurely looking over the newspaper. His mother,* **Otaka**, *is sewing. At about 7:00 on an early October evening, it is dark outside.*)

Ken'ichirō   Mama, where's Otane gone?

Mother   To deliver some sewin'.

Ken'ichirō   Why's she still making clothes? She shouldn't be working for other people any more. There's just no need.

Mother   I know your right, but come time for her ta wed, she'll be better off for every extra kimono she's got.

Ken   (*Turning the pages of the newspaper.*) What happened to that talk about a match a while back?

Mother   That sister of yours, Otane, somehow or other she just didn't take to him. It's no use, even though his family asked over and over for her hand just as nicely as you please.

Ken   And rumor had it he's a man of property. He would've been a good match.

Mother   Maybe, but once a fortune of ten or twenty thousand's gone, ain't no good at all. When your Ma come here ta marry your Pa, he had twenty or thirty thousand in bonds and real estate, but squandered it on high livin'. It were no more'n dust in the wind.

Ken   (*Reminded of some disquieting memories, he remains silent.*) . . . .

Mother   'Cause a my own bitter experiences, I think Otane should take good character over good fortune. Even without property, she can face adversity her whole life long if she has a devoted husband.

Ken   Wouldn't a good man with a fortune be best?

Mother   If wishes were horses. . . . No matter how beautiful Otane is, this family don't have any money. The way things are these days, even a modest wedding ceremony'll soak up three hundred, or even five hundred yen in th' wink of an eye.

Ken   Even Otane suffered a lot as a child because of Dad. We all have to do as much as we can to help out with her hope chest. When we've a thousand yen saved in the bank, we can use half for her wedding.

Mother   That'd be fine an' dandy, but really, three hundred yen's good enough. An' after Otane's weddin', gettin' you married off'd set my heart at ease. Everyone says my husband were a curse, but my children are blessin's. When your Pa left, I just didn't know what I were goin' ta do. . . .

Ken   (*In an attempt to change the subject.*) Shin's pretty late.

Mother   He's evening monitor. Shin said he's gettin' a raise again this month.

Ken   Did he now? He did so well in middle school, teaching primary school's not likely to satisfy him. He's bound to go far if he pushes himself to study more.

Mother   We've got ta start lookin' for a bride for you. I hope there's somebody suitable. The Sonodas' daughter, maybe, but they're a bit more respectable than us, so I doubt they'd have you.

Ken   We've still two or three years, don't we?

Mother   But once I've set Otane on her way, I've got to find you a bride for sure. That way everythin'll be all set. When your Pa ran off, I was left holdin' three babes and wonderin' what were ta become a' me.

Ken   There's no use in bringing up the past.

(*The sliding front door opens.* **Shinjirō** *has come home. He is a primary school teacher and has remarkable boyish good looks.*)

Shinjirō   I'm home!

Mother   Welcome back.

Ken   You're getting back awfully late.

Shin   I had a lot of lesson plans to do, so I was the last one out the door. My shoulders are so stiff.

Mother   Thought we might go ahead and eat, but decided we'd wait.

Ken   We'll eat, then you can go take a bath.[6]

Shin   (*Changing out of his Western-style clothing into informal kimono*) Mama, where's Otane?

Mother   Deliverin' some sewin'.

Shin   (*Relaxing in his Japanese clothes.*) Hey, Ken! I heard a strange rumor today. Mr Sugita, the Principal, said he saw someone who looks a lot like our father over in the neighborhood of Furushin-machi.

Mother & Ken   Wha-a-a-t?

Shin   Mr Sugita was passing along that area there in Furushin-machi where all the inns are lined up, and there was a man of nearly sixty walking in front of him. He took a good look, and it struck him that he'd seen this man before. He got closer, got a look at the man's profile, and says it looked like Father sure enough. He said it seemed awfully like Sōtarō. Said if it was Sōtarō, he'd expect him to have a mole on his right cheek. Mr Sugita was going to call out to the man if there was a mole, but just as he got close enough, he said the man slipped down the alley next to the Suijin Shrine.

Mother   Mr Sugita were one a Pa's best boyhood friends. They did lance trainin' together back then, so it's not likely he'd be mistaken. That said, it's been twenty years, don't ya know.

Shin   That's exactly what Mr Sugita said. They haven't met in twenty years, at the very least, so he can't be absolutely sure. He said the man didn't look a thing like the Sōtarō he used to play with, so Mr Sugita couldn't swear that his eyes weren't betraying him.

Ken   (*Giving **Shinjirō** an anxious glance.*) So, Mr Sugita didn't speak with the man, right?

Shin   He was all set to call out his name if the man had had a mole.

Mother   Well, no doubt Mr Sugita were mistaken. Then again, if your Pa's come back ta town, I'd imagine he'd return to the house 'a his birth.

Ken   Sure, but Father won't dare step an inch over this threshold.

Mother   I just guessed he were dead. It's goin' on twenty years since he upped and run off.

Shin   I heard that some people ran into him in Okayama once.

Mother   Yeah, but that were more'n ten years ago. It were Chōta from over to the Kubō's. That time he went to Okayama.[7] He said Pa was workin' for some sort'a circus or other, with lions and tigers. He took Chōta to a restaurant, treated him to a meal, an' asked him 'bout how things were doin' here at home. Chōta said Pa'd a gold watch tucked in his waistcoat pocket, and was all decked out in silk, actin' hoity-toity. Haven't had a single letter from him since. That were the year after the war,[8] so it must have been twelve or thirteen years ago now.

Shin   Father must have been quite a beau.

Mother   When he were young, he didn't care none for the ol' Confucian Learnin',[9] an' were always tryin' some scheme or other to hit it rich. 'Cause of that, he started takin' loans, on top of which were his debauchery. Then he took a big loss tryin' to export patent medicine to China.

Ken   (*With an uncomfortable expression.*) Lets eat, Mama.

Mother   Yes, yes, lets. I clean forgot. (*She gets up and goes to the kitchen. She continues speaking unseen.*) Mr Sugita said he saw him, but that must a been a mistake. That man were Pa's age – if Pa were alive – but we ain't even had as much as a single postcard.

Ken   (*Fairly seriously.*) When was it that Mr Sugita saw the man?

Shin   He said it was about nine o'clock yesterday evening.

Ken   Did he say anything about how the man looked?

Shin   Fairly. . . . That is . . . not very good. Said he wasn't even wearing a jacket.

Ken   That so?

Shin   What did Father look like, Ken'ichirō?

Ken   I don't remember.

Shin   That can't be true. After all, you were eight, and even though I was only three, I have some vague memories of him.

Ken   I don't remember. I have memories of the past, but I've tried, just as hard as I can, to forget, and I won't go back.

Shin You know, Mr Sugita talks about Father a lot. Father must've been handsome, back in his youth.

Mother (*Bring food from the kitchen.*) Sure was. Pa used to be quite a popular fella. There's a story 'bout when he were workin' as a page for his lordship. They say one a' the housemaids wrote him a love poem and sent it to him inside a chopstick case.

Shin He must have wondered why he was given a chopstick case. Ha, ha, ha, ha. . . .

Mother He were born in the Year of the Ox, that'd make him fifty-eight this year.[10] If he'd just stayed here at home, he could'a been enjoyin' his retirement by now.

(*The three begin eating.*)

Mother Otane ought'a be home soon. It's turned pretty nippy out.

Shin Mama, I heard the shrike calling in the elm at Jōkanji Temple. Autumn's here. . . . Oh, Ken, I've decided to get an English Language certification. I just can't find a good math tutor.

Ken That's fine. So does that mean you'll be going to Mr Erickson's?

Shin Yeah, that's what I thought I'd do. He's a missionary, so there's no charge.

Ken Well, at any rate, you've got to work hard at it. You can't depend on your father's reputation, so study's the only way you're going to be able to show the world you're your own man. You know, I wanted to take the exam for Public Servant First Class, but they've changed the rules and now you have to be a middle school grad. So I've given that up. You graduated from middle school, so throw your heart into it.

(*Just then the front door slides back and **Otane** comes in. She is an exceptionally beautiful, pale-complexioned young woman.*)

Otane I'm home!

Mother You're pretty late.

Otane They asked me to do another job, and I couldn't leave right away.

Mother Come, eat your supper.

Otane (*Sitting, a troubled look on her face.*) Ken, when I came home just now, there was an old man across the street who kept staring hard right at the entryway. (*The other three look concerned.*)

Ken   Oh – ?

Shin   What kind of man was he?

Otane   It was dark, so I don't know, but he was tall.

Shin   (*Stands and goes to the next room to peer out the window.*)

Ken   Anybody there?

Shin   Nope, not a soul.

(*The three siblings are silent.*)

Mother   You know, he left us three days after the Bon celebration.[11]

Ken   Mama, please, could we not talk about the past.

Mother   I know. When I was younger, I wanted to curse this bitterness, too. But somehow my heart softens the older I get.

(*They eat silently. Suddenly, the front door rattles open. The faces of both* **Ken** *and* **Mother** *register extreme agitation. However, the substance of that agitation is remarkably different.*)

A man's voice   Excuse me.

Otane   Coming. (*However, she doesn't get up.*)

A man's voice   I wonder, is Otaka here?

Mother   Yes! (*It's as if suction were drawing her toward the entryway. The exchange below is only heard.*)

Man   That you, Otaka?

Woman   Well! It really is you! My, you've changed!

(*Their voices thick with tears.*)

Man   Yeah . . . and you look . . . well. The kids must be all grown up.

Woman   They're adults. All of 'em are fine grownups. Come in and see for yourself.

Man   Is it all right to come in?

Woman   'Course it is.

(*After twenty years, the* **Father**, *Sōtarō, returns. This haggard man is led into the room by his aging wife.* **Shin** *and* **Otane**, *blinking back tears, stare earnestly at their father's figure.*)

Shin   Father? I'm Shinjirō.

Father   You've grown into a fine young man. When we were parted, you could just barely stand.

Otane   Father, I'm Otane.

Father   I heard there was a girl, and you're quite a beauty.

Mother   Well, Pa, you can say whatever you like, but the children turned out well, and I don't think there's a thing more important than that.

Father   They say children can raise themselves without parents. Don't you hear that a lot? Ha, ha, ha, ha. . . .

(*No one joins the laughter.* **Ken**, *stays silent, leaning forward on the table, staring downward.*)

Mother   Pa. Ken and Shin 're both doin' real well. Ya know, Ken here, he passed the basic civil servant exam at twenty. And Shin never dropped below third in his class the whole time at middle school. Together they're makin' sixty yen a month. Otane is, well, beautiful Otane, but more'n that, we've had proposals from some reputable folks.

Father   That is certainly the best kind of news. Up to about four or five years ago I was touring all over with a troupe of twenty to thirty people. Until we had a terrible loss when our sideshow pavilion burned to the ground over in Kure.[12] After that, nothing went right, and before I knew it, I was old and looking at the little time I had left. I yearned for home with my wife and kids, so I came crawlin' back. I'm beggin' you all, please take me back 'cause I don't expect to live long. (*Gazing steadily at* **Ken**.) Well then, Ken'ichirō! Will you pass me one of those sake cups? Your Old Man doesn't get much good sake to drink these days. Yep, you're the only one I'd expect to recognize me. (**Ken** *doesn't respond.*)

Mother   Come now, Ken. Your Pa's talkin' ta you. It's been ages since you two, father and son, met. You should be celebratin'.

(**Ken** *doesn't respond.*)

Father   Then, Shinjirō, how 'bout you pourin' me a drink?

Shin   Gladly. (*Picks up the cup and starts to hand it to* Father.)

Ken   (*Decisively.*) Leave it! You're not getting any from us.

Mother   What're you sayin'? Ken!

(**Ken** *glares fiercely at his father.* **Shin** *and* **Otane** *stare at the floor.*)

Ken   (*With dignity.*) We do not have a father. Could such dregs be a father?

Father   (*Suppressing furious indignation.*) What's that?

Ken   (*Rather coldly.*) If we had a father, our mother wouldn't have dragged us by the hand to the harbor to attempt suicide when I was eight years old. We survived because Mom misjudged the depth and we jumped into the shallows. If we'd had a father, I wouldn't have had to become an office page at age ten. And because we didn't have a father, we lived joyless lives as children. Shinjirō, do you remember how you cried in primary school because we couldn't afford ink or paper? Have you forgotten how you cried because we couldn't buy proper textbooks and your friends at school teased you for bringing hand-copied ones? We had a father?! With a father, we wouldn't have had that misery.

(**Mother** *and* **Otane** *are crying.* **Shin** *is close to tears, and* **Father**, *in his declining years is angered and saddened.*)

Shin   But, Ken, in the first place, Mama has come to terms with all that, so why can't we buck up and do the same?

Ken   (*More coldly.*) Mama's a woman, so I don't know how she feels, but if I have a father, then he's my foe. When we were little, you know what Mama's stock reply was if we complained we were hungry or things were hard, 'It's all your father's fault, so if you're going to curse someone, curse your father.' If I have a father, he's the bitterest enemy of my childhood. When I was ten I went to work at the Prefectural Office as a page and Mom was gluing matchbooks. Did you forget that time when Mom went a whole month without any work, and we had to skip lunches? I studied for all I was worth just so I could rip that enemy out. I want to triumph over that man who tossed us aside. And even though our father treated us like garbage, I want him to know that I'm building a reputation in society on my own. I don't remember getting one ounce of affection from my father. Until I was eight years old, my father would go out and wander about town getting drunk. In the end, he borrowed bad money from a loan shark, then deserted with his mistress. Even with the affection of a wife and three children, he turned to that woman. What's more, after my father left, he took the sixteen yen from my savings account because Mother entrusted him with the passbook.

Shin   (*Swallowing his tears.*) But, Ken, look at Dad. Look at how old he's become.

Ken   Shinjirō! You say those hypocritical things about Father so often. How can you immediately feel sorry for a stranger who you've never seen before just because he crawls in here saying he's our father?

Shin   But, Ken, he's our flesh and blood . . . no matter how wild, raising its natural offspring is a parent's. . . .

Ken   Duty? Is that what you want to say? Do we have a duty to a wastrel who crawls back in his feeble old age? No matter what you say, I don't have a father.

Father   (*He speaks as if indignant, however, it's anger empty of conviction.*) Ken'ichirō! How dare you speak that way about your natural father!

Ken   You say you're my natural father? The Ken'ichirō you spawned died twenty years ago in the harbor. You abandoned your rights as a father twenty years ago. This here today, is me, brought up myself. I don't owe a thing to anyone.

(*No one says a word. The only sound is the sniffled sobs of* **Otaka** *and* **Otane**.)

Father   So be it. I'm leavin'. I'm a man who's managed tens of thousands of yen. No matter how low I fall, I always find a way to eat. Don't trouble yourself for me. (*Dejected, he starts to leave.*)

Shin   Come now, don't go. Ken may reject you, but I'll do whatever I can. Ken's your son, and I know he'll come round. Don't go. I'll do all I can to take care of you.

Ken   Shinjirō! When have you ever had reason to thank that bastard? At least he cracked me on the head once or twice, but he never raised a finger against you. Who was it paid for your primary school? Who was it that brought you up? It was me, your big brother, who paid your school fees. Have you forgotten how I paid out of my measly salary as a page? You know. Your real father was me. I did the duties of a father. Go ahead and take care of that bastard if you want. And that's what I get thanks for?

Shin   But. . . .

Ken   If you don't like it, you can leave, and take him with you.

(*The two women are still crying.* **Shin** *says nothing.*)

Ken   I suffered because I had no father. But I thought my little brother and sister shouldn't suffer, so I went without sleep to get you two through middle school.

Father   (*Weakly.*) Well, that's it then. My coming back is a bother for you. I won't force a burden on my children. I've got enough wit to take care of myself. So, I'll just go. Otaka! Stay well. You're lucky I tossed you aside.

Shin   (*Following* **Father** *out.*) Do you have any money, sir? Have you eaten supper yet?

Father   (*Entreating* **Shin** *with his eyes.*) I'm all right. I'm all right.

(*Stepping down into the entryway,* **Father** *stumbles, and slumps down on the bench.*)

Mother   Oh! Be careful!

Shin   (*Helping* **Father** *rise.*) Do you have a place to go?

Father   (*Completely dejected, he stays seated.*) You wouldn't want a stray dog dying in your house. (*As if talking to himself.*) You're not obliged to let me set foot in this house, but as I got older and weaker, my feet turned naturally toward my old home. It's been three days since I came back to town. Every evening, I'd come and stand in front of this house. But the threshold was just too high. It would have been better if I hadn't come crawling back. What fool would come home without a single yen to his name? Like anyone else, yearning for my old home came to me in my fifties. But I thought I should at least bring home some money. One or two thousand yen as a gesture of remorse. But I couldn't even muster that much in my old age. (*He finally stands.*) Ah, well, I'll get by somehow. (*He totters to his feet, his aged form turning for one last backward glance, then opens the door and exits. The other four are silent for a while.*)

Mother   (*Pleading.*) Ken'ichirō!

Otane   Ken!

(*There is a tense pause.*)

Ken   Shin! Go and call Dad back!

(**Shin** *leaps out the door. The other three wait steeped in tension.* **Shin** *comes back, his face ashen.*)

Shin   I didn't see him down the street to the south. I'm going to look to the north, so you come too, Ken!

Ken   (*Shocked.*) You didn't find him? How could you not find him?

(*The two brothers dash madly out.*)

CURTAIN

Notes

1   Kikuchi Kan, *History and Trends of Modern Japanese Literature*, trans. S. Sakabe. Tokyo: Kokusai Bunka Shinkokai, 1936, p.8.

2   These three plays along with an early translation of 'Father Returns' were first published in English in 1925 in Kikuchi Kwan (an early transliteration of his name), *Tōjūrō's Love and Four Other Plays*, trans. Glenn W. Shaw. Tokyo: Hokuseido, 1925.

3   Kikuchi 1936, p.8.

4   Takamatsu, Kagawa Prefecture on Shikoku Island, Kikuchi's birthplace, would be just such a town, or small city. The speech of all the characters reflects the provincial setting, but greater education creates a distinct difference between the language use of the parents and children. The translation is a rough approximation of that difference.

5   Standard *tatami*, rice-straw mats, are approximately 3 feet by 6 feet, making the room about 9 by 12, or 108 square feet.

6   At the public bathhouse. For much of the twentieth century in Japan, only the wealthy could afford to have baths in their homes.

7   On the main island of Honshu, just across the Inland Sea from Takamatsu.

8   The First Sino-Japanese War of 1894–5.

9   The Chinese influenced study in samurai households before the Japanese modern era began in 1868.

10 57 by the Western count. In the Japanese count a person is one year old from the minute he or she is born. On the next 1 January, even if it is the next day, the person is counted as two years old because that person is in the second calendar year of his or her life.

11 A Buddhist celebration honouring the spirits of the dead held in late summer.

12 A town near Hiroshima on Honshu, facing the Inland Sea.

Hot Pepper, Air Conditioner and the Farewell Speech

Okada Toshiki

Translated by Aya Ogawa

Born in Yokohama in 1973, Okada Toshiki founded his own company *chelfitsch* (its name is a play on the English word 'selfish' and is never capitalised) in 1997 at the age of twenty-four. He is a playwright, director and a novelist who has very rapidly gained worldwide attention as a unique voice in Japanese theatre and the pre-eminent theatre artist of the economically unstable and socially disconnected millennial generation. Although he has directed for other groups, most notably Beckett's *Cascando* for the Tokyo International Arts Festival/Beckett Centennial Memorial Festival in 2007 and Abe Kōbō's *Tomodachi* (Friends) at the Setagaya Public Theater in 2008, the majority of his work is developed with the members of *chelfitsch*. He has written and directed all of the company's productions.[1]

Okada's work combines choreography and movement, the use of images and a sophisticated, fragmented, abbreviated, idiosyncratic and hyper-colloquial language. His plays have been described as a fusion of drama and abstract dance. Initially, Okada had been reluctant to tour his plays outside of Japan, believing them to be 'uniquely Japanese and untranslatable',[2] but his work has been presented internationally for almost a decade, with performances by *chelfitsch* into Brussels, Vienna, Paris, Cardiff, Salzburg, Singapore, Seattle, Portland, Los Angeles, Pittsburgh, Philadelphia, Minneapolis, Vancouver, Istanbul, Rakvere, and Estonia, among others.

His early works include *Marijuana no Gaini Tsuite* (On the Harmful Effects of Marijuana, 2003) and *Rouku no Owari* (The End of Toil, 2005), but he rose to prominence in Japan with *Sangatsu no Itsukakann* (Five Days in March, 2004), which juxtaposes the beginning of the Iraq war with the brief affair of a couple and won the 2005 Kishida Kunio Prize. Other major works include *Enjoy* (2006), *Watashitachiwamukizunabetsujin de aru* (We Are the Undamaged Others, 2010), *Kaden no yōniwakariaenai* (We Don't Understand Each Other the Way We Don't Understand Home Appliances, 2011), and *Zougame no sonikkuraifu* (The Sonic Life of a Giant Tortoise, 2011)[3] in which thirty somethings reflect upon the lack of happiness and meaning in their lives. Much of his work after this was profoundly shaped by, and in response to, the Tōhoku earthquake and tsunami of 11 March 2011 (known in Japan as 3/11), including plays such as *Genzaichi* (Current Location, 2012), which is an allegorical tale concerning what the Japanese believe about the radiation released from the Fukushima nuclear power plant, and, most recently as of this writing, *Jimen to yuka* (Ground and Floor, 2013), concerning how delicately the vision of the past, present and future of Japan hangs among the Japanese people. Okada also collaborated with the Philadelphia-based Pig Iron Theatre Company to develop his first work written in English, the 3/11-influenced *Zero Cost House* (2012), in which an architect who studies the homes of the homeless declares himself Prime Minister of Japan.

The themes found throughout Okada's work include alienation, the impossibility of direct communication and the life situations of youth who are disengaged, displaced, disempowered and completely unconnected to the world around them. Okada's plays often deal with the disaffected young generation and its place (or lack thereof) in contemporary Japanese society. His play *Hottopeppa, Kooraa, soshite o wakare no aisatsu* (*Hot Pepper, Air Conditioner and the Farewell Speech*) is a triptych – a set of three small, interrelated plays which, performed together, forms a comprehensive picture. *Air Conditioner* was originally an award-winning stand-alone piece written and performed in 2004, but the other pieces were added after the financial meltdown to create a full-length play.

The play takes as its theme the related issues of unemployment and 'non-full-time employees'. As elsewhere in the world after the global financial crisis of 2008, Japanese unemployment grew and many individuals, especially the young, found themselves only able to find temporary or part-time employment, a corporate technique to avoid paying for benefits due to full-time employees. This generation 'endures one of the world's most competitive educational systems' only to transform upon graduation into 'freeters', a term that combines the English 'free' and the German 'arbeiter', meaning worker, a class of temporary worker.[4] The play depicts the crisis of freeters indirectly, showing first a group of co-workers arguing about where to have a goodbye party for a temporary employee who is leaving (*Hot Pepper*), then employees (identified as 'Full-time Worker (Man)' and 'Full-time Worker (Woman)', as if their employment status, not their name, is their true identities) conversing about the temperature in the office in which communication is shown to be impossible (*Air Conditioner*), and finally, Erika, the freeter, whose party was being planned in the first scene, giving a farewell speech in which she discusses a dead cicada on her doorstep, the metaphor for her own situation being readily apparent.

Hot Pepper, Air Conditioner and the Farewell Speech

[*Hottopeppa, Kooraa, soshite o wakare no aisatsu*, 2009]

Subtitles: 'Part 1: Hot Pepper'
Subtitles: 'Three Office Temps'

1.

Temp 1   You know, the farewell party for Erika that's coming up, the three of us temps are supposed to organize it, right, what kind of party do you think it should be? The date hasn't been set yet, has it? Or has the date been set? It hasn't, right, I mean the three of us temps are supposed to organize it, right, and the location of the party, the restaurant, what kind of restaurant it should be in hasn't been decided yet either, right? Or was it decided, what direction we should go in in terms of what kind of restaurant? We haven't decided yet, right, about the farewell party for Erika that's coming up, it would be best, if as the organizers, among the three of us, if anybody has an idea about what kind of restaurant, so anyone? What do you think? Aren't there any strong opinions I mean, as the organizers kind of thing, anything in particular? The three of us temps are supposed to organize it, right, what do you think? If there aren't any like strong opinions, as the organizers, I could, I happen to have a Hot Pepper today, but, it would be best, if as the organizers, among the three of us, if anybody has an idea about what kind of restaurant, is there anyone here who knows what Erika likes to eat? What do you think? Is there anyone here who knows what she doesn't like? Anyone? If there isn't, I happen to have a Hot Pepper today, and in Hot Pepper there are restaurants listed by different categories, like Japanese food, or other Asian food, so among those categories, is there anyone here who knows what Erika likes to eat? The three of us temps are supposed to organize it, right, what kind of party do you think it should be? I've never organized anything like this before so I'm kind of stuck, so it would be best, if as the organizers, among the three of us, if anybody have an idea about what kind of restaurant.

(Subtitles: *Hot Pepper* is a free monthly coupon magazine published by Recruit Company. It is published regionally all over Japan and comes out every last Friday of the month, and distributed on street corners and convenience stores and the like. They also offer the same service online on their web site that can be accessed by computer or cell phone. Most of the coupons are for restaurants and other such dining establishments, but they also have other categories such as beauty-related section for salons and a culture section. [from the Wikipedia Japan entry: *Hot Pepper*])

2.

Temp 2   Well then, may I at least share the information I have about what kind of food Erika likes? But it is pretty old information from a while ago, it's not the latest information but, may I share it with you? I think that it might serve as one clue in terms of what direction we should decide to go, for the restaurant for the upcoming farewell party, as an example, for the three of us as the organizers, so the information I have about what kind of food Erika likes is: *motsu* hot pot, but this is pretty old information from a while ago but, a while back, I can't remember exactly when but, I seem to recall Erika saying something like, 'To tell you the truth, I really love *motsu* hot pot,' so a *motsu* hot pot place may be a good possibility, as one option, in choosing a restaurant, for the farewell party that's coming up, but this is pretty old information from a while ago, it isn't the latest information but, I don't know whether or not she still likes *motsu* hot pot, a *motsu* hot pot place may be a good possibility, as one option, in fact may turn out to be a good choice, in choosing a restaurant, for the farewell party that's coming up, although I don't know whether or not she still likes *motsu* hot pot, but, a *motsu* hot pot place may be a good possibility, as one option, in choosing a restaurant, for the farewell party that's coming up.

(Subtitles: *Motsu* hot pot is a stew-like dish using *motsu*, or beef or pork offal. In a hot pot full of broth, cow or pork intestines are added and boiled until the flavors permeate the stew, and later cabbage and chives are added. The broth is flavored with soy sauce with garlic or chili peppers, or with miso. [from the Wikipedia Japan entry: *motsunabe*])

3.

Temp 3   But see, there's one thing that I find problematic you see, normally the people who are full-time employees at a company take on the organizing of a farewell party, I think, and I just feel like the fact that we, the three of us temps ended up being the ones to organize Erika's party is wrong you know, normally the people who are full-time employees at a company take on the organizing of a farewell party, I think, and it's not at all like we don't wish Erika well or that we don't want to do it or anything like that, but, I just think the role of organizing a farewell party ought to be the responsibility of full-time company employees, and when we accepted the responsibility like OK we'll organize the party thank you, there was this unspoken feeling like, well a farewell party for a temp should be organized by the temps, you know, and at the time I guess we thought that's just the way it is, and that's why I think we agreed to take on the responsibility without question, like OK we'll organize the party thank you, but see, there's one thing that I find problematic you see, normally the people who are full-time employees at a company take on the organizing of a farewell party, I think, and it's not at all like we don't wish Erika well or that we don't want to do it or anything like that, in fact we do wish her well and it's not a chore for us at all, but you see when we accepted the responsibility like OK we'll organize the party thank you, there was this unspoken feeling like, well a farewell party for a temp should be organized by the temps, you know, but now, looking back, I think that, no, that's just not right.

4.

Temp 2   Do you remember, the idea I had a just now, about maybe the possibility of having the farewell party at a *motsu* hot pot place might be a good one? What do you think? Is *motsu* all right? Can you eat it? Do you like *motsu*? Or do you dislike it? I think that the fact that Erika said that she liked *motsu* hot pot is something really crucial as a fact, because I think *motsu* hot pot is not something everybody likes and eats regularly, in fact there are probably more people who don't like it I think, because of its distinct smell, and also the rubbery texture, I think there must be a lot of people who can't eat *motsu*, but is it OK? Do you like *motsu*? Or do you dislike it? I guess some people might think it inappropriate to choose *motsu* for a social event like a farewell party, but what do you think? As the party organizers, a part of me thinks we have to think about all the guests in choosing the restaurant, but, do you remember, the idea I had a just now, about maybe the possibility of having the farewell party at a *motsu* hot pot place might be a good one? I don't want to withdraw that suggestion, what do you think? I think that the fact that Erika said that she liked *motsu* hot pot is something really crucial as a fact, so for this party, I'd really like to decide on *motsu* hot pot.

5.

Temp 1   So, the thing about the farewell party that I think is most difficult is do you know about how much the whole thing should cost, like what is the best estimated budget for these kinds of farewell parties?

If you look at Hot Pepper, they have a, you can see at a glance how much you can expect to pay at each restaurant, and, that's why, that's something we should consider too, when choosing a restaurant, I'd like to choose by how much each person will need to pay approximately? Two thousand would be just too cheap, right, so everyone should expect to pay about five thou per person I guess, but five is, to be honest, actually a substantial amount of money, and on top of that, of course everyone will chip in for Erika's portion, so including that, the total has come to about five per person, of course three would be, honestly, ideal, because five is, to be honest, actually a substantial amount of money, I mean to blow five in one night has got to hurt, I mean it's not at all like we don't wish Erika well or that we don't want to do it or anything like that, in fact perhaps five thou is even too cheap, maybe we ought to go for more, we could easily get to like eight, but that's a little, I'd like to avoid that, so, the thing about the farewell party that I think is most difficult is do you know about how much the whole thing should cost, like what is the best estimated budget for these kinds of farewell parties? Should we temps have to pay the same amount as the full-timers? Or should there be a price difference? I mean, the three of us temps have had to organize this party, so maybe we should set a different price category for the temps and the full-timers? Seven for the legit full-timers and five for us, that would be pretty fair, don't you think? About how much should the whole thing cost, like what is the best estimated budget for these kinds of farewell parties? Do you know? If you look at Hot Pepper, they have a, you can see at a glance how much you can expect to pay at each restaurant, Hot Pepper stays on top of all sorts of details like that, it's really useful, and comes in handy, but, because five is, to be honest, actually a substantial amount of money, I mean to blow five in one night has got to hurt, should there be price difference? I mean, the three of us temps have had to organize this party, so seven for the legit full-timers and five for us, that would be pretty fair, don't you think? Of course the ideal would be about ten and three, but ten and three, is probably too much, although three would be, honestly, perfect but, two would be just too cheap right?

6.

Temp 3   In any case, why is it that Erika was the one whose contract was cut short, before the three of us? It was totally unexpected, it seemed like Erika was really good with Excel and stuff, and without her I think it's going to be really rough, I mean she could actually get a lot of work done, and doesn't agreeing to organize her party really signify a formal expression of gratitude towards her, right? That kind of thing is something that should be taken seriously by the full-timers way more than us, I think, but I guess, I mean, why is it that Erika was the one whose contract was cut short, before the three of us? It was totally unexpected, it seemed like Erika was really good with Excel and stuff, and without her I think it's going to be really rough, I mean she could actually get a lot of work done, and doesn't agreeing to organize her party really signify a formal expression of gratitude towards her, right? Why is it that Erika was the one whose contract was cut short, before the three of us? I wonder if something happened.

(Subtitles: Temp-cutting refers to the massive layoffs that occurred in response to the global financial crisis in November of 2008, when automobile companies and household electronics companies abruptly terminated large-scale contracts with agencies that provided temp workers and the resulting dismissals/hiring freeze of such workers. [from the Wikipedia Japan entry: temp-cutting])

7.

Temp 1   So like, the choice of the restaurant, which restaurant we should have it, the farewell party, should be dictated by the preferences of the person in whose honor the party is, right? I know this because I read an article in Hot Pepper about that, and I read about it, that the choice of restaurant should, as a rule, be chosen according to the taste of the person whose party it is, it was in the March issue of Hot Pepper I think, like my colleague so-and-so is being transferred to the New York branch, and you have been chosen to organize the farewell party, so now what should you do, what should you be careful of, were the kinds of things in the article, like you've gotten all your colleagues to write her a letter or get her a present, and at what moment should you give such gift to the guest of honor, and stuff, and it said that it was a big BZZZZ (*buzzer sound*) for the organizer to choose the restaurant according to his own taste, because the guest of honor is the person who is being bid farewell, so you have to somehow very subtly find out what that person likes and use that as a guideline for choosing the restaurant, and stuff, Hot Pepper stays on top of all sorts of details like that, it's really useful, and comes in handy, so in that sense, I think for this party, a *motsu* hot pot place would actually be OK, if Erika really does like *motsu* hot pot, then we should go with that I think, in choosing the restaurant, because as a rule, to go with the preference of the person in whose honor the party is, they say.

8.

Temp 3 Um you see, I have a suggestion, so, we all know what
happened to Erika, why is it that Erika was the one whose contract was
cut short, before the three of us? It was totally unexpected, but besides
that, it's inevitable that this is going to continue, and we are definitely
going to be laid off, we're going to be the second, and third people to go,
but you just never know when that's going to happen, it could be in the
not-too-distant future, worst case scenario, it could even be next month,
so I think we've got to be prepared, since they say if you're prepared you
have no regrets, so I, that's why I think now, I should make my wishes
very clear, so, by the way, I like Chinese food, so I think we should all
share with each other, what kind of restaurant you'd hope your farewell
party would take place in, just like I did right now, so where would you
like to go? So I think we should all share with each other, what kind of
restaurant you'd hope your farewell party would take place in, since they
say if you're prepared you have no regrets, so, by the way, I like Chinese
food, and if it's a place that has good almond jelly, all the better.

9.

Temp 1 For me I guess, I also would like Chinese too, for my own
farewell party, but then, that would be two Chinese restaurants in a row,
kind of doubled up, and some people might be like, oh God, not two
Chinese restaurants in a row, in which case a regular *izakaya* would
be totally fine but, but then again maybe it's OK to have two farewell
parties in a row at Chinese restaurants, I mean, these farewell parties, it's
not like they'll happen two days in a row, right, I mean 'in a row' could
still mean a month apart, in which case, for me I guess, I also would like
Chinese too, for my own farewell party, but a regular *izakaya* would be
totally fine but, maybe I'll start looking for a good *izakaya* in Hot Pepper
now, I happen to have a Hot Pepper today, but, if it ends up that either
Chinese or an *izakaya* is fine so I can choose, if that happens, then, I'd
like Chinese I guess, so maybe I'll start looking for a good Chinese place
in Hot Pepper now, but, then, that would be two Chinese restaurants in
a row, kind of doubled up, and some people might be like, oh God not
two Chinese restaurants in a row, although I wouldn't mind at all, in
which case a regular *izakaya* would be totally fine but, oh, maybe it's not
really good for me to compromise by saying a regular *izakaya* would be
totally fine, I mean like, the choice of the restaurant, which restaurant we
should have it, the farewell party, should be dictated by the preferences

of the person in whose honor the party is, right? In that case, it'd be up
to me, right, for me I guess, I also would like Chinese too, for my own
farewell party, so maybe I'll look for a good Chinese place in Hot Pepper
now, I happen to have a Hot Pepper today, and Hot Pepper has restaurant
listings like Japanese food, other Asian food, organized in different
categories, so of course they have Chinese, and a category for *izakayas*,
Hot Pepper stays on top of all sorts of details like that, it's really useful,
and comes in handy, Hot Pepper is the best.

(Subtitles: An izakaya (居酒屋) is a type of Japanese drinking
establishment which also serves food to accompany the drinks. The food
is usually more substantial than that offered in other types of drinking
establishments in Japan such as bars or snack bars, [citation needed]
and may be compared to Spanish tapas. [from Wikipedia English entry:
izakaya])

10.

Temp 2   Um, I'm sorry, before I tell you what kind of restaurant I'd
like to go to for my farewell party, there's actually, I'm so sorry, there's
something I have to apologize for, I, just a second ago, I'm sorry, I said
that I had some information about what kind of food Erika likes, and
so I said that Erika said that she likes to eat *motsu* hot pot, but that was
a lie, I was lying, I just have had this unbearable craving for *motsu* hot
pot, and that was because, the day before yesterday, I saw something on
TV, a *motsu* hot pot special, happened to be playing when I turned on the
TV, and I watched it, and thought it looked really delicious, and thought
it also looked really healthy, and so, I just have had this unbearable
craving for *motsu* hot pot, and then, on top of that, *motsu* hot pot has
plenty of chives, and so I have this craving for chives, so I'm sorry, but,
I guess, for my farewell party, I should choose *motsu* hot pot, in the
not too distant future, I'm sorry, so, I'm sure you already understand
but, I, for my own farewell party, in choosing a place, I would like a
motsu hot pot place, but, I guess, I should choose *motsu* hot pot for my
farewell party, in the not-too-distant future, I, by the way, when I think
about it, I haven't had *motsu* hot pot in a very long time, but, and that
is probably definitely not good for my body, and also, I haven't had
any chives in a really long time, chives are really good for you, like all
green leafy vegetables, but that unique smell of chives is this compound
called allicin, I saw that the day before yesterday on TV, as part of the
motsu hot pot special, which happened to be on when I turned on the

TV, chives are a green leafy vegetable from the lily family, and allicin is this chemical that kills bacteria and cleanses the blood, so it's good for like for example hardened arteries, so it's good for your body, and *motsu* hot pot has plenty of chives, so I have this unbearable craving for *motsu* hot pot, but, I guess for my farewell party, I should choose *motsu* hot pot, right, I'm looking forward to it a bit, I can't wait to eat *motsu* hot pot, but, *motsu* hot pot would probably be more delicious in the colder weather than right now, so I hope I don't get laid off until the winter.

(THE END, *Hot Pepper*)

Subtitles: 'Part 2: Air Conditioner'
Subtitles: 'Two full-time workers, a man and a woman'

Full-time Worker (Man)   We're going to do this piece called 'Air Conditioner' now.

Full-time Worker (Man)   This person is Makiko

1.

Full-time Worker (Man)   Hey, Makiko, you know how on Sunday mornings,

Full-time Worker (Woman)   Yes,

Full-time Worker (Man)   they sometimes have those political talk shows on TV

Full-time Worker (Woman)   Yes,

Full-time Worker (Man)   you know? You may be familiar with them but, on TV, when I watch those kinds of shows, the way they talk,

Full-time Worker (Woman)   Yes,

Full-time Worker (Man)   you know how those guys or like, those kinds of people, those people have, how can I describe it, I'm watching them, right, and then, I always think that I can learn something from them, this is what I think while I'm watching, if I may, that I can learn from their relentless, aggressive way of talking, continuous, and they talk without conceding, until they get their point across? Like they know what they want to say and they talk until they've had their say?

Full-time Worker (Woman)   Yes

Full-time Worker (Man)   Like that's their deal? Right and it's like?
You know what I'm talking about right? Like they have their agenda,
right? And like, those kinds of people, so, they have to say what they
have to say, those kinds of people, and even if someone tries to interject,
or comes in shouting from the side, they completely ignore them, they
just keep talking over each other, so aggressively, to the point where it's
totally like 'whoah!' or like 'they've got to be doing that on purpose'
and they go there like it's totally normal, and it's amazing, like do they
really have to take it that far? and I always think, yeah, they do have
to take it that far, and I should too, every time I see them, and there's
always a moment where I'm like, it's OK, right, it's OK, you know, or
like, is it really OK, to be so ruthless, it's like they train themselves to
be that way,

Full-time Worker (Woman)   Yes, I'm kind of cold

Full-time Worker (Man)   They really do train themselves in a sense, at
least that's the way it seems to me you know? When I watch those kinds
of people, on the one hand, I feel that I could really learn something
from them, as a member of society you know? I mean at least a little bit?
That's the impact they have on me, which is pretty deep you know,

2.

Full-time Worker (Woman)   I'm kind of cold, I think it's really
unbelievable but you know how the office air conditioner is set to 23°C,
and it's on high all the time?

Full-time Worker (Man)   Yes

Full-time Worker (Woman)   It's weird, the air conditioner, I mean,
23°C and on high, is too unbelievable, I think, really, I mean it almost
makes me laugh but, um, I'm like, what do you call it, I tend to have
poor circulation a little

Full-time Worker (Man)   Oh, for women, it might be, a little bit
rough, yeah,

Full-time Worker (Woman)   Yes, or like, it's the poor circulation,
really, not that I'm a woman but, you know?

Full-time Worker (Man)   Yes

Full-time Worker (Woman)   Or like. But yes, yes, I am aware of that, I'm conscious of it, I don't know but

Full-time Worker (Man)   Women, yeah, I feel sorry for them

Full-time Worker (Woman)   But, yeah, maybe that is why, I am aware of it, I am conscious of that possibility,

Full-time Worker (Man)   For women

Full-time Worker (Woman)   That's right, yes, I mean not for women but

Full-time Worker (Man)   They really have it rough

Full-time Worker (Woman)   Rough, or like, really it's always, what I'm saying is,

Full-time Worker (Man)   Yes

Full-time Worker (Woman)   when I'm at work, I'm not joking, the state I'm in, I am so cold, I'm miserable, I mean

Full-time Worker (Man)   Oh, but Makiko, your pain is

Full-time Worker (Woman)   Seriously, it's enough to make me quit this job

Full-time Worker (Man)   Oh, Makiko, well I kinda understand what you're saying

Full-time Worker (Woman)   when I'm at work, I'm not joking, the state I'm in, I am so cold, I'm miserable, I mean

Full-time Worker (Man)   Oh, but Makiko, your pain is

Full-time Worker (Woman)   Seriously, it's enough to make me quit this job

Full-time Worker (Man)   Oh, Makiko, well I kinda understand what you're saying

Pause

(Repeat scene 2.)

3.

Full-time Worker (Woman)   I'm kind of cold, I think it's really unbelievable but you know how the office air conditioner is set to 23°C, and it's on high all the time?

Full-time Worker (Man)   Women, yeah, I feel sorry for them

Full-time Worker (Woman)   It's weird, or like, I really, when I'm at work, I'm not joking, the state I'm in, I'm miserable, I mean I'm shivering all day, and my legs are shaking, and like, my lower belly is like, really, you might not understand what I'm trying to say but

Full-time Worker (Man)   No, that's not at all true, it's just a little, well, no not at all

Full-time Worker (Woman)   My stomach really

Full-time Worker (Man)   Yes

Full-time Worker (Woman)   when it gets so cold, I get indigestion and

Full-time Worker (Man)   Yes

Full-time Worker (Woman)   stuff, so I'm always, I'm in the situation all day long where I can't get any work done, I'm miserable, like what am I doing here at work, it's a really miserable feeling, you know?

Full-time Worker (Man)   Well like, Makiko, in my opinion, there's definitely got to be someone who is guilty of always lowering the AC to 23°C, right?

Full-time Worker (Woman)   I mean, I already know who it is, but

Full-time Worker (Man)   Yes, then maybe you should call the police? I feel like maybe that's what you should do, or like, I'm just saying that as it occurred to me just now but, I'm just thinking that as it just occurred to me just now but,

Pause

4.

Full-time Worker (Woman)   I mean, 23°C is like, it's the middle of summer, OK, 23°C is ridiculous, don't you think? I'm seriously totally freezing and like, everyday is like this hellish ordeal, the state I'm living in, like, my desk is, where I sit is pretty much right in front of the air conditioner, the air blows right into my face, like on my forehead, like, I'm in the situation all day long where I can't get any work done at all, I'm miserable, like what am I doing here at work, it's a really miserable feeling, you know what I'm talking about?

Full-time Worker (Man)   Makiko, if it's gotten that bad maybe you should just call the police? I think it's totally fine, I mean since the situation has gotten as far as it has, like it's gotten that bad, I think, you should just call the police, like that would be totally normal

Full-time Worker (Woman)   No it's all right, I haven't called the police yet

Full-time Worker (Man)   Maybe not the police

Full-time Worker (Woman)   Maybe not the police

Full-time Worker (Man)   Maybe not the police

Full-time Worker (Woman)   Maybe not the police

Full-time Worker (Man)   Maybe not the police, but are you going to be OK?

Full-time Worker (Woman)   Yes, for now I'll handle it myself

Full-time Worker (Man)   Yes

Full-time Worker (Woman)   For now, whenever I notice it, I've been turning the setting down myself, I'm like why is it on 23°C I'm thinking, I'm freezing to death, it's really, it's really, it's really been set to 23°C I'm not joking, it's really 23°C, it's always set to 23°C, when I notice it, plus it's on high, and I'm like whoah! so that's why I've been resetting it myself to about 28°C but then before I realize it, someone's set it back to 23°C, plus it's on high, even though I'd set it to low, I'd set it to 28°C on low, but someone resets it high right away, at 23°C no less

Full-time Worker (Man)   Huh, then, you should probably definitely, are you sure you're OK, without calling the police, do you want to call them or like, you should call them, I mean 23°C? That's pretty

Full-time Worker (Woman)   Yes, yes

Full-time Worker (Man)   Huh, I wonder, it's a bit much,

Full-time Worker (Woman)   Yes, yes

Full-time Worker (Man)   or like, well 23°C is really a bit much, I do think it's, I think it's really gotten out of hand, to the point where it's really out of hand

Full-time Worker (Woman)   or like, it's so cold, it's unbelievable, you know, like really 23°C is like, wait, do you really understand what 23°C feels like? You know? Plus it's on high, like whoah! so that's why

I change it myself to about 28°C but then before I realize it, someone's set it back to 23°C, plus it's on high, even though I'd set it to low, I'd set it to 28°C on low, but someone resets it high right away, to 23°C no less

Full-time Worker (Man)   or like, I still think the police, I happen to have my cell phone, I have it on me right now, so (*looking for it*) um, and I also happen to have the number to the police station in my phone, so I can call them right away, but what do you think? What should we do, Makiko, or like in situations like these, I think that calling the police is hands-down the best, most direct way to solving the, well, Makiko, I really think that, but well Makiko, if you don't feel that, oh never mind, but anyway about the air conditioner, the temperature setting, the thermostat yeah, 23°C is really, I feel like, it's really gotten out of hand, to the point where it's really out of hand, I think

Full-time Worker (Woman)   or like, it's so cold, it's unbelievable but

Full-time Worker (Man)   It's unbelievable, totally unbelievable

Full-time Worker (Woman)   or like, really, 23°C is just, it's like, wait, do you really understand what 23°C feels like? Don't you think? Like, whoah!

Full-time Worker (Man)   Makiko, I could help you with this cold AC. . . .

5.

Full-time Worker (Man)   but anyway about the air conditioner, the temperature setting, the thermostat yeah,

Full-time Worker (Woman)   Yes

Full-time Worker (Man)   Hey, Makiko, you know how on Sunday mornings,

Full-time Worker (Woman)   Yes,

Full-time Worker (Man)   they sometimes have those political talk shows on TV

Full-time Worker (Woman)   Yes,

Full-time Worker (Man)   you know? You may be familiar with them but, on TV, when I watch those kinds of shows, the way they talk,

Full-time Worker (Woman)   Yes,

Full-time Worker (Man)   you know how those guys or like, those kinds of people, those people have, how can I describe it, I'm watching them, right, and then, I always think that I can learn something from them, this is what I think while I'm watching, if I may, that I can learn from their relentless, aggressive way of talking, continuous, and they talk without conceding, until they get their point across? Like they know what they want to say and they talk until they've had their say?

Full-time Worker (Woman)   Yes

Full-time Worker (Man)   Like that's their deal? Right and it's like? You know what I'm talking about right? Like they have their agenda, right? And like, those kinds of people, so, they have to say what they have to say, those kinds of people, and even if someone tries to interject, or comes in shouting from the side, they completely ignore them, they just keep talking over each other, so aggressively, to the point where it's totally like 'whoah!' or like 'they've got to be doing that on purpose' and they go there like it's totally normal, and it's amazing, like do they really have to take it that far? and I always think, yeah, they do have to take it that far, and I should too, every time I see them, and there's always a moment where I'm like, it's OK, right, it's OK, you know, or like, is it really OK, to be so ruthless, it's like they train themselves to be that way,

Full-time Worker (Woman)   Yes, I'm kind of cold

Full-time Worker (Man)   They really do train themselves in a sense, at least that's the way it seems to me you know? When I watch those kinds of people, on the one hand, I feel that I could really learn something from them, like, it's OK, right, it's OK, you know, or like, is it really OK, to be so ruthless, it's like they train themselves to be that way, they really do train themselves in a sense, at least that's the way it seems to me you know? When I watch those kinds of people, on the one hand, I feel that I could really learn something from them, as a member of society you know? I mean at least a little bit? that's the impact they have on me, which is pretty deep you know, so I mean about the air conditioner, the temperature setting, the thermostat right,

6.

Full-time Worker (Woman)   I mean, 23°C is like, it's the middle of summer, OK, 23°C is ridiculous, don't you think? I'm seriously totally freezing and like, everyday is like this hellish ordeal, the state I'm living in, like, my desk is, where I sit is pretty much right in front of the air conditioner, the air blows right into my face, like on my forehead, like, I'm in the situation all day long where I can't get any work done at all, I mean, I really focus in on my work right, I don't know but sometimes I can achieve this super-focus when I work and it's like a God-like concentration and I can type at hyperspeed and get all this work done, when I can focus like that, I mean I focus on my work, you know, and sometimes I can achieve this super-focus for a moment, but then, I'm like, um it's really cold, like the tips of my toes are freezing off, and then shivers run up my body, and in that moment all this concentration just flies out the window, you know,

Full-time Worker (Man)   Makiko, I know you really work hard all the time, really I've always thought that, watching you, pretty often, actually, or like

Full-time Worker (Woman)   Or like, I actually think I know who the culprit is,

Full-time Worker (Man)   Or like, Makiko, in my opinion, there's definitely got to be someone who is guilty of always lowering the AC to 23°C, right?

Full-time Worker (Woman)   Or like, I already know who it is

Full-time Worker (Man)   Yes, then maybe you should? Call the police? I feel like maybe that's what you should do, or like, I'm just saying that as it occurred to me just now but, I'm just thinking that as the thought just occurred to me but, it's, Murakami isn't it?

Full-time Worker (Woman)   Or like, I already know who it is, the culprit is just one person

Full-time Worker (Man)   The culprit is Murakami, isn't it?

Full-time Worker (Woman)   There's only one person who is guilty, and he always resets it to 23°C it's just one person, you see, so I already know who the culprit is, and it's the same person who sets it to high

Full-time Worker (Man)   The culprit is Murakami, isn't it?

Full-time Worker (Woman)   Or like, I already know who it is, the culprit is just one person

Full-time Worker (Man)   The culprit is Murakami, isn't it?

Full-time Worker (Woman)   There's only one person who is guilty, and he always resets it to 23°C it's just one person, you see, so I already know who the culprit is, and it's the same person who sets it to high

Full-time Worker (Man)   The culprit is Murakami, isn't it?

Full-time Worker (Woman)   It's really, definitely, but, at first we all thought, at first he definitely couldn't stand the heat so you know there are a number of fat people in the office

Full-time Worker (Man)   Fat or like, I guess there are a few people who tend towards being overweight, Murakami is always drinking energy drinks you know,

Full-time Worker (Woman)   in our office, even among the older guys, so we were saying that it definitely had to be one of the, but we were wrong, but we were wrong, because Murakami isn't particularly fat

Full-time Worker (Man)   Murakami is always drinking energy drinks you know,

Full-time Worker (Woman)   I mean, 23°C and on high, is too unbelievable, I think, really, I mean it almost makes me laugh but, um, I'm like, what do you call it, I tend to have poor circulation a little

Full-time Worker (Man)   Oh, for women, it might be, a little rough, yeah for sure, or like men and women have different sensitivity to that kind of thing which is a point of conflict, I think, so for women, it might be rough

Full-time Worker (Woman)   Yes, or like, it's the poor circulation, really, not that I'm a woman but, you know?

Full-time Worker (Man)   Yes

Full-time Worker (Woman)   Or like? But yes, yes, I am aware of that, I'm conscious of it though I don't know

Full-time Worker (Man)   Women, yeah, I feel sorry for them, yeah,

(THE END, *Air Conditioner*)

Subtitles: 'Part 3: The Farewell Speech'

Full-time Worker (Man)   Now then everyone, shall we begin? (*Everybody gathers around*) Now, Erika, if you could please stand here. Now then, today, Erika will be, as of today, graduating from here, and it's been about two years, since we've had you working, well, very hard for us, but unfortunately, today is really, well, thank you so much for your

hard work, and so, if you could say some final words, I thought I'd like
to ask Erika to speak, so Erika, just a few simple, parting words.

Erika   Um, up until today, it's been about two years, as it was said
before, but to be specific, it's been less than two years, just short of two
years that I've been here and it was really, I can say, a little less than two
years is, when you look back on it, it seems like a long time or a short
time, kind of, but anyway I feel that a little less than two years was
really, I think quite an accomplishment, now, and I really think this office
is a lovely workplace, and everyone here is very, I can say, really, well,
good people and, I guess, to be able to have spent this time surrounded
by such people has been a very, I can say, happy thing for me, I think,
something I feel very grateful for, I think, and perhaps I may never be
this happy again in my life, from here on out, I thought, and I may have
to face a tomorrow like that, I think like this sometimes, and sometimes
not, but anyway, either way, it's like this, today it's sunny outside, there's
a heat wave, it has been scorching since morning, and the cicadas were
crying really loud since morning, and this morning, as always, I had my
alarm clock set to go to work, and when the alarm went off, I woke up
but, by then, the cicadas were already in full force, crying, like at six in
the morning, they're early risers, aren't they, the cicadas, they come
above ground and die in a week, but I wonder how bright it needs to get
for the cicadas to decide to start crying, the dead cicadas cover the
ground these days, it's that time of the season, now, for the cicadas, and
this morning I, was getting dressed for work as always, getting ready
with one thing at a time, and I was pretty much finished, and well, I also
did my make-up, and today, I was trying to do my make-up without any
special feeling, just like normal, just normal, that was my mantra, so I
did but, I think it was normal but, yes, so then, oh, it was about time to
go, so I headed out, and in the foyer, I did take the time to polish my
shoes, but, so then, after that, I was ready to go as soon as I put on
my shoes, so I put on my shoes in the foyer, and started to leave, and
these shoes, they're black and innocuous, they're very ordinary, well,
pumps but, these shoes have lasted a pretty long time, I'd bought them
when I was twenty-three I think, so then, I still wear them, and they've
lasted a pretty long time I think, and I've become attached to them,
before I realized it, even though they are totally ordinary, viewed from
the outside, just ordinary black pumps, right, but for me, they're more
than that, for example, sometimes they remind me of two penguins, when
I look at them like this, so I, sometimes I like pretend I'm a penguin
calling out, when I'm bored, like I pretend to run and slide on the ice,
or pretend like they are having a conversation with each other, the two

guys, I mean, these two birds, penguins, talking to each other, this one is the boy and this one's the girl, and the two of them are just around that age, sitting side by side, like this, and then, at first they seemed to be half like fighting, he was like 'hey man, quit following me' but then before we knew it, they had become friends, and naturally fell in love, yes things like that happened, and then, amazingly, they produced an egg, I thought wow that was fast, she was just a little girl but now she's a mother, but animals mature faster that humans, and in comparison humans are . . . you know, so the little girl who was now a mother now had to keep her egg warm, and then there was a time I, to be honest, I was in the middle of work, but I couldn't move, and I was like, oh no, what if someone asks me to make copies, I'd have to explain this situation, I wonder if they'd understand, no, there's no way, and my heart was pounding, but in the end, nobody came to me with any tasks like that so, it all passed uneventfully, so, these are those shoes, the same shoes I put on this morning, and I opened the door, and it squeaked close, and I tried to leave the house, I mean the foyer of my apartment, and my place is on the fourth floor, and to explain how I usually get to the first floor, in my apartment building, there's an elevator, and when the elevator happens to be stopped on the fourth floor, I'll take it all the way down, but when it's not, I usually take the stairs down to the first floor, and when it happens to be stopped on the fourth floor, I feel as if it's stopped there for me, as if it's been waiting for me, so I feel obliged to take the elevator, even though I feel guilty towards the environment, I feel I shouldn't ignore good will so, I get on the elevator, and then so today, on my last day to go to work, I felt a bit emotional but, in the foyer, I had put on my shoes, and I was about to leave, and so I opened the door, and then, this really crazy thing happened, and the crazy thing was, when I opened the door, right at my doorstep, there was this cicada just lying there, that was clearly on the verge of death, and it seemed to have no ability to move at all, completely debilitated, but, it could somehow still cry, and it was crying 'Meee~n, meee~n,' it was crying pretty loudly, as if it didn't know when to give up, and cicadas, when they're crying so close to you, their cries are like so deafening, they echo in your ear, they like vibrate inside the ears, so that's how it was, an intense vibration in the ear like an electric shock, so then, I thought like, whoah, now, when the first thing I saw when I opened the door was this cicada, I then realized like, oh, a cicada, but at that very moment I was already moving to get out of the apartment, so I had already lifted one leg to take a step forward like this, towards the outside world, the very first step of the day, that's the position my body was in, the first step on my last day to work, with this leg, so then, my raised leg was, no matter how you looked at it,

aiming precisely for the very same spot that this cicada was, that was
dying, and crying, with its belly facing up, and oh, if I kept on this
trajectory, I will squish it for sure, I thought, and I totally panicked, but,
I had already shifted my weight into my foot that was coming down to
the ground, so, really, there was nothing I could do, but you see, when
I think back on it, to tell you the truth, I had a vague sense, around the
moment I started to put on my shoes, I could hear one cicada's cries from
very closeby, even before I opened the door, so I absent-mindedly
thought in the back of my mind that perhaps there was a cicada in the
apartment corridor right outside the door, but, I also wasn't paying that
much attention to it, so you see, I thought then, if only I had really tuned
into my instincts when I heard the cicada, I thought I might have been
able to intuit that there might be a cicada right on my doorstep when I
opened my door, and I should try not to step on it if it's there, I should
have prepared myself, I thought, and then, when you step on something,
there's this like squishy sensation you know, and there was thought that
flashed through my mind that I could have avoided this outcome, but in
that moment it was already too late, when the cicada's belly, you know
how it's round and plump, I'd stepped on that, wouldn't you feel like,
ew! Cockroaches on the other hand have pretty flat bodies, so when you
step on them, it doesn't make leave of an impression, but a cicada's belly,
the way it's plump, there's this squish, and the heel portion of my shoe
sank into it, and made it explode, or implode, as it were, and this really
got me down, first thing this morning, it was that kind of day, gosh, first
thing in the morning, it's over for me, it's a bad luck day, and I thought
I'd ride the elevator down, and because I was going to the first floor I
pressed 1 and I pressed 'door close', and the elevator doors started
closing, very slowly, but then I suddenly realized something, and I
quickly pressed 'door open' and got off the elevator, and what happened
was, I had just left the cicada's carcass out there on my door step, but
today, since it was my last day at work in this office, and I didn't want to
come home at the end of the day, I mean who knows what kind of mental
state I'd be in, I mean not that I'd be so depressed or anything, I mean I
don't think this is something to get depressed over, but realistically, you
just don't know until you get there right, it's like, I'm thinking I'm fine
with finishing up my job here and having nothing planned next, but even
if I think that, there is a chance that it could just be some defense
mechanism, so that is why, I was imagining the worst case scenario, if I
came home tonight in a daze, and saw that dead cicada, it might be really
bad, I thought, that's why I thought I should clean it up before I left in
the morning, in order to protect my future self, I should clean it up,
because it's not like someone else was going to clean it up for me, so

that's why I went back, so then, I couldn't just grab it with my bare hands, so I thought I'd use some disposable chopsticks to grab it and just toss it over the railing in the hallway, but then, as I returned to my apartment, something unexpected was awaiting me, I don't know if any of you have experienced this as well, but there are a lot of stray cats in my neighborhood, and one of these cats, during the less than one minute it had taken for me to leave the house, get into the elevator, and come right back out and return, this cat appeared from nowhere and came to my doorstep, and had started eating the cicada, well the wings had been torn off and cast aside, but, so maybe it wasn't eating it exactly, it may have just been toying with it, but, to me it seemed like the cat was eating it, I think it was probably eating it, and I saw it and thought gross, but then there was a part of me that was like oh, I guess that saved me some trouble, to be honest, I didn't have to squat down and try to handle the cicada, so that's why, in a sense, I didn't want the cat just to play with it, I wanted it to eat the cicada too, because if it was just playing, its scattered remains would probably be left at my doorstep, so I wanted the cat to eat it, every inch of the cicada, so then I was like, all right kitty, I'm counting on you! And then, oh, Mr Kitty, oh, because when I looked at the cat, he had his parts (*testicles*) so, I left the remains to the cat and I came here to the office, so that's how everything resolved, all's well that ends well, as they say, so after that episode, I just headed straight to work this morning, yes, so this is the end, but really, I want to thank each and every one of you, I really ought to have come by your desks one at a time to express my gratitude but, well, that would also be, you know, but so I'd like to thank one person in particular, yes, just one person, and that is, Komatsu, who, like me, at lunch time always brought her own lunch to work everyday and I would always run into her when we would wash our lunch boxes in the kitchen, and when we ran out of dish detergent once, she said that she would notify the general manager Ishihashi, but you know there's always a little bit of residual detergent on the sponge, and it would probably be enough detergent to wash out at least one lunch box, so Komatsu offered me the last bit of detergent to use while she went to get more detergent from Ishihashi and I thought Komatsu was a really good person, I never forgot that, so Komatsu, thank you so much, I think, but here, also I have to point out Ishihashi, who had given me permission to use the detergent, to me who was just a temp, without any hesitation, to give me that permission without any reservation, I really have to thank Ishihashi the general manager, whom I guess isn't here but, it was a coconut-based fragrance free detergent that she let me use, really, thank you very much. . . . Um, that's all, thank you for everything, yes.

Applause

Temp 3 This is from all of us.

Erika Wow, Komatsu, thank you so much.

Temp 3 It's a set of bath salts, an assortment of different scents, I hope you find them healing, Erika, and best of luck to you, sooner or later we will no doubt be following your footsteps so.

Erika Wow, thank you so much.

Applause

THE END

Notes

1   Information about Okada and chelfitsch in English can be found at the
    company's website: http://www.chelfitsch.net/en/index.html.
2   Anne Erbe, 'Translating Indirection: An Interview with Aya Ogawa', *Theatre*,
    Vol. 43, No. 1 (2013), p.99.
3   An English translation of this play is available. Okada Toskihi, *The Sonic
    Life of a Giant Tortoise*, trans. Aya Ogawa, *Theatre*, Vol. 43, No. 1 (2013),
    pp.109–25.
4   Kee-Yoon Nahm, 'Selfless Acts', *Theatre*, Vol. 43, No. 1 (2013), p.127.

Sunrise

Cao Yu
Translated Originally by A. C. Barnes
Retranslated by Amy Dooling

Cao Yu (1910–96) was the most important playwright in modern Chinese theatre known as *huaju* (spoken drama). Born into a high-class family in the northern city of Tianjin, he was active in theatrical productions as a student at Nankai Middle School, one of the earliest huaju training grounds. Before graduation from Tsinghua University in Beijing, he published his first play *Thunderstorm* (*Leiyu*) in 1934. Generally considered a milestone that signalled huaju's maturity, it masterfully blends European dramatic themes and techniques such as the fate and unity of time, place and plot with some of the most urgent issues of modern China – feudal morality versus individual freedom, the old suffocating the young, the haves oppressing the have-nots, to name just a few. It was quickly followed by *Sunrise* (*Richu*, 1936), *The Savage Lang* (*Yuanye*, sometimes translated as *The Wilderness*, 1937) and *Peking Man* (*Beijing ren*, 1941), all of which remain frequently staged and widely studied as best representatives of modern Chinese drama. After 1949, Cao Yu held various leading positions, including artistic director of Beijing People's Theatre, China's best huaju theatre, and president of All-China Dramatic Workers' Association. However, like many writers of his generation, he failed to produce any significant work during this period.

Published in 1936 and premiered in Shanghai the following year, *Sunrise* portrays a kaleidoscope of characters around Chen Bailu, an educated courtesan who is the centre of nightlife in a big hotel. She is supported by a bank manager Pan Yueting and surrounded by other high-society figures, such as a foreign-educated bureaucrat, who readily spouts English words and divorces his wife in pursuit of younger prizes, and a rich widow in pursuit of a young gigolo. We also meet Chen's former friend Fang Dasheng who attempts to lead Chen away from her decadent life and a young girl whom Chen attempts to rescue from the claws of local gangsters. Completing this societal portraiture are Pan's secretary who makes desperate gambles in an effort to climb up the social ladder, a fired clerk in Pan's bank being kicked off that ladder, a prostitute with a compassionate heart and low-life characters such as the hotel steward and gangsters. Compared with *Thunderstorm*'s tight plot, *Sunrise*'s concentric structure centred around Chen provides the reader and audience with panoramic insight into the different strata of life in modern China.

Cao Yu wrote the play when he was teaching in a women's college in Tianjin, China's second largest port city and the economic and financial centre of the north known for its multinational concessions. While he was familiar with decadent lives of the high society, Cao Yu prepared for the play by closely studying life in the brothels, talking to prostitutes and observing their despondent surroundings. His anguish is evident in the play's epigraphs from the Chinese classic *Dao De Jing* by Laozi and

The Bible, especially the first quotation that denounces the way of human beings as 'tak[ing] away from those who do not have enough /In order to give more to those who already have too much.' It is significant that all four acts of the play take place at night, with the ending right before dawn when the heroine is reading the lines from a novel titled *Sunrise*: 'The sun rises, leaving the darkness behind. But the sun is not ours, for we now sleep.' However, the play is not without hope, as dazzling sunlight floods the room as the curtain slowly falls and Fang Dasheng, who is based on one of Cao Yu's writer friends, walks out of the hotel accompanied by the chorus of labourers laying the foundation of a nearby building.

Sunrise

[*Richu*, 1936]

The way of *Tian* is like archers drawing their bows.
To hit something high in the air, they pull the string downward;
To hit something lower, they pull the string upward.
When they have drawn the string too far back, they let some go,
And when they have not drawn far enough, they pull harder.
The way of *Tian* is also to let some go where there is excess
And to augment where there is not enough.
The way of human beings on the other hand is not like this at all.
It is instead to take away from those who do not have enough
In order to give more to those who already have too much.

Lao Zi, Dao De Jing, Chapter 77[1]

. . . God gave them up to a debased mind and to things that should
not be done. They were filled with every kind of wickedness,
evil, covetousness, malice. Full of envy, murder, strife, deceit,
craftiness . . . those that practice such things deserve to die – yet
they not only do them but even applaud others who practice them.

New Testament, Romans, Chapter 1[2]

My anguish, my anguish! I writhe in pain.
Oh, the walls of my heart!
My heart is beating wildly,
I cannot keep silent,
for I hear the sound of a trumpet,
the alarm of war.
Disaster overtakes disaster,
the whole land is laid waste . . .
I looked on the earth, and lo, it was
waste and void,
and to the heavens, and they had no light.
I looked on the mountains, and lo,
they were quaking,
and all the hills moved to and fro.
I looked, and lo, there was no one at all,

and all the birds of the air had fled.
I looked, and lo, the fruitful land was desert,
and all its cities were laid in ruins

> Old Testament, Jeremiah, Chapter 4[3]

Beloved . . . keep away from believers who are living in idleness
and not according to the tradition that they received from us. For
you yourselves know how you ought to imitate us; we were not
idle when we were with you, and we did not eat anyone's bread
without paying for it; but with toil and labor we worked night
and day. . . . For even when we were with you, we gave you this
command: Anyone unwilling to work should not eat.

> New Testament, Thessalonians, Chapter 3[4]

Now I appeal to you brothers . . . that all of you be in agreement
and that there be no divisions among you, but that you be united in
the same mind and the same purpose.

> New Testament, Corinthians, Chapter 1[5]

'. . . I am the light of the world. Whoever follows me will never
walk in darkness but will have the light of life. . . .'

> Gospel according to John, Chapter 8[6]

'I am the resurrection and the life. Those who believe in me, even
though they die, will live . . .'

> Gospel According to John, Chapter 11[7]

. . . Then I saw a new heaven and a new earth, for the first heaven
and the first earth had passed away . . .

> Revelation, Chapter 21[8]

Characters:

CHEN BAILU: A woman living at the X Hotel, twenty-three years old
FANG DASHENG: A former 'friend' of Chen Bailu's, twenty-five years old
ZHANG QIAOZHI: A foreign educated man, thirty-one years old
WANG FUSHENG: A hotel steward
PAN YUETING: Manager of Dafeng Bank, fifty-four years old
MADAME GU: A rich widow, fourty-four years old
LI SHIQING: Secretary at Dafeng Bank, fourty-two years old
MRS. LI: His wife, thirty-four years old

HUANG XINGSAN: A petty clerk at the bank

BLACK SAN: A local gangster

HU SI: An idle gigolo, twenty-seven years old

PIPSQUEAK: A young girl who has newly arrived in the city, fifteen or sixteen years old

(Additional characters appear in ACT III)

Setting:

ACT I   The opulent sitting room of X Hotel; 5:00 a.m. one early spring morning
ACT II   Same as Act I; 5:00 p.m. the same day
ACT III   A low-end brothel; a week later, 11:30 p.m.
ACT IV   Same as Act I; some time after 4:00 a.m. that morning

ACT I

The opulent sitting room of a suite in the X Hotel. The main entrance upstage center opens on to the hotel corridor; on stage right a door leads to the bedroom; on stage left another leads to the parlor. At the back, towards the right-hand corner, is an oblong window which looks out onto high rise buildings that block out the sunlight and keep the interior enshrouded in darkness even in the daytime. Except in the early morning when a few rays of sunshine stream in, not a glimmer of natural light is visible all day long.

The room's irregularly shaped, modernist furniture is rigid and superficial in a way that arouses curiosity but provides little in the way of comfort. In the middle of the room is a small tobacco stand, around which are placed an eclectic assortment of stools – square, round, cube-shaped, and conical ones – and a sofa with randomly colored cushions. Against the window is a curved settee. On the left are a dresser, a sideboard, and a small cosmetic table with women's makeup on it. The walls are hung with a number of risqué pictures of nude women, a calendar poster, and a copy of the hotel regulations. The floor is littered with newspapers, illustrated magazines, wine bottles and cigarette butts. Various articles of feminine attire – hats, scarves, gloves and the like – lie strewn about over the sofa and dresser, among them the occasional male garment. The sideboard is cluttered with liquor bottles, glassware, thermos bottles, and teacups. In the right-hand corner stands a reading lamp, and beside it a small round curio stand with glass shelves displaying ashtrays and trinkets of the sort women find appealing, including a European-style doll and a Mickey Mouse figurine.

In the center of the back wall is a shiny silver clock which reads five-thirty, the time when night is drawing to a close. When the curtain rises it's dark except for a pool of light emanating from the reading lamp by the sofa. The yellow drapes have been drawn, so the décor of the room is not yet clearly discernible, its ugliness and disorder still concealed in the dark.

Slow footsteps approach along the corridor. The main door creaks open halfway and a shapely arm reaches in to switch on the light, instantly illuminating the room. Enter Chen Bailu, dressed in a sheer, colorful evening gown; its many layers and the two long pink ribbons attached to it flowing behind her like a wispy cloud. She wears a red flower in her jet-black hair, which has been permed into cute ringlets that dangle around her ears. Her eyes are bright and attractive; her movements delicate and alert. An aloof smile is always on her lips. But every now and then her expression betrays signs of weariness and dissatisfaction; such ennui is characteristic of unattached women like herself. She loves – but also hates – life. To her, life is but a chain of artificial conventions, and she no longer thinks about the caress of real emotions. Her years of aimless drifting have taught that there's no such thing as the true love of girlish dreams. Life is a steely reality, inherently cruel. She has come to realize that the things in life to which she has grown accustomed are the cruelest shackles of them all and, however much she may admire freedom or long to sacrifice herself for the sake of love (as is so often glamorized in novels and the movies), these shackles will forever prevent her from escaping the clutches of her environment. She tried escaping: once, as a naïve and foolish girl, full of kaleidoscopic wonder and excitement, she flew from this cage with a man who seemed to have stepped out of a work of art. But in the end, like the proverbial bird in the gilded cage that has lost the ability and desire to fly freely, she returned to the sordid confines of her former life, albeit with great reluctance. Of course, she won't be content living like this forever; she has her pride and dreads insult. But all she can do is wait, wait for the day happiness comes knocking at her door, leaving her an unexpected fortune that will enable an independent life. Perhaps the knock she awaits will sound in the middle of the night, and she will open the door to discover a visitor, dressed in black, who comes in without a word. And she will leave with him without a second thought; after all, she knows that unexpected bliss is a rarity, whereas mediocrity, suffering, and death are an inescapable part of life.

She now moves with tired, heavy steps to the center of the stage. She yawns, covering her mouth with her right hand.

Chen Bailu (*Looking back towards the door after a few steps*) Come on in! (*She tosses her purse down and leans back on the sofa in the middle of the room. Frowning, she slips off her silver high heels and gently massages her slender feet with visible relief. Now that she is home she can finally relax on the soft sofa.* 'Hey.' *Suddenly she realizes that the person behind her has not followed her in. Slipping her shoes back on, she jumps up and turns around with one knee still resting on the sofa and smiles towards the door.*) Hey, why won't you come in? (*Now, someone in his late twenties does enter –* **Fang Dasheng**. *Wearing a shabby old Western-style coat, he is frowning disagreeably. Peering in on the cluttered state of the room, he stands in the doorway without uttering a word, though whether from fatigue or repulsion is not clear. But* **Bailu** *misinterprets his hesitation and as she stares intently at him she thinks she detects a look of alarm and suspicion.*)

Bailu Do come in. What are you scared of?

Fang Dasheng (*Calmly*) Nothing. (*Suddenly uneasy*) There's no one else here, is there?

Bailu (*Looking around, teasing him*) Maybe there is. (*Looking at him*) No, probably not.

Dasheng (*With disgust*) I can't stand it. There are people everywhere in this place.

Bailu (*Trying to rattle him, but no doubt also because his attitude annoys her*) Anyway, what if someone were here? You couldn't very well live someplace like this if you detest people!

Dasheng (*Looking over at her, then looking all around*) So this is where you've been living all these years.

Bailu (*Challengingly*) What are you implying, is there something wrong with it?

Dasheng (*Slowly*) Um – (*Feeling that he has no alternative*) no, no, it's alright.

Bailu (*Smiling at his bewilderment*) Why haven't you taken off your coat?

Dasheng (*Suddenly collecting himself*) Oh, er, – my coat? (*Searching for a suitable reply*) Indeed, I haven't.

Bailu (*Amused by his manner*) Precisely. What I mean is, why are you being so polite that you won't even take your coat off without first being asked?

Dasheng (*Unable to find an explanation to offer, somewhat embarrassed*)   Er – perhaps it is because I am not used to taking my coat off the minute I walk in the door. Don't you find it a bit chilly in here?

Bailu   Chilly? It feels pretty warm to me.

Dasheng (*Seeking to deflect attention from himself*)   Perhaps you didn't close the window all the way?

Bailu (*Shaking her head*)   Impossible. (*She goes over and pulls back the curtains to reveal the window with its streamlined frame.*) See, shut tight. (*With sudden delight as she looks out of the window*) Hey, look! Come look!

Dasheng (*Hurries over, not knowing what she means*)   What is it?

Bailu (*Drawing her finger across the glass*)   Look, frost! Frost! Strange having frost when spring's already here.

Dasheng (*Disappointed*)   Oh, frost! You really. . . . (*Naturally what he wants to say next is that she's a bit flighty, but he doesn't and instead just shakes his head*)

Bailu (*With curiosity*)   Why, spring's here yet there's still frost.

Dasheng (*Giving up*)   Yes, very strange.

Bailu (*Elatedly*)   I adore frost! Remember how I liked it when I was little? Isn't it so beautiful, so lovely! (*Pointing suddenly, like a child*) Look, look at that, it's me, isn't it?

Dasheng   Eh? (*Craning forward*) Who?

Bailu (*Pointing excitedly at the window*)   I mean the frost on the window, this here. (*To her annoyance, he looks at the wrong spot.*) No, over here. Look, isn't that a pair of eyes? This poking out is a nose, and the mouth goes in right here, and this patch here is the hair. (*Clapping her hands*) Look at the hair, isn't it just like mine?

Dasheng (*Makes an effort to make a comparison and find the likeness, but –*)   Let me see (*candidly*). No, not really.

Bailu (*Surprised*)   What did you say? (*Like a petulant spoiled child*) It does too. It does. If I say so, it does.

Dasheng (*Obediently*)   It does look like you. A perfect resemblance.

Bailu (*With pride*)   Aha, so you admit it. (*Finding new territory*). And look here. This head looks just like you.

Dasheng (*Points at himself*)   Like me?

Bailu (*Surprised by the question*)   But of course. This here.

Dasheng (*Like a blind man*)   Where?

Bailu   This part, right here.

Dasheng (*After looking for a while, he feels his face, and clearly does not see any resemblance.*)   I, I just don't see it.

Bailu (*Disappointed*)   You! You're impossible.

Dasheng   Am I? (*With a sudden smile*) I've been observing you all night long but just now was the first time you've seemed like your old self.

Bailu   What do you mean?

Dasheng (*An expression of happiness spreads over his face.*)   You're still the girl you used to be.

Bailu (*Her high spirits of a moment ago suddenly pass away like a breath of wind. She sighs and says, as if broken by age.*)   Was there once a time when I was like that, Dasheng? Was I really a happy girl once?

Dasheng (*Understanding her state of mind, encouragingly*)   If only you'd come away with me, you could be as happy and free as before.

Bailu (*Shaking her head, in the voice of someone who has long experienced the hard knocks of life*)   Humph, where is there any freedom?

Dasheng   You – (*He looks at her and thinks better of it. He paces back and forth at times, then stops and looks around.*)

Bailu (*Having recovered her customary air of detachment*)   What are you looking at now?

Dasheng (*With a brief smile*)   This place you've got here, it's, it's (*pointing around, at a loss for words, then suddenly fixing on an innocuous term that would also conceal what he really feels*) quite nice.

Bailu (*Detecting his insincerity*)   Nice, eh? (*She casually picks up a cushion that is lying at her feet and drops it on the sofa, at the same time kicking an empty wine bottle underneath the sofa. She says nonchalantly*): It suffices. (*She yawns involuntarily, which in turn seems to cause **Dasheng** to yawn as well. She smiles at him. The man, like a kid who's been crying, rubs his eyes with the back of his hands.*) Tired?

Dasheng   I'm alright.

Bailu   Do you want to go to bed?

Dasheng   No, I'm all right. I was sitting down the whole time you were dancing.

Bailu   Why didn't you join in the fun?

Dasheng (*Coolly*)   I told you: I don't dance, nor am I one for all that crazy leaping about.

Bailu (*With a somewhat forced laugh*)   Crazy indeed. That's my life, crazy day in, day out! (*The crowing of a rooster can be heard in the distance.*) There's a rooster crowing already.

Dasheng   How odd, hearing a rooster in a place like this.

Bailu   There's a market nearby. (*Glancing at her watch and suddenly looks up again*) Guess the time.

Dasheng (*Concentrating with an effort*)   Must be about five thirty, it'll be light out soon. I checked my watch every five minutes at that dance hall.

Bailu (*Mockingly*)   You *must* have been in quite a state!

Dasheng (*Frankly*)   You know I've been living in the countryside for a quite a while now; I haven't much patience for such noisy, crowded places.

Bailu (*Fixing her hair*)   And now?

Dasheng (*Sighing*)   Naturally I'm feeling more relaxed. Now that we're alone I was thinking I could have a word with you.

Bailu   Yes, but (*Yawning again, her hand over her mouth*) it's almost morning. (*Abruptly*) Why don't you sit down?

Dasheng (*Formally*)   You – you haven't sat down yet.

Bailu (*Laughing and showing her straight white teeth*)   You *are* old-fashioned. None of my other friends ever wait for permission to take a seat (*going over to him and gently pushing him on to an armchair*) Sit down. (*Turning and going over to the sideboard*) I'm dying of thirst, please excuse me for a moment while I get a drink of water. (*Pouring a glass of water and picking up a cigarette box*) Cigarette?

Dasheng (*Staring at her*)   I told you already, I don't smoke.

Bailu (*Good-humoredly mocking him*)   Pity. You *are* a paragon of virtue! (*She deftly lights a cigarette and leisurely exhales a plume of pale-blue smoke.*)

Dasheng (*As he watches her skillfully blow a smoke ring, a sudden sigh escapes his lips and he says sadly and sympathetically*)   I never imagined, Zhujun, that you'd have changed so –

Bailu (*Putting down her cigarette*)   Hang on, what did you call me?

Dasheng (*Taken aback*)   Don't you like hearing your own name?

Bailu (*Nostalgically*)   Zhujun, Zhujun, it's been ages since anyone called me that. Oh Dasheng, do say it again.

Dasheng (*Moved*)   What's the matter, Zhujun?

Bailu (*Pondering the tenderness of having the man say her name*)   It's so sweet, yet so bitter. Say it once more.

Dasheng (*Confused*)   Oh Zhujun, if only you knew how I felt. (*Suddenly*) Are you sure no one else is here?

Bailu   Yes, of course.

Dasheng (*With sorrow*)   It's just when I see you like this, when you don't know how I feel about. . . . (*He stops as a man emerges unsteadily from the bedroom on the right; he is in evening wear with his stiff collar askew. As he staggers forward one of his sleeves, which is hanging loose, swings back and forth.* **Bailu** *and* **Dasheng** *turn around at the same time to find their visitor standing quite unabashed in the doorway with one hand raised to support himself against the doorframe, his face flushed and his hair disheveled. Perched on the end of his nose is a pair of platinum spectacles and he shows the whites of his eyes as he stares over the top of them, hiccupping.*)

The visitor (*In a low, mysterious voice*)   Sh! (*He adjusts his spectacles and points with an erratically moving finger.*)

Bailu (*With great surprise*)   Georgy![9]

Georgy (*Waving his hand, even more mysteriously*)   Sh! (*Of course they stop talking, whereupon he reels across to* **Dasheng** *and says in a low voice*): What did you say? (*Pointing a finger at him*) What was all that about? (*Turning to* **Bailu** *with familiarity*) Who's this, Bailu?

Dasheng (*Displeased but not knowing quite what to do*)   Who's this, Zhujun? Who is this man?

Georgy (*As if to himself*)   Zhujun? (*To* **Dasheng**) You must be mistaken: her name is Bailu. She's our idol here, the queen of them all, the girl I – the girl I most adore!

Bailu (*Exasperated*)   You're drunk!

Georgy (*Pointing to himself*)   Me! (*Shaking his head*) I'm not drunk! (*Pointing unsteadily at* **Bailu**) You're the one who's drunk! (*Pointing at* **Dasheng**) And you! (*As* **Dasheng** *turns away from* **Bailu** *to look at him, his face shows even greater contempt, but their visitor is now directing his remarks at him alone.*) Just look at you, staring blankly in a drunken stupor! Pah! (*Dismissively makes a shooing motion with the snowy white palms of his hands, a gesture of which he is immensely proud and then hiccups again*) I, I can barely stand to look at you.

Bailu (*Now she's the one who can't stand the sight of him.*)   What are you doing here, anyway?

Dasheng (*Emboldened*)   Yes, what *are* you doing here? (*He stares at* **Georgy** *with an inquisitive look.*)

Georgy (*His mind befuddled by alcohol*)   I – er – I was tired, I wanted to sleep. (*As a point suddenly occurs to him*) But wait, what are the two of you doing here?

Bailu (*Glaring at him in irritation*)   I live here, so naturally I am here!

Georgy (*Dubiously*)   You live here? (*In the naughty tone of an incredulous child. First high, then low*) No!

Bailu (*With increasing annoyance*)   And what were you doing in my bedroom?

Georgy What! (*Even more incredulous*) Me in your bedroom? You're mistaken, I wasn't (*Shaking his head*), I wasn't. (*Rubbing his forehead*) But let me have a think . . . (*He gazes up as if mulling it over.*)

Bailu (*Looking over at* **Dasheng** *as if she does not know whether to laugh or cry*)   He wants to think about it!

Georgy (*Waving his hand at them as if telling them to quiet down*) Hold on, give me time, don't rush me. Now, let me figure this out, slowly, slowly. (*He now searches his memory, trying to recall how he walked into the hotel, how he strode through her door and caught sight of that comfortable bed of hers, how he stumbled around, got undressed and plopped down into that soft nest. His lips move as if muttering to himself, while making various gestures as he recollects what just transpired. After some time, he finally says in a low voice*) And then I had a drink and everything was spinning and afterwards I had another drink and everything kept spinning . . . and after that (*Pauses, trying to remember*). . . . I took the elevator . . . (*delightedly, tapping on his* *forehead*) then I came in here, undressed, and got into bed and I was lying there on my back and then I felt nauseous and I– ugh! – (*hits his head with his hand and resuming his normal voice*) yes, that's what happened. And so I couldn't have come out of your bedroom!

Bailu (*Sternly*)   Georgy, you've completely lost your mind tonight.

Georgy (*His forefinger on his lips, like a Hollywood movie star*)   Sh! (*Whispering*). I'm telling you, don't worry, I have not lost my mind, I fell asleep on your bed, I had a bit too much to drink, and I seem to have . . . (*Loudly*) Oh, damn it, I'm going to be sick again. (*Covers his mouth*) Pardon me, Mademoiselle. . . . Please forgive me, miss! My apologies, sir. Pardon, Monsieur. (*As he leaps up he turns and raises his hands, as a famous actor might as he faces his adoring fans, and as his final gesture waves and takes a bow.*) Goodbye, all. Good night! Good night! My lady and gentleman! Oh goodbye, au revoir, Madame, et Monsieur, I – I shall – I shall (*There is a sound of retching as he hurriedly covers his mouth and stumbles out of the room.* **Bailu** *glances at* **Dasheng** *then sits down resignedly.*)

Dasheng (*With disgust*)   What was that?

Bailu (*Sighing*)   Our crème de la crème, entertaining, wouldn't you say?

Dasheng   Entertaining?! Appalling. I don't understand why you mix with this lot. Who is he, and why does he know you so well?

Bailu (*Her cigarette between her fingers*)   You really want to know? Around here he's the best of the best. He studied abroad and earned a Doctorate or Masters or something or other, or so he says. His European name is George and he goes by George Chang when he's overseas and when he's in China he goes by Zhang Qiaozhi. Supposedly he's held several administrative posts since returning from oversees, and made himself a small fortune.

Dasheng (*Approaches her*)   But why are you acquainted with such trash? Can't you see he's an idiot?

Bailu (*Tapping the ash from her cigarette*)   Didn't I just tell you? He's loaded.

Dasheng   You mean, just because he's got money you. . . .

Bailu (*Bluntly spelling it out for him*)   He has money therefore I'm friends with him. When I worked at the dance hall he pursued me for a long time.

Dasheng (*Realizing that the woman in front of him is no longer the same person he once knew*)   No wonder he treats you that way, then. (*He lowers his head.*)

Bailu   You really are a country boy – so serious about everything. Wait till you've been around a few days and you'll realize this is life. Everyone's this way, you needn't be so uptight about everything. Well, now, there's nobody else here, so what was it you were saying?

Dasheng (*Coming out of a reverie*)   What was I saying to you?

Bailu   Fine memory you've got. (*Brightly*) You were telling me about your feelings, were you not? And then our Mr Zhang Qiaozhi showed up.

Dasheng (*Sighing*)   Yes, 'my feelings.' I'm the sort of person, you see, who always lives by his heart. But Zhujun (*Earnestly*), when I see you this way, you cannot imagine how my heart – (*He stops as the door creaks open.*) Mr Zhang again, I suppose.

(*Their visitor is **Wang Fusheng**, a hotel steward, with a crafty demeanor and fawning manner.*)

Fusheng   No, it's not Mr Zhang, it's me. (*With an ingratiating smile*) You're back early, Miss Chen.

Bailu   Did you want to see me about something?

Fusheng   You saw Mr Zhang just now.

Bailu   Well, what about it?

Fusheng   I escorted him to another room and put him to bed.

Bailu (*Annoyed*)   He is free to go wherever he pleases. Why tell me?

Fusheng   I know, but Mr Zhang says he's terribly sorry about getting drunk and barging into your suite and throwing up all over your bed, and –

Bailu   What! He threw up on my bed?

Fusheng   Yes, but don't worry, Miss Chen, I'll tidy it all up for you right away. (**Bailu** *gets up but he bars the way.*) I'd rather you didn't go in there yourself; it'll only upset you to see it.

Bailu   Oh, the brute, he – fine, then, you see to it.

Fusheng   Yes. (*Pausing and turning as he moves away*) You've had quite a few visitors, but you've been out all evening. There's been Fifth Master Li, and Section Chief Fang, and Fourth Master Liu. Mr Pan, the bank manager, stopped by three times. And then there was a phone call from Madame Gu inviting you over to her place tomorrow – er, today, that is – to spend the evening with them.

Bailu   I see. Ring her up later on and invite her here for the afternoon.

Fusheng   And Fourth Master Hu said he'd be stopping by to visit shortly.

Bailu   Tell him he can come if he wants to. Everyone's welcome here.

Fusheng   Then there was the newspaper editor, Mr Zhang –

Bailu   Yes, yes, tell him to come over today if he's free.

Fusheng   Oh yes, and Manager Pan stopped by three times tonight, and at the moment he's . . .

Bailu (*Impatiently*)   Yes, yes, you've said so once already.

Fusheng   But, Miss Chen, now that this gentleman here . . .

Bailu   Oh, that's all right, this gentleman's a cousin of mine.

Dasheng (*Puzzled*)   A cousin?

Bailu (*To* **Fusheng**)   He'll be staying here at the hotel.

Dasheng   No, Zhujun, I won't, I'll be going soon.

Bailu   Very well, then (*Irritated by his sudden obtuseness*), suit yourself. (*To* **Fusheng**) That's all then. Now go get my bed cleaned up. (**Fusheng** *goes into the bedroom.*)

Dasheng   Zhujun, I never imagined you'd become so . . .

Bailu (*Sharply*)   So what?

Dasheng (*Intimidated by her manner*)   E – er – so hospitable, so easy going.

Bailu   Haven't I always been easy going?

Dasheng (*Unwilling to be candid*)   Oh, I, I didn't mean it like that. . . . I mean, you seem much more open-minded than you used to –

Bailu (*Swiftly*)   It's not like I was ever close-minded! Oh, come off it! You needn't beat around the bush. I know what you're thinking: I'm rather too happy-go-lucky, too nonchalant. I'd bet you even think I'm quite depraved, don't you?

Dasheng (*Evasive*)   I. . . . I . . . naturally. . . . I

Bailu (*Presses further*)   Be honest, don't you?

Dasheng (*With a sudden burst of courage*)   Er – yes. You have changed. You're just not the girl I once knew. The way you talk, the way you walk, your whole manner, everything about you, in fact, has changed. I watched you all night long at the dance hall. You're not the innocent girl you once were, you're different. And I'm disappointed, totally disappointed.

Bailu (*Feigning surprise*)   Disappointed?

Dasheng (*Miserably*)   Yes, disappointed. I never expected to come here and find that you've turned into a woman of such loose morals.

Bailu (*Warning him*)   Are you preaching to me? You know I can't stand sermons.

Dasheng   I am not preaching. It's just I can't stand seeing you this way. I heard all sorts of rumors from afar but I didn't believe them. I couldn't believe that the girl I most liked would do anything to make people call her worthless. So I came to see you, and find you living in an establishment like this, an unmarried woman living all alone in a hotel, fraternizing with all sorts of lowlifes – this type of behavior is just – immoral, decadent – what did you expect me to say?

Bailu (*Standing up and putting on a show of being extremely angry*)   How dare you call me decadent to my face! How dare you say you're disappointed in me, in my own home! Who are you to me that you dare preach at *me* like this?

Dasheng (*Aware that he has offended her*)   Naturally there's nothing between us now.

Bailu (*Not letting up*)   Are you suggesting there ever was?

Dasheng (*Faltering*)   I – er – no, of course you can't say there was. (*Looking down*) Though you must remember that you once loved me. And besides, you must know why I'm here.

Bailu (*Stonily*)   No, I don't. Why?

Dasheng (*Pleadingly*)   I do wish you wouldn't act like this, feigning ignorance. You know perfectly well that it's because I want to take you back with me.

Bailu (*Wide-eyed*)   Take me back? Back where? You know perfectly well I've no family left to go back to.

Dasheng   No, no, I mean go back with me. I want you to, I want you to get married.

Bailu (*As if finally comprehending*)   Oh, I see, so the reason you showed up here yesterday is to play matchmaker, to marry me off (*In a tone of voice suggesting that she understands at last what it is all about*) A – a – ah!

Dasheng (*With embarrassment*)   I'm not matchmaking; I want you to marry me. That is, I will be your husband and you will be my –

Bailu   Enough, enough. No need to explain. Women understand what the words 'getting married' mean. But, old friend, why so sudden?

Dasheng (*Taking out train tickets*)   I've got the tickets right here. We can leave once the sun comes up and catch the ten o'clock train to get away from this place.

Bailu   Let me take a look. (*Taking the tickets*) So you really have bought two, a round trip and a one way – you even reserved sleepers, too! (*Smiling*) You think of everything.

Dasheng (*Nervously*)   So you accept, then. That's settled, then. (*picks up his hat*)

Bailu   No, wait a minute. I've got just one question for you.

Dasheng   What?

Bailu (*Unaffected*)   How much money do you have?

Dasheng (*Stunned*)   I don't understand what you mean.

Bailu   No? I mean can you afford to support me? (**Dasheng** *is too surprised to reply, since he has not been thinking in these terms.*) Now what? Don't look at me like that! You think I shouldn't speak like this? Come now. Surely you must understand I want someone who can keep me? Don't you get it? I want comfort. When I go out I'll want to go by car, and when I entertain I'll want nice things to wear, I'll want to have a good time, I'll want to go dancing. Do you understand?

Dasheng (*Coldly*)   Zhujun, you've forgotten who you really are.

Bailu   You ask who I am? Listen up: Background – Miss Chen from a learned family; Education – Aihua Girl's Academy, honor's student; Professional Career – a leading light in society, executive member of various charities and arts organizations; . . . Father deceased, family poor; film actress and cabaret dancer. What, with such a fine resumé, you think I don't know who I am?

Dasheng (*Disdainfully*)   You seem rather proud of yourself.

Bailu   And why not? I've made my own way in the world, without depending on family or friends, on my own to sink or swim. And here I am today, doing just fine, as you can see for yourself, so why shouldn't I be proud of myself?

Dasheng   But do you think there's any honor in making a living this way?

Bailu   I feel sorry for you, Dasheng, you really do live in an ivory tower. Do you think that the money of 'honorable people' is come by honorably, then? We've no shortage of such people here, as you'll see, a great variety of them, bankers, business men, civil servants, the lot. If you think their professions honorable, then the money I earn doing this is far more honorably come by than theirs.

Dasheng   I don't know what you mean, though perhaps our views of what is honorable . . .

Bailu   Yes, perhaps you and I differ in our opinions of honor. I never intentionally hurt anyone; I never snatch food from other people's mouths to put in my own bowl. I like money as much as they do and I make every effort to make money, but I make my money by sacrificing my most precious possession. I don't fleece people's money, I don't extort money by trickery; I live by the generosity of others, because I've sacrificed myself. I perform the most pitiable service a woman can render a man, and I enjoy the privileges that a woman deserves to enjoy!

Dasheng (*Looking into her shining eyes*)   Awful, awful – have you no shame, no scruples whatsoever? Don't you know that once your head is turned by a lust for money, the most precious thing in life – love – will fly away like a bird?

Bailu (*With a touch of sorrow*)   Love? (*Tapping the ash of her cigarette, in a leisurely voice*) What's love? (*She blows the word away into nothingness in a curling wisp of cigarette smoke.*) You're a child! I've nothing more to say to you.

Dasheng (*Undaunted*)   Now Zhujun, I can see that these past two years have practically destroyed you. But I'm here now; I see your lifestyle, and I can't bear to have you go on like this any longer. I'm determined to change your mind, I'm –

Bailu (*Unable to contain her laughter*)   What! You want to change my mind?

Dasheng   Fine, go ahead and laugh; I have no desire to keep arguing with you. I know you think I'm a fool, coming all this way to see you and then coming out with all this nonsense. But I will make one last foolish request.

I repeat, I hope you will marry me; please think it over carefully; I hope you'll have a satisfactory answer for me within the next twenty-four hours.

Bailu (*With a feigned look of alarm*)   Twenty-four hours? You frighten me. But suppose your deadline arrives and my answer is unsatisfactory, what then? Will you force me to marry you?

Dasheng   Well . . .

Bailu   Well what?

Dasheng   If you won't marry me –

Bailu   What'll you do?

Dasheng (*Miserably*)   I – I might commit suicide.

Bailu   What! (*Displeased*) Where did you pick that up?

Dasheng   No (*Feeling he is being rather too trendy in saying this*), no, I won't kill myself. Don't worry, I wouldn't kill myself over a woman; I'll go away, far, far away.

Bailu (*Putting down her cigarette*)   There now, now you sound like an adult. (*Standing up*) Well, my silly boy, you needn't wait your twenty-four hours.

Dasheng (*Stands up*)   What?

Bailu   You can have your answer right now.

Dasheng (*Flustered*)   Now? – No, wait. I am too confused. Don't say anything yet. I have to calm down.

Bailu (*Coolly*)   How about a glass of iced tea to settle down.

Dasheng   No, that's not necessary.

Bailu   Have a cigarette.

Dasheng (*Displeased*)   For the third time, I don't smoke (*feels his heart*). Ok, it's passed. Go ahead, tell me.

Bailu   You've calmed down?

Dasheng   (*With a trembling voice*). Yes.

Bailu   Well (*Handing him his hat*), you can go then.

Dasheng   What?

Bailu   Under no circumstance will I ever marry you.

Dasheng   W-why?

Bailu   There's no why! You really are a fool. One just can't find reasons for this sort of thing, surely you understand that?

Dasheng   Then you feel nothing for me?

Bailu   You could put it that way, I suppose. (**Dasheng** *tries to clasp her hand but she moves deftly to the wall.*)

Dasheng   What are you doing?

Bailu   I am ringing the buzzer.

Dasheng   What for?

Bailu   In case you really do want to kill yourself, I want a witness.

Dasheng (*Looking across at her and slumping listlessly onto the armchair*)   Do you really mean what you just said? You weren't just getting a bit carried away?

Bailu   Do I look like the sort of person who gets carried away by emotion after all this time?

Dasheng (*Standing up again*)   Zhujun! (*He picks up his hat.*)

Bailu   Now what are you doing now?

Dasheng   We must say goodbye now.

Bailu   Yes, goodbye. (*Taking his hand, with exaggerated sorrow*) So it's farewell for always, then.

Dasheng (*On the verge of tears*)   Yes, for always.

Bailu (*Sees him to the door*)   You're actually leaving?

Dasheng (*Like a child*)   Yes.

Bailu   You must have forgotten your tickets, then.

Dasheng   Oh! (*He comes back.*)

Bailu (*Holding up the tickets*)   You're actually leaving?

Dasheng   Yes, Zhujun (*Wipes his uncontrollable tears with a handkerchief*)

Bailu (*Puts her hands on his shoulders*)   What's wrong, you silly boy, can't you feel the tears streaming down your face? Shame on you, tears are for women! Enough (*As if coaxing a little brother*), poor baby, I made you cry. Let me wipe your face, such a big boy, what a laugh. Don't cry, don't cry (*After being comforted, he feels even worse and bursts into louder sobs. Bailu laughs heartily and pushes him down to sit.*). Dasheng, let me be honest with you. Don't be so childish. Do you think you can just leave when you feel like it?

Dasheng (*Looking up*)   Why?

Bailu   Aren't these your tickets?

Dasheng   Yes, what about them?

Bailu   Now watch, first like this (*Tearing the tickets in half*) and then like this (*Tearing them in half again and tossing them into a spittoon*), I'll keep them in there for you. All right?

Dasheng   You – how could you . . .

Bailu   Don't you understand?

Dasheng (*Hope dawning in his face*)   So you accept my offer after all, then, Zhujun?

Bailu   No, no, you've misunderstood, I haven't. I tore up your train tickets not my own bill of sale. This place owns me for life.

Dasheng   Then why won't you let me go?

Bailu (*Earnestly*)   Do you think you're the only one on earth with any feelings? Just because I can't marry you doesn't mean that I despise you, now does it? Don't you have any feelings left for me to spend a few days with me and reminisce about old times? You're so old-fashioned. Do we have to get married to be good friends? Surely something remains of the affection we once felt for each other, something we'd like to share for a while? The minute you stepped through the door, you began looking at me all funny, criticizing this and that. You lectured me, and cursed me, and treated me with disrespect, and then you demanded that I marry you at once. *And* you demanded an answer within twenty-four hours, and want me to go away with you immediately. You may think women are as docile as lambs, but we're not this pathetic.

Dasheng (*Woodenly*)   That's the way I am: I'm no good at declarations of love. If you want me to get down on my knee and make a pretty speech, well, I just can't do it.

Bailu   All right, then, so it won't hurt you to take a few lessons from me; in a few days you *will* be able to do it. Well, now, would you care to spend a couple of days with me or not?

Dasheng (*Bluntly*)   But what would we talk about?

Bailu   Oh, there's plenty to talk about. I'll show you around the city and entertain you in style, and you can observe how people here live.

Dasheng   No, don't bother, the people here are monsters. I am not interested. And anyway, I had my luggage sent to the station yesterday.

Bailu   Is that so?

Dasheng   Why, you know I never – never tell lies.

Bailu   Fusheng.

(*The steward comes out of the bedroom.*)

Fusheng   Don't worry, Miss Chen, I'll have your bed tidied in no time –

Bailu   The luggage I asked you to fetch from the Orient Hotel – I mean the train station – when I went out: have you brought it back?

Fusheng   You mean Mr Fang's, yes, I have. I fetched it from his hotel.

Dasheng   How dare you take my luggage from my hotel, Zhujun!

Bailu   Well, there you have it, I did dare remove it from your hotel. So much for you never telling lies, you dummy. (To **Fusheng**) Where did you put it?

Fusheng   Suite Number 24, East Wing.

Bailu   Is that the best suite?

Fusheng   The best in the hotel apart from this one of yours.

Bailu   Good. Will you show Mr Fang to his suite, then? If it's not to Mr Fang's liking, let me know, and he can have mine.

Fusheng   Very well, Miss Chen. (*He goes out.*)

Dasheng (*Blushing*)   But Zhujun, this is ridiculous.

Bailu   Lots of things in this city are ridiculous. Now that you're here I'm inviting you to take a good look round, so that you can see beyond those old-fashioned lenses of yours. Once you've seen a bit more you'll realize that this is not so ridiculous.

Dasheng   No, Zhujun, I had better think it over.

Bailu   Nonsense. Off you go! (*Pushing him*) Fusheng, Fusheng, Fusheng! (*Enter* **Fusheng**.)

Dasheng   I'll never get any sleep in a hotel like this.

Bailu   In that case, I've got some pills here, a couple of these and you'll sleep through any amount of noise. Want some?

Dasheng   Stop joking, I'm telling you, I have no desire to see this place.

Bailu   But you must, I insist. (*To* **Fusheng**) Show him to his suite. (*Pushing* **Dasheng** *as she speaks*) Hurry up now, have a bath and get some rest. When you get up, change into some fresh clothes and I'll take you out on the town. Now go on then, be a good boy, do as you're told. Don't be naughty, do you hear me? *Good night.*[10] (*A rooster crows in the distance.*) Listen, it really is getting late. Now go along, off to bed.

(**Dasheng** *reluctantly allows himself to be pushed out of the room.*)

(*She closes the door and leans against the door frame momentarily. A night of drinking and smoking and excitement has drained away much of her energy. She yawns and rubs the dark circles under her eyes with the back of her hand, goes over to the table and lights a cigarette. A rooster crows in the distance. She turns her head and looks with fixed attention at the deep blue gradually penetrating the darkness outside. Like a bird, she flits over to the window, and quietly draws on the frosty pane. Stubbing out her cigarette, she presses her face against the glass, half trembling, half-jokingly, and quickly draws back emitting an 'ouch.' Not giving up, she puts her hand flat against the cold pane. She cries out in delight and smiles. She scrapes away a big patch of the frost and peers through with one eye, until it occurs to her to open the window to see the dawn. She is about to turn the metal window crank when she decides she ought to dim the lights, so she glides over to the other side of the room to turn them off. The room is momentarily dark, except for the patch of sapphire blue light, against which can be seen the dark silhouette of the woman opening up the window.*

Outside, in the dark sky a faint light begins to silently creep forth. The outlines of the buildings outside gradually become visible in the grey light that precedes the dawn. She leans out of the window and greedily inhales the cool air of early morning, shivering involuntarily. In the distance comes the mournful cry of a factory whistle.

It is still dark in the room. A figure now steals silently out from behind the food cupboard on the left and stands up holding on to the cupboard, trembling, then tiptoes towards the door, preparing to seize this opportunity to slip away. Sensing a stealthy noise behind her, Bailu all at once turns round. The figure stays rooted to the spot, immobile.)

Bailu (*In a low voice, unable to shout*)   Burglar.

Person (*Holding their breath*)   Don't scream, don't scream!

Bailu   Who is it? (*Frantic*) Who are you?

Person (*Shrinking back, breathing heavily and shivering*)   M. . . .
Miss. . . . Mi. . . . Miss.

Bailu (*Emboldened*)   What are you doing here?

The figure   I. . . . I. . . . (*Sobbing*)

(**Bailu** *slips over to switch on the light, flooding the room with a blaze
of light. Standing before her is a frail, frightened girl, apparently about
fifteen or sixteen years old, two small braids hanging down over her
chest and her hair disheveled, staring at* **Bailu** *in wide-eyed alarm, her
cheeks stained by tears streaming down her face. She is wearing a blue
silk coat, splattered with grease stains, that is far too big for her, its
bottom hem and sleeves hanging almost to the floor. Her trousers are
also enormous, with the bottoms of the legs dragging on the floor around
her feet. Such an outfit makes her look all the more timid and diminutive,
like a baby swathed in adult garments. She is trembling pitifully with
cold and terror, and her bright, clear eyes are innocent and imploring.
Her head lowered, she shuffles backwards inch by inch, nervously
holding up the legs of her trousers with her hands, lest she trip.*)

Bailu (*Looking at the comical yet pathetic creature*)   Why, you're just a
Pipsqueak of a thing after all.

Pipsqueak (*Fearful and shamefaced*)   Yes, Miss. (*She retreats step
by step until, not careful enough, she steps on a trouser leg and almost
tumbles over.*)

Bailu (*Finding it difficult not to laugh, but managing to keep a straight
face*)   Well, and what are you doing here, stealing from me? Eh?
(*Feigning anger*) Now, Pipsqueak, speak up!

Pipsqueak (*Nervously fingering her coat*)   No, I – I didn't steal
anything.

Bailu (*Pointing*)   Then from whom did you get the clothes?

Pipsqueak (*Looking down and examining her clothes*)   From my – my
mother.

Bailu   And who would your mother be?

Pipsqueak (*Giving* **Bailu** *a look and brushing a wisp of hair out of her
eyes*)   My mother! I don't know.

Bailu (*Smiling, but still sizing her up*)   Why, you silly girl, you must know who your own mother is, surely! Where does your mother live?

Pipsqueak (*Pointing to the ceiling*)   Upstairs.

Bailu   Upstairs. (*Suddenly understanding*) Oh, so you're from upstairs. You poor thing. Who told you to run away?

Pipsqueak (*Lowering her voice as to be almost inaudible*)   Me.

Bailu   Why?

Pipsqueak (*Timidly*)   Because . . . they (*Hangs her head.*)

Bailu   What's the matter?

Pipsqueak (*Hesitantly*)   The night before last they . . . (*Fear prevents her from continuing.*)

Bailu   Come now, tell me, there's nothing to be afraid of here.

Pipsqueak   The night before last they wanted me to spend the night with a dark fatso. I was scared, so I wouldn't, and so they – (*She sobs.*)

Bailu   So they beat you.

Pipsqueak (*Nodding*)   Yes, with a whip. Last night they brought me here again and Dark Fatty came back. He really did scare me. I was so frightened that I started screaming, and then the man got angry and left and they – (*She sobs.*)

Bailu   They beat you again.

Pipsqueak (*Shaking her head, tearfully*)   No, there were people next door and they were afraid someone might hear. They put a gag in my mouth, pinched me, and (*Bursting into tears*) . . . and . . . and then jabbed me with an opium needle (*Holding back her tears*), see, look! (*She holds out her arm and* **Bailu** *takes her hand. In her weakness,* **Pipsqueak's** *knees buckle, but as soon her knees touch the ground she lets out a cry and gets to her feet.*)

Bailu (*Hugs her*)   What's wrong?

Pipsqueak (*In pain*)   They jabbed my legs too.

Bailu   Heavens! How did your arms get so. . . . (**Bailu** *uses her handkerchief to wipe her own tears.*)

Pipsqueak   It's ok, Miss. Don't cry. (*Covering up her arms*) They were afraid I would run away, so they took my clothes and forced me to stay in bed.

Bailu   What were they up to when you snuck off?

Pipsqueak   They were smoking opium and playing cards in the other room. That's when I snuck out of bed and put on some of my 'mother's' clothes.

Bailu   Why didn't you keep running?

Pipsqueak (*Sensibly*)   Where to? I don't know anyone, and I don't have any money.

Bailu   What about your mother?

Pipsqueak   She's upstairs.

Bailu   No, I mean your own mother, your real mother.

Pipsqueak   Oh. (*Her eyes welling up with tears*) She died a long time ago.

Bailu   And your father?

Pipsqueak   He died last month.

Bailu   I see. But why did you come in here? They'll find you.

Pipsqueak (*Utterly terrified*)   No, no, no! (*Dropping to her knees.*) Be kind! You can't let them find me, they'll kill me! (*Clutching* **Bailu's** *hand*) Oh, Miss, be kind!

Bailu   Get up (*Helping her to her feet*), I didn't say I was going to send you back. Now sit down while we think about what to do.

Pipsqueak   Thank you, thank you, Miss. (*She suddenly dashes over and closes the door.*)

Bailu   What are you doing?

Pipsqueak   I am shutting the door tight so no one will come in.

Bailu (*Patting her shoulder*)   Don't worry about that. There's nothing to be afraid of yet. (*Pauses*) But weren't you just trying to leave?

Pipsqueak (*Nods her head*)   Yes.

Bailu   Where were you planning on going?

Pipsqueak (*In a whisper*)   I was going back.

Bailu   Going back, going back there?

Pipsqueak (*Lowering her head*)   Yes.

Bailu   But why?

Pipsqueak I'm starved. I thought maybe they hadn't noticed I was gone. I figured they would beat me once the sun came up but they'd also give me some rice porridge to eat. That's more than I'd get anywhere else.

Bailu You still haven't eaten?

Pipsqueak (*Innocently*) If my belly were any emptier I'd be dead; but they don't want me dead, I know that.

Bailu When was the last time you ate? (*Goes over to the sideboard.*)

Pipsqueak More than a day ago. They said they wouldn't give me anything to eat until the dark fatty was happy.

Bailu Here start with some biscuits.

Pipsqueak (*Takes them*) Thank you, Miss. (*Turns her head and wolfs them down.*)

Bailu Slow down, you'll choke.

Pipsqueak (*Suddenly*) Is this all?

Bailu Don't worry, there's plenty more where that came from. (*Compassionately*) Is this what hunger does to people? (*The center door creaks open.*)

Pipsqueak (*Hastily putting down what she is eating and retreating to a corner*) Miss!

Bailu Who is it? (*Enter* **Fusheng**.)

Fusheng It's me, Miss.

Pipsqueak Miss (*Terrified*) He . . . he . . .

Bailu Don't be frightened, Pipsqueak, it's just the hotel steward.

Fusheng Miss, the manager of Dafeng Bank, Mr Pan, came by three times last night.

Bailu I know, I know.

Fusheng He's still here.

Bailu Still here? Why hasn't he left?

Fusheng Well, you know the new high rise going up next door? Well, I suspect Manager Pan's now discussing it with his secretary. But he said that when you returned I was to go and ask him over. He wants to see you.

Bailu   How odd. If they want to put up a new building, fine, but I don't see why they have to come around here in the middle of the night to discuss it.

Fusheng   Indeed.

Bailu   Tell Manager Pan not to come. Tell him I'm off to bed now to get some sleep.

Fusheng   What, why won't you see him? After all, Mr Pan's the manager of a big bank, and . . .

Bailu (*Who has had enough of his verbiage*)   Mind your own business. I don't want to see him. Do you hear me?

Fusheng (*Cringing and smiling obsequiously*)   Very well, but Miss, please don't get upset (*Taking out a huge wad of bills from his pocket*) Now don't panic. Meifeng Jewelers $654.40, Yongchang Silk Shop $355.55, the hotel $229.76, Hongsheng Photography Studio $117.07, Jiuhuachang Shoe Store $91.30, weekly taxi fare $76.50 – oh, and also. . . .

Bailu (*Losing patience*)   Stop, stop there. I don't want to hear it.

Fusheng   It's not that I don't wish to serve you well, Miss, but I can't keep putting your creditors off like this day after day: say what you like, but if you can't come up with the cash again today I'll just have to give up.

Bailu (*With a sigh*)   Money, money, always money! (*With annoyance*) Why are you always trying to frighten me like this.

Fusheng   I wouldn't dare, Miss, but business has been slow these past few years. And who knows what tomorrow has in store.

Bailu   I've never begged anyone for money. It's always been people seeing I can't get by who offer it of their own accord.

Fusheng   There's no doubt about your good standing but Miss –

Bailu   All right, I'll figure out how to settle up somehow; you can tell them to put their minds at ease about that.

Fusheng (*As he is about to leave*)   Why, Miss, what's this girl doing here?

(**Pipsqueak** *looks imploringly at* **Bailu**.)

Bailu (*Going over to* **Pipsqueak**)   Never mind her . . .

Fusheng (*Looking* **Pipsqueak** *up and down*)   She looks familiar. Now Miss, you mustn't go looking for trouble.

Bailu   What do you mean?

Fusheng   There are people looking for her out there.

Bailu   Who?

Fusheng   A bunch of toughs from upstairs. They're dressed in black and wear fedoras tilted to the side. Gangsters, everyone last one of them.

Bailu (*Crying out in fear*)   Oh, Miss. (*Going over to* **Fusheng** *and imploring him*) Oh, Uncle, save me (*Before she can kneel down* **Fusheng** *jumps aside.*).

Fusheng (*To* **Pipsqueak**)   Don't drag me into this.

Bailu (*To* **Fusheng**)   Shut the door! And lock it.

Fusheng   But Miss –

Bailu   Lock the door.

Fusheng (*Locking the door*)   You'll never manage to hide her, Miss. Her parents are ransacking the building for her.

Bailu   Give them some money, surely that'd do the trick?

Fusheng   There you go getting all generous again. Give them money? How many thousands can you spare?

Bailu   What do you mean?

Fusheng   Give them some now and they'll soak you for every dime you've got.

Bailu   Then we'd – (*Sound of footsteps and voices outside.*)

Fusheng   Quiet! Someone's out there. (*Listening briefly*) It's them, they're here.

Pipsqueak (*Unable to restrain herself*)   Oh, what can we do?

Bailu (*Gripping her hand tightly*)   If you make one more peep, I'll throw you out there.

Pipsqueak (*In a hushed voice*)   No, no!

Bailu (*In a low voice*)   Then be quiet.

First male voice (*Explosively*)   The little bitch, she's more trouble than she's worth, running off and throwing away the chance of a lifetime running. Fucking yokel, I'm damned if I know what fathered her.

Woman's voice (*In a shrill voice*)   She offended Master Jin Ba and he ran off.

Second man's voice (*Slow and hoarse voice*)   What, Jin Ba took a liking to her?

Woman's voice   I ask you, here comes someone rolling in money and all this ungrateful kid can do is to take off? That'll take some explaining to do, I'll tell you that much.

First man's voice (*Bellowing impatiently at the woman*)   Stay the fuck out of this. The kid's gone because you didn't keep an eye on her while you were yapping away, and here you are even now with all this fuckin' rubbish. (*No further sound from the woman.*) Hey, Lao San, you don't think she would have gone outside, do you?

Second man's voice (*Black San, the brains of the gang, in a slow and haughty voice*)   No, no chance of that. Cold weather like this, in Auntie's thin gown, where would she go?

Woman's voice (*Chiming in to try to please the first man*)   Yea. She ran off in my gown. She won't get very far like that. But apparently nobody's seen her on the ground floor or on the first. Black San, do you think she might have . . .

Third man's voice (*A tough but completely clueless fellow.*)   Auntie, that steward on this floor said he'd just seen her, so where could she be?

First man's voice (*Harshly authoritative*)   Then she's got to be somewhere on this floor. Come on, let's find her.

Woman's voice (*Snarling*)   She won't get away, the little bitch.

Various male voices   Don't worry, Aunt, we'll find her. Let's split up and search.

(*The three people in the room strain their ears listening as the footsteps of the men and the woman fade away.*)

Bailu   Are they gone?

Fusheng   Yes, probably round to the other side.

Bailu (*Suddenly opening the door*)   Let me take a look. (*Just as she is going to poke her head out, Pipsqueak seizes her by the hand and pulls her back desperately.*)

Pipsqueak (*Shaking her head, pleading*)   Miss! Miss!

Fusheng (*Pushing her, shutting the door, and shaking his head in warning*)   You don't want to get mixed up with them.

Bailu (*To* **Pipsqueak**)   Don't be afraid, it's all right. (*To* **Fusheng**) Now what's all that about . . .

Fusheng   Don't get on their bad side. People like that can be vicious if you provoke them. A wise man does not fight when the odds are stacked against him.

Bailu   What do you mean by that?

Fusheng   They're gangsters and they've got weapons. They kill people for a living.

Bailu   But they can't be completely devoid of reason! Look what they did to her, look (*Holding up* **Pipsqueak's** *arm*), they stabbed her with an opium needle and made her bleed badly. If they insist on making trouble, I'll report them.

Fusheng (*Scornfully*)   Report them? To whom? What good would that do? They're in bed with all the people who matter around here, so how can you turn them in? Even if you did win a law suit against them, what chance would you stand when they show up to even the score?

Bailu   So I'm supposed to just hand the kid over to them?

Pipsqueak (*Hoarse with terror*)   No, don't, Miss. (*She wipes the tears that have begun to trickle down with her oversized sleeve.*)

Fusheng (*Shaking his head*)   It's a tricky situation. I think you'd better do the sensible thing and take the child back to them. I hear she smacked Master Jin Ba on the face and got him mad. Didn't you know?

Bailu (*Taken aback*)   Master Jin Ba? Who's he?

Pipsqueak (*Lifting her head*)   Old Dark Fatty.

Fusheng (*Surprised at* **Bailu's** *ignorance*)   Master Jin, the Godfather of Wealth himself, a man of money and influence, and these gangsters are on his payroll. You haven't heard of him?

Bailu (*Slowly takes a deep breath, with fear*)   Oh, him. What would he be doing in this hotel?

Fusheng   When he's fed up at home, he comes here for a night out, and why not? After all, he's rolling in money.

Bailu (*To herself*)　Jin Ba. (*To* **Pipsqueak**) You really do have bad luck. To think you went and upset a monster like that. You slapped him on the face, Pipsqueak?

Bailu　You mean the dark fatso? Yes. He – he was forcing himself on me – I couldn't get away and somehow I smacked him (*Brightening up at the memory.*) Smacked him right on his fat face.

Bailu (*Gravely to herself*)　You slapped Jin Ba!

Pipsqueak (*Apologetically*)　Yes, Miss, but I won't do it again, not ever.

Bailu (*To herself*)　Good for you! Well done! I hope it hurt!

Fusheng (*Afraid of trouble*)　Miss, I must make it quite clear that I do not want any part of this business. If you want to play the good Samaritan and take the girl in, then you are on your own, I'll have nothing to do with it. If they ask me about. . . .

Bailu (*Bluntly*)　Then you haven't seen her!

Fusheng (*Looking at* **Bailu**, *uneasily*)　Haven't seen her? But –

Bailu　I want you to say you haven't seen her.

Fusheng (*Looking at* **Pipsqueak**)　But –

Bailu　If anything happens, I'll take full responsibility.

Fusheng (*Hoping that she would say this*)　All right, all right, you answer for it, then. (*Glibly*) Witness the lights above and the floor beneath that you yourself said so.

Bailu (*Nodding*)　Yes, of course, and when I say something I mean it. Now go ask Manager Pan in.

Fusheng　But didn't you just say that you didn't want him to come?

Bailu　Just do as I tell you and stop with all your nonsense.

Fusheng (*In a drawl*)　Very well – very well – very well – (*He goes off in a huff.*)

Bailu (*To* **Pipsqueak**)　Had enough to eat?

Pipsqueak (*Dazedly*)　I only had a couple.

Bailu　Hmmm?

Pipsqueak　I. . . . I . . . I'm still hungry.

Bailu　Eat as much as you like.

Pipsqueak   No, I can't eat anymore.

Bailu   What's the matter?

Pipsqueak   I can't, I'm too scared – (*She bursts out crying.*)

Bailu (*Goes over to her to comfort her*)   There, there, don't cry!

Pipsqueak   Miss, you won't take me back there, will you?

Bailu   No, I won't. Now stop crying, stop crying. Listen, someone's outside!

(**Pipsqueak** *stops at once and stares at the door with bated breath.*)

(*Enter* **Master Pan**, *the bank manager. He is a massive creature with graying hair and ponderous movements, but when he sees* **Bailu** *his years seem to fall away and he suddenly becomes youthful and lively in his actions and manner, though in fact his youngest son is in his twenties. He has a shiny balding head, his eyes are narrow slits, and his nose like a Pekinese dog's; he has a thin drooping moustache, a large mouth, and a gold tooth that gleams ostentatiously when his lips part in a jocular smile. He is wearing a dark brown gown lined with otter fur with a sleeveless satin jacket over the top, from which dangles a gold watch-chain and an emerald pendant. He seems to have just dressed, for his collar button has not yet been fastened and part of the collar is stuck inside his clothes. He holds a cigar in one hand and although his brows are creased into a frown he cannot keep a smile from his lips. Such is the graceless manner with which he greets* **Bailu**.)

Pan   Bailu, I knew you'd send for me! I've been waiting all night long. Fortunately, Li Shiqing turned up to go over some bank affairs. Otherwise I wouldn't have known how to kill the time. I sent someone up several times to see if you'd gotten back. Well, now, I invite you out to dinner and you decline; I invite you dancing and you decline; but when I ask you to . . . (*with great satisfaction*) I knew you'd send for me sooner or later.

Bailu (*Sliding him a look out of the corner of her eye*)   You're very sure of your powers of seduction, aren't you?

Pan (*Self-confidently*)   Pity you didn't know me when I was younger. In those days (*Suddenly turns to* **Fusheng**) Since that's all, why are you still here? Get out!

Fusheng   Yes, Manager Pan. (*Exit* **Fusheng**.)

Pan (*In a low voice*)   I knew you were thinking of me (*with deliberate sentimentality*), weren't you? Tell me now, you've been thinking of me, haven't you? (*Guffaws loudly.*)

Bailu   Oh yes, I was thinking of you –

Pan   There you are, I knew it. (*Gesturing towards her*) Your heart's in the right place.

Bailu   Yes, I was thinking you and I could take on a little project together.

Pan (*Putting on a frown*)   Another project. Is that all you can think of when you see me? No time for anything but getting mixed up in things that don't concern you.

Bailu   How do you know about this?

Pan   Fusheng told me everything.

Bailu   Will you help or not?

Pan (*Going across to* **Pipsqueak**)   So this is Pipsqueak.

Bailu   Look at the poor thing, she –

Pan   All right, all right, I get it. Anyway, it's always the same old story.

Bailu (*Menacingly*)   Well, Yueting, will you help or not?

Pan   Yes, I will!

Bailu   Well, Pipsqueak, aren't you going to thank Master Pan?

(**Pipsqueak** *is about to kneel down to him.*)

Pan (*Stopping her*)   No, no, don't start that. Bailu, you are always getting me in trouble.

Bailu   Listen! (*Voices outside.*)

Sounds like they're back. Pipsqueak, go in there. (*She indicates the door on the right.*) (**Pipsqueak** *goes into the next room.*)

Black San's voice (*From outside*)   This door?

Second man's voice   That's the one.

Bailu (*To* **Pan**)   They probably mean my door.

Pan   Yes.

Black San's voice   You're sure this was the door you saw her go in?

Second man's voice   Yes.

Black San's voice   And she didn't come back out?

Woman's voice What's wrong with you? You find the door and then just stand there twiddling your thumbs.

Third man's voice No, we've got to be sure, we can't go in the wrong place.

(*Muffled confused sound of men's voices.*)

Bailu You shouldn't wait for them to come in, Yueting. Open the door and go out there to tell them to go away.

Pan They probably know me, these fellows, so I shouldn't have much trouble getting rid of them.

Bailu That's good, Yueting, thank you, thank you, you're a good man.

Pan (*Smiling naively*) That's the first time since I've known you that you've ever thanked me for anything.

Bailu (*Teasing him*) That's because it's the first time you've been a good man.

Pan There you go again, Bailu, making fun of me, you . . .

Bailu Now stop talking and go send them away.

Pan Very well. (*Just as he is about to go out –*)

Bailu You are aware, of course, Yueting, that it was Jin Ba who took a fancy to the girl.

Pan Jin Ba? (*He lets go of the door knob.*)

Bailu She offended Jin Ba.

Pan What? This is someone Jin Ba's taken a fancy to?

Bailu Didn't Fusheng tell you?

Pan No, he didn't; look here, Bailu, that was a close call. (*He shrinks back.*)

Bailu Don't tell me you've changed your mind, Yueting?

Pan You must know, Bailu, that this fellow Jin Ba is a ruthless creature who could care less about face.

Bailu You won't help then?

Pan It's not that I won't: I can't. Anyway, for the sake of a mere country girl like this, why do you have to go and –

Bailu Yueting, don't stand in my way. If you won't help, fine, but don't try to stop me.

Pan   Now, now.

Third man's voice outside (*Roughly*)   Knock on the door, she's in there all right.

Black San's voice   Hmmm?

Third man's voice   Look, isn't that Aunty's handkerchief? Well, the girl was wearing her clothes when she escaped, wasn't she?

Woman's voice   Yea, that's right, that's my handkerchief.

Black San's voice   Then this must be the door, she's gotta be here. Open up in there! Open up!

Bailu (*Teasing* **Pan**)   Now don't be afraid, Yueting! (*She goes to open the door.*)

Pan (*Grasping* **Bailu's** *hand*)   Ignore them.

Voices outside   Open up in there! We're looking for someone.

Bailu   Yueting, go in there to spare yourself the embarrassment. I'm opening the door.

Pan   No, Bailu, don't.

Bailu   In you go. (*Pointing to the door on the left*) Go – don't make me mad.

Pan   All right, I'm going.

Bailu   Hurry up now!

(**Pan** *goes into the room on the left and* **Bailu** *immediately pulls the main door wide open.*)

Bailu (*To those outside*)   Come on in. Who are you looking for? (**Black San** *is standing outside the door dressed in black and sporting a black fedora.*)

Black San   None of your business. (*Boisterously, to his colleagues outside*) Come on in, all of you, search the place.

Bailu (*A sudden tone of outrage in her voice and expression*)   Stop right there! All come in? Who said anything about you all coming in? Just who do you think you are, anyway? If you're going to be so unreasonable, you'll find your most unreasonable ancestor at this port of call. (*Smiles*) You're after contraband? I've got opium, guns too (*squaring her shoulders*). I'm not kidding (*Points to the left-hand room*). There's 500 kilos of opium in there (*Points to the right-hand room*) and in here I've got 80 revolvers. So tell me, what is it you want? There ought to be plenty for you to amuse yourselves with. (*The men in the doorway have been* *brought to a halt by this outburst, and she continues speaking through the doorway.*) Do come in, gentlemen! (*With a great show of politeness*) Won't you come in? Big fellows like yourselves, what are you scared of?

Third man (*In his bovine manner*)   Come on, let's go in. What's the big deal?

Black San   You morons, who told you to come in? Stay the hell out!

Third man (*Dully*)   Out, then, if that's what you want. It's all the same to me.

Black San (*Smiling*)   Now don't – don't upset yourself. No need to fly off the handle. Don't think we'd come and disturb you for no good reason. We've had a girl run away from us, a girl new to the business, and so we've come looking for her, in case she's hiding in here somewhere and startles you later on.

Bailu   Oh, I see. (*As if she suddenly understands*) So all you fellows here are looking for one little girl!

Black San (*With sharpening interest*)   Then I expect you must have seen her come in.

Bailu   I'm sorry, I have not.

Black San   But look, we found a handkerchief she'd dropped right outside your door.

Bailu   Well, it's not my problem that she dropped it.

Black San   Ah, but let me tell you something else: someone saw her come in here a short while ago.

Bailu   If she's been in my suite I'll tell you this right now: if she stole anything of mine you'll have to pay for it.

Black San   Cut out the funny stuff, please. Seems we're in the same racket, so you might give us a hand. I can see that you and Master Jin Ba are . . .

Bailu   Master Jin? Oh, you're friends with Jin Ba too?

Black San (*Smiling*)   Not exactly friends, but we do the odd job for him.

Bailu   Well, that's all right, then. Jin Ba was just now telling me to tell you to clear off.

Black San   Just now, you say?

Bailu (*Who has no alternative but to go through with her plan now that she has gone this far*)   Master Jin's right in there, as it so happens.

Black San (*Dubious*)   In there? But we saw Master Jin Ba off just now.

Bailu   What you didn't see is that he came back in.

Black San   Came back in? (*Pausing and sensing the lie*) Then we'd better see him and tell him how we're getting on. (*Turning and speaking through the doorway*) Hadn't we?

Voices from the doorway   Yes, yes, we've got to see him.

Bailu (*Calmly*)   I'm sorry, but Jin Ba said no visitors.

Black San   He can't refuse to see me. I must see him.

Bailu   Well, you can't.

Black San   It's not a matter of can't, it's a matter of must. (*Seeing* **Bailu** *head towards the room on the right where* **Pipsqueak** *is hiding*) Master Jin Ba's probably in there.

Bailu (*Suddenly dashing across to the door of the room on the left where* **Pan** *is hiding and standing in front of it*)   Sure, you go in that room, just don't come in here.

Black San   Aha – so Mrs Jin is playing tricks again, is she? (*Smiling mirthlessly at* **Bailu** *as he comes across to her, then, fiercely*) Out of my way!

Bailu   You'll get your head bitten off, I expect. (*Turning and speaking through the door*) Master Jin, Master Jin, come on out and teach this gang of bastards a lesson.

(*The door opens and* **Pan Yueting** *emerges in a dressing gown.*)

Pan (*Pointing inside the room and speaking in a low voice*)   What's all this ruckus, Bailu? Master Jin's asleep. (*Looking at the man*) Why, it's you, Black San! What are you doing here?

Black San   Oh (*taken aback*), so you're here, too, Fourth Master Pan.

Pan   I came with Jin Ba to rest my legs for a moment and have a smoke, and here you are causing mayhem. What is going on?

Black San (*Faltering*)   Oh, Master Jin Ba *is* here after all. (*Laughing nervously*) Uh-uh, he's sleeping here, is he?

Pan   Did you want to come in for a chat? Then by all means come right in and sit down, then! (*Throwing the door wide open*) I'll heat up a bead of opium and wake Jin Ba up to entertain you, shall I?

Black San (*Smiling obsequiously*)   Don't kid around like this, Master Pan.

Pan   You won't sit down? Won't those gentlemen in the doorway there come in for a rest?

Black San   No, no, we're still on a job –

Pan   Excellent. If you're busy, then please be so good as to piss off instead of standing there talking nonsense.

Black San (*Obediently*)   Very well, Master Pan, but please don't be so angry. I hope you'll forgive us if we've offended you. (*Suddenly turning his head and addressing those in the doorway*) What are you gawking at? Go on, get out of here, scumbags! Fucking lowlifes (*turning back with a smile*) See that? What can you do with a bunch like that? Master Pan, when Jin Ba wakes up please don't, under any circumstances, let him know that we were here. And you must put in a good word for us, Miss. Please don't breathe a word about what happened just now. We were just having a laugh. I don't deserve to live. (*Striking himself across the mouth*) I don't deserve to live.

Bailu   Okay, okay, now hurry up and get out.

Black San (*Obsequiously*)   You're not mad anymore? It's all right, we're going now. (*He goes out.*)

Bailu (*Closing the door*)   That's that, then. (*To herself*) I've never done anything so satisfying in my life.

Pan   That's that. I've never done anything so foolish.

Bailu   Well, now you can go and ask the almighty Jin Ba to resume his throne.

Pan   Humph! 'Easier to raise the Devil than to send him away.' We got rid of them by invoking the devil easily enough, but next time I see Jin Ba there'll be hell to pay.

Bailu   We'll worry about that tomorrow. In any case, that was great fun.

Pan   Fun?

Bailu   Anything can be fun. Don't you think? (*Yawning*) I *am* tired. (*Suddenly catching sight of the sunlight on the floor*) Look! Look at that!

Pan   Eh? What?

Bailu   The sun, the sun's up. (*She hurries over to the window.*)

Pan (*Drily*)   Yes, the sun has risen. Hardly worth shouting about.

Bailu (*Looking out of the sun-filled window, through which comes the faint chirping of sparrows*)   Look at all the clouds in the sky, and the sunlight. And listen, sparrows! (*The chirping of sparrows can be heard outside the window.*) Spring's here. (*With great feeling, her heart filled with joy*) Oh! I love the sun, I love the spring, I love being young, I love being me. Oh! I love it! (*She takes in a deep breath of the chilly air.*)

Pan (*Uninterested*)   Well, good for you, though I don't see what all the fuss is about. (*Suddenly*) Bailu, it's too cold in here. You'll freeze. Let's close the window.

Bailu (*Obstinately*)   No, I won't! I won't!

Pan   All right, all right, leave it open if you want. I don't know what to do with you, kiddo; I don't even indulge my own daughter this much.

Bailu (*Looking round*)   What's so unusual about that? Would you indulge me if I were your daughter?

Pan   I asked for that, a very penetrating remark. (*Imploringly*) Come on, then, shut the window or I'll be ca . . . catching . . . (*Mouth open and eyes wrinkled as if he's about to sneeze*) catching a . . . (*a violent sneeze*) there, now I've caught a cold.

Bailu (*Suddenly coming back from the window*)   You silly boy, why didn't you say so before?

Pan (*With satisfaction*)   Now perhaps you'll shut the window.

Bailu (*Shaking her head*)   No, I won't, I'll get you some extra clothes to put on. Come along now, sit down, with my coat around your shoulders, and my scarf round your neck, and this fur-lined gown over your legs, and you can have this hot-water bottle of mine, too. There, that's better now, isn't it? (*Arranging the old man in a bizarre-looking heap on the sofa*) I really am fond of you, you're just like a father to me. My dear old Daddy, we do treat you badly here, don't we!

Pan (*Pushing her away*)   Bailu (*Trying to get up*), I won't have you calling me Daddy.

Bailu (*Pushing him till he topples back on to the sofa again*)   I will if I want to. My dear old Dad.

Pan (*Protesting*)   I'm not old, why call me your dear old dad?

Bailu (*Smiling, she nuzzles up to him like a cat*)   That's what I'm going call you, so there! My dear old Dad! My dear old Dad!

Pan (*In a better humor now*)   Go ahead, then, I don't mind! I like it, I like it. (*He beams with delight.*)

Bailu (*Suddenly*)   Now sit still, Yueting (*She straightens out his bundle of clothes.*). You're like my little baby, so I'm going to sing you a lullaby.

Pan (*Confused*)   A lullaby? (*Feels his white beard*) No, don't do that.

Bailu   Then I'll read you a story. (*She picks up a handsomely bound book.*)

Pan (*Reading out the title of the book* **Bailu** *is holding*)   *Sunrise*, no, that's no good, I can tell just from the title.

Bailu (*Like a spoiled child*)   Even so, you must listen carefully.

Pan   I am not listening, I am not interested.

Bailu (*Again willfully*)   I insist.

Pan (*Looking woefully at* **Bailu** *and heaving a sigh*)   All right, all right, then read.

Bailu (*Turning to a page and reading aloud*)   '. . . The sun rises, leaving darkness behind.'

Pan (*Yawning and stretching*)   Doesn't make any sense, no sense at all.

Bailu (*Ignoring him and reading on*)   '. . . But the sun is not ours, for we now sleep.'

Pan (*Yawning deeply*)   That doesn't make sense either, though there's something in that last bit.

Bailu (*Closing the book impatiently*)   Oh, you're impossible. Another word and I'll – (*She raises the book as if to hit him.*)

(*From the bedroom on the right comes the yapping of a Pekinese dog mingled with cries of alarm from* **Pipsqueak**.)

Pan   What was that? (**Bailu** *gets up.*)

(**Pipsqueak** *dashes out of the bedroom. She closes the door in alarm, leaving the dog barking on the other side.*)

Pipsqueak (*Panic-stricken*)   Miss, Miss!

Bailu   What's the matter?

Pipsqueak   He . . . he's after me. He . . . he's awake.

Bailu (*In consternation*)   What! Who? Who?

Pipsqueak (*Breathless with fright*)   Your dog woke up. (*Looking behind her*) And he bit me and won't let me stay in there.

Bailu (*Relaxing*)   You silly child! For a moment there I thought that those people were coming in through the bedroom window!

Pan   I told you this wouldn't be easy. (*A knock on the door.*)

Bailu (*Looking at* **Bailu**)   Someone's at the door.

Pan   Not them again, I hope?

Bailu (*Going to the door*)   Who is it?

(*The door opens and* **Fang Dasheng** *enters.*)

Dasheng   It's me, Zhujun.

Bailu (*Taken aback*)   Why aren't you in bed?

Dasheng   I can't sleep in this place, it's too noisy. The steward's been telling me you've just acquired a foster daughter.

Bailu   A foster daughter?

Dasheng   Yes.

Bailu   Oh, I see what you mean. (*Indicating* **Pipsqueak**) Here she is. What do you think? My foster daughter.

Dasheng (*Interested*)   Such a young little thing.

Pan (*Rising from his heap of clothes in a brightly-colored scarf and a coat which almost completely envelops him*)   Now, now, Bailu, don't just stand there chatting away like that. And who would this gentleman be?

Bailu (*Feigning surprise*)   Don't you know? Let me introduce you. This is my cousin.

Pan (*Surprised*)   Your cousin?

Dasheng (*Realizing for the first time that there is another man in the room, to* **Bailu**)   What's this, you already have another . . .

Bailu (*Keeping a perfectly straight face*)   Why, don't you know who this is? My Dad.

Pan (*Happily*)   Dad!

Dasheng (*Taken aback*)   Dad?

Pan (*To* **Bailu**, *jokingly*)   One happy family! (*Suddenly, pointing to the window*) But do hurry up and shut . . . shut . . . (*Gesturing towards the* *window*) . . . shut . . . (*sneezing.*) There, I really have caught a cold this time. (*The three of them all look at* **Pipsqueak** *standing there listlessly.*)

(*The curtain falls quickly.*)

ACT II

The scene is the same as Act I, still the opulent sitting room of a suite in the X Hotel. It's almost night time and the setting sun can be seen through the window. Inside the room itself it is dark, and the lamp must be turned on to see anything clearly. From outside comes the rhythmical sound of pile-driving songs of the laborers laying the foundations of the new building next to the hotel. The sound, gradually receding into the distance, is intermingled with the trampling of many feet and the heavy thud of the stone rammers against the earth. The laborers here sing two different songs officially known as 'The Calling': One is 'The Little Sea,' the other is 'The Zhouhao.' At this moment they are singing the 'The Little Sea' with one shrill voice taking the lead and twenty or thirty low and somber voices answering in chorus. Sandwiched between the two, as the voices pause momentarily, comes the earth-ramming chant of several teams of men with 'rammers.' The heave-ho'ing sounds of work are heard throughout this act, from beginning to end, like the depressed howls of wronged souls, brimming with threats and admonitions. They use a primordial language to sing out their misery, suffering, and grief, and the gravity of their struggle. 'Little Sea,' therefore, contains no words, as it would be foolhardy and futile to use words to express their thoughts and feelings. Each phrase ends on a certain note of Northern coarseness and ferocity.

There's a pause midway through the song, when you can hear the heave-ho'ing of the workers moving past. Just when they can no longer be heard, they return once more. When the curtain rises **Fusheng** *is alone in the room tidying up the ashtrays, cigarette boxes and so forth, an expression of tremendous impatience on his face; he constantly glances over at the window and yawns. But outside the sound of the workers' heng-heng-hei grows more vigorous and row upon row of wooden rammers hit the damp soil with heavy, solemn thuds, as if they were a battalion of puppet soldiers marching in unbelievably orderly formation.*

Fusheng (*Fed up, he turns toward the window and spits with contempt*)   Bah! 'Hai-hai!' Nothing but the same damned 'hai-hai.' We'll be dead from all this racket by the time the building's up. (*Now comes* *the distant sound of the laborers heaving their stone rammers against the ground and singing the 'Little Sea' song.*)

Fusheng (*After listening briefly, viciously*)   Still at it! I'm lucky if I can catch a couple of winks during the day, but those damned fellows won't let up. It's nearly dark out but they're still singing and working, working and singing. You'd think they'd get fed up with it: born to eat millet cakes and salted pickles. Humph, if I ever have a son, he'd be better off starving to death than doing this (*he spits again*).

(*The chanting grows louder and louder and now they change the tune and begin singing 'The Zhouhao':*

> *'The sun sets in the west.*
> *Causing our hearts to worry.*
> *If we don't work ourselves to the bone*
> *No one will be spared.'*

Fusheng (*Listens momentarily, then all of sudden sits down and removes two wads of paper that he has stuffed into his ears; he rubs the insides of his ears with his fingers. Challengingly*)   Come on, then! Keep it up! Let's hear your hai-hai-ing. Belt it out! Now that I'm stuck with you, I'll listen and you sing, and we'll fuckin' see who gives in first! (*Closing his eyes determinedly*) See who gives in first! (*Naturally, the singing grows stronger.*)

(*Enter* **Fang Dasheng***; the singing begins to fade*)

Fusheng (*Rising and looking round when he becomes aware of someone behind him*)   Oh, Mr Fang. Up so early?

Dasheng (*The meaning of this escapes him*)   Why, of course – it's nearly dark out.

Fusheng (*Glad to have an audience to whom to air his grievances*)   No wonder you're up! No chance of sleeping with all the racket out there. Need their necks wringing –

Dasheng (*Gesturing towards the window*)   Sh! Listen!

Fusheng (*Misunderstanding*)   Don't worry, I'm not afraid of them. I'm up all night and need to get some sleep during the day, but they just go on and on, making noise all day long. Dammed . . .

Dasheng (*Pointing towards the window, his interest fully aroused*)   Listen, listen to them singing, be quiet!

Fusheng (*Taken aback*)   You want me to listen to them sing?

Dasheng (*Curtly*)   Correct.

(*Outside they are singing:*

'*The sun sets in the west.*
Causing our hearts to worry.
If we don't work ourselves to the bone
No one will be spared.'

As the last line ends, for some reason there is a roar of laughter, but immediately the steady, rhythmical heng-heng-hei heng-heng-hei *of the laborers is heard again as they move on pounding the earth with their rammers.*)

Dasheng (*Leaning against the window and looking down below with delight*)   What splendid singing!

Fusheng (*Puzzled*)   Did you say splendid?

Dasheng (*Sighing, but happily*)   They are so happy. Just look at them, their faces streaming with sweat, yet singing away with such joy.

Fusheng (*With a sardonic smile*)   Born to slave away in poverty. Otherwise, you think they'd spend their lives pile-driving, as coolie laborers, building places for other people to live in?

Dasheng   Who's putting up the place?

Fusheng   People with money, that's who. It's being built by Dafeng Bank, by Fourth Master Pan, and our very own Madame Gu (*Pointing to the room on the left*) probably even has a share in it. (*Dispiritedly*) What do they do with their money! (*Gesturing at random*) Put up big foreign buildings like that. (*Feeling sorry for himself like Ah Q*)[11] The more money they have, the more they make!

Dasheng   Madame Gu? You mean the old dame who wears all the makeup?

Fusheng   Yes, that's the one! Dresses way too young for a woman of her age; but she's loaded, so of course everybody complements her on her youth and beauty. Even Master Pan flatters her, to say nothing of all the others. You saw Manager Pan go in there (*Pointing to the room on the left*) with Miss Chen and Madame Gu to play mahjong, didn't you? I'm telling you, she's rolling in it.

Dasheng   But I left ages ago. You mean that these (*Distastefully*) people are still in there playing mahjong? They're not gone yet?

Fusheng   Gone? Gone where? It's almost dark out and there'll be even more people showing up, and then they'll be even less likely to go . . .

Dasheng (*Pacing up and down the room a couple of times*)   I can't stand how stuffy it is in here. And so dark.

Fusheng   The only time there's any sunlight in this room is early morning, so of course it's dark.

Dasheng (*Nods*)   True, the sun seldom shines in here.

Fusheng   It wouldn't really matter if it did since they'd sleep through it anyway. They don't come to life until night time. During the day they're dead asleep. We're like little ghosts who don't require sunlight.

Dasheng   True, the sun is not for us. (*Murmurs*) But then who is it for?

Fusheng (*Not comprehending*)   Who? (*smirking*) I couldn't care less.

Dasheng (*Picking up the thread*)   So what, right?

Fusheng   Exactly. So what, haha. (*There is a knock on the door.*)

Dasheng   Someone's at the door.

Fusheng   Who is it? (*He goes to open the door.*)

Dasheng (*Stopping him*)   Wait a moment, I don't feel like seeing anyone, I'm going in there.

(*He goes through the door on the right into* **Bailu's** *bedroom, as* **Fusheng** *opens the middle door.* **Huang Xingsan** *enters timidly with a look of great embarrassment and terror on his face. His pale face is devoid of color and his lips purple with cold. He is wearing only a pair of lined black trousers that gather at the ankle and a faded brown gown covered in grease stains. He holds a black wool scarf in his hand. He glances all around with pitiful nervous eyes. He is skinny as a rail, with throbbing serpentine-like veins on his forehead. He is a shy and anxious man and he wears the same forlorn expression even when he smiles. On occasion one is hard pressed to know if he is laughing or crying. It takes him considerable effort to blurt out a sentence – and when he finally does he coughs involuntarily a few times, albeit very weakly. In his humility and insecurity, he fears that the very sound of his voice will try other people's patience. He is not particularly old, but years of worry and toil, insomnia and malnutrition have left him frail as an old man. He retains certain middle-aged features but we wonder why at his age his back is so hunched over, his hands shake, and his hair has turned so white. He stands apprehensively in the doorway peering all around.*)

Fusheng   You again! (*Seeing that* **Huang** *doesn't recognize him, his face stiffens.*) What are you doing here?

Huang (*His voice trembling*)   I'm sorry! (*With a self-effacing laugh*) I – I'm sorry! (*Bowing*) I – I must have come in the wrong door. (*He coughs and turns to leave.*)

Fusheng (*Grabs him*)   Come back here! Where do you think you're going?

Huang (*His face flushing and the veins on his forehead twitching, as he hastens to excuse himself*)   I've come in the wrong door, sir.

Fusheng   Wrong door or not, back you must come. Think you can just barge in anywhere you like?

Huang   But sir, I made a mistake, and I – I apologize.

Fusheng   Don't you realize there are all kinds of people in this hotel? Why didn't you knock first before just barging straight in?

Huang (*With a nervous smile*)   I – I did knock, sir.

Fusheng (*Prevaricating*)   Then how come I didn't hear you?

Huang (*Smiling miserably*)   What am I to do, sir, if you didn't hear? (*Pitifully*) Shall I knock again for you? Let me go now, sir.

Fusheng   Idiot! Who are you here for, anyway?

Huang (*Fumbling uneasily with his scarf*)   I've – I've come to see Mr Li.

Fusheng (*Antagonistically*)   There are dozens of Li's; which Mr Li?

Huang   No (*Hastening to explain*): No, I mean I was looking for number fifty-two.

Fusheng   This is room number fifty-two.

Huang (*Unable to conceal his delight*)   Then, then I have come to the right place. (*Turning to* **Fusheng** *again, politely*) I'm here to see Mr Li Shiqing.

Fusheng   He's not here.

Huang (*After hesitating a long time finally blurts out*)   Then if Manager Pan isn't busy I'd like to see him instead. Would you mind letting him know, sir?

Fusheng (*Sizing him up*)   Well, there *is* a Manager Pan, but (*acerbically*) you? You'd like to see Manager Pan? (*Snickers loudly*)

Huang (*Desperately*)   I'm – a clerk at the Dafeng Bank.

Fusheng (*Icily*)   A clerk? Even your most illustrious ancestors would stand no chance of seeing a man like Manager Pan. He comes here to enjoy himself and he never takes visitors.

Huang   But (*Imploringly*), sir, you must just go and ask him if he'll see me, please?

Fusheng   He's not here! (*Losing patience*) I'm telling you Manager Pan's not here. Out! Out! Out! Stop making a nuisance of yourself. You show up here a complete stranger, butting in trying to see people, there's no telling what you're up to!

Huang (*In another attempt to explain*)   But sir, I – I was a clerk at the Dafeng Bank, the name's Huang. . . .

Fusheng (*Suddenly turning squarely to* **Huang** *and pointing to himself*)   Do you or do you not know who I am?

Huang (*After looking at him for a while*)   No, I can't say I do.

Fusheng   In that case, march! (*Pushing him*) Go on, out!

Huang   But sir, my name's Huang . . .

Fusheng (*Opening the door and pushing him outside*)   Go on, out! Out! Stop bothering me. And if you come back again I'll –

Huang (*Over his shoulder as he is pushed out*)   Sir, my name's Huang, Huang Xingsan. I used to be. . . .

Fusheng (*Arrogantly*)   I know, you used to be a clerk, your name's Huang Xingsan, you want to see Mr Li, you want to see Manager Pan, in fact you'll see anyone from Dafeng Bank. You're going round everywhere pretending to be something you're not and trying to get a job. You think I don't know all about it? Think I don't know who you are?

Huang (*So upset his hands tremble*)   If you know me, sir (*smiling submissively*), that's even better.

Fusheng (*Happily abusing him*)   I've seen you here at the hotel time and again but you don't even recognize me. You imagine you're going to find a job with a son-of-a-bitch memory like that? (*Seizing hold of* **Huang** *and giving him no chance to explain as he shoves him forcibly outside*) Now get out of here, go to hell!

Huang (*Staggering and falling over, almost paralyzed, emitting a dry cough*)   Why call me names? I know I'm poor, but you can't call me a cuckold, I am not a cuckold, I tell you, I am not. Why are you. . . .

Fusheng (*Playing with him maliciously*)   You'd better ask your wife about that, how should I know? (*Clapping him on the shoulder and grinning sardonically*) All right, then, you're not a cuckold but your son is certainly a bastard how's that?

Huang (*Suddenly stands up furiously and raises his hand as if he intends to hurl the entire weight of his body on this creature before him and crush him to death*) You – you – I'll. . . .

Fusheng (*Every inch the thug, he shoots up his eyebrows, puffs up his chest and seizes* **Huang** *by the front of his gown, and says in a low threatening voice*) You'll do what? If you so much curse me one time or lift one finger I'll kill you! (*A pause.*)

Huang (*With eyes like a madman, fixes his gaze on* **Fusheng** *with a mixture of fear and fury as his hands shake uncontrollably. After a while he speaks in a soft feeble voice*)   Let – me – go! Let – me – go!

(**Fusheng** *releases him and he slinks out. Outside, the* heng-heng-hei-heng-heng-hei *of the laborers is heard again, brimming with righteous anger.*)

(*The telephone rings.* **Fusheng** *turns his head, goes to the small table by the sofa, picks up the receiver, answering irritably.*)

Fusheng   Yea, who is it? Who is it? Who do you want? Tell me who you want!. . . . Who are you calling a bastard. . . . You're the. . . . What's that? The name's Jin. . . . Oh. . . . So. . . . Oh, I see, sir, it's Master Jin Ba. . . . Yes. . . . Yes. . . . Yes. . . . This is room number 52. . . . I didn't recognize the voice, I didn't know it was you, sir. . . . (*With an obsequious smile*) Call me what you like, sir! (*He stands to attention bobbing and bowing repeatedly albeit quite unconsciously, listening with a beaming face to the stream vile abuse that is being poured into his ear.*) Indeed. . . . Indeed. . . . I deserve every word of it! You're quite right sir!

(**Pan Yueting** *comes in through the door on the left.*)

Pan (*To* **Fusheng**)   Who is it? Who's calling? Is it Mr Li Shiqing?

Fusheng (*Upset, uncertain which of the two he should pay attention to. Smiling obsequiously into the receiver*)   No, I wouldn't dare. . . . No, I won't dare do it again. . . . Yes. . . . Now please don't get angry, sir . . .

(*Shakes his head to indicate that the call is not from Li Shiqing, at the same time frowning as the cursing clearly intensifies.*) Yes, this is Fusheng . . . yes, I am that turtle egg Fusheng, please don't be angry, please sir, don't upset yourself (*It would appear the caller's anger has begun to subside.*). Yes, I am a bastard. You wanted Manager Pan? Just a moment, sir, he's coming right away. (*To* **Pan**) For you . . . sir. (*He is about to hand over the receiver when the voice starts again. He hastily puts it to his ear.*) Yes, yes, I'm not of human parentage. (*Heaves a long sigh and hands over the receiver*)

Pan (*His hand over the mouthpiece, in a low voice*)   You moron! Who is it?

Fusheng (*In such a state that he cannot think clearly*)   Who? Who is it?. . . . Oh, er, it's Jin Ba, Master Jin Ba.

Pan (*To* **Fusheng**)   Has Mr Li Shiqing arrived yet?

Fusheng   No, not yet.

Pan   Go ask Mrs Li what time her husband said he'd be here.

Fusheng   Very well, sir. (*He goes out.*)

Pan (*Clearing his throat*)   Is that Master Jin?. . . . Yueting here. . . . Yes . . . yes, there shouldn't be any problem with your account. If you'll just sit tight for three days, and then come for it, I can definitely let you have it. . . . Yes . . . yes . . . business is just fine at the bank these days, we've done well on government bonds – Salt-tax and Disbandment, so don't worry, three days, and your funds at the bank will definitely be repaid in full. . . . What?. . . . Nonsense!. . . . Not on your life, a run on the bank!. . . . Who's saying that?. . . . Uh, er, rumors, just rumors, don't believe them. Now Master Jin, hasn't the bank invested in an enormous new building next door to the hotel at this very moment?. . . . Why build?. . . . Why, naturally, when the market's strong one likes to keep one's money on the move. Relax! The bank's reserves are solid . . . three days. Just hold on for three days, for old times' sake, and you'll get every penny back. . . . Yes (*Laughing*), Master Jin . . . any particular news about government bonds? . . Ah, yes, so I hear, the market's up. A rally . . . are you buying?. . . . Yes . . . yes. . . .

Fusheng (*Coming in through the door on the left*)   Mrs Li says Mr Li is on his way. (*Looking over his shoulder*) Manager Pan's here, Madame Gu.

(*Enter* **Madame Gu**, *a fat and vulgar woman. She is wearing an exceedingly tight patterned qipao with gilded borders, so garish it's hard on the eye. She walks like a baby whale; her enormous buttocks sway back and forth, boggling the mind as to what else might be enveloped within that layer of clothing besides flesh and vileness. Her face is*

*wrinkled, but she conceals the deep creases beneath with thick layers
of powder and makeup. She's always guffawing with laughter. This
has several advantages: firstly, it makes her seem a bit more youthful;
secondly, in her opinion, she's more attractive when laughing; and thirdly,
only when she laughs are her gold teeth displayed in all their dazzling
splendor. So she puckers up her mouth, eyes, and nose all together and
laughs and laughs ad nauseam. Her eyebrows are drawn in thin lines and
she wears diamond earrings that exude wealth; when she talks it is always
with excited gesticulations and considerable bodily movement, and then the
jewels on her sausage-like fingers and her earrings flash and sparkle until
one's nerves are set on edge. She's as fit as an ox though for some reason
she is forever ailing and the slightest thing sets off bouts of dizziness,
nausea and an interminable sequence of aches and pains. But she can
also be quite flirtatious, under the false impression that her girlhood
charms remain undiminished by the passage of time. When she's in one
of those moods, one really cannot help admiring the patience of* **Hu Si**, *
her latest beau – although sometimes even he turns away in disgust.
Yet* **Madame Gu** *is in her own world, blissfully ignorant of people's
ridicule; for she is alive, happily and youthfully alive, after all, or so she
claims, she only turned thirty the year before last, though this year she
inexplicably became twenty-eight, and though she does have a daughter
who has graduated from college. When* **Hu Si** *is in a good mood he plays
along and tells her that she doesn't look nearly as old as that, and this
encourages her even more to feign innocence in male company.*)

(*The sound of talking and laughter can be heard emanating from the next
room and when* **Madame Gu** *pushes open the door on the left the clatter
mahjong tiles and the din of noisy conversation get even louder. She
appears to be making an escape, as she treads in a determined attempt to
tiptoe quietly, smiling and panting.*)

Gu (*Facing back toward the other room*)   No, I'm quite exhausted;
I couldn't possibly play another round. (*She looks round and says
gushingly, as if noticing* **Pan Yueting** *for the first time.*) Why, Manager
Pan! What are you doing here all alone?

Pan (*Bowing*)   Madame Gu. (*Pointing to the telephone, motioning that
he has nearly finished.*)

(**Fusheng** *exits through the center door.*)

Gu (*Nodding to him and turning to look in through the doorway
again*)   No, Mr Wang, no, I'm exhausted. No, Bailu, it's my heart, if I
keep playing my ailment might flare up again.

(*She turns again and goes over to* **Pan** *like a gust of wind, still addressing her remarks to the other room.*) You must let me rest now. (*Dropping ponderously down onto the sofa*) I'm not well.

Pan   . . . . Yes, all right, goodbye then, goodbye. (*Putting down the receiver*) Well, now, Madame Gu . . .

Gu (*Volubly*)   Now that was very naughty of you, Manager Pan, leaving your game of mahjong and your cigar to slip out here all alone to chat on the phone! (*Lowering her voice with exaggerated gravity*) You'd better be more careful, with Bailu right there playing mahjong. (*The would-be confidante*) But here you are making secret phone calls. You can tell me: who is she? Why did she call you here? I know all about you men; you're experts at making money and spending it, but none of you understand a thing about love, what a wonderful and splendid thing love is.

Pan   Madame Gu, you're the most sentimental woman on earth!

Gu (*Gratified*)   That's why I'm the most tragic, the most tormented, the most passionate, the most vulnerable.

Pan   Well, why did you suddenly stop playing? You're not vulnerable at the mahjong table.

Gu (*Suddenly reminded*)   Aiya, I'm sorry, could you pour me a glass of water, Manager Pan? I've got to take some medicine (*She sits down and takes out some pills from her handbag.*)

Pan (*Pouring water*)   What's the matter now? Do you need anything else?

Gu   Don't ask. Quickly, hand me the water. I must take this first. (*She feels her heart and thumps herself gently.*)

Pan (*Handing her the glass*)   Are you all right? Bailu's got all sorts of medicine here.

Gu (*Swallows the pills*)   That's a bit better.

Pan (*Standing beside her*)   If not, why not take one of Bailu's sleeping pills and sleep it off?

Gu (*Making the most of it*)   No, that won't be necessary. I've got chest pains! The reason I stopped playing just now was that I suddenly got to thinking about that ungrateful creature Hu Si and it made my heart start aching again. You feel it if you don't believe me!

Pan (*Reluctant to touch her*)   I believe you.

Gu (*Obstinately*)   Come on, feel this!

Pan (*Resignedly stretching out his hand*)   All right, then. (*In a cursory manner*) Seems all right to me.

Gu (*Put out*)   What do you mean, 'all right'! I'm on the brink of death! My heart's palpitating so hard it's nearly bursting through my chest. I went to one doctor after another and they all said there's nothing wrong with me, but I didn't believe it! So I spent two hundred dollars on a consultation with the famous French doctor, Dr Ledoux, and he diagnosed what was wrong straight away: heart disease. No wonder I often suffered from heartache, since there was something wrong all along. Feel again if you don't believe me and listen to the way it keeps pounding away. (*She grabs* **Pan's** *hand.*)

Pan (*Having no alternative but to put his head down and listen*)   All right, I will. (*Nodding his head repeatedly*) Yes, it really is pounding, isn't it? (**Bailu** *comes in through the door on the left; she is in high spirits.*)

Bailu (*Taken aback at seeing them and not knowing quite what to say*)   Oh! So you're here too, Yueting?

(**Pan** *stands up and walks over to the table to light a cigarette.*)

Gu (*Embarrassed*)   Did you see that? Mr Pan is giving me medical attention!

Bailu   Your heart again? (*Looking back toward the open door, through which still comes the sound of conversation and mahjong tiles*) Mr Liu, you can take those rounds. You must forgive me running off like this, Mrs Li. If you want anything, just ask. I must entertain my new friend.

Pan   New friend?

Gu   What new friend?

Bailu   I thought Dasheng was out here.

Pan   Are you referring to that cousin of yours Fang?

Bailu   Yes, he was here just now.

Gu   Bailu, you mean that gentleman who grimaces whenever he sees anyone? You mustn't invite him here again! He gives me the creeps! (*She goes towards the window.*)

Bailu   He lives here.

Gu   Here?

Bailu (*With a smile*)   Yes – Dasheng! Dasheng!

(**Dasheng** *Comes in through the right hand door.*)

Dasheng (*Pausing in the doorway*)   Oh, it's you. Did you want me for something?

Bailu   What are you up to? Why don't you come out here and socialize?

Dasheng   I've been chatting with your foster daughter Pipsqueak. (*Happily*) What a sweet kid.

Bailu   And now how about coming out here and chatting with us. (*Going over to him*) Come and join us, don't be so anti-social.

Dasheng (*Sizes up* **Pan** *and* **Madame Gu**, *and as if talking to himself*)   Oh, I see your dad is here (*Pauses, looks at* **Gu**) and from the look of it, your mom too. (*Suddenly turns to* **Bailu**). No, I'd rather keep talking to the girl. (*He turns and closes the door behind him.*)

Bailu   It's simply hopeless trying to get him to do anything.

Pan   By the way, Madame Gu, Hu Si hasn't turned up for work at the bank the last few days again.

Gu   I scolded him and he went off in a huff. Don't take it personally, Manager Pan, he – he –

Pan   All right, enough about him. (*Standing beside* **Madame Gu** *at the window*) Look, they've already started construction on the bank's new building. Once they've laid the foundation they'll have the building up in no time. A great location like this we've only got to lease it out and we're guaranteed fifteen per cent interest at the very least. And if the market picks up we'll make twenty, perhaps even thirty, per cent.

Gu   Listen to the wonderful schemes Manager Pan's got, Bailu. Now what was it you were saying, Mr Pan? When the market is something-or-other and the economy is something else, you – what was it you said one should do?

Pan   I said when the market is volatile and the economy unstable one should invest in real estate.

Gu   That's it; you see, Bailu? If I don't spend money now on putting up buildings my market will become unstable, you see? So you were quite right when you had the idea of putting up this big building, Manager Pan. Twenty per cent interest, that'll bring in two or three thousand dollars a month, not bad pocket money. (*Enter* **Fusheng**)

Fusheng   Mr Zhang from the newspaper office is here, Sir.

Bailu   What would he want with you all of a sudden?

Pan   I asked him over to find out what's been happening the past few days.

Fusheng   Shall I see him in?

Pan   No, take him along to room thirty-four.

Fusheng   Miss, Mrs Dong has arrived, and Miss Liu, too.

Bailu   Take them all in there. They've come for mahjong. Say I'll be right in.

Fusheng   Very well, Miss. (*Exits.*)

Pan   Well, Madame Gu, that's settled then, I'll have your funds transferred.

Gu   I leave it all to you. If it's in your hands nothing can go wrong.

Pan   Good, I'll discuss it with you later.

Bailu   Just a moment, Yueting. Don't forget what I asked you to do.

Pan   About what?

Bailu   About Pipsqueak. I want to take her in as my foster daughter. I need you to mention it to Jin Ba and set it right.

Pan   All right, don't worry, I'll see to it.

Bailu   Thank you.

Pan   No need to thank me; just stop calling me dad, and I'll be happy. (*Exits through the center door.*)

Gu (*She watches* **Pan** *jauntily depart, then looks round again and unleashes another torrent of words*)   I do admire you, Bailu! I really don't know how to do you justice. You're a work of art! Charming, beautiful, romantic, voluptuous. On your own in a place like this, yet with friends everywhere. Take Manager Pan, for instance: he doesn't approve of anyone, but he approves of you. Mr Pan's a fine and capable man, to quote a modern phrase, he's a 'unique and unprecedented first class product.' Real estate, stocks, government bonds, is there anyone better than him? That's why I leave my money in his hands for him to invest on my behalf. And this is the man you've fallen for, you've hooked him, when you say yes he daren't say no, that why I'm always saying you're a girl with the most wonderful prospects.

Bailu (*Lighting a cigarette*)   I didn't hook Pan, he's the one who wants to come here, what can I do about it?

Gu (*Making an effort to please her*)   In any case, it's a case of 'beauty is in the eye of the beholder.' No, that's not quite what I meant to say (*Smugly makes an attempt to cover up her mistake*). You know, with all these modern friends of mine and their newfangled phrases, I sometimes get mixed up. . . . What I meant to say is that you two are just like Maurice Chevalier and Jeanette MacDonald,[12] tweedle dee and tweedle dum, a match made in heaven.

Bailu (*Willfully*)   You really do have a way with words. I'm always at a loss for words when I'm with you, since you've said it all already.

Gu (*Preening herself*)   Do you mean that? (*Can't help swinging her legs back and forth.*)

Bailu   Absolutely.

Gu   I'd have to agree with you. Ever since my old man passed away it's like my mouth has been switched on like a record player; I've suddenly gotten so much smarter and I have something to say about everything. (*With a mixture of satisfaction and self-pity*) But what's the use of a clever tongue? One still can't control a man's heart with it. I'm now realizing for the first time, Bailu, that men have absolutely no conscience. However well you treat a man it's all in vain.

Bailu (*Looks at her in amusement*)   Oh? What's Hu Si been up to now?

Gu (*With a long sigh*)   Who knows? I haven't even seen him in whole two days. I've phoned, I've written, I've gone to *see* him myself, but he's never in. What do you think, after all the money I've spent on him and after lavishing my affection on him, now look what he does: at the first little thing that upsets him he storms off and ignores me for days on end.

Bailu   In that case you mustn't fret over him anymore and save yourself a lot of bother.

Gu   But . . . you can't put it like that. I think that however modern a woman may be she ought to pay some heed to the 'three obediences and four virtues.' So no matter how poorly Hu Si treats me I shall always have a certain amount of affection for him.

Bailu   Bravo, my dear!

Gu (*Taken aback*)   What do you mean?

Bailu Bravo for leading such a principled life! Fancy you and Hu Si embracing notions of 'submission and propriety'!

Gu (*With an indignant flash of her eyes*) What! You think I'm a woman with no character or principles?

Bailu But my dear Madame Gu, if you're going to go on about 'submission and propriety' you'll have to get back into that bridal sedan-chair again and officially marry Hu Si!

Gu Hu Si and I get married? (*Shaking her head vigorously*) That would never do. If this is the way he treats me before we're married, he'd treat me a lot worse afterwards – I'd be worse off than a worn out shoe! And this newfangled marriage is just useless: if he ever changed his mind all he'd have to do is hire a divorce lawyer. Not like before when I was married to my dearly departed: for better or worse I was his wife! And a wife who'd been brought in on a bridal chair, too, so he had to behave himself and worship me and pay my bills. Couldn't he divorce me, you say? Get rid of his own lawfully wedded wife? In his dreams! But now . . . (*Gloomily*) ah. . . . Bailu, you're a smart girl, think about it, what's the point of getting married? What's the point?

Bailu (*With a sigh*) There's nothing in it either way. (*Thoughtfully*) Though I've always thought forcing one's lover to become one's husband does seem a great pity.

Gu (*Not quite understanding* **Bailu**, *yet guessing the gist of her meaning*) That's just what I was trying to say! Going out to dinner, for instance, or going out dancing: as long as two people aren't married they'll always have a good time, but as soon as they tie the knot, humph. (*Her feelings getting the better of her, as if she can already see Hu Si turning into a callous husband.*) No, it can't be done, not if you talk till the cows come home. Hu Si can say what he likes; if he proposes, I shall refuse. And besides, I'm afraid of him: once we were married he'd show his true colors; and you know that daughter of mine –

Bailu The college graduate?

Gu Yes, that's the one.

Bailu What about her?

Gu (*Launching into her second objection*) You know what a free-and-easy spirit I am; well, I certainly don't take after my daughter. She's quite the intellectual, she's a Christian, enjoys charity work, and puts on all sorts of airs. Not like me. Once I'd set my heart on my Qiu, nothing else mattered to me but him; now that I've set my heart on Hu Si, all I live for is Hu Si. Funny, isn't it, my daughter being like that when I'm like this? Must have something to do with heredity! (*Proud that she has utilized another new word; unconsciously begins to cough*)

Bailu   But what's your daughter got to do with your getting married?

Gu   Oh, yes, I always get carried away and forget what I was going to say. (*Dropping her voice and speaking close to* **Bailu's** *ear with animated gestures*) I'll tell you, my daughter's quite opposed to Hu Si – though naturally I understand completely: she's afraid Hu Si is going to spend all my money; furthermore, if I did marry him, you see, their ages would be . . . well, er, there wouldn't be that much difference between them, and as her mother you can imagine how awkward it would be to tell her what to call him!

Bailu (*Yawning and growing bored of this tiresome topic*)   I don't see why you're so stuck on to Hu Si when he treats you so badly.

Gu (*With a great show of pride*)   That's love for you! Obviously I know perfectly well he's lazy and lacks ambition. I had to beg Manager Pan to give him a job. Manager Pan said that business was bad, but for my sake he dismissed fifteen, or was it twenty? No fifteen, no twenty, in any case, quite a few people from the bank so that he could squeeze him in. And what does Hu Si do? He complains that the salary's too low and the work boring and after showing up for a couple of days he's now stopped going in regularly. Lazy, good-for-nothing, helpless, – ah, poor boy, it's his nature. If I don't take him under my wing, who will? (*As if having discovered a universal truth*) Ah, love! I never understood what the word really meant till now.

Bailu (*Mockingly*)   No wonder you've become so clever.

Gu   I'll tell you, love is when you willingly give a man money to spend and don't mind how he squanders it – *that's* what love is! – Yes, that's love!

Bailu   That explains why they say love has its price. I finally understand what this actually means.

Gu   Yes, there's no doubt whatsoever about that. I'd like to get Manager Pan to find him a job with a film studio. Now, Bailu, considering what good friends we are, couldn't you have a word with Manager Pan for me? I really feel I can't bother him again myself.

Bailu   What, you mean you want him to be a film star?

Gu (*Fervently*) Yes, and what a sensation he'd be! Don't you see, he's every inch the film star! Physique, features, nose, eyes, all pretty good, in my opinion.

Bailu But aren't you afraid other women will chase after him?

Gu No, that's one thing I am not concerned about. Whatever his faults at least he's devoted to me – follows me around like a little puppy. (*Suddenly realizing that this statement is slightly inconsistent with reality*) Of course, he hasn't come to see me these past few days, but you can hardly blame him; you see, he asked for three hundred dollars and I wouldn't let him have it. He wanted me to buy a new car, a Chevrolet, but I didn't have the money just then so I said no. Then he proposed to me – for the umpteenth time, I'm telling you – but I turned him down again, so no wonder he's mad.

Bailu So you want to find him a better job to restore his good mood.

Gu I promised him this time that if he becomes a movie star I will marry him. I'm telling you; I've thought the whole thing through; we're sure to have our photos in all the magazines, great big spreads, of me, of Hu Si, of the two of us together. And the papers will be full of the news of our honeymoon every day. What's more . . .

Bailu Congratulations! So now you do want to get married. I shall have to drink a toast in your honor! But what about your daughter the college graduate? What will you do about her?

Gu (*Confidently*) Oh, it'll all be different once Hu Si becomes a star. I'll get him to attend her charity events and perform a couple of romantic songs (*Gestures with her hand*), dance the hulla-hulla, and she'll be delighted, you see if she isn't!

Bailu All right, my dear, I promise. Clever you, you really do think of everything. I'll ask Manager Pan about it and tomorrow we'll get him into a film company. All right?

Gu (*Overcome with gratitude*) Thank you! Thank you! There, didn't I say you were a genius, and I was absolutely right.

(**Fusheng** *comes in through the center door holding a stack of bills.*)

Fusheng Oh, I didn't realize you were here, Madame Gu.

Gu What do you want?

Fusheng I am here to see Miss Chen.

Bailu About those bills you have there?

Fusheng   Yes, Miss. Master Pan's covered the bills that were due yesterday, Miss, and told me to bring these to you.

Bailu   Burn them.

Fusheng   Very well . . . er, but there are (*Reaching into his pocket*) there are some more –

Bailu   More?

Fusheng   If you don't believe me I'll tell you (*About to recite them to her.*)

Bailu   Can't you see I've got company?

Fusheng   Pardon me, Miss. (*Enter* **Georgy Zhang** *through the door on the left. He is in evening wear and is carrying a top hat, white gloves, an ivory walking stick, and a bouquet of flowers. He enters the room with a pompous swagger.*)

Georgy (*Glowing with enthusiasm and heartiness*)   Bonjour! Bonjour! I knew you two would be out here! (*Shaking hands*) Bonjour! Bonjour (*He grips their hands tightly.*)

Gu   Evening, Dr Zhang!

Georgy   Madame Gu! (*Looking her up and down*) You really do get lovelier by the day.

Gu (*Enraptured*)   Really?

Georgy (*Looking at* **Bailu**)   Oh my, my little Lulu, that dress of yours is . . .

Bailu (*Imitating his manner*)   Tout simplement ravissant!

Georgy   Absolutely right! You're brilliant, you always know what I'm going to say. (*Turning to* **Fusheng**) By the way, er, garçon!

Fusheng   Ye-si, si-a!

Georgy   Tell them in there that I won't be joining them for mahjong.

Fusheng   Ye-si, si-a! (*He goes out through the door on the left.*)

Bailu   Settle down, will you? Do take a seat.

Georgy   Excusez-moi, ma cherie, Lulu.

Gu   Hey, will the two of you refrain from all that foreign gibberish.

Georgy   Oh, je m'excuse, pardonnez-moi. I'm terribly sorry, but you see my Chinese has gotten so rusty that I find it more convenient to express myself in French. It's coming back now, but at first I could barely manage a whole sentence in Chinese, that's how powerful foreign languages are, you see.

Gu   Professor Zhang you really are fortunate, having gone abroad, what with the supremacy of foreign languages. Poor me, my whole life I'd never manage to forget Chinese.

Bailu   Georgy, why are you all dressed up today?

Georgy   Ah, you've no idea the things one gets roped into working for the government. One day it's some ceremony or other, the next it's a wedding one has to attend. Liu, our department head at the ministry, got married today, and I was his best man. Afterwards I suddenly thought of you and I couldn't even wait to change, I just had to see you straight away. . . . Oh, yes, I've brought you these flowers, to express my wish that you will always be as beautiful as you are today and to apologize. My intentions last night when I went into your room were. . . .

Gu   What happened last night?

Bailu   (*Giving him a meaningful look*) It was nothing.

Georgy   It was nothing, you say? Fantastic, you're always such a good sport.

Gu   Professor Zhang, you haven't been spending time with Hu Si the past few days, have you?

Georgy   Hu Si? I saw him at the club the other day, being all lovey-dovey with a . . .

Gu (*Excited*)   A what?

Georgy   The dog he was walking.

Gu   The callous creature, he'd rather take his dog out than me.

Georgy   Why, what's the matter, have you two fallen out again? Then what's he doing sitting in a car out front?

Gu   What! You say he's outside?

Georgy   Didn't you know? That's odd.

Gu   Professor Zhang, no one would think you're an educated man, honestly. Why didn't you say so before?

Georgy   I don't see how an education is any guarantee of being able to divine your desire to see Hu Si.

Gu   Well, I am not going argue with you, I must be off. (*Hurries to the center door then turning around*) Oh, and Bailu, don't forget the favor I asked. Remember to put in a word for me when you see Manager Pan.

Bailu   All right.

Gu   Professor, Gu-da-bai! Bai-Bai! (*Exits*)

Georgy   Whew! Gone at last, the dear thing. (*Turning warmly to* **Bailu**) Bailu, I must tell you the good news.

Bailu   Good news? Has your wife blessed you with another son?

Georgy (*With his usual smug wave of the hand*)   Pah! Ridiculous.

Bailu   Then you must have been promoted again.

Georgy   As wonderful as that. This is it. (*Taking* **Bailu's** *hand and speaking intimately and happily*) Yesterday afternoon I officially divorced my wife!

Bailu   Divorced her? But hasn't she given you three children? And now you don't want her anymore? She struggled to raise your children while you went overseas to study and then you turn around and divorce her as soon as you get back?

Georgy   What do you mean? I paid her, I made her a proper settlement. What's with you, how can you be so unkind?

Bailu   All right then, please enlighten me.

Georgy   No, Lulu, let's not talk about her, forget her. Let me tell you my other piece of good news.

Bailu   You're just brimming with good news today.

Georgy (*With a look of great tenderness*)   Lulu, do you know why I came here last night?

Bailu (*Mockingly*)   Don't tell me you came to propose to me as well?

Georgy (*Taken aback*)   *Oh la la! Juste ciel!* You really are divine, how can you guess what's going on in my heart?

Bailu (*Alarmed*)   What! You –

Georgy   Now, Lulu, you must take pity on me, take pity on a recent divorcee, a man with no one to love him. You must say yes.

Bailu   You mean that when you showed here and made that scene last night (*With utter disgust*), and threw up all over my bed, you were here to propose to me?

Georgy   That was because I was drunk.

Bailu   Obviously.

Georgy   And because I was so overjoyed. Because I suddenly realized that I was going to be the luckiest man on earth, because I knew you'd accept.

Bailu   Strange, why is it men all have such extraordinary self-confidence?

Georgy   Lulu, I've got a house now on Guangdong Road, stock in Daxing Coal Corporation, tens of thousands in savings at Dafeng Bank, and then of course there's still my government job. Down the road, if I play it smart, I shouldn't have the slightest difficulty securing an income of three or four thousand dollars a month. On top of all this, I didn't do so badly for myself overseas: I have a Ph.D. and an M.A. in political science, a B.A. in economics, and on top of that . . .

Bailu (*Shouting*)   Dasheng, Dasheng, come out here.

(**Dasheng** *emerges from the bedroom on the right.*)

Dasheng (*Seeing the two of them sitting together*)   Oh, pardon me, you two are here. I must have misheard. (*He turns to go.*)

Bailu   No, I called you, open the window, quickly.

Georgy   What for?

Bailu   I want a breath of fresh air. There's quite a stench in here all of a sudden.

Dasheng   Stench?

Bailu (*Scathingly*)   Why, yes, don't you smell it? (*Changing the subject.*) And Pipsqueak?

Dasheng   In the room. The kid is so amusing. I quite like her.

Bailu   Then why don't you take her with you?

Dasheng   Fine, I've always wanted a little sister like her.

Bailu   She's yours.

Dasheng   Thank you. It's settled.

Georgy (*Looking at* **Dasheng**)   Hh, hm, Bailu, aren't you going to introduce us? Where are your manners?

Bailu   Oh, haven't you two met?

Georgy (*Looking at* **Dasheng**)   Your face looks familiar. Have we met somewhere?

Dasheng   Mr Zhang, I have met you, you're Georgy Zhang, Zhang Qiaozhi. You've some sort of PhD. or M.A., you've held various posts . . .

Georgy (*Suddenly*)   Why, of course, of course. We have met before, we're old friends!

Bailu (*Stifling a laugh*)   Really? Where did you meet?

Georgy   Yes, we're old friends. I remember now, five years ago it was, we came back aboard the same ship from Europe. (*Suddenly going up to* **Dasheng** *and gripping him firmly by the hand, warmly*) Already so many years ago. Excellent, excellent. Do sit down. (*He turns to get a cigar.*)

Bailu (*In a low voice*)   What's he talking about?

Dasheng (*With a smile*)   Your guess is as good as mine.

(*Enter* **Li Shiqing** *from the door to the left. A former clerk at the Dafeng Bank, through sheer cunning and a gift for flattery he has now risen to the position of Pan Yueting's secretary. He is a wizened little man who strives to imitate the manner of the important personage he imagines himself to be, though he can never quite conceal his humble origins and constantly surveys the expression on people's faces and smiles with fawning attentiveness. When he assumes a serious look we discover on his forehead a great many wrinkles of long standing, one fine furrow upon another, laden with all the humiliation, poverty, and degradation that he has suffered in life. When in the company of all these personages of 'wealth and rank' that he so admires and envies he often feels ashamed of his own inferiority, and fearful of being looked down upon, brags of purely fictitious achievements, though when he remembers his family, old and young, he can't help but hang his head in mortified silence. He despises those above him yet feels obliged to serve them. All he can do is swallow his indignation and vent on his poor wife and children when he gets home. Such is his detestable yet pathetic character. He has rat-like eyes, thinning hair, faint nearly invisible eyebrows, and a few stray whiskers; he has a flat nose and stubby chin, and a mouth full of rotten teeth; his voice is always shrill. His small, thin frame is clad in* *a faded yellow gown. Over this he wears a brand new black satin jacket. His entrance is heralded by the tapping of his patent-leather shoes, the laceless kind; though worn out they've been polished to a shine. His trousers are bound at the ankles.*)

Li   Good evening, Miss Chen! (*To* **Georgy**) Professor! (*He bows.*)

Georgy   Ah, what perfect timing. Mr Li, I'd like you to meet an old friend of mine.

Li   Yes, yes, yes.

Georgy (*Turning to* **Dasheng**)   This is Mr Li Shiqing, secretary of Dafeng Bank, Mr Pan's right-hand man.

Li   You are too kind, too kind. And this gentleman would be . . .

Georgy   This is an old classmate of mine who travelled back from Europe with me. Mr – er, Mr –

Dasheng   Fang.

Georgy (*Striking the side of his head*)   Of course, what a terrible memory I've got, yes, Fang. Mr Fang.

Li   A pleasure to meet you.

Bailu   You'd better watch out, Mr Li. Mrs Li's been looking for you, says she wants to see you about something.

Li   Did she? (*Smiling*) She's busy playing mahjong so I can't imagine she has the time.

Bailu   Still? She told me earlier she wasn't going to play anymore. How's she doing, winning or losing?

Li   My wife's not that good at mahjong so naturally she's losing, though she keeps her losses down, only three or four hundred dollars, hardly . . .

Bailu (*Saying it for him*)   Hardly much.

Li   You're a clever one, Miss Chen, the way you take the words right out of one's mouth. (*With a forced smile*) Really, though, it's a pleasure even to lose when we come to your place for mahjong.

Bailu   Thanks, but you needn't flatter me. I hardly deserve it.

Georgy   You haven't seen Manager Pan, have you?

Li   I was hoping to find him, as a matter of fact.

Bailu   He's probably in room thirty-four. Fusheng will know.

Li   Thank you, Miss Chen, in that case I hope you don't mind if I take my leave, excuse me, Professor. Excuse me, Mr Fang.

(*Just as* **Li***, bowing and nodding, is about to depart,* **Madame Gu** *enters in through the middle door shepherding* **Hu Si** *in front of her. He is just what one would expect: pale complexion, a high-bridged nose, thin lips, straight white teeth, sleekly combed back hair, a thin moustache which is quite enchanting when, on the rare occasion, he smiles, and a pair of melancholic eyes. He never looks directly at anyone but gives them a sidelong glance then quickly looks away as if he does not want to be seen looking; this mannerism of his is universally held to be an endearing one. He seldom laughs, giving the impression of being rather sad; nor does he speak much, though when the occasional phrase or two escapes him it comes as a shock, for no one expects that such a pretty exterior could harbor such a multitude of crass thoughts and feelings. Yet he makes no attempt to disguise them nor does he consider them ugly; on the contrary, he prides himself on being, as many people praise him, 'the most handsome fellow in China.' He is forever gazing in the mirror, fixing his hair and adjusting his clothes; clothes are his life, sacred, inviolable treasures. At present he is wearing a European-style outfit: black shirt, white silk tie, a flamboyant polka-dotted lavender suit. He carries a short exquisitely-made cane with a glittering silver chain.*)

(*As he comes in he wears a nonchalant expression devoid of emotion, he shows neither apprehension nor politeness, nor does he so much as nod a greeting when he sees people. He just walks in 'mysteriously,' as* **Madame Gu** *puts it.*)

Li   Good evening, Madame Gu. (*With familiarity*) Good evening, Mr Hu.

Gu (*To* **Li**)   Help me drag him in.

Li   What's happened this time?

Hu Si (*Glancing at* **Madame Gu** *then turning unconcernedly to* **Li**)   Don't mind her.

Li   You must excuse me, I have to see Manager Pan. (*He goes out.*)

Gu (*Petulantly, like a naïve girl, obviously in imitation of* **Bailu**)   Now you're to stay with me! I won't have you looking! (*Pushing* **Hu Si** *into the room and speaking triumphantly, half to* **Hu Si** *and half to the others*) When I say you can't look, you can't! Do you hear me?

Hu Si (*Distastefully acquiescing*)   All right, all right, I heard you. Now look what you've done! (*With a frown he wrestles free of her grasp and points to his sleeve, which is now creased by the pressure of her large mantou-like hand.* **Madame Gu** *feigns an indifferent laugh as she lets go.*) Good clothes ruined! (*He brushes himself off and straightens his tie.*)

Gu (*Smiling uneasily, yet feeling obliged to be angry with him since there are other people present*)   Oh, you!

Bailu   Now what's all this about?

Hu Si   Nothing. (*Astutely realizing the situation could turn ugly, takes* **Madame Gu** *by the hand and smiles in a captivating manner*) Oh, you! (*He was going to say 'What are you so frantic about?' but changes his mind and smoothes back his sleek shiny hair. The two burst into laughter and* **Madame Gu's** *good mood is restored.*)

Gu (*Herself again, to* **Bailu**)   We do have fun, don't we, bickering all day like this?

Bailu   You're like a couple of youngsters, making scenes like that in public.

Gu   But we *are* a couple of youngsters! (*To* **Hu Si**) Aren't we? Now I ask you, why did you insist on looking at that woman? It's not as if she were beautiful. Coarse, fat, common, uneducated –

Hu Si   Oh, enough already, why must you keep on about it? (*He sits down without waiting to be asked, takes out a handkerchief and wipes his face, then produces a small mirror and looks at himself in it.*) I came when you told me to, didn't I? (*Suddenly noticing* **Georgy** *and bowing*) Hello, you're here early, Professor.

Georgy   Hu Si, long time no see. What have you been doing with yourself lately?

Hu Si   Not much. Larking about at the club, hanging out with the dance-hall girls, nothing too exciting.

Gu   Humph, some slut's got her claws into you again, I suppose.

Hu Si   There you go again! (*Indifferently and unhurriedly*) If you say so.

Gu (*Annoyed*)   I didn't say you had for certain.

Hu Si (*With the same expression of indifference*)   All right then, isn't it?

(**Fusheng** *enters from the left.*)

Fusheng   The refreshments are ready, Miss, in room fifty-one. Would you like to take a look at them first?

Bailu (*Turning from talking with* **Dasheng**)   All right, I'll be right there.

Fusheng   Very well, Miss. (*Exits left.*)

Bailu   Hu Si, have you met my new guest? (**Hu Si** *rises languidly.*) Mr Fang, just arrived here, a cousin of mine. (*To* **Dasheng**) This is Hu Si, the most handsome fellow in China.

Gu (*Turning elatedly from talking to* **Georgy**)   You mustn't compliment him so, he'll only go making my life miserable again.

Bailu   Well, why don't you two chat while I go in there to make sure everything's all right. (*Exits left.*)

Hu Si (*Unconsciously smoothing his hair again, he turns to look in the mirror on the wardrobe. After standing by* **Dasheng** *for a while without speaking, he suddenly blurts out.*)   I've been looking forward to meeting you; be nice and look out for me.

Dasheng (*Not knowing quite how to respond*)   Er – well –

Hu Si   You look familiar.

Dasheng   Do I?

Hu Si   How old are you?

Dasheng (*Taken aback*)   Eh?

Hu Si   You're quite good-looking, not bad at all. You'll do well here. Hey, Professor, don't you think Mr Fang looks like that friend of mine, Huang Yunqiu? (*He scans* **Dasheng** *up and down.*)

Georgy   Huang Yunqiu?

Hu Si   The female impersonator who plays the noblewoman at the Grand Stage.

Dasheng (*With distaste*)   And I'll bet you play the flirtatious young woman.

Hu Si   How observant of you – well, actually, I just dabble a bit. Madame Gu is my student, and Bailu's had lessons from me, too.

Dasheng (*To himself*)   Who does he think he is? (*A pause.*)

Hu Si (*Puzzled, then suddenly serious*)   Feel like something to eat, Professor?

Georgy (*Startled*)   Eh? – No, I'm not hungry!

Gu (*Also puzzled by this unexpected question from* **Hu Si**)   Are you –
are you hungry?

Hu Si   I – er – (*Glancing at* **Dasheng**) no (*Shaking his head*), no, me
neither.

Dasheng (*Looking at the three of them, with a sigh*)   If you'll excuse
me, I think I'll go for a walk.

Georgy   But, Mr Fang, you –

Dasheng   You must excuse me.

(**Dasheng** *exits through the center door. The three of them watch him
leave, then exchange meaningful glances.*)

Hu Si   What's he so stuck-up for?

Gu   Bailu must really be bored to have brought an idiot like this from
who knows where to amuse herself with.

Georgy   Strange, come to think of it I'm not so sure that I have met him
before.

Hu Si (*Lighting a cigarette*)   Professor, I've learned to drive.

Gu   Yes, you haven't seen him drive yet, have you? He goes awfully fast.

Hu Si   And you know what, Professor? I've been asked to join a film
company. They want me for the young male parts. So now I've started
learning how to ride, and swim, and dance, and dress in European style.
Speaking of which, Professor, what do you think of my western suit?
Pretty sharp, don't you think?

Georgy   It'll do, it'll do. Though at the very least you should have
your suits made in Hong Kong, and don't pay less than one hundred and
seventy dollars for them.

Hu Si (*Looking at* **Madame Gu**)   Hear that? And you'd have me
working at Dafeng Bank on a monthly salary that wouldn't get me even
one suit!

Gu   Don't be so greedy. Li Shiqing is at it from morning till night and
he only makes two hundred a month, and that's only because Bailu was
kind enough to put in a word with Manager Pan on his behalf.

Hu Si   And that's because he won't stand up for himself. Nobody sells
themselves as cheaply as that. (*Enter* **Bailu** *from the left.*)

Bailu (*Standing in the doorway*)   This way, the refreshments are served. Come on in, everyone, and have something to eat. Make yourselves at home. (*Looking over her shoulder*) Look, here's *Georgy*, Miss Liu.

Georgy (*Catching sight of Miss Liu at a distance through the open door, he goes across, his hand already extended, exclaiming loudly*)   Bonjour, bonjour, mademoiselle. (*With a wave of greeting*) – Ah, my dear Miss Liu. Don't get up. Let me come over and keep you company. (*He goes in still talking loudly and an exchange of greetings can be heard from within.*)

Hu Si (*Unhurriedly adjusts his belt and straightens his clothing, then turning to* **Madame Gu**, *with his usual air of languid nonchalance*)   Come on! I've been starved ever since I arrived.

Gu (*Darting him a glance*)   Why didn't you say so before? Hurry up, then! (*She stomps forward.*)

Hu Si (*With a sideways glance at her, more slowly than ever*)   Oh, you!

Gu (*Having now reached the door on the left she looks round and, seeing* **Hu Si** *still standing there, she extends a hand and beckons to him, smiling*)   Come along now, Hu Si.

Hu Si (*Rolls his eyes, as if in triumph*): Ha!

(*With ease he moves through the doorway on the left, flashing* **Bailu** *an entrancing smile as he goes.*)

Bailu (*Looking all round*)   Hey, what happened to Dasheng? (*Looking over her shoulder and suddenly seeing Mrs Li behind her*) Why, Mrs Li, aren't you having something to eat?. . . . Oh, I see, please come in.

(*Enter* **Mrs Li**, *a gaunt woman with sedate movements and not very elegantly dressed. Her expression is gentle but suffused with sorrow. Apart from a dusting of face powder she is devoid of makeup. She seems to have come with great reluctance. She talks with* **Bailu**; *she is courteous yet ill at ease.*)

Bailu (*Amicably*)   You wanted to have a word with Mr Li?

Mrs Li   Yes, Miss Chen.

Bailu (*Ringing the bell*)   You *are* an affectionate couple, can't bear to be parted for even a short while. I do envy you. (*Enter* **Fusheng**.)

Bailu   Fusheng, go and ask Mr Li to come. Tell him Mrs Li would like a word with him.

Fusheng   Very well.

Bailu   Oh, and is Mr Fang out there?

Fusheng   I haven't seen him.

Bailu   That'll be all, then. (**Fusheng** *goes out.*)

Bailu   Will you excuse me a moment, Mrs Li, I must attend to something. (*Going towards the door on the right*) Dasheng, Dasheng!

(**Pipsqueak** *comes out of* **Bailu's** *bedroom. Her appearance has been completely transformed from twelve hours ago. She is wearing an old rose-colored qipao of* **Bailu's**, *which is still too loose and clearly not her own. Her jet-black hair is down, and she has two large circles of rouge on her fair-complexioned cheeks. Her eyes are bulging out like a goldfish, partly on account her excessive weeping over the past few days and partly because she is so bewildered by the strangeness and novelty of her surroundings. She looks at* **Bailu** *and* **Mrs Li** *without uttering a sound, like a painted doll.*)

Bailu   Is Mr Fang in there?

Pipsqueak   Mr Fang?

Bailu   The gentleman who was talking with you just now.

Pipsqueak   Oh, him. No, he's not in there.

Bailu   He's run off again, then. (*Suddenly, to* **Pipsqueak**) Hey, who told you to come out?

Pipsqueak (*Alarmed*)   I – I came out because I heard you calling.

Bailu (*Teasing her*)   Have you already forgotten who was here last night, then?

Pipsqueak (*Immediately turning and going back through the door*)   All right, Miss.

Bailu   Come back. (**Pipsqueak** *returns*) There's a window in there that opens on to the hallway. Now, don't forget to keep it closed tightly, do you hear?

Pipsqueak   Yes, all right. (*She runs back into the bedroom.*)

(*Enter* **Li Shiqing** *through the center door.*)

Bailu   Wait, come back here (**Pipsqueak** *returns and* **Bailu** *uses a handkerchief to even out her makeup, and to dry her tears, and smiles kindly.*). There, off you go! (**Pipsqueak** *goes back into the right room.* **Bailu** *turns.*)

Bailu   Ah, so there you are at last, Mr Li. Your wife insists on seeing you. You really are a devoted couple.

Li (*Politely keeping up the spirit of her bantering remark*)   I tell you, Miss Chen, we're as much in love as we ever were. My wife gets quite miserable if an hour passes without whispering sweet nothings to me.

Bailu   Is that so? Then I'll leave you to talk to your hearts' content without disturbance. (*She exits left.*)

Li (*He bows as he watches* **Bailu** *leave, then pauses momentarily. Having looked all round his face hardens and he speaks in a harsh tone*)   Well, how did it go? Did you win or lose?

Mrs Li (*Pitifully*)   Won't you let me go home now, Shiqing?

Li   You lost?

Mrs Li (*Hanging her head*)   Yes.

Li (*Showing signs of agitation*)   You lost the entire hundred and fifty dollars I gave you?

Mrs Li (*In a subdued voice*)   Not all of it, but almost.

Li (*Pausing, at a loss*)   But how could you lose so much?

Mrs Li   I was nervous, and that made me play even worse than usual.

Li (*Losing his temper*)   Nervous? It's just a game. What's there to be nervous about? You're so . . . so ignorant.

Mrs Li (*Unable to bear his reproach, begins to cry*)   I didn't want to play mahjong in the first place, but you insisted. You made me come here, and so I did as you said, and played for high stakes with this rich crowd – and when I lose money you go and – (*She weeps aloud.*)

Li (*Glares at her and becoming more angry still*)   Cry! Cry! That's all you ever do! This is no place to cry! Making a spectacle of yourself! Now stop crying. (*Irritably*) I've plenty of money here, so enough of this nonsense.

Mrs Li   I don't want any money.

Li   Then what do you want?

Mrs Li (*Meekly*)   I want to go home.

Li   Don't be ridiculous. I've got more money here. (*Taking out his wallet to comfort her*) See, look, I've a hundred dollars here. Take eighty for now, how's that?

Mrs Li   Where did you get all this?

Li   Never mind.

Mrs Li (*Suddenly*)   Where's your fur coat?

Li   At home, I didn't wear it this evening.

Mrs Li (*Noticing a receipt rolled in with the cash in his hand*)   Shiqing, what do you have there?

Li (*Hurriedly*)   It's a – (*But **Mrs Li** has already snatched it from him.*)

Mrs Li (*Looking at the receipt and then handing it back to him*)   You've gone and pawned your coat again.

Li   Don't shout at the top of your lungs like that!

Mrs Li   Oh, Shiqing, is it worth it?

Li (*Angrily*)   It's none of your business, I'm telling you, it's none of your business.

Mrs Li   Shiqing, I've really had enough. Let me go home, alright? We don't belong in an establishment like this. No respectable company, not a decent word spoken –

Li   What do you mean, no respectable company! Isn't Manager Pan respectable? Look at all the schools, and workhouses for the poor, and factories he's opened are these not the deeds of a decent man?

Mrs Li   But haven't you seen the way he carries on with this Miss Chen?

Li   Of course I have. That's because he fancies her and because he's got tons of money and likes spending it; what's that got to do with respectability?

Mrs Li   Fine, it has nothing to do with us. (*Begging him*) But you must realize that on our meager income we can't afford to socialize with the likes of Miss Chen or a such a well-heeled crowd?

Li   How many times have I told you to keep that kind of remark at home, if you must make them at all? Don't come out with them here. You'll be a laughing stock if people hear you.

Mrs Li (*Aggrieved*)   I think they already laugh at us.

Li (*Indignantly*)   How dare they? Our money's as good as theirs, and we spend hundreds playing mahjong just like them, do we not?

Mrs Li   But what for? We've got all those children at home! There's Ying's schooling to be paid, and Fang on the point of getting engaged, and Little Five's ill again. And Mother doesn't have a single piece of decent winter clothing. And yet you neglect all that and instead come here and spend our hard-earned money playing mahjong with them, paying our dues, a hundred dollars at a time, how – how *can* I go on playing?

Li (*Banging his head*)   Stop talking about it.

Mrs Li   Isn't it hard enough being a bank clerk, running yourself ragged from morning till night on a salary that doesn't even get us through to the end of the month? But you still have to socialize with your superiors and play mahjong with them? We can't afford school tuition, the rent at the end of the month, or even a good doctor when the kids get sick, yet you are still obligated to socialize . . .

Li (*Bursting out*)   Stop! I won't have you talking like this! (*Bitterly*) Can't you see how bad I feel? That I'm fully aware that I'm a poor man? I hate the fact that I didn't have a good father to raise me in more comfortable circumstances, so that I could hold my head up with confidence? I'm not inferior to them, that lot, you know that. They're no better than me. They've got no brains, no guts, no heart. The only difference is that they were born into money and status and I wasn't. I am telling you, there's no justice, no equality, in this society. So-called morality and public service are just a big con. Even if you follow all their rules, you'll still die a pauper. So all you can do is throw caution to the wind and take them on in the hope that one day you'll come out on top.

Mrs Li   You're so busy taking them on, Shiqing, that you've forgotten your own children. What will become of them?

Li (*With a sigh*)   Children! Humph, if it weren't for our poor children, do you think I'd swallow my pride and drag you to a place like this? What is Chen Bailu, anyway? A quasi-dancing girl-prostitute-concubine, piece of trash! Yet the old bastard fancies her, and since the old bastard's rolling in money, I am obliged to address her as 'Miss' and agree with whatever she says. You may think I kowtow to them as if they were my own ancestors. But Suzhen, you don't realize how I loathe myself sometimes for sacrificing my self-respect and lowering myself to curry favor with them. Here I am, a man in his forties, bowing and scraping, day in day out, mixing with these bastards, even garbage like that Hu Si – I have to flatter them and be sociable with each and every one of them, I, Li Shiqing, a man, I – (*He drops his head in silence.*)

Mrs Li   There, there, Shiqing, don't feel bad, don't be so down on yourself. I do know how you feel with all you have to put up with.

Li I don't feel bad. (*He slowly raises his head and says indignantly.*) I will stand up, I will change my lot. I'm going to turn as hard as a stone, with no more room for sentiment, no more feeling sorry for people. I want to be completely selfish. I want revenge.

Mrs Li Revenge? Who has bullied you? Who do you despise?

Li They all bully me; and I despise them all. Twenty years I've worked here and how much crap have I put up with? Sooner or later I will stand up and let it all out, you'll see.

(**Pan Yueting** *comes in through the center door.*)

Pan Ah, Shiqing! You're back, then.

Li (*Deferentially*) For quite some time now. I was told you were conversing with someone from the newspaper so I didn't dare interrupt you.

Pan Does Mrs Li need you for something?

Li No, no (*To Mrs Li*) You'd best get back to your mahjong game. (*Exit Mrs Li to the left.*)

Li Any news from the newspaper office about the political situation?

Pan That's none of your business. Did you purchase the government bonds as I instructed?

Li Yes, two million altogether, this month's issue.

Pan What did you get them for?

Li Seven seventy-five.

Pan And what did the market do once you'd bought them?

Li Wasn't a very favorable reaction, I'm afraid. What with rumors flying and money tight and share prices dropping all the time and holders of government bonds dumping them, but then you went and –

Pan I went and bought in.

Li On the assumption of a rally, of course.

Pan Well, it wouldn't very well be in anticipation of a downturn, now would it!

Li (*Deferentially*) Ordinarily, Manager Pan, there's not much risk in bonds: in a pinch one can always cash them in and buy them back later. But . . . the current situation seems different. Prices are plummeting.

If they were to stabilize there's always hope that they'll come up again and then you'll make a fortune. But we have no control over that.

Pan (*Taking a cigar*)   How do you know you can trust such rumors?

Li (*Smiling deferentially*)   I see, I see. So you are suggesting is this all a ruse on the part of investors who'd like to buy in?

Pan   Ruse or not, I'd like to think I am able to spot a reliable piece of information when I hear it, after all the years I've been dealing in government bonds.

Li (*Ingratiatingly*)   Yet Jin Ba always has the best inside information, and I hear he's not buying at all. What's more. . . .

Pan (*Annoyed*)   It's always best, Mr Shiqing, to mind one's own business. At the bank, you are to do what's asked of you; otherwise, butt out and don't start asking questions. That's our policy at the bank.

Li (*Greatly put out by this rebuff, yet doing his utmost to control himself*)   Of course, Manager Pan, I mention it merely to remind you of this fact.

Pan   The bank's affairs are not open to discussion, and I certainly don't need any reminders from you.

Li   Very well, sir.

Pan   You've been to see Jin Ba, then?

Li   Yes. We discussed the matter of the new Dafeng building that the bank's financing. He said he didn't see how the bank could afford it just now. And then he went on about the terrible state of the market and the drop in real estate, and said that as construction has only just gotten underway, it would be advisable to halt it at once.

Pan   But didn't you tell him the contract for the building has been signed and the deposit already paid?

Li   Of course, I told him the job had been taken by a foreign contractor and that there was no question of asking for our money back, which meant that for the moment it would be virtually impossible to free Mr Jin's accounts with us, so could he give us a couple of days' grace.

Pan   How did he respond?

Li   He mulled it over for a moment then said 'Later then,' though from the look on his face I wouldn't be surprised if he were to change his mind.

Pan   That hooligan! Not an ounce of decency in him!

Li (*Sneaks a glance at* **Pan**)   Oh, and he also asked whether all the bank's real estate holdings had been mortgaged yet.

Pan   What! Why would he ask that?

Li   Yes, I wondered myself, though I didn't say anything.

Pan   What did you tell him?

Li   Naturally I told him that none of the properties had been mortgaged. (*After a moment's pause, he casts another surreptitious glance at* **Pan**, *and then plucks up his courage.*) Though I am aware that every one of the bank's properties *has* been mortgaged.

Pan (*Taken aback*)   You – who told you that?

Li (*Looking up*)   Isn't it a fact, sir, that a few months ago you mortgaged the bank's last piece of property, extending from Changxing Lane to Huangren Lane?

Pan   Ridiculous. Who told you that?

Li   Manager Pan, haven't you mortgaged it all to the Youhua Company?

Pan   Oh, er. (*Pacing a few steps*) Now, Shiqing, where did you get such information? (*Sitting down*) You mean to say that people know about this?

Li (*Realizing he has put his finger on his opponent's weak spot*)   No, no, sir, relax, nobody else knows. I myself saw the contracts you signed.

Pan   Where?

Li   In your desk drawer.

Pan   How dare you –

Li   The truth is (*With a crafty smile*), I was rather puzzled by the goings on at the bank, suddenly constructing a huge building and buying up government bonds at the same time, and so one day when you were busy seeing a client I took the liberty of looking in your desk. (*Smiling*) I do realize, though, that it was a bit nosy on my part.

Pan (*Staring blankly momentarily*)   Shiqing, no, no, that's quite all right. I wouldn't call it nosy. (*With an uneasy smile*) Good thing to keep an eye on each other, you know. Please sit down, won't you? We can talk this over.

Li   That's too kind of you, sir.

Pan   Not at all, sit down, make yourself at home. (*Sitting down*) Now that you know about this matter, you understand, of course, that it's all strictly confidential and must not under any circumstance be divulged to anyone, otherwise it will be very inconvenient for the bank.

Li   Yes indeed. I'm aware that there have been a number of substantial withdrawals recently.

Pan   Right, then, so we are all in this together. We'll have to help each other and combine forces to keep the bank afloat. There have been a lot of rumors lately about the bank, and now there's uncertainty about our reserves.

Li (*Deliberately interjecting*)   Whereas in actual fact not only are our reserves running low, but our cash flow is in trouble. Isn't Master Jin's withdrawal a case in point?

Pan (*Uneasily*)   But, Shiqing –

Li (*Interrupting him*)   But, sir, sir, ever since you made it public that the bank is making a profit and announced plans for the new building, the run on the accounts has slowed a bit.

Pan   You're quite astute, you've figured out what I am doing. So the building must go up. It makes no difference when it's done: what matters is that we can afford to have it done. It shows that the bank's got plenty of reserves and that it's on a firm footing.

Li   The thing about making money, though: the bank staff knows we're not.

Pan   Hence the utmost importance of keeping quiet about the mortgages and about Master Jin's withdrawal. News of either could cause a panic, so you must be very careful.

Li   Naturally I shall be careful. All the time I've served under you I've been very discreet, and there's no reason why I should fail you now.

Pan   I'm working on another plan as well. If we can make a bit on these government bonds, it'll tide us over for the time being. Once we get through this I'll see to it that your loyalty is properly rewarded.

Li   You can always count on me, sir. I – er – I recently heard that the assistant manager Mr Zhang is to be transferred.

Pan (*Hesitantly*)   Er, yes, the assistant manager, yes, he is. Well, if you don't think the position beneath you, I'm quite prepared to help you out.

Li Thank you, sir, thank you. Don't worry, you can always count on me to do my utmost on your behalf.

Pan That's that, then. Good. By the way, have you brought the pink slips?

Li Yes.

Pan About how much will we save with these cuts?

Li Only five hundred dollars a month or so.

Pan Every little bit helps. Did you reduce the wages of the construction workers at the building site last payday?

Li Yes, by two hundred dollars, I've got it with me.

Pan As much as that?

Li It's not that much really. I only deducted ten cents per worker.

Pan All right, we'll deal with that later. (*He takes a couple of steps towards the door on the left, then suddenly looks round.*) Oh yes, I knew there was something else: when you saw Jin Ba did you mention the matter of that young girl last night?

Li Yes, I said Miss Chen had taken a great fancy to the child, so would he save us some face and step aside.

Pan What did he say?

Li He shook his head and said he knew nothing about it.

Pan The bastard. Feigning ignorance. Not a shred of decency in him. Oh, well, let him have his way, she's nothing but a peasant girl after all.

Li Yes, sir.

(**Pan** *exits.*)

Li (*Paces a few steps, then hears the chanting of the workers outside, and the sounds of labor, suddenly bursts out*) Go ahead and chant, you'll work like this your whole lives, stupid sons of bitches. I loathe your earnestness.

(*Suddenly the telephone rings.*)

Li (*Picking up the receiver*) Hello, who's calling? Oh! I see, Mr Zhang from the newspaper office. You'd like a word with Manager Pan? He's not here . . . this is Shiqing. You can tell me, it's all the same. I see. What's that? Jin Ba's buying the same issue as us? How much? Three million! That's strange, yes . . . yes, no wonder our manager's been buying them up too! . . . . Yes, you're right about that, government bonds are practically Jin Ba's own private property, since they're under his control. . . . Yes, I agree, looks like the market will rally after all . . . right you are. . . . I'll go tell the manager straight away. Goodbye, Mr Zhang. Goodbye!

(*He puts down the receiver, pauses a moment, then turns to go out by the door on the left.*)

(**Huang Xingsan** *comes in through the middle door.*)

Huang (*Timidly*)   Mr – Mr Li.

Li   You again. Who told you to come to see me here?

Huang (*Weakly*)   We're hungry. My family's at home with nothing to eat.

Li (*Coldly*)   And you think you'll get something by coming here? This is a hotel, not a soup kitchen.

Huang   Mr Li, I've pawned everything that can be pawned. I really don't know where else to turn, otherwise I wouldn't dare come back and bother you.

Li (*With contempt*)   What am I, a relative of yours? An old pal? Perhaps I owe you from some former debt? Just what do you think you're doing, following me around wherever I go?

Huang (*With a wry smile, bleakly*)   You're quite right, I've no such claims on you, but Mr Li, when I worked at the bank I only cost you thirteen dollars a month. When you let me go, where was I to go? By turning me out, the bank's as good as telling me to stop living.

Li (*With annoyance and distaste*)   So, according to you, the bank can't fire anyone. Once the bank hires you, you're as good as guaranteed food for life, is that it?

Huang (*Twisting his scarf in his fingers*)   No, no, that's not what I meant, Mr Li, I – I realize the bank treated me well; I'm not being ungrateful. But . . . you haven't seen the houseful of energetic children at home that I have to find food for every day. Now that the bank's fired me I've no money coming in, and we've got no rice, and they're all crying from hunger. The rent's six weeks late, so pretty soon we won't even have a roof over our heads. (*Brokenly*) Mr Li, you haven't seen what a

large brood of children I've got. I truly don't know where else to turn –
all I can do is . . . cry.

Li (*Coldly*)   And who made you have so many kids?

Huang   Mr Li, when I was at the bank I never made a single mistake.
I always went to work at the crack of dawn and I never got home till late
at night. I worked all day long, Mr Li –

Li (*Losing patience*)   All right, all right, I know you were a conscientious
worker, content with your lot and never making trouble. But surely you
realize that there's been a downturn in the market, an economic crisis? It's
not as if I didn't warn you. I told you time and again that the bank would
be downsizing the staff and cutting back on salaries. You can't say I didn't
warn you!

Huang (*Hesitantly*)   But Mr Li, isn't the bank putting up a huge new
building at the moment? And they're still taking on people at the bank,
new people.

Li   That's none of your business! It's all part of the bank's policy, to
improve business. As for taking on new people after you were laid off,
I would have thought that after all the years you've been in the business
you'd have learnt that much at least about the ways of the world.

Huang   Yes, I – I have, Mr Li. (*Pitifully*) I realize I've got no backers.

Li   There you are, then.

Huang   But I've always believed that Providence doesn't let down a
man who does his best, so if I work hard I may be able to make up for
this particular shortcoming.

Li   And that's why the bank kept you on for four or five years. If you
hadn't worked hard you wouldn't have lasted that long.

Huang (*Pleading*)   But Mr Li, I beg you, please help me out just this
once. Won't you *please* have a word with Manager Pan, and ask him to
take me back? I'll do anything, willingly, even if it means extra hours,
extra tiredness, even if I have to work myself to death.

Li   You really are a nuisance. You think the manager is going to bother
with your troubles? You people all have the same problem: you always
attach far too much importance to yourselves. In other words, you're just
plain selfish. Do you really think a busy man like Manager Pan has time for
your petty problems? But what I don't understand is how come you have
worked for us all these years without setting aside at least some savings?

Huang (*With a wry smile*)   Savings? What, on thirteen dollars a month and a large family to feed? Savings?

Li   I don't mean from of your salary. Naturally you couldn't squeeze anything extra out of your salary. But – in other ways, surely you made a little something for yourself on the side?

Huang   No, Mr Li, I always kept my conscience clear.

Li   I mean – surely you made something for yourself from the office supply purchases?

Huang   Never, my conscience would never allow it. You can ask the chief clerk, Mr Li.

Li   Humph! You are a fool going on about your conscience in times like these! No wonder you're in such a pitiful state now. All right then, off with you.

Huang (*In a panic*)   But Mr Li –

Li   If anything turns up we can reconsider the matter. (*Waving him away*) At the moment there's absolutely nothing I can do for you. Go on then.

Huang   Mr Li, Sir, you can't –

Li   And let me be clear, if you come hounding me like a little dog again, following me everywhere I go, you'll find I won't be so polite next time.

Huang   Then you mean there's absolutely no hope whatsoever?

Li   Get moving! The ladies are due to arrive any minute, and if they find you here it will be very awkward.

Huang   All right, then. (*With his eyes welling up with tears, he hangs his head low.*) Mr Li, Sir, please accept my sincere apologies. (*With a bitter smile*) Coming here bothering you all the time. I'll go now.

Li   Go on, then, and good riddance.

Huang (*He heaves a long sigh and begins to move away but after a couple of steps he suddenly turns and comes back. He says miserably*) But where can I go? Where can I go? My family has broken up. I'll swallow my pride and tell you, my wife left me. We had nothing to eat and she couldn't bear our miserable lot any longer, so she ran off with another man. I've got three kids at home waiting to be fed.

At the moment I've got just twenty cents in my pocket and I'm not well (*Coughing*). I cough all day long. Mr Li, where can I go? Where can I go?

Li (*Sorry for him, but also despising his weakness*)   Wherever you please. Though I'd like you to know that it's not that I don't *want* to help you out; I'm in no position to be a philanthropist and I can't start with you.

Huang   I'm not asking for a handout. All I'm asking you is to be so kind as to give me a job. I must survive, for the sake of my children!

Li (*Thinking a moment, then looking disdainfully at* **Huang**)   The fact is, there are plenty of jobs to be had as long as you're willing to do them.

Huang (*A spark of hope reviving in him*)   You mean that?

Li   For one, you could go pull a rickshaw.

Huang (*Disappointed*)   I – I could never manage that. (*Coughing*) I'm ill, you know. The doctor says the lung on this side is already (*Coughing*) – useless.

Li   I see, in that case you could always go out on the streets to beg –

Huang (*Flushing, uneasy*)   Mr Li, I'm educated man, you know. I couldn't just –

Li   You just couldn't bring yourself to beg from people, is that it? Well, there is one other path you could go down, an extremely easy and comfortable path: you could break into people's houses and (*Seeing* **Huang's** *lips moving soundlessly*) – that's right, you've guessed it.

Huang   What, you mean – (*With trembling lips*) you mean I should go – (*One sees his lips move but the words are inaudible.*)

Li   Say it out loud, what are you afraid of? 'Steal.' 'Steal.' Why not, after all? The rich grab money by the fistful right from people's pockets so it must not require much courage!

Huang   To tell you the truth, Mr Li, in my desperation the thought had crossed my mind.

Li   Is that so?

Huang (*Terrified*)   But I'm afraid, I'm afraid, I could never bring myself to do it.

Li (*Exasperated*)   Well, if you don't even have the guts to steal, what do you expect me to do about it? You've got no influential relatives, no influential friends, nor any outstanding abilities. So there you have it: I say beg, but your pride gets in the way; I say pull a rickshaw, but you haven't got the strength; I say steal, but you haven't got the guts. You keep whining about conscience and altruism and morality as if one could support a wife and children on honesty and humility; but you couldn't even provide for your own wife, you pathetic imbecile, you're not fit to raise a family! I tell you, this world is not meant for – people like you. (*Pointing out of the window*) See that high-rise over there? That's the Xinhua Department Store, thirteen stories tall. I think that would be your best way.

Huang (*Uncomprehending*)   Which way, Mr Li?

Li (*Going up to* **Huang**)   Which way? (*With a devilish smile*) I'll tell you. You climb up one flight at a time. And when you reach the top you step over the railings and stand on the edge. Then all you have to do is to take one step forward, into thin air. Your heart may pound momentarily, but it will only last a second, only one second, and you'll be out of your misery, no more worries about food and clothing.

Huang (*Dumbfounded, his voice almost inaudibly low*)   But Mr Li, do you mean I should commit – (*Suddenly in a tragic voice*) no, no, I cannot die, Mr Li, I must survive! For my children's sake, for my motherless children, I must keep living: My Wangwang, my Little Yun, my – yes, I've contemplated it. But Mr Li, you must let me stay alive! (*Grasping* **Li's** *hand*). You must help me, just this once, I can't die, no matter how hard it gets, I can't die. I must find a way to keep living! (*He coughs.*)

(*The door on the left opens wide. Through it comes the laughter of* **Madame Gu**, **Hu Si**, **Georgy Zhang** *and the others.* **Pan Yueting** *half appears, speaking back into the other room: 'Keep on playing, I'll be right back.'*)

Li (*Jerking* **Huang's** *hand away*)   Let go of me. Someone's coming, so behave yourself.

(**Huang** *can only stand there, leaning against the wall, as* **Pan Yueting** *enters.*)

Pan   Ah?

Huang   Sir!

Pan   Shiqing, who is this? And what's he doing here?

Huang   My name's Huang, sir. I was a clerk at the bank.

Li   He's one of those who's just been dismissed.

Pan   What are you doing here? (*To Li*) Who let him in?

Li   I'm not sure how he found his way in.

Huang (*Going up to* **Pan**, *piteously*)   Be kind, sir. If you have to let somebody go, don't let it be me. I've got three young children, I can't be without work. I'm on my knees begging you sir, you must let me go on living.

Pan   Preposterous! How dare you come here asking me for a job, you – (*Furiously*) beat it!

Huang   But sir –

Li   Get up! Up! Go on, get out of here! (*Sending him sprawling with a shove*) If you keep this up I'll have somebody kick you out.

(**Huang** *looks from* **Li** *to* **Pan**.)

Pan   Out, get out, now! This is absurd!

Huang   All right, I'm getting up, you don't have to punch me. (*Slowly getting to his feet*) So you'd have me stop living. You! (*Pointing at* **Pan**) You (*Pointing at* **Li**), both of you would just have me stop living. (*Sobbing hysterically, halfway between tears and laughter*) Oh, the injustice! How heartless of you. A measly thirteen dollars a month you paid me, though after all your deductions for this and that in fact I was left with just ten dollars and twenty-five cents. And for my miserable ten dollars and twenty-five cents I wrote all day long, all day long, hunched over a desk working for you; I wrote on and on and so without so much as lifting my head or catching my breath; I wrote from morning till night; even when I broke into a cold sweat and the words began to blur I still had to keep on writing; through wind and rain I came to the bank to write for you! (*With a gesture*) Five years! Mr Pan! Look at what those five years did to me! (*Thumping his chest with his hands*) A walking skeleton, a man at death's door! I tell you both, my left lung's shot, yes, the doctor says it's completely useless! (*In a shrill voice, past caring now*) I tell you, I'm at death's door, I'm on my knees begging you, for the sake of my poor children. Let me keep on writing and writing and writing for you – for one more bowl of rice to eat. Ten dollars and twenty-five cents in exchange for my worthless life. But you won't allow it! You won't! You want to make money for yourselves, so you fire your staff, you fire me! (*Brokenly*) What can you do with ten dollars and twenty-five cents? I am not asking for a handout: I am giving you my life in exchange! And without it, I am done. (*Bitterly*) There's not an ounce of decency between you, the way you've treated me – you thieves, you robbers, you monsters! You've got less humanity in you than wild beasts –

Pan   Son of a bitch! Get out of my sight this instant!

Huang (*Weeping*)   I'm not afraid of you now! I'm not afraid! (*Seizing* **Pan's** *clothing*) I've been wronged and I swear I'll kill –

Pan (*Swiftly punching* **Huang** *in the chest*)   What! (**Huang** *at once falls to the floor.*)

(*A pause.*)

Li   He meant he's going to kill himself, sir. A man like that would never hurt anyone.

Pan (*Brushing off his hands*)   Doesn't matter now, he's out cold. Fusheng! Fusheng!

(**Fusheng** *comes in.*)

Pan   Take him away. Put him in another room and have Master Jin's men deal with him till he comes to then give him a couple of bucks and send him away.

Fusheng   Very well, sir. (*He drags* **Huang** *out of the room.*)

Li   Mr Zhang phoned.

Pan   What about?

Li   The bonds you bought – Jin Ba's bought three million's worth.

Pan (*His face lighting up with delight*)   I knew it! He must expect the market to rally.

Li   Assuming that the information is reliable, and that Jin Ba did in fact buy in, then yes he's expecting the market to rally.

Pan (*Pacing up and down*)   It must be reliable, it must be.

(*The door on the left swings open and* **Georgy Zhang**, **Hu Si**, **Madame Gu** *and* **Bailu** *burst in and stand in the doorway, while female guests can be heard conversing and laughing behind them.*)

Georgy (*In the highest of spirits, a cigar in his hand*): . . . So that's why I maintain that it's not easy living in China, there's not a comfortable place to be found. You only have to look at my Jacky (*To* **Hu Si**) – the hunting dog I brought back from America – just finding beef to feed him is a great headache for me every day. It's dirty, neither clean nor nourishing, and at fifty cents a pound, why it's inedible. I tell you, I put four pounds of raw beef in front of him every day (*Putting his nose forward and sniffing*), he gives it a sniff then goes off with his tail between his legs, won't even look at it. Just think, even the animals in China are feeling the pinch, not to mention the people! And as for folks like us, well! (*He shakes his head and shrugs, and everyone bursts out laughing.*)

(*Outside,* **Dasheng** *can be heard shouting* '**Pipsqueak! Pipsqueak!**')

Bailu   Hey, listen, what's Dasheng shouting about? (**Dasheng** *bursts into the room.*)

Dasheng   Pipsqueak! Have you seen Pipsqueak, Zhujun?

Bailu   She's in there, isn't she?

Dasheng (*Incredulous*)   In there? (*Dashes into the room on the right, bellowing.*) Pipsqueak!

Gu   Has he lost his mind?

(**Dasheng** *reappears.*)

Dasheng   No, she's not in there, she's gone. As I was coming up the stairs just now I thought I saw her go down in the elevator with two or three men. I only caught a glimpse of her and then she disappeared, I could barely believe my eyes, but now that I'm here I see that someone has abducted her after all. (*Picking up his hat*) Goodbye, I'm going after her.

(*He rushes out.*)

Bailu (*Going up to* **Pan**)   See what happens when I ask you for a small favor, Yueting! (*Suddenly*) Wait for me, Dasheng! I'm coming with you! (*She throws a coat around her shoulders and heads towards the door.*)

Pan   Bailu! (*She runs out, ignoring him.*)

Georgy (*Becoming caught up in the excitement*)   Really, she too has lost . . .

Hu Si and **Gu** (*Speaking together*)   Her mind! (*Everyone bursts into laughter.*)

(*The curtain falls quickly.*)

ACT III

Characters:

CUIXI: An older hooker in her thirties
LITTLE SHUNZI: An attendant at the Precious Harmony Brothel
PIPSQUEAK: Little Cui, a new arrival of three days
NEWSPAPER MAN: A mute
WANG FUSHENG
HU SI
BLACK SAN
FANG DASHENG

Characters Offstage:

FATTY and HIS PALS
GRAMOPHONE PLAYER MAN
NEWSPAPER VENDOR
FRUIT PEDDLER and OTHER SNACK PEDDLERS
CRIES OF A BABY
STREET SINGER and STRING INSTRUMENT PLAYER
ATTENDANT WHO CALLS OUT THE PROSTITUTE'S NAMES
TWO BEGGARS WHO PERFORM SHULAIBAO[13]
VAGRANT WHO SINGS CHINESE OPERA
WATCHMAN WHO BEATS THE CLAPPER
HEARTY MALE and FEMALE LAUGHTER
SHORTCAKE SELLER
PATRON WHO SINGS 'CALL ME DARLING' in the final scene
WOMAN QUIETLY WEEPING

One night a week later, around midnight, in a low-end brothel called the Precious Harmony where the noise of peddlers hawking their wares, shrill conversation, women cursing, and all the sounds of busy whoredom boil and bubble in hellish commotion. The main entrance is plastered with New Year's couplets such as 'Southern women are natural beauties; Northern girls are rouged by nature,' while across the center beam are horizontal inscriptions such as 'A Paradise for Lovers' or

'The Wonderland of the Peach-blossom Spring.' At the front entrance
stand two or three attractive girls making eyes and provocative gestures
at the lecherous onlookers who stare with feigned interest at the red
glossy paper tariff of charges, blackened with dirt, on the wall (On it are
scrawled four items: 'Quickie . . . cents; all night . . . dollars . . .; shared
room . . . cents; light entertainment . . . cents'), then pass lewd remarks at
the heavily made up women until the latter, thinking there is a chance of
doing business, approach to invite them inside, whereupon the onlookers
disperse, roaring with laughter. This back-alley teems like an ant colony
with the so-called dregs of humanity. The women here struggle on the
brink of starvation, but unlike others who wince and grimace from hunger
pangs these women must suffer with smiles on their faces.

Inside the courtyard, the whorehouse is like a pigeon coop with row upon
row of tiny compartments, and when business is booming there is an endless
stream of men of every description coming and going: petty merchants,
electricians, ordinary clerks, waiters from steamships, servants from foreign
companies, and some hulking lads in short jackets with an ostentatious
display of buttons, left undone to bare their chests. One may come and go
as one pleases in the courtyard, and upon entry a lame doorman hollers
'Out front! A patron!' A small copper bell on a rope begins to ring and from
the various little coops there emerge one after the next unnaturally pale
creatures. They automatically cluster together amid giggles and shouting.
The 'patron' has of course been shown inside by now. His eyeballs flit this
way and that as he takes in the sight. Now an attendant shouts in a shrill,
piercing VOICE 'Greet the customer'. Fat ones and skinny ones, they
step forward in turn, as the attendant calls out their professional names,
to parade swiftly in front of the 'patron' with smiles and sidelong glances.
Those standing at the back begin whispering and chattering with their heads
together, until one of the creatures is selected, to her ostensible delight,
whereupon the rest of them return from whence they came.

Surprisingly enough, for all the sweet nothings being whispered and
various excesses taking place within the little pigeon coops, out in the
courtyard is a continuous babel of noise: Sing-song girls, beggars going
from door to door reciting folktales, tramps humming snatches of Beijing
opera, gramophone dealers, vendors of fruit, peanuts and chestnuts,
'lucky dip' men, hoarse newspapermen, string instrument players, sellers
of hot tea-eggs . . . common entertainers of every description and hawkers
pushing their wares, each of them going along the rows of small windows
shouting at the top of their lungs, sometimes even lifting the door curtains
and going right in, insisting that the 'patron' do business with them.

But all the audience sees is one such little coop – a small room, long,
narrow, dark and dingy. There are two doors against the rear wall of

the room, one to the left and one to the right, both opening on to the courtyard, each draped with a tattered blue screen to keep out the wind. Between the two doors is a curtain hanging from a wire; when drawn across it divides the space into two rooms. When it's busy, unacquainted patrons are put on either side of the curtain, so that they can sit and drink tea and chat without disturbing one another; in this way a poor creature entertain two patrons at once, economizing on space and saving her legs, while also saving on lighting and heating. At the moment the curtain, discolored at the top with yellow stains and frayed along the bottom, is pushed back against the wall; indicating of course that the occupant is not too busy just now.

On the right is a wooden bed covered with a thin, worn-out sheet with quilts piled at the end. The wall to the right of the bed is covered with pictures – 'Pigsy's Wedding,' 'New Year Festivities,' 'Chubby Cherub Picking a Lotus-Flower' and a number of cigarette advertisements featuring pin-up girls. By the door is an upside down Fu character in red meaning 'happiness is here.' Near the bed is a rickety old dressing table with a cracked wash basin and a couple of small decorated bowls. Several pairs of embroidered shoes lie scattered beneath the bed; beside the bed are several chairs. On the left next to wall stands a square table with a chair on each side; on the table are an incomplete tea-service and a battered round cigarette tin. To the right hangs a pair of scrolls mottled with black smudges; the left-hand one reads 'Her beauty is that of Xi Shi reborn' and the right-hand one 'Hers is the face of Diaochan come back into the world again.'[14] *Between the two scrolls is a dressing-mirror which produces distorted reflections, across the top of which is the inscription reading 'A thousand pieces of gold for a smile.' A couple of canvas chairs are scattered about the room.*

On both the left and right sides there is a window, each covered with a small red curtain; beneath the left window there is an iron stove in which the fire is dying out. By the table stands a stove burning coal briquettes, of which there is a pile under the table. Above the small door on the left hangs a picture frame enclosing three characters, **Hua Cuixi**, *presumably the professional name of the girl occupying the room.*

When the curtain rises, **Cuixi** *is standing in the doorway to the left, her back to the audience, holding back the door curtain and peering out. She is about thirty years old, a creature degraded and bullied to the point of utter numbness. She is not the least bit attractive, being somewhat pudgy, and her face is caked in powder with a thick layer of rouge on her eyelids. Her hair is shoulder length, her forehead purposely pinched into purple patches running straight across like a cluster of flower petals and her temples are even more horrifyingly purple. She is wearing a*

*reddish-purple padded gown with a sleeveless velvet jacket over the top,
cloth slippers, and cotton-padded trousers gathered at the ankles with
black satin ribbons. She holds the stub of a cigarette in her right hand
and from time to time she blows the ash off it and puts it to her lips. Every
now and then she scratches her head with the same hand. She is laughing
and calling out, as if in conversation with someone outside. The various
sounds outside mingle in a confused medley of noise.*

First voice (*Shrilly*)   Oranges and bananas! Peanuts and chestnuts!

Second voice (*Weakly*)   Gramophone!

A little girl's voice (*To the lilting, swerving sound of a two-stringed
instrument*)   Sing you a song!

(*The sound of men's and women's laughter, beatings, curses.*)

Cuixi (*Waving out of the door*)   See you tomorrow, Fatty! See you
tomorrow, Second Master Zhang! Bye, Master Chen!

The voices of fatty and his friends (*Muffled*)   See you tomorrow, Cuixi.

Cuixi (*Suddenly standing on tiptoe and raising her voice*)   Fatty, it's
chilly out there, keep wrapped up, don't catch cold.

Fatty's voice (*As he comes back and takes* **Cuixi's** *hand, speaking with
affection albeit somewhat in jest*): Why, my dear Cuixi, you love me
more than my old lady! Come here, my love! (*As he says this he seems to
give* **Cuixi** *a sudden tug.*)

Cuixi (*Almost falling through the curtain in the doorway into* **Fatty's**
*arms, she holds on to the doorframe for support and pulls herself up
straight again, then pushes* **Fatty's** *hand away and says laughing and
panting for breath*)   You wicked rascal, Fatty, let go of me. You'd better
get home and suck on your wife's tits instead of pestering me!

One of fatty's friends (*Smacking his lips and speaking with a note of
admiration to tease them*)   Hey, hey, get a load of these two youngsters,
just raring to go. Hey, Fatty, you might as well stay put if the woman is
going to keep getting you all worked up like this.

Fatty's voice (*Playing the infatuated fool*)   He's right, my love, I won't
leave after all.

Cuixi (*Well aware that they are teasing her, and pushing them away*)   Go
on, off you go, out! Stop fooling around. Come back tomorrow, Fatty, and
make sure you *do* come. And you two gentlemen come with him!

The men's voices (*Muffled*)   All right, Cuixi, we'll be here.

The voice of a newspaper vendor (*Deep and hoarse*)   Get your paper, evening paper! Entire family swallows opium. Read all about it. Clerk jumps in the river. Read all about it.

Cuixi (*She turns to look at the newspaperman, and when she looks round again she finds that* **Fatty** *and his companions are almost out of the gate. She suddenly shouts*): Fatty, you be sure to come back tomorrow! If you don't, may your children be born without assholes, d'you hear? (*She laughs.*)

(*She swings round, throws away her cigarette butt, clears her throat and goes to the square table on the left. She picks up money left by* **Fatty**, *counts it, then puts it back down on the table with a sigh.*)

Cuixi (*Sitting down on the chair by the table*)   Fuck, it gets worse every day. Don't know how much longer I can take it. (*She picks up a cigarette butt from the table and lights it. Outside can be heard all kinds of peddlers plying their wares. She turns towards the little room on the left.*) Little Cui! Little Cui! (*She goes to the doorway and pulls back the curtain.*) Are you getting up, or what, Little Cui? If you don't do as you're told – (*Suddenly*) oh, that stubborn kid, I don't have time for this.

(*Enter a dwarf wearing a short jacket and carrying a kettle. His thick lips curl back to reveal two large buck teeth. He speaks with a slight lisp and a stammer. He goes to the table, sets down the kettle, counts the notes and looks suspiciously at* **Cuixi**.)

Cuixi   What are you looking at, Shunzi?

Shunzi   Is this what the f – f – fat fellow left?

Cuixi   Why, don't you think it's enough? Must be saving his dough for his funeral, that's his trouble.

Shunzi (*Shaking his head*)   Are you ha – handing it all over?

Cuixi   Do I have a choice? The boss has got to have his dollar a day, you know that.

Shunzi   But h – how are you going to eat?

Cuixi   Eat? Don't make me laugh! I'll fill up my belly on northwest air. (*She goes to the stove burning coal-dust briquettes and warms herself.*)

Shunzi (*Turning round, as if reluctant to speak*)   Yo – yo – your old man's here a – a – again.

Cuixi   He's wasting his time. He couldn't beat any money out of me if
he tried. If business were better I'd be happy to send a dollar home, two
or three even, to make things easier for the family. But why keep coming
here to see me? (*Lowering her head in thought, then, suddenly*) By God,
when I first came here to work business was so brisk that I'd have two
dozen customers a day, and even you, Shunzi, picked up nearly a buck a
day in my room, didn't you? Humph (*Shaking her head*), it's no use, I'm
too old.

(*Under the window there is a beggar singing shulaibao and beating
two bamboo clappers that go 'di-di-da, di-di-da, di-di-da, di-di-da,
di-di-da.'*)

The beggar (*With a cough, singing in a quick, lively voice*):

'Oh, we rattle 'em fast and we rattle 'em slow,
As up to the Hall of Beauties we go.
Two scrolls hang beside the door,
Writ by a master's hand, I'm sure.
And what do they say?
All day the cups go from hand to hand,
And every night brings a different man.
(*Di-di-da, di-di-da, di-di-da-di-da-di-da.*)
With a one and a two and a three,
You make less on your back than you do on the tea,
So it's tea for the ugly ones, the handsome boys for me.
The ladies treat their guests in style,
Melon seeds and sugar plums all the while.
Then it's "Come here, my darling, come here, my sweet,
Come to my arms and I'll give you a treat"'

The beggar's voice (*Resuming his feeble speaking voice*)   Mr Manager,
ladies, take pity on a poor blind man.

Cuixi   Go on, beat it. Don't come round here with your screeching,
we've got no money. (*Taking the cigarette from her lips and throwing it
out the door*) There, a cigarette butt for your trouble. (*Seeing the beggar
pick it up*) Hey! Things are looking up these days: when a blind man sees
a cigarette butt now, all he's got to do is reach out and pick it up!

The beggar (*Grinning broadly*)   Ah, I'm only blind in one eye. See you
later, ma'am.

Shunzi   Your – your man wants you to get the baby and go back home to him.

Cuixi (*Clearing her throat contemptuously*)   Go back home? What for, so I can freeze to death in this weather? At least the baby won't die if it's here. Tell the cripple I'm busy with a customer and that I won't be out till later. He's standing at the gate?

Shunzi   I asked him in but he wouldn't come. He says, he – he's too ashamed.

Cuixi   Humph! Ashamed of what? He's the one who can't even support his own wife, and has shared me with other men all these years!

Shunzi (*Wiping down the table*)   Where's the new girl?

Cuixi   You mean Little Cui? In there.

Shunzi (*Lowering his voice*)   I reckon Black San'll be back soon.

Cuixi (*With a sigh*)   I'm telling you, she hasn't sold a single thing all night long. When Black San gets back he'll thrash her, mark my words. (**Pipsqueak** *now emerges slowly from the room on the left.*)

Pipsqueak (*Now quite changed, hardened, and says slowly and unswervingly*)   He can thrash me to death if he likes, I've only got to die once.

Cuixi (*Taken aback*)   Why, Little Cui, what's come over you?

Shunzi   So you've ch – ch – changed your tune, Little Cui. Not afraid of Black San anymore, are you?

Pipsqueak (*Wiping her tears*)   I've had enough the last three days. What's the use of being scared?

(*She is now wearing a lined blue jacket and black trousers; who knows what became of the old qipao she had been wearing. Her previous childish naiveté has been covered over by a thick layer of seriousness and gloom. She now looks like a grown up woman.*)

Shunzi   You're an odd one, won't do business when you can, won't do nothing but cry all day long. If you don't powder your face, and put on some makeup, how – how do you expect to get any customers?

(**Pipsqueak** *sits down by the table with her head down, fiddling with her clothes and ignoring him.*)

Cuixi (*To* **Shunzi**)   Never mind, the kid's a pain in the neck. You can talk to her till you're blue in the face. Might as well talk to a brick wall. Dumb as they make 'em.

(**Shunzi** *goes out through the front door on the left, taking the kettle with him.*)

(*A pause.*)

Pipsqueak   Will Black San be back soon?

Cuixi   Soon enough, don't you worry! Now listen, three days you've been here, without snagging a single customer. And every one of these days Black San's made your life miserable. Don't think you're so high and mighty just because you came from a big hotel with a better class of customer. You're here now and there are rules to follow. Think that son-of-a-bitch Black San's going to let you off, do you, when he finds you've gone another day without any business?

Pipsqueak   A person can only take so much.

Cuixi   Only so much? Not in this line of work. I'm telling you, we're not together in this room because we're friends or sisters: fate brought us together here. You somehow wound up sharing my room, where you've been for the last three days: that's your fate. I'm not blowing my own trumpet, now, but when I first got into this business, I was the queen of whores and saw shiny silver dollars by the thousand. But a woman past her prime is like a tarnished pearl, no longer worth much. When you get on in years you can't take the pace and you end up in a place like this. You've got to stick it out or else go under. I'm telling you, my Little Cui, once you end up in a place like this, forget about respectability. God knows, you're smothered in men all the time. Whoever comes to you, doesn't matter who he is, whether you know him or not, if he says bed then bed it must be; it's off with your trousers and let him have his way with you. How the fuck can you worry about respectability when you have to go on like that?

Pipsqueak (*On the verge of tears again*)   But – but . . .

Cuixi   But what? Men – there's not a single decent one. Every last one that comes here is after sex. They fool around, laughing and joking all the time, but when the rich guys have finished amusing themselves, once they've had their fun and gone home, we're left with our own heartaches, and in the middle of the night we think to ourselves: every one of us had a father and a mother. Every one of us was once some mother's precious baby. And which one of us won't have children of our own one day, and have a family to look after. Humph! We're all human beings, none of us was born into filth and none of us makes a living in this hellhole because we want to! (*Her head sinks forward as if she is going to cry.*)

Pipsqueak (*Taking out a handkerchief and offering it to her*)   Here . . . wipe your eyes.

Cuixi   I'm not crying. (*With a sigh*) My crying days are gone, long gone. I'm telling you, we are all flesh and blood. But I'm getting old and sooner or later I'm going to die from exhaustion trying to keep my family alive, and then I'll get rolled up in a piece of matting and buried out in the fields, and that'll be that. But you're young and still have plenty to look forward to. Stick it out a few years and you can find yourself a husband; then you can turn your back on all this and start a family and make a comfortable life for yourself. Don't be so stubborn with Black San: give in a bit. Otherwise you'll only be making things harder for yourself. Once we end up here we're stuck, and the worst that can happen to us is death. Where else is there to go? What's the point of getting yourself thrashed by Black San, the bastard? You know what they say about women like us: 'Resentment in our hearts but a smile on our lips.' No need to show your hand. When he says something nice to you, listen up; when he says something mean, let it slide off you like water on a duck's back, just pretend he hasn't said a thing. That's the only way to stay sane.

Pipsqueak   I – I just can't take it.

Cuixi   Come on, sure you can. The sun will set in the west today and tomorrow it'll rise in the east, the same as always. Only fools moan about not being able to take it. Shit (*Sighing*), people are a sorry lot, afraid of the slightest suffering, but when it comes down to it they *have* to put up with it. You can't just quit living for a day!

The voice of a newspaper man   Paper, evening paper, read all about it. Clerk jumps in the river. Paper, evening paper. Entire family swallows opium. Read all about it.

Pipsqueak   Listen!

The voice (*Fading into the distance*)   Read all about it, clerk jumps in the river.

Cuixi   Don't waste your time listening to that. You know the saying: 'Spend all your time listening to the crickets and the crops'll never get planted.' Now put on some makeup so you're ready for customers.

(*The crying of a waking child comes from the small door on the left.*)

Pipsqueak   The baby's awake. You'd better go in and feed him.

Cuixi   Yes. (*Exits.*)

(*Peddlers' cries can be heard outside; from beyond the inner room comes the crying of the child and* **Cuixi's** *soothing murmurs as she rocks him back to sleep.*)

(**Pipsqueak** *sits down on the bed silently. From next door comes the sound of a woman singing lasciviously to the accompaniment of a Sihu.*[15] *After a few bars she stops and she and the men roar with laughter.*)

'Call me baby,
Gaze at me till dawn.
When morning came,
you leave my bed.
Little darling, I can't bear to lose you;
one night together
and I love you forever more.

I sit in my room
while the lonesome hours drag on,
thinking of you
in love with another girl.
Little darling,
I can't bear to lose you;
my heartless love,
how can you be so cruel?'

(**Pipsqueak** *throws herself face down on the bed and begins to sob.* **Shunzi** *enters through the door on the left and goes over to her.*)

Shunzi (*Looking at her*)   I. . . . I think, Little Cui, if you carry on like this you'll just be . . .

(**Pipsqueak** *looks up at him.*)

Shunzi (*With a sigh*)   Little Cui, what – what are you going to do?

Pipsqueak   I don't know.

Shunzi (*His thick lips curling back*)   Why do you have to be so headstrong? We're not living on the farm where all you need to do is to work hard to eat and be happy. You – you can't be fussy when you come to a place like this. Just look at – at how Black San's been cl – clobbering you the last three days.

Pipsqueak (*Suddenly*)   Why did my dad have to go and get himself crushed to death by that iron piling?

Shunzi   If your dad were alive he'd still be treated like shit; who'd listen to him? A miserable footings-rammer, what could he have done for you?

Pipsqueak (*Thinking*)   Well, I might not have wound up here. He was a lot stronger than Black San – and bigger. If he'd seen Black San put me in a brothel he'd have punched the living daylights out of him. A decent man, my dad.

Shunzi (*His eyes shifting from side to side*)   Yes – but, but – isn't he dead?

Pipsqueak (*In a soft voice*)   Yes, he's dead. Saw it with my own eyes, the huge iron piling – I saw it crush him to death. (*Flinging herself face down on the bed again*) Oh, Dad! (*Sobbing*) Dad!

Shunzi   Now, now kid. You'd be better off trying to get a customer than crying over your dad.

Pipsqueak (*In tears*)   Who says I don't want a – a customer? But when I try, they all – they say I'm too young, and they don't pick me, so what can I do?

(**Shunzi** *sits down at the table. Beyond the window is someone giving a stylish rendition of 'The Exile of Qin Qiong' to the accompaniment of castanets made from pieces of broken ceramic.*

'*Here I stand before you in the street; good people, hear my tale.*
No highwayman am I, nor armed robber chief,
*   nor am I an outlaw come to surrender.*
Yang Lin accused me of collaborating with robbers,
*   and so I am exiled to Dengzhou.*
'*Tis hard to leave the prefect who has shown me such great kindness,*
Hard to leave my fellow officials in the Yamen,
Hard to leave all my neighbors and friends,
Hardest of all to leave my white-haired mother.
As mother and son we are truly as one flesh,
*   and my banishment of thousand miles will cause her grief*
With the red sun sinking behind the western hills,
I ask my escorts to find me lodging for the night.')

The singer (*Clanging loudly on his castanets at the end of his song, then resuming his usual doleful voice*)   Wealthy sirs, take pity on a poor fellow. I'm a long way from home and stuck in a strange city. It's bitterly cold, so spare me the price of a bed, wealthy sirs.

Pipsqueak   What time is it?

Shunzi   Past midnight

Pipsqueak   Then work is over?

Shunzi   Well, the lights'll be out soon, but who knows, we might get a whole bunch of customers showing up.

Pipsqueak (*Looking at* **Shunzi** *for a moment and sighing*)   A bit longer, then, a bit longer and then that'll be it.

Shunzi (*Not understanding her meaning*)   Humph, you can't very well go off to bed before all the patrons have gone. And you never know, any minute there might be a customer for the night, and if he takes a liking to you and decides to spend the night with you, then you will get to bed early.

A shrill voice outside   Up there! This way, sir. Clear a room there!

Shunzi   Customer. (*Towards the inner room*) Auntie, there's a customer.

(**Shunzi** *goes out with the kettle and* **Cuixi** *enters from the room on the left.*)

Cuixi   What are you doing just sitting there?

Pipsqueak (*Wiping away her tears*)   Nothing. Did the baby go back to sleep?

Cuixi   Yes, he's asleep.

The shrill voice outside   Attend the visitors!

Cuixi (*To* **Pipsqueak**)   Go on, see what you can do. Get yourself a nice customer for the night and save yourself another thrashing tonight.

(**Pipsqueak** *dazedly stands up.*)

The shrill voice   Attend the visitors! Come out, all of you, front and courtyard! Come attend the visitors!

(**Pipsqueak** *is shepherded out by* **Cuixi**.)

The shrill voice (*Pausing after each girl's name*)   Precious Orchid, Golden Cassia, Turquoise Jade, Cherry Apple, Black Jade. . . .

(*The sound of a small bell.*)

Another voice   Clear the room. Clear the room. This way, Second Master. Come and sit down in here.

(**Shunzi** *lifts the door curtain aside and shows* **Fusheng** *and* **Hu Si** *into the room.* **Hu Si** *is wearing a fur coat, a sleeveless purple woolen jacket and high-collared lined gown of crackle-patterned grey satin, patterned silk stockings, and black satin shoes. He wears his melon-shaped cap tilted slightly to one side and an inch or so of white shirtcuffs showing; he comes in with a carefree air.* **Fusheng** *is also in high spirits, his face glowing; he wears an old sheepskin gown beneath which can be seen the edge of his uniform, giving the impression that he must have left the hotel in a rush and thrown it on. As they come in through the door,* **Hu Si** *glances around and takes out a handkerchief, which he holds over his nose.*)

Fusheng   What's the matter?

Hu Si   It reeks in here. (*As he says this he leans back against the edge of the table.*)

Fusheng (*Wiping the table with his hand*)   Watch your clothes.

Hu Si (*Springing up and brushing off his coat*)   Shit! What a dump.

Fusheng (*Smooth-tongued*)   Well, now that I've escorted you here, Mr Hu, I'll be getting back to the hotel.

Hu Si (*Grabbing hold of him*)   Oh no, you don't. You're staying right here with me and keeping me company.

Fusheng   My dear sir, it's busy at the hotel at the moment. Manager Pan's in the middle of entertaining guests and I've got to get back to attend to them.

Hu Si   But surely you got somebody else on the staff to fill in for you?

Fusheng   No, no one knows I'm here with you. If Madame Gu finds out, it's all on you, you came on your own.

Hu Si   Relax, I'll keep you out of it.

Fusheng   All right, then, I'll stay a while, but I have to get back soon.

Hu Si   Me too.

Shunzi (*To* **Fusheng**)   Second Master, sir, you haven't been to see us in quite a while. Your usual girl's been moved, so I'm afraid it'll have to be someone else.

Fusheng   No, it's not for me, it's for the gentleman here. (*Indicating* **Hu Si**) Master Hu has dropped by to have a look and have some fun.

Shunzi   Shall I fetch a few for you to have a look at, then?

Hu Si (*Very much the man of the world*)   Yes, let's see a few for starters.

Shunzi   Very well, Mr Hu. (*Going out*) Visitors, come meet the visitors!

Fusheng   So after all the trouble of getting me to come here and show you this Pipsqueak, you now change your mind and don't want her after all?

Hu Si (*Rolls his eyes*)   And why not? I paid good money, why not look a few of them over, you idiot? We can still get Pipsqueak to entertain us. (**Shunzi** *pulls back the curtain across the front doorway on the right, though he does not enter.*)

Shunzi (*To the creatures*)   Come stand here. (**Hu Si** *and* **Fusheng** *go up to the doorway, and peer out.*)

Another voice   Come meet the visitors! All of you, from the front and back, come out all of you! Jade Orchid! (*A prostitute flits past the doorway.*)

Hu Si (*Sticking out his tongue in disapproval*)   Old pumpkin.

The other voice (*Rattling the names off quickly*)   Turquoise Jade! Golden Cassia! Cherry Apple! Black Jade! (*As their names are called the girls flit past the doorway, giggling among themselves.*)

Hu Si (*Making various gestures and comments as each creature parades before him, as if inspecting cattle*)   No good, no good at all; that one's not bad, a pity she's so skinny (*With a leer at* **Fusheng**) What a fat pig! They're getting worse and worse! – Nice name that one's got, but not the looks. (**Fusheng** *obliges him.*)

The voice   Cuixi

Hu Si (*Looking at* **Cuixi**)   Impressive.

The voice   Little Cui.

Fusheng (*To* **Hu Si**, *in an undertone*)   That's her, that's the girl.

The voice   Feng'e! Bitsy! Yueqing!

Shunzi (*To* **Hu Si**)   That's the lot, sir. Apart from the ones that are ill or on leave, that's it.

Hu Si (*To* **Shunzi**)   Cuixi and Little Cui are sisters?

Shunzi   Yes, they're in the same room.

Hu Si   We'll take those two, then.

Shunzi   Miss Cuixi and Little Cui. (*Enter* **Cuixi** *and* **Pipsqueak**. **Shunzi** *goes out.*)

Cuixi (*In a very experienced manner*)   Which of you two gentlemen am I to entertain?

Hu Si (*Pointing to himself*)   Me.

Cuixi   And my young friend? (*Indicating* **Pipsqueak**)

Hu Si (*Pointing to himself*)   Me as well.

Cuixi (*Tittering*)   Is this alright?

Fusheng   Anything wrong with it? (**Pipsqueak** *recognizes* **Fusheng**.)

Cuixi (*To* **Hu Si**)   And what's your name, sir?

Hu si   Hu, Hu Si.

Cuixi (*To* **Hu Si**)   Pleased to meet you, Master Hu. (*Indicating* **Fusheng**) Won't you introduce me to your friend?

Hu Si   Oh, this is Master Wang, the Eighth.

Fusheng   The Wang part's correct, but I am not the eighth.[16]

(**Shunzi** *comes in with a kettle. He produces a packet of melon seeds from his pocket, which he opens and places on metal dish on the table, then waits for an attendant to bring in hand towels.*)

Cuixi (*Offering the melon seeds*)   Fourth Master, Eighth Master. Now, aren't you going to take off your coat, Master Hu?

Hu Si   No, I don't like the cold. (*He brushes off the covers on the bed with a handkerchief before sitting down.*)

Cuixi (*To* **Pipsqueak**)   Well, don't just stand there staring. (*Turning to* **Hu Si**) You must forgive her, Master Hu, she's just a kid. Only started working a few days ago.

Fusheng (*Answering for* **Hu Si**)   No need to tell us.

Hu Si (*Taking* **Pipsqueak** *by the hand*)   Let's have a look at you. Not bad at all, no wonder Jin Ba took a fancy to her.

Fusheng (*Pointing to himself*)   Recognize me?

Pipsqueak (*Gritting her teeth*)   I'd recognize you if you were ground to dust.

Fusheng (*Amused*)   Will you listen to that! Here just three days and already she's got a mouth on her.

Hu Si (*Appraising her*)   The kid's got a good head on her shoulders all right! Dress her up a bit – I could choose her clothes myself – take her out to the Jockey Club, and in less than three days she'd be the talk of the town.

Fusheng   Naturally, but do you think she deserves such a stroke of good luck?

Hu Si   But . . . (*Suddenly, to* **Pipsqueak**) weren't you the one who slapped Jin Ba?

(**Pipsqueak** *flashes* **Fusheng** *a look of hatred, then lowers her head without a word.*)

Cuixi   Master Hu's speaking to you, you silly girl. (**Pipsqueak** *stands there like a statue.*)

Fusheng   Look at her, like a block of wood.

Hu Si (*Lighting a cigarette*)   I can't figure it out, such a wisp of thing daring to have a go at Jin Ba.

Fusheng   What do you expect from a country bumpkin? Innate irrationality. Just think, Jin Ba fell for her, the chance of a lifetime. She could have had whatever her heart desired: clothing, food, parties, the lot. Shit (*Looking around at* **Pipsqueak**), she's got it into her head that she's going to remain a virgin, won't sell at any price. (*Pointing at* **Pipsqueak**) But who's your father, a bank manager? Or the owner of a gold mine? Big money comes her way and she shoves it away, I ask you, now (*To* **Cuixi**), isn't that the height of peasant irrationality?

Cuixi   Ah well, we all get what we deserve, it must be in her stars, she doesn't deserve such good fortune.

Fusheng (*Becoming more irate the longer he looks at* **Pipsqueak**)   Fuck, how much longer are you going to keep this up? Think they'll let you stay in this city after this, do you? Shit, if I had a daughter who behaved like you and drove away a goldmine like that, I'd *kay* –[17] her, I'd wring her neck, I'd eat her alive. (*Pointing at* **Pipsqueak**). You are a fucking da-ma fu-lu.[18] (*He pronounces these English words with great pride.*)

Hu Si   What's the big deal, Fusheng?

Fusheng   I – (*With a smile*): I get worked up thinking about how stubborn the silly little bitch is.

Pipsqueak (*Going to the other end of the room and turning to* **Fusheng**): Come over here.

Fusheng   What now? (*Glancing at* **Hu Si** *with a knowing wink, then swaggering up to her*) What did you say?

Pipsqueak (*Coldly*)   You tricked me the other day to get me out of the hotel.

Fusheng   So what?

Pipsqueak   And now Black San is guarding me like a hawk so I'll never make it back there.

Fusheng   But Miss Chen at the hotel hasn't asked for you back.

Pipsqueak (*Trembling from head to foot*)   I only barely escaped and then you had to go throw me right back into Black San's hands.

Fusheng   Damn it, Pipsqueak, we brought you here to find you a mother-in-law, and you're still fucking ungrateful. And now you complain!

Cuixi (*To* **Pipsqueak**)   Have you lost your mind again?

Pipsqueak (*Ignoring her*)   I – I hate you.

Hu Si (*Walks up to* **Pipsqueak** *and teases her*)   Now don't go hating people. You'd be better off doing a bit of loving! (*He pulls her by the hand and tries to make her sit on his lap.*)

Pipsqueak (*Throwing off* **Hu Si** *hands and rushing towards* **Fusheng**) I'll – (*She slaps his face twice in a row and hurls herself at him.*)

Fusheng   The little bitch! (*He tries to fend her off.*)

Cuixi (*Dragging her away*)   You're out of your mind. (*Enter* **Shunzi**)

Shunzi   What the . . .

(*As he pushes open the door and comes in,* **Black San** *appears in the doorway wearing a fur jacket inside out, his face is covered in a thick beard and his eyes are savage.*)

Cuixi (*To* **Pipsqueak**)   Black San's here!

Pipsqueak (*Immediately dropping her hands, paralyzed like a mouse spotting a cat*) Oh!

Black San (*Smiling viciously and beckoning* **Pipsqueak** *with a great show of politeness*) Come here. (**Pipsqueak** *looks from one face to another, all round the room, but doesn't dare go over to* **Black San**. *There is a moment's silence.*)

Fusheng Go on, girl! (*He gives her a shove.*)

Black San (*Even more amiably*) Won't you come here?

(**Pipsqueak** *approaches him slowly.*)

Black San (*Seizing her by the hand and turning to* **Hu Si**) I'm sorry about the disturbance, Master Hu. She hasn't quite learned the rules yet. (*To* **Cuixi**) You attend to Master Hu, then, Cuixi. Show him a good time. Sorry, Fusheng, brother, treating you like this.

(*Like a wolf with a chicken clenched in its jaws,* **Black San** *drags* **Pipsqueak** *out of the room. As the door closes behind them we hear:*

Black San's voice (*Viciously*) Fucking take that! (*He slaps* **Pipsqueak**.) And that! (*Slapping her again.*) (*We hear* **Pipsqueak** *let out cries of pain following each heavy blow.*)

(*A pause.*)

Black San's voice (*To* **Pipsqueak**) Now get in that room! Go on, in! (*It seems that* **Pipsqueak** *is going with him, whimpering yet hardly daring to cry.*)

Cuixi I don't know what to say. I've never known such a strange kid. She didn't hurt you, did she, Mr Wang? I'm sorry about this.

Fusheng Oh, it doesn't matter, don't worry about it.

Shunzi (*Smiling*) After all, she's just a kid. You have to make allowances for children.

Hu Si Fuck off, who asked you?

Shunzi Sorry. Nobody. Forget I said anything. (*He exits, flustered.*)

Hu Si How are you feeling, Fusheng? Did it hurt?

Fusheng Oh, I'm all right! She slapped Jin Ba himself so I can't very well complain, now can I? (*The small bell outside rings.*)

A voice outside Prepare a room! Visitors!

Hu Si   That's life. If you don't enjoy yourself when you can, you're a fucking idiot. What's a couple of slaps?

Fusheng   Let's go, Master Hu. I think you ought to be getting back to the hotel.

Cuixi   Says who! (*To* **Fusheng**) Hey, hey, what's the big rush?

Fusheng   Well, I know when I'm not wanted. I can take a hint when I've had my face slapped.

Cuixi   Now, Master Wang, it's not easy for any of us in this profession. You have to make allowances sometimes. (**Shunzi** *enters*)

Shunzi   I'm afraid we'll have to squeeze you in here, Second Master. I'll pull the curtain across.

(**Shunzi** *moves the furniture across to the right and draws the curtain across the middle of the room, thus partitioning it into two halves. He goes to the door on the left and opens it to admit* **Fang Dasheng**. **Dasheng**, *wearing a blue padded gown, trudges in wearily.*)

Shunzi (*To* **Dasheng**)   Please make yourself comfortable here, sir.

Dasheng   Yes.

Shunzi   If you have a regular girl just tell me her name.

(**Dasheng** *looks all round. Overwhelmed by the stench, he covers his nose with a handkerchief. He shakes his head.*)

Shunzi (*Unconvinced*)   Just let me know, sir, if there's a regular girl you get.

Dasheng   No, there's not. (*He coughs.*)

Shunzi   A bit chilly in here, sir.

(*Meanwhile on the right-hand side of the room* **Hu Si** *draws* **Cuixi** *to one side.*)

Hu Si   I want a word with you.

Cuixi (*Smiling*)   What for?

Hu Si (*Taking her by the hand*)   Come over here. (*He whispers to her.*)

Cuixi (*Tittering*)   Go to hell!

Hu Si   You mean that? (*He whispers again.*)

Cuixi (*She pinches* **Hu Si** *and he yelps*)   Hungry, are you?

Hu Si (*Winking at her*)   I am (*He whispers again.*)

Cuixi (*Pretending to be angry*)   The very idea! If you want to do that, go fly an airplane.

Hu Si   What do you mean?

Cuixi   To make you think you're in heaven!

(**Hu Si** *roars with laughter and playfully pinches* **Cuixi** *so that she cries out, then the two of them giggle together. Meanwhile,* **Fusheng's** *attention has increasingly been drawn to the visitor in the left half of the room.*)

(*On the other side of the dividing curtain the action is continuing simultaneously.* **Dasheng** *stands there frozen, looking extremely uncomfortable. Finally –*)

Shunzi   I'll call them out so that you can see them.

Dasheng   I've been to many establishments.

Shunzi (*Casually*)   Oh, I see, out for a good time, eh, sir?

Dasheng (*As if to himself*)   And I still haven't found her.

Shunzi   Oh, you're –

Dasheng   I'm looking for someone.

Shunzi (*Puzzled*)   Loo – loo – looking for someone?

Dasheng   Yes, a girl who's just recently come to this district.

Shunzi   Well, there're hundreds of girls round here. Have you got a name?

Dasheng (*Embarrassed*)   Her – her name's – er – she, er, she hasn't got a name.

Shunzi   That makes it difficult. How old is she?

Dasheng   Fifteen or sixteen.

Shunzi   Well, there's several that age. I'll call some out for you to see.

(*Meanwhile, on the other side of the room –*)

Fusheng (*Stealthily pulling back one corner of the curtain and spying through the gap into the other side, suddenly, in a whisper*): Master Hu! Master Hu! Mr Fang has shown up.

Hu Si   Who?

Fusheng   Mr Fang.

Hu Si   What? (*Hurrying over and peeking through*) Well, if it isn't that lunatic! Fancy running into him here of all places!

(**Fusheng** *suddenly rushes out of the front door on the right.* **Hu Si** *stands next to the curtain peeking through, then* **Cuixi** *goes over to him, apparently asking him who it is and so on, but he just grins and waves a hand at her, waiting inquisitively for the people on the other side of the room to say something. When she sees that she will get nothing out of him,* **Cuixi** *goes disconsolately across to the dressing table and lights a cigarette, then saunters up to the front door and leans idly against the door frame.*)

(*On the left,* **Black San** *can be heard outside yelling 'Shunzi! Shunzi!'*)

Shunzi   Coming! (*To* **Dasheng**) I'll go and fetch them for you, sir.

Dasheng   All right. (*Exhausted he sits down at the table.*)

(*After a moment* **Shunzi** *returns.*)

Shunzi   The girl you're looking for probably isn't here, sir.

Dasheng   How can you say that when I haven't seen anybody yet?

Shunzi   Then I can call out a few that age, if you like.

Dasheng   Go on, then. (**Shunzi** *goes out again.*)

(*A pause.*)

(*Meanwhile, from outside comes the sound of a beggar singing shulaibao to the accompaniment of ox bones with small bells attached.*)

The beggar (*Shaking the ox bones, di-di-da, di-di-da, di-di-da-di-da-di-da*):

> '*Here I come a jingle-jang-a-jingling with my bells.*
> *The boss stands at the gateway touting for his gals.*
> *And very nice it is when trade begins to boom:*
> *Is this a new customer? Good! Clear a room!*
> *There's Cuixi and Xiaoda and also Baolan,*
> *And each of them as lovely as the famous Diaochan.*
> *But it'll cost you a dollar*
> *to take 'em to bed.*'

The beggar (*Resuming his feeble speaking voice*)   Wealthy sirs and ladies, spare me a dime, help me get the price of a bed.

Cuixi (*Standing in the doorway*)   Unbelievable. You again?

The beggar   Have a heart, lady. Do a good deed today and tomorrow you'll find yourself a husband and have a chubby baby.

Cuixi   Go to hell. And you'll freeze to death . . . you bastard.

(*Enter* **Black San** *from the left.*)

Black San   Here you go, sir! Here's two to look at.

(*He lifts aside the curtain over the door.*) (**Dasheng** *gets up and peers out.*)

Black San   Either of them her?

Dasheng (*After glancing at them*)   No, neither of them. She's pretty young, this girl, round face, big eyes, very blunt manner of speaking.

Black San   Oh, you mean the one who just started the other day?

Dasheng   Yes, only a few days ago: let me see, yes, about four or five days ago, I think.

Black San (*Gesturing with his hands*)   About so tall, so thin, round face, big flat feet, little round eyes, short hair?

Dasheng   Yes, that's her.

Black San   I'll go and fetch her for you if you'll just wait a moment. (*Exits.*)

(*Meanwhile, on the other side of the curtain:*)

The beggar (*Striking his ox bone, di-di-da, di-di-da, di-di-da-di-da-di-da*):

> 'I come with my bells, as jolly as can be;
> A maiden fair before me I do see.
> With long black braids and curly tresses,
> Her pointed chin and her lips so red,
> She'll have you on your knees without a word said.'
> (*Di-di-da, di-di-da, di-di-da-di-da-di-da*)
> 'I come with my bells all a-tinkling away,
> My lady is dressed all in silk today,
> Lovely to see and in rich; array.
> Without a word she smiles so gay,
> They'll come back to see you day after day!'

The beggar   Spare me a dime, lady!

Cuixi (*Unrelenting*)   You won't get anything out of me!

The beggar (*Teasing her*)   In that case I'll keep on singing.

Cuixi   Go ahead. Who's stopping you?

(**The beggar** *strikes his ox bone, di-di-da, di-di-da, di-di-da-di-da-di-da.*)

(*Meanwhile on the other side of the room the door opens and a newspaper vendor enters. Unlined trousers, a tattered padded jacket, a bearded face. Deftly he extracts a newspaper and puts it on the table. His gestures indicate that he wants money for it, he salutes like a foreigner, stands to attention, bows, and makes inarticulate noises.*)

Dasheng   I don't have any change. (*The* **mute** *points to the paper and begins explaining the latest news through various miming gestures.*)

Dasheng   I've already read about it. (*The* **mute** *thrusts the paper into his hands, so he has no choice but to read it as the* **mute** *continues miming.*) You're saying there is a clerk . . . he had no food to eat. (*The* **mute** *nods his head.*) What, oh, you're saying, he had lots of kids (*The* **mute** *nods*) . . . what, what, oh, the clerk was laid off, so he bought some opium, eh? The kids refused to eat it, so he mixed it in some brown sugar and fed it to them (*Sighs*) and they all died. Oh, there was no more opium left so he himself was about to jump in the river (*Reads*) but right at that moment the cops came and arrested him. (*To the* **mute**) You don't need to explain further, I've read it. The cops took him in and charged him with homicide and want to put him in jail.

Mute (*Nods his head, and stretches out his hand*)   Ah . . . ah

Dasheng (*Murmuring*)   He was a clerk at the Dafeng Bank, Manager Pan's clerk. So unfair (*Stands up*).

Mute (*Sticks his hand out for money*)   Ah . . . ah (**Dasheng** *gives him a ten-cent note but won't take the change. The* **mute** *again bows and salutes, then goes out, overcome with gratitude.*)

(*Meanwhile on the other side the room:*)

Hu Si (*To himself*)   He really is crazy!

(*The* **beggar** *is still beating out the same di-di-da, di-di-da, di-di-da-di-da-di-da on his ox bone. He sings:*

'I've sung her praises till my throat is hoarse,
But Madam still won't open her purse.

Don't think beggary is something low:
It's none of your 'nine lower trades' you know!
From the families of generals and priests we came,
And we beg from those with a sage's name.
We've made our speeches, read poetry.
We know the Five Bonds and the Duties Three.
We know how to read, we can handle a brush,
And the Five Constant Virtues are all known to us.'

The beggar How about it, lady? Aren't you going to give me a dime?

Cuixi With weather this cold, and times as hard as they are, I wouldn't give you money even if I had any! (**The beggar** *quickly improvises a reply:*

'Times are hard, you say? Quite right,
But yours and mine is a different plight.
The trouble with you is that trade is slack,
But I haven't got the price of a snack.
If I had two hundred cash or so
I wouldn't be telling you a tale of woe.'
Di-di-da, di-di-da, di-di-da-di-da-di-da.

The beggar Now –

Hu Si Go on, get lost! (*Throwing him a penny*) Now leave us alone.

The beggar Much obliged, sir. (*The sound of footsteps, then he begins banging on his ox bone and singing next door.*)

(*Enter* **Fusheng**)

Hu Si (*Pointing towards the left*) What now?

Fusheng (*With a sneaky smile*) Take a look. (*They both go over to the curtain and peek through.*)

(*On the other side,* **Black San** *and* **Shunzi** *come in.*)

Black San Here you are, sir, this must be your girlfriend.

Dasheng (*Going to the doorway to look but greatly disappointed*) No, that's not her.

Shunzi You've got to give us a name.

Dasheng (*Suddenly*) Have you got one here called Pipsqueak?

Shunzi Pipsqueak?

Dasheng   That's right.

Shunzi   Nope.

Black San (*With a crafty smile*)   That's an unusual name.

Dasheng (*Picking up his hat*)   Sorry to have troubled you.

(*With his head hanging, he is about to leave the room, when* **Black San** *blocks him, thrusting out his hand.*)

Dasheng   What's this?

Black San   For all our trouble, don't we get something?

Dasheng (*Staring in surprise*)   You charge even for that?

Black San   What sort of a joint do you think this is? Think we live on air?

Dasheng (*With a pitying smile at* **Black San's** *desperate expression, taking out some money*)   Here, take this.

Shunzi (*Hurriedly stretching out his hand*)   Thank you.

Black San (*Opens* **Shunzi's** *hand*)   Is this some kind of a joke? You're not throwing pennies to a beggar, you know.

(*In the side-room to the left the baby begins to cry,* **Cuixi** *pulls aside the dividing curtain across the center and heads in that direction. Seeing* **Dasheng** *she stops and stares at him.* **Dasheng** *turns away in distaste and begins coughing, then, covering his nose with one hand and throwing some money on the table with the other, he rushes out.*)

(*Puzzled* **Cuixi** *goes into the side-room on the left and again begins soothing the baby back to sleep.*)

(**Black San** *breaks into coarse laughter.*)

(**Shunzi** *draws the center curtain back.*)

Black San   If you'll make yourself at home for a minute, Mr Hu, I'll fetch Little Cui to entertain you.

Fusheng   Don't bother, Black San, we have to get going.

Hu Si   We've been here a long time.

Black San   Now don't go rushing off before you've had a chance to enjoy yourself. (*He hurries out shouting 'Little Cui!'*)

Fusheng   We'd better get back, you really ought to show your new outfit off to Madame Gu.

Hu Si (*Remembering his nickname of 'China's most handsome fellow,' brightening up*) By the way, don't you think this suits me?

Fusheng I do indeed! I think it's your best one yet.

Hu Si (*Unconsciously beginning to preen himself again, smoothes his clothes, self-satisfied*) Not bad, if I do say so myself. (*Enter* **Black San**, *followed by* **Pipsqueak**.)

Black San Now come and take care of Master Hu properly. Then perhaps he'll take kindly to you. Say how do you do to Master Hu.

Pipsqueak (*Sobbing out the words*) How – how – how d'you do, Master Hu?

Black San And apologize to Master Wang. (**Pipsqueak** *just stands there looking at* **Fusheng**.)

Black San Go on, say 'I wouldn't dare do it again, Master Wang.'

Pipsqueak (*Sobbing out each syllable*) I – I – I – wouldn't dare do it again. Master – Master – Master Wang.

Fusheng That's quite all right.

Black San (*Very pleased with himself*) Now pour Master Hu a cup of tea and ask Mr Wang if he'll come again tomorrow with Master Hu.

Hu Si All right, tomorrow, then. (*Getting up*) Now enough of the formalities. Everything's all right. (**Cuixi** *emerges from the side-room.*)

Cuixi What's all this talk about leaving? I'm not letting either of you go. What was it you were saying just now, Master Hu? (*She whispers in his ear.*)

Hu Si (*Nodding repeatedly*) Yes, that's right. (*With a wicked smile*) But I really am busy. Tonight's no good. See you tomorrow.

Fusheng (*Smiling*) Yes, we are busy. We'll see you tomorrow.

Black San This time she found herself with Fourth Master Hu, who's a very reasonable sort. But what happens if she rubs a difficult customer up the wrong way? Before we knew it, we'd be out of business!

Cuixi (*Clinging to* **Hu Si**) Promise you'll come tomorrow, then?

(**Hu Si** *nods, smiling insincerely.*)

(*By now* **Pipsqueak** *has poured the tea and is bringing a cup over to* **Hu Si**.)

Fusheng (*Teasing her*)   Careful now, don't burn yourself, Miss. (**Pipsqueak** *goes up to* **Hu Si** *with her head down and eyes welling up with tears.*)

Fusheng   See that, Master Hu? Little Cui's winking at you. (**Pipsqueak** *darts an angry glance over her shoulder at* **Fusheng**.)

Hu Si (*Delighted*)   Is she? (*Trying to pinch her cheek*) So the little pipsqueak likes me, does she?

Pipsqueak (*Not expecting to find* **Hu Si** *so near her when she turns her head all of a sudden, the cup collides with* **Hu Si's** *hand and the tea splashes on his outfit*): Oh!

Hu Si   Now look what you did!

Black San (*Bellowing*)   What the hell do you think you're doing!

Pipsqueak (*So scared her hand slips and the whole cup of tea spills on* **Hu Si's** *new clothes.*)   Oh!

Hu Si (*His face dark with rage*)   Damn it! You little idiot, you! (*He hurriedly mops himself with a handkerchief.*)

Black San (*Lunging across to where* **Pipsqueak** *is standing, his hand raised to strike her*)   You fucking little – (**Pipsqueak** *takes refuge behind* **Cuixi**.)

Cuixi (*Restraining* **Black San**)   Don't hit her now!

Fusheng (*Also restraining* **Black San**)   Hang on, Black San, take care of his clothes first.

Black San (*In a flurry*)   Quick, grab a towel, Shunzi. (**Shunzi** *dashes in with a cloth. Everyone is dabbing the clothes all at once except for* **Pipsqueak**, *who stands petrified with fright.*)

Hu Si (*Infuriated*)   Get off! Get off! Don't wipe them like that! (*He goes and inspects his clothes under the light.*) Just look, my whole outfit practically ruined. Damn it. (*To* **Fusheng**) Come on, we're leaving! (*Suddenly strides over to* **Pipsqueak**) Worthless piece of shit, I'll – (*He makes as if to slug her, but* **Pipsqueak** *backs away and he swings round away from her.*) Trash! (*Suddenly taking out a wad of cash from his pocket and turning back to* **Pipsqueak**) See this? I've loads of money. But for a stupid little idiot like you (*Turning to* **Black San**), I wouldn't give a penny! (*Turning to* **Shunzi**) Give this to Cuixi for looking after us. (*He gives him a bank note.*) And this is for the people outside. (*He gives him another note.*)

Shunzi Thank you.

Hu Si (*With a nod*) Come on. (*To* **Fusheng**) Let's get back to the hotel. (*He storms out.*)

(**Fusheng** and **Shunzi** *follow him out.*)

Cuixi (*Seeing them out*) Come back tomorrow, Master Hu! Don't forget! (*She comes quickly back into the room.*)

Black San (*Glaring at* **Pipsqueak** *like a wild beast, his voice low*) Come here, you. We're going in there. (*He indicates the small side room on the left.*)

(**Pipsqueak** *takes a few steps, but her legs give out and she collapses to her knees with a thud.*)

Black San (*Going over to* **Pipsqueak** *and yanking her up by the arm*) Come!

Cuixi (*Putting her arms round* **Pipsqueak**) Don't hit her, Black San! (*Imploring*) It wasn't her fault, you mustn't hit her!

Black San (*Pulling out a whip from under the table*) Butt out!

Cuixi Black San, she can't take another beating.

Black San (*Pushing her down*) Stay the hell out of this, you!

(**Cuixi** *cries out in pain, then begins rubbing her injured hand.*)

Black San Come on! (*He drags* **Pipsqueak** *into the next room and locks the door.*)

Cuixi (*Suddenly remembering her baby, she rushes over and bangs on the door*) Open up, Black San, the baby's in there. Open the door, open the door!

(*There is no reply from* **Black San**, *who is busy whipping and cursing* **Pipsqueak**; *the latter seems to be taking each lash of the whip in silence.*)

Cuixi (*Hammering at the door, panic-stricken*) Open the door, open up! You'll frighten my baby. My baby! (*The child begins to cry.*)

Cuixi (*Shouting desperately*) Open the door, open the door, Black San! Don't be frightened, my darling, Mama's coming!

(*Unable to withstand the pain,* **Pipsqueak** *begins to wail, and this combined with the crying of the baby attracts several curious onlookers outside.* **Shunzi** *hurries in.*)

Cuixi (*Frantically*)   Open up the door! (*She beats on it wildly.*) Open the door! Black San! If you don't open up right now, I'll call the police.

Shunzi   Black San, there's somebody outside to see you.

(**Black San** *opens the door and comes out holding the whip, his face drenched with sweat.*)

Black San (*Over his shoulder*)   I'm letting you off easy this time, you little bitch.

(**Cuixi** *dashes into the room, where the baby's crying and* **Pipsqueak's** *wails can be heard.*)

Black San (*To* **Shunzi**)   Who is it? Who's here?

Shunzi   Somebody from the hotel. (*The small bell outside rings.*)
(*A pause.*)

Black San   About what?

Shunzi   Says Jin Ba wants to see you about something.

Another voice   Visitor staying the night! Outside, everyone not fixed up for the night!

Black San   Let's go see him, then. (*Towards the small door on the left*) Come on out! Outside! (**Pipsqueak** *drags herself painfully out.*)

Black San (*Pointing with the whip*)   I'm letting you off this time. There's somebody spending the night. Go out and see them. If you don't fucking land a customer again tonight don't bother coming to see me in the morning. D'you hear me?

Pipsqueak (*Sobbing*)   Yes.

Black San Now go. Wipe your eyes and go see the customer.
(**Pipsqueak** *goes out with her head down.*)

Black San   I'm leaving now, Shunzi. See ya in the morning.

Shunzi   All right then. See you tomorrow. (**Black San** *goes out.*)

Shunzi   Here, Cuixi, come out here. The cripple's tired of waiting. Hurry up and go see him. (**Cuixi** *appears through the small doorway on the left.*)

Cuixi   Whew! What a life!

(**Cuixi** *and* **Shunzi** *exit together, leaving the room empty.*)

The voice of an attendant outside   Lights out! Lights out!

The voice of a hawker (*Bleakly*)   Sweet buns! Sweet buns!

(*The sounds of watchman's hollow wooden gong pass by.*)

Another attendant's voice (*Calling out the girls' names in a lowered voice since the visitors have now gone to bed*)   Precious Orchid, Turquoise Jade, Cherry-apple, Little Cui.

(**Shunzi** *comes in and turns off the lamp, then lights a candle from the drawer. It is nearly dark in the room. Just as* **Shunzi** *is leaving,* **Pipsqueak** *returns slowly.*)

(*Next door and across the courtyard men and women are laughing and conversing in subdued voices.*)

Shunzi   Well, did you hook him?

Pipsqueak (*Shaking her head*)   No.

Shunzi   How come?

Pipsqueak (*With a sob*)   Said I was too young.

Shunzi (*Sighing*)   Then you might as well go to bed alone.

Pipsqueak   Yes.

Shunzi (*Consoling her*)   Fuck that. Tomorrow is tomorrow; d – d – don't think about it.

(*In the distance* **Cuixi** *is weeping and shouting.*)

A man's voice   Are you coming home or not, you? Eh?

Cuixi's voice   Go ahead, hit me, then! Hit me! If you don't kill me today you're a bastard.

Pipsqueak (*Standing up*)   Who's that?

Shunzi   Cuixi. Her hu – hu – sband's giving it to her. (*Looking out of the window*) Poor thing. Such a hard life she's had. Her husband got the pox after they got married and now he's a cripple. Two babies, b – b – blind from birth. Then there's his mother, paralyzed and bedridden. And so the whole family scrapes by on wha – what they can get out of this joint.

Pipsqueak (*Sitting down again, staring blankly*)   Yes, mm, yes.

Shunzi   Here she comes. (*Shouting out of the door*) Cuixi (**Cuixi** *comes in sobbing.*)

Shunzi   What happened?

Cuixi (*To herself*)   What the hell, I'll go home with you! Right now! But once I get home we're splitting up. There's no sense going on like this. (*Muttering, she goes into the room on the left.*)

Shunzi (*Watching her*)   Tut. (**Cuixi** *returns with the baby in her arms.*)

Pipsqueak   Is he asleep?

Cuixi (*Choked with sobs*)   Yes, Little Cui, he . . . he . . . is. (*With a sob between each word*) That . . . that . . . all-nighter . . . just now, did . . . did you get him?

(**Pisqueak** *hangs her head but doesn't reply.*)

Shunzi (*Shaking his head*)   No, she didn't.

Cuixi   How . . . how come?

Shunzi   The usual. Thought she was too young.

Cuixi (*Stroking* **Pipsqueak's** *face*)   You . . . you poor kid. Still, never mind, you can have the bed all to yourself tonight. You won't have me taking up half of it. It gets cold at night, so put on plenty of covers. Don't . . . don't catch cold. Don't start worrying about tomorrow now. Take care of yourself while you can, because if you get sick in this place no . . . nobody gives a damn.

Pipsqueak (**Pipsqueak** *looks at her, then overcome, flings her arms around* **Cuixi** *and bursts into tears*)   My, my . . .

Cuixi (*Shedding tears of anguish and hugging her tightly*)   Little Cui, Little Cui, don't . . . don't cry. I'm . . . going . . . now. First thing . . . tomorrow morning I'll. . . . I'll come and visit.

(**Pipsqueak** *sobs.*)

Cuixi   I'm. . . . I'm going, then.

Pipsqueak   Yes.

Shunzi   You'd better get to bed yourself.

Pipsqueak   All right.

(**Cuixi** and **Shunzi** *exit together.*)

A voice outside   Lights out! Lights out!

(*The wooden gong sounds. The stage grows even darker.*)

The hawker's voice (*Bleakly*)   Sweet buns! Sweet buns!

(**Pipsqueak** *suddenly stands up and goes silently into the side-room on the left.*)

(*The stage is now empty.*)

(*The sound of laughter from a couple in a room across the courtyard.*)

The woman's voice   Go. Go, go. What are you doing coming twenty miles to see me for, when you've got girls back home?

The man's voice (*Muffled*)   . . . I

The woman's voice   Stop it, don't do that! (*Giggling*) Aren't you shy, this being your first time?

The man's voice (*Still muffled*)   Mm. . . .

(**Pipsqueak** *reappears from the side-room dragging her slippered feet, a hempen rope in one hand. She stands next to the table wide-eyed as if seeing a vision, nodding her head. Trancelike she goes to each of the front doors in turn, closes them, and turns the locks. She begins to tremble, then summoning up her courage goes to the small doorway on the left, where she stops. She moves a chair over, stands on it, and ties the rope to the upper door post in the form of a small noose. Then she steps back down. She paces distractedly back and forth, then suddenly stops.*)

Pipsqueak (*In a soft choking voice*)   Oh, Father! (*She kneels down facing the noose and kowtows three times, then gets to her feet. With a sigh she climbs back up on the chair, slips her head through the noose, and kicks the chair away. . . . Such a tiny, such a weak, pathetic little life now hangs from the lintel.*)

The hawker's voice (*Desolately*)   Sweet buns!

(*Meanwhile, apart from the sound of the wooden gong, come voices:*)

A man's voice (*Singing suggestively*):

'You called me your little sweetheart.
sleepless until the dawn.
When morning came,
you left my bed.
Lover,
I can't bear to lose you;
one night together,
and I love you forever more.'

(*The sound of a woman weeping softly, as if far off in the distance.*)

(*As* **Pipsqueak** *hangs there, the flickering candlelight dances around her feet. One of her backless slippers drops quietly to the floor, and there is now not a single person in the room.*)

(*The stage gradually blacks out.*)

(*The curtain falls.*)

ALTERNATIVE ENDING TO THIS ACT

The ending of this Act might be considered too harrowing, so, for the purpose of stage presentation, I have changed it as follows:

[From the second half of the previous page to the end of the Act.]

(**Pipsqueak** *reappears from the side-room dragging her slippered feet, a hempen rope in one hand. She stands next to the table wide-eyed as if seeing a vision, nodding her head. Trancelike she goes to each of the front doors in turn, closes them, and turns the locks. She trembles all over, holding back her tears, then with an expression of alarm she goes to the side-door on the left and stops.*)

The hawker's voice (*Desolately*)   Sweet buns!

Sweet buns!

(*A watchman's wooden gong sounds in the distance.*)

(*She moves a chair over to the door, stands up on it, and ties the rope to the upper door post in the form of a small noose.*

She calms herself to carry out the deed . . . but with a shiver of terror she climbs back down again and stands there in a daze.)

A man's voice (*Singing softly and suggestively*):

> 'You called me your little sweetheart,
> sleepless until the dawn.
> When morning came,
> you left my bed.
> Lover.
> I can't bear to lose you;
> one night together.
> and I love you forever more.'

(*Sounds of a woman weeping softly, as if far away.*)

(*Undecided,* **Pipsqueak** *takes a few shaky steps in time with the woman's weeping, then, unable to bear her inaction any longer, suddenly throws herself down on to the floor and weeps broken-heartedly.*)

The hawker's voice (*Desolately*)   Sweet buns! Sweet buns!

(*The watchman's wooden gong sounds far off in the distance.*)

(*The stage gradually blacks out.*)

(*The curtain falls.*)

ACT IV

The same night as Act III, around four a.m. In the opulent sitting room of a suite in the X Hotel. The curtains have been drawn, and in the harsh glare of the lamp light the bizarre furnishings of the room assault the eyes. The air is thick with cigarette smoke and the stench of face powder. Bottles are strewn across the floor, liquids dripping from them, precious as gold, soaking unheeded into the carpet, staining the plush upholstery of the armchair's yellow and running off the marble top of the small tea-table. In the middle, by the legs of a small armchair, are the shards of a broken champagne glass. The hands of the shiny clock on the wall point to four o'clock. The hubbub of a mahjong game still emanates from the left-hand room, with spells of quiet broken only by the occasional crisp clickety-clack of mahjong tiles, now a period of chatter and joking, curses and exclamations, slaps of annoyance on the mahjong table, and derisive laughter . . . all mingled with the sound of the tiles being shuffled on the surface of the table. When the curtain rises, **Bailu** *is standing alone at the window, her back to the audience, holding the curtains back and looking out. She is wearing a black velour dress edged with a patterned orange border with black polka dots. The fact that she is dressed in black lends severity to her appearance. She stands alone at the window, and there is not a sound from anything in the room. A pause.*

The left-hand door swings wide open and immediately a torrent of laughter and noise from the mahjong players floods into the room.

Voices from the next room   Lulu! Lulu! (**Bailu** *ignores them, standing there motionless.*)

Georgy's voice   Lulu! Lulu!

Georgy (*To the people inside the room as he emerges*)   No, no, I'll be right back. (*Self-confidently*) Look, I'll get her and then come back. (**Georgy** *now emerges. He is wearing an impeccable European-style suit with his tie loosened and his waistcoat buttons undone. In one hand he holds a champagne bottle, in the other a glass. He approaches* **Bailu** *in a boisterous mood.*)

Georgy (*Staggering across to* **Bailu**, *the spirit suddenly moving him*)   Ah! My little Lulu! (*Looking her up and down and gesticulating, as if reciting poetry*) Si belle! Si charmante! et si melancolique![19] (*Getting carried away*) So beautifully bewitching! And so bewitchingly beautiful! (**Bailu** *continues to gaze out of the window, motionless, and as though she hasn't heard him.*)

Georgy (*Going up to her*)   As I was saying, you are beautiful! You are beauty incarnate this evening! (*With an air of complacency, he closes his eyes in rapturous appreciation.*) Beautiful! Absolutely beautiful! You really do know how to dress, with such melancholy and such allure! *And* you know how to wear perfume, it smells so – (*Sniffing and making a long-drawn-out 'Mm!'*) – so delicate, yet so mysteriously distant! Ah! The moment I smell the fragrance of your perfume – oh no, the pure fragrance that emanates from your beautiful body, it transports me back to Paris. . . . (*Floating away on the mists of memory*) Ah, those Paris nights! Paris at night! (*With an appreciative sniff*) Mm, *Exquise!*

Bailu (*Still not turning around*)   You're drunk, I suppose.

Georgy   Drunk? I feel absolutely splendid tonight! Did you see Miss Liu just now? Says she wants to marry me, insists on marrying me, but I told her – (*Haughtily*) I said: 'You? (*Contemptuously*) You marry me? You stand there and tell me you want to marry me? You?' She hung her head pathetically and said (*In a tearful voice*) 'Georgy, I'm willing as long as you are.' She went on and on, almost in tears, but (*Tugs at* **Bailu**, *who still does not turn around*) See, this is how I looked at her (*Raises his head and gives a sideways glance*) I said, 'You? You want to marry Georgy Zhang? Pah! The only woman in the world worthy of Georgy Zhang is Chen Bailu!' (*He waits for* **Bailu** *to laugh, but she doesn't.*) Why, Lulu, why don't you laugh?

Bailu (*Her attitude unchanged*)   What's so funny about that? (*In an undertone*) Any champagne left?

Georgy (*Surprised*)   You fancy another drink?

Bailu   Yes.

Georgy   See how I wait on you? I've come prepared. (*As he pours her a drink,* **Madame Gu's** *voice comes from the right-hand room calling* **Bailu's** *name. When he hands the glass to* **Bailu** *she gulps it down and hands the glass back without so much as glancing at him.*) (**Madame Gu** *emerges from the room on the right. Dressed in her usual gaudy fashion she enters imperiously.*)

Gu (*In the doorway*)   Where *are* your sleeping pills, Bailu?

(*Suddenly noticing* **Georgy**) Oh! Professor Zhang. So the two of you have snuck out here to chat.

Georgy   Two of us? Why I must be drunk.

Gu   What?

Georgy   Strange. I was under the impression I was here ranting to myself.

Gu   Oh please, I simply do not comprehend your academic jargon. Bailu, quick, where are your sleeping pills?

Bailu   In the small cabinet beside my bed.

Georgy   What's the matter Mrs Gu?

Gu (*Rubbing her heart*)   My heart aches. I'm suffering.

Georgy   What is it this time?

Gu   It's that unfeeling creature again. An upset like this will lose me three nights' sleep. I really must take some sleeping pills home. But enough about this: you two get back to your conversation.

(*She turns to go back through the door.*)

Georgy   Hey, don't go. Come and sit with us for a while and chat.

Gu   No, no, impossible. I'm in agony with this heart of mine. I must go and take some of Doctor Ledoux's medicine.

Georgy   Yes, but look, you can do that just as easily in here, can't you?

Gu   Just listen to my heart, though. It is pounding away again. (*Clutching her heart with both hands and grimacing as if in agony*) Ooh! I must lie down for a while.

(*Suddenly the door on the left opens wide unleashing the clamor of noise and laughter is again into the room.*)

Miss Liu's voice   Georgy!

Gu (*Looking at* **Miss Liu** *standing in the doorway to the left, beaming*): Miss Liu, you're still here playing mahjong? (*to* **Georgy**) Fine, Miss Liu's here, why don't you three have fun? (**Madame Gu** *exits left.*)

Miss Liu   Georgy! GEORGY (*Puts his finger up to his lips as a sign*) Shh! (*He motions in the direction of* **Bailu** *and signals to* **Miss Liu** *to come in to join the conversation.*)

Miss Liu's voice (*Severely*)   Georgy!

Georgy (*Motioning to her to not shout, his finger still on his lips, and appears to indicate to her that* **Bailu** *is for some reason unhappy and in tears, and that* **Miss Liu** *should come in to keep them company*):

Miss Liu's voice (*Hardly the pathetic creature he has made her out to be*)   I am not going in there, I won't.

Georgy (*Shrugging his shoulders as if there's nothing he can do, then gesticulates again that she should come in the room*)

Miss Liu's voice (*With even more severity*)   Georgy!!! Are you coming or not?

Georgy (*Overcome with fear by the ultimatum that has apparently been issued by the one at the door*)   No, please don't! I'm coming! I'm coming! I'm coming! Right away! (*Smiling nervously, he goes through the left hand door.*)

Miss Liu's voice (*In a low but urgent tone of voice*)   I am leaving. When you are here on your own, I won't have you flirting with the ladies, do you hear me?

Georgy's voice   I haven't been flirting with anyone.

Bailu (*She slowly turns round, with a dismal look on her face. She has had too much to drink and her face is flushed. She lightly pats her chest a few times and then lets her hand swing limply down as if in despair. She heaves a sigh*): U-u-uh. (*She lifts her head. Tears trickle down from the corners of her eyes. She covers her eyes with her handkerchief. A knock on the door.*)

Bailu (*Removing the handkerchief and drying her eyes*)   Who is it?

Fusheng's voice   It's me, Miss.

Bailu   Come in.

(*Enter* **Fusheng**. *Having returned to the hotel earlier, he is now back in uniform.*)

Fusheng Miss.

Bailu What do you want?

Fusheng (*Noticing that* **Bailu** *has been crying*)   Oh, didn't you call for me?

Bailu No.

Fusheng Oh, all right, very well . . . (*Looking at* **Bailu**) You've had a bit too much to drink this evening, Miss.

Bailu I know.

Fusheng (*Looking all round*)   Isn't Mr Fang around?

Bailu He's not back yet. Why, did you want to see him?

Fusheng Nothing urgent. Another telegram came for him a short while ago.

Bailu Same as this morning?

Fusheng Yes.

Bailu Where is it?

Fusheng (*Producing it from a pocket*)   Do you want it?

Bailu I'll give it to him myself. (**Fusheng** *hands her the telegram.*) Anyway, it's still early.

Fusheng Early! It's after four!

Bailu (*Absently*)   Haven't those people left yet?

Fusheng (*Looking at the door on the left*)   They're all eating and drinking and have plenty to amuse themselves with here, so who'd want to leave?

Bailu (*Nodding sadly*)   So this is their playground.

Fusheng (*Not understanding*)   Hmm? Well, of course!

Bailu And what happens when they've been sufficiently amused?

Fusheng Well, naturally they'll go home. They've all got homes of their own to go to – who would want to spend their whole life in a hotel?

Bailu Then why don't they leave?

Fusheng Miss, you're saying . . . um, um, no doubt they haven't been sufficiently amused.

Bailu (*In the same flat tone*)   Why not?

Fusheng (*Perplexed and can't help laughing*)   They just haven't.

Bailu (*Suddenly walks up to* **Fusheng** *and spits out*)   I am asking you, why not? (*Loudly*) Why not? (*Even louder*) Why don't they finish amusing themselves and go back to their own homes. Go! Go! (*Irate*) Why don't they just . . . (*Suddenly aware that she has lost her normal composure and forces herself to stop talking, hanging her head down*)

Fusheng (*Looks at* **Bailu's** *face, as if with great understanding, pours a cup of water and brings it over to her*)   Miss.

Bailu (*Looking at the glass in his hand*)   What's this?

Fusheng   You've probably just had too much to drink.

Bailu (*Takes the glass*)   No, no. (*Shaking her head and lowering her voice*) I've probably just had all the amusement I want. (*Sitting down*) Yes, I've had enough (*Pensively*), I'd like to go home myself, back to my old home.

Fusheng (*Astonished*)   But Miss, you mean you've got a home here?

Bailu   Yes, that's correct. (*Sighs*) Everyone has a home of their own. Who'd want to spend their life in a hotel?

Fusheng   Are you serious, Miss?

Bailu   Yes, I think about it often.

Fusheng (*Hurriedly*)   Look, Miss, if you are really considering going home, what about all your unpaid bills here? You'll have to –

Bailu   Yes, I know I'm deep in debt. But surely I've paid my dues over the years?

Fusheng (*Pragmatically*)   Now look, Miss, you've just paid off eight hundred but you still owe another two thousand. If you keep throwing money around like this you won't ever get out of debt the rest of your life. And more bills came this afternoon. See all these invoices (*Taking some from his pocket*) altogether, they come to . . .

Bailu   No, don't bother getting them out. I don't want to see them.

Fusheng   But they say you must pay up without fail by tomorrow afternoon. I did my best to explain –

Bailu   Who asked you to explain? 'Every injustice has its perpetrator, every debt its debtor.' I don't go begging for help myself, so why should you?

Fusheng   But, Miss –

Bailu   I know, I know. Stop talking about it. Money! Money! Money!
Why do you always keep on at me like this?

(*The telephone rings.*)

Fusheng (*Picking up the receiver*)   Hello . . . Who's calling? Oh . . . this
is Suite 52, Miss Chen's.

Bailu   Who is it?

Fusheng (*Covering the mouthpiece with his hand*)   Mrs Li. (*Speaking
into the receiver again*) Oh, I see, yes. Mr Li's not here. He was here this
afternoon, but he left a long time ago. . . . Yes . . . yes. . . . Mr Li phoned
Manager Pan here not long ago and asked him to be so kind as to wait
for him as he'd be over again soon. . . . Well, why not give us another
ring later on? (*He puts down the receiver.*)

Bailu   What was all that about?

Fusheng   Mr Li's son is quite sick and Mrs Li wants him back home at
once.

Bailu   I see. All right, then, you may go.

(**Manager Pan** *enters through the main entrance, his oily face beaming
with joy, eyes half closed and mouth agape. He holds a cigar in one
hand, while he strokes his mustache with the other.* **Fusheng** *steps aside
as he enters, then exits through the center door.*)

Pan   Lulu, Lulu, your visitors haven't left, have they?

Bailu   No.

Pan   Splendid. Don't let any of them leave. We must make this a party
to end all parties.

Bailu   What for?

Pan   I think a real stroke of fortune has finally come my way. I've got
some good news.

Bailu   What good news? Why, has Jin Ba agreed to give you another
week to return his deposits?

Pan   No, no – he agreed to that several days ago. Now let me tell you:
government bonds are going up after all. Way up. Higher than they've
ever been. And that's going to put me on my feet again! You know I
suddenly heard this morning that the news of a rally was merely a rumor

being spread on purpose by Jin Ba. That he was saying that he's buying up quite a bundle himself so that everybody else would buy, whereas in actual fact he was dumping his own holdings and merely wanted to create a favorable selling market. When I heard that I was in an absolute panic! I thought I'd fallen for his trap and that the value of my holdings was going to plummet, so that my every last penny and a whole lot more would be called for on settlement day, thanks to him. You can well imagine my panic at the thought of being ruined, with all my business interests and my big family, especially at my age. I tell you, Lulu, I even had a revolver ready, I – (*He starts coughing.*)

Bailu (*Hands him a handkerchief*)   You poor thing, my poor old dad.

Pan (*Perking up*)   You really mustn't call me that anymore. I am not that old. When I heard the news I must have shed twenty years. I'm telling you, one must have money. Without money, life's not worth living. But now, Lulu, I really am rich. In a couple more days, I'll have piles and piles of money, and a few days after that I may well have even more, a great deal more. (*With sudden generosity*) And from now on I'm going to do more charity; store up some good credits to make amends for the past –

Bailu   You let Jin Ba have Pipsqueak back without a second thought. That's something that's going to take a lot to make up for.

Pan (*Suddenly remembering*)   Oh, what became of Pipsqueak? You mean to say you haven't got her back yet?

Bailu   Got her back? She might as well have jumped into the ocean. I've searched for her, and so has Dasheng, but there's no sign of her anywhere.

Pan   Don't worry. I'm rich now, with plenty of money. I can bring Pipsqueak for you alive and kicking just like that. That ought to cheer you up.

Bailu (*With despair*)   All right, then. Oh, by the way, are you aware that Li Shiqing is on his way to come see you?

Pan   Yes. He says he's got good news for me. He's a son of bitch, though, and thinks he can treat me anyway he likes and get away with it. I'll show him this time, though.

Bailu   What do you mean?

(**Madame Gu** *enters from the left.*)

Madame Gu   Lulu! Lulu! – Why, Manager Pan, where have you been all evening? (*Coyly*) Really now, abandoning us here, ignoring us, you men really are something! Oh, yes, I know what I was going to tell you, Manager Pan you should see the way Hu Si's behaving himself now that he's started working at the film studio. You were right, you know. One can always trust you to suggest the right thing and recommend the right person for the job, Manager Pan. (*Before* **Pan** *can reply she slips over to the dressing mirror on the wardrobe on the left to inspect herself, then suddenly spins around to face* **Bailu**.) Lulu, has my color improved any? Not too ghastly, I hope?

Pan (*Having no alternative*)   You keep Mrs Gu company, Lulu, while I go in the other room to see the others. (*He goes out left.*)

Gu   Are you leaving us, Mr Pan? (*Hurriedly*) Bailu, I can't sleep. (*Self-pityingly*) The more I lie there, the worse I feel.

Bailu   What's wrong?

Gu (*Rashly*)   Do you suppose he ever will come? The heartless creature, he told me to wait for him here at your place. He was going to teach me some opera – *Staying the Night and Killing Xijiao*, it was. It's nearly dawn and still no sign of him (*Points to her red nose*). Look, I've gone through two handkerchiefs with all my crying. (*In reality, fake crying*) Oh, I really – I – I really think I should call Fusheng and ask him –

Bailu (*Out of patience with her, she calls him before she has finished speaking*)   Fusheng! Fusheng! (**Fusheng** *enters through the center door.*)

Bailu   Do you know where Master Hu Si has gone?

Fusheng   No, I don't.

Gu (*Ill-humoredly*)   He'd never admit to knowing anything.

Fusheng   I assure you . . . (*With an ingratiating smile*) I really don't know. Though I seem to recall him saying that first he'd have to go and –

Gu (*Explosively*)   Change his clothes!

Fusheng (*With an assumed smile, simultaneously*)   Change his clothes.

Gu (*Annoyed and upset*)   Change his clothes! Change his clothes! Is that all you can ever tell me?

Bailu   What is going on? (*To* **Fusheng**) Do you know where Hu Si has gone?

Fusheng (*Humbly*)   Madame Gu has asked me four or five times already, so no wonder the venerable old madam is fed up with hearing it over and over again. After all, the venerable old madam does tend to get anxious about things, and for another thing –.

Gu (*Suddenly flushing with anger*)   Fusheng, I don't like all your 'old madam' this 'old madam' that! I don't like people calling me that. I don't like it.

Fusheng   Yes, Madame Gu.

Gu   Get out! Get out! The very sight of you infuriates me. Who told you to come in here and make me feel worse?

Fusheng   Very well, as you wish. (*He goes out through the center door.*)

Gu (*Thumping her heart*)   There goes my heart aching again. And on top of that, Hu Si's taking his new job less and less seriously, even though he's only been at the film company for two days. I feel like dying! Lulu! I'm taking all your sleeping pills home with me.

Bailu (*Slightly alarmed*)   Why, you're not going to take sleeping pills, are you?

Gu   Yes, I must.

Bailu (*urging her*)   I don't think you really need to. You'd better let me have them back. (*She holds out her hand.*)

Gu (*Oblivious*)   No, I absolutely must take some. If I can get a good sleep I'll recover my temper. Dr Ledoux says that a good hour of sleep is as good as a square meal. And I'll have a square meal, as well! I'll show that Hu Si!

Bailu   Oh, I see. (*Reassured*) But I must warn you: these sleeping pills are very potent. If you take ten you won't be here in the morning. Do be careful.

Gu (*Inspects the bottle of tablets*)   Well, so ten of them will kill you.

Bailu   Yes, ten will do it.

Gu   Well . . . in that case, I'll. . . . I'll just take one pill, no, half a tablet, no, just a third. That should do it for me.

Bailu   Oh, I thought you . . .

Gu   Oh, I see (*Suddenly understanding*), you thought I wanted to do myself in? No way. I'm not stupid. I intend to enjoy life for a few more years! Hmm. I'm just beginning to understand a thing or two, I've – humph! If

Hu Si's going to leave me one day, I'll leave him. I'll find somebody else, I'll – I'll make him really mad! (*All the exertion makes her tremble and shake her head.*)

Bailu (*Looking at her dispassionately*)   Aren't you tired?

Gu   Why, yes, I am rather tired. I'd better have a few more rounds of mahjong to rest my brain. Join me.

Bailu   No, you go on without me. I'd like to sit here on my own for a while.

(**Gu** *goes out left.*)

(*A knock on the center door.*)

Bailu   Who is it? (*Enter* **Dasheng**, still wearing his blue fur coat. He has a clouded expression that brightens up at the sight of **Bailu**.)

Bailu   Just getting back?

Dasheng   A little while ago. But when I got to your door I heard Madame Gu so I didn't come in.

Bailu (*Looking at him*)   Well? Did you find Pipsqueak?

Dasheng (*Shaking his head*)   No. I searched every last one of those places, but she wasn't anywhere.

Bailu (*Losing hope*)   That's what I thought. (*A pause, then she takes his arm and sits him down.*) Tired?

Dasheng   A little, though my mind is very much awake. I've been busy thinking. The last day or two I've been thinking hard about something.

Bailu (*With a smile*)   What, thinking about that again?

Dasheng   I can't help myself; That's just the way I am. I've been thinking, especially tonight. (*Suddenly*) Tell me, why must people be so cruel to one another?

Bailu (*Smiling*)   That's what you've been thinking about?

Dasheng   No, not exactly. I've been thinking about a much larger, much more concrete problem. I can't figure out why you people allow a beast like Jin Ba to go on living.

Bailu   Why, you really must be naïve. I tell you, the question is not whether we allow Jin Ba to go on living: it's whether he'll allow us to go on living.

Dasheng   I don't believe he really wields so much power. He's just one man.

Bailu   How can you be so sure?

Dasheng (*Deep in thought*)   Hey. . . . (*Suddenly*) have you ever met him?

Bailu   Never had the good fortune. Why, do you want to meet him?

Dasheng (*With meaning*)   Yes.

Bailu   That shouldn't be too hard. There are a great many Jin Bas around here. Big ones, little ones, medium-sized one, sometimes they're everywhere, like bedbugs.

Dasheng (*Deep in thought*)   Precisely. Just like bedbugs! But the vileness of bedbugs is obvious at a glance, whereas the horror of Jin Ba is not, making him far worse.

Bailu (*Staring at* **Dasheng**)   You seem different, somehow.

Dasheng   I think so too, and for that I have you to thank.

Bailu (*Baffled*)   For what?

Dasheng (*Solemnly*)   For giving me this opportunity.

Bailu   I don't follow. From the sound of it you have some regrets.

Dasheng (*Affirmative*)   No, I have no regrets, I don't regret spending a few extra days here. You were right that I really ought to study this lot, for now I do understand them. What I don't understand is you and why you mix with them. Can't you see they are demons, monsters? Zhujun, I can see in your eyes that you detest them too, yet day after day you feign that air of indifference, day after day deceiving yourself.

Bailu (*Looking intently at him*)   You –

Dasheng   Why are you looking at me like that?

Bailu (*Bristling with sudden sarcasm*)   You think you're so smart, don't you?

Dasheng   There you go again, Zhujun. No, I don't. But I've great faith in your intelligence. Now don't try to deceive me. You're unhappy. Remember we're old friends . . . so please stop being so stubborn. I know you've learned to keep a stiff upper lip and to lie in order to make people think you're happy, but your eyes can't hide your fear, your doubt, your dissatisfaction. A person might fool others, Zhujun, but he cannot fool himself. If you carry on this way you'll die of frustration.

Bailu (*With a sigh*)   So what would you have me do, then?

Dasheng   Simple. Leave with me and get away from this place.

Bailu   Leave?

Dasheng   Yes, and get far, far away from these people.

Bailu (*Raises her head*)   But . . . but . . . but where would I go? I'm the kind of person who craves peace and quiet when things get rowdy, but misses the action when it gets quiet. I don't know what I want. Where would you have me go?

Dasheng   You ought to get married, Zhujun. You need to get married. You ought to come with me.

Bailu (*Suddenly starts laughing*)   Here comes your favorite part of the script again.

Dasheng   No, you misunderstand. I am not asking you to marry me. I didn't say I wanted to marry you. I said I would take you with me. I'd like to find you a husband.

Bailu   You want to find me a husband?

Dasheng   Yes. Women all know about getting married; what you don't know is what kind of man to marry. So this time, I will take you and help you find a real man. Come with me.

Bailu (*Laughing*)   So you'll pull me along with one hand and beat a gong with the other, searching the land for a man for me?

Dasheng   What's wrong with that? Zhujun, you ought to marry a *real* man. He should be solid, somewhat naïve, and hardworking, like those construction workers here these past few days.

Bailu   Are you saying I should marry a construction worker?

Dasheng   What's wrong with that? They are men through and through. Zhujun, you should get married. You should get away from this place at once.

Bailu (*Meditatively*)   Get away – yes. But – get married? (*Lets out a sigh.*)

Dasheng   Zhujun, you are still so young, you ought to give it a try. Living is an endless adventure, and marriage is the most adventurous part of all.

Bailu (*Pauses, then suddenly turns away and speaks slowly, one word at a time*)   I've tried it.

Dasheng (*Shocked*)   What? You've tried it?

Bailu (*Indifferently*)   Yes, and it wasn't an adventure at all. (*Sighing*) It was dreary and dull, and rather ridiculous, when I think back on it.

Dasheng   Zhujun, you, you've already been married?

Bailu   Why are you so surprised? Why, was I supposed to wait for your help before embarking on this adventure?

Dasheng (*Softly*)   Who was he?

Bailu (*Cryptically*)   Someone rather like you.

Dasheng (*Pricking up his interest*)   Like me?

Bailu   Yes, very much so – He was a fool.

Dasheng (*Disappointed*)   Oh.

Bailu   He was a poet, you see. (*Recalling memories*) He . . . he was so smart when it came to thinking, but an idiot at doing anything. He was charming as long as you let him talk away on his own, but as soon as anyone else joined the conversation he became so unbearable that it gave one a headache just to listen to him. He was a most loyal friend, but a most inconsiderate lover. He swore at me and beat me too.

Dasheng   But (*Looks afraid to say it*) you loved him?

Bailu (*Emphatically*)   I did! When he asked me to leave this place and marry him, I did, and when he wanted me to move to the countryside, I did. He said I should have a kid, so I did. The first few months after we got married were heaven. He loved to watch the sunrise and every morning he'd get up as soon as it was light out and make me watch the sunrise with him. He was just like a child, so earnest about it all! And so happy! Sometimes he'd get so excited that he'd do somersaults in front of me, and he was always saying, 'The sun has risen, and the darkness will soon be past.' He was an eternal optimist, and even wrote a novel called *Sunrise* because he believed that there was hope for everything.

Dasheng   But – afterwards?

Bailu   Afterwards . . . (*Lowering her head*) What's there to say?

Dasheng   Why can't you share some of his hope with me?

Bailu (*looking straight ahead of her*)   Afterwards he began to pursue his hopes alone.

Dasheng   How do you mean?

Bailu   You wouldn't understand. Afterwards the novelty gradually wore off. The longer we were together the more dull and dreary it got. Still we put up with it. But then one day, he called me a burden, and I couldn't help telling him he was annoying. After that we stopped bickering and quarreling; he stopped cursing and beating me.

Dasheng   Wasn't that a good thing?

Bailu   No, no, you don't understand. Let me tell you, the most awful thing about marriage is not poverty or jealousy or quarrelling, but dullness, boredom and getting fed up with each other. Two people both feeling that the other is a burden. We no longer cared enough to quarrel and just hoped the sky would fall one day, waiting to die. At first we just made faces and frowned whenever we saw each other, and we weren't on speaking terms. In the end he did everything in his power to make my life a misery, and I did the same back. If he wanted to do anything I'd try to stop him, and if I wanted to budge an inch he'd hold me back. It was as if we had been bound together and thrown into the sea, sinking down . . . down . . . down.

Dasheng   And yet you both escaped.

Bailu   Only because the rope snapped.

Dasheng   What do you mean?

Bailu   The child died.

Dasheng   And so you separated.

Bailu   Yes, he went off to pursue his hopes.

Dasheng   Where is he now, then?

Bailu   Who knows.

Dasheng   Perhaps one day he'll come back for you.

Bailu   No, he'll never come back. He's no doubt happy doing his work now. (*Her head drooping*) He would think I'd now sunk so low that I'm beyond rescue. (*Bitterly*) Humph! He's long since forgotten me.

Dasheng (*Suddenly*)   But you don't seem to have forgotten him.

Bailu   No, I can't forget him. I won't ever be able to forget him for as long as I live. Hey, do you like this? 'The sun rises, leaving the darkness behind; but the sun is not ours, for we now sleep.' Like it?

Dasheng   I'm not quite sure what it means.

Bailu   An old man utters this line on his death bed in his novel.

Dasheng   Why are you suddenly bringing it up?

Bailu   Because I. . . . I. . . . I often think about such people.

Dasheng (*Suddenly*)   I think you're still in love with him.

Bailu (*Her head bowed*)   Yes, I am.

Dasheng   You really love him.

Bailu   I do. But why are you asking me all this?

Dasheng   No reason . . . perhaps if I get matters straight I can set my mind to rest and stop thinking about you all the time. Thank you, Zhujun, for your honesty. (*Getting up*) Well, Zhujun, I must go and pack now.

Bailu   You're not going already? Oh, there's a telegram for you here. (*She takes it out and hands it to him.*)

Dasheng (*Tearing it open and reading it*)   Mm, yes. (*He crushes it up into a ball.*)

Bailu   Telling you to hurry back home?

Dasheng   Yes. (*After a pause*) Well, goodbye, Zhujun! (*Extends his hand*)

Bailu   What's the big hurry? Surely you're not leaving at the crack of dawn?

Dasheng   I intend to leave the hotel at the crack of dawn.

Bailu   Which train are you taking?

Dasheng   No, I don't mean I'm going back home. I'm just moving somewhere else.

Bailu   You're not leaving?

Dasheng   No, I'm not going back home. But I may not be able to come and see you very often.

Bailu (*Surprised*)   Why not? This is all very mysterious.

Dasheng   I'm going to stay in the city for a few more days. I've got some business to take care of.

Bailu   You mean you're going to look for a job?

Dasheng   Oh, there's plenty to do. I may contact Jin Ba; I may keep running around in search of Pipsqueak; I may do something for people

like that bank clerk. I don't really know yet. I just feel there's a lot that
could be done.

Bailu   In other words, you're taking the same path as him.

Dasheng   Who?

Bailu   Him – my poet.

Dasheng   No, I won't become a poet. But I may become a fool.

Bailu (*Sighing*)   Go on! Go on, both of you! I know I'll be forgotten by
both of you.

Dasheng (*Suddenly*)   But why won't you come with me, Zhujun?
(*Taking her by the hand, warmly*) Come with me. Come with me.

Bailu   But (*Staring blankly ahead*) where would I go? I've told you
once that I've been sold to this place.

Dasheng (*Releasing her hand and looking at her with compassion*)   Fine,
then. You – ah . . . you . . . you're too proud, too stubborn. (*A knock on the
door.*)

Bailu   Who is it?

(*Enter **Li Shiqing** through the center door. His demeanor has changed
and he looks very pleased with himself. His jacket has been replaced by
a sleeveless one, and his thinning hair is combed across in shiny streaks,
though his eyes dart about suspiciously. His former deferential manner
has been replaced by a certain air of haughtiness.*)

Bailu   Ah, Mr Li. (**Fusheng** *follows him in.*)

Li (*Glancing at **Dasheng** and **Bailu***)   Good morning, Miss Chen.
(*Turning to **Fusheng**, who has remained in the doorway*) Fusheng, go
down and tell my driver to wait as I may be going home after I've had a
word with Manager Pan.

Fusheng   Very well, Mr L – (*Suddenly*) Assistant Manager Li, sir. Your
wife just rang to say –

Li (*Testily*)   I know, I know. Go down and tell him, then.

Bailu   Is your son feeling better, Mr Li?

Li   Ah, he's all right, well enough. Is Yueting in there?

Bailu   I think so.

Li   I have something confidential to discuss with him.

Bailu (*Annoyed*)   So did you want us to get out of the way?

Li (*Realizing he has overstepped the mark*)   No, no, that won't be necessary. I can talk it over with him in there. Well, pardon me for running off like this. (*He struts into the room on the left.*)

Bailu (*Watching him go, with a snort of amusement*)   Well!

Dasheng   He's suddenly – what's happened?

Bailu   You didn't know? He's assistant manager now.

Dasheng (*Suddenly understanding*)   Ah, I see! How funny!

Bailu   Very.

(*Enter **Hu Si** through the center door. He has changed his outfit, and looks more elegant than ever. With his coat over his arm and a cigar in his hand, he opens the door humming a popular tune.*)

Hu Si (*As if coming into his own home he tosses his hat and coat on to an armchair, whistling away to himself oblivious that there is anyone else in the room. He goes straight up to the dressing mirror on the left and inspects himself in it, then addresses **Bailu** with a yawn*)   Where is she?

Bailu   Who?

Hu Si (*His face as immobile as ever*)   The old she-devil.

Bailu   No idea.

Hu Si (*With another yawn*)   Tired?

Dasheng (*With distaste*)   Whom are you asking?

Hu Si   Oh, Fang – Mr Fang. Just got back? Can't get away from each other, can we? Second time we've met this evening.

Dasheng (*Ignoring him*)   Why don't you come sit in my room for a while, Bailu?

Bailu   Yes, all right.

(*The two of them go out through the center door.*)

Hu Si (*Watching them leave*)   Fucking waste of space! A sourpuss and a nut case rolled into one.

(*He straightens his clothes, turns towards the mirror again, and pushes the front of his hair into place. He is about to go into the room on the left when the door opens and **Pan Yueting** and **Li Shiqing** appear.*)

Li (*To* **Pan**)   Too crowded in there, we'd better talk out here.

Pan   All right, if you like.

Hu Si (*With great familiarity*)   You're still here, Shiqing? Not gone home yet?

Li   No. No.

Hu Si   Manager Pan.

Pan   You'd better hurry up, Hu Si. Madame Gu's is still in there waiting for her opera lesson.

Hu Si   I was just going. Hey, Shiqing, come here a minute so I can tell you something.

Li   What is it?

Hu Si (*Mischievously*)   Saw your wife on the street again yesterday (*In an undertone in* **Li's** *ear*), she's real pretty!

Li (*Long accustomed to having* **Hu Si** *speak to him in this manner, he now finds it difficult to be stiff and formal with him. With embarrassment*)   Nonsense! Nonsense!

Hu Si   Ah, well, that's it. See you later, Shiqing.

(*He goes out briskly through the door on the left.*)

Pan   Take a seat. Something you wanted to see me about?

Li (*Sitting down, very self-satisfied*)   Of course.

Pan   What is it?

Li   Yueting – (*As if finding the name does not come easily to his tongue*) Manager, are you aware of what's happening in the market?

Pan (*Pretending*)   Not really. Let's hear it.

Li (*In a low, secretive voice*)   I found all this out from a very confidential source. You can set your mind at rest now; it seems we did the right thing by buying those bonds. Jin Ba really is buying in this time, and the rumor that it's just a ruse so he can unload is quite wrong – pure jitters. So it seems we've done the right thing this time. I've just worked it out that you're holding four and a half million altogether at the moment, so it looks as if we might make three hundred thousand on this transaction.

Pan (*Pretending to agree with him*)   Yes . . . you're right. Yes. (*But before* **Li** *can finish he suddenly interrupts.*) By the way, I heard Fusheng saying your wife –

Li (*Who cannot be bothered with such trifles*)   I know, I know. As I was saying, it looks as if we might make three hundred thousand. That's on the assumption that prices keep rising at the current rate. But in a day or two, when people begin to realize what's happening, the bears will be scrambling to pick up whatever they can, and this will give a boost to the market. I'm telling you, within ten days there'll be a further profit of a hundred or two hundred thousand for us, just for the picking up, simple as that.

Pan (*Stopping him*)   Yes, yes, but isn't your wife anxious for you to get home?

Li   Forget her, forget her for the moment. What I suggest, Yueting, is that under no circumstances should we sell our holdings now. I'm telling you, this time the prices are going to go up and keep going up, not just reach a certain point and then stop. In fact (*Very excited*), if you'll take my advice, Yueting, the best thing to do is to buy more as we see fit tomorrow. There's still time tomorrow; we can't go wrong.

Pan   Shiqing, do you realize that your son's ill?

Li   That's all right, don't worry about that – (*More excited than ever*) I think we should keep buying. Yes! That's settled, then. This is the chance of a lifetime, Yueting. After we've pulled this off successfully I don't think the bank should take any more risks of this kind. Whatever happens we should never again act in such an unethical manner: in the future we must keep faith with our investors. But this time, having burnt our bridges, we should look at the market first thing in the morning and buy more.

Pan   But –

Li   We should take another half million to bring it to a round figure. Can't go wrong, in my view. I've worked it all out, the first thing that we should do is to put the bank's credit on a firm footing, which means: first, the deposits should be –

Pan   Shiqing! I do think you'd best get home and see how things are. Don't you realize how ill your son is?

Li   Why must you keep on bringing up such a depressing subject?

Pan   I think you're being altogether too cheerful.

Li Yes, I am. I think I've helped you handle this bit of business in a way that does us credit. Naturally I'm cheerful!

Pan I'm sorry. I was forgetting that you've been my assistant for all of two days.

Li What do you mean by that, sir?

Pan Nothing at all. Mr Li, these bonds I'm holding are now money?

Li Of course.

Pan And this little bit of profit will be enough to repay Jin Ba in full?

Li According to my calculations there'll be some over.

Pan Excellent. Now, think: with this surplus, plus the influence and ability I possess, is it likely that I'm going to stand for nonsense from anybody?

Li I'm afraid I don't quite see what you're driving at sir.

Pan It's possible that someone might start a rumor that that my bank has insufficient reserves –

Li Eh?

Pan Or go around saying I've mortgaged all the bank's properties.

Li What. . . .

Pan Or else that my bank hasn't earned any money all year long and is on the verge of closing.

Li (*With an ingratiating smile*) What's the point of bringing this up, sir? It's not –

Pan I'm certainly not eager to bring the subject up, but there's always a chance that someone else will insist on doing so.

Li That's rather far-fetched, sir.

Pan (*Looking at him coldly*) Not at all. Why just six or seven days ago a certain someone was saying as much to my face, Mr Li.

Li Now, don't vex yourself over it, sir. To quote the Classics 'If one is not patient in small affairs one will never be able to control great ventures.' It's always better for a man in charge of great affairs to be patient, rather than impatient.

Pan (*With a glare at him*) I think I've been patient enough these last few days. Let me tell you quite plainly, though, I dislike intensely having smart-alecks blow their own trumpets at me; and I don't at all like having people think I'm easy meat, and imagining that I'm going to submit willingly to blackmail. But what's most detestable is when my own colleagues at the bank call me a blind old bastard behind my back because I have a third-rate nincompoop for an assistant.

Li (*Controlling himself with a great effort*)   It wouldn't hurt to be a little more polite, sir. You might weigh your words a bit more carefully before coming out with them.

Pan   I've weighed my words with the greatest care.

Li (*With a mirthless smile*)   All right, then; the actual words you've been using are not so very important. After all, first-raters and third-raters are much the same, very little difference between them really. The point is, sir, we're both men with a great deal of public responsibility, and I think the least one can do, when it comes to issues large and small, is to keep one's word.

Pan (*Looking at* **Li**)   Keep one's word? (*Laughing out loud*) Is that what you're worried about, keeping one's word? It's not that I never keep my word, but it depends on to whom. And after being around all these years I ought to know to whom to keep my word and to whom not.

Li   Then it appears, sir, that you're not prepared to keep your word to me.

Pan (*Acidly*)   That's not the sort of remark one would have expected from a smart man like yourself.

Li   Well, of course, you're much smarter than the rest of us, sir.

Pan   Not necessarily. But perhaps I do grasp one very important minor principle: I may sometimes utterly refuse to keep my word to self-opinionated scoundrels. (*Suddenly*) Do you realize that your wife has been phoning you?

Li (*Confused*)   I know, I know.

Pan   Your son's gravely ill, on the brink of death. Mrs Li wants you home urgently.

Li (*Staring intently at* **Pan**, *says in a low voice*)   I'm going.

Pan   Glad to hear it. Your car's waiting for you outside. (*Harshly*) It won't take you long to get home by car. And when you do get home you might get in a bit of practice with your cleverness. I can't see a shrewd go-getter like you being without a job. When you do get a job, I suppose you can always open people's drawers in order to see, for example, whether their property has been mortgaged or not, or to check up on the actual amount of their deposits. Oh, and I might as well tell you, while we're on the subject, that in order to spare you any further anxiety on my account I've now taken the documents out of my drawer and stored them in the safe.

Li (*Staring and gaping*)   Oh!

Pan (*Taking an envelope out of his pocket*)   This, Mr Li, is the remainder of your salary. Let's just work it out. The salary of a director's assistant is two hundred and seventy-five dollars a month. You were on the job for three days and the accountant informs me you've already drawn an advance of two hundred and fifty dollars, but I think we ought to treat you decently, so I'm paying you a full month's salary. So please accept the remaining twenty-five dollars. Though the bank won't be able to cover today's car fare.

Li   But Manager Pan – (*He suddenly breaks off and thrusts out his hand, glaring at* **Pan** *with animosity.*) All right, give it here, then. (*Takes the money.*)

Pan (*Starts to leave then turns around*)   Well, I'm off. Drop in for a chat when you're free sometime. And you can address me however you please, Yueting, as you've just been calling me, is fine, or you can you can drop the sirs and call me 'old chap' if you like, since we're now on an equal footing! Goodbye. (*He goes out left.*)

Li (*Speechless for a long time, then emits several cold, nasal laughs*)   Fine! (*Clutching the notes tightly, his voice low with indignation*) Twenty-five dollars! (*His voice sinking even lower*) Twenty-five dollars. (*Grinding his teeth*) I'll get you for this! (*The telephone rings but he ignores it.*) For the sake of these measly bonds of yours, I've neglected my family, even my sick child, and spent my own money on bribes to get you information. But now that you've hit the jackpot, you're suddenly finished with me. (*With a mirthless smile*) Finished with me. You treat me like a thief, and call me names right to my face, insult me, and look down your nose at me! (*Touching on a sensitive spot, raising his voice*) Yes, you look down on me! (*Pounding his chest*) You look down on Li Shiqing. Yes, you had me on a piece of string this whole time: Fine. (*The telephone rings again. He laughs shrilly, saying sarcastically*) So I'm 'a smart-aleck,' I'm 'a nincompoop!' Well, you flatter me by calling me a bastard, because I am a bastard, I am third-rate! (*An unnatural laugh, then the telephone rings again.*) Think I'm going to let you get away with this just like that? Think I'm scared of you? – Huh! (*His eyes flash with indignation.*) Today I'm going to finish you off, the whole lot of you. I won't leave one of you standing, not a single one.

(*Suddenly there is an urgent knocking on the center door.*)

Li   Who is it? (**Mrs Li** *comes in with great agitation. She looks more haggard than ever. Her clothing is rumpled and tears are in her eyes.*)

Mrs Li   Shiqing! What's gotten into you? You've been out all day long and you still haven't come home!

Li (*Looking fixedly at her*)   I'm not going home!

Mrs Li (*Breaking down*)   It won't be long now for Little Five, his tongue's gone cold already, Shiqing. I hired a car and Mother and I have taken him to three hospitals, but none of them will admit him.

Li   Won't take him? Is he past treating, then?

Mrs Li   They want money. They all want cash down, no credit. Even the cheapest one wants a fifty dollar deposit. And all we've got at home is fifteen dollars, so even if I spent our last penny it still wouldn't be enough. (*Sobbing*) Shiqing, you must find a way to save him.

Li (*Feeling in his pockets and producing a few small notes*)   Here, take it all.

Mrs Li (*Hurriedly counting them*)   There's – there's only seventeen dollars and a bit here.

Li   Then – in that case there's nothing we can do.

Mrs Li (*Wiping her eyes*)   Shiqing (*Looking at him*), our Little Five –

Li (*Indignantly*)   Why did we have to have all these children? (*Nevertheless, he finds himself picking up the notes he has just been given, clutching them tightly in his hand. Then, swallowing his resentment, he hands them to his wife, his voice full of bitterness.*) Take it, take it! Twenty-five dollars, the price of my self-respect.

Mrs Li (*Quickly taking the money, urgently*)   Aren't you coming with me?

Li   You go on ahead. I'll be there later.

Mrs Li   You can't do that! You must come with me!

Li (*Bellowing*)   When I tell you to go on ahead, go on ahead. Don't stand there arguing! Go on, hurry up! Don't make me mad!

(*A knock at the door.*)

Mrs Li (*Imploring him*)   Shiqing – (*Another knock on the door.*)

Li   Who is it? (*No reply. Another knock.*) Come in! Who is it? (*Still another knock.*) Who is it? (*He goes across to the center door and yanks it open violently. He is shocked.* **Huang Xingsan** *stands like a skeleton in the doorway, looking at him with glittering eyes.*)

Li (*In a low voice*)   Oh you again! (*Snickering*) Perfect timing.

(*He enters gloomily, like a blast of cold wind, like a ghost or a stiff corpse that has crawled out from a tomb at midnight. His gown is nowhere to be seen. On top, he wears only a blue, almost black, tattered padded jacket with the collar unbuttoned to reveal the jutting bones of his neck. Below the jacket he wears nothing but a pair of unlined trousers. His hair is disheveled and his body is more hunched than ever, though he does not seem as timid as before. His face is dispirited and expressionless, incapable of laughing or crying. He gazes dully at* **Li Shiqing** *as if possessed by an evil spirit.*)

Li (*To his wife*)   You'd better go. There's somebody here.

Mrs Li   Shiqing – you . . . (*Throwing him a look of despair, she exits through the center door sobbing.*)

Li (*Watching her out, angrily*)   Humph, I won't leave. I won't leave. I'll die before I leave here without finding a way to get even with him. (*He paces to and fro, forgetting that* **Huang Xingsan** *is with him.*)

Huang   Manager Pan, sir!

Li (*Stopping in his tracks*)   You – you tramp. Why are you back pestering me again?

Huang   Manager!

Li (*Suspicious*)   What do you mean, 'Manager Pan'? Who told you to call me that?

Huang (*Still woodenly as if reciting a text from memory*)   Manager, I'm a petty clerk at the bank. My name's Huang, Huang Xingsan, and I make ten dollars twenty-five cents a month. I've three children, sir . . . and I earn ten dollars twenty-five a month! My name is Huang, Huang Xingsan.

Li (*Looking at him and suddenly understanding*)   You! (*With distaste*) What are you doing coming round here for me again? Do you know who I am? Who am I? What are you coming to me for?

Huang   Manager Pan! I beg you, I beg you!

Li (*Irascibly*)   I am not Manager Pan, damn you! My name's not Pan, it's Li! (*Pointing to himself*) Don't you recognize me? Don't you?

Huang (*Nodding*)   Yes, I recognize you.

Li   Who am I then?

Huang   You are Manager Pan.

Li   Bah! What's wrong with you? Why do you have to choose this of all times to come to play with me?

Huang (*Still in the same dull voice*)   They won't let me die! They won't let me die.

Li   You can die if you like. Why won't they let you?

Huang   Those people, those officials and those gentlemen, they insisted on letting me go.

Li   So they released you.

Huang   They insisted that my mind was deranged at the time. They insisted that I was innocent. (*Earnestly*) I beg you, please, do me one favor; punch me again hard (*Indicating his chest*), here; just one punch, please. Manager Pan, please.

Li   Really! I am not Manager Pan. Take a good look at me. My name's not Pan, it's Li, Li Shiqing. You don't recognize me? (*A pause.*)

Huang (*Suddenly beginning to sob like a woman*)   My children, my poor children, I killed you, your daddy forced you to die.

Li   You mean your children are all –

Huang   All gone to heaven. (*Suddenly*) Why won't you all let me die? (*His mind is wandering and he thinks he is still in the courtroom.*) I'm not insane! I'm telling you, Your Honor, I'm really not. My mind was quite clear, I bought the opium myself with the money Manager Pan gave me: two dollars went on the rent and one on the opium, Your Honor. I bought the brown sugar myself to mix with it. I made the children take it, I poisoned them with my own hands. Why wouldn't you let me jump in the river? I didn't have the money to buy any more opium. Why won't you just let me die? My mind's quite clear, I'm not in the least bit insane. We have laws in this country, you can't just let me go. (*Grasping* **Li** *by the hand*) Your Honor, I committed murder with my own hands, I poisoned my children, my Wang Wang, my Little Yun, my . . . (*Throwing his arms round* **Li**) Put me to death, Your Honor!

Li (*Struggling free with a violent effort*)   Get away, take your hands off
me, you fucking moron! Look where you are. (*Shaking him violently*)
Look at me, who am I?

Huang (*Looking first at* **Li**, *then around the room, he pauses for a
moment. Suddenly*)   Manager – Manager Pan, where am I?

Li   Bah! Why do you keep bothering me, you bag of bones! Go, get out,
get out or else I'll send for the police to take you away. (*He goes to ring
a bell.*)

Huang   No, don't, don't send for the police. (*In an anguished voice*)
Manager Pan, people can't treat each other like this, they just can't!
A few days ago my children were alive and I wanted to keep living;
I begged you to let me stay alive, but you wouldn't. Now (*Weeping*)
they're dead, and I want to die. I'm begging you to let me die but you
won't let me.

We're all human beings, Manager Pan. Human beings can't treat each
other this way! (*Hopelessly*) They can't treat each other this way!

Li   Bah! . . . You stupid bastard! You're getting on my nerves. Out, get
out before you drive me insane as well. Out, you tramp, out.

Huang   No, please, Manager Pan, have a heart. I can't go on any
longer. I am on my knees begging you, take pity on me, don't force me
any longer. (*Sinks to his knees*) Let me take the easy road.

Li (*Pulling him up*)   All right, all right, I'll let you die. But first get
up. First recognize who I am. My name's Li. Now listen carefully once
more: my name's Li. Li. Li. Li.

Huang (*Unable to recall the name*)   Li?

Li   Don't you remember coming here to see me the other
day?. . . . When I. . . . I advised you to become a rickshaw driver?

Huang   Huh?

Li   And I also urged you to become a beggar?

Huang   Huh?

Li   And I also urged you to steal?

Huang   That's right, you also urged me to throw myself off the top of
a building! (*With a sudden frenzied delight he looks all round and as his
eye falls on the window he runs straight over to it.*)

Li (*Pulls him back with one hand*)   Fusheng! Fusheng! (*Enter* **Fusheng** *through the center door.*)

Li   Get him out of here. He's insane.

Fusheng (*Grabs him and pulls him out of the room, as* **Huang** *struggles like a chick*)   You here again!

Huang   Mr Li, I'm not insane! You must save me, save me. I'm not insane! (*He is dragged outside by* **Fusheng**.)

Li   Good God! (*Indignantly*) That stupid bastard, why go mad? Why let yourself be driven mad? You let him off too easily! (*The telephone rings urgently again.*)

Li (*Picking up the receiver*)   Hello? Who? Mr Zhang from the newspaper? Oh, this is Shiqing. What? You tried calling earlier? No one picked up. . . . Oh. . . . I see . . . you've already sent a message by courier. I see. . . . What? Bad news? Says who? . . . You mean the information was leaked out by Jin Ba's people? Impossible! But these past few days we've heard that Jin Ba's been buying in himself! . . . Eh? He hasn't bought a single share?. . . . Ah, so the rally we've been expecting this week is nothing more than one of his rumors. . . . Eh? He started dumping his holdings yesterday?. . . . Is that really true? (*So pleased his hands begin to shake*) What? So the news has already been leaked, has it?. . . . Yes, yes, that means the market will fall sharply tomorrow as soon as the session opens. By how much, do you think? . . . (*Slapping the table*) What? No trading after the second session? (*Sitting down on the table*) Ah. . . . I see . . . (*Slapping his buttocks*). You say that. . . . The Dafeng Bank's been taken in nicely by Jin over these bonds, you say. . . . Yes . . . yes, that's what I think: chances are Jin Ba will demand his deposits back . . . how terrific. . . . I mean, rather . . . how terrible. Right you are . . . yes, I see, the message already been sent over by hand. Right. See you later. Yes, I'll be sure to give it Manager Pan. (*He replaces the receiver and goes hurriedly to the door.*)

Li   Fusheng, Fusheng! (*Enter* **Fusheng**)

Li   Mr Zhang from the newspaper sent a messenger here with a letter for Manager Pan a little while ago. Have you seen it?

Fusheng   Yes, it came earlier.

Li   Where is it?

Fusheng   Here it is. (*He produces it from a pocket.*)

Li   Give it here! Why didn't you say so before? (*He snatches it from* **Fusheng** *and hurriedly reads it.*)

Fusheng (*Giving his explanation while* **Li** *is reading*)   I was going to give it to Manager Pan a moment ago, but I found him busy playing mahjong. He was doing well and had a winning hand, so I didn't want to disturb him.

Li   Oh, go away! Go away! Just shut your mouth already.

Fusheng   Very well, sir. (*He goes out.*)

Li (*Finishes reading the letter, draws a long sigh, beside himself with excitement*)   What perfect timing! Just perfect! This couldn't have come at a better moment. (*Enter* **Bailu** *through the center door.*)

Li (*His face wreathed in smiles*)   Ah, Miss Chen. Your guests still haven't left?

Bailu   They'll be going any minute now. I've come out to see them off. Why, Assistant-Manager, suddenly you're all smiles.

Li   Ah, good news makes one happy. And right now, well, very shortly, I will be getting some very good news.

Bailu   Promotion to Vice-Manager?

Li   Well, as good as that. If you're going in there, Miss, I wonder if I could trouble you to ask Manager Pan to come out here for a moment as soon as he can. There's a message here for him that's just been sent over, something extremely important has happened. So could you ask him to come out at once and give instructions on what should be done about it?

Bailu   How odd. You've suddenly gotten all formal again.

Li   One should always be a formal in the presence of a lady (*Bows*) (**Bailu** *goes out left.*)

Li (*Trembling with excitement*)   Ah . . . oh. . . . I must get a hold of myself. (*He paces back and forth.*)

(*Enter* **Pan Yueting** *from the left.*)

Pan   Oh, you still haven't gone home?

Li   No, sir, I keep worrying about your bank's affairs, so I didn't want to go home.

Pan   What did you want me for?

Li (*In a low, self-effacing voice*)   How's your mahjong game going?

Pan (*Looking at him*)   Not too badly at all!

Li   I hear you're in fine form tonight.

Pan   Not bad, I must admit.

Li   How many rounds have you won?

Pan (*Disdainfully*)   I knew you'd come looking for me, but I didn't think you'd want to talk about this sort of thing.

Li   You thought I'd come looking for you, begging for a bowl of rice to eat. And it's true, I've got no money, since I made my living at the bank. Think about it, just now . . .

Pan (*Suddenly*)   Where's the letter?

Li   Which letter?

Pan   Bailu said you had a note in your hand addressed to me.

Li   Oh yes, would you like to see it?

Pan   Who's it from?

Li   Mr Zhang at the newspaper. He sent a messenger over with it.

Pan   Hurry up and hand it over then.

Li   I was afraid the shock would be too great once you've read it, so I didn't dare send it in.

Pan   What, bonds are going up again . . .

Li   It is about the bonds, of course. It came as a very great surprise to me when I saw what was in it.

Pan   Splendid, if it's about bonds, then it must be good news. I really got it right this time. Hurry up and hand it over.

Li   But, manager, I've already opened it.

Pan   What? How dare you?

Li   But, Manager, if I hadn't opened it, how would I have known if there was good news to report to you?

Pan (*Anxious to read the letter*)   Fine, fine. Give it to me, quickly now.

Li   You won't get mad, and call me a meddlesome nincompoop? (*Takes the letter out and spreads it out on the table, deliberately taking his time*) Read it carefully, sir.

Pan (*Seems to sense that something strange is going on. He looks distrustfully at Li, then hastily picks up the note.*) Fine.

Li (*Next to him, interrupts in an irritatingly slow manner*)   I never would have expected this; things just don't work out as neatly as this; it's too good to be true. It's got to be a rumor. See, Manager, I do have a habit of interrupting and gossiping, you don't mind, do you?

Pan (*A great change coming over his face as he finishes reading the letter*)   I – I don't believe it. It can't be true. (*Rereading the letter*) This information can't be reliable. (*Hurries to the telephone and dialing a number*) Hello, Xin Newspaper? My name's Pan, Pan Yueting. . . . I want to speak to the editor, Mr Zhang. And hurry, it's urgent!. . . . What? He's gone out? But he just . . . Oh, I see, he just left. . . . Do you know where he's gone?. . . . You don't? Idiot, why didn't you ask him? (*He hangs up the receiver and pauses a moment before dialing another number.*) Hello, is this the Huixian Club? I'd like to speak to Mr Ding. . . . Jin Ba's private secretary. Mr Ding Muzhi. . . . What? Gone home? How could he have gone home already? It's only (*Looking at his watch*) only . . .

Li   It's only just after five. Almost dawn.

Pan (*Glancing at **Li**, then into the receiver*)   What's his home number, then, 43543, yes . . . all right . . . (*Hangs up the receiver*) This lot, you can never find them when you want them in a hurry . . . (*Dialing another number*) Hello . . . hello . . . hello . . . is this the Ding residence? Hello? Hello? Hello. (*To himself*) Why isn't anyone picking up?

Li   The servants are probably all asleep by now.

Pan (*Slamming the receiver down*)   Dead asleep! (*Sitting down weakly*) It's ridiculous! Just ridiculous! This information can't be reliable. It's impossible. Impossible. (**Li Shiqing** *fixes his gloating eyes unwaveringly upon him.*)

Pan   Lulu, Lulu! (*Enter **Bailu** from the left.*)

Bailu   What is it, Yueting?

Pan   Could I trouble you for a glass of water?

Bailu   What's the matter?

Pan   I've got a bit of a headache. (**Bailu** *goes to pour some water.*)

Li   I agree his information must be unreliable. (*With feigned earnestness*) Didn't you ask all around this morning?

Pan (*To himself*)   It must be a joke, it must be.

Bailu (*Handing him a glass of water*)   What's the matter, Yueting?

Pan (*Hand her the letter*)   Read it! (*He sits there in a stupor.*)

Li (*Going over to* **Pan** *and lowering his voice*)   The fact of the matter is, sir, it wouldn't be such a terrible blow. You wouldn't lose much if prices only dropped by a couple of cents. Did you read the letter carefully, sir, to see whether it actually says how big the drop will be?

Pan (*Suddenly stands up*)   Ah, yes. Lulu, give me the letter. (*He snatches it from her and quickly reads.*)

Li (*Standing behind him and pointing*)   No, not there, it's on this page, here.

Li & Pan (*Reading the note in low voices*)   '. . . This information has already leaked out, and prices are bound to plummet tomorrow. No doubt about it. . . .'

Bailu   He says quite plainly the market will take a huge dive.

Pan (*Staring dazedly at the note*)   Yes. What he means is that trading will close as soon as the session opens tomorrow.

Li   Mr Zhang also phoned after he sent this over.

Pan (*Seeing a glimmer of hope*)   He phoned? Well, what did he say?

Li   He said there was nothing we could do about it. Jin Ba is behind this so there's not the slightest thing we can do.

Pan (*Brokenly*)   That lowlife bastard! (**Fusheng** *pushes open the center door and comes in.*)

Bailu   What is it?

Fusheng   Mr Zhang from the newspaper's here.

Bailu   Show him in.

Fusheng   He says there are too many people here, so he's waiting in Room 10.

(**Pan Yueting** *at once makes for the door.*)

(*Just as* **Fusheng** *is coming in the telephone rings.*)

Li (*Answering the telephone*)   Hello, who's calling. . . . This is Room 52. Oh . . . this is Shiqing. . . . Oh, you want Manager Pan? He's right here. (*Stopping* **Pan**) Jin Ba's secretary, Mr Ding, wants to have a word with you.

Pan (*Taking the receiver*) Mr Ding? Yueting here. I've been searching
high and low for you . . . yes . . . yes . . . yes . . . don't worry, not
at all. . . . What! He wants to withdraw it. . . . What! All of it,
tomorrow morning? Yes, but listen, he and I clearly agreed on a week
extension. . . . Then he's . . . why, he must be joking with me, that's
all I can say! . . . (*Exasperatedly*) Now listen, Mr Ding. He can't go
back on his word like this. He gave me his word, tell him. He agreed
to give me another week, and now he suddenly. . . . Now listen
here . . . listen. . . . I'd like to talk this over with him. What? He's not
seeing anyone just now?. . . . Listen, tell me this, Muzhi: has Mr Jin
bought any government bonds the last few days?. . . . What?. . . . He
can't unload them fast enough?. . . . I see. . . . Hello! You listen to me.
You listen . . . (*Getting no response, he hangs up.*) Bastard, getting drunk
at some girl's house and waiting until it's this late before he tells me.
(*He collapses exhaustedly into a chair.*)

Fusheng   Sir, Mr Zhang's. . . .

Pan   Oh, get out! And don't come bothering me again, any of you.

Li   But, sir –

Pan (*Bellowing*)   Go on, get out! (*To* **Li Shiqing**) Get out of here! (*Exit*
Li *through the center*)

Pan (*To* **Bailu**)   If you would just leave me alone here to rest. . . .

Bailu   Yueting, you –

Pan (*Waving his hand*)   You'd better go see to your guests. They're
probably ready to leave. (**Bailu** *exits left*)

Pan (*Pacing to and fro, too restless to sit or stand still*)   It's hopeless.
A dead end. Jin Ba intends to do me in.

(*The center door opens slightly.*)

Pan (*Startled*)   Who is it?

Li   Me, sir. The smart-aleck scoundrel back again.

Pan   What – what do you want?

Li   I thought it would be more pleasant for the two of us to talk alone.

Pan   What more is there to talk about?

Li   Nothing. Just a third-rater coming to see how the first-rater's
doing now.

Pan (*Springing to his feet*)   Bastard!

Li (*His eyebrows shooting up*)   Bastard yourself!

Pan   Get out of here!

Li (*With equal vehemence*)   You get out! (*A pause; then, with an icy smile*) You forget we're on an equal footing now.

Pan (*Reigning in his temper and sitting down*)   Be careful. Be careful how you speak to me.

Li   I don't have to be careful. I don't have a penny to my name and my pockets are full of pawn slips. No need for *me* to be careful!

Pan   You'd better watch out that somebody doesn't take you to court to sue you, you pauper.

Li   As you say, pauper. But take a good look at yourself, my dear Manager Pan. I don't have any debt, tens of thousands of dollars of debt. I don't have people after me for money. And I haven't had money snatched from under my own nose just as I was thinking it was mine. You'd better start feeling sorry for yourself, Mr Pan. You're worse off than a pauper. I've been had by a scoundrel, and now I'm poor, but you've been had by an even greater scoundrel, and he's after your life! (*Bitingly*) Yes, you wouldn't keep your word to an opinionated scoundrel, and now you've been paid in your own coin! You may go back on your word but other people can play that game even better. You thought you were so smart, but somebody was even smarter than you! You called me names, mocked me, insulted me, yes, and looked down on me, too. (*Raising his voice*) But now I'm so happy, so pleased! For tomorrow morning I'm going to watch the run on your bank with my own eyes, I'll see you unable to pay up, I'll see the small depositors with nine or ten dollars of savings in your bank, looking down on you, calling you names, cursing you – yes, they'll kill and cannibalize you. You've ruined them! You've ruined them, and they'll want to skin you alive and gouge out your eyes! The only thing that will appease them will be your demise! Death is your only escape!

Pan (*Banging the table with irritation*)   Stop it! Stop it!

Li   No, I'll say it, with relish – you old bastard, you piece of shit, you blind fool. . . .

Pan (*Springing up*)   I'll – I'll kill you (*He struggles with **Li**, grabs him by the throat, and is about to –*)

(**Bailu** *bursts in.*)

Bailu   Yueting! Yueting! Let go of him!

Li (*Struggling, with* **Pan** *still clutching his throat*)   Kill me, then! Kill me! But Jin Ba won't let you get away with this: the door, the door . . .

Bailu   Let him go, Yueting.

Pan (*Lets go*)   What about the door?

Li   Black San's waiting for you at the door. Jin Ba sent him over to keep an eye on you.

Pan   Why – what for?

Li   He's afraid you might try to escape. So he's sent Black San and his gang to follow you.

(*There is a pause while* **Pan** *hangs his head.*)

Bailu (*In an undertone*)   Jin Ba! Jin Ba! How can he everywhere?

Pan (*With his head bowed*)   He'll kill me. (*Suddenly smiles wanly at Li*) I suppose you're satisfied now!

(**Li** *looks at him but does not speak.*)

(*The telephone rings urgently.*)

Pan   Answer it for me, Bailu. It's probably Jin Ba.

Li   Let me get it.

Bailu   No, no, I'll get it. (*She has already picked up phone and* **Li** *and* **Pan** *stand either side of her looking anxiously at her.*) Hello, who's calling? This is suite 52. Chen Bailu. Ah, Mrs Li. I see . . . you want Mr Li? He's right here. (*Turning to Li*) It's Mrs Li, phoning from the hospital.

Li (*Taking the receiver*)   Shiqing speaking. You made it to the hospital, then? Oh, I see. . . . Little Five's what? (*Agitated, in complete contrast to his nonchalance a moment ago*) What? Say it again. . . . I can't hear you very clearly. . . . What! Little Five passed . . . passed out? Then – then get a doctor! (*Slapping the table in his anguish*) Get a doctor! You've got the money with you, haven't you? Pay them! Give them the money!. . . . What? He . . . he passed away on the . . . on the way there? . . . (*The tears running down his cheeks*) He was calling for me, calling 'Daddy' . . . and then he stopped breathing . . . (*He lets the receiver fall and begins to weep.*) Oh, my boy! My Little Five. (*Suddenly picking up the receiver again*) I'm coming! Right away!

(*As Shiqing grabs his hat he wipes his tears and looks at* **Pan**, *who returns the look with a dazed glance;* **Li** *then exits through the center door.*)

Bailu   Poor thing. What was all that about, Yueting? (*A rooster crows in the distance.*)

Pan   Have your guests left, Bailu?

Bailu   Yes, they all left a while ago except Hu Si and Madame Gu.

Pan   To think that I would ever live through such a day! Wait for me, Bailu, I think I'll go discuss this with Mr Zhang from the newspaper.

Bailu   Feeling better now, Yueting?

Pan   Well enough. I'll be back later.

Bailu   Are you leaving me now?

Pan   No, I'll be back later.

Bailu   All right, off you go, then. (*Exit* **Pan** *through the center door.*)

(*Again a rooster crows in the distance.* **Bailu** *walks over to the window and slowly pulls back the drapes to reveal a pale blue sky. She gazes at it for a moment, then sighs and slowly paces back. A rooster again crows in the distance. She stands in the center of the stage staring into space deep in thought.*)

Bailu (*Murmuring to herself in a dismal voice*)   Bailu, It's nearly dawn. (**Hu Si** *and* **Madame Gu** *enter on the left.* **Hu Si's** *face has the glow of an opium smoker. He continues with what he is saying while mopping his face with his hand.* **Madame Gu** *follows him in, worshipping her hero.*)

Hu Si (*Having just smoked a bowl of opium, the taste of which still lingers in his mouth, he smacks his lips contentedly*): What a fine smoke that was. It really picked me up! (*Continuing what he was saying before*) Then straight after that comes the introduction on the drum. And the large gong and the small one both join in: ba-la-da-chang, ba-la-da-chang, ba-la-da-chang, chang-chang-ling-chang, ba-la-da, da, da . . . (*He coughs and spits on the floor.*)

Gu   Again with the spitting! Come on, keep going with the lesson. (*Quite oblivious to* **Bailu's** *state of mind at the moment. With pride*) Listen, Lulu. Listen, Hu Si is teaching me *Staying the Night and Killing Xijiao.* (*Showing off*) That introduction was called 'Rushing wind.'

Hu Si (*His voice hoarse from too much opium, yet very vivaciously, rolling his eyes in despair*) 'Rushing wind,' she says! With a memory like that you'll never master opera.

Gu (*Trying to cover up her mistake*) No, I meant it's the 'Long Slow Stab.'

Hu Si Oh forget it! It's not called the 'Long Slow Stab.' Now let's get on with it. Just pay attention to the rhythm: (*Repeating it*) ba-la-da-chang, ba-la-da-chang, ba-la-da-chang, chang-chang-ling-chang . . . Ba-la-da! (*He suddenly stops, then, dramatically, he strikes downwards three times with his right hand to represent the drum.*) Da! Da! Da! (*Then a downward blow for the gong*) Chang! (*His whole body alive, his face exuding the enthusiasm with which he is throwing himself into the part, his words tumbling out with great rapidity*) Now, watch: after the introduction the old man character swings his beard, knits his brow, glares, and his whole body trembles. Then, with the drum accompanying him, the old man grinds his teeth, points, and shouts (*His pointing finger, almost touching the tip of* **Madame Gu's** *nose*): 'You cheap whore! . . .'

Gu Can't we have something else besides 'cheap whores' all the time? I don't want to hear the 'old man' part; it's the beautiful young female role that I want to learn.

Hu Si (*Contemptuously*) The huadan? You? (*A pause.*) Well, all right, but you'll have to tell me which passage you want to do.

Gu (*As if racking her brains*) That bit that goes 'Suddenly I hear . . .' or something or other, after the part where somebody sings 'I'll ask her to open the door.'

Hu Si (*Showing off*) Oh, that's easy!

Gu Then act it out with me with all the movements, then.

Hu Si Easy. Nothing to it. The huqin plays the *Siping* melody: yi-ge-long-ge-li-ge-long-ge-long-ge-long. Sing: (*With liberal bodily movement*) 'Young Lady, open the door quickly!' Back to speaking voice 'My dear young lady, come and let me in!'

Gu I want to be the young heroine.

Hu Si Patience! Immediately afterwards, the curtain is lifted and the huadan comes on. (*Already acting it out bashfully with a handkerchief in his hand*) Your steps must be light and graceful, your eyes lively, and when you come out on to the stage you strike a pose – like this! (*Looking* *coy and inviting*) Yi-ge-long-ge-li-ge-long-ge-long-ge-long. (*In a falsetto*) 'Suddenly I hear' – (*Resuming his normal voice*) long-ge-li-ge-long-ge-long-ge-long-ge- (*Throwing himself into it whole-heartedly*) 'there's someone calling me at the door.' Long-ge-long-li-ge-long-ge-ge-long-ge. . . .

(*A rooster crows in the distance.*)

Bailu   Listen, listen to that.

Hu Si   What?

Bailu   A rooster crowing.

(*The rooster crows again in the distance.*)

Gu   Why, so it is! (*Suddenly looking out of the window*) Why, it'll soon be light. (*To* **Hu Si**) Come on, we must get going! Time for bed. We've stayed longer than usual tonight.

Hu Si (*With an air of complete unconcern*)   By the way, what about that bill of mine for five hundred dollars?

Gu   I'll write you a check from my account at Dafeng Bank as soon as I get home. Though you –

Hu Si (*Obediently*)   I'll be good. No more going to see that horrible woman.

Gu   Now then, don't make a fool of yourself in front of Lulu. Hurry up and get your things on and we'll be going. Now tomorrow – or rather today, haven't you got to go to the studio to make a movie?

Hu Si (*The perfect yes-man, lying easily*)   Yes, I have. The director said if I don't turn up today they can't shoot it.

Gu   Then hurry up and get your things on and get home to bed. I'm going with you to the studio myself today to have a look round.

Hu Si (*Taken aback*)   Oh, are you? I – er. . . . (*But he prefers to pass the subject over for the moment: slowly and with infinite care he puts his coat on.*)

Gu (*Turning to* **Bailu**, *very smugly*)   You know, Lulu, Hu Si's going to be a great film star. Before you know it he'll be a great success. The Company says he's a unique, unprecedented genius, and they want him to do three films in a row. The film magazines will all be featuring his photograph in a matter of days. They'll probably print mine as well.

Bailu   Yours?

Gu Yes, mine, one of me and Hu Si. One of Madame Gu with Hu Si, that superstar of the silver screen, the greatest in China. You see (*Lowering her voice and speaking with shyness and embarrassment like a young girl*) I'm going to. . . . I've said yes after all. I'm hoping. . . . I'm hoping that the day after tomorrow we'll . . . we'll be getting married. There, Lulu, don't you think that will be nice?

Bailu Yes, very nice. But . . .

Gu Lulu, you must be one of my bridesmaids.

Bailu (*Her voice becoming lower*) All right, then, but . . .

Gu What?

Bailu I was going to ask whether your savings are with Dafeng Bank at the moment.

Gu Of course. Why do you ask?

Bailu Oh, no reason. Just curious.

Gu (*Gazing at* **Hu Si** *in admiration*) Ah! (*She opens her purse and takes out a powder-compact. She is just about to put some on when she catches sight of the bottle of sleeping pills.*) Look at that, Lulu! What do I need these for! (*Taking the bottle out of the bag*) I'd better return this. I won't be needing any after all, thanks all the same.

Bailu Thank you. (*Taking them*) I was about to ask for them back.

Gu Good, I'd rather you kept them.

Hu Si (*Now dressed up and ready to go*) Come on, then, let's go.

Gu Don't rush me. I've still got to do my face yet.

Hu Si (*Pulling on her arm*) Oh, don't bother. Who's going to see you at this time of morning? Come on, let's go! (*He steers her towards the center door.*)

Gu (*To* **Bailu**, *proudly*) See how he bosses me around? (*As* **Hi Si** *drags her forward another step or two*) Goodbye, then!

Hu Si Bye, Bailu.

(**Hu Si** *puts on his hat and tugs the brim down, then departs with* **Madame Gu** *through the center door.*)

(*Left alone,* **Bailu** *goes to the window and opens it. In the stillness the silhouette of the buildings opposite can be seen emerging slowly from* *the darkness. Everything is identical to Act One: outside is a world of stillness and solitude, and in the far off distance comes the faint mournful cry of a factory whistle, mingling with the crowing of roosters that can be heard now and then from the market. It is the hour when darkness gives way to the glow of morning, before the sun has appeared.*)

(*There is a knock at the center door.*)

Bailu (*Without turning her head*)   Come in. (*Enter* **Fusheng**, *stifling a yawn.*)

Bailu (*Still not turning*)   Can anything be done, Yueting?

Fusheng   Miss.

Bailu (*Turning*)   Oh, it's you.

Fusheng   Mr Pan sent me to tell you he won't be returning after all.

Bailu   I see.

Fusheng   He says he doesn't think he'll be able to come the next few days, either.

Bailu   I understand.

Fusheng   He told me to tell you to look after yourself, and said you must always be careful and take good care of yourself. He said . . .

Bailu   I understand. He won't be coming round to see me anymore.

Fusheng   That's right. But Miss, why did you have to go and offend a wealthy man like Manager Pan?. . . . Isn't it enough to have offended Jin Ba, without . . .

Bailu (*Shaking her head*)   You don't understand. I haven't offended him.

Fusheng   But when I handed him the bills you owe just a minute ago, all he did was shake his head and sigh, then he left without saying a word.

Bailu   Why did you have to go give him my bills again?

Fusheng   But Miss, they absolutely must be paid today. They said no excuses this time. The total comes to two thousand five hundred dollars, and they won't take a penny less. You don't want to ruin your reputation by having them take you to court! If you can't find some way of getting the money out of Manager Pan, do you think it's just going to fall out of the sky?

Bailu (*Deep in thought*)   It might.

Fusheng   Oh well, it's up to you to do what you can in the next few hours. I've done all I can; I can't keep them at bay for you any longer.

Bailu (*Picking up the bottle of sleeping pills and clenching it tightly in her hand*)   All right, you can go now.

(*Just as* **Fusheng** *exits through the center door, there is a loud knocking on the door to the left and a voice shouting 'Open the door, open up!'* **Fusheng** *comes back into the room and goes over to the door. When he opens it,* **Georgy Zhang** *bursts in, his face bathed in perspiration.*)

Georgy (*Distraught*)   Hey, why was the door locked?

Fusheng (*Smiling*)   It wasn't locked. Who would lock it?

Georgy (*Clutching his heart*)   I had a dream, Bailu. *J'ai fait un rêve.* It was horrible, ghastly! *C'etait affreux! Affreux!* I dreamed this building was overrun by ghosts, jumping and leaping all over the place, on the stairs, in the dining room, on the beds, under the armchairs, on top of the tables, all gnawing on the heads of the living, gnawing on their arms and thighs, laughing and making noises, tossing human skulls back and forth, croaking and snarling. Suddenly there was a great crash and the whole building collapsed, crushing you and me beneath it, along with a whole lot of other people too . . .

(**Fusheng** *exits through the center door.*)

Bailu   Georgy, where have you been?

Georgy   I've been asleep.

Bailu   You didn't leave?

Georgy   Well, if I had, would you be seeing me here now? I had too much to drink and fell asleep in an armchair in there. You didn't see me, and I had such a terrible dream. Simply terrifying!

Bailu   You really did have quite a bit to drink.

Georgy   Yes, I don't deny it. I had a drop too much and it upset my nerves. That's what made me have this nightmare. (*Yawning*) I'm tired. I'm going home now. Oh, yes (*Suddenly becoming animated*), I wanted to tell you something.

Bailu   No, first, I've got a favor to ask.

Georgy   Go ahead. Anything you like.

Bailu   There's someone who, who . . . wants me to lend them three thousand dollars.

Georgy   Oh?

Bailu   But at the moment I don't have that much at my disposal.

Georgy   I see.

Bailu   Georgy, could you find three thousand dollars for me, to lend this person?

Georgy   Well . . . er . . . of course . . . that's rather a different matter. I've always been a generous man. But it depends on who's involved. No, I can't lend money to your friend, because . . . because I'm jealous of him, whoever he is. Though of course if it were someone as intelligent as yourself who wanted to borrow such a paltry sum for their own use, then I wouldn't hesitate for a moment.

Bailu (*Reluctantly*)   All right, then: let's suppose I'm borrowing it from you myself.

Georgy   You? Lulu borrow money from me? Borrow money from Georgy Zhang?

Bailu   Yes, why not?

Georgy   No, no, I refuse to believe that. Lulu borrow a measly sum like that? *Ah non,* I refuse to believe that! You're teasing me (*Laughing aloud*) You'll be the death of me. Lulu borrowing money from me, and borrowing such a paltry sum! Oh, my little Lulu, you're an intelligent girl, you've got a wonderful sense of humor. There's not another girl in the world as clever as you. Ah well, I'll say goodbye now. (*He picks up his hat.*)

Bailu   Goodbye, then. (*With a faint smile*) You're the intelligent one.

Georgy   Thanks for the compliment! (*Going to the door*) Oh yes, before I forget, there's something I wanted to tell you. I couldn't hold out any longer, so I've accepted her after all. I'm thinking – we're thinking – of getting married tomorrow. But I told her we must have you as a bridesmaid.

Bailu   You want me for a bridesmaid?

Georgy   Of course you. It would be impossible to find anyone as good.

Bailu   All right, then. Well, goodbye.

Georgy   Goodbye. So that settled. *Bonne nuit!* I mean: good morning, my little Lulu. (*With a wave of his hand he exits through the center door.*)

(*The glow of morning gradually filters in through the window, and the first glint of sunlight begins to touch the rooftops.*)

Bailu *shuts the door and goes and sits down at the table in the middle. After staring vacantly in front of her for a moment she gets up and paces back and forth a few steps, surveying the room with the regret of parting. Then she goes to the small side table by the sofa, picks up a bottle and pours herself a drink. She takes several large gulps, then stands by the sofa lost in thought.)*

(The center door creaks open and **Fusheng** *comes in.)*

Bailu *(In a low, strained voice)*   What do you want?

Fusheng   Aren't you going to bed yet? It's light, and the sun's already up.

Bailu   Yes, I know.

Fusheng   Shall I get you a drink of soy milk before you go to bed?

Bailu   No, don't bother. You needn't stay.

Fusheng *(Taking a bundle of bills out of his pocket)*   Er, Miss, these are the bills that must be paid today. I'll – I'll leave them here, so that you can add them all up. *(He puts the bills on the center table.)*

Bailu   All right, leave them there, then.

Fusheng   Will that be all? (**Bailu** *nods her head.*)

(**Fusheng** *turns his back to* **Bailu** *and yawns wearily, then exits by the center door.)*

(**Bailu** *finishes her drink and puts down the glass. She goes to the center table and slowly goes through the bills, tossing each one on the floor after she's looked at it, until the floor around the table is littered with them.)*

Bailu *(Heaving a sigh)*   Yes. *(She picks up the sleeping pills from the table and goes over to the settee under the window. She removes the lid and begins tipping out the tablets one or two at a time, then suddenly pauses undecided and collapses weakly in the settee, where she sits for a moment staring ahead blankly. She looks up and catches sight of her reflection in the dressing mirror on the door of the wardrobe to the left. She stands up and approaches the mirror.)*

Bailu *(She turns this way and that as she examines the beautiful woman in the mirror, then slowly turns to face her reflection squarely. She shakes her head and sighs. Bleakly)*: Hardly unattractive. *(After a pause)* And you couldn't call her old. Yet. . . . *(She heaves a long sigh. Unable to bear the sight any longer, she walks slowly back to the center table and begins* *counting out the pills from the bottle, a faint smile on her lips. Her voice and her manner both evoke that of a young orphan girl alone in a small courtyard, eating sweets to console herself, pitying herself with immense tenderness and anguish.*) One, two, three, four, five, six, seven, eight, nine, ten. (*Clutching the ten small tablets tightly in her hand, she tosses the empty bottle with a crash into a spittoon. She spreads her arms out flat on the table and stretches them out to their full length, looking in front of her, nodding her head slightly and speaking sadly.*) So – young, and – so – beautiful, so – (*Silent tears stream down her cheeks. She musters her courage and stands up. She picks up a teacup, turns, and downs the tablets in two gulps.*)

(*A ray of sunlight now filters into the room and falls on the littered floor. The sky is now brilliant, and outside the window the laborers laying the foundation of the new building have already assembled and now, with the sun on their faces, draw closer and closer with even, somber footsteps, their 'heng-heng-yo, heng-heng-yo' sounding in the distance. Team by team the wooden rammers pound the earth and the heavy stone rammers fall with muffled echoes; the heavy 'heng-heng-yo heng-heng-yo' is followed by the soldier-like march of the laborers at work. They have not yet begun singing their pile-driving song.*)

Bailu (*Tossing the cup aside, her attention fixed on the sound of the wooden rammers outside. She straightens her shoulders and goes to the window. She draws back the curtains and the sunlight illuminates her face as she looks out, speaking in a soft voice*): 'The sun rises, leaving the darkness behind.' (*She takes a breath of the cool morning air, shivers, and looks around.*) 'But the sun is not ours, for we now sleep.' (*Suddenly she turns off the light and draws the curtains so that the room is plunged back into darkness, except for a ray or two of sunlight quivering through the gap between the curtains. She thumps her chest as if she feels pain or tightness there. She picks up the copy of* Sunrise, *then lies down on the sofa, preparing to read quietly . . .*)

In the far distance come the faint voices of the laborers begin a pile driving song – But we cannot make out the words.)

Dasheng's voice (*Outside*)   Zhujun! Zhujun! (*The voice approaches the door.*)

(**Bailu** *quickly puts the book down, stands up, and goes to the door. Realizing who it is, she glances around, then at once picks up the bills on the table, crumples them into a ball in her hand, then picks up the book and hurries into the room on the right, her footsteps already showing signs of heaviness. She closes the door behind her and locks it.*)

Dasheng's voice (*Subdued*)   Zhujun! Zhujun! Is there someone with you? Zhujun! Zhujun! I'm about to leave! (*Getting no reply*) I'm coming in, then, Zhujun.

(*The chirping of a sparrow can be heard outside the window.*) (**Dasheng** *pushes open the door and comes in.*)

Dasheng (*Looking around the room*)   Zhujun! I'm telling you . . . (*Suddenly realizing how dark it is in the room, he goes to the window and draws back the curtains again. Sunlight floods in, and with it the twittering of birds.*) I don't get it, why don't you let the sunlight in? (*Going to the door of the bedroom*) Listen to me, Zhujun. Going on like this will be the death of you. Listen to me, you're better off coming with me; don't associate with those people anymore, OK? Look (*Pointing out of the window*), the sun's shining, it's spring.

(*The singing of the laborers now draws nearer. They are singing: 'The sun comes up from the east; the sky is a great red glow . . .'*)

Dasheng (*Knocking on the door*)   Listen! Listen! (*Rapturous*) The sun's out. The sun is shining down on them. Come with me, together we can accomplish something. We can take on the Jin Bas, we could – (*Realizing that he is being ignored*) Zhujun, why do you ignore me? (*Tapping lightly on the door*) Zhujun, why don't you say something? You – (*Turning away with a sigh*) You're too smart. You wouldn't want to do something foolish like me (*Suddenly gathers himself*) Fine, I'll go. Farewell, Zhujun. (*Still getting no reply from the other room, he turns his head to listen to the pile-driving song outside the window, then exits through the center door, his head held high and the sunlight on his face.*)

(*The room is flooded with the sunlight streaming in through the window, and outside everything is dazzlingly bright. The laborers are singing a resounding chorus:*

   'The sun comes up from the east;
   the sky is a great red glow!
   If we want rice to eat
   we must break our backs in toil.'

(*The heavy stone rammers thud steadily into the earth with a sound that hits the audience's ears as that of a great surge of life advancing in a mighty tide, flooding the whole universe with its power.*)

(*The light begins to fade in the room, but outside it shines brighter still.*)

(*The curtain slowly falls.*)

Notes

1   Translation taken from Roger Ames and David Hall, *Dao De Jing:*
    A Philosophical Translation. New York: Ballanite Books, 2003, p.196. *Tian*
    is generally translated as heaven.
2   Translation here and below from *New Revised Standard Version Bible:*
    Pocket Edition. New York: Oxford University Press, 2006, p.162.
3   p.738.
4   p.221.
5   p.176.
6   p.107.
7   p.111.
8   p.279.
9   Translator's note: Original in English.
10 Translator's note: The original is in English here.
11 Translator's note: The name of the notoriously self-deluding and narrow-
    minded title character of Lu Xun's novella *The True Story of Ah Q*, written in
    the early 1920s.
12 Translator's note: These are Hollywood movie stars known for their roles in
    musicals in the 1930s.
13 Translator's note: A traditional rhythmic storytelling to the accompaniment
    of clappers.
14 Translator's note: Diaochan and Xi Shi were two of the four renowned
    beauties of ancient China, and thus the subject of many works of art and
    literature.
15 Translator's note: A four-stringed instrument played with a bow.
16 Translator's note: Hu Si is making a joke at Fusheng's expense by calling
    him Wang the Eighth, or Wang Ba, which sounds identical in Chinese to the
    term for cuckold.
17 Translator's note: Fusheng's Chinglish for 'kill'.
18 Translator's note: Fusheng's Chinglish for 'damned fool'.
19 Translator's note: The original terms here in English. I've translated into
    French to retain their foreign flavour.

I Love XXX

Meng Jinghui, Huang Jingang, Wang Xiaoli, Shi Hang
Translated and Introduced by Claire Conceison

Meng Jinghui has been the most influential experimental theatre maker in Mainland China since the early 1990s, when his productions like *I Love XXX* began attracting young audiences back to the theatre. His work over the past two decades includes original plays, literary collaborations with his wife Liao Yimei and other writers, and adaptations of non-Chinese works, including Western classics like *The Bald Soprano, Waiting for Godot, The Balcony, The Accidental Death of an Anarchist, Dr. Faustus* and *Twelfth Night*, as well as more unusual choices including Mayakovsky's *The Bedbug* and Hanoch Levin's *Ya'akobi & Leidental*, and stage adaptations of films such as Billy Wilder's *The Apartment* and Rainer Fassbinder's *Love is Colder than Death*. Meng is known for taking both political and artistic risks, and his style has become so distinct that the work of subsequent directors imitating it is called 'Meng-style' (*Mengshi*). Rossella Ferrari insightfully labels his aesthetic 'pop avant-garde', a phenomenon that exhibits constant evolution and experimentation along with a successful combination of critical acclaim and market appeal.[1]

In the case of *I Love XXX*, an 'anti-play' first staged in 1994 and 1995, Meng uses repetition, rhythm and word play to deconstruct both language and historical events, expressing the angst, nostalgia and contradictions of his generation in a poetic, playful, darkly satirical manifesto. The script originated from Meng and friends Shi Hang, Wang Xiaoli and Huang Jingang in a student dormitory at the Central Academy of Drama playing a word game that began with the phrase 'I love . . .'. Collaboratively written in a manner that recalls collective art creation during the revolutionary period of their childhood in the 1960s, the play addresses China's unique transition to 'post-socialism' in the 1990s and the coming of age of their generation amidst tumultuous events during the 1970s, along with the onslaught of materialist capitalism and its spoils that captivated their peers in the wake of the idealism of the 1980s. The resulting path-breaking production challenged the notion of character and plot as the core of drama, a form of experimentation that was still new in China in 1994 and carried great risk, particularly in this play with its overt political references and powerful eroticism. Removal of plot and character and emphasis on word play allowed Meng to further hone his craft in formal techniques such as the arrangement of actors' bodies and voices on stage and the employment of multimedia. Repetition in the text was echoed in visual iteration in the production's mise-en-scène: television sets of varying shapes and sizes were scattered about the space and a chain of identical images of a human silhouette resembling a target formed the primary backdrop for the ensemble of eight actors. Incorporation of multimedia included large-scale video projections: in Part Two, the lines are not spoken by actors, but rather projected onto the back wall, and in the beginning of Part Three, the first six lines of the play are repeated over and over, accompanied by video projections of the documentary footage of the Cultural Revolution era.

In the play, a litany of world events, people and sociopolitical movements of the twentieth century is spoken aloud, along with mention of common objects, entities and ideas. The citations are both global and domestic, ranging from international wars and upheavals to Chinese political references. Inevitably, about halfway through the play, comes the anticipated 'I love Tiananmen Square' – this utterance contains a double referent: the revolutionary song that every Chinese citizen knows, and the tragic controversial events of five years prior that had taken place in the enormous public square. Although the line appears only once in the script, it was repeated consecutively twenty times in performance, increasing its power (particularly in its signification of June Fourth). If the political content did not push the boundaries enough, the erotic recitation of body parts in a section echoing Walt Whitman's poem *I Sing the Body Electric* challenged morés and invited censorship. The fact that the play is framed by the concept of 'love' does not exclude the listing of unbearable attributes of modern society that are disdained, many of which are commercially successful aspects of popular culture. Here, another of Meng's traits emerges – that of goading the audience, purposefully teasing young urbanites and challenging prevailing norms to expose hypocrisy (even his own). In that same spirit, many of the events and phenomena listed in the play actually did not occur or exist. As Ferrari points out in her analysis of the play, this 'historical rewriting' subverts grand historical narratives, particularly of the party-state, and calls attention to atrocities that happened by stating that they did *not* happen, while also satirically inventing new histories and assigning significance to bizarre occurrences that are not conventionally privileged.

I Love XXX premiered in Beijing on 26 December 1994 with six unadvertised performances in a small space at the China Acrobat Troupe. A subsequent public run at the Haidian Theatre in May 1995 was halted due to the absence of a performance permit. Three months later, without securing permission from his official work unit (Central Experimental Theatre), Meng brought the production to the Tiny Alice Festival in Tokyo, Japan. As in many of Meng's productions, the actors were from a variety of local institutions, and several would continue to work with him, most notably Guo Tao. The play has been published in Chinese in an anthology of Meng's plays, and video of the production is included in DVD collections of his works.

After almost 20 years, Meng Jinghui restaged *I Love XXX* in June 2013 in Beijing, retaining about two-thirds of the text's original material (including intertextual citations from classical poetry and other sources) and creating new text with his new group of actors that brought the witty puns and topical references more into step with current events, popular trends and personal experiences of the ensemble.[2] The actors in 2013 were born in the 1980s or after 1990, whereas members of the ensemble in 1994 (and their audiences) who were born just before or after 1970 during the Cultural Revolution, came of age during China's opening and reform, and were deeply affected by the government crackdown in Tiananmen Square in 1989, about which the actors and audience in 2013 knew little if anything. From Meng's perspective, this shift is from his own 'angry' generation to the current generation that he hopes will be 'brave'. His 2013 revival of *I Love XXX* was an attempt to bridge the divide and find a cross-generational collective voice that could reignite the passion of his generation in step and in chorus (both literally and figuratively) with the young artists and audiences of today.

This translation of the original 1994 version of *I Love XXX* is the first of Meng's plays to ever be anthologised or published in English. Although the director's inventive use of actors' bodies, choral vocal arrangements and multimedia are integral to the play, the text provided here can be interpreted freely by individual readers and subsequent stage directors, who are invited to imagine and invent movement, style, vocal techniques and visual elements of their own design.

I Love XXX, directed by Meng Jinghui, Beijing, December 1994.
(Photo: Li Yan; Courtesy: Meng Jinghui Studio.)

I Love XXX, directed by Meng Jinghui, Beijing, December 1994.
(Photo: Li Yan; Courtesy: Meng Jinghui Studio.)

I Love XXX, directed by Meng Jinghui, Beijing, December 1994.
(Photo: Li Yan; Courtesy: Meng Jinghui Studio.)

2013 version of *I Love XXX* at Beehive Theatre in Beijing, directed by Meng Jinghui. (Photo by Liu Haiyang; Courtesy: Meng Jinghui Studio.)

2013 version of *I Love XXX* at Beehive Theatre in Beijing, directed by Meng Jinghui. (Photo by Liu Haiyang; Courtesy: Meng Jinghui Studio.)

I LOVE XXX[3]

[*Wo ai XXX*, 1994]

Part One: The Less Said the Better

I love light
I love and so there was light
I love you
I love and so there was you
I love myself
I love and so there was myself

I love the year 1900
I love the ringing in of the new year 1900
I love the beautiful new century that began in the year 1900
I love this carefree society, this liberating society, this gleeful society,
　　this complacent society of 1900
I love the sun shining down on the earth in 1900
I love the rain pouring down on everything in 1900
I love the bounty brought by the sun and rain for the beautiful new
　　century in 1900
I love the beginning of 1900
I love the air of splendor and glory and romance at the beginning of
　　1900
I love every minute of the beginning of 1900: morning, afternoon, evening,
　　midnight, one o'clock, two o'clock, three o'clock, four o'clock[4]
I love every spot at the beginning of 1900: New York, London, Paris,
　　Havana, Beijing, Rome, Berlin, Moscow
I love each and every person at the beginning of 1900: Tom, Mary, Peter,
　　Michelle, Henry, George, Lavsky, Novic
I love the times, places, people, events, causes and effects at the
　　beginning of 1900
I love 1900, 1900
I love the ringing in of the new year 1900, the ringing in of the new year
　　1900

I love the beautiful new century that began in 1900, the beautiful new century that began in 1900

I love that those great masters died, all those great masters died, each and every one of those great masters died at the beginning of the beautiful new century in 1900

I love that German philosopher Frederich Nietzsche died

I love that French writer Emile Zola died

I love that Russian playwright Anton Chekhov died

I love that Czech composer Antonin Dvorak died

I love that American authors Mark Twain, O. Henry, and Jack London died

I love that Russian literary giant Leo Tolstoy died

I love that Russian socialist theorist Vladimir Plekhanov died

I love that French painter Paul Gauguin died

I love that Norwegian composer Edvard Grieg died

I love that Norwegian playwright Henrik Ibsen died

I love that French sculptor Auguste Rodin died

I love that German bacteriologist Robert Koch died

I love that French science fiction writer Jules Verne died

I love that those great masters died, all those great masters died, each and every one of those great masters died, and that those stars were born, all those stars were born, each and every one of those stars was born

I love that this is an age when great masters die and stars are born

I love the stars born in 1900

I love that star American film actors Clark Gable and Gary Cooper were born

I love that star British novelist Graham Greene was born

I love that star French philosopher Jean-Paul Sartre was born

I love that star American athlete Jesse Owens was born

I love that star Brazilian soccer player Pelé was born

I love that star French dramatist Samuel Beckett was born

I love that star British film actor Laurence Olivier was born

I love that star Italian director Bernardo Bertolucci was born

I love that star Chinese Emperor Aixin Jueluo Puyi was born[5]

I love that star Romanian dramatist Eugene Ionesco was born

I love that star Romanian politician Nicolae Ceaucescu was born

I love that star American film actor Ronald Reagan was born
I love that star American politician John Kennedy was born
I love that star American oilman John Rockefeller was born
I love that star American warmonger West Point Patton was born
I love that star Spanish peacemaker Pablo Picasso was born
I love that star Indian politician Indira Gandhi was born
I love that star German conductor von Karajan was born
I love that star American cartoonist Walt Disney was born
I love that star American fitness guru Jane Fonda was born
I love that star French world viewer Albert Camus was born[6]
I love that star Swiss comedian Charlie Chaplin was born
I love that star Chinese actor Mei Lanfang was born
I love that those stars were born, all those stars were born, each and every one of those stars was born

I love all of you in the audience, men in the audience, women in the audience

I love making you watch a play, watch a play that nothing can be done about

I love raising the curtain and starting the show

I love proclaiming to the audience the news of the top ten world events of 1900

I love the top ten world events of 1900

1. On 15 April, the 1900 World's Fair opens in Paris. It covers 547 acres, larger in scale than any previous exposition in Europe.[7]

2. New York City Mayor Van Wyck breaks ground with a silver spade, digging up the first shovel of dirt at the opening ceremony of the first Rapid Transit Tunnel.

3. The Boxer Rebellion breaks out in China and the Eight-Nation Alliance invades Beijing.

4. Engineer John Browning invents the Browning pistol. Swedish scientist Alfred Nobel invents the Nobel Prize. Someone named Tango claims he invented the Tango.

5. After two fatal incidents, the state of Ohio passes a law prohibiting college upperclassmen from hazing freshmen.

6. On 1 November, a group of medical doctors in Barcelona make the following announcement: X-rays can be used for effective treatment of breast cancer and to increase milk production in cows.

7. On 2 November, because of the critical increase in the homosexual male population, the women of Greece hold a massive assembly calling for the reinstatement of polygamy.

8. High brow art goes from Paris to the Bund for the first time when the opera *Madama Butterfly* is performed in Shanghai. Meanwhile in European countries, fourteen politicians engage in 'peachy' sex scandals.[8]

9. On 19 September, police in Paris kill and injure seventy eight demonstrators when they mistake the command 'open the road' for 'open fire.'[9]

10. On 4 May 1900, the play *Romeo and Juliet* is staged in London, the opera *Romeo and Juliet* is staged in Paris, and the ballet *Romeo and Juliet* is staged in Warsaw.[10]

Part Two (Surtitles)[11]

I love that all this happened

I love that all this never happened

I love that those absurd realities didn't happen

I love that those evil realities didn't happen

I love that those absurd predictions didn't happen

I love that those evil predictions didn't happen

I love that World War I didn't happen

I love that World War II didn't happen

I love that World War III didn't happen

I love that World War X didn't happen

I love that the assassination of the Archduke didn't happen

I love that abuse of prisoners of war didn't happen

I love that Haley's Comet blazing towards earth didn't happen

I love that ten million people dying of war and twenty million people dying of influenza didn't happen

I love that Junkers dropping bombs and the formula for the atom bomb didn't happen[12]

I love that the invention of radium, the invention of Hollywood, the invention of anarchy, the invention of government, the invention of multiple governments didn't happen

I love that the era of utilizing poison gas didn't happen

I love that the era of the scientific assembly line didn't happen

I love that the revelries of Pearl Harbor, Hiroshima, and Auschwitz didn't happen

I love that Lenin's death didn't happen

I love that Trotsky's exile didn't happen

I love that the Moscow Trials didn't happen

I love that the Pope leaving the Vatican didn't happen

I love that the Yalta Conference didn't happen

I love that the Reichstag fire didn't happen

I love that Arab rebels protesting against Jews didn't happen

I love that the mayor of New York drowning his sorrows in drink didn't happen

I love that the building of the Berlin wall, the Paris wall, the Korea wall, the London wall didn't happen

I love that one U.S. dollar being equal to forty trillion Deutsch marks did not happen

I love that thousands upon thousands of bankrupt people committing suicide by leaping off buildings didn't happen

I love that the strike that ends strikes because salaries go up didn't happen

I love that female competitors being forbidden to wear bikinis while playing in the Wimbledon Championship didn't happen

I love that the obscene rock 'n roll singer Presley becoming US Army Private 53310761 didn't happen

I love that on his way back to Beijing the famous love poet Xu Zhimo being lost in a plane crash, being lost in a train crash, being lost on the operating table, and 'Saying Goodbye to Cambridge Again' didn't happen[13]

I love that Karl Liebknecht and Rosa Luxemburg being murdered in Berlin didn't happen

I love that the invention of sulfonamide, the invention of penicillin, the invention of streptomycin, the invention of cortisone, the invention of ACTH, the invention of tobramycin, the invention of aureomycin, the invention of the polio vaccine didn't happen

I love electric guitars and all guitars that are electric

The Beatles' song 'Revolution' plays.

Blackout.[14]

On 9 November 1965, the northeast states of the U.S. and part of Canada suddenly fall into darkness. It is the most severe accidental black out to happen up to that point in history. Off-duty policemen and the National Guard are ordered to the streets of every city, where they control traffic and prevent looting of stores. Most of the twenty four million citizens remain calm during the darkness. At 5.17 p.m., a switch unexpectedly malfunctions at a power plant near Niagara Falls and the lights instantly go out in every city in the northern part of New York State. The power in Massachusetts immediately goes out, and Connecticut, Rhode Island, Vermont, Maine, New Hampshire and two provinces in Canada immediately lose electricity as well. Most parts of New Jersey and Pennsylvania also go dark. It is said that traffic lights went out, and gridlock ensued. It is said that elevators in sky scrapers stopped between floors, and since it was late at night, countless people were stuck inside. It is said that lights went out in operating rooms, so hospitals had to start automatic generators. It is said that many airplanes had to circle aimlessly over pitch-dark runways. It is said that some romantic lovers hid in cozy places and fully took advantage of the wonderful moment. It is said that a full nine months after the blackout, all hospitals reported a spike in births.

At about the same time, on the other side of the world in Beijing, approximately seventy percent of women of childbearing age are using birth control, two-thirds of them taking contraceptive medicine (the Pill). In communes often rural counties around Beijing, approximately forty percent of women of childbearing age are taking the Pill. According to the renowned Chinese doctor Dr Lin Qiaozhi, her research team called the Birth Control Battalion is testing a kind of pill taken once every three months. And now they believe they can come up with a pill or injection that can last about a year. The Pill is in high demand and short supply. China has about seventy to eighty million women of childbearing age, which means that every year approximately seventeen billion of the pills taken twenty-two days a month have to be produced.

Enter any hospital ward in China and you will notice a significant change in health care: increasingly strong promotion and application of all practical approaches to family planning.

But the famous Dr Lin Qiaozhi and her staff still have to spend even more time delivering babies into the world.

Part Three: Better Said Than Sung

I love light

I love and there was light

I love you

I love and there was you

I love myself

I love and there was myself[15]

I love that when I was born a million people hailed Eisenhower

I love that when I was born a million people hailed Khrushchev

I love that when I was born a million people hailed Dubcek

I love that when I was born a million people, a million people hailed
  Chairman Mao

I love that when I was born a million people in Europe clashed with police

I love that when I was born a million people in America occupied college
  campuses

I love that when I was born a million people in South America engaged
  in guerilla warfare

I love that when I was born a million people in the Middle East
  overthrew kings

I love that when I was born a million people's determination triumphed
  over heaven[16]

I love that when I was born a million people took collective action

I love that when I was born a million people collectively degenerated

I love that when I was born a million parks had hallucinating youth

I love that when I was born a million electric guitars blasted from
  amplifiers

I love that when I was born a million Red Guards wept passionately

I love that when I was born a million Berlin Walls went up between people

I love that when I was born a million KGB agents were waiting to spy
  on me

I love that when I was born a million Nixons were waiting to take over
  America

I love that when I was born a million Dr Lins were delivering babies
  from a million women

I love that when I was born a million Dr Lins and a million women were
  staring at me

I love the fatherland[17]
I love the people
I love the teachers
I love my classmates
I love the collective
I love honor
I love civilization
I love good manners
I love studying
I love working
I love science
I love public property
I love the Four Modernizations
I love being a successor[18]
I love politics
I love discipline
I love organizations
I love principles
I love order
I love morality
I love cleanliness
I love hygiene
I love exercise
I love field trips
I love dictation
I love school duty
I love white shirts
I love blue pants
I love red kerchiefs
I love blackboard bulletins
I love white sneakers
I love red-tasseled toy spears
I love green book bags
I love purple tincture of iodine
I love morning study sessions
I love evening study sessions

I love the Five Emphases and Four Beauties[19]
I love 'Friendship Comes First'[20]
I love *The Country Schoolteacher*
I love *Lenin in October*
I love *Ali Baba and the Forty Thieves*
I love *For the Sake of Sixty-One Class Brothers*[21]
I love *Two Hundred Foreign Folk Songs*
I love *Three Hundred Tang Dynasty Poems*
I love *Four Hundred Song Dynasty Poems*
I love *Five Hundred Yuan Dynasty Poems*
I love *One Thousand and One Nights*
I love *Eight Thousand Miles of Clouds and Moon*[22]
I love *One Hundred Thousand Whys*[23]
I love Xu Guozhang's *English Book One*[24]
I love moral, intellectual, physical education
I love math, physics, chemistry
I love male classmates, female classmates
I love substitute teachers and classroom monitors
I love sport competitions
I love children's palaces
I love passing love notes
I love keeping a diary
I love coming late
I love leaving early
I love morning exercise
I love young love
I love side burns
I love bell bottoms
I love Sanyo tape recorders
I love Teresa Teng's 'Fine Wine and Coffee,' 'When Will You Return to Me'
I love midterm exams, final exams, school entrance exams, college
    entrance exams
I love applications, transcripts, parent signatures
I love Beijing's Chang'an Avenue
I love Beijing's Tiananmen Square[25]
I love Beijing's Friendship Store

I love Wangfujing Street, the Labor Union Building

I love Beijing Hotel, National Hotel

I love Zhongshan Park, Beihai Park

I love Hepingmen roast duck, Qingfeng steamed buns[26]

I love the Capital Theatre, the Xishiku Cathedral[27]

I love Peking Union Medical College Hospital, People's Liberation Army Number 301 Hospital[28]

I love the National Art Museum of China, National Music Museum of China, National Dance Museum of China, National Theatre Museum of China[29]

I love East Xiushui Street, West Xiushui Street, South Xiushui Street, and North Xiushui Street[30]

I love Blue Sky Kindergarten, the CCTV Galaxy Children's Choir

I love the Central People's, Beijing People's, Capital People's, Regional People's Broadcasting Station[31]

I love teachers, but I love truth more

I love knowledge, but I love isms more

I love realism

I love neorealism

I love socialist realism

I love magical realism

I love surrealism

I love the fusion of modernism and realism

I love the fusion of postmodernism and realism

I love the fusion of classicism and realism

I love the fusion of neoclassicism and realism

I love the fusion of romanticism and realism

I love the fusion of expressionism and realism

I love the fusion of neo-expressionism and realism

I love the fusion of symbolism and realism

I love the fusion of existentialism and realism

I love the fusion of primitivism and realism

I love the fusion of Dadaism and realism

I love the fusion of nihilism and realism

I love the fusion of humanism and realism

I love the fusion of pragmatism and realism

I love the fusion of futurism and realism

I love the fusion of impressionism and realism

I love the fusion of naturalism and realism

I love the fusion of structuralism and realism

I love the fusion of formalism and realism

I love Scar Literature[32]

I love Search-for-Roots Literature[33]

I love Misty Poetry[34]

I love Stream of Consciousness

I love the literature of the New Era decade[35]

I love the non-literature of the New Era decade

I love the avant-garde, avant-gardism, avant-garde novels, avant-garde poetry, avant-garde films, avant-garde theatre, avant-garde dance, avant-garde music, avant-garde pioneers, and Pioneer stereos[36]

I love Third Generation poets[37]

I love Fifth Generation filmmakers[38]

I love Eighth Generation rock 'n' roll[39]

I love Twelfth Generation criticism

I love collectivism

I love collective classification

I love the collective unconscious

I love the collective conscious

I love collective dance[40]

I love that era of collective dance

I love this era of collective dance

I love that right after that there was collective dance, and when there was collective dance, there was us

I love collective dance of Mayakovsky full of secrets of youth[41]

I love collective dance flaunting fashion and swirling skirts down tree-lined boulevards on lovely spring evenings[42]

I love collective dance at new construction sites, we climbed up the scaffolds

I love collective dance at ancient Beidahuang, we sat in the drivers' seats[43]

I love collective dance in boundless clouds, we ride on flying silver swallow planes

I love collective dance in surging seas, our swift boats come and go[44]

I love collective dance in noisy factories, we make our own steel

I love collective dance in expansive fields, we sow our own seeds

I love collective dance on quiet campuses, with sounds of reading books in the libraries

I love collective dance in bustling mountains, the young people full of joy

I love collective dance

I love collective dance in celebration of the thirty-fifth birthday of the republic

I love collective dance in celebration of the thirty-fifth birthday of collective dance

I love collective dance ever youthful, like a round red sun emerging from the sea

I love collective dance ever strong, like rows of poplars that will become timber

I love collective dance ever passionate, like the rolling tide and raging flames

I love collective dance ever pure, like the color of the blue sky and white clouds

Even if tomorrow morning / the muzzle and bleeding sun / make me surrender freedom, youth and pen / I will never surrender this evening / I will never surrender you[45]

China, I've lost my collective dance[46]

I hope to meet a collective dance that carries its worries like lilacs[47]

Near and far, high and low, the surface of the winding lotus pond is covered with collective dance[48]

Confucius says: When three men are walking, one is bound to be collective dance[49]

Since I could not sleep anyway, I read intently half the night, until I began to see words between the lines, the whole book being filled with the two words 'collective dance'[50]

Half is sea water half is collective dance[51]

There is no royal road to science, and only those who do not dread the fatiguing climb of its steep paths have a chance of gaining the luminous summits of collective dance[52]

I love collective dance

I love that right after that, there was collective dance, and when there was collective dance, then there was us

I love that right after that, there was us, and when there was us, then there was love

I love that right after that, there was love, and then there was I love, then came I love you, I love you

I love your body

I love your body electric[53]

I love your body electric and electric poetry

I love that you irrepressibly attract my body electric

I love that it's always low tide receiving the climax of high tide's stimulation, always high tide receiving low tide's stimulation of love's body

I love that it's always bright trembling love serum

I love that it's always sweet, gentle, milky-ecstasy love serum

I love that it's always the rising and setting sun

I love that it's always victory and freedom that come from revelry

I love that it's always my two hands lightly tracing your whole body, my fingers running through your hair and inside your lips

I love that it's always like drunk infatuation, passing out from so much good sex

I love that it's always passionate kisses and embraces coming from your quivering lips

I love that it's always poetry that comes from eyes and hands and breasts and buttocks

I love that it's always brides and grooms making love in the night

I love that it's always electric brides and grooms making love in the night

I love that it's always the body electric and electric poetry

I love that it's always ignorant love

I love that it's always flagrant love

I love that it's always anxious love

I love that it's always sublime love

I love you and your body and your love

I love your head and your hair

I love your ears, your earlobes, your eardrums

I love your eyes

I love your eyelashes

I love your eyeballs

I love your eyebrows

I love your eyelids

I love your tongue

I love your lips

I love your teeth

I love your nose, your nostrils, the bridge of your nose

I love your forehead, your cheeks, your temples, your chin, your neck,
your throat, your nape, your spine

I love your strong shoulders, your delicate shoulders

I love your sharp shoulder blades, powerful shoulder blades

I love your heaving chest, beautiful chest

I love your broad back, burly back

I love your firm breasts

I love your plump breasts

I love your smooth breasts

I love your sweet breasts

I love your breast milk

I love your nipples

I love your areolae

I love your warm bosom

I love your upper arm

I love your armpit

I love your elbow

I love your forearm

I love your arm

I love your wrist and your wrist joint and hand and palm and knuckles
and thumb and index finger and middle finger and ring finger and
pinky finger and fingernails

I love your curly chest hair

I love your breastbone

I love your ribs

I love your spongy lungs

I love your waist

I love your tummy

I love your clean fragrant guts

I love your belly

I love your belly button

I love your backbone

I love your tailbone

I love your hucklebone and sciatic nerve
I love your bottom, your beautiful buttocks
I love your testicles, your beautiful penis
I love your pubic hair, your beautiful vagina
I love your labia, your beautiful uterus
I love your thigh, your knee, your kneecap, your calf, your calf muscle
I love your feet, your toes, your toenails, your soles, your arches, your
    heels, your ankles
I love your five senses
I love your sense of touch
I love your sense of taste
I love your sense of smell
I love your beating heart
I love your hot desire
I love your maternal instinct
I love your voice, the sound of your words
I love your words, what you say
I love your sounds and your furies
I love your shouts and whispers
I love you and your body and your love
I love your body electric and your electric poetry
I love your soul
I love that your body is your soul
I love you, if your body is not your soul, then what is a soul
I love you, if your soul is not your body, then what is a body
I love that your body is precisely your soul's body
I love that your soul is precisely your body's soul
I love that your body is precisely your body's body
I love that your soul is precisely your soul's soul
I love you
I love you
I love you
I love you
I love you
I love you
I love you

Stage Directions

We come upon a relatively fresh atmosphere, an early morning, with both sunshine and dust particles; there is a single sound that immediately grabs one's attention, not an alarm clock, but rather water dripping on the surface of steel or ceramic tile. Then we see a pair of lovers cleaning a room. They convey the excitement of love and joy by the way they move furniture around, wipe things, pick things up; then we see another person crashed in bed, continually surfing television channels, and from bed, he repeatedly helps the lovers move chairs around and hands them things, and his face bears a smile and a touch of weariness; (he even insists on brushing his teeth in bed). Meanwhile, someone in a hurry grabs his suitcase while looking for his airline ticket, of course continually messing up the room just cleaned by the pair of lovers, and he is making loud noise; at this moment we find a door, through which someone returns still bearing the tipsiness and music of the previous night out, he may bring back the first sunflower, slurring his speech; he needs to speak with another person, energetic and slightly neurotic, who is diligently preparing breakfast, and at this moment we again notice the water (note: up to here, the bustling atmosphere should not be too noisy, everything should be cool and relaxed); then we see a journalist who is on the phone getting the latest news while flipping through a stack of newspapers on the table. He turns up another sunflower from the stack of papers and hands it over to a yuppie who is calmly reading all kinds of news, but this person is fidgeting the whole time, looking down and fiddling with his cell phone, he shouldn't speak; finally a big bearded man returns from his morning jog, should he take home all the sunflowers? The relationship of these people emerges through the process of arranging several chairs in just the right way, then they sit down together, and sing.

Part Four: No Sooner Said than Done

I love tonight here and now
I love you all here tonight
I love you all here in the audience tonight
I love this expressive era of love, I love you
I love this bountiful era of love, I love you
I love this carefree era of love, I love you
I love this liberating era of love, I love you
I love this gleeful era of love, I love you

I love this complacent era of love, I love you
I love Pierre and Marie Curie
I love Karl and Jenny Marx
I love Sergei Yesenin and Isadora Duncan
I love Xu Zhimo and Lu Xiaoman[54]
I love Wang Gui and Li Xiangxiang[55]
I love Guo Jing and Huang Rong[56]
I love Ingrid Bergman and Roberto Rossellini
I love John Lennon and Yoko Ono
I love Auguste Rodin and his lover
I love Jean-Paul Sartre and Simone de Beauvoir
I love Laurence Olivier and Vivian Leigh
I love Mr. Rochester and Jane Eyre
I love Yamaguchi Momoe and Miura Tomokazu[57]
I love John Hinckley and Jodie Foster
I love Vincent Van Gogh and prostitute Rachel
I love the Duke of Windsor and Mrs. Simpson
I love Marilyn Monroe and the Kennedy brothers
I love you, love genius
I love you, love prodigy
I love you, love tutor
I love you, love singer
I love you, love pyramid
I love you, Mount Everest of love
I love you, love of love's love
I love you, love marathon
I love you, love manifesto
I love you, love seeding-machine[58]
I love you, masterpieces
I love you, character actors and typecast actors
I love you, performers of the world
I love you, performers of love
I love you, worshippers of eternity
I love you, illustrated collectors' editions[59]
I love you, plagues
I love you, immortal souls

I love you, heroes
I love you, anti-heroes
I love you, heroes of the times
I love you, epistemic authorities
I love you, upper crust
I love you, blips in history
I love you, ambitious guys, brilliant guys, optimistic guys
I love you, noncommittal people
I love you, people who reject other people
I love you, people out for yourselves
I love you, people living open and civilized lives
I love you, people right here[60]
I love you, people with bright futures
I love you, people with big ideals
I love you, people with clear-cut personalities
I love you, people with great acting skills
I love you, methodical people
I love you, consistent people
I love you, kind gracious people
I love you, people who believe in the future
I love you, people with smiling faces
I love you, popular people
I love you, knowbots
I love you, dirty thinkers
I love you, sound of mind and body
I love you, trend followers
I love you, old schoolers
I love you, social animals
I love you, playboys
I love you, boasters
I love you, capitalists
I love you, hypocrites
I love you, pretty boys
I love you, back-stabber guys
I love you, smoke-blower guys
I love you, bull-shitter guys

I love you, gaping-mouthed guys
I love you, well-bred guys
I love you, wishy-washy guys
I love you, guys not worth mentioning
I love you, pessimists
I love you, pacifists
I love you, nihilists
I love you, individualists
I love you, collectivists
I love you, intellectual paupers
I love you, grand-standers
I love you, by-standers
I love you, applause-stealers
I love you, stand-takers
I love you, paupers and misers
I love you, show-offs
I love you, sick people
I love you, cancer patients
I love you, tuberculosis patients
I love you, syphilis patients
I love you, heart disease patients
I love you, liver disease patients
I love you, edema patients
I love you, stroke patients
I love you, diabetes patients
I love you, AIDS patients
I love you, people right here
I love you, ladies and gentlemen
I love you, brothers and sisters
I love you, comrades
I love you, darling comrades in the audience
I love you
I love you
I love you
I love you
I love you

I love you
I love you
I love you

I love tonight right here and now
I love all of you here tonight
I love all of you sitting here in the theatre tonight
I love all of you who have had enough
I love the quick wit from Jiangnan who has had enough
I love the father of folk songs from Xibei who has had enough[61]
I love the prophet of the literary world who has had enough
I love the scientific pioneer[62] who has had enough
I love the movie stars who have had enough
I love the white collar beauty who has had enough
I love the workday lunch that has had enough
I love the campus ballad that has had enough
I love the CCTV Chinese New Year Celebration broadcast that has had
    enough
I love the television serials that have had enough
I love the qigong master who has had enough
I love the ideal husband who has had enough
I love the producer who has had enough
I love the agent who has had enough
I love the emcee who has had enough
I love the publicist who has had enough
I love the rock star who has had enough
I love the corporate star who has had enough
I love the lucky spectator who has had enough
I love the lucky listener who has had enough
I love the honorary consultant who has had enough
I love the columnist who has had enough
I love the tabloid journalist who has had enough
I love the cleaning person who has had enough
I love the radio broadcast serial stories and karaoke that have had
    enough[63]

I love the quack doctors and psychiatrist hotlines who have had enough
I love the cover girls and calendar girls who have had enough
I love Richard Clayderman and Milan Kundera who have had enough[64]
I love the drivers who have had enough
I love the ticket vendors who have had enough
I love the office workers who have had enough
I love the unemployed who have had enough
I love the scholars who have had enough
I love the filmmakers who have had enough
I love those filing lawsuits who have had enough
I love those filing for divorce who have had enough
I love those playing the stock market who have had enough
I love those compiling dictionaries who have had enough
I love those who overeat who have had enough
I love those who overdo it who have had enough[65]
I love that we haven't even started yet and we've had enough
I love that we don't plan to stop yet and we've had enough
I love that I do what I say
I love when you crash to the ground
I love when you're crashing to the ground
I love when you're all crashing to the ground
I love when we're all crashing to the ground
I love when playwrights crash to the ground
I love when directors crash to the ground
I love when the lights crash to the ground
I love when the set crashes to the ground
I love when the curtain crashes to the ground
I love when the theatre crashes to the ground
I love when the earth crashes to the ground
I love when the sky crashes to the ground
I love when the evening breeze crashes to the ground
I love when the clock's chime crashes to the ground
I love when the roadway crashes to the ground
I love when the footsteps crash to the ground
I love when the staircase crashes to the ground
I love when the doorway crashes to the ground

I love when you all crash to the ground
I love when you all storm off
I love when you all crash to the ground on your way home
I love when you all crash to the ground on your beds tonight
I love when you all smile when you're on the road tomorrow
I love that you all hate while you're smiling tomorrow
I love that while you're hating you eat up all the chocolate and burgers
    you can find
I love that you all think lofty thoughts while taking your medicine
I love that you all miss us when you are studying
I love that you make fun of yourselves when you are missing me
I love that you are all restless when you make fun of me
I love that you all secretly make private copies of my scripts
I love that you all secretly circulate copies of my diary
I love you all, clap for me
I love you all, take photos of me
I love you all, give me flowers
I love you all, give me hugs
I love you all, kill me
I love you all wiping your mouths and going off to pray
I love you all, forget me
I love you all wiping your eyes and looking around dazed
I love light
I love and so there was light
I love you
I love and so there was you
I love the stage
I love and so there was the stage
I love leaving
I love and so there was leaving

END OF PLAY

Notes

1 Rossella Ferrari, *Pop Goes the Avant-garde: Experimental Theatre in Contemporary China*. Calcutta: Seagull Press, 2013. The play *I Love XXX* is discussed on pages 191–207.

2 For more on the 2013 production of *I Love XXX*, see Conceison, "China's Experimental Mainstream: The Badass Theatre of Meng Jinghui" in *TDR* (*The Drama Review*), Vol. 58, No. 1 (2014): 64–88.

3 In Chinese, 'XXX' is pronounced '*cha cha cha*'. According to Meng Jinghui, the repetition of capital 'X' expresses opposition/negation (*fouding* 否定), while also having the feel of an ellipsis . . ., and in Chinese, as in English, carries a sexual connotation as well. For a Chinese speaker, the title is playful, subversive, intriguing and suggestive. This text is forthcoming in Claire Conceison (ed.), *Longing for Worldly Pleasures and Other Plays of Meng Jinghui* (Seagull Books). This original translation completed in 2012–3 is independent of an earlier translation by Nancy Tsai; the translator wishes to express her appreciation for Tsai's 1994 unpublished version, which was helpful in identifying intertextual citations and sources in Part Three and in decoding Western names from their transliterations in Chinese characters throughout the play.

4 In the original Chinese script, almost all lines beginning with 'I love . . .' throughout the play have no punctuation. This English translation has adopted the convention in the original script of not ending sentences with periods, but, in consultation with Meng Jinghui, the translator has chosen to add commas within lines. Lines in the play that do not begin with the words 'I love . . .' do have punctuation in the original Chinese script.

5 The spelling of the Manchu surname (clan name) of China's last emperor Puyi (1906–67, ruled 1908–12) varies; it appears here in standard Pinyin Romanisation of the four characters 爱新觉罗, but is also commonly found with the spelling Aisin Gioro.

6 In the original Chinese text, 'star' (*mingxing* 明星) is used as a noun in this section – and Camus is playfully described as a '*shijieguan mingxing*' (世界观明星) or 'world view star'. The translator employs 'star' as an adjective to maintain the repetition, meaning and word play of this section and the invented term 'world viewer' to echo the playfulness of the original line about Camus.

7 The original 1994 Chinese text says 14 April, but the 1900 World Expo opened on 15 April, so the date is changed here with Meng Jinghui's permission.

8 In Chinese, reference to the scandals as '*taose*' (桃色 peach-coloured) indicates sex or infidelity.

9 Here '*kailu*' (开路) and '*kaihuo*' (开火) are translated literally as 'open the road' and 'open fire' to maintain the repetition, pun and meaning of the original Chinese line; however, Chinese readers would also recognise '*kailu*' 开路 as the pidgin Japanese phrase for 'get going', often said by Japanese soldiers in Chinese movies set during the Japanese invasion of China.

10   The date 4 May has a particular connotation in China. Chosen in 1949 as the
     date to celebrate China's annual Youth Day (still observed), it commemorates
     the date of patriotic student demonstrations in 1919 triggered by China's
     weak response to the Treaty of Versailles – the May Fourth movement and
     era (of roughly 1915–21) take their name from this date/event.

11   For this section in performance, the full text is not spoken, but is projected
     on the back wall (or screen) and continuously scrolls for the audience to
     read, while music plays (tune to *Greensleeves* in 1994 Beijing production)
     and actors are visible in dim light.

12   Junkers were German bomber planes (the first all-metal aircraft) originally
     designed by engineer Hugo Junkers in 1915 and used with varying success
     during World War I and World War II. More than one hundred different
     models were manufactured between 1915 and 1940, named sequentially
     (Junkers J 1 to Junkers Ju 390 etc).

13   See note 54 for more on Xu Zhimo.

14   There is a blackout at this point, and, though not indicated in the script, the
     production video indicates that the section that follows is called 'Blackout'.
     When the play was performed, the lines that follow were delivered in the
     darkness by the ensemble, alternating between male and female actors (in
     chorus and individually), sometimes holding lighters.

15   The first six lines are repeated several times (isolated and then overlapping)
     in the original production, first in total darkness and then while documentary
     footage of Mao meeting with world leaders and of the mass demonstrations
     in Tiananmen Square during the Cultural Revolution are projected on a huge
     screen (actors remain in darkness with lighters aflame raised in the air above
     their heads).

16   Allusion to a popular slogan in New China preceding the Cultural
     Revolution: 'Man is sure to triumph over heaven' (人定胜天) that refers to
     the ability of mankind and technology to overpower nature (this carries tragic
     irony in the light of events like the disastrous Great Leap Forward of 1958).

17   In Meng's 1994 production of the play, just before this line, there is a long
     pause during which one actress whistles the well-known tune *Farewell* (送别
     songbie, by Li Shutong, 1927) while standing downstage with remaining
     actors seated in a row on chairs upstage behind her; the next 24 lines are
     spoken by one of the seated actresses and repeated in unison by the ensemble
     (like a teacher and students) while the actress standing downstage in front
     of them remains silent. Then the lines are repeated (beginning with 'I love
     the fatherland') up until 'I love exercise' (with the lines regarding principles,
     discipline, morality and hygiene being negated in repetition – for example,
     'I love morality / I love immorality'), after which a long game of leap frog
     ensues, and the remaining lines up until 'I love Beijing Tiananmen' are uttered
     rapid-fire and increasingly overlapping, merging into a cacophony.

18   Allusion to the first line of *China Youth Vanguard Song*
     (中国少年先锋队队歌): 'We are the Successors of Communism'
     (我们是共产主义接班人).

19 'Five Emphases, Four Beauties, and Three Loves' (五讲四美三热爱) was
    a political policy implemented in 1981: the five emphases (also translated
    as 'five stresses') stressed decorum, manners, hygiene, discipline
    and morals; four beauties were of the mind, language, behaviour and
    environment; three loves were of the fatherland, socialism and the Chinese
    Communist Party.

20 The first part of a familiar slogan used in sports in the 1970s: 'Friendship
    comes first, competition second' (友谊第一，比赛第二).

21 *The Country School Teacher* (1947, also known in English as *A Village
    Schoolteacher*) and *Lenin in October* (1937) are both Soviet films; *Ali Baba
    and the Forty Thieves* (1954) is a German film; *For the Sake of Sixty-One
    Class Brothers* (1960) is a mainland Chinese film. Of the five lines that
    follow, three are titles of well-known books (*Two Hundred Foreign Folk
    Songs, Three Hundred Tang Dynasty Poems, and One Thousand and One
    Nights*), while the other two distort the titles of well-known books in order
    to add "four hundred" and "five hundred" to the playful sequencing – the
    real titles are *Three Hundred Song Dynasty Poems* (宋词三百首 *Songci
    sanbaishou*) and *A Collection of Yuan Dynasty Poems* (元曲选 *Yuanqu xuan*).

22 A 1947 film set in Shanghai and the interior during and after the
    Japanese occupation, its title taken from a line in the famous set of lyrical
    poems *Man jianghong* (满江红) attributed to Song dynasty poet Yue Fei
    (1103–41).

23 China's most popular science book for children (fondly recalled by the
    playwrights during their childhood in the 1970s) offers answers to about
    3,000 questions on 'the mystery of life'. Originally published in 1961, it
    has sold over 100 million copies in China, with the latest edition published
    in 1999 and an updated edition scheduled to be released in 2013. Another
    reason it may have been topical in 1994 when this play was written is
    because popular Hong Kong singer Faye Wong (Wang Fei) released an
    album with the same title (*100,000 Whys*) in 1993.

24 The English language instruction books of famous structural linguist Xu
    Guozhang (1915–94) have sold millions of copies in China since first being
    published in the early 1960s. Meng Jinghui notes that it was rare before the
    Cultural Revolution for an individual like Xu to use his own name as a brand
    this way, and that the books were extremely influential when he and his peers
    were in high school and college during the 1980s.

25 The opening line of a short patriotic song from the revolutionary era
    familiar to all Chinese (followed by the lines 'The sun rises above
    Tiananmen/The great leader Chairman Mao/Leads us forward' In
    Chinese: 我爱北京天安门 / 天安门上太阳升 / 伟大领袖毛主席 /
    指引我们向前进). In Meng's 1994 production of the play, the frenetic action
    ceases just before this line when one actor whistles and the group assembles,
    standing still in a tight formation; after a brief pause, the ensemble repeats
    the line 'I love Beijing Tiananmen' twenty times (the first six times very
    slowly, then progressively faster until it reaches a crescendo). In the context

of the original production occurring five years after the spring 1989 events in Tiananmen Square, the repetition of the line 'I love Beijing Tiananmen' in performance shifts from a nostalgic upbeat song to a painful remembrance of recent local events in which many cast and audience members themselves participated.

26 Hepingmen translates literally as 'Peace Gate' and is a famous roast duke restaurant in Beijing. Qingfeng is a brand of pork-filled steamed buns that go back to just before founding of the People's Republic and have become a popular chain.

27 Xishiku, a Roman Catholic church officially named Church of the Saviour but locally referred to as *Beitang* ('north cathedral'), was founded by Jesuits in 1703 near Zhongnanhai (originally imperial gardens, and now the headquarters of the communist government), then moved to Xicheng district in 1887.

28 PUMCH is a hospital founded by the Rockefeller Foundation in 1921. PLA No. 301 hospital was affiliated with PUMCH until 1953, and is the army's largest general hospital.

29 The first of these, *Zhongguo meishuguan* 中国美术馆 exists, whereas the others are not actually existing museums called by the names given here.

30 East Xiushui Street, known in English as Silk Street or the Silk Market, is a shopping market near many of the international embassies in Beijing, known for knock-off Western fashion items as well as silk garments. The other three streets named here do not actually exist.

31 The first two of these exist and the second two are invented. They allude to various levels of China's national public radio (the national level was first established as Yan'an Xinhua [New China] Broadcasting Station by the Communist Party at Yan'an in 1940 and took its current name in Beijing in December 1949, two months after the establishment of the PRC).

32 Also called Wound Literature (*shanghenwenxue*), the genre emerged in 1977 just after the Cultural Revolution and lasted for two years. Typified by Liu Xinwu's story 'Class Teacher' and Lu Xinhua's 'The Scar', Scar Literature recounted personal tales of suffering during the chaos of the previous decade.

33 Also referred to as the Root-seeking School, Search-for-Roots Literature (*xungenwenxue*) emerged in the 1980s. Defined by essays such as Han Shaogong's 'The Roots of Literature', these works utilised a variety of indigenous Chinese forms and cultures to comment on the present modern condition.

34 The Menglong (or 'misty') poets, such as Bei Dao and Gu Cheng, of the period just after the Cultural Revolution, were so called because their poems were often designated as hazy or obscure, reacting to the previous era of strict socialist realism.

35 The New Era decade was 1979–89.

36 The term for 'avant-garde' in Chinese is *xianfeng* 先锋, which is also the brand name for Pioneer electronics, popular at the time. Meng Jinghui was branded 'avant-garde' in the 1990s and celebrates that status with this self-referential pun.

37 A term coined in 1985 to categorise young poets who had grown up in the 1970s and expressed their voices in the mid-1980s (and distinguished themselves from the Second Generation poets such as the Misty poets). Meng Jinghui collaborated with one of these poets, Xi Chuan, on an experimental production in 2006.

38 A term that refers to a small but influential group of film directors that graduated from the Beijing Film Academy in the early 1980s, including Chen Kaige, Tian Zhuangzhuang and Zhang Yimou.

39 This line and the next one do not refer to actual colloquial terms for recognised collective categories like the previous two lines, but are added as playful inventions.

40 Collective dance, composed of prescribed synchronised movements (some derived from traditional Chinese folk dance), was popular during the Cultural Revolution, and taught to children but also practiced by adults. The best-known example is the 'Loyalty Dance' expressing devotion to Mao Zedong.

41 Allusion to the poem *The Secret of Youth* by Vladimir Maykovsky (1893–1930), one of Meng Jinghui's muses (see especially Meng's film *Chicken Poets*).

42 Allusion to a line from Mayakovsky's poem *The Secret of Youth*. (English translation here is from the Chinese translation of the Russian). The translator thanks Radik Lapushin for assistance in locating the line in the original Russian poem.

43 Beidahuang is a vast agricultural region in Liaoning, northeast China (sometimes referred to as wasteland), and is usually mentioned in the context of youth being sent there during the Cultural Revolution. The drivers' seats referred to here are of tractors.

44 This line and the preceding line refer to China's airforce and navy.

45 Allusion to the line that begins the third and final verse of the poem *Rainy Night* (雨夜) written sometime between 1979 and 1983 by 'misty poet' Bei Dao (1949–), as translated by Bonnie McDougall (*The August Sleepwalker*, New Directions, 1990: 51):

即使明天早上
枪口和血淋淋的太阳
让我交出青春、自由和笔
我也决不会交出这个夜晚
我决不会交出你

46 Allusion to the title and first line of Liang Xiaobin's 1980 poem *China, I've Lost My Key* (中国我的钥匙丢了). The poem exhibits the nostalgia for days of youth during the Cultural Revolution reflected in this 'collective dance' section of the play and also the previous section from the lines 'I love the fatherland' through 'I love Beijing Tiananmen'.

47 Allusion to the line in the poem *Rainy Alley* (雨港) by symbolist poet Dai Wangshu (1905–50): 我希望逢着一个丁香一样地结着愁怨的姑娘 'I hope to meet a girl who carries her worries like lilacs'.

48 Allusion to two lines in the lyrical essay *Lotus Pond by Moonlight*
(荷塘月色) by modernist poet and essayist Zhu Ziqing (1898–1948):
曲曲折折的荷塘上面，弥望的是田田的叶子 'The surface of the winding
lotus pond is covered with fields of leaves' and 荷塘的四面, 远远近近,
高高低低都是树, 而杨柳最多 'Surrounding the lotus pond, near and far,
high and low, trees are everywhere, mostly willows'.

49 Allusion to a famous saying by Confucius: 三人行, 必有我师焉 'When
three men are walking, one is bound to be my teacher'.

50 Allusion to the line in the short story *A Madman's Diary* 狂人日记 by
China's best-known modern writer Lu Xun (1881–1936): 我横竖睡不着,
仔细看了半夜,才从字缝里看出字来, 满本都写着两个字是
'吃人'！ 'Since I could not sleep anyway, I read intently half the night, until
I began to see words between the lines, the whole book being filled with the
two words – "Eat people"!'

51 Allusion to the title of the novel *Half Flame, Half Seawater*
(一半是火焰一半是海水) by Wang Shuo (1958–).

52 The original lines in Chinese are an allusion to the Chinese version of Marx's
preface in *Das Kapital* – the most common English translation is used here.

53 Allusion to the poem *I Sing the Body Electric* by American poet Walt
Whitman (1819–92).

54 Xu (1897–1931) was an early twentieth-century Chinese poet; Lu (1903–65),
a painter, was his second wife. Xu died in a plane crash while flying from
Nanjing to Beijing. A memorial stone to Xu bearing the first and last two
lines of his poem 'Saying Goodbye to Cambridge Again' is on the campus of
King's College, Cambridge, UK.

55 Li Ji (1922–80) wrote the epic ballad-poem *Wang Gui and Li Xiangxiang*
in 1945. It is set during the civil war between the Nationalists and the
Communists and written in the folk song style of Northern Shaanxi province
(Xintianyou); the title names of the couple who are the two main characters.

56 The couple Guo Jing and Huang Rong are the protagonists of the martial arts
novel *The Legend of the Condor Heroes* by Jin Yong (1924–). Huang Rong is
first seen disguised as a beggar after fleeing her father, who raised her alone
on an island and trained her in martial arts.

57 Yamaguchi (1959–) is one of Japan's most popular singers from the 1970s;
at the height of her fame at age 21, she retired to marry movie star Miura
(with whom she had co-starred in several films) and never made a public
appearance or performed again.

58 This line and the preceding line in Chinese (我爱你这个爱情的宣言书 /
我爱你这个爱情的播种机) are allusions to Mao's remarks in a speech
on 27 December 1935 in which he posed a rhetorical question regarding
the significance of the Long March and replied: 'We answer that the Long
March is the first of its kind in the annals of history, that it is a manifesto,
a propaganda force, a seeding-machine' (宣言书、宣传队、播种机),
proceeding to explain further the three analogies. (See http://www.marxists.
org/reference/archive/mao/selected-works/volume-1/mswv1_11.htm.)

59 These special editions (图文并茂的珍藏本) were fancy printings of books (often in a series) with attractive bindings and high-quality illustrations.

60 This line and others in this section refer in the second person collectively to the audience.

61 Jiangnan refers to the area south of the lower Yangtze River. Xibei is Northwest China.

62 The Chinese term here is 报春鸟 (bao chun niao), a bird that announces the coming of spring, so a more playful term such as 'scientific nightingale' could be used if the symbolic meaning of nightingale as a muse or literal meaning as a European early morning and early spring bird would come across in English.

63 Radio serial dramas and karaoke were popular trends in the 1990s.

64 Clayderman (1953–) is a French pianist extremely popular in Asia; Kundera (1929–) is a Czech novelist living in exile in France since 1975.

65 The preceding line uses the phrase 吃饱了 (chi baole) meaning that one has eaten to the point of being full, and this line puns on the one before it by using the phrase 吃饱了撑的 (chi baole chengde) which is usually said to someone who does something impulsive or outrageous, such as kicking over a trashcan.

Bicycle

O Tae-sŏk

Translated by Ah-jeong Kim and R. B. Graves

Korea is the 'shrimp between two whales', positioned geographically between China and Japan. The Korean language 'is the foundation of a national culture' that has been influenced by China and Japan, including Confucian ethics and enforced colonial modernity under Japanese occupation, but has remained unique and distinctive.[1] At the end of the nineteenth century, the land was a unified kingdom called Chosŏn (from the Chinese name Chaoxian – 'Land of Morning Calm').[2] In 1895, China gave up its stake in Chosŏn following its defeat in the Sino-Japanese war. In 1905, similarly, Russia was forced to give up its interest in the kingdom following defeat by Japan. In the same year, Japan declared Korea a protectorate, finally annexing and colonising it in 1910.

Japan's colonisation lasted until 1945 and defeat in World War II. Korea was then partitioned between the Soviet-occupied North and the American-occupied South. In 1948 this division was made permanent into the Republic of Korea (South Korea) and the Democratic People's Republic of Korea (North Korea). In 1950 the North invaded the South, launching the Korean War, which lasted until a ceasefire in 1953. In South Korea, a military dictatorship controlled the nation from 1961 to 1993, followed by democratic civilian rule until the present. This legacy of oppression, colonisation and tragedy manifests itself in Korean culture, including theatre.

Shingŭk, the modern Korean theatre, was patterned after shingeki, the modern Japanese theatre, as part of Japan's aggressive cultural colonisation. Nevertheless, shingŭk also became a form of resistance literature. Much of twentieth-century South Korean theatre is a search for Korean identity and a form of nationalism that both resist the oppression of the dictatorship while also resisting communism of the North.

O Tae-sŏk, postwar Korea's leading (and arguably most innovative) playwright, was born in 1940 in rural central South Korea, studied philosophy at Yonsei University, but became an experimental theatre artist in the sixties despite having no formal theatrical training, except for a brief period in New York City in which he encountered avant-garde and experimental theatre. He founded Mokwha (Raw Cotton Repertory Company) in 1984, which he still serves as artistic director, chief playwright, acting teacher and director. His plays are avant-garde, combining Western drama and traditional Korean performance and rooted in a search for 'Korean-ness', a particularly Korean ethos. In particular, he explores Korean history through hybrid theatre, combining shamanic rituals, traditional Korean theatre elements, Western dramaturgy and an inventive theatricality.

As an adapter and director, O has blended Shakespeare on stage, and his productions of *Romeo and Juliet* and *The Tempest* have been performed internationally. His aesthetic is both visual and physical, seeking to use movement and powerful images to convey emotion and meaning. He rejects Western-style pictorial realism and has argued that a play does not need to follow a linear, logical story line but rather should unfold in image, language and moment. His directing and playwriting shape each other profoundly, and rehearsal is the final step in textual creation. The play is not complete until O has explored it extensively with actors, finding the final form once it reaches an audience.

His significant works include *T'ae* (Lifecord, 1974), *Ch'unp'ung ŭi ch'ŏ* (Ch'unp'ung's Wife, 1976), *Pujayujin* (Intimacy Between Father and Son, 1987), *Shim-ch'ŏngginŭn wae indangsue tubŏn ŭl tŏnjŏt nŭnga* (Why Did Shim Chong Plunge into the Indang Sea Twice?, 1990) and *Toraji* (Bellflower, 1992), all of which have been staged multiple times since their initial productions.

Chajŏngŏ (Bicycle) was written in 1983, based on an event that happened in Oh's home village of Sŏch'ŏn during the Korean War. In September 1950, retreating North Korean People's Liberation Army troops rounded up 127 suspected anti-communists, locked them in the town registry building, then set the building on fire, burning all inside to death. Rather than dramatise the incident, O presents a stream-of-consciousness ghost story that moves back and forth between past and present on bicycles. This journey is not meant to be read literally – time and place are always fluid on O's stage.

The play begins in 1980, on the thirtieth anniversary of the massacre, with Yun Chin and his colleague returning from work. Yun reports encountering a ghost and we learn of his family history, in which one of his uncles was a local soldier ordered to start the fire which also killed Yun's father. The audience also encounters a family dealing with a legacy of leprosy and the fears and pariah status the disease conveys. O uses these two plots and the recurring image of the bicycle to interrogate Korean history and the scars (in this case literalised on the face of Yun Chin's uncle) of the Korean War.

Bicycle

[*Chajŏngŏ*, 1983]

Cast of Characters:

YUN CHIN, *a clerk of the town registry office*
KU, *another clerk of the town registry office*
IM, *a schoolteacher*
HAN, *a villager, father of the House of Geese*
YOUNG WOMAN, *thought to be the eldest daughter of the House of Geese*
CHILD, *thought to be the second daughter of the House of Geese*
Man from SOLMAE, *a leper*
His WIFE, *also a leper*
An herbal DOCTOR, *now deceased*
OLD MAN
HWANG SOK-KU, *a crippled liquor distiller*
Two GRAVE DIGGERS
YOUNG MAN, *a mourner*
OWNER *of Persimmon-Tree House*
His SERVANT
VOICE *of a North Korean soldier*
YUN CHIN'S UNCLE *from Yesan, a survivor of the registry fire*
SO KWAN-HO, *the other survivor of the registry fire*

TOWN REGISTRY OFFICE

Yun How about writing an absence report for me?

Ku What do you want me to say?

Yun Well, listen, here's a rough draft. (*Reading from a note in his hand*) 'One night I fainted because the ghost of a young woman called out to me from her grave by the side of the road. I was so scared that I began to shake and, later, I got sick. Because of this, I missed forty-two days of work. Whereupon I submit this report of absence.'

Ku   You're going to send that in?

Yun   Well, I guess I have to, unless I make up some outright lies, because that's what happened. This is why I really need your help.

Ku   But what happened? You've got to tell me the whole thing.

Yun   (*Pause*) I was having a rough day. I'd turned in my high school friend to the police for practicing medicine without a license. He was just a quack. All he knew about medicine was what he had learned in the army as a nurse. I couldn't let him keep doing that. So, I sent a report about him to the police station. I was about to have a cigarette when I found this girl about fourteen or fifteen standing right in front of me holding a medical report issued by the Provincial Hospital. Said she came to register the death of her sister. But the family registry worker had already left for the day. I asked where she came from. 'Munjang Village,' she said. She'd come a long way, so I handled her case and did the paperwork. Her sister had died of tuberculosis at age nineteen, worst luck . . .

Ku   Was that the girl? The ghost you ran into? You said somebody called to you.

Yun   (*Shaking his head*) I'm not sure if I heard a voice. I was totally discombobulated. It was like I was drowning in water.

Ku   Wait a second. You're skipping part of the story. I don't follow you. So what happened after you took care of the death certificate at the office?

Yun   I had a couple of drinks at Naesan's. I was feeling real out of sorts. For the first time in my life I had turned in someone knowing that it would hurt a lot of people. So, I had a few drinks. Later, the Naesan woman told me to leave my bicycle behind, since it would be difficult to drag along. But I felt sort of empty without it, so I decided to push it beside me as I walked. I thought I walked pretty far, but in fact I'd barely climbed over Nokpae Hill. (*He starts walking, dragging along his bicycle which has been parked beside him.* KU *follows.*)

NOKPAE HILL

(**Im**, *an elementary school teacher, approaches from one side, dragging his bicycle. He is holding a flashlight.* **Ku** *steps to the other side.* **Yun** *and* **Im** *park their bicycles in one corner of the stage.*)

Im   On your way home now? It's real late.

Yun   How about you? You on night duty?

Im   Oh, no, the family's holding the memorial service at the big house, you know. I guess you'll be having a memorial service tonight, too, eh?

Yun   Is tonight the eighth? I almost forgot.

Im   (*Lighting a cigarette, squats down*) They delivered the memorial stone to the town registry building. Said it came from Hongsong. Anyhow, it's a black stone.

Yun   Black, you say? Must be obsidian, after all the talk about marble.

Im   It's good, hard stone. Besides, black's right for a memorial.

Yun   They're supposed to have it up before the end of the year, I hear.

Im   It took them three years just to decide on the stone. (*Holding the cigarette in his mouth, starts off with his bike*) We might have frost tonight, what with all this fog. Down below there's a hut near the stone bridge. You'll see a light there, but watch your step in the dark.

Yun   I see. Goodbye. You take care of yourself, too.

(**Im** *exits.*)

Ku   (*Coming forward*) What are they building at the registry?

Yun   The memorial, you see. Don't you know about it? During the occupation, the town registry – that's where the town registry building used to be before the war. They say a hundred twenty-seven people, most of them pretty well known in this town, were locked up inside it, accused of being anticommunists. The nationalist army was pushing up from the south. The bastards from the north were in the middle of retreating, so they set fire to the building with everyone inside. Tonight, at least a hundred families are holding memorial services for the dead. No, not this way, it'll only confuse you. Why don't we do it like this? I'll do exactly what I did that night, so you won't have to try to figure out what it was like. Just imagine it's happening tonight.

Ku   All right. We'll pretend it's all happening tonight. Then what?

Yun   I thought about taking a nap in a seedbed of rice. But I couldn't because I remembered that my uncle from Yesan would be making a scene at my house, cutting his face with a piece of glass and . . . (*Shaking his head*) He was there at the registry building, you see, the night of the fire. Just two men survived, and he happened to be one of them. Let's see, my father's his older brother. My uncle says it's shameful he came out alive – that he didn't save his brother. On each anniversary night, he takes over the living room and cuts his face with a piece of glass. (*With his finger, he mimes cutting across his forehead*) He gouges in, line by line, like the furrows of a rice field . . . the blood dripping down his face. (*Shakes his head and pushes the bicycle along*) If we go down a little more, it's only three miles to Shintulmae Gully. There's a couple of houses there. The house of lepers is farther on in Solmae, and right before an intersection that leads up a hill called Saengbae is another house. The family there's called the House of Geese because they raise geese. His name's Han, though – he's a good man, a living Buddha, to tell the truth, but his wife's got a bad case of epilepsy. He and his wife haven't lived near a soul for some twenty years now. Once he wanted to plant some things in a small lot out behind his house, so I helped him get a permit to work it. Somehow or other Han thinks I gave him the land. Every day he comes out to say hello. Look at him. Even this late at night, he's waiting for me.

THE HOUSE OF GEESE

(**Han** *has been looking over a fence made of trifoliate orange trees. Seeing* **Yun** *approaching,* **Han** *walks around the fence to greet him.* **Han** *holds a small box which he ties to the rear set of* **Yun**'s *bicycle.* **Ku** *steps aside.*)

Yun   Now, what are you tying on there?

Han   I gathered some *todok* roots for you. But I don't think they're big enough to put on the memorial altar.

Yun   But I could be fired for taking a bribe, you know.

Han   (*Taking out a small folded note from his sleeve*) Just a while ago, back home, my kids read this note for me. I couldn't imagine the little one would do such a thing. (*Lights a match so that* **Yun** *can read the note*)

Child's voice   (*As* **Yun** *reads the note*) Weather, clear. I helped my sister Chi-yong with her homework in handicrafts by cutting up two potatoes. I hear the sound of a train coming from town. Is that train going up north or going down south? Which train should I take? I don't know.

Han   That's my number two. She's only fourteen.

Yun   She ran away? When?

Han   After lunch, nobody saw her. If she took the train like she says here, she must've gone to the city. But I never thought she could do such a thing.

Yun   Does she know anyone in the city?

Han   Nobody. Who would she know? She's never been outside this town, not even to the market.

Yun   But who gave you this note? What did your oldest one say?

Han   All she can do is choke back tears.

Yun   Let me talk to her for a second.

Han   (*Calling over the fence*) Hey! Are you there? (*Goes around the fence into the house*)

Yun   (*To* **Ku**.) You've got to promise me something now. Don't tell anyone what you're going to hear – what the oldest one and I talked about. Just listen and think about it.

(**Ku** *nods. Suddenly, there is the sound of honking as* **Han**, *chasing geese in one direction, goes away into the backyard of the house. The sound of two people talking is heard. A* **young woman**, *about twenty years old, comes out. One notices her peculiar demeanor even before her shabby clothes. She neither bows nor looks at* **Yun**. *As a consequence, she may appear to be a person of low intelligence who is stubborn and insensitive. She speaks as if she were talking to herself, unaware of* **Yun's** *presence.*)

Young woman   (*Pause*) I sent my sister away.

Yun   What do you mean, 'sent her away'?

Young woman   Last year they brought us a newborn baby from the house across the way.

Yun   From the house of lepers?

Young woman   My sister would have been shocked to find out that we adopted the baby. One day last month, she asked me if she came from the same family.

Yun   Did anyone else come from that house?

Young woman   (*Pause Nods*) A boy. He started grammar school this year. My sister didn't know anything about us taking him in because she was too young then even to know what adoption was.

Yun   So what happened? Did she figure out she came from the same house?

Young woman   Their house is a lot farther away than it looks. But whenever she saw anything in front of it, she started shaking – like my mom does in one of her fits. At night, when I'm sleeping, she comes over and examines my face, feels it with her hand, over and over, and then checks her own face. Then she stares into my eyes, and that scared me to death. (*She shudders*) I drove her out because I was scared. Anyway, she couldn't live that way. Neither could I.

Yun   But where could she have gone? How could you drive her away like that? Do you mean to the lepers' house?

Young woman   (*Startled, crouches down, embracing herself by grabbing her elbows. She gags several times as if something were caught in her throat.*) I wonder if she did go to the house over there. Once I saw her grab a goose by the neck and twist it. She said that in a dream her mom came to see her and that a goose bit off her mom's finger. Now she was twisting the goose for the finger, because she wanted to give it back to her mom.

Yun   Did she come from the lepers' house, then?

Young woman   She came along when I was six. I don't know. (*Suddenly stares at him*) Did she come from there, too?

Yun   I asked you that question.

Young woman   In my dream, I. . . . I. . . . I set fire to that house. In a dream . . .

Yun   Are you all right? Is she all right now?

Young woman   I can't even hang the wash up on the line. When I see clothes swaying in the wind, I feel sick because they look like the people from that house. While making a fire, if I hear wood cracking, I count the fingers on my hand, because I think a finger broke off and is burning like a stick of kindling. If *I'm* like this, can you imagine what was going through that little girl's mind? Poor thing. I didn't drive her away to die. I didn't. I wanted her to live. I wanted her to go far away and forget mom and me and . . . live!

Yun   But you're old enough to know what the world's like. How could you chase her out of the house like that? Did you reckon she could beg meals out there? She can't beg for food, you know.

Young woman   But that's her fate.

Yun   I can't believe what she's saying. Do you think your father gets anything for raising you children?

Young woman   (*Quivers in anger*) The girl who ran away didn't think so. She washed the little ones and rocked them to sleep. She loved them very much. She was simply scared. She ran away out of fear. Fear.

(*She turns away to go inside the house. The sound of geese erupts several times and then subsides. A sense of gloom falls over the stage.*)

Yun   (*To* **Ku**.) I'd gotten into it this far, so I decided to walk toward the house at Solmae.

Ku   To the lepers' house – so late at night? To do what?

Yun   Well, what else could I do? I had this sinking feeling in my chest, thinking about the little girl, nowhere to be found, far away from home. (*Walks his bicycle. A bell attached to the wheels rings a couple of times. As if in response to this, geese honk wildly, but then their sounds rapidly subside.*) You see? These days, the most common thing in the world around here is a runaway kid. And once a kid runs away, she's gone, and that's it. At least you can do something about a quack who cuts open people's guts without knowing the first thing about medicine. All you have to do is turn him in. but with a runaway child, it's different. What drove her away from home? – I just had to find out, don't you see? And whose kid is she anyway? – That's what I had to find out first. So I started walking toward Solmae. And I saw the man from Solmae coming from the opposite direction. Like he was waiting for me.

(*Out of the darkness, the man from the Solmae house of lepers emerges. He is wearing a worn-out plastic bag over his clothes tied around his waist with a string, like fishermen are normally dressed. A towel is wrapped around his face and a straw hat sits on top of his head, over the towel. He offers* **Yun** *two boxes of candles by politely extending both hands, on which he wears long, red plastic gloves.*)

Solmae   I heard you were holding a memorial service tonight.

Yun   (*Takes the candle boxes and tucks them under straps on the rear carrying-rack of his bicycle*) How are you doing these days?

Solmae   Well, it looks like we'll be doing so-so this year. Peppers may be okay, but the cabbages don't look good at all. Maybe the seeds were bad; the cabbage leaves are all turning kind of yellow. Seems like they won't do as good as other people's, anyway. Now, watch your step as you go.

(As he disappears into darkness, the rustling noise of his plastic clothes trails behind him.)

Ku   You know, you seem to get more respect around here than a cabinet minister. I don't think most people would bring out a box of candles on a night like this, even if a damned cabinet minister walked by.

Yun   It's only because the man is lonely.

Ku   But, by the way, you forgot to ask him whose child the girl was.

Yun   I couldn't, what with him popping out like that all of a sudden. Anyway, I felt somehow it wasn't the right moment.

Ku   Yeah, you're right. Besides, it's really the House of Geese's problem. *(Starts rolling the bicycle beside him. The bell on the bicycle wheel rings.)*

Yun   Over there, sitting in the outhouse by the three-way intersection, is the herbal doctor who passed away at the time of the registry fire.

Ku   What?

Yun   At first I thought some guy from another town had taken one drop too many. *(He parks his bicycle and sits on its seat.)*

THREE-WAY INTERSECTION

(A small, temporary outhouse for farmers is seen. Without a roof, it consists entirely of three walls of sedge mat only waist-high. An apparition of a **doctor***, once a practitioner of Chinese herbal medicine, is seated inside the outhouse with only his face showing. He wears a traditional outer coat, as he did while alive. As the heavy fog gathers, he appears at first glance to be bathing in a muddy lake, with his head just above water.)*

Doctor   Got a light?

*(***Yun*** gets off his bicycle, his head darting in all directions. He listens.* **Yun's** *movements are slightly confused in this scene; the confusion is particularly evident in how he gauges distance and direction.)*

Doctor   Got a light?

Yun   Yes.

Doctor   It's me. Me.

Yun   But . . . who are you?

Doctor   Give me a light.

Yun   Yeah. . . . I'm just looking for a match here.

(*He strikes a match, but his shaking hands cause the matches remaining in the match box to rattle. The burning match illuminates the* **doctor's** *face, which does not yet have a cigarette in its mouth. The* **doctor** *blows it out again.* **Yun** *lights yet another match.*)

Yun   Ouch! It's hot! Are you drunk or something? (*Rubs the inside of his hand.*)

Ku   What do you keep striking matches for? You've been drinking too much lately. If you keep tossing it down like that, you'll have a hell of a time when you're old, you know.

Yun   (*To the* **doctor**.) Did you get the light?

Doctor   Are you the grandson of Se-hwan from Hangaengee?

Yun   Yes, I am. But who are you?

Doctor   Riding on a bike like that, you look exactly like your grandfather. Just like him.

Yun   How did you know my grandfather?

Doctor   I left your dad just now. Your dad must be home by now. You should hurry, it's late.

Yun   Where did you two go?

Doctor   We went to the market to get some arrowroots. We couldn't find anything good, though. There was only a handful of them and they were only the size of my finger. Much too small. Why are you standing there like that? Go home. Hurry up, now!

Yun   Okay, okay, I'm going. Take care.

Doctor   Go on. I'm done here, too.

(**Yun** *unlocks the bicycle and lifts it up to put on his shoulder as if he were crossing a stream. He falters backwards a few steps. The* **doctor** *stands up, pulls up his trousers, and wraps a belt around his waist. The old man is quite meticulous in carefully unwrapping the straw string that had been holding the long outer clothes around his waist. Coming out of the outhouse, he tucks a broken straw broom [which he had put aside] in a cleft of the sedge mat of the outhouse and walks* *away leisurely.* **Yun**, *still holding his bicycle on his shoulder, watches as the old man disappears.* **Ku**, *who has been hidden by fog, emerges. In this scene,* **Ku** *has not been able to see the* **doctor**. *He can only conjecture from* **Yun**'s *strange behavior that* **Yun** *has encountered an apparition.*)

Ku   So you stood there like that the whole time?

Yun   (*Parks his bicycle*) You saw the old man, didn't you? He was having a grand old time here in the outhouse. (**Ku** *shakes his head.*) Didn't you hear us talking?

Ku   I did, but I only heard you say, 'Who are you? . . . Yeah, I'm just looking for a match here. . . . Did you get a light?' What did he say?

Yun   He's already gone.

Ku   (*As if warming his hand over a fire, he stretches his hand to touch the broken broom tucked in the cleft of the outhouse.*) But what does your grandfather have to do with it? You were talking to him, too.

Yun   Yosubaemi Lake is on the way to the Saengbae fields, isn't it? My grandfather drowned in the lake on his way back from seeing his mistress in town. He was talking about it.

Ku   Is the lake deep enough to drown in?

Yun   Oh, no. Even when the lake's high, the water only comes up to your chest. Even so, my grandfather died mysteriously with his head above water, sitting on his bike. He died sitting straight up, pretty as a picture.

Ku   The bike was on top of the water?

Yun   (*Parks his bicycle.*) Well, they say the bike was standing just like this, right in the middle of Yosubaemi Lake.

Ku   But who did it?

Yun   We don't know. Everybody felt it was some sort of foul play, but there was never any evidence. We always thought someone might have done something to him because, before independence, he'd been a policeman at the station. I pass by the lake all the time, but I've never seen him. Then this doctor was telling me that I look exactly like my grandfather.

Ku   Look here, do you see these ghosts a lot?

Yun   The souls are busy tonight.

Ku   You know, you need to find yourself a goat, a whole goat, cook it real good, and eat it like medicine. And if I were you, I wouldn't eat just one, but a whole lot of them.

Yun   Didn't you hear me screaming 'It's hot!' after lighting one of the matches? I thought the head of a match had stuck to the palm of my hand. But it didn't. Later I found a scratch from somebody's fingernail. (*Opening his palm*) Here. Ah, it's healed now. This is the scratch.

Ku   It works, you know. Goat's the only cure for this.

Yun   I saw a lot of blood on my palm.

Ku   It's not good to see ghosts so much. Have a goat or two before things get out of hand. I know a guy who was guarding a melon patch at night who saw some ghosts. He raced out of the shed to catch them. They found him later – drowned in the reservoir. In fact, it was Brother Il-yol who died that way.

Yun   Is that right? He died like that, huh?

(*They both walk their bicycles, and the bells on the wheels ring. In the distance, an* **old man** *is seen crouching down, hanging a small lantern in a crab-fishing hut.*)

Ku   Well now, somebody's taking some time off. Free time like that's hard to come by these days.

Yun   That man closed his cloth shop last year after he got robbed walking back from P'angyo Market. He sits there hoping to catch the robber. The district manager says he'll catch him someday.

CRAB-FISHING HUT AT THE STONE BRIDGE

(*A humpbacked stone bridge only ten feet long and four feet wide; although quite small, it is made of a single huge stone. It is old and magnificent, as though someone long ago had sculpted a turtle-shaped memorial stone and placed it across the river. Under one end of the bridge is a crab-fishing hut made of straw, shaped like a kitchen drainer turned upside-down. An* **old man** *arranges a lantern in the hut so that its light lures crabs into a net as they crawl up toward the rice fields. The* **old man** *is a rural villager who has managed to purchase a rice field by peddling cloth in the city. Used to a life of wandering, he habitually leaves home to visit the hut.* **Yun** *parks his bicycle and approaches the hut, while* **Ku** *sits on the stone bridge.*)

Yun   You've caught quite a few crabs this evening.

Old man   Who are you? – Hush, listen to that! Did you hear it?

Yun   What?

Old man   (*Listens*) They must be butchering something down in the valley – on the sly. They were making noises like that the other night, and they're doing it again tonight.

Yun   Butchering down in the valley?

Old man   Sure, they do it there because it's near the river spring but far away from people passing by.

(*The two men listen for a moment.* **Yun** *catches a crab, takes it from the net, and puts it in a bucket.*)

Yun   Ah, this one keeps running away from me.

Old man   It mustn't be.

Yun   I hear someone coming.

(*A crippled liquor distiller,* **Hwang Sok-ku***, emerges from the darkness. Infuriated about something, he is breathing hard and also drags a bicycle. On the rear of his bike are two white plastic liquor barrels hanging on either side of the rear wheel.*)

Hwang   No one's going to believe this. Who could believe that I, Hwang Sok-ku, just took a dive into the manure pile because a cow kicked me in the butt? Not one soul in this town would believe such a story except me, Hwang Sok-ku. Damn it!

Old man   What's that smell? Why the hell did you come around here smelling like that? Get out of here!

Hwang   Well, thanks a lot! If I go to the shop like this, it'll stink up the liquor.

Old man   So, instead, you decide to splash shit around here when I'm trying to catch crabs?

Hwang   You know the Persimmon-Tree House over at Sondong Village? With an outhouse right beside the cow shed? I was in the outhouse minding my own business. The plank under my left foot creaked – it wasn't put in right. So I bent over to fix it, and, god almighty, this thing called a cow must have thought my butt was a barn or something. It bumped me hard right in the ass. I could easily be dead by now with my nose stuck in a pile of shit. I was so pissed off, I decided to show it who was boss – me, Hwang Sok-ku. So I say to the cow, 'Now, you're dead!' And I grabbed that cow by the horns and kicked it hard, right in the stomach. It started jumping around, all over the place, till it leaps out of the shed, smashing up everything. So I shout, 'The cow's jumping! The cow's jumping!' And the whole family runs out of the house and chases after it.

Yun   Good heavens! What a mess for them!

Hwang   Who gives a damn about somebody else's troubles around here? There was a big fuss tonight at your house, too, you know.

Yun   Was our cow jumping around, too?

Hwang   The old man's face . . . oh, god . . . it looked like a snake shedding its skin. The blood poured down his face . . . over his eyes and nose. His whole face was red, covered with blood. I can't describe it.

(**Yun** *climbs up the stone bridge where* **Ku** *is standing;* **Hwang** *and the* **old man** *freeze.*)

Yun   (*To* **Ku**) Here now, remember that part of the story – when the cow was running wild, 'cause I think I heard the sound of a cow jumping myself.

Ku   A cow jumping at night?

Yun   Farther away, though, over in Shintulmae Gully.

Ku   Then the guy's story isn't hogwash, is it?

Yun   Well, I don't know about that.

Ku   But the Old Man said something about a cow, too, didn't he?

Yun   Eh?

Ku   Didn't he say something about people making noise, butchering something? That there was some funny business going on across the gully?

Yun   All he saw was a couple of guys putting sod on a grave. A couple of days later, I found out they were secretly burying someone – the dead girl from Munjang Village. I ran into them later.

(**Yun** *steps down to the hut, and* **Hwang** *resumes speaking in his previous manner.*)

Hwang   And this guy was having a big fight with Tong-son's mother. Tong-son's family farmed a small field right over your father's grave, didn't they?

Yun   Yeah, I know this spring they worked some land – no bigger than the back of my hand.

Hwang   Tong-son's family must have been fertilizing it. This guy was complaining that putting fertilizer on top of a grave was disrespectful to the dead. But who was that guy? Is he related to you?

Yun   He's my uncle from Yesan. Every year on the anniversary night of my father's death, he cuts his face with a piece of broken glass.

Hwang   Come to think of it, tonight's the memorial night for the old registry building.

Old man   Hush. . . . Listen to that.

Hwang   What is it?

Old man   Don't you hear a noise from the gully?

Hwang   On the way over here I saw some people putting sod on a grave.

Yun   Sodding a grave – at night?

Old man   I thought they were secretly killing something.

Hwang   I'm gonna catch those guys. Just you wait and see.

Old man   But how can you with your legs?

Hwang   What do you mean with my legs? These legs did just fine when I was the first nationalist solider to make it back to town after we pushed the North Koreans out. I rode into town with Korean flags stuck all over my bicycle.

Yun   You don't say! Flags flying on your bike, eh?

Hwang   You bet. The mayor of Kilsan had fixed up a bike with flags all over it to welcome us. I asked him if my brother was okay, and he gave the bike to me. Told me to go home. I was peddling it across Saengbae field. People had just begun harvesting the rice. I could see my house in the distance. (*He shouts an exclamation of tearful relief.*) Aigoo! I was crying like a baby. I yelled out at the top of my lungs, 'I'm coming home! I'm coming home alive!' I saw the townspeople running toward me, and I got off the bike. Then I felt this sharp pain in my leg. It was a bamboo knife, wider than my hand, sticking out of my leg like a cow's horn. Somehow his gigantic knife got stuck deep in my leg. *Aigoo!* I fainted when I saw it. (*He pulls up his pants to show the scar.*)

Yun   I never knew that before. I always thought you got hurt in the war. But who would do such a thing?

Hwang   The old man, Chi-hwan. He died soon after that.

Old man   He'd been tortured for keeping the night school going during the occupation and went crazy.

Hwang   Damn it all! I was so sad when Chi-hwan passed away. (*Blows his nose*) Well, what are you standing around here for? Get home fast. Your uncle was starting to calm down, but who knows what he's up to by now.

(**Yun** *rolls along on his bicycle. The bell from the bicycle rings.*)

SHINTULMAE GULLY

Ku   Do you remember your father?

Yun   Not at all. I was barely a year old when he passed away.

Ku   So you don't have any memories of him?

Yun   I'm just like my mom. I think of my uncle from Yesan as my father, just like she does.

Ku   What did your father do for a living?

Yun   He was assistant principal at the school. Once he fell out of a persimmon tree at school and broke his foot. So every day he had to stick his foot in the damn urine bucket. My mom says his left shoulder got permanently bent out of shape – like this. She does a good imitation of him, but I can't.

(*At this moment, two* **grave diggers** *emerge from the darkness at the other side of the stage. One is carrying a small coffin in his traditional backpack [A-frame carrier], while the other's backpack is empty. A* **young man** *wearing a mourner's hemp cap follows the* **grave diggers**. **Yun** *and* **Ku** *step aside to allow them to pass by.*)

Yun   Where are you all going?

Young man   To Oejang.

Yun   Where's Oejang?

Young man   Past Kwiam.

Yun   That's a long way to go, did you know that?

Young man   And we have to take the back roads.

Yun   It'll take you a lot longer that way. You'll have to hurry to get there before dawn.

(*The* **grave diggers** *quickly disappear.*)

Yun   From the looks of them, I think they're grave diggers.

Ku   If they aren't, what's that coffin for?

Yun   To trick people like me. I turned the corner, see? Here we are. Now you take the bicycle – it'll make it easy to explain exactly what happened. (**Ku** *takes over the bicycle.*) I came around the corner and thought I saw a fox in the distance. But it vanished just like that. A second later the girl from the House of Geese steps up behind my bicycle.

(*A* **child**, *the second daughter of the House of Geese, sits on the rear rock of* **Yun's** *bicycle.* **Ku** *acts as* **Yun** *in this scene, while* **Yun** *continues to explain the situation.*)

Ku   Good heavens! What's this now? Where did you come from?

(*The* **child** *freezes catatonically as if she were a stage prop. Not even a hair moves. Her face is frozen with fear. It is clear that* **Yun** *must have used a great deal of patience to coax her into speaking.*)

Ku   So she didn't go to the train station after all?

Yun   She was scared.

Ku   Well why didn't she go home?

Yun   She was scared.

Ku   But what was she going to do?

Yun   Nothing. She was just trembling. She'd been in the graveyard all by herself. Can you imagine what it must have been like? When she heard the sound of my bike, she ran down to the road thinking it might be her schoolteacher or the town clerk. She just started running down here. But I worked on her, coaxed her little by little. Finally I talked her into going back home. Then I turned the bike in the other direction. Now, turn the bike around.

(**Ku** *turns the bike. The* **child** *sits on the rear rack. A strange and subtle change comes over her. She straightens from the waist up and leans forward, staring ahead.*)

Yun   I lit the candles on the bike to calm her down. Light two candles, please.

(**Ku** *stations the bicycle so he can take candles out of the box that the Solmae leper gave to* **Yun**. **Yun** *makes a fire with some paper taken from a plastic bag.* **Ku** *attaches the two candles to the handlebars by tying them with straw. The candles swing enchantingly. Completely lost in thought, the* **child** *stares at the candle flames.*)

Yun   I asked if she knew who I was, and I told her that I was the town clerk, Yun. She nodded. I told her not to worry about her dad because I'd tell him nice things about her. Then I was hoping to bring her out of it, so I told her the story of the bicycle with the Korean flags. I said, 'There was a big war a long time ago. A soldier was coming home from battle after winning the war. He rode across Saengabe field riding a bike with Korean flags on each handlebar. They say he shouted, "I'm coming home! I'm coming home alive!" Well now, you're riding with candles instead of flags. So why don't you yell like the soldier? "I'm coming home! I'm coming back home!"'

(*At this moment the* **child** *lets out a shriek, jumps down from the bicycle, and starts pulling it backwards as if she were in a rope-pulling contest. She screams with fear, and with her finger indicates that someone is coming from the direction the bicycle faces.* **Ku** *and the bicycle tumble down together,* **Ku***'s body intertwined with the bicycle. The child quickly disappears into the darkness.*)

Ku   Where's she going? Why's she doing that?

Yun   She grabbed my waist. Said someone's coming. I couldn't hear a thing, but she was sure somebody was coming – that we had to run away from whoever it was. I tried to calm her down, but she bit my hand and ran away. So I said, 'Stop,' and turned my bicycle around to find a man standing in my way.

(*From the side opposite to the direction in which the* **child** *ran, there is a rustling of a plastic garment. The Solmae leper appears as before.*)

Ku   Where are you going?

Solmae   I heard my kid ran away from home.

Yun   I asked what he was talking about as he didn't have any kids.

Ku   Your kid? You don't have any children, do you?

Solmae   I mean the child of the House of Geese. She ran away.

Yun   (*Prompting* **Ku**.) 'But she's not the House of Geese's kid, is she? I know all about it.' You see, I was trying to pressure him.

Ku   But she's not really the child of the House of Geese, is she? You put her up for adoption when she came along, didn't you? I know all about it!

(*The Solmae leper collapses to the ground as if someone had kicked him in the stomach. From the ground he bows twice and murmurs the following speech while rubbing his hands together, still wearing red plastic gloves. His murmuring is such that it is not clear whether he is speaking or weeping.*)

Solmae   Please forgive me! We only wanted her to live a normal life. To live like a normal person. I did it – a damned leper, living in hell – I did it, and I wasn't afraid of god at all.

Yun   'But it's not just the one kid,' I said. 'It's all the children.' I bullied him – said that if he really wanted to see his children have a normal life, he should just disappear, burn his house down, and go far away.

Ku   (*Acting as* **Yun**, *addresses the leper*) You've got to leave the children alone. Only if you leave them alone can they live like ordinary people. Listen to me. Set your house on fire and leave town tonight.

Yun   As I was speaking, I saw a red flame from the direction of Solmae.

(*In the distance, the night sky grows red.*)

Ku   What's that fire? Isn't that your house?

Solmae   Oh, my lord! My wife! Get out of there! You've got to get out! Please forgive me. Oh, no. What am I going to do?

(*Clutching at the air, he disappears into the darkness.*)

Ku   What's that fire all about? Who set the fire?

Yun   I knew we would lose the girl for good if I didn't catch her. So I rode back on the bike. Turn the bike around.

Ku   Was it the girl – the girl from the House of Geese who set the fire?

Yun   As soon as I turned the bike around, I heard a woman's voice.

(**Ku** *parks the bike and sits on it. The feeble voice of a woman is heard from a distance.*)

Voice of the wife from Solmae   Yon-ji! Hey! It's me!

Yun   Put out the lights!

(**Yun** *pulls the candles off the bicycle and stamps them out. The sky over Solmae glows red like a sunset.* **Yun** *is struck by something and falls to the ground, letting out a sharp scream. The red flames in the sky over Solmae die down rapidly, and the sounds of a cowbell and the galloping of a cow continue in complete darkness. The sound resembles that of rocks rolling. It recedes into the distance. Silence.*)

(**Ku** *strikes a match to light a candle from the candle box.* **Yun** *straightens up.*)

Ku   So what happened?

Yun   I passed out. Later they found my bicycle hanging on a branch of the pine tree down there. A whole boxful of burnt matches was spread around on the ground like a spider's web. And where the lines of matches were broken, I was lying with my arms and legs spread-eagled. – So can you guess what it was?

Ku   (*Pause*) Could it be a cow? A cow, maybe, went by?

Yun   But was it that cow?

Ku   Well, there was a cowbell and the sound of hoofbeats. So we can say that you were struck by a cow – that makes the story more believable. But that's different from your first report. Before, you said that you were stopped by a ghost – a woman calling you.

Yun   That's right! That's what I think I heard. But I don't remember anything else except that something hit me from behind. Now I wonder if it was a cow that hit me. You see, if it was a cow, I would have got over it in just a couple of days, but I was sick for a long time. I'd sit staring into space. I'd feel fine one moment, then suddenly my heart would start racing. It felt like I was possessed by something.

Ku   Well, old friend, why don't you lie down again?

Yun   Lie down here?

Ku   Let's see if we can hear what might have happened that night again. Maybe someone else can tell us a different story.

Yun   What do you mean?

Ku   You said you heard a voice, a woman's voice looking for the child. And without thinking, you put out the candles to see who it was.

Right then you were hit by the cow . . . and while you were unconscious maybe the woman came here to see you. Let's see if this gets us anywhere.

Yun   You're right. The woman could have come here. She must have spotted me by the candlelight.

Ku   Lie down here. Now, you're unconscious.

(**Yun** *lies down. As if a film were being rewound and then replayed, the situation that occurred just before Yun blew out the candles resumes. The night sky glows red in the far distance.*)

Yun   What's that fire? Isn't that your house?

Solmae   Oh, my lord! My wife! Get out of there! You've got to come out! Please forgive me. Oh, no. What am I going to do? (*Grasping the air, he disappears into the darkness.*)

(**Yun** *turns the bike around and rides on it. In the distance, the feeble voice of a woman is heard.*)

Voice of the wife from Solmae   Yon-ji! Where are you? It's me! Yon-ji! Hey, where are you? It's me!

(**Yun** *pulls the candles from the wheel and stamps them out. The sound of rocks falling is heard in the darkness. The sound turns into the hoofbeats of a cow. The sound of a cowbell is heard. After a while, someone carefully breaks a pine branch, as if to see what effect the sound might produce. After the sound of breaking branches has been heard several times, footsteps are heard walking on the dried branches. It is the **wife** of the Solmae leper. She looks like her husband, although her leprotic symptoms are more advanced than his. She moves slowly and is so tiny that she looks like the second-eldest daughter of the House of Geese. She notices **Yun**, shakes him, and lights a match to look closely at the ground. She picks up the candles **Yun** had put out and relights them. She swings the candles in all directions as if wanting to let people know where she is rather than to look about the area. She speaks to herself, but loudly enough to be heard from a distance.*)

Wife   Yon-ji-ya! Go home. Don't you see the fire? The fire! Your mother's house is on fire. I'm leaving, I can't stay here. Don't you see, sweetheart? It's bad to run away from home. You won't survive away from your home. Do you see the fire? Mommy can't come back again. Please, go home. You've got to listen to me. Your mother at the House of Geese will be looking for you. Don't run away, go home. Yon-ji-ya! Take good care of the little ones and don't tell them about me. Even if it means dying, never tell them about me. A sickness like mine doesn't give me much time. I won't come back to you. Don't worry, and go home. Don't run away, my little baby!

(*She flashes the lighted candles in all directions in an act of cleaning the area, then extinguishes them with a bowing motion. She disappears as if she had been sucked into the dark. The rustling sound of her plastic garment lingers for quite a while and then stops abruptly. Silence. The red sky over Solmae rapidly darkens.* **Ku** *comes out and* **Yun** *sits up straight.*)

Yun   The wife of the Solmae leper died that night in the town hospital. Severe burns, they said.

Ku   Hush! Someone's coming. Lie back down!

(**Yun** *lies down and* **Ku** *hides himself. From the direction in which the* **wife** *from Solmae disappeared comes the sound of men exchanging whispers. Soon, the* **owner** *of the Persimmon-Tree House and his* **servant** *appear. The* **servant** *stumbles over* **Yun**'*s body and falls down.*)

Servant   Ouch! What's this? (*The* **owner** *of the Persimmon House lights a match.*) Isn't that Yun, the town clerk? Oh my, he must have been kicked by a cow.

Owner   Nonsense. He's only drunk. Must've passed out from too much to drink.

Servant   (*Lights a match to see the cow footprints*) The cow ran this way, I'm pretty sure.

Owner   Don't worry about it. He'll make it home after he wakes up.

(*The two men quickly disappear into the dark.*)

Ku   Who are those people?

Yun   They're from Persimmon-Tree House. (*Pause*) 'I was in bed for forty-two days after being hit by a cow.' But I should have some injuries, don't you see? Some open wounds or broken bones, something like that. It's maddening because I don't have any of those.

(*He puts his arms around his chest.*)

Ku   When did you wake up after passing out?

Yun   Not till the next day at home. Hwang – the wine maker – found me and brought me home.

Ku   Hold on, aren't you skipping something here?

Yun   (*Pause*) Well, no, I . . . don't think I missed anything.

Ku   What about the sound of the young woman?

Yun   The young woman?

Ku   Yeah! You said the young woman followed you from the beginning. As I see it, seems like you felt this woman hanging around you till you saw the fire at the Solmae house, and then all of a sudden she vanished. Let's go back to the beginning. Let's trace what happened step by step. Stop me if I leave anything out or if you remember something. (*Takes out the draft of the absence report from his pocket*) This is your absence report. You fainted one night because the ghost of a young woman called out to you from a hidden grave. A young woman who was recently buried at the side of a road is the one who appears in your report. Then, you met a second woman: the young woman of the House of Geese.

THE HOUSE OF GEESE

(*Suddenly, the loud sound of geese is heard inside the fence. The* **young woman** *appears.*)

Young woman   I sent my sister away.

Yun   What do you mean, 'sent her away'?

Young woman   Last year they brought us a newborn baby from the house across the way.

Yun   The house across the way? You mean . . . from the lepers?

Ku   And you ask her if the girl who ran away was also from the lepers' house. Then, she asks you the same question.

Young woman   She came along when I was six. I don't know. (*Suddenly.*) Did she come from there, too?

Yun   I asked you that question.

Young woman   In my dream, I. . . . I. . . . I set fire to that house. In a dream . . .

Yun   Are you all right? Is she all right now?

Ku   When the Solmae house was burning, wouldn't it be natural to think of the young woman as you watched the fire?

SHINTULMAE GULLY

Ku   So, in Shintulmae Gully, you hear a woman's voice following you. Later it turns out to be the wife of the Solmae leper. But since you could only *hear* the voice, you might have thought it was the young woman from the House of Geese. Let's go over the part where you lit the candles to calm the little girl down – when she was riding on the back of your bike.

(**Yun** *lights the candles and puts them on the bike. The* **child** *sits on the rear rack of the bicycle.*)

Yun   There was a big war a long time ago. A soldier was coming home from battle after winning the war. He rode a bike with Korean flags on each side. They say he shouted, 'I am coming home! I come home alive!' Well, now you're riding with candles instead of flags. So why don't you yell like the soldier? 'I'm coming home! I'm coming back home!'

(*At this moment the* **child** *lets out a shriek, jumps down from the bicycle, and starts pulling it backwards as if she were in a rope-pulling contest. The Solmae leper appears.*)

Yun   Where are you going?

Solmae   My kid ran away from home.

Yun   Your kid? You don't have any children, do you?

Solmae   I mean the child of the House of Geese.

Yun   But she's not really the child of the House of Geese, is she? I know all about it! You put all of your children up for adoption, including the oldest and the newborn.

Solmae   Please forgive me. I only wanted to see them live like normal people.

Yun   If you want to see them live a normal life, you've got to go away. Burn your house down and disappear.

(*The fire at the Solmae House flames up.*)

Solmae   Oh, my lord! My wife! Please get out! (**Solmae** *exits.*)

Yun   (*Abruptly*) I went there to tell him to burn the house and disappear.

Ku   Went where?

Yun   Over to Solmae.

Ku   But when did you go? Did you follow him?

Yun   No.

Ku   Was it after the cow hit you?

Yun   I don't remember. But I'm sure I went over there.

Ku   And?

Yun   I found the young woman there. She was there.

THE HOUSE AT SOLMAE

(*A small hut is on fire. The hut is only the size of a cow shed with its roof hanging so low that it nearly touches the ground. The* **young woman** *is crying and screaming on the ground. Then, in an effort to put out the fire, she repeatedly approaches the house and then retreats.*)

Young woman   Mama! *Aigoo!* Mama! Oh my god, fire! What are you doing? Mama! Get out of there. No, no, my mama's burning to death – why's there no sound? Mama! Oh my god! I'm killing my mother. I set the fire. Yes. I lit it to burn your disease away. To heal you, Mama. To burn everything and to heal. *Aigoo!* Mother, I only did it 'cause I was afraid. What are you doing? Mama, get out of there. Now we can live together. I'll take you in. But you've got to get out of there. What's she doing in there? She's burning to death! My mother's dying. Get out quick, or you'll die. What am I gonna do? I started the fire. *Aigoo!* Mama! *Aigoo!* Mama! I killed my mother! What can I do? My own mother! My mother!

(*The* **young woman** *freezes. The flame freezes. Like an auditory hallucination, a voice calling the names of people is heard. A picture of a crowd of people who died in the registry building fire is projected on the screen of flames.*)

Voice of a North Korean soldier   Pak Pyong-hun, Song Ki-man, Yu Sok-jun, Ch'oe Hui-bok, Cho Chun-gol, Kim Young-sop, Kim Chae-il, Yi Pang-hui, Yi Won-baek, Yi Pang-jin, Chang Tong-su, Kim Ch'on-ui, Pak Sang-sok, Yu Sun-hon, Yi Pyong-jun, Yi Yong-hwan, Cho Chong-do, Pak Chung-won, Shin Song-u, Ho Song-sok, Ch'oe Ch'ang-hwan, Im Hong-sun, Pak Song-gon, Kim Myong-hak, Kim Yong-gyun, Yi Su-wung, Chong Ch'a-ryang, Yi Chong-il, Im Tae-ch'ol, Song Hong-gu, Yi Kon-ch'ol, Yi Si-bok, Chong Kwang-il, Ch'on Tu-sok, Hyun Ch'ang-uk, Yun Chong-p'il, Yi Chong-baek, Yi Sang-dae, Yi Nae-won, Kim In-gwan, Chong Chin-gol, Chong Chin-yong, Ho Kwang-mun, Shim Kun-sok, Hwang Hon-yon, Chong Kwang-su, Chong Kwang-yi, Yi Sang-lae,

Om Chong-won, Mun Paek-hyon, Chang Kum-yong, Yun Chong-t'ae, Yun Chong-mok. Yun Chong-mok! Set the fire, get your bag, and follow us!

(Yun's **uncle***, who has been sitting in one corner of the stage, breaks a glass bowl into pieces. He picks up a piece of glass and cuts his forehead.)*

Uncle   I set the fire! Yes, I did it! Please, let this living man live!

Voice of a North Korean soldier   Kim Chung-gil, Pak Sang-sun, So Nam-sun, Cho Yong-ho, Ch'oe Yong-bin, Yi Song-gyun, Shim Hui-jun, Chang Kum-yong, Chang Kum-yop, Ch'oe Chong-yon, Ho Kwang-gu, Song Hong-gyong, Kim Hak-su, Yu Ui-hwan, Kim Won-man, Kim Tong-ch'ol, Yu Kyong-sok, Yi Pang-jae, Pyon Yong-hwan, Kim Chun-hoe, Kim In-shik, Pak Chae-hwan, Shin Kyu-jong, Yi Nam-hui, Yi Wu-kyong, Kim Chung-gi, An Chong-ch'ol, Cho Yang-il, Hong Chong-ok, Chu Chong-gun, Yi Yong-gil, So Ki-yong, No Chong-yun, Pyon Yong-hun, Yi Pan-bok, Chong Yong-il, Kim Won-p'yong, Ho Hyok, Ch'oe T'ae-hwa, Yi Chun-nam, Yi In-jae, Won Chong-guk.

So Kwan-ho! Set the fire, pick up your bag, and follow us.

(So Kwan-ho*, who has been sitting in another corner of the stage, breaks a glass bowl into pieces. He picks up a piece of glass and cuts his forehead.)*

So Kwan-ho   I set the fire! Yes. I did it! Please, let this living man live!

Voice of a North Korean soldier   Kim Wi-song, Kim Su-hwang, Kwon T'ae-mu, Kang Si-jin, An Yong-sang, Ch'on Kil-bon, Cho Kyong-su, Chong U-bok, Yi Chae-gun, Yang T'ae-o, Shin Yong-gil, Pae Su-byong, Ko Song-jin, An Ui-gyong, Shin Chong-guk, Cho Po-gun, Yi Chin-ho, Mun Paek-son.

(Everything stops. Everything turns to the color of ashes.)

TOWN REGISTRY OFFICE

Yun *and* **Ku**.

Ku   *(Reading a draft of the absence report)* On the eighth of last month, on my way home after working the night shift, I passed out in Shintulmae Gully where I was run over by a three-year-old cow. I recovered the next day, but the severe headache, along with high fever and loss of consciousness, made it impossible for me to work. Whereupon I submit this report of absence. Respectfully, Yun Chin.

(The lights fade.)

Notes

1 Donald N. Clark, *Korea in World History*. Ann Arbor: Association for Asian Studies, 2012, p.1.
2 The English name for Korea comes from Koryŏ, the name of the kingdom from 918 to 1392.

The Post Office

Rabindranath Tagore
Translated by Sagaree Sengupta

Bengal, on the Northeast coast of India, was the headquarters of the East India Company and the site of the first British colony on the subcontinent in the eighteenth century. Exposed to British spoken drama, Bengal thus also became the site of the oldest modern theatre building in India and, in fact, in all of Asia, as well as a strong modern drama tradition. It is also the home of the man considered by many to be the Father of modern Indian theatre.

Born in Kolkata (known in English at the time as Calcutta and the capital city of the Bengali Presidency), Rabindranath Tagore (1861–1941) grew to be a poet, essayist, philosopher, director, actor, choreographer and the father of Bengali drama. Tagore won the Nobel Prize for Literature in 1913, the first non-European to do so. He made his acting debut at age sixteen in his family's Jorasanko Theatre, leaving the following year to study in England for several years. Over the course of his life he travelled the globe to Ireland, the United States, China and Japan. He was friends with W. B. Yeats, telling the Irish poet and playwright that Ireland was 'a part of Asia', identifying the Irish cultural experience of creating a modern culture after British colonisation as similar to that of India. Tagore sought to develop a modern poetic idiom for Indian drama in resistance to colonialism. Although initially accepting a knighthood in 1915, he declined it subsequently in protest to the slaughter of Punjabi protestors by British troops.

Tagore wrote over sixty plays, beginning under the influence of his older brother Jyotirindranath. Tagore experimented with drama, influenced by Sanskrit drama, naturalistic drama and other forms, freely mixing elements of Eastern and Western drama and performance. He wrote in Bengali, often translating his own work into English. His remarkable output included verse plays such as *Prakritirpratishodh* (Nature's Revenge, 1884) about a monk's love for an orphan girl and *Malini* (1896) in which the eponymous princess works to bring peace between Hindus and Buddhists, social dramas such as *Raktakarabi* (Red Oleanders, 1924) in which a young woman opposes a king's oppression as a critique of mining practices in contemporary India, and musical plays, such as his opera *Balmiki Protibha* (The Genius of Vālmīki, 1881), in which the eponymous bandit gives up bloodshed in his quest for the goddess of poetic inspiration. In its original production, Tagore played the title character.

In 1901 Tagore founded an experimental school for boys and wrote plays to be performed by his students. Arguably the best known of these is *Dak Ghar* (The Post Office, 1912). This play, written in just four days, is from his *Gitanjali* period ('Songs of Offering'), which had among its dominant themes death and passage into the next life. In this one-act, Amal is a sick child watching life pass, seeing the construction of a modern post office and imagining that he might someday receive a letter from the king. The play was first performed by and for schoolboys at Tagore's school in Santiniketan. The first western performance was just two years later in 1914 at the Abbey Theatre in Dublin. It has subsequently been translated into many languages and performed throughout the world. Its themes of liberation and transcending difficult situations through imagination, creativity and love of life made the play a favourite during the Second World War, with famous productions in Polish in the Warsaw Ghetto and a Paris radio production on the eve of the Nazi invasion.

Tagore himself explained the meaning of the play to C. F. Andrews, an English friend, stating:

> Amal represents the man whose soul has received the call of the open road. But there is the post office in front of his little window, and Amal waits for the King's letter to come to him direct from the King's own physician and that which is death to the world of hoarded wealth and certified creeds brings him awakening in the world of spiritual freedom. The only thing that accompanies him in his awakening is the flower of love given to him by Shudha.[1]

In other words, though influenced and inspired by naturalism and the modern theatre movements of the west, the play itself is rooted not in a celebration of modernity in and of itself but in the spiritual and creative freedom one finds in leaving concern for the material world behind. The play remains one of Tagore's most popular.

The Post Office

[Dak Ghar, 1912]

Cast of Characters:

Madhab Datta, businessman
Amal, young boy
Kobiraj, Ayurvedic doctor
Yogurt-seller
Village watchman
Panchanan, Village headman
Sudha, a village girl
Group of village boys
Grandpa (dressed as a fakir, or wandering ascetic), an elderly man
of the neighborhood
Royal messenger
Royal kobiraj (the king's Ayurvedic doctor)

Scene 1

[**Madhab's** *house.* **Madhab Datta** *is speaking with the visiting* **Kobiraj.**]

Madhab Datta   Now I'm in trouble. I didn't care about him before he
began living here, and I wouldn't have missed him – I had no worries.
Then he came out of nowhere – and settled in. He filled my house with
life. If he leaves us, this house won't feel like home any more. Kobiraj
Sir, is there anything we can . . .?

Kobiraj   If it's written in his fate, he might even live a very long life;
but according to the Ayur Veda he . . .

Madhab Datta   What do you mean?!

Kobiraj   In says in the Shastra that *bile, mucus and wind give rise to
intermittent disease* . . .

Madhab Datta   Oh, never mind. Please don't recite those ancient
verses again – they frighten me even more. Just tell me what we need to
do for him.

Kobiraj   [*inhaling snuff*] You will have to keep extremely close watch over him.

Madhab Datta   That may be true, but please tell us exactly what we have to watch for!

Kobiraj   As I told you earlier, don't let him go outside – at all!

Madhab Datta   But he's a child – it's going to be hard to keep him in day and night.

Kobiraj   Then, what can you do? This early autumn sunlight and breeze are both like poison for the boy – because in the ancient text, it says, *during fever and coughing if you forget the something or . . .*

Madhab Datta   Oh, please, never mind your ancient text. Then I've got to keep him shut up inside? Isn't there any other way?

Kobiraj   No, because *indeed, wind and heat both do . . .*

Madhab Datta   What will I do with all your 'indeeds'? Just leave that gibberish aside and tell me what to do. Your prescriptions are too harsh for him. It's bad enough to see the poor boy quietly endure the suffering of his illness – but it's watching him take your medicine that really breaks my heart.

Kobiraj   *The greater the suffering, the better the result.* That's why Maharishi Chyavan said, *Both bitter herbs and bitter words of advice yield the speediest results. . . .* Well, that's all today. I'll be on my way, Mr Datta.

[**Kobiraj** *exits.* **Grandpa** *enters.*]

Madhab Datta   Oh no! Grandpa is here! Now you've done it!

Grandpa   Why, what's the matter? Why are you so afraid of me?

Madhab Datta   Because you're an expert in getting children riled up.

Grandpa   You're not a child, and there aren't any children in your house. And you're well past the age of getting riled up yourself – what are you worried about?

Madhab Datta   But I've brought a boy into my house.

Grandpa   How's that?

Madhab Datta   My wife was wild to adopt a boy.

Grandpa   I've been hearing that for ages, but I didn't think you wanted to.

Madhab Datta   My friend, you know that I worked really hard to make my money. I used to feel awful even thinking that some other man's offspring could suddenly show up from God knows where, and without contributing any labor at all, waste the wealth I sweated to build up. But I've gotten attached to this boy, so much so that . . .

Grandpa   . . . that it seems the more money you spend on him, the more those clinking coins seem grateful to be put to that use . . .

Madhab Datta   It was like an addiction when I made money before – there was no way I could stop myself. But now my greatest joy is knowing that the boy will get whatever money I do earn.

Grandpa   Fine, fine, my friend. Tell me, where did you find the boy?

Madhab Datta   He's a boy from my wife's village, a kind of nephew to her. The poor child had lost his mother already, and just the other day his father passed away too.

Grandpa   Oh! Then I need him!!

Madhab Datta   The kobiraj says that there's not much hope left, what with the way the four humors are all mixed up and roused in his little body. The only thing left to do now is to keep him inside the house – keep him protected from the sunlight and air of the harvest season. I'm afraid of you exactly because it amuses you, in your old age, to tempt youngsters to sneak out of the house.

Grandpa   You're right there! I've become as terrifying as the harvest sunlight and autumn air myself! But my friend, I know some ways to keep youngsters amused indoors too! I've got some business to look after first, so I'll strike up a friendship with your boy on my way back. [*Exits.*]

[**Amal Gupta** *enters.*]

Amal   Uncle!

Madhab Datta   Hello there, Amal.

Amal   Can't I even go as far as the courtyard?

Madhab Datta   No, son, you can't.

Amal   Over there, where Auntie shells the dried lentils – look, look over there! There's a squirrel sitting up on its tail and it's picking up pieces of broken lentil from the ground with its little paws, and nibbling on them – can't I even go that far?

Madhab Datta   No, son.

Amal   I wish I was a squirrel. But uncle, why won't you let me go outside?

Madhab Datta   Because the kobiraj says that if you go outside, you'll get sick.

Amal   How does the kobiraj know?

Madhab Datta   What do you mean, Amal? Why wouldn't the kobiraj know? He's read all kinds of enormous old books.

Amal   Can people learn anything by just from reading old books?

Madhab Datta   Why, that's just wonderful! – You didn't even know that?!

Amal   [*sighing*] I haven't read a single old book. That's why I didn't know.

Madhab Datta   Listen, those big scholars are all just like you – they don't go outside the house either.

Amal   They don't?

Madhab Datta   No – and tell me, when could they go out, anyway? They just sit and read gigantic old books all day – they don't have eyes for anything else. Mr Amal, when you grow up, you'll be a scholar too. You'll sit there and read all *kinds* of enormous old books, just like that, and everyone will be very impressed.

Amal   No, no, Uncle! I beg you – please – I don't want to be a scholar, Uncle, I never want to be a scholar!

Madhab Datta   What kind of talk is that, Amal?! I would have given anything to become a scholar!!

Amal   I want to see everything there is out there in the world – I want to travel around just seeing things!

Madhab Datta   Listen for a minute – what is it that you will see out there? What's out there that's so worth seeing?

Amal   You know that far off mountain we can see out our window? I want to go far, far past that mountain.

Madhab Datta   What kind of crazy talk is that? There's no rhyme or reason here – suddenly you want to go 'far past that mountain'! There's no sense in what you're saying. Since that mountain stands so high and keeps us in like a fence, we've got to accept that it's forbidden to go past it. Why else would giant boulders and such be gathered up to build a huge thing like that in the first place?

Amal   But Uncle, do you really think it's forbidding us? I feel like the earth can't really speak, so it's raising an arm towards the sky to call out to it. People far away, sitting inside by their windows in the quiet of the afternoon, can hear that call. I suppose learned people can't hear things like that.

Madhab Datta   They're not nutty like you – they don't even want to hear such things.

Amal   I did see someone yesterday who was nutty like me.

Madhab Datta   Is that right? Can you tell me about it?

Amal   He had a bamboo pole on his shoulder. There was a little bundle tied at its tip. He had a waterpot in his left hand. He wore a pair of curly tipped[2] shoes and was walking along the track in the field, right towards that same mountain. I called out to him and asked, 'Where are you going?' He said, 'Who knows – wherever I end up.' I asked him, 'Why are you going?' He answered, 'I'm looking for work.' Uncle, can you tell me, do people have to *look* for work?

Madhab Datta   Indeed they do. There are lots of people who go around looking for work.

Amal   In that case, I want to go looking for work too.

Madhab Datta   What if you go looking but you don't find any?

Amal   If I don't find any at first, then I'll look again! Then that man in the curly-tipped shoes went away – I stood in the doorway and watched him. You know that place where a waterfall flows by the base of the fig tree? He put his pole down there and washed his feet slowly in the spring water, and then he took his chickpea paste out of his bundle, kneaded it and began to eat. When he was done, he tied his bundle up again and put the pole on his shoulder. He tucked the cloth up around his legs and managed to wade across the water to the other bank. I told Auntie that one day I'm going to go over to that waterfall and to eat some chickpea paste.

Madhab Datta   And what did Auntie say to that?

Amal   Auntie said, First get well, and then I'll take you to that waterfall so you can sit and eat some chickpea paste – right in that spot!

When am I going to get well, Uncle?

Madhab Datta   It won't be long now, son.

Amal   Really, it won't be long? I'm going to go as soon as I'm better.

Madhab Datta   Where will you go?

Amal   I'm going to wade across ever so many streams with meandering waterfalls, with my clothes tucked up. I'm going to go off looking for work ever so far away in the afternoons, when everyone else is napping behind closed doors.

Madhab Datta   Alright, that's fine. First get well, and then you can –

Amal   Then – please don't tell me to become a learned man, Uncle!

Madhab Datta   Alright, you tell me what you want to be.

Amal   I can't remember anything now – let me think and then I'll tell you.

Madhab Datta   But next time, don't go calling out to any old fellow who comes from somewhere far away.

Amal   But I like people from faraway places!

Madhab Datta   What if one of them kidnapped you and carried you off?

Amal   Oh, that would be wonderful! But nobody carries me anywhere! All they do is make me sit right here.

Madhab Datta   I've got work to do, I'm going – but son, be sure not to dash out.

Amal   I won't go out. But Uncle, I want to stay in this room because it's right by the street.

[*Exit* **Madhab Datta**.]

Scene 2

[*Enter* **Yogurt seller**.]

Yogurt seller   Yo – gurt! Wonderful yo – gurt!

Amal   The yogurt seller! It's the yogurt seller! Hey there, Yogurt Seller!

Yogurt seller   Why're you calling me? Are you going to buy some yogurt?

Amal   How can I? I don't have any money.

Yogurt seller   What kind of boy are you, anyway? You're not going to buy anything, but you're slowing me down.

Amal   If I could go with you, I would.

Yogurt seller   With me?!

Amal   Yes. When I hear you go by, calling from far off, I feel so wistful.

Yogurt seller   [*lowering his wares, carried in two sets of pots balanced at the two ends of a pole*] Son, what are you doing sitting here?

Amal   The doctor says I can't go out, so I just sit here all day.

Yogurt seller   Oh that's too bad, sonny. What kind of sickness do you have?

Amal   I really don't know. I haven't studied any books, so I don't know what the matter is with me. Yogurt seller, where are you coming from?

Yogurt seller   I'm coming from our village.

Amal   Your village? Is your village fa – ar away?

Yogurt seller   Our village is at the foot of that Five-Peak Mountain, near the Shamoli River.

Amal   Five-Peak Mountain. . . . Shamoli River . . . who knows, maybe I've seen your village, but I can't tell you when.

Yogurt seller   You've seen it? Have you been to the foot of the mountain, then?

Amal   No, I never have. But it seems to me as if I've seen the place. Your village sits in the shade of many huge old trees, next to a red dirt road, doesn't it?

Yogurt seller   That's right, my son.

Amal   The cows go grazing on the slopes of the mountain there.

Yogurt seller   That's amazing! You're absolutely right! The cows in our village do indeed graze, they graze a lot!

Amal   And the women fill their waterpots at the river and carry them home with the pots balanced on their heads. They have red saris on.

Yogurt seller   Oh! That's exactly right! All the women from our cowherd quarter do go to the river to get water. But I can't say they *all* wear red saris – but sonny, you must have gone to the village some time for an outing.

Amal   I'm telling you the truth, Yogurt Seller – I've never been there, not even once. The day the kobiraj says I can go outside again, will you take me with you to your village?

Yogurt seller   I will indeed, son – I'll take you for sure.

Amal   Please teach me how to sell yogurt door to door too, the way you do . . . balancing that pole and with those clay pots hanging from on my shoulder, going along that far path just the way you do . . .

Yogurt seller   Oh goodness! Why would you want to sell yogurt? You'll read a ton of big books and become a learned man!

Amal   No, I'll never become a learned man. I'm going to take yogurt from your cowherd village that's under the old banyan tree, next to the redclay road, and sell it far and wide in other villages. How do you say that? – 'Yo – gurt. Yo – gurt. Really good yo – gurt!' Please teach me how it goes!'

Yogurt seller   Oh woe is me! That's not something worth learning!

Amal   No, no, I love hearing that call. You know how your heart suddenly becomes sad when you hear a bird calling from the very ends of the sky? When I heard your call today, coming from the far-off crossroads through that row of trees, I felt, I felt . . . who knows what I felt!

Yogurt seller   My child, why don't you eat a little cup of yogurt now?

Amal   But I don't have any money.

Yogurt seller   No no no – don't mention money. It's going to make me so happy if you eat a little of my yogurt.

Amal   Did I hold you up too long?

Yogurt seller   Oh, you didn't hold me up at all. No, no, there's been no loss to my business. From you, I just learned what a pleasure it is to sell yogurt! [*Exits*.]

Amal   [*calling out in a singsong way*] Yo – gurt! Yo – gurt! Really good yo – gurt! Yogurt from the cowherd village at the foot of Five-Peak Mountain, by the River Shamoli!! Every morning they stand their cows under the trees to milk them! And in the evening they make the yogurt – that yo – gurt! Yo – gurt! Yo – gurt! Really good yo – gurt!. Oh, look! The watchman is pacing up and down the street!

Oh, Watchman, come here a minute, will you?

[*Enter* **Watchman**.]

Watchman   Why are you summoning me like that? Aren't you afraid of me?

Amal No – why should I be afraid of you?

Watchman What if I arrested you and carried you off to jail?

Amal Where would the jail be? Would it be far away? For instance, beyond that mountain?

Watchman What if I took you straight to the king?

Amal To the king? Why *don't* you take me to him! But the kobiraj said I can't go out. No one can carry me off anywhere – I can't budge from here; I'm stuck here day and night.

Watchman The kobiraj won't allow it? Poor thing, I can see – your face looks pale. You have dark circles under your eyes. I can see the veins in the backs of your hands.

Amal Aren't you going to ring your bell, Watchman?

Watchman It isn't time yet.

Amal Some people say 'time is passing,' and some say 'it isn't time yet'. So, if you just ring the bell, it *will* be the time, won't it?

Watchman How can that be? When it's time, then I ring the bell.

Amal I like that bell of yours – I love the way it sounds. In the afternoon at our house, when every last person is done with their luncheon, and Uncle goes off somewhere to work, and Auntie falls asleep while reading her *Ramayana* and our little dog goes to sleep in that shady corner of the courtyard, with its nose tucked into its tail , that's when your bell rings – Bo-ong Bo-ong Bo-ong! Bo-ong Bo-ong Bo-ong! Why does your bell ring?

Watchman The bell tells everyone that time isn't sitting still, that time is always moving along.

Amal Where is it moving to? What country?

Watchman No one knows that.

Amal Why, hasn't anyone ever traveled there? I wish so much that I could run off along with time – off to that far-off country no one knows about.

Watchman So, everyone will have to go there *some* day.

Amal Will I have to go too?

Watchman Of course you will!

Amal   But the kobiraj has forbidden me to even go outside.

Watchman   Who knows, one day the kobiraj himself will take you by the hand and lead you to that place!

Amal   No, no, you don't know him – he just holds you back.

Watchman   But there's a better doctor than him, and he comes to release people.

Amal   When will that good doctor come to see me? I don't feel like waiting here any longer.

Watchman   Don't say things like that, my son!

Amal   No – I'm still sitting here waiting – once they put me down somewhere, I don't budge. But that bell of your sounds – Bo-ong! Bo-ong! Bo-ong! – and it makes me so wistful. Listen, Watchman?

Watchman   What, my son?

Amal   You see those pennants flying on that big house over there across the road, where there are a lot of people coming and going constantly – what's going on there?

Watchman   There's a new Post Office there.

Amal   A Post Office? Whose Post Office?

Watchman   Who else? It's the King's Post Office, of course? – [*Aside*] This child is a funny one!

Amal   Do all letters from the king come to the King's Post Office?

Watchman   Indeed they do. You'll see, one day there'll be a letter for you.

Amal   There will be a letter for me too? But I'm a child!

Watchman   The king writes tiny little letters to children.

Amal   Oh, that would be a fine thing! When will I get a letter? And how do you know that he'll write me a letter too?

Watchman   Then why else would he get them to put up such a great big golden pennant and set up a new Post Office right in front of your window? – [*Aside*] I rather like this youngster!

Amal   Now, if a letter comes from the king, who's going to bring it to me?

Watchman   The king has many mail-runners. Haven't you seen them going around with those golden medallions on their shirts?

Amal   Alright, but what places do they go to?

Watchman   They go from house to house, from land to land – this boy's questions make me laugh!

Amal   When I grow up, I'm going to be a mail-runner.

Watchman   Ha ha ha! A mail-runner! That's a huge job! It doesn't matter if the sun is hot, or if it's raining; it doesn't matter if the people he delivers to are rich or poor – he goes from door to door distributing letters everywhere. It's a hard job, my boy!

Amal   Why are you laughing? I think I would like that job the best. No, no, you have a fine job too – because when the sun is harshest during the afternoons, your bell goes Bo-ong Bo-ong Bo-ong. And then sometimes I wake up in the middle of the night and see that the oil lamp in the corner has gone out, but far away through the darkness outside that bell is sounding – Bo-ong Bo-ong Bo-ong!

Watchman   Oh, here comes the village headman – I better slip off now. He'll get me into a heap of trouble if he sees me chatting with you.

Amal   Where's the headman? Where? Where?

Watchman   Look over there, far away. He's carrying a big round leaf to shade his head.

Amal   I suppose the king made him headman?

Watchman   Oh no, not at all. He just decided that for himself. If anyone objects, he harasses them day and night so now everyone's afraid of him. He keeps himself in business by picking fights with everyone. That's enough for today – I've been missing too much work. I'll come again tomorrow morning and bring you news of the whole town. [*Exits.*]

Amal   It would be lovely if I got a letter from the king every day – I'd sit here by the window and read it. Except that I can't read! Who could read it to me? Auntie just reads the *Ramayana*. Would she be able to read the king's writing? If there's no one to read the letter to me, I'll just put it away carefully and read it when I grow up. But what if the mail-runner doesn't recognize me? Mr Headman, hey there, Mr Headman – come here for a minute! I've got something to ask you.

[*The* **Headman** *enters.*]

Headman   Who's that? Who is calling me like that out of the blue? What kind of rudeness is this?

Amal   You're Mr Headman. Everyone respects you.

Headman   [*pleased*] Yes, yes, that they do indeed. They respect me alright.

Amal   Does the king's mail-runner obey you?

Headman   Would he live to see another day if he didn't? Of course he does! He doesn't have a choice!

Amal   Please tell the mail-runner for me that it's *my* name that is Amal, and that I sit here by this window.

Headman   And can you tell me why I should do this?

Amal   In case a letter comes for me . . .

Headman   A letter . . . for you? Who's going to write you a letter?

Amal   If the king writes me a letter then . . .

Headman   [*laughing*] Ha ha ha ha! What a child! Ha ha ha ha ha! The king's going to write you a letter? Oh, I'm sure he is, too! Because you're his closest friend! In fact, I've heard that he's just wasting away because he hasn't heard from you in several days! It won't be long now – the letter could be here any day, today or tomorrow!

Amal   Why are you talking like that, Mr Headman? Are you angry at me?

Headman   Come now. Angry at you? Would I dare be angry at you? When you have a regular correspondence going with the king! I can see that Madhab Datta is getting a little ahead of himself. He's saved up a few coins and now there's nothing but talk of kings and emperors at his house! Now just wait and see – I'll teach him a lesson! Hey, boy, it's alright, I'll arrange for the king's letter to arrive here soon, very soon indeed.

Amal   No, no, you don't have to do anything.

Headman   Why not, now? I'll let the king know all about you, and then he won't be able to hold back – he'll send a messenger just to get news of you people, I'm sure! No, Madhab Datta has been getting too insolent – it will all get straightened out once the king hears of it. [*Exits*.]

Amal   Who's that going by with jingling anklets – won't you stop a minute?

[*A village* **girl** *enters*.]

Girl   Oh, there's no way I can stop. It's getting late.

Amal You don't feel like stopping, and I don't feel like sitting here anymore.

Girl When I look at you, the faint morning star comes to mind – can you tell me what the matter is with you?

Amal I don't know. The kobiraj told me not to go outside.

Girl Poor thing, then don't go outside. People have to listen to the kobiraj. You can't be restless, or people will say that you're naughty. If looking outside makes you want to go out, why don't I shut this half-door for you?

Amal No, no, please don't close it. Everything else here is closed for me, just this one thing is open. Why don't you tell me who you are? I don't think I know you.

Girl I'm Sudha.

Amal Sudha?

Sudha Don't you know? I am the daughter of the garland maker here.

Amal What do you do?

Sudha I pick baskets full of flowers and then I make garlands with them. I'm on my way to pick flowers now.

Amal You're off to pick flowers? That's why your feet sound so happy – the more you walk, the more your anklets go jingle, jingle, jingle! If I could go with you then I'd climb all way up into the branches so high that you can't even see them, and I'd pick the flowers that are up there for you.

Sudha Is that right? As if you know more about flowers than I do!

Amal But I do – I know a lot about them. I know the story about the Seven Champa Brothers who were reborn as flowers. I think that if they let me out, I could go deep into the forest where there aren't any paths. There, I could blossom as a champa flower on the very tip of a delicate swaying branch where the *monua* bird sits. Would you be my big sister Parul, like the Champa brothers had?

Sudha Some idea you've got! How could I be your big sister Parul? I'm Sudha, the daughter of Shashi the garland-maker. I've got to make an enormous bunch of garlands every day. How fun it would be if I could just sit here like you do!

Amal What would you do all day then?

Sudha   I've got a groom doll and a bride doll, and I could have play weddings for them. I've got a pet cat, and I could. . . . Oh, I've got to go! If I'm late, there won't be any flowers left!

Amal   Why don't you stay and talk with me a while? I would like that.

Sudha   Alright then. Don't be naughty. Be good and sit still right here, and I'll stop and chat with you on my way back from picking my flowers.

Amal   And will you give me a flower?

Sudha   I can't just give you a flower, you know. You've got to pay.

Amal   I'll pay you when I'm grown up. I'm going to go look for work on the other side of that waterfall, and I'll bring you the money then.

Sudha   Well, then it's fine.

Amal   Then you'll come after you pick your flowers?

Sudha   I will.

Amal   You'll come?

Sudha   I will.

Amal   You won't forget about me? My name is Amal. Will you remember it?

Sudha   I won't forget it. You'll see, I'll remember.

[**Girl** *exits*.]

[*A group of* **boys** *enters*.]

Amal   Friends, where are you all going? Won't you stop here for a minute?

Boys   We're going off to play.

Amal   What are you going to play?

Boys   We're going to play being farmers.

First Boy   [*showing* **Amal** *a stick*] This is our plow.

Second Boy   The two of us are going to be the two bulls pulling the plow.

Amal   Are you going to play all day?

Boys   Yes, a – ll day!

Amal   And then are you going to go back home along the riverbank at twilight?

Boys Yes, we'll go back home at twilight.

Amal Please go back home this way my friends, by my house.

Boys Why don't you come out? Come with us to play!

Amal The kobiraj told me not to go out.

Boys The kobiraj! Do you really listen to what he says? Come on, brother, come on – we're getting late.

Amal No, friends. Why don't you play here in the road, in front of my window, for a while? I could watch you.

Boys What could we play with here?

Amal Look. All my toys are lying around here. You should take them. It's no fun playing by myself inside the house. They just lie here in the dust. I have no use for them.

Boys Oh, look! Oh, look! What wonderful toys! Look at this toy ship! Look at this old grandma doll with the topknot! Do you see? What a lovely toy soldier! You're really giving these to us? Don't you feel bad?

Amal No, I don't feel bad about it at all. I give them all to you.

Boys We won't give them back, then.

Amal No, you don't have to give anything back.

Boys Will anyone scold us?

Amal No, no, no one. But please play with them a little bit every morning right here, in front of my window, will you? And when these toys get old I'll get you new ones.

Boys That's fine, my friend, we'll come by here to play every day. Hey, let's set up all the soldiers and have a play battle! Where can we find some guns? Look, there's a big stick lying there – we could break it up into little pieces and use them for guns. But, Amal, you're falling asleep!

Amal Yes, I'm getting sleepy. I don't know why I suddenly get sleepy every once in a while. I've been sitting for a long time, and I just can't sit any more – my back is starting to hurt.

Boys The morning has hardly begun! Why are you sleepy already? Listen, there's the midmorning bell!

Amal Yes, it's going Bo-ong, Bo-ong, Bo-ong – it's calling me to go to sleep.

Boys   Then we'll be on our way. We'll come again tomorrow morning.

Amal   My friends, before you go, there's something I want to ask you. You all are outside all the time – do you know any of the mail-runners that belong to the king's post office over there?

Boys   Yes, of course we know them – we know them well!

Amal   Who are they then? What are their names?

Boys   There's one that's called Badal-runner, and another runner called Sharat – there are lots more, too.

Amal   If there's a letter with my name on it, will they be able to find me?

Boys   Of course they will! If your name is on the letter, they'll identify you for sure!

Amal   When you come tomorrow morning, could you please bring one of them over and introduce me?

Boys   Sure, we'll do that.

Scene 3

[**Amal** *is lying in bed.* **Madhab Datta** *is at his side.*]

Amal   Uncle, won't you even let me go near that window of mine today? Did the kobiraj forbid that too?

Madhab Datta   That's right, son. I'm sure you made yourself sicker going over there to look outside all day.

Amal   No, uncle, no – I don't know anything about my illness but I know that when I'm there I feel very well.

Madhab Datta   You've sat there by the window and made friends with every sort of young and old person that might wander by. It's as if there's a country fair setting up at our door every day. That alone can't be good for your health. Just look at how your face is all pale today!

Amal   But Uncle, that fakir friend of mine might go away if he doesn't see me at the window.

Madhab Datta   Now who's this fakir of yours?

Amal   It's that man who comes everyday to tell me about all kinds of faraway places. I love listening to him.

Madhab Datta   But, I don't know of any fakir.

Amal   Oh, it's exactly the time for him to come, right now – please, Uncle, please, please go tell him to come to my room to visit me.

[**Grandpa** *enters, dressed as the* **Fakir**.]

Amal   Hey there! Oh Fakir – please come here and sit at the edge of my bed for a minute!

Madhab Datta   What's this?! But he's. . . .

Grandpa [*grandly addressing* **Madhab**]   I am a fakir!

Madhab Datta   What I can't figure out is if there's anything that you *aren't*.

Amal   Fakir, where did you go this last time?

Grandpa/Fakir   I went to Crane Island.

Madhab Datta   Did you say Crane Island?

Grandpa/Fakir   Why are you so surprised? Do you think I'm like you all? It doesn't cost me a penny to go anywhere. I can go wherever I like.

Amal   [*clapping his hands*] Oh, you have so much fun! Fakir, do you remember that you said that when I got well, you would make me your disciple?

Grandpa/Fakir   I remember very well. When we are wandering around, I'll teach you all kinds of fabulous mantras so that nothing can obstruct you whether you're at sea, up in the mountains, or deep in the jungle,

Grandpa/Fakir   My son Amal, I'm not afraid of hills and mountains and oceans, but my mantras will have to bow down in defeat if the Kobiraj comes again and gangs up with this Uncle of yours.

Amal   No, no, uncle, don't say anything to the Kobiraj. I'm only going to lie here – I won't move a hair. But the day I get well, I will take the fakir's mantra and take off – no river or mountain or ocean will be able to hold me back.

Madhab Datta   Shame, my son. It's not nice to keep talking about leaving your home. I get sad when I hear you talk this way.

Amal   Fakir, tell me what kind of place Crane Island is!

Grandpa/Fakir   Oh, it's an amazing place. It's a land of birds – there are no humans there at all. They don't talk, they don't walk; they just sing their birdsongs and fly around.

Amal   How wonderful! Is it by the ocean?

Grandpa/Fakir   Of course it's by the ocean.

Amal   Are all the mountains blue there?

Grandpa/Fakir   The blue mountains is where birds have their nests! When the rays of the setting sun fall on those mountains in the evening, and the sky teems with green birds returning to their homes, it's spectacular to see the color of the sky and the color of the birds and the color of the mountains, all against each other!

Amal   Is there a waterfall on that mountain?

Grandpa/Fakir   Of course! There has to be a waterfall! And this one is just like a lot of molten diamonds flowing together! And what a dance that waterfall does! It rushes along, dashing pebbles against each other so that they ring out! It gurgles and flows along until it reaches the ocean, and then it leaps right into its heart! No Kobiraj on earth could hold it back for a single hour. If those birds weren't so scornful of me for being a mere human, I'd make myself a home right there by the waterfall, near those thousands and thousands of birds' nests and I'd spend the whole day gazing at the ocean waves.

Amal   If I were a bird, then . . .

Grandpa/Fakir   Then there would be big trouble. I heard that you told the yogurt seller that you were going to sell yogurt when you grew up – now that business is not going to be very successful if you have *birds* for customers! I have a feeling you'll be operating in the red.

Madhab Datta   I can't bear this anymore. I can see that you are going to drive *me* mad as well! I'm off – goodbye.

Amal   Uncle, did my yogurt seller already come and go?

Madhab Datta   He certainly did. No one would ever eat around here if we were all flitting around the birds' nests of Crane Island in our minds, with that amateur fakir's bundle in tow. He's left a little pot of yogurt for you. He told me to tell you that his niece's wedding is taking place in his home village, and that's why he had to go to Kolmipara to order some bamboo flutes. That's why he's been so busy.

Amal   But he told me that he was going to marry *me* to his youngest niece . . .

Grandpa/Fakir   Then there is a huge problem.

Amal   He told me I was going to have a lovely young bride, wearing a bright nose-ring and a striped red sari. Every morning, she'd milk the black cow with her own hands and then bring me an earthen cup of foaming fresh milk. In the evenings she would take the puja lamp to the cowshed for a moment, and then she would come sit down next to me and tell me the story of The Seven Brothers Champa.

Grandpa/Fakir   Oh, that sounds like a *fine* wife! Even a wandering fakir like me could feel tempted! But don't you worry – let him marry this one off *this* time, but I can tell you that if you need a bride in the future, there will never be a shortage of nieces in his family.

Madhab Datta   [*exasperated*] Now go on! – I can't stand it anymore. [*Exits.*]

Amal   Hey Fakir, Uncle has left – can you quietly tell me if a letter has come for me at the King's Post Office?

Grandpa/Fakir   Now what I've heard is that his letter has been *dispatched*. It's on its way now.

Amal   Its way? What way? You mean the path over there that goes through that thick jungle far in the distance – the one you can just barely see after a heavy rain, when the sky is crystal clear? That way?

Grandpa/Fakir   I can see that you already know everything – yes, that's the very path.

Amal   Fakir, I know everything!

Grandpa/Fakir   So I can see! How did you manage that?

Amal   I don't know the answer to that. I can see things in front of my eyes . . . as if I've seen them many times before . . . way long ago. . . . I can't remember . . . how long ago. Shall I tell you about it? I can see a king's mail runner coming down and down the mountain, all by himself, with a lantern in his left hand and a sack of letters on his shoulder. He works his way down the same slope for days and days and nights and nights. And then at the foot of the mountain where the waterfall-path ends, there he takes up the path along the meandering river, getting closer and closer; he comes down the narrow paths that go through that millet field near the river. Then, there's a cane field – he gets closer, walking along the high earthen ridge that borders that cane field. He walks alone night and day, day and night. The crickets call in the field, and there isn't a single human being down by the river, only snipes sashaying around and showing off their tail feathers – I can see everything. I feel waves of gladness filling me up the closer he gets.

Grandpa/Fakir   I don't have young eyes like you but I can see all that along with you.

Amal   Listen, Fakir? Do you know the king that the Post Office belongs to?

Grandpa/Fakir   Of course I do. I beg alms from him every day.

Amal   Now, that's a fine thing! When I get better, I'll beg from him too! I'll be able to go, won't I?

Grandpa/Fakir   Son, you won't need to beg. Whatever he has to give you, he'll give you freely.

Amal   But no, I'll stand in the street in front of his house and beg, crying out 'Victory to the King!' I'll play my finger cymbals and dance – that would be good, wouldn't it?

Grandpa/Fakir   Oh, that would be grand. I'll get plenty of alms and fill my stomach if I take *you* along with me! What are you going to beg from the king?

Amal   I'm going to say, Please make me your mail-runner. I want to deliver your letters house to house with a lantern in my hand. Did you know, Fakir, that somebody told me that when I got well, he would teach me how to beg? I will go around begging with him whenever I please.

Grandpa/Fakir   And who was that?

Amal   Chidam.

Grandpa/Fakir   Which Chidam?

Amal   You know, that blind lame man. He comes to my window every day. A boy just like me pushes him around in his wheeled cart. I told him that when I get better, I'll push him around.

Grandpa/Fakir   That would be fun to see!

Amal   He's the one who told me that he'll teach me how to beg. I tell Uncle to give him alms, but Uncle says that he's a fake blind man and that he's faking his lameness too. So listen, even if he's fake blind, he really can't see, can he?

Grandpa/Fakir   You are right, son – this much is true that he can't see, whether you call him blind or not. So if no one gives him anything here, why does he spend time sitting with you?

Amal   It's because I tell him all about what you find where. The poor man can't see. I tell him all about the different lands you tell me about. The other day you told me about that light-weight land – where nothing has any weight at all, where if you just jump up a little you can cross right over mountains. He really loved hearing about that place. Listen, Fakir, which way do you go to get there?

Grandpa/Fakir   There's an inner route to that place – it might be hard to find.

Amal   But the poor man is blind – maybe he wouldn't find the way, and he'll end up wandering around begging. He was so sad about that, but I told him that he gets to see so many different places while begging – not everyone gets to do that.

Grandpa/Fakir   So what's so sad about staying home, anyway?

Amal   No, I'm not sad. When they first told me I had to stay in the house, it felt like the days would never end. But since the King's Post Office appeared, I feel good every day – I feel good even sitting in this room. Some day my letter will come, and I can sit happily here, very quietly, just thinking about it. But I don't know what will be written in the king's letter to me.

Grandpa/Fakir   That doesn't matter. As long as your name is on it – that's the only important thing.

[**Madhab Datta** *enters.*]

Madhab Datta   Now tell me what kind of trouble have the two of you cooked up?

Grandpa/Fakir   Why, what's the matter?

Madhab Datta   I hear you've spread the rumor that the king started the Post Office just so he could write to you two?

Grandpa/Fakir   So?

Madhab Datta   The village headman Panchanan has sent off an anonymous complaint letter to the king about that.

Grandpa/Fakir   The king hears about everything in the land – don't we already know that?

Madhab Datta   Then why don't you reign yourself in a bit? Why do you even utter such nonsense about kings and emperors and all? You two are going to get me into trouble too.

Amal   Fakir, is the king going to be angry?

Grandpa/Fakir   Just like that?! Angry? Let's just see how angry he can get! We'll just have to see what kind of kingly temper he dares show to a fakir like me, and to a boy like you!

Amal   Listen, Fakir, ever since this morning I have been feeling like a darkness comes over my eyes from time to time. Everything seems like a dream. I want to be completely still. I don't feel like talking. Isn't the king's letter going to come? What if this room fades away . . . what if . . .

[**Kobiraj** – *the Ayurvedic Doctor – enters.*]

Kobiraj   How do you feel today?

Amal   Kobiraj sir, I feel really fine today. It seems like all the pain is gone.

Kobiraj   [*a little apart, privately to* **Madhab Datta**] That smile of his doesn't seem healthy. And did you hear? He said he felt fine – that's a bad sign right there. Our great Chakradhar Datta has written . . .

Madhab Datta   I beg you, Kobiraj Sir, let's leave Chakradhar Datta aside. Tell me what the matter is with Amal.

Kobiraj   It seems like we can't hold on to him any longer. I had forbidden it, but it seems like he's been exposed to some outdoor air.

Madhab Datta   No, Kobiraj Sir, I have kept him under close watch. I don't let him go outside – I've kept the door closed most of the time.

Kobiraj   Suddenly there is a new sort of breeze today. I just saw it blowing into your house, right through the main entrance. That is not a good thing at all. You must close that door up and padlock it very securely. So what if people are hampered and can't come and go for a few days? If someone does show up, there's always the small cut-in doorway. See those rays of the setting sun coming in through that window? You should put an end to that too – they have a way of keeping the patient too wakeful.

Madhab Datta   Amal's eyes are closed; I think he's asleep. When I look at his face, Kobiraj, it seems as if – as if – I brought home someone who didn't belong to me, then I loved him, and now it seems like he's leaving me.

Kobiraj   What's that!! The village headman is headed this way. What a bother!! I'll be on my way, my friend! But you go – go close that door firmly. I'll go home and send over a poison pill – give that to Amal and see. If he's to live, it's that pill that will pull him back. [**Madhab Datta** *and* **Kobiraj** *exit.*]

[*The* **Village Headman** *enters.*]

Village Headman   Hey boy, how're you doing?

Grandpa/Fakir   [*scrambling to get up*] Hush, hush now.

Amal   No Fakir, you thought I was asleep? I don't sleep. I listen to everything. It's as if I can hear words being spoken way far off too. It seems to me like my mother, my father, are at the head of my bed . . . talking.

[**Madhab Datta** *enters.*]

Headman   Look here, Madhab Datta – it seems like you're connected to some pretty big people these days!

Madhab Datta   What are you saying, Headman? Don't mock me. We are just ordinary people.

Headman   But this boy of yours has been waiting for a letter from the king.

Madhab Datta   He's a child! He's crazy! You shouldn't take him seriously.

Headman   No, no, what's so surprising about that? Where would the king find as worthy a family as yours? That's why, don't you see, the king's new Post Office has been set up right across from your parlor window? Hey, kid, there's a letter in your name from the king.

Amal   [*startled*] Really?

Headman   What else? You've got that great friendship going with the king! [*Handing him a blank sheet of paper*] Ha ha ha ha – here's his letter.

Amal   Don't make fun of me. Fakir, Fakir – please tell me – is this really his letter?

Grandpa/Fakir   Yes, son. [*Grandly*] I, the Fakir, am telling you that this really is his letter!

Amal   But I don't see anything there. Everything looks white to me now. Headman Sir, will you please tell me what is written there?

Headman   The king writes, 'I'll be arriving at your home today or tomorrow. Please have a feast of puffed rice ready for me – I don't feel like staying in the royal palace even an hour longer!' Ha ha ha ha!

Madhab Datta [*joining his hands in supplication, (as in 'namaste')*]
Dear Headman Sir, I beg you, please don't make a mockery of such things.

Grandpa/Fakir Mockery! Mockery of what?! Does he have the wits
to mock anything?

Madhab Datta Stop! Grandpa, have you gone mad!?

Grandpa/Fakir Yes, that's right. I have gone mad! That's why I can see
the letters written on this white paper. The king writes that he's coming
himself to see Amal, and he's bringing his royal kobiraj with him.

Amal Fakir! There, Fakir, I hear the sound of his musicians! Can't you
hear them?

Headman Ha ha ha ha! He won't be able to hear them until he's one
degree crazier!

Amal I used to think that you were angry at me, that you didn't care
for me at all. I never thought that you would really bring me the king's
letter – please, let me touch the dust of your feet.

Headman I've got to say, this boy has some respect for his elders! No
brains at all, but he's got a good heart.

Amal I think it must be dusk by now. There's the bell ringing – Bo-ong
Bo-ong Bo-ong – Bo-ong Bo-ong Bo-ong. Fakir, has the evening star
risen yet? Why can't I see it?

Grandpa/Fakir It's because they closed that window – wait, I'll open
it for you.

[*Banging on the door, from outside*]

Madhab Datta What is it? Who's there? What kind of trouble is this?

[*Voice from outside*] Open the door!

Madhab Datta Who are you all?

[*Voice from outside*] Open the door!

Madhab Datta It's not robbers, is it, headman?

Headman Who are you? I'm Headman Panchanan. Aren't you people
afraid of anything? Now go look – they've stopped banging. The minute
they hear Panchanan's voice, there's no escape, no matter what caliber
robber or highwayman it might be . . .!

Madhab Datta   [*looking out of the window*] They've broken the door down, that's why there's no more knocking.

[*The* **Royal Messenger** *enters.*]

Royal Messenger   The king will arrive tonight.

Headman   Oh no! What misfortune!

Amal   How late, Messenger, how late tonight?

Royal Messenger   At midnight tonight.

Amal   When my friend the night watchman rings the bell at the main town gate – Bo-ong Bo-ong Bo-ong, Bo-ong Bo-ong Bo-ong – then?

Royal Messenger   Yes, then. The king has sent his best Kobiraj of all to examine his young friend.

[*The* **Royal Kobiraj** *enters.*]

Royal Kobiraj   What's this?! Why is everything shut up like this? Open it all up! Open it all up! Open up every door and window! – [*Placing his hand on* **Amal**] Son, how do you feel?

Amal   Very well, very well, Kobiraj Sir. My sickness has all gone away. My pain has all gone away. Look! You've opened all the doors and windows! I can see all the stars! All the stars on the other shore!

Royal Kobiraj   When the king arrives at midnight, will you be able to get up from your bed and go out with him?

Amal   I will, I will! I'd give anything to go out! I'll ask the king to show me the pole star in this dark sky. I've seen that star ever so many times but I still don't know how to pick it out.

Royal Kobiraj   He'll show you all of them. [*To* **Madhab**] You should clean this room up and decorate it with flowers to welcome the king. [*Pointing to the headman*] You've got to get that man out of the house.

Amal   No, no, Kobiraj Sir – he's my friend. He brought me the king's letter when you all hadn't arrived yet.

Royal Kobiraj   That's fine, son, that's fine then. If he's your friend, then he can stay in the house.

Madhab Datta   [*speaking low in* **Amal's** *ear*] Son, the king is fond of you, and he's coming in person today – please ask him for something. We are not doing so well. You know all about that.

Amal   I've already decided that, Uncle – you've got nothing to worry about.

Madhab Datta   What is it that you've decided, son?

Amal   I'm going to ask him to make me a mail-runner for his Post Office – I'll go from land to land distributing his letters.

Madhab Datta   [*striking his forehead*] My wretched luck!

Amal   Uncle, the king is going to come – are you going to have a feast ready for him?

Royal Messenger   He said that he would have a puffed rice feast here.

Amal   Puffed rice! Headman, you told us before that you knew all about the king. We didn't know anything about him at all!

Headman   If you send someone over to my house, I could have some good things sent over for the king –

Royal Kobiraj   There's no need. Now all of you quiet down. Look, he's falling asleep. I'll sit at the head of his bed – he's going to sleep now. Put out the lamps – let the starlight shine on him, he's going to sleep.

Madhab Datta   [*to* **Grandpa**] Grandpa, why are you standing there silently with your hands joined? I am a little afraid. Is all this a good sign? Why are these people darkening my home? Of what use is starlight to me?

Grandpa/Fakir   Be quiet, you faithless one! Don't speak!

[**Sudha** *enters.*]

Sudha   Amal.

Royal Kobiraj   He's gone to sleep.

Sudha   But I've brought him some flowers – can't I put them in his hands?

Royal Kobiraj   Alright then, give him your flowers.

Sudha   When is he waking up?

Royal Kobiraj   Soon, when the king comes and calls him.

Sudha   Will you whisper something in his ear then for me?

Royal Kobiraj   What is that?

Sudha   Please say, 'Sudha has not forgotten you.'

[*Curtain.*]

Notes

1 Quoted in Krishna Dutta and Andrew Robinson, 'Drama' in Krishna Dutta
   and Andrew Robinson (eds), *Rabindranath Tagore: An Anthology*, New York:
   St. Martin's Griffin, 1998, p.22.
2 As worn at traditional royal courts – not everyday Bengal village footgear at
   the time.

Hayavadana[1]

Girish Karnad
Translated by Girish Karnad
Introduced by Erin B. Mee

*My generation was the first to come of age
after India became independent of British
rule. It therefore had to face a situation
in which tensions implicit until then had
come out in the open and demanded to be
resolved without apologia or self-justification:
tensions between the cultural past of the
country and it colonial past, between the
attractions of Western modes of thought and
our own traditions, and finally between the
various visions of the future that opened up
once the common cause of political freedom
was achieved. This is the historical context
that gave rise to my plays and those of my
contemporaries.*

Girish Karnad[2]

Girish Karnad was born in 1938 in Matheran, near Mumbai. He was educated at the Karnatak University, Dharwad, and at Oxford, where he was a Rhodes scholar from 1960 to 1963. After working as an editor at Oxford University Press for seven years, he resigned to concentrate on writing and film-making. Karnad served as the director of the Film and Television Institute of India and, from 1988 to 1993, as the chairman of the Sangeet Natak Akademi. He was the recipient of a Homi Bhabha fellowship (1970–2), the Kamaladevi Chattopadhyaya Award, the Padma Shri (in 1974), the Padma Bushan (in 1992), and in 1999, he received the Bharatiya Jnanpith Award, India's highest literary award. His plays, which have been produced all over India and abroad, include *Yayati* (named for a character from the *Mahabharata*, 1961), *Tughlaq* (about Sultan Muhammad bin Tughlaq, 1964), *Naga-Mandala* (Play with a Cobra, 1988), *Tale-Danda* (Death by Beheading, 1989), *Agni Mattu Male* (The Fire and the Rain, 1993), *The Dreams of Tipu Sultan* (1997), *Bali, The Sacrifice* (2000), *Flowers* (2004) and *Broken Images* (2005).

When *Hayavadana* was published in 1971, it was immediately taken up as a 'poster play' for the emerging theatre of roots movement.[3] Suresh Awasthi credited Karnad with having evolved 'a new dramatic form' and singled out *Hayavadana* as an example of what could be done creatively with 'folk forms' in an urban setting (in SNA 1971: 5, 29). Later, in his famous article on the roots movement, Awasthi said that the 1972 production by B. V. Karanth (1929–2002) in Delhi 'reversed the colonial course of contemporary theatre'.[4] Five different directors in five different cities staged productions of *Hayavadana* in 1972. In his review of Karanth's Delhi production, J. N. Kaushal hailed *Hayavadana* as 'not only an event of Delhi's theatre season but an event of the Indian theatre itself'. He said the production 'was a pointer towards the form the emerging [Indian] theatre may take'.[5] While Panikkar created a hybrid theatre in his attempt to create a 'decolonized' modern Indian theatre, Karnad consciously set out, in almost all of his plays, including *Naga-Mandala* (Play with a Cobra, 1988) and *Agni Mattu Male* (The Fire and the Rain, 1994), to create a hybrid theatre that reflects the complex subjectivities of post-Independence reality. For Karnad, erasing all the effects of colonial theatrical culture was neither possible nor desirable. In *Hayavadana* Karnad employs a linear narrative structure, the proscenium stage, the fourth wall and human characters, strategically placing them in a play with a structure of concentric circles, several nonhuman characters, an acting style that occasionally breaks the fourth wall and references to *darshan*, a way of seeing that operates in Hindu ritual practice. By weaving structures, aesthetics and techniques of Western theatre together with structures, aesthetics and techniques from traditional Indian performance, specifically *yakshagana*, a well-known genre of dance-drama performed in Karnataka,[6] Karnad creates a play that is *neither* 'Western' *nor* 'Indian', *both* 'Western' *and* 'Indian'; a new theatre that is more than and different from the sum of its parts. With *Hayavadana* Karnad created a hybrid dramaturgical structure, acting style and visual practice that offers spectators a model for practising cultural ambidexterity – the ability to successfully and easily operate simultaneously in two or more cultural systems without privileging either one over the other.

The central plot in *Hayavadana* is based on a tale found in the *Kathasaritsagara* (The Ocean of Story),[7] a collection of Sanskrit stories dating from the eleventh century, and on its further development in Thomas Mann's 1940 German novella *The Transposed Heads*. Thus *Hayavadana*'s origins are intergeneric (a folktale transformed into a novella into a play) and intercultural (the story travelled from India to Germany and back again). 'Inter-ness' pervades *Hayavadana* at every level, from its origins to its thematic content to its production history.

Hayavadana focuses on Padmini, who is attracted to Kapila, her bookish husband Devadatta's sexy friend. In a jealous fit, Devadatta cuts off his own head. Kapila finds the body and, knowing he will be blamed for Devadatta's suicide, beheads himself. Padmini, terrified of the gossip that will surely ensue, appeals to the goddess Kali for help. Kali agrees to restore the men to life, and tells Padmini to put the heads back on their bodies. But Padmini, desiring the man of her dreams – one with Devadatta's mind and Kapila's body – 'accidentally' switches the heads, leading to the central question of the story: which man is her husband, the one with Devadatta's head or the one with his body? When a *rishi* (great sage) announces that the head is the supreme limb of the body and that the man with Devadatta's head is therefore her husband, Padmini feels that she has the best of both worlds, and happily goes home with the new Devadatta. Kapila exiles himself to the forest. Eventually, unable to tolerate an 'other' body as their own, the two men kill themselves/each other. In the *Kathasaritsagara*, this head/body split occurs between body and soul; in Mann's novella the dichotomy is between intellect and emotion; in Karnad's play the conflict is between self and other. In the *Kathasaritsagara* and in Mann's novella, the split is dealt with philosophically; in *Hayavadana* it is placed in the social and political context of post-Independence India.

Hayavadana

[Hayavadana, 1971]

ACT ONE

The stage is empty except for a chair, kept centre stage, and a table on stage right – or at the back – on which the **Bhagavata** *and the musicians sit.*

At the beginning of the performance, a mask of Ganesha is brought on stage and kept on the chair. Pooja is done. The **Bhagavata** *sings verses in praise of Ganesha, accompanied by his musicians. Then the mask is taken away.*

O Elephant-headed Herambha
whose flag is victory
and who shines like a thousand suns,
O husband of Riddhi and Siddhi,
seated on a mouse and decorated with a snake,
O single-tusked destroyer of incompleteness,
we pay homage to you and start our play.

Bhagavata May Vighneshwara, the destroyer of obstacles, who removes all hurdles and crowns all endeavors with success, bless our performance now. How indeed can one hope to describe his glory in our poor, disabled words? An elephant's head on a human body, a broken tusk and a cracked belly – whichever way you look at him he seems the embodiment of imperfection, of incompleteness. How indeed can one fathom the mystery that this very Vakratunda-Mahakaya, with his crooked face and distorted body, is the Lord and Master of Success and Perfection? Could it be that this Image of Purity and Holiness, the Mangalamoorty, intends to signify by his very appearance that the completeness of God is something no poor mortal can comprehend? Be that as it may. It is not for us to understand this Mystery or to try to unravel it. Nor is it within our powers to do so. Our duty is merely to pay homage to the Elephant-headed god and get on with our play.

This is the city of Dharmapura, ruled by King Dharmasheela whose fame and empire have already reached the ends of the eight directions. Two youths who dwell in this city are our heroes. One is Devadatta.

Comely in appearance, fair in colour, unrivalled in intelligence, Devadatta is the only son of the Revered Brahmin, Vidyasagara. Having felled the mightiest pundits of the kingdom in debates on logic and love, having blinded the greatest poets in the world with his poetry and wit, Devadatta is as it were the apple of every eye in Dharmapura.

The other youth is Kapila he is the only son of the ironsmith, Lohita, who is to the King's armoury as an axle to the chariotwheel. He is dark and plain to look at, yet in deeds which require drive and daring, in dancing, in strength and in physical skills, he has no equal.

(*A scream of terror is heard off-stage. The* **Bhagavata** *frowns, quickly looks in the direction of the scream, then carries on.*)

The world wonders at their friendship. The world sees these two young men wandering down the streets of Dharmapura, hand in hand, and remembers Lava and Kusha, Rama and Lakshmana, Krishna and Balarama.

(*Sings.*) Two friends there were

– one mind, one heart –

(*The scream is heard again. The* **Bhagavata** *cannot ignore it any more.*)

Who could that be – creating a disturbance at the very outset of our performance? (*Looks.*) Oh – It's Nata, our Actor. And he is running. What could have happened, I wonder?

(*The* **Actor** *comes running in, trembling with fear. He rushes on to the stage, runs round the stage once, then sees the* **Bhagavata** *and grabs him.*)

Actor   Sir, Bhagavata, sir –

Bhagavata (*trying to free himself*)   Tut! Tut! What's this? What's this?

Actor   Sir . . . oh my God! – God! –

Bhagavata   Let me go! I tell you, let go of me!

(*Freeing himself.*) Now what's this? What . . .

Actor   I – I – I – Oh God! (*Grabs him again.*)

Bhagavata   Let me go!

(*The* **Actor** *moves back.*)

What nonsense is this? What do you mean by all this shouting and screaming? In front of our audience too! How dare you disturb . . .

Actor   Please, please, I'm sorry. . . . But – but . . .

Bhagavata (*more calmly*)   Now, now, calm down! There's nothing to be afraid of here. I am here. The musicians are here. And there is our large-hearted audience. It may be that they fall asleep during a play sometimes. But they are ever alert when someone is in trouble. Now, tell us, what's the matter?

Actor (*panting*)   Oh – Oh – My heart. . . . It's going to burst . . .

Bhagavata   Sit down! Sit. Right! Now tell me everything quietly, slowly.

Actor   I was on my way here. . . . I was already late . . . didn't want to annoy you. . . . So I was hurrying down when. . . . Ohh!

(*Covers his face with his hands.*)

Bhagavata   Yes, yes. You were hurrying down. Then?

Actor   I'm shivering! On the way . . . you see. . . . I had drunk a lot of water this morning . . . my stomach was full . . . so to relieve myself . . .

Bhagavata   Watch what you are saying! Remember you are on stage . . .

Actor   I didn't do anything! I only wanted to . . . so I sat by the side of the road – and was about to pull up my dhoti when . . .

Bhagavata   Yes?

Actor   A voice – a deep, thick voice. . . . It said: 'Hey, you there – don't you know you are not supposed to commit nuisance on the main road?'

Bhagavata   Quite right too. You should have known that much.

Actor   I half got up and looked around. Not a man in sight – no one! So I was about to sit down again when the same voice said . . .

Bhagavata   Yes?

Actor   'You irresponsible fellow you, can't you understand you are not to commit nuisance on the main road?' I looked up. And there – right in front of me – across the fence . . .

Bhagavata   Who was there?

Actor   A horse!

Bhagavata   What?

Actor   A horse! And it was talking.

Bhagavata   What did you have to drink this morning?

Actor   Nothing, I swear. Bhagavata sir, I haven't been near a toddy-shop for a whole week. I didn't even have milk today.

Bhagavata   Perhaps your liver is sensitive to water.

Actor (*desperate*)   Please believe me. I saw it clearly – it was a horse – and it was talking.

Bhagavata (*resigned*)   It's no use continuing this nonsense. So you saw a talking horse? Good. Now go and get made up . . .

Actor   Made up? I fall to your feet, sir, I can't . . .

Bhagavata   Now look here . . .

Actor   Please, sir . . .

(*He holds up his hand. It's trembling.*)

You see, sir? How can I hold up a sword with this? How can I fight?

Bhagavata (*thinks*)   Well then. There's only one solution left. You go back . . .

Actor   Back?

Bhagavata   . . . back to that fence, have another look and make sure for yourself that whoever was talking, it couldn't have been that horse.

Actor   No!

Bhagavata   Nata . . .

Actor   I can't!

Bhagavata   It's an order.

Actor (*pleading*)   Must I?

Bhagavata   Yes, you must.

Actor   Sir . . .

(*The **Bhagavata** turns to the audience and starts singing.*)

Bhagavata   Two friends there were

– one mind, one heart –

Are you still here?

(*The* **Actor** *goes out looking at the* **Bhagavata**, *hoping for a last minute reprieve. It doesn't come.*)

Poor boy! God alone knows what he saw – and what he took it to be! There's truth for you . . . Pure illusion.

(*Sings.*) Two friends there were

– one mind, one heart –

(*A scream in the wings. The* **Actor** *comes rushing in.*)

Now look here . . .

Actor   It's coming. Coming . . .

Bhagavata   What's coming?

Actor   Him! He's coming . . . (*Rushes out.*)

Bhagavata   Him? It? What's coming? Whatever or whoever it is, the Actor has obviously been frightened by its sight. If even a hardened actor like him gets frightened, it's more than likely that our gentle audience may be affected too. It's not proper to let such a sight walk on stage unchallenged. (*To the wings.*) Hold up the entry curtain!

(*Two stagehands enter and hold up a half curtain, about six-feet in height – the sort of curtain used in Yakshatgana or Kathakali. The curtain masks the entry of* **Hayavadana**, *who comes and stands behind it.*)

Who's that?

(*No reply. Only the sound of someone sobbing behind the curtain.*)

How strange! Someone's sobbing behind the curtain. It looks as though the Terror which frightened our Actor is itself now crying!

(*To the stagehand.*) Lower the curtain!

(*The curtain is lowered by about a foot. One sees* **Hayavadana's** *head, which is covered by a veil. At a sign from the* **Bhagavata**, *one of the stagehands removes the veil, revealing a horse's head. For a while the horse-head doesn't realize that it is exposed to the gaze of the audience. The moment the realization dawns, the head ducks behind the curtain.*)

Bhagavata   A horse! No, it can't be!

(*He makes a sign. The curtain is lowered a little more – just enough to show the head again. Again it ducks. Again the curtain is lowered. This goes on till the curtain is lowered right down to the floor.* **Hayavadana,** *who has a man's body but a horse's head, it sitting on the floor hiding his head between his knees.*)

Incredible! Unbelievable!

(*At a sign from the Bhagavata, the stagehands withdraw. The* **Bhagavata** *goes and stands near* **Hayavadana.** *Then he grunts to himself as though he has seen through the trick.*)

Who are you?

(**Hayavadana** *lifts his head, and wipes the tears away. The* **Bhagavata** *beckons him to come centre stage.*)

Come here!

(**Hayavadana** *hesitates, then comes forward.*)

First you go around scaring people with this stupid mask. And then you have the cheek to disturb our show with your clowning? Have you no sense of proportion?. . . . Enough of this nonsense now. Take it off – I say, take off that stupid mask!

(**Hayavadana** *doesn't move.*)

You won't? – Then I'll have to do it myself!

(*Holds* **Hayavadana's** *head with both his hands and tries to pull it off.* **Hayavadana** *doesn't resist.*)

It is tight. Nata – My dear Actor . . .

(*The* **Actor** *comes in, warily, and stands open-mouthed at the sight he sees.*)

Why are you standing there? Don't you see you were taken in by a silly mask? Come and help me take it off now.

(*The* **Actor** *comes and holds* **Hayavadana** *by his waist while the* **Bhagavata** *pulls at the head.* **Hayavadana** *offers no resistance, but can't help moaning when the pain becomes unbearable. The tug-of-war continues for a while. Slowly, the truth dawns on the* **Bhagavata.**)

Nata, this isn't a mask! It's his real head!

(*The* **Actor** *drops* **Hayavadana** *with a thud.* **Hayavadana** *gets up and sits as before, head between knees.*)

Truly, surprises will never cease! If someone had told me only five minutes ago that there existed a man with a horse's head, I would have laughed out in his face.

(*To* **Hayavadana**.) Who are you?

(**Hayavadana** *gets up and starts to go out. The* **Actor** *hurriedly moves out of his way.*)

Wait! Wait! That's our green room there. It's bad enough that you scared this actor. We have a play to perform today, you know.

(**Hayavadana** *stands, dejected.*)

(*Softly.*) Who are you?

(*No reply.*)

What brought you to this? Was it a curse of some *rishi*? Or was it some holy place of pilgrimage, a *punyasthana*, which you desecrated? Or could it be that you insulted a *pativrata*, dedicated to the service of her husband? Or did you . . .

Hayavadana   Hey . . .

Bhagavata (*taken aback*)   Eh?

Hayavadana   What do you mean, Sir? Do you think just because you know the *Puranas* you can go about showering your Sanskrit on everyone in sight? What temple did I desecrate? What woman did I insult? What . . .

Bhagavata   Don't get annoyed . . .

Hayavadana   What else? What *rishi*? What sage? What? Whom have I wronged? What have I done to anyone? Let anyone come forward and say that I've caused him or her any harm. I haven't. Yet . . .

(*He is on the point of beginning to sob again.*)

Bhagavata   Don't take it to heart so much. What happened? What's your grief? You are not alone here. I am here. The musicians are here. And there is our large-hearted audience. It may be that they fall asleep during a play sometimes . . .

Hayavadana   What can anyone do? It's my fate.

Bhagavata   What's your name?

Hayavadana   Hayavadana.

Bhagavata   How did you get this horse's head?

Hayavadana   I was born with it.

Bhagavata   Then why didn't you stop us when we tried to take it off? Why did you put up with our torture?

Hayavadana   All my life I've been trying to get rid of this head. I thought – you with all your goodness and *punya* . . . if at least you manage to pull it off . . .

Bhagavata   Oho! Poor man! But, Hayavadana, what can anyone do about a head one's born with? Who knows what error committed in the last birth is responsi . . .

Hayavadana (*annoyed*)   It has nothing to do with my last birth. It's this birth which I can't shake off.

Bhagavata   Tell us what happened. Don't feel ashamed.

Hayavadana (*enraged*)   Ashamed? Me? Why should I . . .

Bhagavata   Sorry. I beg your pardon. I should have said 'shy.'

Hayavadana (*gloomy*)   It's a long story.

Bhagavata   Carry on.

Hayavadana   My mother was the Princess of Karnataka. She was a very beautiful girl. When she came of age, her father decided that she should choose her own husband. So princes of every kingdom in the world were invited – and they all came. From China, from Persia, from Africa. But she didn't like any of them. The last one to come was the Prince of Araby. My mother took one look at that handsome prince sitting on his great white stallion – and she fainted.

Actor   Ah!

Hayavadana   Her father at once decided that this was the man. All arrangements for the wedding were made. My mother recovered – and do you know what she said?

Actor, Bhagavata   What?

Hayavadana   She said she would only marry that horse!

Actor   What?

Hayavadana   Yes. She wouldn't listen to anyone. The Prince of Araby burst a blood-vessel.

Actor   Naturally.

Hayavadana   No one could dissuade her. So ultimately she was married off to the white stallion. She lived with him for fifteen years. One morning she wakes up – and no horse! In its place stood a beautiful Celestial Being, a *gandharva*. Apparently this Celestial Being had been cursed by the god Kubera to be born a horse for some act of misbehavior. After fifteen years of human love he had become his original self again.

Bhagavata   I must admit several such cases are on record.

Hayavadana   Released from his curse, he asked my mother to accompany to his Heavenly Abode. But she wouldn't. She said she would come only if he became a horse again. So he cursed her . . .

Actor   No!

Hayavadana   He cursed her to become a horse herself. So my mother became a horse and ran away prancing happily. My father went back to his Heavenly Abode. Only I – the child of their marriage – was left behind.

Bhagavata   It's a sad story.

Actor   Very sad.

Hayavadana   What should I do now, Bhagavata Sir? What can I do to get rid of this head?

Bhagavata   Hayavadana, what's written on our foreheads cannot be altered.

Hayavadana (*slapping himself on the forehead*)   But what a forehead! What a forehead! If it was a forehead like yours, I would have accepted anything. But this!. . . . I have tried to accept my fate. My personal life has naturally been blameless. So I took interest in the social life of the Nation – Civics, Politics, Patriotism, Nationalism, Indianization, the Socialist Pattern of Society. . . . I have tried everything. But where's my society? Where? You must help me to become a complete man, Bhagavata Sir. But how? What can I do?

(*Long silence. They think.*)

Bhagavata   Banaras?

Hayavadana   What?

Bhagavata   If you go to Banaras and make a vow in front of the god there . . .

Hayavadana   I've tried that. Didn't work.

Bhagavata   Rameshwaram?

Hayavadana   Banaras, Rameshwaram, Gokarn, Haridwar, Gaya, Kedarnath – not only those but the *Dargah* of Khwaja Yusuf Baba, the Grotto of Our Virgin Mary – I've tried them all. Magicians, mendicants, maharshis, fakirs, saints and sadhus – sadhus with short hair, sadhus with beards – sadhus in saffron, sadhus in the altogether – hanging, singing, rotating, gyrating – on the spikes, in the air, under water, under the ground – I've covered them all. And what did I get out of all this? Everywhere I went I had to cover my head with a veil – and I started going bald. (*Pause. Shyly.*) You know, I hate this head, but I just can't help being fond of this lovely, long mane. (*Pause.*) So – I had to give the miss to Tirupati.

(*Long silence.*)

Bhagavata   Come to think of it, Hayavadana, why don't you try the Kali of Mount Chitrakoot?

Hayavadana   Anything you say.

Bhagavata   It's temple at the top of Mount Chitrakoot. The goddess there is famous for being ever-awake to the call of the devotees. Thousands used to flock to her temple once. No. No one goes now, though.

Hayavadana   Why not?

Bhagavata   She used to give anything anyone asked for. As the people became aware of this, they stopped going.

Hayavadana   Fools!

Bhagavata   Why don't you try her?

Hayavadana (*jumps up*)   Why not? I'll start at once . . .

Bhagavata   Good. But I don't think you should go alone. It's a wild road. You'll have to ask a lot of people, which won't be easy for you. So . . .

(*To the* **Actor**.) You'd better go with him.

Actor   Me?

Bhagavata   Yes, that way you can make up for having insulted him.

Hayavadana   But, Bhagavata Sir, may I point out that his roadside manners . . .

Actor   There! He's insulting me now! Let him find his own way. What do I care?

Bhagavata   Come, come, don't let's start fighting now. (*To* **Hayavadana**) Don't worry. There's no highway there. Only a cart track at best.

(*To the* **Actor**.) You've no reason to feel insulted. Actually you should admire him. Even in his dire need, he doesn't lose his civic sense. Be off now.

Hayavadana (*to the* **Actor**)   Please, don't get upset. I won't bother you, I promise.

(*To the* **Bhagavata**.) I am most grateful . . .

Bhagavata (*blessing him*)   May you become successful in your search for completeness.

(*The two go.*)

Each one to his own fate. Each one to his own desire. Each one to his own luck. Let's turn now to our story.

(*He starts singing. The following is a prose rendering of the song.*)

Bhagavata (*sings*)   Two friends there were – one mind, one heart. They saw a girl and forgot themselves. But they could not understand the song she sang.

Female chorus (*sings*)   Why should love stick to the sap of a single body? When the stem is drunk with the thick yearning of the many-petalled, many-flowered lantana, why should it be tied down to the relation of a single flower?

Bhagavata (*sings*)   They forgot themselves and took off their bodies. And she took the laughing heads, and held them high so the pouring blood bathed her, coloured her red. Then she danced around and sang.

Female chorus (*sings*)   A head for each breast. A pupil for each eye. A side for each arm. I have neither regret nor shame. The blood pours into the earth and a song branches out into the sky.

(**Devadatta** *enters and sits on the chair. He is a slender, rather good-looking person with a fair complexion. He is lost in thought.* **Kapila** *enters. He is powerfully built and darker.*)

Kapila (*even as he is entering*)   Devadatta, why didn't you come to the gymnasium last evening? I'd asked you to. It was such fun . . .

Devadatta (*preoccupied*)   Some work.

Kapila   Really, you should have come. The wrestler from Gandhara – he's one of India's greatest, you know – he came. Nanda and I were wrestling when he arrived. He watches us. When I caught Nanda in a crocodile-hold, he first burst into applause and said . . .

(*Notices that* **Devadatta** *isn't listening and stops. Pause.*)

Devadatta (*waking up*)   Then?

Kapila   Then what?

Devadatta (*flustered*)   I mean . . . what did Nanda do?

Kapila   He played the flute.

Devadatta (*more confused*)   No. . . . I mean . . . you were saying something about the wrestler from Gandhara, weren't you?

Kapila   He wrestled with me for a few minutes, patted me on the back and said, 'You'll go far.'

Devadatta   That's nice.

Kapila   Yes, it is. . . . Who's it this time?

Devadatta   What do you mean?

Kapila   I mean – who – is – it – this – time?

Devadatta   What do you mean who?

Kapila   I mean – who is the girl?

Devadatta   No one. (*Pause.*) How did you guess?

Kapila   My dear friend, I have seen you fall in love fifteen times in the last two years. How could I not guess?

Devadatta   Kapila, if you've come to make fun of me . . .

Kapila   I am not making fun of you. Every time, you have been the first to tell me about it. Why so reticent this time?

Devadatta   How can you even talk of them in the same breath as her? Before her, they're as . . .

Kapila   . . . as stars before the moon, as the glow-worms before a torch. Yes, yes, that's been fifteen times too.

Devadatta (*exploding*)   Why don't you go home? You are becoming a bore.

Kapila   Don't get annoyed. Please.

Devadatta   You call yourself my friend. But you haven't understood me at all.

Kapila   And have you understood me? No, you haven't. Or you wouldn't get angry like this. Don't you know I would do anything for you? Jump into a well – or walk into fire? Even my parents aren't as close to me as you are. I would leave them this minute if you asked me to.

Devadatta (*irritated*)   Don't start on that now. You've said it fifty times already.

Kapila   . . . And I'll say it again. If it wasn't for you I would have been no better than the ox in our yard. You showed me that there were such things as poetry and literature. You taught me . . .

Devadatta   Why don't you go home? All I wanted was to be by myself for a day. Alone. And you had to come and start your chatter. What do you know of poetry and literature? Go back to your smithy – that's where you belong.

Kapila (*hurt*)   Do you really want me to go?

Devadatta   Yes.

Kapila   All right. If that's what you want.

(*He starts to go.*)

Devadatta   Sit down.

(*This is of course exactly what* **Kapila** *wants. He sits down on the floor.*)

And don't speak . . .

(**Devadatta** *gets down on the floor to sit beside* **Kapila**. **Kapila** *at once leaps up and gestures to* **Devadatta** *to sit on the chair.* **Devadatta** *shakes his head but* **Kapila** *insists, pulls him up by his arm.* **Devadatta** *gets up.*)

You are a pest.

(*Sits on the chair.* **Kapila** *sits down on the ground happily. A long pause.*)

Devadatta (*slowly*)   How can I describe her, Kapila? Her forelocks rival the bees, her face is . . .

(*All this is familiar to* **Kapila** *and he joins in, with great enjoyment.*)

Both   . . . is a white lotus. Her beauty is as the magic lake. Her arms to the lotus creepers. Her breasts are golden urns and her waist . . .

Devadatta   No. No!

Kapila   Eh?

Devadatta   I was blind all these days. I deceived myself that I
understood poetry. I didn't. I understood nothing.

Tanvee shyama –

Both   . . . *shikharidashana pakvabimbadharoshthee – Madhyekshama
chakitaharinee prekshana nimnanabhih.*

Devadatta   The Shyama Nayika – born of Kalidasa's magic
description – as Vatsyayana had dreamt her. Kapila, in a single
appearance, she has become my guru in the poetry of my love. Do you
think she would ever assent to become my disciple in love itself?

Kapila (*aside*)   This is new!

Devadatta (*his eyes shining*)   If only she would consent to be my Muse,
I could outshine Kalidasa. I'd always wanted to do that – but I thought it
was impossible. . . . But now I see it is within my reach.

Kapila   Then go ahead. Write . . .

Devadatta   But how can I without her in front of me? How can I
concentrate when my whole being is only thinking of her, craving for her?

Kapila   What's her name? Will you at least tell me that?

Devadatta   Her name? She has no name.

Kapila   But what do her parents call her?

Devadatta (*anguished*)   What's the use? She isn't meant for the likes of
me . . .

Kapila   You don't really believe that, do you? With all your qualities –
achievements – looks – family – grace . . .

Devadatta   Don't try to console me with praise.

Kapila   I'm not praising you. You know very well that every parent of
every girl in the city is only waiting to catch you . . .

Devadatta   Don't! Please. I know this girl is beyond my wildest
dreams. But still – I can't help wanting her – I can't help it. I swear,
Kapila, with you as my witness I swear, if I ever get her as my wife, I'll
sacrifice my two arms to the goddess Kali, I'll sacrifice my head to Lord
Rudra . . .

Kapila Ts! Ts! (*aside*) This is a serious situation. It does look as though this sixteenth girl has really caught our Devadatta in her net. Otherwise, he isn't the type to talk of such violence.

Devadatta I meant it! What's the use of these hands and this head if I'm not to have her? My poetry won't live without her. The *Shakuntalam* will never be excelled. But how can I explain this to her? I have no cloud for a messenger. No bee to show the way. Now the only future I have is to stand and do penance in Pavana Veethi . . .

Kapila Pavana Veethi! Why there?

Devadatta She lives in that street.

Kapila How do you know?

Devadatta I saw her in the market yesterday evening. I couldn't remove my eyes from her and followed her home.

Kapila Tut! Tut! What must people have thought?

Devadatta She went into a house in Pavana Veethi. I waited outside all evening. She didn't come out.

Kapila Now tell me. What sort of a house was it?

Devadatta I can't remember.

Kapila What colour?

Devadatta Don't know.

Kapila How many storeys?

Devadatta I didn't notice.

Kapila You mean you didn't notice anything about the house?

Devadatta The door frame of the house had an engraving of a two-headed bird at the top. I only saw that. She lifted her hand to knock and it touched the bird. For a minute, the bird came alive.

Kapila (*jumps up*) Then why didn't you tell me before? You've been wasting precious time . . .

Devadatta I don't understand . . .

Kapila My dear Devadatta, your cloud-messenger, your bee, your pigeon is sitting right in front of you and you don't even know it? You wait here. I'll go, find out her house, her name . . .

Devadatta (*incredulous*)   Kapila – Kapila . . .

Kapila   I'll be back in a few minutes . . .

Devadatta   I won't ever forget this, Kapila . . .

Kapila   Shut up!. . . . And forget all about your arms and head. This job doesn't need either Rudra or Kali. I'm quite enough. (*Goes out.*)

Devadatta   Kapila – Kapila. . . . He's gone. How fortunate I am to have a friend like him. Pure gold. (*Pause.*) But should I have trusted this to him? He means well – and he is a wizard in his smithy, in his farm, in his fields. But here? No. He is too rough, too indelicate. He was the wrong man to send. He's bound to ruin the whole thing. (*Anguished.*) Lord Rudra, I meant what I said. If I get her, my head will be a gift to you. Mother Kali, I'll sacrifice my arms to you. I swear . . .

(*Goes out. The* **Bhagavata** *removes the chair.* **Kapila** *enters.*)

Kapila   This is Pavana Veethi – the street of merchants. Well, well, well. What enormous houses! Each one a palace in itself. It's a wonder people don't get lost in these houses.

(*Examines the doors one by one.*)

Now. This is not a double-headed bird. It's an eagle – This? A lotus. This is – er – a lion. Tiger. A wheel! And this? God alone knows what this is. And the next? (*In disgust.*) A horse! – A rhinoceros – Another lion. Another lotus! – Where the hell is that stupid two-headed bird? (*Stops.*) What was the engraving I couldn't make out? (*Goes back and stares at it. Shouts in triumph.*) That's it! Almost gave me the slip! A proper two-headed bird. But it's so tiny you can't see it at all unless you are willing to tear your eyes staring at it. Well now. Whose house could this be? (*Looks around.*) No one in sight. Naturally. What should anyone come here for in this hot sun? Better ask the people in the house.

(*Mimes knocking. Listens.* **Padmini** *enters humming a tune.*)

Padmini   . . . Here comes the rider – from which land does he come? . . .

Kapila (*gapes at her. Aside*)   I give up, Devadatta. I surrender to your judgment. I hadn't thought anyone could be more beautiful than the wench Ragini who acts Rambha in our village troupe. But this one! You're right – she is Yakshini, Shakuntala, Urvashi, Indumati – all rolled into one.

Padmini   You knocked, didn't you?

Kapila   Er – yes . . .

Padmini   Then why are you gaping at me? What do you want?

Kapila   I – I just wanted to know whose house this was.

Padmini   Whose house do you want?

Kapila   This one.

Padmini   I see. Then who do you want here?

Kapila   The master . . .

Padmini   Do you know his name?

Kapila   No.

Padmini   Have you met him?

Kapila   No.

Padmini   Have you seen him?

Kapila   No.

Padmini   So. You haven't met him, seen him or know him. What do you want with him?

Kapila (*aside*)   She is quite right. What have I to do with him? I only want to find out his name . . .

Padmini   Are you sure you want this house? Or were you . . .

Kapila   No. I'm sure this is the one.

Padmini (*pointing to her head*)   Are you all right here?

Kapila (*taken aback*)   Yes – I think so.

Padmini   How about your eyes? Do they work properly?

Kapila   Yes.

Padmini (*showing him four fingers*)   How many?

Kapila   Four.

Padmini   Correct. So there's nothing wrong with your eyes. As for the other thing, I'll have to take you on trust. Well then. If you are sure you wanted this house, why were you peering at all those doors? And what were you mumbling under your breath?

Kapila (*startled*)   How did you know?

Padmini   I am quite sane . . . and I've got good eyes.

Kapila (*looks up and chuckles*)   Oh, I suppose you were watching from the terrace . . .

Padmini (*in a low voice, mysteriously*)   Listen, my father could be a servant in this house. Or the master of this house could be my father's servant. My father could be the master's father, brother, son-in-law, cousin, grandfather or uncle. Do you agree?

Kapila   Er – yes.

Padmini   Right. Then we'll start again. Whom should I call?

Kapila   Your father.

Padmini   And if he's not in?

Kapila (*lost*)   Anyone else.

Padmini   Which anyone?

Kapila   Perhaps – your brother.

Padmini   Do you know him?

Kapila   No.

Padmini   Have you met him?

Kapila   No.

Padmini   Do you know his name?

Kapila (*desperate*)   Please, please – call your father or the master or both, if they are the same, anyone. Please call someone!

Padmini   No. No. That won't do.

Kapila (*looking around; aside*)   No one here. Still I have to find out her name. Devadatta must be in agony and he will never forgive me if I go back now. (*Aloud.*) *Madam*, please. I have some very important work. I'll touch your feet . . .

Padmini (*eager*)   You will? Really? Do you know, I've touched everyone's feet in this house some time or the other, but no one's ever touched mine. You will?

Kapila (*slapping his forehead as he sinks to the ground*)   I'm finished – decimated – powdered to dust – powdered into tiny specks of flour. (*To Padmini.*) My mother, can I at least talk to a servant?

Padmini   I knew it. I knew you wouldn't touch my feet. One can't even trust strangers anymore. All right, my dear son! I opened the door. So consider me the door-keeper. What do you want?

Kapila (*determined*)   All right! (*Gets up.*) You have no doubt heard of the Revered Brahmin Vidyasagara.

Padmini   It's possible.

Kapila   In which case you'll also know of Devadatta, his only son. A poet. A pundit. Knows the Vedas backwards. Writes the grandest poetry ever. Long, dark hair. Delicate, fair face. Age twenty. Height five feet seven inches. Weight . . .

Padmini   Wait a minute! What's he to you?

Kapila   Friend. Greatest in the world! But the main question now is: What's he going to be to you?

(*Sudden silence.*)

Padmini (*blushing as the import of the remark dawns on her*)   Mother!

(*Runs in.* **Kapila** *stands, staring after her.*)

Kapila   Devadatta, my friend, I confess to you I'm feeling uneasy. You are a gentle soul. You can't bear a bitter word or an evil thought. But this one is fast as lightning – and as sharp. She is not for the likes of you. What she needs is a man of steel. But what can one do? You'll never listen to me. And I can't withdraw now. I'll have to talk to her family . . .

(*Follows her in.*)

Bhagavata   Need one explain to our wise and knowing audience what followed next? Padmini is the daughter of the leading merchant in Dharmapura. In her house, the very floor is swept by the Goddess of Wealth. In Devadatta's house, they've the Goddess of Learning for a maid. What could then possibly stand in the way of bringing the families together? (*Marriage music.*) Padmini became the better half of Devadatta and settled in his house. Nor did Devadatta forget his debt to Kapila. The old friendship flourished as before. Devadatta – Padmini – Kapila! To the admiring citizens of Dharmapura, Rama – Sita – Lakshmana.

(*Enter* **Devadatta** *and* **Padmini**.)

Padmini   Why is he so late? He should have been here more than an hour ago.

(*Looks out of a window.*)

Devadatta   Have you packed your clothes properly?

Padmini   The first thing in the morning.

Devadatta   And the mattresses? We may have to sleep out in the open. It's quite chilly. We'll need at least two rugs.

Padmini   Don't worry. The servant's done all that.

Devadatta   And your shawl? Also some warm clothes . . .

Padmini   What's happened to you today? At other times you are so full of your books, you even forget to wash your hands after a meal. But today you've been going on and on and on all morning.

Devadatta   Padmini, I've told you ten times already I don't like the idea of this trip. You should rest – not face such hazards. The cart will probably shake like an earthquake. It's dangerous in your condition. But you won't listen.

Padmini   My condition! What's happened to me? To listen to you, one would think I was the first woman in this world to become pregnant. I only have to stumble and you act as though it's all finished and gone . . .

Devadatta   For God's sake, will you stop it?

Padmini (*laughs*)   Sorry! (*Bites her tongue in repentance.*) I won't say such things again.

Devadatta   You've no sense of what not to say. So long as you can chatter and run around like a child . . .

Padmini (*back at the window*)   Where is Kapila?

Devadatta   . . . and drool over Kapila all day.

Padmini (*taken aback*)   What else should I say? The other day I wanted to read out a play of Bhasa's to you and sure enough Kapila drops in.

Padmini   Oh! That's biting you still, is it? But why are you blaming me? He was your friend even before you married me, wasn't he? He used to drop in every day even then . . .

Devadatta   But shouldn't he realize I'm a married man now? He just can't go on as before . . .

Padmini   Don't blame him. It's my fault. He learnt a bit about poetry from you and I thought he might enjoy Bhasa. So I asked him to come. He didn't want to but I insisted.

Devadatta   I know that.

Padmini   Had I realized you would be so upset, I wouldn't have.

Devadatta   I'm not upset, Padmini. Kapila isn't merely a friend – he's like my brother. One has to collect merit in seven lives to get a friend like him. But is it wrong for me to want to read to you alone? Or to spend a couple of days with you without anyone else around? (*Pause.*) Of course, once he came, there wasn't the slightest chance of my reading any poetry. You had to hop around him twittering 'Kapila! Kapila!' every minute.

Padmini   You aren't jealous of him, are you?

Devadatta   Me? Jealous of Kapila? Why do you have to twist everything I say . . .

Padmini (*laughs. Affectionately*)   Don't sulk now. I was just trying to be funny. Really you have no sense of humour.

Devadatta   It's humour for you. But it burns my insides.

Padmini   Aw, shut up. Don't I know how liberal and largehearted you are? You aren't the sort to get jealous. If I were to fall into a well tomorrow, you wouldn't even miss me until my bloated corpse floated up . . .

Devadatta (*irritated*)   Padmini!

Padmini   Sorry, I forgot. I apologize – I slap myself on the cheeks. (*Slaps herself on both cheeks with her right hand several times in punishment.*) Is that all right? The trouble is I grew up saying these awful things and it's become a habit now. But you are so fragile! I don't know how you're going to go through life wrapped in silk like this! You are still a baby . . .

Devadatta   I see.

Padmini   Look now. You got annoyed about Kapila. But why? You are my saffron, my marriage thread, my deity. Why should you feel disturbed? I like making fun of Kapila – he is such an innocent. Looks a proper devil, but the way he blushes and giggles and turns red, he might have been a bride.

Devadatta (*smiles*)   Well, this bride didn't blush.

Padmini   No one taught this bride to blush. But now I'm learning from that yokel.

(*They both laugh. She casually goes back to the window and looks out.*)

Devadatta (*aside*)   Does she really not see? Or is she deliberately playing this game with him? Kapila was never the sort to blush. But now, he only has to see her and he begins to wag his tail. Sits up on his hind legs as though he were afraid to let her words fall to the ground. And that pleading in his eyes – can't she really see that? (*Aloud.*) Padmini, Kapila isn't used to women. The only woman he has known in his life is his mother.

Padmini   You mean it's dangerous to be with him? The way you talk one would never imagine he was your friend.

Devadatta (*incensed*)   Why do you have to twist everything I say . . .

Padmini (*conciliatory*)   What did I say? Listen, if you really don't want to go to Ujjain today, let's not. When Kapila comes, tell him I'm ill.

Devadatta   But . . . you will be disappointed.

Padmini   Me? Of course not. We'll do as you feel. You remember what the priest said – I'm your 'half' now. The better half! We can go to Ujjain some other time. . . . In another couple of months, there's the big Ujjain fair. We'll go then – just the two of us. All right? We'll cancel today's trip.

Devadatta (*trying to control his excitement*)   Now – if you aren't going to be disappointed – then – truly – that's what I would like most. Not because I'm jealous of Kapila – No, I'm not, I know that. He has a heart of gold. But this is your first baby . . .

Padmini   What do you mean first? How many babies can one have within six months?

Devadatta   You aren't going to start again?

Padmini   No, no, no, I won't say a word.

Devadatta (*pinching her cheek*)   Bad upbringing – that's what it is. I don't like the idea of your going out in a cart in your present condition, that's all.

Padmini   Ordinarily I would have replied I had a womb of steel, but I won't – in the present condition.

(*Both laugh.*)

All right. If you are happy, so am I.

Devadatta (*happy*)   Yes, we'll spend the whole day by ourselves. The servants are going home anyway. They can come back tomorrow. But for today – only you and me. It's been such a long time since we've been on our own.

Kapila (*off-stage*)   Devadatta . . .

Padmini   There's Kapila now. You tell him.

(*She pretends to go in, but goes and stands in a corner of the stage, listening.* **Kapila** *enters excited.*)

Kapila   I'm late, ain't I? What could I do? That cartman had kept the cart ready but the moment I looked at it, I knew one of the oxen was no good. I asked him to change it. 'We won't reach Ujjain for another fortnight in this one,' I said. He started . . .

Devadatta   Kapila . . .

Kapila   . . . making a scene, but I stood my ground. So he had to fetch a new one. These cart-hirers are a menace. If ours hadn't gone to Chitrapur that day . . .

Devadatta   Kapila, we have to call off today's trip . . .

Kapila (*suddenly silenced*)   Oh!

Devadatta (*embarrassed*)   You see, Padmini isn't well . . .

Kapila   Well, then of course . . .

(*Silence.*)

I'll return the cart then.

Devadatta   Yes.

Kapila   Or else he may charge us for the day.

Devadatta   Uhm.

Kapila (*aside*)   So it's off. What am I to do for the rest of the day? What am I to do for the rest of the week? Why should it feel as though the whole world has been wiped out for a whole week? Why this emptiness? Kapila, Kapila, get a tight hold on yourself. You are slipping, boy, control yourself. Don't lose that hold. Go now. Don't come here again for a week. Devadatta's bound to get angry with you for not visiting. Sister-in-law will be annoyed. But don't come back. Go, go! (*Aloud.*) Well then – I'll start.

Devadatta   Why don't you sit for a while?

Kapila   No, no. We might upset sister-in-law more then with our prattle.

Devadatta   That's true. So come again. Soon.

Kapila   Yes, I will.

(*Starts to go.* **Padmini** *comes out.*)

Padmini   Why are you sitting here? When are we going to start? We are already late . . .

(*They look at her, surprised.*)

Kapila   But if you aren't well, we won't . . .

Padmini   What's wrong with me? I'm in perfect health. I had a headache this morning. But a layer of ginger paste took care of that. Why should we cancel our trip for a little thing like that?

(**Devadatta** *opens his mouth to say something, but stays quiet.*)

(*To* **Kapila**.) Why are you standing there like a statue?

Kapila   No, really, if you have a headache . . .

Padmini   I don't have a headache now!

Devadatta   But, Padmini . . .

Padmini   Kapila, put those bundles out there in the cart. The servant will bring the rest.

(**Kapila** *stands totally baffled. He looks at* **Devadatta** *for guidance. There's none.*)

Be quick. Otherwise I'll put them in myself.

(**Kapila** *goes out.* **Padmini** *goes to* **Devadatta**. *Pleading.*)

Please don't get angry. Poor boy, he looked so lost and disappointed, I couldn't bear to see it. He has been running around for us this whole week.

Devadatta (*turning his head away*)   Where's the box in which I put the books? Let me take it.

Padmini   You are an angel. I knew you wouldn't mind. I'll bring it. It's quite light.

(*Goes out.*)

Devadatta (*to himself*)   And my disappointment? Does that mean nothing to you? (*Aloud.*) Don't. I'll take it. Please, don't lift anything.

(*Goes in after her.*)

Bhagavata Why do you tremble, heart? Why do you cringe like a touch-me-not bush through which a snake has passed? The sun rests his head on the Fortunate Lady's Flower. And the head is bidding goodbye to the heart.

(**Kapila**, *followed by* **Padmini** *and* **Devadatta**, *enters miming a cart-ride.* **Kapila** *is driving the cart.*)

Padmini How beautifully you drive the cart, Kapila! Your hands don't even move but the oxen seem to know exactly which way you want them to go.

(**Kapila** *laughs happily.*)

Shall we stop here for a while? We've been in this cart all day and my leg feel like bits of wood.

Kapila Right! Ho – Ho . . .

(*Pulls the cart to a halt. They get down. She slips but* **Devadatta** *supports her.*)

Padmini What a terrible road. Nothing but potholes and rocks. But one didn't feel a thing in the cart! You drove it so gently – almost made it float. I remember when Devadatta took me in a cart. That was soon after our marriage. I insisted on being shown the lake outside the city. So we started, only the two of us and Devadatta driving – against my advice, I must say. And we didn't even cross the city gates. The oxen took everything except the road. He only had to pull to the right, and off they would rush to the left! I've never laughed so much in my life. But of course he got very angry, so we had to go back home straight!

(*Laughs. But* **Kapila** *and* **Devadatta** *don't join in.*)

Kapila, what's that glorious tree over there? That one, covered with flowers.

Kapila Oh that! That's called the Fortunate Lady's Flower – that means a married woman . . .

Padmini I know! But why do they call it that?

Kapila Wait. I'll bring you a flower. Then you'll see.

(*Goes out.*)

Padmini (*watching him, aside*) How he climbs – like an ape. Before I could even say 'yes', he had taken off his shirt, pulled his *dhorti* up and swung up the branch. And what an ethereal shape! Such a broad back: like an ocean with muscles rippling across it – and then that small, feminine waist which looks so helpless.

Dedvadatta (*aside*)   She had so much to talk about all day, she couldn't wait for breath. Now, not a word.

Padmini (*aside*)   He is like a Celestial Being reborn as a hunter. How his body sways, his limbs curve – It's a dance almost.

Devadatta (*aside*)   And why should I blame her? It's his strong body – his manly muscles. And to think I had never *ever* noticed them all these years! I was an innocent – an absolute baby.

Padmini (*aside*)   No woman could resist him.

Devadatta (*aside*)   No woman could resist him – and what does it matter that she's married? What a fool I've been. All these days I only saw that pleading in his eyes stretching out its arms, begging for a favour. But never looked in her eyes. And when I did, took the whites of her eyes for their real depth. Only now I see the depths. Now I see these flames leaping up from those depths. Now! So late! Don't turn away now, Devadatta, look at her. Look at those yellow, purple flames. Look how she's pouring her soul into his mould. Look! Let your guts burn out. Let your lungs turn to ash, but don't turn away. Look and don't scream. Strangle your agony. But look deep into these eyes – look until those peacock flames burn out the blindness in you. Don't be a coward now.

Padmini (*aside*)   How long can one go on like this? How long? How long? If Devadatta notices . . .

(*Looks at* **Devadatta**. *He is looking at her already and their eyes meet. Both look away.*)

Padmini (*aloud*) , There he comes. All I wanted was one flower and he's brought a heap.

(**Kapila** *comes in, miming a whole load of flowers in his arms and hands. He pours them out in front of her.*)

Kapila   Here you are. The Fortunate Lady's flowers.

Padmini   And why a 'Fortunate Lady', pray?

Kapila   Because it has all the marks of marriage a woman puts on. The yellow on the petals. Then that red round patch at the bottom of the petals, like on your foreheads. Then, here, that thin saffron line, like in the parting of your hair. Then – uhm . . . oh yes – here near the stem a row of black dots, like a necklace of black beads –

Padmini   What imagination! (*To* **Devadatta**.) You should put it in your poetry. It's good for a simile.

Devadatta   Shall we go? It's quite late.

Padmini   Let's stay. I have been sitting in that cart for I don't know how long. I didn't know the road to Ujjain was so enchanting.

Kapila   The others take a longer route. This is a more wooded area, so very few come this way. But I like this better. Besides, it's fifteen miles shorter.

Padmini   I wouldn't have minded even if it were fifteen miles longer. It's like a garden.

Kapila   Isn't it? Look there, do you see it? That's the river Bhargavi. The poet Vyasa had a hermitage on its banks. There's a temple of Rudra there now.

Devadatta (*suddenly awake*)   A temple of Rudra?

Kapila   Yes, it's beautiful. And – there – beyond that hill is a temple of Kali

(*Two stagehands come and hold up a half-curtain in the corner to which he points. The curtain has a picture of Goddess Kali on it. The* **Bhagavata** *places a sword in front of it.*)

It was very prosperous once. But now it's quite dilapidated.

Devadatta (*as though in a trance*)   The temple of Rudra!

Kapila   Yes, that's old too. But not half as ruined as the Kali temple. We can have a look if you like.

Padmini   Yes, let's.

Devadatta   Why don't you go and see the Kali temple first?

Kapila   No, that's quite terrible. I saw it once: bats, snakes, all sorts of poisonous insects – and no proper road. We can go to the Rudra temple, though. It's nearer.

Padmini   Come on. Let's go.

Devadatta   You two go. I won't come.

Padmini (*pause*)   And you?

Devadatta   I'll stay here and watch the cart.

Kapila   But there's no fear of thieves here. (*Sensing the tension.*) Or else. I'll stay here.

Devadatta   No, no. You two go. I'm also a little tired.

Padmini (*aside*)   He has started it again. Another tantrum. Let him. Why do I care? (*Aloud.*) Come, Kapila, we'll go.

Kapila   But perhaps in your condition . . .

Padmini (*exploding*)   Why are you two hounding me with this condition? If you don't want to come, say so. Don't make excuses . . .

Kapila   Devadatta, it's not very far. You come too.

Devadatta   I told you to go. Don't force me, please.

Padmini   Let's not go. I don't want the two of you to suffer for my sake.

Devadatta (*to* **Kapila**)   Go.

Kapila (*he has no choice*)   Come. We'll be back soon.

(**Kapila** *and* **Padmini** *go out.*)

Devdatta   Goodbye, Kapila. Goodbye, Padmini. May Lord Rudra bless you. You are two pieces of my heart – Live happily together. I shall find my eternal happiness in that thought. (*Agonized.*) Give me strength, Lord Rudra. My father, give me strength. I'm already trembling, I'd never thought I would be so afraid. Give me courage, Father, strengthen me.

(*He walks to the temple of Kali. It's a steep and difficult climb. He is exhausted by the time he reaches the temple. He prostrates himself before the goddess.*)

Bhavani, Bhairavi, Kali, Durga, Mahamaya, Mother of all Nature, I had forgotten my promise to you. Forgive me, Mother. You fulfilled the deepest craving of my life. You gave me Padmini – and I forgot my word. Forgive me, for I'm here now to carry out my promise.

(*Picks up the sword.*)

Great indeed is your mercy. Even in this lonely place some devotee of yours – a hunter perhaps or a tribesman has left this weapon. Who knows how many lives this weapon has sacrificed to you. (*Screaming.*) Here, Mother Kali, here's another. My head. Take it, Mother, accept this little offering of my head.

(*Cuts off his head. Not an easy thing to do. He struggles, groans, writhes. Ultimately succeeds in killing himself. A long silence.* **Padmini** *and* **Kapila** *return to the cart.*)

Padmini (*enters talking*) . . . he should have come. How thrilling it was! Heavenly! But of course he has no enthusiasm for these things. After all . . .

(*Notices* **Devadatta** *isn't there.*)

Where's Devadatta?

(*They look around.*)

He said he'd stay here!

Kapila (*calls*) Devadatta – Devadatta –

Padmini He's probably somewhere around. Where will he go? He has the tenderest feet on earth. They manage to get blisters, corns, cuts, boils and wounds without any effort.

Kapila (*calls*) Devadatta.

Padmini Why are you shouting? Sit down. He'll come.

(**Kapila** *inspects the surrounding area. Gives a gasp of surprise.*)

What's it?

Kapila His footprints. He has obviously gone in that direction. (*Pause.*) But – that's where the Kali temple is!

Padmini You don't mean he's gone there! How absurd!

Kapila You stay here. I'll bring him back.

Padmini But why do you have to go? There's nothing to fear in this broad daylight!

Kapila (*hurrying off*) It's very thickly wooded there. If he gets lost, he'll have to spend the whole night in the jungle. You stay here. I'll come back in no time.

(*Runs out.*)

Padmini (*exasperated*) He's gone! Really, he seems more worried about Devadatta than me.

(*She sits down.* **Kapila** *goes to the Kali temple – but naturally faster than* **Devadatta** *did. He sees the body and his mouth half opens in a scream. He runs to* **Devadatta** *and kneels beside him. Lists a truncated head and moans.*)

Kapila   You've cut off your head! You've cut off your head! Oh my
dear friend, my brother, what have you done? Were you so angry with
me? Did you feel such contempt for me, such abhorrence? And in your
anger you forgot that I was ready to die for you? If you had asked me
to jump into fire, I would have done it. If you had asked me to leave
the country, I would have done it. If you had asked me to go and drown
in a river, I would have accepted. Did you despise me so much that
you couldn't ask me that? I did wrong. But you know I don't have the
intelligence to know what else I should have done. I couldn't think – and
so you've pushed me away? No, Devadatta, I can't live without you. I
can't breathe without you. Devadatta, my brother, my guru, my friend . . .

(*Picks up the sword.*)

You spurned me in this world. Accept me as your brother at least in the
next. Here, friend, here I come. As always, I follow in your footsteps.

(*Cuts off his head. It's an easier death this time.* **Padmini**, *who has been
still till now, moves.*)

Padmini   Where are they? Now Kapila's disappeared too. He couldn't
still be searching for him. That's not possible. Devadatta's too weak to
have gone far. They must have met. Perhaps they're sitting now, chatting
as in the old days. For once, no bother of a wife around. No, more like
Devadatta's sulking. He's probably tearing poor Kapila to shreds by just
being silent and grumpy. Yes, that would be more like him.

(*Pause.*)

It's almost dark. And they aren't back. Shameless men – to leave me
alone like this here! No, it's no use sitting here any longer. I had better go
and look for them. If I die of a snake bite on the way, serve them right.
Or perhaps, so much better for them.

(*Walks to the temple, slowly. Rubs her eyes when she reaches there.*)

How dark it is! Can't see a thing. (*Calls.*) Kapila – Kapila – Devadatta
isn't here either. What shall I do here? At this time of the night! Alone!
(*Listens.*) What's that? Some wild beast. A hyena! It's right outside –
what shall I do if it comes in? Ah! It's gone. Mother Kali, only you can
protect me now.

(*Stumbles over the bodies.*)

What's this? What's this?

(*Stares at the bodies and then lets out a terrified scream.*)

Oh God! What's this? Both! Both gone! And didn't even think of me
before they went? What shall I do? What shall I do? Oh, Devadatta, what
did I do that you left me alone in this state? Was that how much you
loved me? And you, Kapila, who looked at me with dog's eyes, you too?
How selfish you are, you men, and how thoughtless! Where shall I go?
How can I go home?

(*Pause.*)

Home? And what shall I say when I get there? What shall I say
happened? And who'll believe me? They'll all say the two fought and
died for this whore. They're bound to say it. Then what'll happen to me?
No, Mother Kali, no, it's too horrible to think of. No! Kapila's gone,
Devadatta's gone. Let me go with them.

(*Picks up the sword.*)

I don't have the strength to hack off my head. But what does it matter
how I die, Mother? You don't care. It's the same to you – another
offering! All right. Have it then. Here's another offering for you.

(*Lifts the sword and puts its point on her breast when, from behind the
curtain, the goddess' voice is heard.*)

Voice   Hey . . .

(**Padmini** *freezes.*)

Put it down! Put down that sword!

(**Padmini** *jumps up in fright and, throwing the sword aside, tries to run
out of the temple. Then stops.*)

Padmini   Who's that?

(*No reply.*)

Who's that?

(*A tremendous noise of drums.* **Padmini** *shuts her eyes in terror. Behind
the curtain one sees the uplifted blood red palms of the goddess. The
curtain is lowered and taken away and one sees a terrifying figure, her
arms stretched out, her mouth wide open with the tongue lolling out. The
drums stop and as the goddess drops her arms and shuts her mouth, it
becomes clear she has been yawning.*)

Kali (*completes the yawn*)   All right. Open your eyes and be quick.
Don't waste time.

(**Padmini** *opens her eyes and sees the goddess. She runs and falls at her feet.*)

Padmini   Mother – Kali . . .

Kali (*sleepy*)   Yes, it's me. There was a time – many years ago – when at this hour they would have the *mangalarati*. The devotees used to make a deafening racket with drums and conch shells and cymbals. So I used to be wide awake around now. I've lost the habit. (*Yawns.*) Right. What do you want? Tell me. I'm pleased with you.

Padmini   Save me, Mother . . .

Kali   I know. I've done that already.

Padmini   Do you call this saving, Mother of all Nature? I can't show my face to anyone in the world. I can't . . .

Kali (*a little testily*)   Yes, yes, you've said that at once. No need to repeat yourself. Now do as I tell you. Put these heads back properly. Attach them to their bodies and press that sword on their necks. They'll come up alive. Is that enough?

Padmini   Mother, you are our breath, you are our bread – and – water . . .

Kali   Skip it! Do as I told you. And quickly. I'm collapsing with sleep.

Padmini (*hesitating*)   May I ask you a question?

Kali   If it's not too long.

Padmini   Can there ever be anything you don't already know, Mother? The past and the future are mere specks in your palm. Then why didn't you stop Devadatta when he came here? Why didn't you stop Kapila? If you'd saved either of them, I would have been spared all this terror, this agony. Why did you wait so long?

Kali (*surprised*)   Is that all you can think of now?

Padmini   Mother . . .

Kali   I've never seen anyone like you.

Padmini   How could one possibly hide anything from you, Mother?

Kali   That's true enough.

Padmini   Then why didn't you stop them?

Kali   Actually if it hadn't been that I was so sleepy, I would have thrown them out by the scruff of their necks.

Padmini   But why?

Kali   The rascals! They were lying to their last breaths. That fellow
Devadatta – he has once promised his head to Rudra and his arms to me!
Think of it – head to him and arms to me! Then because you insisted
on going to the Rudra temple, he comes here and offers his head. Nobly
too – wants to keep his word, he says – no other reason!

Then this Kapila, died right in front of me – but 'for his friend'. Mind
you! Didn't even have the courtesy to refer to me. And what lies! Says
he is dying for friendship. He must have known perfectly well he would
be accused of killing Devadatta for you. Do you think he wouldn't have
grabbed you if it hadn't been for that fear? But till his last breath – 'Oh
my friend! My dear brother!'

Padmini   It's all your grace, Mother . . .

Kali   Don't drag me into it. I had nothing to do with it. You spoke the
truth because you're selfish, that's all. Now don't go on. Do what I told
you and shut your eyes.

Padmini   Yes, Mother . . .

(*Eagerly,* **Padmini** *attaches the severed heads to the bodies of the men.
But in her excitement she mixes them up so that* **Devadatta's** *head goes
to* **Kapila's** *body and vice versa. Then presses the sword on their necks,
does* namaskara *to the goddess, walks downstage and stands with her
back to the goddess, her eyes shut tight.*)

Padmini   I'm ready, Mother.

Kali (*in a resigned tone*)   My dear, daughter, there should be a limit
even to honesty. Anyway, so be it!

(*Again the drums. The curtain is held up again and the goddess
disappears behind it. During the following scene, the stagehands, the
curtain as well as the goddess leave the stage.*

Padmini *stands immobile with her eyes shut. The drums stop. A long
silence follows. The dead bodies move. Their breathing becomes loud
and laboured. They sit up, slowly, stiffly. Their movement is mechanical,
as though blood circulation has not started properly yet. They feel their
own arms, heads and bodies, and look around, bewildered.*

Henceforth the person with the head of **Devadatta** *will be called*
Devadatta. *Similarly with* **Kapila**.

They stand up. It's not easy and they reel around a bit.

Padmini *is still.*)

Devadatta   What – happened?

Kapila   What happened?

(**Padmini** *opens her eyes, but she still doesn't dare look at them.*)

Padmini   Devadatta's voice! Kapila's voice!

(*Screaming with joy.*) Kapila! Devadatta!

(*Turns and runs to them. Then suddenly stops and stands paralyzed.*)

Kapila   Who . . .?

Devadatta   Padmini?

Kapila   What – happened? My head – Ooh! It feels so heavy!

Devadatta   My body – seems to weigh – a ton.

Padmini (*running around in confusion*)   What have I done? What have I done? What have I done? Mother Kali, only you can save me now – only you can help me – What have I done? What have I done? What should I do? Mother, Mother . . .

Devadatta (*a little more alive*)   Why are you – crying?

Kapila   What's – wrong?

Padmini   What shall I tell you, Devadatta? How can I explain it, Kapila? You cut off your heads. But the goddess gave you life – but – I – I – in the dark. . . . Mother, only you can protect me now – Mother! I – mixed up your heads – I mixed them up! Forgive me – I don't deserve to live – forgive me . . .

Kapila (*looking at* **Devadatta**)   You mixed up . . .

Devadatta   . . . the heads?

(*They stare at each other. Then burst into laughter. She doesn't know how to react. Watches them. Then starts laughing.*)

Devadatta   Mixed-up heads!

Kapila   Heads mixed up!

Devadatta   Exchanged heads!

Kapila   Heads exchanged!

Devadatta   How fantastic! All these years we were only friends!

Kapila Now we are blood relations! Body relations! (*Laughing.*) What a gift!

Devadatta Forgive you? We must thank you . . .

Kapila We'll never be able to thank you – enough . . .

Devadatta Exchanged heads!

(*They roar with laughter. Then all three hold hands and run round in a circle, singing.*)

All three (*together*) What a good mix!

No more tricks!

Is this one that

Or that one this?

Ho! Ho!

(*They sing this over and over again until they collapse on the floor.*)

Kapila Oooh – I'm finished!

Padmini . . . Dead!

Devadatta Nothing like this could have ever happened before.

Padmini You know, seeing you two with your heads off was bad enough. But when you got up it was terrible! I almost died of fright . . .

(*They laugh.*)

Kapila No one will believe us if we tell them.

Padmini (*suddenly*) We won't tell anyone.

Devadatta We'll keep our secrets inside us.

Padmini 'Inside us' is right.

(*Laughter.*)

Kapila But how can we not tell? They'll know soon . . .

Devadatta No one'll know.

Kapila I'm sure they'll . . .

Devadatta I'll take any bet.

Kapila But how's that possible?

Devadatta   You'll see. Why worry now?

Padmini   Come. Let's go.

Kapila   It's late.

Devadatta   No Ujjain now. We go back home!

Kapila   Absolutely.

Padmini   This Ujjain will last us a lifetime. Come.

(*They get up. Every now and then someone laughs and then all burst out together.*)

Padmini   Devadatta, I really don't know how we're going to keep this from your parents. They'll guess as soon as they see you bare-bodied.

Devadatta   They won't, I tell you. They take us too much for granted.

Kapila   What do you mean?

Devadatta   Who ever pays attention to a person he sees every day?

Kapila   I don't mean that . . .

Padmini   I'm not so sure. I'm afraid I'll get the blame for it ultimately.

Devadatta   Stop worrying! I tell you it . . .

Kapila   But what has she got to do with you now?

Devadatta (*stops*)   What do you mean?

Kapila   I mean Padmini must come home with me, shouldn't she? She's my wife, so she must . . .

(*Exclamations from* **Devadatta** *and* **Padmini**.)

Padmini   What are you talking about, Kapila?

Kapila (*explaining*)   I mean, you are Devadatta's wife. I have Devadatta's body now. So you have to be my wife.

Padmini   Shut up!

Devadatta   Don't blather like an idiot! I am Devadatta . . .

Padmini   Aren't you ashamed of yourself?

Kapila   But why, Padmini? I have Devadatta's body now . . .

Devadatta   We know that. You don't have to repeat yourself like a parrot. According to the Shastras, the head is the sign of a man . . .

Kapila (*angry now*)   That may be. But the question now is simply this: Whose wife is she? (*Raising his right hand.*) This is the hand that accepted her at the wedding. This the body she's lived with all these months. And the child she's carrying is the seed of this body.

Padmini (*frightened by the logic*)   No, no, no. It's not possible. It's not. (*Running to* **Devadatta**.) It's not, Devadatta.

Devadatta   Of course, it isn't, my dear. He is ignorant. (*To* **Kapila**.) When one accepts a partner in marriage, with the holy fire as one's witness, one accepts a person, not a body. She didn't marry Devadatta's body, she married Devadatta – the person.

Kapila   If that's your argument, I have Devadatta's body, so I am Devadatta – the person.

Devadatta   Listen to me. Of all the human limbs the topmost – in position as well as in importance – is the head. I have Devadatta's head and it follows that I am Devadatta. According to the Sacred Texts . . .

Kapila   Don't tell me about your Sacred Texts. You can always twist them to suit your needs. She married Devadatta's body with the holy fire as her witness and that's enough for me.

Devadatta (*laughs*)   Did you hear that, Padmini? He claims to be Devadatta and yet he scorns the texts. You think Devadatta would ever do that?

Kapila   You can quote as many Texts as you like, I don't give a nail. Come on, Padmini . . .

(*Takes a step towards her. But* **Devadatta** *steps in between.*)

Devadatta   Take care!

Padmini   Come, Devadatta. It's no use arguing with this rascal. Let's go.

Devadatta   Come on.

Kapila (*stepping between them*)   Where are you taking my wife, friend?

Devadatta   Will you get out of our way or should . . .

Kapila   It was you who got in my way.

Devadatta (*pushing* **Kapila** *aside*)   Get away, you pig.

Kapila (*triumphant*)   He's using force! And what language! Padmini, think! Would Devadatta ever have acted like this? This is Kapila's violence.

Devadatta Come, Padmimi.

Kapila Go. But do you think I'll stay put while you run away with my wife? Where will you go? How far can you go? Only to the city, after all. I'll follow you there. I'll kick up a row in the streets. Let's see what happens then.

(**Devadatta** *stops.*)

Padmini Let him scream away. Don't pay him any attention.

Devadatta No. He's right. This has to be solved here. It'll create a scandal in the city.

Padmini But who'll listen to him? Everyone will take you for Devadatta by your face.

Kapila Ha! You think the people in Dharmapura don't know my body, do you? They've seen me a thousand times in the wrestling pit. I've got I don't know how many awards for body building. Let's see whom they believe.

Padmini (*pleading*) Why are you tormenting us like this? For so many years you have been our friend, accepted our hospitality . . .

Kapila I know what you want, Padmini. Devadatta's clever head and Kapila's strong body . . .

Padmini Shut up, you brute.

Devadatta Suppose she did. There's nothing wrong in it. It's natural for a woman to feel attracted to a fine figure of a man.

Kapila I know it is. But that doesn't mean she can just go and live with a man who's not her husband. That's not right.

Padmini (*crying out*) How can we get rid of this scoundrel! Let's go – Let's go anywhere – to the woods – to the desert anywhere you like.

Kapila You'll have to kill me before you'll really escape me. You could. I don't have the strength to resist Kapila.

Padmini (*using a new argument*) But I gave you life –

Kapila That was no favour. If you hadn't, you would have been a widow now. Actually he should be grateful to me because my wife saved his life. Instead, he's trying to snatch you away.

(**Padmini** *moans in agony.*)

Devadatta   This way we won't get anywhere, Kapila.

Kapila   Call me Devadatta.

Devadatta   Whatever you are, this is no way to solve the problem.

Kapila   Of course not. If marriage were a contract, it would be. But how can Padmini's fancy be taken as the solution?

Devadatta   Then what is the solution to this problem?

(*They all freeze.*)

Bhagavata   What? What indeed is the solution to this problem, which holds the entire future of these three unfortunate beings in a balance? Must their fate remain a mystery? And if so shall we not be insulting our audience by tying a question mark round its neck and bidding it good-bye? We have to face the problem. But it's a deep one and the answer must be sought with the greatest caution. Haste would be disastrous. So there's a break of ten minutes now. Please have some tea, ponder over this situation and come back with your own solutions. We shall then continue with our enquiry.

(*The stagehands hold a white curtain in front of the frozen threesome, while the* **Bhagavata** *and others relax and sip tea.*)

ACT TWO

The white curtain is removed.

Bhagavata   What? What indeed is the solution to this problem, which holds the entire future of these three unfortunate beings in a balance?

Way back in the ages, when King Vikrama was ruling the world, shining in glory like the earth's challenge to the sun, he was asked the same question by the demon Vetala. And the king offered a solution even without, as it were, batting an eyelid. But will his rational, logical answer backed by the Sacred Texts appeal to our audience?

(*Sings.*)

The future pointed out by the tongue safe inside the skull is not acceptable to us.

We must read the forehead which Brahma has disconnected from the entrails.

We must unravel the net on the palm disclaimed by the brain.
We must plumb the hidden depths of the rivers running under
our veins.

Yes, that would be the right thing to do.

So our three unfortunate friends went to a great *rishi* in search of a
solution to their problem. And the *rishi* – remembering perhaps what
King Vikrama had said – gave the verdict:

(*In a loud, sonorous voice.*)

As the heavenly Kalpa Vriksha is supreme among trees, so is the head
among human limbs. Therefore the man with Devadatta's head is indeed
Devadatta and he is the rightful husband of Padmini.

(*The three spring to life.* **Devadatta** *and* **Padmini** *scream with delight
and move to one corner of the stage, laughing and dancing.* **Kapila**,
brokenhearted, drags his feet to the other corner.)

Devadatta (*embracing* **Padmini**)   My Padmini . . . my lovely Padmini . . .

Padmini   My King – My Master . . .

Devadatta   My little lightning . . .

Padmini   The light of my joy . . .

Devadatta   The flower of my palm . . .

Padmini   My celestial-bodied Gandharva. . . . My sun-faced
Indra . . .

Devadatta   My Queen of Indra's Court . . .

Padmini (*caressing his shoulders*)   Come. Let's go. Let's go quickly.
Where the earth is soft and the green grass plays the swing.

Devadatta   Let us. Where the banyan spreads a canopy and curtains off
the skies.

Padmini   What a wide chest. What other canopy do I need?

Devadatta   My soft, swaying Padmini. What other swing do I want?

Padmini   My Devadatta comes like a bridegroom with the jewelry of a
new body . . .

Devadatta (*a manly laugh*)   And who should wear the jewelry but the
eager bride?

Padmini   Let's go. (*Pause.*) Wait. (*She runs to* **Kapila**.) Don't be sad, Kapila. We shall meet again, shan't we? (*In a low voice, so* **Devadatta** *can't hear.*) It's my duty to go with Devadatta. But remember I'm going with your body. Let that cheer you up. (*Goes back to* **Devadatta**.) Goodbye, Kapila.

Devadatta   Goodbye.

(*They go out, laughing, rubbing against each other.* **Kapila** *stands mute for a while. Then moves.*)

Bhagavata   Kapila – Kapila . . . (*No reply.*) Don't grieve. It's fate, Kapila, and . . .

Kapila   Kapila? What? Me? Why am I Kapila?

(*Exits.*)

Bhagavata   So the roads diverged. Kapila went into the forest and disappeared. He never saw Dharmapura again. In fact, he never felt the wind of any city again. As for Devadatta and Padmini, they returned to Dharmapura and plunged into the joys of married life.

(**Padmini** *enters and sits. She is stitching clothes,* **Devadatta** *comes. He is carrying in his hands two large dolls – which could be played by two children. The dolls are dressed in a way which makes it impossible to decide their sex.*

Devadatta *comes in quietly and stands behind* **Padmini**.)

Devadatta   Hey!

Padmini (*startled*)   Oh! Really, Devadatta. You startled me. The needle pricked me! Look, my finger's bleeding.

Devadatta   Tut – Tut! Is it really? Put it in my mouth. I'll suck it.

Padmini   No, thanks. I'll suck it myself. (*Sees the dolls.*) How pretty! Whose are those?

Devadatta   Whose? Ours, of course! The guest is arriving soon. He must have playmates.

Padmini   But the guest won't be coming for months yet, silly, and . . .

Devadatta   I know he isn't, but you can't get dolls like these any time you like! These are special dolls from the Ujjain fair.

Padmini   They are lovely! (*Hugs the dolls.*) They look almost alive – such shining eyes – such delicate cheeks. (*Kisses them.*) Now sit down and tell me everything that happened at the fair. You wouldn't take me with you . . .

Devadatta   How could I – in your condition? I went only because you insisted you wanted to keep your word. But I'm glad I went. A very funny thing happened. There was a wrestling pit and a wrestler from Kamarupa was challenging people to fight him. I don't know what got into me. Before I'd even realized it, I had stripped and jumped into the pit.

Padmini (*fondling the dolls*)   You didn't! You've never even wrestled before . . .

Devadatta   Didn't think of anything. I felt 'inspired'! Within a couple of minutes, I had pinned him to the ground.

Padmini (*laughs out*)   What would your father say if he heard of this?

Devadatta   My few acquaintances there were quite amazed.

Padmini (*caressing his arm*)   That day in the gymnasium you defeated the champion in a sword fight. Now this! Don't overdo it: people may start suspecting.

Devadatta   Of course they won't. I was standing there bare-bodied and not a soul suspected. A friend even asked me if I'd learnt it from Kapila.

Padmini   You have, after all!

(*They laugh.*)

Devadatta   You know, I'd always thought one had to use one's brains while wrestling or fencing or swimming. But this body just doesn't wait for thoughts – it acts!

Padmini   Fabulous body – fabulous brain – fabulous Devadatta.

Devadatta   I have been running around all these days without even proper sleep and yet I don't feel a bit tired. (*Jumps up.*) Come on, we'll have a picnic by the lake. I feel like a good, long swim.

Padmini (*mocking*)   In my condition?

Devadatta   I didn't ask you to swim. You sit there and enjoy the scenery. Once our son's born, I'll teach you to swim too.

Padmini   You go on about it being a son. What if it's a daughter?

Devadatta   If it's a daughter like you, I'll teach the two of you together.

Padmini   Ready!

(*He pulls her to him.*)

Now – now – what about the picnic?

Devadatta   Quite right. First things first.

Padmini (*pause*)   Devadatta . . .

Devadatta   Yes?

Padmini   Why do you – have to apply that sandal oil on your body?

Devadatta   I like it.

Padmini   I know, but . . .

Devadatta   What?

Padmini (*hesitating*)   Your body had that strong, male smell before – I liked it.

Devadatta   But I've been using sandal oil since I was a child!

Padmini   I don't mean that. But – when we came back from the temple of Kali – you used to smell so manly . . .

Devadatta   You mean that unwashed, sweaty smell Kapila had? (*Incredulous.*) You liked that?

Padmini (*pause. Then lightly*)   It was just a thought. Come on, let's start. We'll be late.

(*They go out. A long silence.*)

Doll I   Not a bad house, I would say.

Doll II   Could have been worse. I was a little worried.

Doll I   This is the least we deserved. Actually we should have got a palace. A real palace!

Doll II   And a prince to play with. A real prince!

Doll I   How the children looked at us at the fair! How their eyes glowed!

Doll II   How their mothers stared at us! How their mouths watered!

Doll I   Only those beastly men turned up their noses! 'Expensive! Too expensive!'

Doll II   Presuming to judge us! Who do they think they are!

Doll I   Only a prince would be worthy of us.

Doll II   We should be dusted every day . . .

Doll I   . . . dressed in silk . . .

Doll II   . . . seated on a cushioned shelf . . .

Doll I   . . . given new clothes every week.

Doll II   If the doll-maker had any sense, he'd never have sold us.

Doll I   If he had any brains, he should never have given us to this man . . .

Doll II   . . . with his rough labourer's hands.

Doll I   Palms like wood . . .

Doll II   A grip like a vice . . .

Doll I   My arms are still aching . . .

Doll II   He doesn't deserve us, the peasant.

(**Devadatta** *comes running in, tosses the dolls in the air, catches them and kisses them.*)

Devadatta   My dolls, your prince has arrived! The prince has come!

Doll I (*in agony*)   Brute! An absolute brute!

Doll II (*in agony*)   Beast! A complete beast!

Devadatta (*runs to the* **Bhagavata**)   Here, Bhagavata, Sir, take these sweets. You must come to the feast tomorrow at our house.

Bhagavata   What's it for?

Devadatta   Haven't you heard? I've got a son like a gem – a son like a rose – Yippeee . . .

(*He goes out dancing some* Lezim *steps. A long silence.*)

Doll I   Is that little satan asleep yet?

Doll II   Think so. God! It's killing me . . .

Doll I   . . . crying, all day . . .

Doll II   . . . making a mess every fifteen minutes.

Doll I   What have we come to! One should never trust God.

Doll II   It's our fault. We should have been wary from the moment we saw that child in her dreams.

Doll I   We should have noticed she was bloating day by day.

Doll II   We should have suspected foul play then.

Doll I   It wasn't our fault. How could we know she was hiding this thing inside her?

Doll II   How she was swelling! Day by day! Week by week! As though someone were blowing air into her . . .

Doll I   How ugly she looked . . .

Doll II   . . . not to her husband, though!

Doll I   When they were alone, he would place his hand on her belly and say, 'Is he kicking now?'

Doll II (*seriously*)   We should have been on our guard.

Doll I (*dispirited*)   We should.

Doll II   And then comes this little monster.

Doll I   . . . this lump of flesh . . .

Doll II   it doesn't even have proper eyes or ears . . .

Doll I   . . . but it gets all the attention.

Doll II (*in disgust*)   Ugh . . .

Doll I (*sick*)   Awk . . .

(**Devadatta** *and* **Padmini** *enter with the child, for which a wooden doll may be used. They walk across the stage, engrossed in talking to and about the child, and go out.*)

Doll I   A spider's built its web around my shoulders.

Doll II   Yesterday a mouse nibbled at my toe.

Doll I   The other day a cockroach ate my left eye.

Doll II   Six months – and not a soul has come near us.

Doll I   Six months – and not a hand has touched us.

Doll II   Six months and we reach this state. What'll happen in a year's time?

(**Padmini** *and* **Devadatta** *enter.*)

Padmini   Listen.

Devadatta   Yes.

Padmini   You mustn't say 'no' – at least this time.

Devadatta   To what?

Padmini   We'll take him to the lake.

Devadatta   In this cold?

Padmini   What if it's cold? He's older now. There's no need to mollycoddle him. I grew up running around in heat and cold and rain – and nothing happened to me. I'm all right.

Devadatta   No, it's unnecessary trouble for everyone.

Padmini   What do you mean trouble? What's happened to you these days? You sit at home all day. Never go out. You've forgotten all your swimming and sports.

Devadatta   I'm a Brahmin, Padmini. My duty . . .

Padmini   I've heard all this!

Devadatta   It was fun the first few days because it was new. All that muscle and strength. But how long can one go on like that? I have a family tradition to maintain – the daily reading, writing and studies.

Padmini   I don't know.

Devadatta (*affectionate*)   Now look here, Padmini . . .

(*Puts his hand round her shoulder. She suddenly shudders.*)

Why? What happened?

Padmini   Nothing – I don't know why – I suddenly had goose flesh.

(*Pause.*)

Devadatta (*withdrawing his hand*)   Do you know where I've kept the copy of *Dharma Sindhu*? I've been looking for it.

Padmini   I think I saw it on the shelf. Must be there . . .

(**Devadatta** *goes to* **Doll I**, *moves it aside and picks up the book.* **Doll I** *shudders.*)

Doll II   Why? What happened?

Doll I   He touched me, and . . .

Doll II   Yes?

Doll I   His palms! They were so rough once, when he first brought us here. Like a labourer's. But now they are soft – sickly soft – like a young girl's.

Doll II   I know. I've noticed something too.

Doll I   What?

Doll II   His stomach. It was so tight and muscular. Now . . .

Doll I   I know. It's soft and loose.

Doll II   Do you think it'll swell up too?

(*They laugh.*)

Doll I (*holding its hands in front of its stomach to suggest a swollen belly*)   It'll swell a little.

Doll II (*holding its hands a little farther in front*)   – then more . . .

Doll I (*even further*)   – more and . . .

Doll II (*even further*)   – and more until . . .

Doll I   . . . if it's a woman . . .

Doll II   . . . there'll be a child . . .

Doll I   . . . and if it's a man . . .

Doll II   BANG!

(*They roll with laughter.* **Padmini** *comes in with the child. She sings a lullaby.*)

Padmini   Here comes a rider!
From what land does he come?
Oh his head a turban
with a long pearly tail.
Round his neck a garland
of virgin-white jasmines.
In his fist a sword
with a diamond-studded hilt.
The white-clad rider

rides a white charger
which spreads its tossing mane
against the western sky,
spreads its mane like breakers
against the western sky.
Sleep now, my baby
and see smiling dreams.
There he comes – here he is!
From which land does he come?
But why are the jasmines on his chest
red O so red?
What shine in his open eyes?
Pebbles O pebbles.
Why is his young body
cold O so cold?
The white horse gallops
across hills, streams and fields.
To what land does he gallop?
Nowhere O nowhere.

(*Halfway through the lullaby,* **Devadatta** *comes in and sits by* **Padmini's** *side, reading. They don't look at each other. At the end of the lullaby, they fall asleep.*)

Doll I (*in a hushed voice*)   Hey.

Doll II   Yes?

Doll I   Look.

Doll II   Where?

Doll I   Behind her eyelids. She is dreaming.

Doll II   I don't see anything.

Doll I   It's still hazy – hasn't started yet. Do you see it now?

Doll II (*eagerly*)   Yes, yes.

(*They stare at her.*)

Doll I   A man.

Doll II   But not her husband.

Doll I No, someone else.

Doll II Is this the one who came last night?

Doll I Yes – the same. But I couldn't see his face then?

Doll II You can now. Not very nice – rough. Like a labourer's. But he's got a nice body – looks soft.

Doll I Who do you think it is?

Doll II I – It's fading. (*Urgently.*) Remember the face!

Doll I It's fading – Oh! It's gone!

Doll II And she won't even remember it tomorrow.

(**Padmini** *and* **Devadatta** *sit up.*)

Padmini Are you ill?

Devadatta Why?

Padmini You were moaning in your sleep last night.

Devadatta Was I?

Padmini Aren't you feeling well?

Devadatta Who? Me? I'm fine.

(*Gets up energetically to show how well he feels. Suddenly grabs his shoulder with a groan.*)

Padmini What's wrong? Tell me.

Devadatta (*avoiding her eyes*) Nothing. I went to the gymnasium yesterday morning. Then went swimming.

Padmini To the gymnasium? After all these years? But why?

Devadatta I just felt like it. That's all. Don't go on about it.

Padmini (*without irony*) Are you going again today?

Devadatta (*flares up*) No, I'm not. And there's no need to laugh. I know I've made a fool of myself by going there. I won't again.

(*Goes out. Long pause.*)

Padmini What are you afraid of, Devadatta? What does it matter that you are going soft again, that you are losing your muscles? I'm not going to be stupid again. Kapila's gone out of my life – forever. I won't let him come back again. (*Pause.*) Kapila? What could he be doing now? Where could he be? Could his body be fair still, and his face dark? (*Long pause.*) Devadatta changes. Kapila changes. And me?

(*Closes her eyes.*)

Doll I   There he is again.

Doll II   In the middle of the day?

Doll I (*doubtful*)   I'm not sure this is the usual visitor. This one looks rougher and darker.

Doll II   It's him all right. Look at his face.

Doll I   He goes to her . . .

Doll II   . . . very near her . . .

Doll I (*in a whisper*)   What's he going to do now?

Doll II (*even more anxious*)   What?

(*They watch.*)

Doll I (*baffled*)   But he's climbing a tree!

Doll II (*almost a wail of disappointment*)   He's dived into a river!

Doll I   Is that all he came for?

Doll II   It's going . . .

Doll I   . . . going . . .

Doll II   Gone! Wretched dreams! They just tickle and fade away.

(**Padmini** *wakes up and mimes putting the crying child to sleep.*)

Padmini (*suddenly vicious*)   Change! Change! Change! Change! Change! The sand trickles. The water fills the pot. And the moon goes on swinging, swinging, swinging, from light to darkness to light.

(**Devadatta** *comes in. He is now completely changed to his original self.*)

Devadatta   A pundit's coming to see me. He wants me to explain some verses to him. Can you keep some sweets and lime juice ready?

Padmini   Yes. (*Pause.*) Did you hear . . .? The maid was telling me.

Devadatta   What?

Padmini   Kapila's mother died this morning. (*Pause.*) Poor thing! She'd been bedridden all these years, ever since . . .

Devadatta (*snapping at her*)   What did you expect me to do about it? (*Then embarrassed.*) Get the lime juice ready soon.

(*They go out.*)

Doll I   Each one to his fate!

Doll II   Each one to her problems!

Doll I   As the doll-maker used to say, 'What are things coming to!'

Doll II   Especially last night – I mean – that dream . . .

Doll I   Tut! Tut! One shouldn't talk about such things!

Doll II   It was so shameless . . .

Doll I   I said be quiet . . .

Doll II   Honestly! The way they . . .

Doll I   Look, if we must talk about it, let me tell.

Doll II   You don't want to talk about it. So.

Doll I   You don't understand a thing. They . . .

Doll II   What do you know? Last night . . .

Doll I   Let me! In that dream . . .

Doll II   I'm . . .

Doll I   Shut up!

Doll II   You shut up!

(*They start arguing, then fighting. They roll on the ground, on top of each other, biting, scratching, hitting each other. They shout, scream and giggle. As they fight, the giggles become louder and more frantic. Their clothes get torn. At last they lie side by side panting, bursting with little giggles. Then they sit up.* **Padmini** *enters, looks at them.*)

Padmini   Just look at the dolls! The baby's really torn them to rags. How long can we go on with them! (*Calls.*) Listen.

Devadatta (*entering*)   Yes.

Padmini   We must get new dolls for our baby. These are in tatters.

Devadatta   You're right. I hadn't noticed.

Padmini   The Ujjain fair is to be held in another four days. Why don't you go and get new dolls there? If you start today you'll be there in time for it. It's unlucky to keep torn dolls at home.

Doll I (*to* **Doll II**)   Did you hear that? She wants to throw us out . . .

Doll II   She wants new dolls.

Doll I   The whore.

Doll II   The bitch.

Doll I   May her house burn down.

Doll II   May her teeth fall out.

Devadatta (*to* **Padmini**)   It'll take me more than a week to go to Ujjain and come back. Shall I ask one of the neighbours to get them for us?

Doll I (*to* **Devadatta**)   You wretch – before you throw us out watch out for yourself.

Doll II   Cover your wife before you start worrying about our rags.

Padmini (*to* **Devadatta**)   Who knows what sort of dolls they'll get for us? We must bring things ourselves for our baby.

Devadatta   But . . .

Padmini   If you don't want to go, say so. Don't . . .

Devadatta   Shall I ask one of the servants to come and sleep here at night while I'm away?

Padmini   No need. We are not in the middle of a forest.

Doll I (*to* **Devadatta**)   Watch out, you fool . . .

Doll II   Refuse, you idiot . . .

Devadatta   All right. I'll start at once. Take care of yourself. (*He drags the dolls out.*)

Doll I   Villain . . .

Doll II   Rascal . . .

Doll I   Swine . . .

Doll II   Bastard . . .

(*One can hear them screaming curses as he takes them out.* **Padmini**
stands watching him go. Then to the child in her arms.)

Padmini   My poor child, you haven't seen the witching fair of the
dark forest, have you? Let's go and see it. How can I describe it to you?
There's so much. Long before the sun rises, the shadows of twigs draw
alpanas on the floor. The stars raise *arati* and go. Then the day dawns
and the fun begins. The circus in the treetops and the cockfights in a
shower of feathers. And the dances! The tiger dance, and the peacock
dance, and the dance of the sun's little feet with silver anklets on the
river. In the heart of the forest stands the stately chariot of the shield-
barer. It's made of pure gold – rows of egrets pull it down the street, and
rows of flames of the forest salute it with torches. Then the night comes,
and our poor baby is tired. So we blow gently and out goes the moon.
But before we leave, there's one more thing to do. Right outside the fair,
watching it from a distance, stands the tree of the Fortunate Lady. It's an
old tree, a close friend of ours. We have to say 'hello' to it. All right?

(*She goes out with the child. A long silence.* **Kapila** *enters. He too is as
he was at the beginning of the play, tough and muscular.*)

Bhagavata   Who? Kapila?

Kapila   Yes.

Bhagavata   It's such a long time since we met.

Kapila   Yes.

Bhagavata   Where are you now?

Kapila   Here.

Bhagavata   Here? In this jungle! It's difficult to believe any man could
live here.

Kapila   Beasts do. Why not men?

Bhagavata   What do you do?

Kapila   Live.

Bhagavata   Have you had any news from the city?

Kapila   Long ago. Father sent word asking me to come back. I said,
'I won't come. No need for you to come here either!' That's all.

Bhagavata   You mean – you don't know your father died last year?
Also your mother . . .

Kapila (*expressionless*)   No.

Bhagavata   And Padmini has a son.

Kapila   I see.

Bhagavata   Why this anger, Kapila?

Kapila   What anger?

Bhagavata   It shows in the way you stand, you move.

Kapila   All that is your poetry.

(*Moves on.*)

Bhagavata   Kapila! Kapila!

(**Kapila** *goes round the stage once. He mimes picking up an axe and felling a tree. A long silence. Only the soundless image of* **Kapila** *cutting the tree.*

Padmini *enters, child in arms. She is scared and walks in rapidly. She sees* **Kapila** *and stands transfixed.* **Kapila** *doesn't see her for a while and when he does, stands paralysed. A long silence.*)

Kapila (*slowly*)   You?

Padmini   Yes.

Kapila   Here?

Padmini   My son had never laughed with the river or shivered in the wind or felt the thorn cut his feet. So I brought him out. I lost my way in the woods.

Kapila   You shouldn't have lost it this far.

Padmini   The wrong road stuck to my feet; wouldn't let go.

Kapila   You shouldn't have lost it this far. Wild beasts – robbers – pathless paths – all sorts of dangers.

Padmini   I asked the villagers. And the pilgrims. And the hunters. And the tribesmen. When there wasn't anyone any more, I asked myself. Everyone saw to it that I didn't lose the wrong road.

(*Pause.*)

Kapila   Is that your son?

Padmini   Yes. And yours.

Kapila Mine?

Padmini Your body gave him to me.

Kapila Mine? (*Erupting.*) Not mine. I'm Kapila, Padmini. I didn't accept it that day. But I accept it now, I'm Kapila.

Padmini (*softly*) And how's Kapila?

(*The* **Bhagavata** *sings. The following is a prose rendering of the song.*)

Bhagavata Once I spread my wings, and kicked away the earth and flew up. I covered the seven continents, the ten shores and measured the sky.

Now because you have a child at your breast, a husband on your thighs, the red of rust on the lips of your late-opening mouth, I pick a picture here, and there a card of fate, and live for the grace of a grain – an astrologer's bird.

Kapila Can I look at him?

Padmini That's why I brought him.

(**Kapila** *looks at the child.*)

Kapila What's wrong with me? You've come so far and I haven't even asked you to sit down. Why don't you go in and take a little rest?

(*She goes in with the child. He stands as in a daze. She comes out without the child.*)

Kapila Why . . .

Padmini I don't need any rest.

(*Long silence.*)

Kapila How are you?

Padmini I'm well. No illness, problems or difficulties.

Kapila Your son looks exactly like you.

Padmini (*a slight pause*) And you.

(**Kapila** *doesn't reply.*)

He has the same mole on his shoulder.

Kapila What mole?

(*She comes to him and points out the mole on his shoulder.*)

Padmini   This one. Which other could it be? That's the only one you have on your shoulder.

Kapila   Oh! I hadn't seen it. I don't look much at this body.

Padmini (*quietly*)   Do you despise it that much?

(*No reply.*)

Why have you tortured it so?

(*Takes his hand in hers.*)

When this went to you, it was so soft, like a prince's. These arms were so slender and fair. Look at them now. Why have you done this to yourself?

Kapila   When this body came to me, it was like a corpse hanging by my head. It was a Brahmin's body after all: not made for the woods. I couldn't lift an axe without my elbows moaning. Couldn't run a length without my knees howling. I had no use for it. The moment it came to me, a war started between us.

Padmini   And who won?

Kapila   I did.

Padmini   The head always wins, doesn't it?

Kapila   Fortunately, yes. Now I can run ten miles and not stop for a breath. I can swim through the monsoon floods and fell a banyan. The stomach used to rebel once. Now it digests what I give. If I don't, it doesn't complain.

Padmini   Must the head always win?

Kapila   That's why I am Kapila now. Kapila! Kapila with a body that fits his face.

Padmini   What a good mix
No more tricks
Is this one that
Or that one this?
Do you remember the song we sang in the Kali temple?

Kapila   So?

Padmini   Nothing. I often remember it. It's almost my autobiography now. Kapila! Devadatta! Kapila with Devadatta's body! Devadatta with Kapila's body! Four men in a single lifetime.

Kapila (*suddenly*)   Why have you come away from him?

Padmini   What do you want me to say?

(*They freeze.*)

Bhagavata   How could I make you understand? If Devadatta had changed overnight and had gone back to his original form, I would have forgotten you completely. But that's not how it happened. He changed day by day. Inch by inch. Hair by hair. Like the trickling sand. Like the water filling the pot. And as I saw him change, I couldn't get rid of you. That's what Padmini must tell Kapila. She could say more, without concealing anything. 'Kapila, if that *rishi* had given me to you, would I have gone back to Devadatta someday exactly like this?' But she doesn't say anything. She remains silent.

Kapila (*to* **Padmini**)   Why have you come here?

Padmini   I had to see you.

Kapila   Why? (*No reply.*) Why? Why did you have to come just when I thought I'd won this long and weary battle? Why did you have to pursue me just when I had succeeded in uprooting these memories? I am Kapila now. The rough and violent Kapila. Kapila without a crack between his head and his shoulders. What do you want now? Another head? Another suicide? Listen to me. Do me a favour. Go back. Back to Devadatta. He is your husband, the father of this child. Devadatta and Padmini! Devadatta and Padmini! A pair coupled with the holy fire as the witness. I have no place there, no peace, no salvation. So go. I beg of you. Go.

(*A long silence.*)

Padmini   I will. If you want me to.

Kapila (*almost a moan*)   Oh God!

Padmini   Why?

Kapila   Nothing. Another memory – when I too was asked to go – Yes, go back. Now.

Padmini   I will. But can I ask a little favour? My son's tired. He's asleep. He has been in my arms for several days now. Let him rest a while. As soon as he gets up I'll go. (*Laughs.*) Yes, you won, Kapila. Devadatta won too. But I – the better half of two bodies – I neither win nor lose. No, don't say anything. I know what you'll say and I've told myself that a thousand times. It's my fault. I mixed the heads up. I must suffer the consequences. I will. I'm sorry I came. I didn't think before I started. Couldn't. But at least until my child wakes up, may I sit here and look at you? Have my fill for the rest of my life? I won't speak a word.

(*Long pause.*)

Kapila   What does it matter now whether you stay or go? You've done the damage. I had buried all those faceless memories in my skin. Now you've dug them up with your claws.

Padmini   Why should one bury anything?

Kapila   Why shouldn't one? Why should one tolerate this mad dance of incompleteness?

Padmini   Whose incompleteness? Yours?

Kapila   Yes, mine. One beats the body into shape, but one can't beat away the memories trapped in it. Isn't that surprising? That the body should have its own ghosts, its own secrets? Memories of touch – memories of *a* touch – memories of a body swaying in these arms, of a warm skin against this palm – memories which one cannot recognize, cannot understand, cannot even name because this head wasn't there when they happened.

Padmini   Kapila . . .

Kapila (*without anger*)   Why did you come? You came. You touched me. You held my hand, and my body recognized your touch. I have never touched you, but this body, this appendage, laughed and flowered out in a festival of memories to which I'm an outcaste.

Padmini   Poor Kapila!

Kapila   Don't pity me.

Padmini   Be quiet, stupid. Your body bathed in a river, swam and danced in it. Shouldn't your head know what river it was, what swim? Your head too must submerge in that river: the flow must rumple your hair, run its tongue in your ears and press your head to its bosom. Until that's done, you'll continue to be incomplete.

(**Kapila** *raises his head and looks at her. She caresses his face, like a blind person trying to imprint it on her finger tips. Then she rests her head on his chest.*)

My Kapila! My poor, poor Kapila! How needlessly you've tortured yourself.

(**Kapila** *lifts her up and takes her in.*)

Bhagavata   You cannot engrave on water
nor wound it with a knife,
which is why
the river
has no fear
of memories.

Female chorus   The river only feels the
the pull of the waterfall.
She giggles, and tickles the rushes
on the bank, then turns
a top of dry leaves
in the navel of the whirlpool, weaves
a water-snake in the net of silver strands
in its green depths, frightens the frog
on the rug of the moss, sticks and bamboo leaves,
sings, tosses, leaps and
sweeps on in a rush –

Bhagavata   While the scarecrow on the bank
has a face fading
on its mudpot head
and a body torn
with memories.

(**Devadatta** *enters. He is holding a sword in one hand, and in the other,
two dolls, made of cloth.*)

Bhagavata   Who! Devadatta?

Devadatta   Where does Kapila live here?

Bhagavata   Uhm – well – Anyway, how are . . . you . . .

Devadatta   If you don't want to tell me, don't. I can find out for
myself.

Bhagavata   There. Behind those trees.

Devadatta   How long has Padmini been here?

Bhagavata   About four or five days.

Devadatta   Amazing! Even a man like me found the road hard. But how quickly she covered it – and with a child in her arms.

Bhagavata   Devadatta . . .

(**Devadatta** *moves on.*)

Devadatta moves on. There are only two words which make sense to him now – Kapila and Padmini! Kapila and Padmini! The words sweep him along to the doorstep of Kapila's hut. But suddenly he stops. Until this moment he has been rearing to taste the blood of Kapila. But now he is still and calm.

(**Kapila** *comes out.*)

Kapila   Come, Devadatta. I was waiting for you. I've been expecting you since yesterday. I have been coming out every half an hour to see if you'd arrived. Not from fear. Only eager.

(**Padmini** *comes out and stands watching them.*)

Kapila (*to* **Devadatta**)   You look exactly the same.

Devadatta (*laughs*)   You too.

Kapila (*points to the sword*)   What's that?

Devadatta (*extending the hand which holds the dolls*)   Dolls. For the child. I came home from the fair. There was no one there. So I came here.

(**Padmini** *steps forward and takes the dolls. But neither speaks.* **Padmini** *goes back to her place and stands clutching the dolls to her bosom.*)

Kapila   Come in and rest a while. There'll always be time to talk later.

(**Devadatta** *shakes his head.*)

Why? Are you angry?

Devadatta   Not any more. (*Pause.*) Did my body bother you too much?

Kapila   It wasn't made for this life. It resisted. It also had its revenge.

Devadatta   Did it?

Kapila   Do you remember how I once used to envy your poetry, your ability to imagine things? For me, the sky was the sky, and the tree only a tree. Your body gave me new feelings, new words. I felt awake as I'd never before. Even started writing poems. Very bad ones, I'm afraid.

(*They laugh.*)

There were times when I hated it for what it gave me.

Devadatta   I wanted your power but not your wildness. You lived in hate – I in fear.

Kapila   No, I was the one who was afraid.

Devadatta   What a good mix. No more tricks.

(*They laugh.*)

Tell me one thing. Do you really love Padmini?

Kapila   Yes.

Devadatta   So do I.

Kapila   I know.

(*Silence.*)

Devadatta, couldn't we all three live together – like the Pandavas and Draupadi?

Devadatta   What do you think?

(*Silence.* **Padmini** *looks at them but doesn't say anything.*)

Kapila (*laughs*)   No, it can't be done.

Devadatta   That's why I brought this. (*Shows the sword.*) What won't end has to be cut.

Kapila   I got your body, but not your wisdom.

Devadatta   Where's your sword then?

Kapila   A moment.

(*Goes in.* **Padmini** *stands looking at* **Devadatta.** *But he looks somewhere far away.*)

Bhagavata   After sharing with Indra
   his wine
   his food
   his jokes
   I returned to the earth
   and saw from far –

a crack had appeared
in the earth's face –
exactly
like Indra's smile

(**Kapila** *returns with his sword. They take up positions.*)

Kapila   Are you still in practice?

Devadatta   Of course not. But you'd learned well. And you?

Kapila   I learnt again. But one's older now – slower at learning.

Devadatta (*pause*)   You realize it's immaterial who's better with a sword now, don't you?

Kapila   Yes, I do.

Devadatta   There's only one solution to this.

Kapila   We must both die.

Kapila   With what confidence we chopped off our heads in that temple! Now whose head – whose body – suicide or murder – nothing's clear.

Devadatta   No grounds for friendship now. No question of mercy. We must fight like lions and kill like cobras.

Kapila   Let our heads roll to the very hands which cut them in the temple of Kali!

(*Music starts. The fight is stylized like a dance. Their swords don't touch. Even*)

Bhagavata (*sings*)   Like cocks in a pit
we dance – he and I,
foot woven with foot
eye soldered to eye.
He knows and I know
all there's to be known:
the witch's burning thirst
burns for blood alone.
Hence this frozen smile,
which cracks and drips to earth,
and claw-knives, digging flesh
for piecemeal death.

The *rishi* who said 'Knowledge gives rise to forgiveness' had no knowledge of death.

(**Kapila** *wounds* **Devadatta** *who falls to his feet and fights. He stabs* **Kapila**. *Both fight on their knees, fall and die.*

A long silence. **Padmini** *slowly comes and sits between the bodies.*)

Padmini   They burned, lived, fought, embraced and died. I stood silent. If I'd said, 'Yes, I'll live with you both', perhaps they would have been alive yet. But I couldn't say it. I couldn't say, 'Yes'. No, Kapila, no, Devadatta. I know it in my blood you couldn't have lived together. You would've had to share not only me but your bodies as well. Because you knew death you died in each other's arms. You could only have lived ripping each other to pieces. I had to drive you to death. You forgave each other, but again, left me out.

Bhagavata (*without leaving his seat*)   What is this? It's a sight to freeze the blood in one's veins. What happened, child? Can we help you?

Padmini (*without looking at him*)   Yes, please. My son is sleeping in the hut. Take him under your care. Give him to the hunters who live in this forest and tell them it's Kapila's son. They loved Kapila and will bring the child up. Let the child grow up in the forest with the rivers and the trees. When he's five take up to the Reverend Brahmin Vidyasagara of Dharmapura. Tell him it's Devadatta's son.

Bhagavata   And you?

Padmini   Make me a large funeral pyre. We are three.

Bhagavata   You mean you are performing *sati*? But why, child?

Padmini (*puts the dolls on the ground*)   Give these dolls to my son. I won't see him. He may tempt me away from my path.

(*At a sign from the* **Bhagavata**, *two stagehands come and place a curtain in front of* **Padmini**.)

Kali, Mother of all Nature, you must have your joke even now. Other women can die praying that they should get the same husband in all lives to come. You haven't left me even that little consolation.

(*Does* namaskara. *The stagehands lift the curtain, slowly, very slowly, very slowly, as the song goes on. The curtain has a blazing fire painted on it. And as it is lifted, the flames seem to leap up. The female musicians sing a song. The following is a prose rendering of it.*)

Female chorus (*sings*)   Our sister is leaving in a palanquin of sandalwood. Her mattress is studded with rubies which burn and glow. She is decked in flowers which blossom on tinderwood and whose petals are made of molten gold. How the garlands leap and cover her, aflame with love.

The Fortunate Lady's procession goes up the street of laburnums, while the *makarandas* tie the pennants and the jacarandas hold the lights.

Goodbye, dear sister. Go you without fear. The Lord of Death will be pleased with the offering of three coconuts.

Bhagavata (*picks up the dolls and comes downstage*)   Thus Padmini becomes a *sati*. India is known for its *pativratas*, wives who dedicated their whole existence to the service of their husbands; but it would not be an exaggeration to say that no *pativrata* went in the way Padmini did. And yet no one knows the spot where she performed *sati*. If you ask the hunting tribes who dwell in these forests, they only point to a full-blossomed tree of the Fortunate Lady. They say that even now on full moon and on new moon nights, a song rises from the roots of the tree and fills the whole forest like a fragrance.

Female chorus (*sings*)   Why should love stick to the sap of a single body? When the stem is drunk with the thick yearning of the many-petalled, many-flowered lantana, why should it be tied down to the relation of a single flower?

A head for each breast. A pupil for each eye. A side for each arm. I have neither regret nor shame. The blood pours into the earth and a song branches out in the sky.

(*When the song ends, the* **Bhagavata** *does a* namaskara *to the audience. The audience should get a definite feeling that the play has ended when a scream is heard in the wings.*)

Bhagavata   What's that? Oh! Nata, our Actor!

(**Actor II** *comes rushing out. He doesn't even see the* **Bhagavata** *in his desperate hurry.*)

Why is he running? Where's the National Anthem?

(**Actor II** *suddenly stops in his tracks.*)

Actor II   The National Anthem!

Bhagavata   What?

Actor II   How did you know?

Bhagavata   Know what?

Actor II   Please, Bhagavata Sir, how did you know . . .

Bhagavata   Know what?

Actor II   About the National Anthem.

Bhagavata   What do you mean?

Actor II   Please, Sir, I beg of you. I implore you. Don't make fun of me. How did you know it was the National Anthem . . .

Bhagavata   Why? Haven't you seen an audience . . .

Actor II (*relieved*)   Phew! That! Ram Ram!

Bhagavata   Why? What . . .

Actor II   I almost died of fright . . .

Bhagavata   Really?

Actor II   I was coming down the road, when I heard someone singing at a distance, at the top of his voice. He was singing, *Jhanda Ooncha Rahe Hamara* (May our flag fly high!) Then he proceeded to *Sare Jahan se Acchha Hindostan Hamara* (Our India is better than the whole world). Then *Rise, Rise my Kannada Land.* Then *Vande Mataram* . . .

Bhagavata   Then?

Actor II   I was baffled. A true patriot at this time of the night? I had to find out who it was. A house – a big, thick fence around with not a gap in it. But I managed to find a hole to crawl through. I was just half-way in when I saw . . .

Bhagavata   What?

(*The* **Actor** *wipes his brow.*)

Come on, what did you see?

Actor II   A horse!

Bhagavata (*eager*)   A horse?

Actor II   Yes. It turned to me and in a deep, sonorous voice said, 'Friend, I'm now going to sing the National Anthem. So please do stand up to attention!'

Bhagavata   Listen, Nata, are you sure . . .

Actor II   I swear . . .

Bhagavata   No, no, what I mean is . . .

(*Commotion in the wings.*)

What's that now?

(**Actor I** *enters with a boy of about five. The boy is very serious, even sulky. There's not a trace of laughter on his face. He is holding the two cloth dolls which we have already seen, but the dolls are dirtier now. The commotion come from* **Actor I**, *who is so busy trying to make the child laugh – making faces at him, clowning, capering, and shouting – he doesn't notice the* **Bhagavata**.)

Bhagavata (*delighted*)   Oh! Nata! You again!

Actor I (*turns around and sees the* **Bhagavata**)   Oh, Sir, it's you!

Bhagavata   Well, well, you'll live to be a hundred.

Actor I   Why? What have I done?

Bhagavata   I was just thinking of you and you turned up. Just now this Nata (*pointing to* **Actor II**) was saying he saw a horse-headed man and I wondered if it was Hayavadana. So I remembered you.

Actor II   Bhagavata Sir . . .

Actor I (*ignoring* **Actor II**)   There's an actor's fate in a nutshell for you. Always remembered for someone else.

Bhagavata   Where's Hayavadana now? Has he come back?

Actor I   I don't know, Sir. He chased me away the moment we reached the Kali temple. Wouldn't let me stay there a minute longer.

Bhagavata   Oh! I very much hope the goddess granted him what he wanted. (*Sees the child.*) Who's this child?

Actor I   Him? Well? (*To the child.*) Go on, tell him. (*The child remains silent. Doesn't answer any questions.*)

Bhagavata   Who are you, child? What's your name? Where are your parents?

Actor I   You see? Not a word. Children of his age should be outtalking a dictionary, but this one doesn't speak a word. Doesn't laugh, doesn't cry, doesn't even smile. The same long face all twenty-four hours. There's obviously something wrong with him.

(*Bends before the child and clowns a bit.*)

See? No response – no reactions. When he grows up, he should make a good theatre critic.

Actor II (*restless*)   Bhagavata Sir . . .

Bhagavata (*to* **Actor I**)   Where did you find him?

Actor I   In a tribal village of hunters. On my way back I had to stay a night there and a tribal woman brought him to me. Said, 'This is not our child. It's from the city. Take it back'.

Bhagavata   A child of this city? (**Actor I** *nods.*) How strange! (*Notices the dolls.*) But – but – these dolls . . .

(*Tries to touch the dolls. The child reacts violently and moves away angry, terrified.*)

Actor I   I was about to warn you! Whatever you do, don't touch his dolls! At other times he'll starve and freeze to death rather than say a word. But touch the dolls and he'll bare his fangs. He almost bit off my finger once.

Actor II   Bhagavata Sir . . .

Bhagavata (*to* **Actor I**)   But Nata – (*Pause.*) Child, let me see your shoulder.

(*The child moves back.*)

No, no, I won't touch the dolls. I promise you. Just your shoulder.

(*Inspects his shoulder. Then with a cry of triumph.*) Nata . . .

Actor II   Bhagavata Sir . . .

Actor I   Yes . . .

Bhagavata   Look, the mole. It's Padmini's son. . . . There's no doubt about it.

Actor I   Padmini? Which . . .

Actor II (*shouting at the top of his voice*)   Bhagavata Sir!

(**Actor I** *and the* **Bhagavata** *react.*)

Bhagavata   Yes? Why are you shouting?

Actor II   I have been calling you for the last half-an-hour . . .

Bhagavata   Yes, yes. What's it?

Actor II   You said I'd seen a horse-headed man. I didn't. What I saw was a complete, perfect, proper . . .

(*A voice is heard off-stage singing the third stanza of 'Jana Gana Mana'.*)

There it is!

(*All stare in the direction of the song. A horse enters the stage singing.*)

Horse   *Tava Karunaruna Rage*

Nidrita Bharata Jage

Tava Charane Nata Matha

Jaya Jaya Jaya He Jaya Rajeshwara

(*Comes and stands in front of them.*)

Hohoo! What's this? Mr Bhagavata Sir! My Actor friend! Well, well, well! What a pleasant surprise! Delightful! How are you, Sir, how are you?

Bhagavata   It's not – not Hayavadana, is it?

Hayavadana   Your most obedient servant, Sir.

Bhagavata   But what . . .

Actor II   You mean you know this horse?

Bhagavata (*bursts into a guffaw*)   We're old friends.

Actor I (*laughing*)   Fellow pilgrims!

Hayavadana   But not fellow travelers. What?

(*They roar with laughter. Suddenly the boy too starts laughing. Doubles up with laughter. The dolls fall out of his hand as he claps his hands.*)

The boy (*clapping his hands*)   The horse is laughing! The horse is laughing!

Actor I (*jumping with delight*)   The boy is laughing!

Hayavadana (*goes to the boy*)   Why, my little friend, you may laugh, but I may not?

(*The boy is in hysterics.*)

Devadatta   That's Padmini's son, Hayavadana.

Hayavadana Padmini? I am not aware of . . .

Bhagavata You don't know her. But this poor child – he hadn't laughed, or cried, or talked in all these years. Now you have made him laugh.

Hayavadana Delighted. Delighted.

Bhagavata But tell me: you went to the goddess to become a complete man, didn't you? What happened?

Hayavadana Ah! That's a long story. I went there, picked up a sword which was lying around – very unsafe, I tell you – put it on my neck and said: 'Mother of all Nature, if you don't help me, I'll chop off my head!'

Actor I Then?

Hayavadana The goddess appeared. Very prompt. But looked rather put out. She said – rather peevishly, I thought – 'Why don't you people go somewhere else if you want to chop off your stupid heads? Why do you have to come to me?' I fell at her feet and said, 'Mother, make me complete'. She said 'So be it' and disappeared – even before I could say 'Make me a complete man!' I became a horse.

Actor I I am sorry to hear about that . . .

Hayavadana Sorry? Whatever for? The goddess knew what she was doing. I can tell you that. Ha Ha! Being a horse has its points. (*Pause.*) I have only one sorrow.

Bhagavata Yes?

Hayavadana I have become a complete horse – but not a complete being! This human voice – this cursed human voice – it's still there! How can I call myself complete? What should I do, Bhagavata Sir? How can I get rid of this human voice?

Bhagavata I don't know what to advise you, Hayavadana.

Hayavadana That's why I sing all these patriotic songs – and the National Anthem! That particularly! I have noticed that the people singing the National Anthem always seem to have ruined their voices, so I try. But – but – it – it doesn't seem to work. What should I do?

(*He starts to sob.*)

Boy Don't cry, horse. Don't cry. Stop it now.

Hayavadana No, I won't cry. The boy's right. What's the point of shedding tears?

Boy   Don't cry. You are nice when you laugh.

Hayavadana   No, I won't cry. I won't give up trying either. Come, little friend, let's sing the National Anthem together.

Boy   What is that?

Bhagavata   How could he? He has been brought up in a forest.

Hayavadana   Then sing some other song. Look, if you sing a song, I'll take you round on my back.

Boy (*excited*)   Yes – please.

Hayavadana   Well, then, what are we waiting for? Get on my back. Quick.

(*The* **Bhagavata** *seats the child on the horse's back.*)

Boy   Hiyah – Hiyah –

Hayavadana   No, no. You sing first. Then we start.

Bhagavata   Sing, son.

(*The boy sings and the horse goes around in a slow trot.*)

Boy   Here comes a rider.
　　　From what land O what land?
　　　On his head a turban.
　　　Sleep now, sleep now.
　　　Why his chest?
　　　Red O red?
　　　Why his eyes
　　　Pebbles O pebbles?
　　　Why his body
　　　Cold O cold?
　　　Where goes the horse?
　　　Nowhere O nowhere.

(*As the song ends, the horse comes and stands in front of the* **Bhagavata**.)

Hayavadana   Mr Bhagavata Sir . . .

Bhagavata   Yes.

Hayavadana   It seems to me the rider described in the song is dead. Am I right?

Bhagavata   Er – I think so – yes.

Hayavadana   Who could have taught this child such a tragic song?

Boy   Mother . . .

Bhagavata   What's there in a song, Hayavadana? The real beauty lies in the child's laughter, in the innocent splendor of that laughter. No tragedy can touch it.

Hayavadana   Is that so?

Bhagavata   Indeed. What can match a child's laughter in its purity?

Hayavadana   To be honest, Mr Bhagavata Sir, I have my doubts about this theory. I believe – in fact I may go so far as to say I firmly believe – that it's this sort of sentimentality which has been the bane of our literature and national life. It has kept us from accepting Reality and encouraged escapism. Still, if you say so, I won't argue. Come, child, let's have another song.

Boy   I don't know . . .

Hayavadana   Then sing the same song again.

Boy   You laugh first.

Hayavadana   Laugh again? Let me try. (*Tries to laugh.*) Ha Ha Ha! No, it's not easy to laugh – just like that.

Boy (*mimes whipping*)   Laugh – laugh . . .

Hayavadana   All right. All right. I'll try again. Ha! Ha! Ha! Ha! – Huhhuh . . . heahhh . . .

(*His laughter ends up as a proper neigh.*)

All   What's that?

Bhagavata   Hayavadana – Hayavadana . . .

Hayavadana   Heahhh . . .

(*His human voice is gone now. He can only neigh and leaps around with great joy.*)

Bhagavata   Careful – careful. Don't drop the child . . .

(*But the horse is too happy to listen. It prances around, neighing gleefully. The boy is also enjoying himself, singing bits of the song and urging the horse on.*)

Bhagavata   So at long last Hayavadana has become complete. (*To the* **Actors**.) You two go and tell the Revered Brahmin Vidyasagara that his grandson is returning home in triumph, riding a big, white charger.

Actor II   And the dolls?

Bhagavata   Throw them away. There's no further need for them.

(*The* **Actors** *go out with the dolls.*)

Unfathomable indeed is the mercy of the elephant-headed Ganesha. He fulfills the desires of all – a grandson to a grandfather, a smile to a child, a neigh to a horse. How indeed can one describe His glory in our poor, disabled words?

Come, Hayavadana, come. Enough of this dancing. Our play is over and it's time we all prayed and thanked the Lord for having the ensured completion and success of our play.

(**Hayavadana** *comes and stands by the* **Bhagavata**. *The* **Bhagavata** *helps the child down. At this point the curtain, with the fire painted on it – which has been there all the time – is dropped and* **Padmini**, **Kapila** *and* **Devadatta** *step forward and join the* **Bhagavata** *in prayer.*)

Grant us, O Lord, good rains, good crop,

Prosperity in poetry, science, industry and other affairs.

Give the rulers of our country success in all endeavours,

and along with it, a little bit of sense.

END OF PLAY

Notes

1 Reproduced by permission of Oxford University Press India © Oxford University Press 1997. Unauthorized copying is strictly prohibited.

2 Girish Karnad, 'Introduction' in *Three Plays*, Delhi: Oxford University Press, 1994, p.1.

3 See Erin B. Mee, *Theatre of Roots: Redirecting the Modern Indian Stage*. London: Seagull Books, 2007, which dedicates an entire chapter to Karnad and *Hayadavana*, as well as chapter seven in *Modern Asian Theatre and Performance* by Siyuan Liu, Kevin J. Wetmore, Jr. and Erin B. Mee, London: Methuen, 2014.

4 Suresh Awasthi, 'Theatre of Roots: Encounters with Tradition', *TDR*, Vol. 33, no. 4 (1989), p.48.

5 J. N. Kaushal, 'Last Month in Delhi: *Hayavadan*', *Enact*, 63 (1972), n.p.

6 Yakshagana is popular in the coastal areas of Karnataka, a state in the southwest of India. *Yaksha* means celestial being, and *gana* means music; the term 'yakshagana' originally referred to a particular style of 'celestial', or good, music. Plays written to this style of music were known as yakshagana *prasangas* (a prasanga is, in this context, a theme or story). Eventually, however, the term yakshagana no longer referred to the music itself but came to refer to the plays involving yakshagana-style music. See K. Shivaram Karanth, *Yakshagana*, Delhi: Abhinav Publications 1997, pp.82–4.

7 In the *Kathasaritsagara*, Padmini is torn between her brother and husband, but the element of incest has dropped out of both the Mann and Karnad versions. Other versions of the same story appear in the *Vetal Panchavimshati* and in other sources as well, but Karnad used the version from the *Kathasaritsagara*, which he first heard about from his friend and colleague, the folklorist and poet A. K. Ramanujan, who has collected, edited and retold a number of folk tales from India.

The Struggle of the Naga Tribe

W. S. Rendra
Translated and Annotated by Max Lane

W. S. Rendra (1935–2009), the son of a Roman Catholic missionary and a dancer at the court of Surakarta, is the best known modern Indonesian playwright and theatre maker.[1] At the age of thirteen he wrote his first play *Kaki Palsu* (False Foot, 1948). His actual theatre career, however, did not begin until the fifties. In 1954 the Department of Education and Culture in Yogya granted him its literature prize for *Orang, Orang Ditikungan Djalan* (People at the Curve of the Road), the first of many prizes, awards and honors for Rendra's work. In that same decade, he also published award-winning short stories and poems.

It was, however, in the sixties that Rendra rose to prominence. He was imprisoned in 1962 and 1963 due to his political statements through his art. He left the country in 1964 to visit New York City and remained there during the failed coup and purges of 1965. He studied at New York University and subsequently received his only formal training in theatre at the American Academy of Dramatic Arts. In 1967 he returned to Indonesia and, according to Evan Darwin Winet, 'began to produce a kind of modern theatre Indonesia had not seen before: ensemble-based, improvisational, abstract, and theatrical, a theatre that privileges action over text, visual over linguistic composition and the company over the individual actor.'[2] He began to produce a series of popular performances. Again, however, politics interfered and in 1978 he was arrested on 1 May and banned by the government from performance for 7 years. After the resignation of Suharto he rose in public prominence again, remaining a vital and important figure in Indonesian culture until his death in 2009.

Rendra has written a variety of types of plays, from *minikata* ('mini word'), developed from improvisational exercises with actors, to adaptations of Western classical dramas, such as *Oedipus Rex*, *Lysistrata*, *Hamlet*, *Macbeth* and even an Indonesian *Waiting for Godot*, to his powerful, satirical dramas such as *Mastadon dan Burung Kondor* (The Mastadon and the Condors, 1973) and *Sekda* (Province Secretary, 1977), all of which covertly criticised the government, frequently leading to censorship. Winet notes, 'Rendra viewed theatre as a form of cultural resistance through which clowns spoke truth to the authorities.'[3] This approach places him in a long line of dramatists, from Aristophanes through Beckett and several other playwrights in this volume.

Arguably his greatest work, *Kisah Perjuangan Suku Naga* (The Struggle of the Naga Tribe) was written in 1975 and almost immediately encountered censorship. The play, as translator Max Lane observes in his original introduction to the play, 'is both a reflection upon Indonesia's [then] current national reality and a response to that reality'.[4]

The play itself is also profoundly rooted in Indonesian culture, employing *wayang* structure and opening with a prologue by a *dalang*, a *wayang* puppeteer. Rendra uses *wayang* structure and the comments of the *dalang* to offer a (not very disguised) critique of Indonesian society. In the very first lines the audience is told 'this story does not . . . take place in Indonesia'. But obviously the fictitious setting of Astinam serves as plausible deniability that the play concerns Indonesia. Indeed, the prologue itself begins the satire by apologising for any satire, then immediately stating 'satire does not break the law and is a healthy element of society'. As Evan Darwin Winet observes, the play contains Rendra's argument that 'an enlightened nation respects the criticism of its artists rather than insisting that artists act as spokesmen for official policies'.[5] It is the role of the fool (in the Shakespearean sense) to remind the audience that the emperor has no clothes.

The play was written and rehearsed by Rendra and his actors while visiting rural villages and involved the villagers in the evolution of the piece. The play thus was born out of an experience of working with the rural poor in order to promote social justice. A tension is present in the play between the village people and 'townspeople', with Rendra coming down firmly on the side of the former. The struggle of the Naga tribe is no less than a liberation struggle, not merely in the political sense but also in a spiritual one, what Max Lane calls 'a humanist radicalism'.[6] The members of the Naga seek to liberate themselves from a society that demands subjugation and subservience of nature and of humanity to the state.

Note: The footnotes in the play are the original footnotes to the 1979 text. As a result, some are dated and refer to events and situations now past.

The Struggle of the Naga Tribe

[Kisah perjuangan suku Naga, 1975]

Characters:

DALANG

CHORUS OF MACHINES

CHORUS OF AMBASSADORS (Herr Schmits Schmerrrr, Mr Joe, Gregory Marakasov, Horomoto, and the Ambassador with no name but a Chinese accent)

ABISAVAM, Chief of the Naga tribe

ABIVARA, his son

CARLOS, a young journalist from across the sea

UNCLE, of Abivara

SUPAKA, a woman of the Naga tribe

SETYAWATI, Abivara's *fiancée*

SRI RATU, Queen of Astinam

PRIME MINISTER, of Astinam

COLONEL SRENGGI, Minister of Security

CHORUS OF PARLIAMENTARY FACTION CHAIRMEN

PRESIDENT OF PARLIAMENT

MINISTER OF MINES

ENGINEER, a European

BIG BOSS, an international millionaire

VILLAGERS

PROLOGUE

Enter **Dalang**.[7]

Dalang   Good evening everybody!
    Allow me to begin my story.
    This story does not – I stress once again – does not –
    take place in Indonesia,

So don't get uptight and censor the story.[8]
But I must proffer my sincere apologies for any satire that appears,
whether intended or, as it were, not intended.
You see satire does not break the law and is a healthy element
in society.

Now the story:

There is a kingdom called Astinam[9]
Situated in the Imagination
To the South of Prejudice
To the West of Fantasy
Bordering on Nonsense Sea
In short, it's strategically situated.
Astinam is ruled by a Queen.
She is assisted by a Prime Minister and Cabinet.
The Kingdom also has a Parliament and Constitution.
The Kingdom is supposed to be a democracy.

Me, I'm from Astinam.
My name is . . . oh, I'd better not give my name,
Or next you'll be asking for my address.

But return to our story.
This is a story of society.[10]
People cannot live alone. They must mix with others.
And relationship between people can be just or unjust.
This is what we wish to talk about.

Meanwhile, across the sea, in the lands of the ogres –
I mean Europe and America, and Japan too: Life is different.[11]
We are an agricultural country rich in produce and minerals.
They are industrial countries, rich in capital and in machines
that produce commodities.
To make these differences clearer we will examine them in the
various scenes.
And we'll look at the nature of their society.

(*A* **chorus of machines** *enter, moving in a jerking mechanical fashion.*)

> Ah, this is an industrial country.
> The machines are now expressing themselves.

THE MACHINES' CHORUS

Chorus   Boom! Boom! Boom!
Jas-Jis-Jos
Machines moving go gedeboom
People moving pant hongos-hongos.

Dalang   Come on machines, show us how you work!

Chorus   (*lining up at front of stage*): Jegler. Jegler. Jegler.
Ketpak. Ketipak. Ketipung.
The warehouses overflow
We've got nowhere to store our goods.
Sah-Soh-Sah
Ketoprak gebyar gebyar
We sell our products cheaply
We must have a huge market.

Dalang   How huge?

Chorus   Working fast requires a big market.
Cheap goods can be sent far and wide.

Dalang   Oh God! They could ask for the whole world!

Chorus   Tertam! Tertam! Tertam!
Tertum Tertum Tertum
Don't be so uptight.
We like working with a smile on our face.

Dalang   Wow! Incredible! Who owns you?

Chorus   The Big Boss.[12]

Dalang   You must make quite a profit for him?

Chorus   One million. . . . Two million . . .

One billion. . . . Two billion.
Whew, it's exhausting counting.

Dalang   Where does it all go?

Chorus   Profit increases capital.
Capital increases profit.
More money means more schemes.
We can't be held up, we can't be interrupted.

Dalang   What do you mean?

Chorus   Money must circulate
Money creates money
Money must circulate
Time is money
Goods are money
We call this economics.

Dalang   Wah! I give up!
Money goes round and round
Money circulates
Round and round in the sky
Up towards heaven.
Ah, but from there
It never comes down to earth.

The god of money gets richer
The poor remains coolies
For all eternity.
The people are cultivated, schooled and moulded
To be nothing but consumers.

Chorus   Boom! Boom! Boom!
Jas-Jis-Jos
Machines moving go gedeboom gedeboom
People moving pant hongos-hongos

If you disturb us
The economy will collapse.

If you disturb us
Unemployed workers will bite their nails.

Sah-soh-sah
Ketoprak kepri kepri
Give us raw materials
So that we can run.

Dalang   Wah! They want huge markets. They want raw materials.
What else do they want?

Chorus   Progress! This is the age of progress!
We are the leaders of progress.
The age of agriculture we leave behind.
The age of industry we make a reality.

THE AMBASSADORS' CHORUS

Enter five **Ambassadors** *carrying canes and wearing bow-ties.*

Chorus   Hallelujah! Hello! Hello! Hallelujah!
We are here, hallelujah!
We are progress, hallelujah!
We are friends of the world!

Prosperity we dispense
Progress we teach
Help we offer.
We are ambassadors of peace.

Dalang   A very impressive introduction, Gentlemen.

1st Ambassador   Call me Mr Joe.

When you speak to me, say: Hello! Hello!

Dalang   Hello! Hello!

Chorus   Hallelujah! Hello, hello, hallelujah!

2nd Ambassador   I am Herrrr Schmits Schmerrrr,
We must be cleverrr; yes, fairrrr,
Forward unhaltingly just like a panzerrr.

Dalang   Yes, cleverrr; yes, fairrrr – fly shit isn't too bad eitherrr.

Chorus   Hallelujah! Hello, hello, hallelujah!

3rd Ambassador   Melinovitch Marakasov.
   All the world must progress . . . must be tov!
   All must wear uniforms
   All must be international . . .

Chorus   Hallelujah! Hello, hello, hallelujah!

4th Ambassador   Ah-so! My name is Horomoto! Ah – so!
   I don't want anything –
   But only to say – Harro, harro, harro!!!

Dalang   Horrotonoyo![13]

4th Ambassador   Let's just play.

   (*The* **4th Ambassador** *then goes through the motions of riding a
   motor bike and then driving a car.*)
   Ah – so! Rrum – rrum – rrumm . . . magic![14]
   Ah – so! Brum – brum – brrumm . . . magic!
   Ah – so! Cheap! Practical! Cheap!

Chorus   Hallelujah! Hello, hello, hallelujah!

5th Ambassador   Nihao-maa?

Dalang   Bakso![15]

5th Ambassador   I am a simple person
   No need to tell my name.
   I like simple and cheap goods:
   Shirt buttons, scissors, knives, bobbypins,
   Combs, toothbrushes, soap, lamps, buckets,
   In short:
   Everyday goods.
   Excellent for friendship – hallelujah.[16]

Chorus   Hallelujah! Hello, hello, hallelujah!
   We are ambassadors, hallelujah!
   We laugh but are not happy.
   We pray but only get influenza
   An Ambassador's task couldn't be heavier.

Developing countries' ambassadors
Their task is to look for debts.
Hallelujah!
Developed countries' ambassadors
Their task is to sell goods.

Markets! Markets! After markets!
Cut down forests!
Dig up mines!
Empty the seas!
Grab up raw materials!
These are our first tasks.

Hello! Hallo! Hello! Harro! Hayo!
Hallelujah!
(*Linking arms*:) We all share a single fate.
(*Toasting together*:) Hahaha! Hihihi! Hahaha!
Off to work!
One two hallelujah!
Three four hallelujah!
(*The chorus of* **Ambassadors** *moves around the stage lining up at front centre stage again.*)
(*Bowing to imagined Royal presence*)
Your Highness,
We surrender our Letters of Accreditation.
We pass on our countries' greetings.
We all love your country.
Its culture is ancient and refined.
It is now, without a doubt, developing.
Progress – that is the key to this century!
This nation will not be left behind by another,
We are prepared to assist your country's holy efforts.
Loans can be negotiated.
One billion. Two billion. Three billion.[17]

1st Ambassador   Ten billion!

2nd Ambassador   20½ billion!

4th Ambassador   50 billion!

5th Ambassador   70 billion! Plus 10 per cent commission!!

Chorus   Your Highness,
Loans can be arranged.
All for progress,
For culture and humanity.
To achieve this, loan money
Must genuinely be used to benefit the people.
The people need 'Shopping Centres'[18]
We have the experts
The steel girders,
And the commodities
To be sold inside them.

Dalang   Ah! So that's what they're up to!

Chorus   Your Highness, supermarkets are progress!

Dalang   Rubbish!
The concrete is from over there,
The girders from there,
Hinges and handles from there
Screws from there.
The commodities for sale are from over there.
Everything is imported, because that is progress!

Chorus   Health must be advanced.[19]
People need Tonikum.

Dalang   Rice and plant root tonic![20]

Chorus   They need synthetic vitamins.

Dalang   Gado-gado! Gado-gado![21]

Chorus   And powdered milk.[22]

Dalang   Mothers' milk! Mothers' milk!
Green pea porridge! Green pea porridge!

Chorus   And ice-cream free from dust.

Dalang   Yes, but it's all from chemicals.[23]

Chorus   Onwards to progress, our friends!
   To make progress a reality:
   You must become the same as Japan, Europe, Russia, and America.
   We will arrange scholarships.[24]
   Send the hope of your nation's youth to study in our countries.
   They will become progressive.
   They will be able to use a refrigerator,
   Make-up,
   Air-conditioning;
   And yes, sit on a porcelain toilet.
   Yes, yes! This is progress,
   And we have the goods!

Dalang   More sales talk!

Chorus   Hallelujah, onward, forward, to work we go!
   An Ambassador's task is heavy,
   He eats well but gets diabetes.
   Cool weather gives him influenza.

Dalang   Always sitting on soft chairs, he gets piles.

(**Ambassadors** *exit.*)

Dalang   We have just heard the Ambassadors from across the sea.
   Hidden intentions behind every word!

Now let's return to Astinam.

In the mountain ranges of Astinam, to the north . . . ah, east . . . wait
a minute, is it north or east? Oh, I've got it now, to the west . . . there
can be found a beautiful and cool valley. This valley is situated
between mountains rich in copper. In this valley is the village of the
Naga Tribe.

Ever since ancient times, the Naga have been content as Astinamese,
adhering, like other tribes, to the principle of Astinamese national unity.[25]
Since those ancient times, the Naga have been farmers and have
made great progress in developing their agriculture.

Their irrigation system has been perfected and their cattle raising
methods improved. They produce enough food to fulfill their own
needs, and yet not enough if they also have to supply the capital city.

THE NAGA

Enter **villagers** *and* **Abisavam**, *Tribal Chief.*

Villagers   The Sun sends out its rays,
    The world is caught in its net.
    Children are out climbing the mango trees.
    The ancestors' spirits extend their blessings.
    (**Abisavam** *moves to front centre of stage.*)

Abisavam   Yesterday and tomorrow
    Are today.
    Disaster and good fortune
    Are the same.
    Horizons beyond us
    Horizons within us
    Uniting in the soul.

Dalang   This we call 'total'.

Villagers   The Sun sends out its rays.
    The lake's water sparkles.
    We greet mother earth (*patting the ground*)
    We take the benefits given.

Abisavam   I call out to the *mlinjo* tree:
    'This season you will bear much fruit.
    My son Abivara has returned home.
    I will pick your fruit,
    And make him his favourite biscuit.'[26]

Villagers   Fruit trees
    Timber trees,
    All types of trees
    Are our brothers.
    One gives food
    Another materials for tools
    And still another shelter.
    We must protect them.
    This is the way of nature
    According to karma.[27]

Dalang   Nah! Don't be so greedy with nature!

Laying forests bare just as you like!

Forests polluted!

Rivers polluted!

Even the seas are sold![28]

Abisavam   The rooster crows: cock-a-doodle-doo!

The goat joins in: embeek!

The cow adds: moooo!

And I call out to my son:

Abivara, come out now

Work in the fields awaits us!

Villagers   And at the river women launder.

Eels and snails sleep in paddy field canals.

The *tekubur* bird sings in cemeteries.

While in the heavens with the Sun.

Ancestor spirits play the *gamelan*.

Ayo! Come on!

All nature linked in mutual effort

All striving together.

Abisavam   Today we are going to open up new fields.

We will burn the weeds and underbrush.

We will share out the land and then it will be irrigated and developed and kept in order.

You all know the basic principle to which we hold:

Every farmer must own land. So when we share out these new fields, priority will be given to those who have no land: our young people who need land to work.

People who already own land, such as myself, will be considered last of all. We also emphasize that land owned by a person must be worked by that person. Land cannot be worked from outside the village. In order to own land in this village, people must come and live here.

The land that people receive from the sharing out of these new fields may not be sold before it is worked by that owner for at least ten years.

People who do not participate in the clearing of these new fields will not receive any even if they have enough money to buy some.[29]

Now, what do you all say to that?

Villagers   We agree, Abisavam.

> Indeed that is what our tradition decrees.
> Farmers must protect their land.
> Without land, farmers are only tools of the landlord
> Like oxen or cattle.
> Probably, in the eyes of the landlord,
> Farmers compared to cattle,
> The cattle would be more valuable.

Abisavam   I, Abisavam, head of your tribe, will maintain this principle in the name of the continuing integrity of our society. You all saw what happened in the village of the Kariman tribe. They have already sold two-thirds of their land to townspeople. The result? Every harvest brings forth at least three times their basic needs, yet the Kariman remain short of food. This is because a large part of their harvest is no longer owned by them but by people in the town. The Kariman themselves are only paid as labourers. And they aren't even paid enough to buy the food they need. That is why, in this village, we have the rule:

> Whomsoever leaves this village must return his land to the village
> and may not sell it to anyone else.

In other words:

> Land is the basic need of a village society, and because of that,
> ownership of land must be organised and controlled by the village
> concerned.

Villagers   So runs the traditions of our ancestors

> Who protected our villages wisely.
> A farmer who sells his land brings down disaster
> Upon his fellow farmer.
> Why must you sell your land?
> To buy bracelets and ear-rings?
> They do not grow.
> They give forth no fruit.
> Do you do it to build a brick house?
> A brick house is not progress.
> It produces nothing,
> Indeed, with just a small mistake, it can become Full of mould and
> mildew.

A progressive farmer is one who loves his land.

A progressive farmer is one who is able to protect his fellow farmers.

A progressive farmer is one who can lead his village to prosperity.

A progressive farmer is one who quickly discovers new plants and new ways to protect his environment.

Abisavam   Good! But look, it's Abivara, my son, coming with a friend.

ABIVARA COMES HOME TO HIS VILLAGE

Enter **Abivara** *with* **Carlos.**

Abivara   My father, uncles and all my friends, I, Abivara, son of Abisavam, have now returned from studying across the sea to work in my village.

Abisavam   Good! Good! Doesn't he speak well? Don't you agree? Simple, but to the point.

Uncle   Indeed! I'm happy that he wanted to come home. And I'm glad too that he hasn't forgotten the customs of his village.

Abivara   I want to take this opportunity to introduce a friend of mine. I came to know him in the town across the sea where I studied. He works for a newspaper, and he is my good friend. He is interested in the fate of the people of developing societies. And now he is here as my guest and wants to write about our village for his newspaper, and for a special book he is preparing. His name is Carlos.

Uncle   Can he speak. . . . Indon. . . . I mean, Astinamese?[30]

Carlos   Yes, but still not very well, I, Carlos, friend of Abivara, son of Abisavam, pay my respects to the members of the Naga tribe.

Abisavam   Eh, Carlos, your Astinamese is excellent, very fluent.

Carlos   Thank you. Your praise encourages me greatly. I must also apologize for making Abivara arrive late in the fields. He has just taken me to see the irrigation system which was built by your ancestors. I became absorbed in my inspection of this nature-supporting technology. It is basic and simple, yet we can see from the results that it fulfills its purpose very satisfactorily. This sort of technology helps conserve the environment and doesn't destroy It. I truly praise it.[31]

Abisavam   Our ancestors would he happy to hear such praise.

Uncle   One thing of which we must be proud is that Abivara wanted to return home to build up his village.

Abivara   And why not? You yourself, Uncle, returned home to the village after studying in the capital. There are many other young people who have returned home after their studies.[32]

Abisavam   This is what makes our village so special when compared with the others.

Carlos   Why is this village so special?

Abisavam (*reflecting*)   What is the reason?
>   Perhaps tradition
>   But then what is tradition?
>   Tradition is the reality of the expression of society's soul.
>   Tradition is the inner feeling.

Villagers (*gathering around* **Abisavam** *to advise him*)   Perhaps the inner feeling.
>   But then what are inner feelings?
>   (**Abisavam** *listens attentively.*)
>   Society's inner feelings are the expression of society's soul.
>   Society has a soul and a body.
>   Society's body is custom, institutions and law.
>   Society's soul is the common instinct which can only be realized in symbol and legend.
>   This is the sacred path via which society's soul is joined with the Spirit of the One.[33]

Abisavam   The unity of soul and body in this village is still strong. Our whole way of life is still tied strongly to the worship of the One. Abivara came home because of his desire to worship. Here work and worship are one and the same.

Abivara   Other fields other grasshoppers.
>   Other waterholes other fish.
>   Were I a grasshopper, here would be my field.
>   Were I a fish, here would be my waterhole.[34]

Supaka   Abivara, don't you want to become an 'important person' in the capital?[35]

Abivara   No, Aunt, I'm not the 'important person' type.

Supaka   Don't you want to get ahead in life?

Abivara   Oh yes! I want to be a person who is useful. But to be an 'important person' is, on the contrary, not to get ahead, not to progress. I want to be a leader. The 'important persons' always defend the status quo; leaders are willing to go forward.

Carlos   Big shots are afraid of criticism. Leaders learn to go forward from criticism.

Abivara   Exactly!

Supaka   Have you brought home any woolen coats or sunglasses?[36]

Abivara (*laughing*)   No, Aunt. Woolen clothes are too hot for wearing Astinam. And across the sea sunglasses are only worn on the beach. The only people who wear dark glasses in town are gangsters.[37]

Supaka   Why didn't you bring home a car, Abivara?

Abivara   Indeed, as I lived modestly, I could have easily saved enough to buy two cars. But we don't need cars here. What we need are trucks. Cars aren't progress – they're just a luxury. On the other hand trucks can fulfill our basic needs. They can carry both more goods and more people. But first, the roads between the villages must be improved. To bring in trucks before the roads are improved is to show that you don't understand technology.[38]

Abisavam   So it's important that our village also builds roads?

Abivara   Yes father. Our village will then be able to run its own transport which can take our produce straight to the market.

Abisavam   There is a lot to be done in the time ahead. But now we must finish clearing this field.

Carlos   If you think I won't be a hindrance, I'd also like to help.

Abisavam   O.K.!

Ayo everyone, off to work!

THE ASTINAMPURAM SCENE[39]

Dalang   We now move to the capital of Astinam – Astinampuram. This is the residence of the Queen of Astinam, Sri Ratu, – beautiful, secure, and prosperous.

(**Sri Ratu** *enters. She is dressed in a* kebaya, *the Indonesian national dress for women, with a large red and white sash; red and white being the Indonesian national colours.*

Her hair is done in a sanggul, *the traditional hair-do of Central Japanese ladies.*[40])

Ah, here is Her Majesty now.

(**Dalang** *looks the queen over.*)

Her gait isn't bad.

The gait of a hungry tiger, I'd call it.

Funny isn't it, every tiger always seems to be hungry.

(**Sri Ratu** *stops and poses.*)

This is the pose of a queen. Nose somewhat thrust upwards to create the impression of being above other people. This is called the Aristocrat's Pose.

(**Sri Ratu** *takes out a pair of sunglasses. She carefully polishes the lenses on her* kebaya, *looks again at the lenses and then purposefully puts them on.*)

Those dark glasses are always worn; they are the symbol of progress. Nine out of eleven Hollywood film stars wear such glasses.

(**Sri Ratu** *begins to arrange her hair.*)

The hair is arranged . . . then it is sprayed . . . scattered with gems of all kinds.

(**Sri Ratu** *makes up her face.*)

Now it's the face's turn . . . first foundation is put on – then mascara . . . powder . . . Lipstick . . . all foreign made, that's progress.[41]

(**Sri Ratu** *breathes in and puts on her girdle.*)

This is to slim in the body . . . before it's too late.

Unlike a beauty queen, real queens are usually not pretty, so she must try hard to look like a queen.

(**Sri Ratu** *looks this way and that way.*)

Her Highness Sri Ratu is ready. She confronts the world with style.

Sri Ratu   It seems that today is going to be terrible.

The sun is shining too strongly.[42]

Nature is cruel.

We must domesticate it with advanced technology.

Dalang   Listen to her accent, will you? Unnatural, artificial. The Menteng style.

In Astinampuram there is a suburb called Menteng.

Sri Ratu   Heh you! Heh you!

(**Dalang** *isn't aware that* **Sri Ratu** *is addressing her*.)

Heh, are you deaf or something!?!

Dalang   Oh, me?

Sri Ratu   You deaf?[43]

Dalang (*to* **Sri Ratu**)   Aduh! I'm sorry, Your Majesty, your servant misunderstood . . .

(*to audience*) It seems I was the one she was calling 'Heh you! Heh you!'

(*to* **Sri Ratu** *again*): Your servant waits upon Your Majesty's words, be they an order, a communiqué, regulations, or even indoctrination.

Sri Ratu   Come on you, I want to hear your honest opinion of me.

Dalang (*to audience*)   This is an order to praise her.

– Yes, Your Majesty, honesty and faithfulness are indeed my main characteristics.

Sri Ratu   Aren't my clothes very nice?

Dalang (*to* **Sri Ratu**)   Oh, an exact fit. It reflects exactly Your Highness's character.

(*to audience*)   The character of a clothes line, nothing to it except what's hung on it.

Sri Ratu   Now I am ready to start today's work.

Call in the Prime Minister.[44]

Dalang   Will the Prime Minister please attend the Queen!

(*The* **Prime Minister** *enters, takes out a pair of dark glasses, carefully polishes them, and then – with a flourish – puts them on*.)

Sri Ratu   How are things today Mr Prime Minister?

Prime Minister   In general, everything is fine; the Kingdom is solid, safe and secure. But in particular, my piles are acting up again.

Sri Ratu   Oh well yes, what can we do? Nature is indeed stubborn. It creates so many irritations for us. I myself, at the moment, have a very disturbing condition. My blood pressure is up again. You know we're lucky this is the age of progress. For every illness there is a medicine. How many medicines must you take?

Prime Minister   I must take seventeen pills three times daily and must have an injection every two days.

Sri Ratu   Oh, I have to take more pills than that!! Wah! Doctors these days are really wonderful. Our nation must not be left behind in developing modern medical science.

Prime Minister   No need to worry, Your Majesty. Happily there are many foreign companies who want to invest here and build pharmaceutical factories.

Sri Ratu   Their requests must be given priority – providing, of course, they show sufficient 'understanding'.

Prime Minister   Their 'understanding' is quite large. They are going to keep aside ten percent of the capital for unforeseen matters, the use of which will be entirely up to Your Majesty, and will be directly deposited in Your Majesty's bank account in Hong Kong.

Sri Ratu   Excellent!

Prime Minister   Moreover, the Wijaya Kusuma Hospital Project is ready to begin.[45]

Sri Ratu   Have my latest suggestions been implemented yet?

Prime Minister   Yes, Your Majesty. Every cell and room will be air-conditioned and all the toilets will be of porcelain, and every patient, in line with advanced societies, will be taught to use toilet paper.[46]

Prime Minister   In every room there will be a telephone.

Sri Ratu   Are the laboratories good?

Prime Minister   Excellent! Don't worry, it will be the most modern hospital in all Southeast Asia. It will be able to cater for plastic surgery, will have enough heart pump machines, lots of medicines, the largest blood storage facilities, and also artificial lung machines.

Dalang   Nothing is as it should be!!!!

Prime Minister   Everything is as it should be!!!!

Dalang   What's the use of all this for the ordinary people? Most people in this country still live in poverty. What they need is not the most modern hospital in all Southeast Asia, but more small hospitals in each district. One luxury hospital could mean fifty simple hospitals available to all.[47]

Prime Minister   Your Majesty, we must have Progress!

Dalang   Progress does not mean living in luxury! Progress means an increasingly equal level of prosperity and welfare. What is not useful for the majority is wasteful. There is no need to give it priority.

Prime Minister   Your Majesty, to ensure the security of development, the people must be further put in order. Colonel Srenggi, Minister of Security, wishes to see you to put forward his plans for security.

Sri Ratu   Ah, show him in!

Dalang   Colonel Srenggi, Minister of Security, please enter.[48]

(**Colonel Srenggi** *enters, takes out a pair of dark glasses, polishes the lenses on his sleeves, looks to the right and left holding the glasses up to the light, and then slowly and carefully puts them on.*)

Sri Ratu   Good morning, Colonel Srenggi.

Colonel Srenggi   Good morning, Your Majesty. Good morning, Mr Prime Minister.

Prime Minister   Ho ho, you've got a new pair of sun glasses!

Colonel Srenggi   Yes, the brand is 'Cool Magic', for 'night and day'. Very modern.

Sri Ratu   Do they have a feminine version?

Colonel Srenggi   Yes, Your Majesty. I will arrange a dozen for Your Majesty.

Sri Ratu   Thank you. Now, how are things Colonel?

Colonel Srenggi   In general, quite good Your Majesty, but in particular. . . . I'm in the middle of an attack of diabetes.

Sri Ratu   Colonel Srenggi, everyone has their trials. Piles, diabetes, high blood pressure. If we dwell on them all the time, we'll become very despondent. But these are modern times. Our nation, in its development, will not forget the health field. There is a lot of foreign capital which is in sympathy with our goals in this area. They are going to invest millions in vitamin pill and tonic factories. Besides that, there is the Wijaya Kusuma Hospital project. It will be the largest and most modern hospital in all Southeast Asia.

Colonel Srenggi   This will really bring prestige to our people.

Sri Ratu   Yes. But it's a pity everyone doesn't think this way.

Dalang   What's wrong with thinking differently?

Prime Minister   Yes, there are many viewpoints which object to Progress.

Sri Ratu   And they disturb our development efforts.

Colonel Srenggi   In short, they're a nuisance!

Sri Ratu   While I've got this blood pressure condition, their comments only serve to make things worse, they only make trouble.

Colonel Srenggi   Of course that's what they do. Just imagine someone sweeping up a yard while someone else goes around disturbing him, commenting and talking just as he likes. This is simply worrying someone who is trying to work.[49]

Dalang   What sort of logic is this? Making cheating comparisons! Is running a government the same as sweeping up a yard? If that's what he thinks, let him become a sweeper rather than a minister.

Prime Minister   We must secure and safeguard development, Your Majesty.

Colonel Srenggi   As Minister of Security I will issue a statement decreeing that to criticise development is sabotage, and that sabotage is subversion.

Prime Minister   Ah, then there will be no more opposition.

Colonel Srenggi   Opposition is our enemy!

Sri Ratu   Excellent! Now we will be able to develop with ease and speed.

Dalang   They're uncontrolled. Free to do as they like. This is anarchy. Regulations are only used to control the people, but can't be used to control those above. We call this situation primitive.

Colonel Srenggi   Those who wish to speak must remember the proper channels. Isn't that what order is?

Dalang   Channels which don't channel – more like dams.

Colonel Srenggi   Sacrifice and obedience are the beginnings of Preofress.

Dalang   That's what the colonizers of earlier times also said!

Colonel Srenggi   Don't let's always be suspicious of each other. Suspicion is the enemy of development.[50]

Dalang   Control is not needed because there is suspicion. Control is needed to safeguard balance and justice.

Colonel Srenggi   This nation has a Council of People's Representatives. It is the living witness to the democracy we are building.

Prime Minister   Your Majesty, it appears that it is necessary to call in the Heads of the Parliamentary Factions.[51]

Sri Ratu   Good! Call them!

Prime Minister & Colonel Srenggi   Heh you! Yes, you! Come and report!

THE PARLIAMENTARY FACTION CHAIRMEN

Enter five dapperly dressed members of parliament. They are the **President of Parliament** *and the four* **Faction Chairmen***. They twist and turn as they walk as if they were drunk or drugged.*

Faction Chairmen and President of Parliament:

We have been summoned by Her Majesty.
This is indeed an honour.
We are all men of quality.
Our clothes make this very clear.

As soon as we took up our jobs
Clothes were made for us.
In past times we were activists and protesters
Now we're cautious in what we say –
This because we must defend our positions.
Indeed this is politics, to whose rules we are bound.[52]

If 'recalled', oh what a horrible plight!
Okay then, let's just be polite.
If 'recalled', we lose our ties and medals –
This makes us feel embarrassingly bare.

Our first and main task
Is just to talk a lot.
It must be talk that approves
But avoids debate.
Inside Parliament
Unity is more important than debate.
And the prime promoters of unity
Are orders from above.

We are channels
Channels of officialisation.
We are given clothes and procedures
Just like those of Europeans.
We have been prepared for Progress.
But the people are still ignorant.[53]
They must always be given direction.

Council of Representatives really means Council for Direction
Opponents' proposals may be debated
Superiors' proposals must quickly be passed.
When this principle is erred against
It is a sign there are subversives amongst us.

Sri Ratu   Heh, how come you're walking like that?

Faction Chairmen and President of Parliament   We're stoned, Sri
Ratu. We're possessed by Development.

Sri Ratu   Heh, I thought it was only Colonel Srenggi's son who gets
stoned.[54]

Dalang   What they mean is that the word 'development' has become so
cheap, that after a while they become confused themselves as to what it
means.

Sri Ratu   I like people who love development. I hope you all don't forget to repeat the word 'development' very frequently, as if you were praying. It's very good for the soul. Before long, when you really understand it, Development becomes mystical.[55]

Faction Chairmen and President of Parliament   In general, excellent, but in particular . . .

Sri Ratu   Stop! (*to* **President of Parliament**) In particular, what's wrong with you?

President of Parliament   Stomach ulcers, Your Majesty.

Sri Ratu (*to* **1st Faction Chairman**)   And You?

1st Faction Chairman   Gout.

Sri Ratu (*to* **2nd Faction Chairman**)   You?

2nd Faction Chairman   Piles.

Sri Ratu (*to* **3rd Faction Chairman**)   You?

3rd Faction Chairman   High blood pressure.

Sri Ratu   Same as me. How does it feel?

3rd Faction Chairman (*making faces*)   Painful, painful, painful.

Sri Ratu   And you?

4th Faction Chairman   Diabetes.

Sri Ratu   Yes, yes, yes!! – Indeed health services need to be urgently developed and upgraded. The Wijaya Kusama Hospital Project has begun. It will be the most modern hospital in all Southeast Asia. Is this not what the people desire?

President of Parl.   Exactly! The people need a strong nation, a nation worthy of pride, where progress is taking place, a nation that won't be left behind by Europe and America. How could anyone possibly disagree with such a laudable project as this? Are they against progress? Being against progress means being against development. Opposing development is subversion.[56]

Sri Ratu   Excellent! And what do you think about it?

1st Faction Chairman   Idem.

Sri Ratu   You?

2nd Faction Chairman   Idem.

Sri Ratu   You?

3rd Faction Chairman   Ditto.

Sri Ratu   And you?

4th Faction Chairman   Ditto.

Prime Minister   Ah, united!

Colonel Srenggi   This is the result of guided election implementation.[57]

Sri Ratu   Yes! They are brilliant, all of them!

Colonel Srenggi   Just recently I have noted signs[58] of a group who are always making demands, and are always being suspicious. Their criticisms are deflecting us from the road to development. I call them the 'spoilt group'. I ask you: why should people be able to make these criticisms when we have an official channel in the Parliament?

President of Parl.   How will we ever be able to get credit from overseas for Development if we can't show them that their capital here is safe. For this reason our thinking must be tidied up. Indeed this is what Parliament is for!

    (*to* **Faction Chairmen**) Agreed?

1st Faction Chairman   Agreed!

2nd Faction Chairman   Agreed!

3rd Faction Chairman   Idem!

4th Faction Chairman   Ditto!

Prime Minister   Wah! nice and tidy!

Sri Ratu   I just feel that they are so clever, all of them!

Colonel Srenggi   In order to safeguard development we must pass new laws stating that the time of Parliament's meeting to enact the Four Year Development Plan approaches, there may be no negative voices which try to influence the outcome of the session.

3rd Faction Chairman   What do you mean by 'negative voices'?

Colonel Srenggi   Indeed, quite a lot of things.

President of Parl.   In short, anything subversive.

3rd Faction Chairman   What do you mean by 'subversive'?

President of Parl.   Indeed a lot of things. – In short, this concept must be sufficiently broad so it can be used wherever and whenever. Eh, are you a subversive?

3rd Faction Chairman   Oh no!!

President of Parl.   Ahh, good!

Colonel Srenggi, laws such as you mentioned will be passed.

Colonel Srenggi   Excellent, excellent!

Ah . . . there is something else. Later when the Four Year Development Plan is passed and its implementation begins, people should still not be able to criticise it.

Dalang   This is total silencing!

President of Parl.   This is a brilliant defence tactic.

It's a tremendous strategy.

Dalang   They want to run a government in the same way as they would wage a war!?!

President of Parl.   This way we can really protect stability.

Prime Minister   This is excellent; everything is running well.

President of Parl.   Mr Prime Minister, in the end culture is tidiness. So our thinking must also be tidied up. Ideas and actions must all be tidied up, so that national unity can be created.[59]

Sri Ratu   Truly brilliant!

Prime Minister   Indeed, Your Majesty. All his pronouncements calm our hearts. This is what we call a positive attitude.[60]

Colonel Srenggi   Now security can be safeguarded even more. I am also very pleased with him – now we're ready to move onto new matters – Your Majesty, an Ambassador from across the sea is waiting. His name is Mr Joe.

Sri Ratu   Ah, Mr Joe! I've been expecting him for some time. Call him in!

All   Hello, Mr Joe!

Hello, hello, hallelujah!

Mr Joe, – 'please, come in.'

(**Mr Joe** *enters accompanied by the* **Minister of Mines**.)

Mr Joe   I pay homage to Your Most Praiseworthy and Sparkling Majesty, Queen of Astinam.

Sri Ratu   Good! Welcome. Your Astinamese is very fluent.

Mr Joe   Such praise reflects the generous heart of a queen of great wisdom.

Sri Ratu   Thank you! – Ah, I see that you are accompanied by our Minister of Mines.

Minister of Mines   Yes, I attend to pay homage to Your Majesty and there are also some matters that I wish to bring to Your Majesty's notice.

Mr Joe   He has gone out of his way for me, for it is rather I who wish to discuss some matters with Your Majesty that indeed are related to his Department.

Sri Ratu   Good. It just so happens that there are many people here at the moment. Big fish, too!

Mr Joe   Greetings to their Excellencies, the Prime Minister, the Minister of Security, the President of Parliament and the other important gentlemen.

All   Hell! Salam! Hallo! Hullo! Helo! Salam! Hello!

Mr Joe   Ah, a very joyful greeting.

Prime Minister   But Your Excellency looks a little pale?

Mr Joe   Yes, in fact . . . hmm, in general my condition is good, but in particular . . . well . . .

Sri Ratu   What?

Mr Joe   Stomach ulcers, Your Majesty.

Sri Ratu (*to* **Minister of Mines**)   And you?

Minister of Mines   Gout, Your Majesty.

Sri Ratu   So how many have gout?. . . . Stomach ulcers?. . . . Diabetes?. . . . Piles?. . . . High blood pressure?. . . . Yes, add me, that makes two there. . . . Yes, yes, yes. . . . I become more and more convinced that our war against disease must be intensified. (*to* **Mr Joe**) Our plan for the construction of the most modern hospital in all Southeast Asia with credit from Your Excellency's country must soon be implemented.

Mr Joe   All arranged! You can rely upon my country as a friend. As long as we aren't caused any trouble, we will certainly be friends, always ready to help you. But if we are caused trouble, we will of course withdraw all our aid!

Co-operation! That's the key. In co-operation 'mutual understanding' is
what is important.

Prime Minister   Agreed! I really like that. Your Majesty, I myself am
prepared to guarantee that Mr Joe is truly full of 'understanding'.

Sri Ratu   That is very gratifying. And what matters might you wish to
discuss, Mr Joe?

Mr Joe   There are two things, Your Majesty.
   Firstly, a matter of money.
   Secondly, a matter of money.
   That is, if credit is indeed needed, as the Astinamese
   Ambassador has made known to our government.

Sri Ratu   Certainly we need credit for the smooth progress of
Development.

Mr Joe   One loan will be given, but it will have the following
condition: namely, that it be used genuinely to fulfill the people's food
needs.

Prime Minister   That is a priority of Development.

Mr Joe   As a sign of the genuineness of this intention, 40 per cent of
this loan must be used to buy wheat from us.

Dalang (*to audience*)   That is the wheat surplus from their harvest last
year! Rather than let it rot, better to dump it on us! What sort of help is
that?[61]

Prime Minister   Wheat contains many nutrients.

Colonel Srenggi   So it must be good for the people's health.

Faction Chairmen   Wheat can be made into bread.
   Bread with butter – ah, very nice!
   Bread goes well with cheese
   Goes well with ham
   Goes well with jelly
   And other foods in a can,
   Imported from overseas
   In accordance with what is Progress.

Sri Ratu   We agree to accept this credit.
   It will be excellent for health.

Prime Minister   Excellent, Your Majesty.

Colonel Srenggi   Bravo!

Dalang (*to audience*)   This is nutrition the European way. Are our stomachs indeed European stomachs?

Sri Ratu   Now the second matter?

Mr Joe   Yes, this is the major matter. There is a company in my country which wishes to invest a large amount of capital in the mining industry here. (*To* **Faction Chairmen**:) Of course, it will use the official channels. Because it always places a high value on official channels. I am only concerned to give support, because I really know the character of the President Director of this company. He is a million – million – millionaire who has reached the highest level of knowledge about life. Besides mining, he also has interests in pharmaceuticals, hotels, and . . . spiritual affairs. He has built many churches, mosques and monasteries all over the world. Just recently he has built his own monastery on a beautiful mountain. There he also has lessons in yoga, samadhi, silat, tai chi and so on.[62] Yes, I can whole-heartedly guarantee this businessman.

Sri Ratu   As long as a person is full of understanding we will certainly respect him.

Mr Joe   Indeed, he is truly understanding.

Minister of Mines   Excuse me, Your Majesty. I would also like to support him. His understanding is quite great. And to prove he is an expert in mining, he has chosen something which he has himself mined as a gift for Your Majesty – this diamond.

Sri Ratu   A diamond?

Minister of Mines   It's worth at least two million dollars – a fantastic jewel of nature.

Sri Ratu   Thank you. I'm very pleased. This is truly 'art'.

Minister of Mines   Your Majesty, the Big Boss, as we call our friend, greatly admires the beauty of our country's natural environment. Spurred on by this admiration he has long been making a survey of our minerals. Now he has discovered a copper load of considerable value on Mt. Saloka in the region of the Naga tribe. To further the progress of our country he will invest considerable capital to mine this copper.

His machines are so modern!

Prime Minister   I think this must be considered seriously.

Faction Chairmen   Minerals in the ground
   Have no value
   Rather than remain unmined
   Let them be mined
   Then we will all be busy
   And in this business
   There will be additional income

Minister of Mines   So it's productive. The money could also be used to finance the other ministries.

Sri Ratu   If that's so, we must consider it seriously.

Mr Joe   Hallelujah!

All Together   Hullo, hullo, hallelujah!

ABIVARA AND SETYAWATI[63]

(**Abivara** *and* **Setyawati** *enter together.*)

Abivara   Setyawati, have you received the gifts from my mother?

Setyawati   Yes, I'm very happy.

Abivara   In a short while we'll be married.

Setyawati   After getting married will we move to the town?

Abivara   No, I will work here in the village. Besides rice farming, I want to develop some animal husbandry. Bee-keeping amongst other things.

Setyawati   I'm thinking about our children's future.

Abivara   What about their future?

Setyawati   They'll be far away from progress.

Abivara   What do you mean by 'progress'?

Setyawati   Well, there are various things – If you live in the village it's difficult to get to see films.

Abivara   The cinema is only entertainment, it's not a tool of progress.

Setyawati   Yes, but there are some good quality films.

Abivara   Sure, but only one or two. We can go into town to see them. But the other films, they're nothing more than the purveyors of a life whose character is very shallow and false. A life whose character is dependent on imports. Is this progress?

Setyawati   Yes, but living in the village there's not much social life.

Abivara   Is it really true that there is more social life in the towns? Good God! Townspeople hardly ever know the names of their own neighbours. Social intercourse between friends has become expensive in the towns. All social intercourse must be related to some practical interest. It doesn't matter if it's a business or sexual interest, or some other material concern. It's only one-sided social intercourse, not total. So in fact, it's really the townspeople who lack a social life.

Setyawati   Abivara!

Abivara   That means you're dispirited.

Setyawati   I'm dejected. I don't want my children to be left behind by fashion.

Abivara   What is 'fashion'? Is fashion 'progress'? Fashion is nothing more than new habits and customs. Fashion only binds people.

Setyawati   Abivara!

Abivara   You're angry!

Setyawati   I'm dejected. I don't want my children to feel inferior when they grow up.

Abivara   Why should they feel inferior?

Setyawati   You know how townspeople view villagers!

Abivara   Their view is an uneducated view. They should know that village people are more productive than townspeople. Villagers produce things from the earth. But what do townspeople produce? All they can do is import. Their economy is a hawker's economy. Or the most they're capable of producing is bureaucracy. And bureaucracy is an obstacle to progress.

Setyawati   What must I say?

Abivara   Your opinion.

Setyawati   I'm confused.

Abivara   Think on it for two or three days.

Setyawati (*crying*)   Abivara!

Abivara   I'm not going to console you. I believe you will be able to digest all this. – now go home, I will take you.

Setyawati   (*gazes at* **Abivara**)

Abivara   (*gazes at* **Setyawati**)

Setyawati   (*suddenly turns around and runs away*)

Abivara   (*suddenly stops still, strikes the air, runs off*)

ABISAVAM DEBATES WITH AUNT SUPAKA

Enter **Abisavam** *and* **Supaka**.

Supaka   I want to talk with you again.

Abisavam   Good.

Supaka   So use your mind. Listen to me.

Abisavam   Use your mind? Why are you yelling?

Supaka   Because you're being obstinate!

Abisavam   I think I'm being 'relaxed' enough.[64]

Supaka   I know what you're up to. You want to make me cry.

Abisavam   Good heavens!

Supaka   I want to sell my rice lands.

Abisavam   You can't. You can't sell your land to outsiders because that will mean the beginning of landlords in the village. And you can't sell it to people within the village both because everyone already has sufficient land, and because the village needs to be able to control the price of land.

Supaka   Abisavam.

Abisavam   What is it?

Supaka   Did not my beloved late husband get this land legally?

Abisavam   Yes, legally.

Supaka   And now I'm a widow.

Abisavam   Yes, a young widow.

Supaka   I don't understand farming.

Abisavam   You haven't received a good education then.

Supaka   I'm not a farmer.

Abisavam   If that's the case you shouldn't be living in a village.

Supaka   But I came to the village with my late beloved husband.

Abisavam   Your late beloved husband should have taught you farming.

Supaka   But I was always busy back and forth to town trading. My aptitudes are more fitted to trading.

Abisavam   They are worthy aptitudes.

Supaka   Farming is not suitable for me.

Abisavam   Indeed not.

Supaka   So it's reasonable that I sell the land from my husband to add to my trading capital.

Abisavam   Oh, that's not allowed. So says our tradition. Because that would mean transferring the wealth of the village to the town. This would be the beginning of the exploitation of the village by the town.

Supaka   You! You!

Abisavam   You're going to use your last weapon. You're going to cry.

Supaka (*crying*)   You're mean.

Abisavam   Ah, what did I say!

NEWS FROM UNCLE[65]

A villager, **Uncle***, enters running just as Aunt* **Supaka** *is crying.*

Uncle (*calling out*)   Abisavam! Abisavam!

Abisavam   What's wrong? What is it?

Uncle (*puffing, gasping for breath*)   Wait a minute, wait a minute!

Abisavam   What's up?

Uncle   Out of breath.

Abisavam   Tired?

Uncle   In a panic!

Supaka   Huh! Why are you panicking?

Uncle   Oh no!

Supaka   Why did you say 'Oh no'.

Uncle   You're a foolish nuisance.

Supaka (*approaching* **Uncle** *threateningly*)   Who's foolish, you or me?

Abisavam (*intervening*)   Enough! Enough! Break it up – How's your breath now?

Uncle   OK

Abisavam   Still panicking?

Uncle   Ah, this is the problem.

Abisavam   Tell us!

Uncle   We are going to be moved from this village.

Abisavam (*laughing*)   Ha, ha, ha! – Get your breath again.

Uncle   It's OK.

Abisavam   Good. Speak again.

Uncle   We're going to be moved from this village.

Abisavam (*laughing again*)   Ha, ha, ha! Who's going to move us?

Uncle   Her Majesty.

Abisavam   Which Her Majesty?

Uncle (*waddling to imitate the Queen's movements*)   Our Her Majesty.

Abisavam   This is looking serious.

Uncle   I've been serious all along.

Abisavam   I'm still not clear on what's happening.

Uncle (*pointing*)   Look, what mountain is that?

Abisavam   Mt Saloka.

Uncle   There are unmined minerals there.

Abisavam   Yes, copper.

Uncle   Now they want to mine it.

Abisavam   So?

Uncle   Our village will be turned into a mining town.

Abisavam   And us?

Uncle   Transmigration.

(**Abisavam** *squats down*.)

Uncle   Are you in a panic or just tired.

Abisavam   Shit!

(*Enter villagers,* **Abivara** *and* **Carlos**. **Abisavam** *stands up*.)

Abivara   Father? They are going to move us!

Abisavam   I've heard.

Villagers   Who do they think they are? – Mad! – I won't accept it!!!

Abisavam (*squatting down again*)   Calm down everyone!

Uncle   What are you going to do?

Abisavam (*pausing a moment*)   I don't know.

Supaka (*coming forward*)   I'm going to sell my land to them!

Abisavam (*standing up and approaching* **Supaka**)   You want to make a hole in our defences? Are you so greedy for riches that you're prepared to get it in a way that means disaster for others? Profit gained from the suffering of others, is that proper commerce?

(**Supaka** *bows her head.*)

The villagers, **Abivara**, **Abisavam** *and* **Carlos**, *are still on stage. A European engineer enters and starts making measurements. He moves clumsily in contrast with the energetic and rhythmical movements of the villagers in earlier scenes. The villagers watch him; politely move out of the way to let him survey the area. Then a conversation takes place.*

Uncle   Heh Albino! Can you speak Astinamese?

Engineer   Yes. But I'm not an albino, I'm a white person.[66]

Uncle   Oh yes. I'm sorry. What are you doing?

Engineer   Measuring, drawing and planning.

Abisavam   What for?

Engineer   This village is to be made into a mining town.

Abisavam   Who wants to do this?

Engineer   A 'Joint Venture'.[67]

Abisavam   Very interesting.

Engineer   This is a Queen's Order Project.[68]

Abisavam   I see! And what will happen to the villagers here?

Engineer   They will be moved to some other place.

Abisavam   I am Abisavam, head of the village.

Engineer   So you're the one who'll be leading the transmigration.

Abisavam   We'll see, we'll see.

Engineer   Have you got some other idea?

Abisavam   Yes. What do you think of this valley and this village?

Engineer   It's beautiful. Wonderful!

Abisavam   Wonderful! That's right. Our ancestors, the ancestors of the Naga people, chose this place very carefully. For centuries we have lived here. Look at that! That is the cemetery of our ancestors. Yes, on that slope over there.

And over there, on that rocky plain is where, we carry out our fertility Ritual. For us the fertility deity is very important.

And his lake is sacred to us, because it is where we go to wash and purify ourselves before the beginning of our annual forty days fast. You can see the many water lilies which are symbols of purity for us.

You see, all this is not just 'some place'.

But one part of the totality of life. This is a culture.

It can't just be leveled to make way for a town.

Do you understand?

Engineer   This is the age of progress. Things like that aren't binding any more.

Abisavam   Why not?

Engineer   They're not 'efficient'.[69]

Abisavam   Everything must be efficient, eh! Astonishing!
Do you also fall in love efficiently!
Do you also worship efficiently!

Engineer   I am not a psychologist or religious expert; I'm an engineer.

Abisavam   You just blindly follow your superiors.

Engineer   Yes indeed! I do have superiors.

Abisavam   Have you got haemorrhoids?

Engineer   I'm quite healthy – just got a little bit of gout, that's all.

Abisavam   Just as I expected.

Carlos (*to engineer*)   Why didn't you choose to build over the other side, why do you have to build it here?

Abisavam   Yes, why not?

Carlos   For efficiency? So that you don't have to make a winding road! To save a few million dollars you want to wipe out a whole culture?

Abivara   Yes, father, they should build their factories and housing over the other side of Mt Saloka.

Abisavam   It is my duty to protect the integrity of our culture – I'm in favour of new developments. But new developments shouldn't always mean the annihilation of other things. That's oppression, not society.

Carlos   I will write a report about this. I will give as comprehensive a picture as possible. In the country of these companies the people's voice is heeded. Their parliaments are real parliaments. So through the newspapers there I will make known what one of their giant corporations is doing in Astinam. The people and parliament there will not let this go on. They will protest and ask for an accounting.

Supaka   Abisavam, this village must be defended. My husband's grave and those of my ancestors are in this village. Don't let them turn those graves into casinos, stations or hotels.[70]

Abisavam   Good, Supaka. I didn't expect your awareness to increase so quickly.

Supaka   Don't be so stubborn!

Abisavam   Heh!?

Supaka   I don't really understand farming, I don't know how to defend my land in this situation. So that I now hand my land back to the village.

Uncle   That is indeed in accordance with our traditional law.

Supaka   Shut up!

Uncle   I'm just commenting.

Supaka   I'm not talking to you.

Abisavam   Enough! Enough! – Supaka, we accept you surrender of the land back to the village. We will guard it to the best of our ability.

Supaka (*to villagers*)   Don't any of you here be forced into selling your land.

Abivara   In the village of the Kariman tribe, through using both force and manipulation, they succeeded in buying all the fertile land.

Abisavam   That happened because the Kariman people fought as individuals. We must struggle together, only then will we succeed. I feel strong enough to lead you. Tonight we will hold a night of meditation.[71]

Carlos   Your struggle will be in accordance with civilised values. The outside world will support a struggle like yours. The methods they use here are even opposed by their own people! Nowadays they think they can easily put it over developing countries. (*to the engineer*) Don't pretend you don't know all about this!

Engineer (*in English*)   Who are you?

Carlos (*in English*)   I am Carlos. And I am their friend. But speak in Astinamese!

Engineer (*in English*)   I'll remember you.

Carlos   You'd better.

Engineer   Goodbye.

Carlos   Goodbye.

Abisavam   Yes!! Goodbye!!!!!!

CARLOS'S WITNESS

Carlos   *Report from Astinam*:

The Big Boss's Corporation has established a joint venture with an Astinamese company, to mine and refine copper on Mt Saloka, near a village of the Naga tribe.

The Astinam government is going to empty the village and turn it into a mining town, complete with housing for the mine workers, places of entertainment for them, mosques, churches, garages, repair shops, refineries, warehouses and so on.

This will mean the disappearance of the places of worship of the Naga people. Their holy places will be desecrated. Their traditional houses will be swept away. This seeking for profit that in the end will be used to increase inequality, is destroying a whole minority group and its culture.

Copper, whose factory refinement requires much acid, will cause pollution which could end up turning the Naga's village into desert. A factual example of such negligence is available: look at Copper Basin in Tennessee, U.S.A. Now it is a desert, before it was a dense forest. This is the result of acid pollution caused by their copper factory disposing the factory waste just as it pleased.

Destruction of the environment always begins with grass and small bushes; then it spreads to insects, the fish in rivers, and other small animals, which are in fact agents in the process of renewing the environment. Finally this small destruction will develop into the destruction of the forests. Without the chlorophyll of the forest leaves the purification of the atmosphere will decrease. Earth, water and air become unclean, until finally man also suffers.

This chasing after profit, sacrificing nature and culture, is in essence not development but rather destruction. This cannot be allowed to continue.

The culture of the Naga people is more mature than the culture which is to be forced upon them.

HER MAJESTY IS ANGRY

Enter **Sri Ratu**, **Ministers** *and the* **Dalang**.

Her Majesty is carrying several newspapers.

Sri Ratu   What's this? What's this?

Prime Minister   Calm down, Your Majesty. Newspapers like this can't have any great effect.

Sri Ratu   What did you say? Can't do much? These are the top foreign newspapers. Already the UNESCO people are beginning to criticise our development programme! Can't do much you say? At the very least my blood pressure is rising again.

Colonel Srenggi   Your Majesty, we never rest. All foreign newspapers and magazines which contain reports about the Naga people have been stopped. I have ordered that editions which contain such reports be seized.[72] My men then cut out the offending sections and burn them. The rest we sell by the kilogram as wastepaper.

Prime Minister   Brilliant!

Sri Ratu   What's so brilliant about it? All the foreigners here are increasingly commenting upon the disappearance of several magazine editions. I see that as time goes on your tactics are becoming less and less refined.

Colonel Srenggi   I request advice from Your Majesty.

Sri Ratu   We must use methods which . . . .(*waving hands*). . . . Understand me?

Colonel Srenggi   Understand, Your Majesty. Well, a little . . . but in fact . . . in fact . . . actually what do you mean?

Sri Ratu   That's what you must work out.

Minister of Mines   May I dare to make a suggestion?

Sri Ratu   Yes, speak!

Minister of Mines   Let's invite Muhammad Ali to contest his title here!

Sri Ratu   What are you getting at?

Minister of Mines   Both foreign and local journalists will be interested in such an event. That sort of happening will seize their attention and for days the papers will be full of nothing else but Muhammad Ali.

Now, in these conditions, we can make another approach to the Naga people. We can take care of other troublesome matters too.

Indeed if we are to make a few arrests at such a time very few people would notice.

Sri Ratu   An excellent idea!

Minister of Mines   Thank you.

Sri Ratu   Your proposal is accepted. What are your opinions?

All   We agree!

Sri Ratu   United! Ah, you arrange the discussions with the Naga, Minister.

Minister of Mines   Ready and willing, Your Majesty.

Sri Ratu   The President of the Parliament will help you in dealing with any trouble.

President of Parl.   Good, Your Majesty. But I will need funds to assist in giving direction to some of the journalists and to some members of parliament.

Sri Ratu   Agreed. Funds will be made available. But be careful. Don't attract the attention of the foreign press. Only recently the Foreign Minister called upon me. He looked very tired. It's fortunate that he has also invested a lot of capital in national development projects. So we don't have to worry about losing his support.

Minister of Mines   Everything will go smoothly, Your Majesty.

President of Parl. and Minister of Mines:

> Everybody wants to be happy,
> Is prepared to pay to be happy.
> No need to oppose people so quickly.
> Lick arses and hearts will open.

THE MINISTER OF MINES' STYLE

Enter the Naga villagers, **Abisavam**, **Carlos** *and the* **Minister of Mines**.

Minister of Mines   Honoured Chief of the Naga Tribe, honoured ladies and tribal elders, brothers: Greetings!

(*His greeting obtains no response. Everyone is quiet.*)

Yes, yes – well, I'm very pleased to be here.

Abisavam   What is it that you like about us?

Minister of Mines   I like your dances, I like the shape of your houses. I like the culture and the character of the Naga tribe.

Abisavam   That will all disappear if this village is turned into a mining town.

Minister of Mines   Disappear! No need for it to disappear! Oh no, don't let it disappear! All of it can be saved. Just imagine: In the middle of this mining town full of modern buildings, you will be able to find an ancient cemetery and traditional houses complete with all the materials needed for your rituals and everything else. Your places of worship, your sacred lake, sacred tree, all will be 'upgraded' so they can be enjoyed by many people.[73]

Abisavam   You mean by 'upgrading' they'll be made into tourist objects, don't you?[74]

Minister of Mines   Tourism adds to the national outcome.

Abisavam   I know what tourism is. It's praying while being stared at, right? If necessary the ceremony can be shortened and 'popped up' right? Religious devotion turned into a commodity, isn't that what you mean?[75]

Minister of Mines   Oh, all the authenticity can be retained.

Abisavam   Rubbish! The integrity of such a ritual is always lost. Only its dramatic element is retained.

You don't really like our culture. You want to put our culture in a museum.

Minister of Mines   Let us not be lax in sacrificing for the national interest.

Abisavam   It is also in the national interest to foster the development of regional culture. The national interest shouldn't be measured by profit alone.

Minister of Mines   We must all participate in the government's development programme.

Abisavam   To participate also means to have an opinion, to join in evaluating and controlling development. It doesn't mean just being apathetic.[76]

Minister of Mines   I will report all this conversation to my superiors.

Abisavam   Excellent. But don't forget to report to the people as well.

Abivara   I will report it to my friends.

Carlos   And I will report it to my friends.

Abisavam   Mr Minister, we are busy people. We want to get on with preparing fresh fields. Would you like to help us?

Minister of Mines   Why not? But other matters await me. We'll arrange such co-operation at another time. You must now allow me to return to the capital.

(**Minister of Mines** *leaves to the laughing of the villagers. The villagers then go off to work.*)

THE WITNESS OF FOREIGN NEWSPAPERS

Enter **Carlos**, **Abivara** *and* **Abisavam** *carrying newspapers.*

Abivara   Look Father, all these foreign newspapers have published reports about the disaster that may be descending on our village. Carlos's friends have been able to smuggle them in.

Abisavam (*inspecting the papers now laid out on the floor*)   Good! Good! – Carlos, all of this is a result of your efforts.

Carlos   Ah, I was only doing my duty as a journalist.

Abisavam   Right, Carlos, right. (*to* **Abivara**:) And what do our own papers say?

Abivara (*laughing*)   They haven't reported anything about it. Not even in a back page corner, let alone an editorial.

Abisavam   Yes, just a while ago when the National Pergasmina Corporation ran into financial troubles, we also first heard about it via the foreign press. What's the use of all these journalist-upgrading programmes? It looks like they are not taught to report the truth but rather to hide the truth.[77]

Abivara   They call it 'Guidance'.

Abisavam   Guidance which avoids the truth is contrary to justice.[78]

(**Setyawati** *enters.*)

Setyawati   Abivara! Abivara! – The army! The army is here!

Abivara   Calm down. What's wrong?

Setyawati   There are trucks full of soldiers. Tanks. Jeeps. They're all carrying rifles.

Abivara   What are they like?

Setyawati   They're terrifying!

Abivara   No, I mean: What are they doing?

Setyawati   I don't know. They're coming now.

(*Other villagers enter running.*)

Uncle   Abisavam, soldiers! Lots of soldiers!

Abisavam   We know. Setyawati has told us. What are they doing?

Uncle   Marching! Hup-two, Hup-two, hup-two!!!

(*Marching in an exaggerated manner*)

Abisavam   And then?

Uncle   Just more marching! (*marching*) Turn right, march! Turn left, march! And then – Preseeent arms!!

Abisavam   After that?

Uncle   They march again. Hup-two, hup-two, hup-two.

Abivara   They're trying to frighten us!

Uncle   The bloody hide! Come on friends, we can't just take this lying down. Let's bare our teeth to them.

(*Villagers move to front of stage and bare their teeth to the audience.*)

Abivara   Bare your teeth? Don't be like Dracula!? Calm down everyone. Just because the army has come, there's no need to copy them, Hup-two, hup-two – present hoes – plotat-plotot! No! don't be cajoled into joining in creating an atmosphere of war. We just remain as we are. We just remain farmers.

A problem, solve it with reason.

A quarrel, solve it with negotiations.

If oppressed, don't just sit and take it.

If deceived, don't just be silent.

Squat down calmly and say to whoever has dealings with you: 'OK mate, just stay calm if you have any dealings with us!'

THE PRESIDENT OF PARLIAMENT MAKES A VISIT

Villagers remain on stage. **President of Parliament** *enters.*

President of Parl. (*to villagers*)   Greetings, brothers.

Uncle (*pointing to the troops*)   He came with them!!

President of Parl.   Brothers, I am the President of Parliament. Perhaps, brothers, you have already seen my photo in the papers.

Abivara   What do *you*[79] want here, eh?

President of Parl.   Huh, are *you* the village head?

Abivara   No. Do *you* want to meet him?

President of Parl.   Heh, who do *you* think you're talking to?

Abivara   To *you*!

President of Parl.   Oh, ah, yes, brother, I would like to meet brother's village head.

Abivara   Good, brother. Wait a minute, brother.

President of Parl.   Thank you, brother.

Abivara   My pleasure. Father, there is someone here who wants to talk to you. He is the President of Parliament.

Abisavam (*having squatted down earlier*)   Ohh, President of Parliament. Then he is a representative of the people? Hmmmm. We are the people. So then he's a representative of us?

Abivara   Yes, father.

Abisavam   Just let him wait a moment. I want to light a cigarette. (*lights cigarette, takes a puff*) Nah, if this person is our representative I have some business with him, namely, to criticise him. (*to the* **President of Parliament**) Are you the one?

President of Parl.   Yes, I am the President of Parliament.

Abisavam   The people's representative?

President of Parl.   Already installed.

Abisavam (*pointing to bow-tie and cane*)   How come you're dressed like that?

President of Parl.   I beg your pardon?

Abisavam   I thought you were an ambassador from Europe.

President of Parl.   I'm making an inspection tour.[80]

Abisavam   Why the soldiers?

President of Parl.   Just for company on the journey.

Abisavam   Maybe you are also from the army?

President of Parl. (*slightly embarrassed*)   But already functionalised![81]

Abisavam   Please sit down.

President of Parl.   On the ground?

Abisavam   Yes. I am sitting on the ground.

President of Parl. (*having sat down*)   I'm so happy to be amongst the people again.

Abisavam   No? Really?

President of Parl.   Really. This is terrific. I like you all very much.

Abisavam   Oh yes? I don't like you.

President of Parl.   You are very honest.

Abisavam   Thank you. I don't like the way you came here or the way you introduced yourself. You gave the impression you were trying to be intimidatory.

President of Parl.   But that was not my intention.

Abisavam   Then it must just be a part of your character. You are a representative of the people, you should respect those you represent!

President of Parl.   Please excuse the misunderstanding.

Abisavam   You're dressed like a gangster from Europe.

President of Parl.   Different people have different preferences.

Abisavam   Then if someone expresses a different preference don't go around banning them.

President of Parl.   Yes, yes, although sometimes 'guidance' is necessary.

Abisavam   Who decides what sort of guidance?

President of Parl.   Why, our superiors of course?

Abisavam   Ah, but we are your superiors – the people.

And we are mostly poor – remember that! You are a representative of the people – so it is the people who are your superiors.

President of Parl.   You speak very honestly.

Abisavam   What's so unusual about being honest. That's something natural, normal. No need to give praise because of that.

President of Parl.   Yes, yes. But I mean, besides being honest, people must also be careful in what they say.

Abisavam   Yes. I'm always careful that I don't betray my inner feelings, and that I don't violate my religious beliefs.

President of Parl.   But in political matters one must also be careful.

Abisavam   Yes, I'm always careful that I don't betray the interests of the poor masses, and end up only crawling to a small minority of the rich and powerful.

President of Parl.   Well, I'd better pass on my messages.

Abisavam   Don't tell me you came all this way just to do that?

President of Parl.   It would be a great pity if people such as yourself were considered anti-government.

Abisavam   Just a moment ago, you were calling me honest; now you're worrying that I'm anti-government. Honest people, I would have thought, would be considered useful to the government!

I want justice – not a change of government.

President of Parl.   It's very difficult to debate with you.

Abisavam   Alas, you, a people's representative and member of parliament, should be clever at debating. It's a pity all you can ever say is 'I agree'.

President of Parl.   Excuse me, I'll go. Goodbye.

(*Exits to laughter of villagers.*)

THE BIG BOSS

Enter the **Big Boss** *and* **Mr Joe**.

Mr Joe   Welcome, Big Boss.

Big Boss   Good day, Joe. How's your stomach?

Mr Joe   Still got ulcers. And yours, Boss?

Big Boss   I've just been operated on. A little cancer. And now there's something wrong with my left eye. The doctor says there's a kind of . . . hm . . . growth there. As you see Joe, I'm truly a veteran of life's struggle.

Mr Joe   I have to acknowledge you are heroic, Boss.

Big Boss   I like what you say, Joe.

Mr Joe   How's your monastery project, Boss?

Big Boss   Success, Joe, success! Many executives are going there to find peace of mind. I know that they want to get rid of their feelings of guilt. So I charge high prices and they are willing to pay.

Joe, these days, as long as we retain their sweeter aspects, religion and yoga are becoming good saleable commodities.

Mr Joe   I see your tourist interests are doing well too, Boss.

Big Boss   Going smoothly, Joe. It's only your project that isn't going well, Joe.

Mr Joe   Things are different here, Boss.

Big Boss   Nothing's going right, Joe!

Mr Joe   This problem isn't so simple, Boss. There are a lot of complications. We can't just impose our will as we would like.

Big Boss   But a lot of money has already been made available. Surely the complications can be smoothed out.

Mr Joe   In fact, Boss, all the channels in Astinam are already pretty smooth. I can usually push the government into . . . well . . . we call it here – creating 'tidiness for development'.[82] . . . And yes, you could also say that all opposition has been silenced. There remains only the Naga.

Big Boss   Send their youth overseas. Teach them skills in such a way that they can only work if they have modern tools made by us.

Mr Joe   The son of the village chief has just returned from our country. But he has rather grown closer to his environment. He doesn't need electric guitars, air-conditioning and porcelain toilets. He talks about pollution. And about the importance of architects considering ventilation systems like those designed by Spanish and Portuguese architects in the seventeenth century, and then further developed by Dutch architects in the nineteenth century in their tropical colonies.

Big Boss   Get him appointed as a Secretary General of a Department.

Mr Joe   He doesn't want to be a VIP, he wants to be a leader.

Big Boss   Get him a mass following. Encourage him to set up an organisation, then get rid of him via the officials of his own organisation.

Or get him to lead a mass demonstration. Then get some people to burn shops and create havoc. After the demonstration, its leaders can be arrested as the trouble makers.[83]

Mr Joe   No, that won't work either. He doesn't like organisations. He doesn't like mass followings. He hates anarchy and chaos, but rather likes to discipline himself by meditating, admires tenacity at work, and the courage to create new ideas. . . . No, there is only one way to get rid of him . . .

Big Boss   Yes?

Mr Joe   Accuse him of subversion!!

Big Boss   How is that possible? He hasn't tried to organise a power change in the government.

Mr Joe   Ha! Ha! Ha! Boss! People here are still primitive. Words can be turned into invulnerable charms. That person has made trouble. Now, brand him on his forehead. It doesn't matter if the brand is true or not, but whether it is official or not.

Big Boss   Can that still be lawfully arranged here, Joe?

Mr Joe   Law? What law? There is no law here, only power. And the powerful here are pretty clever. They're not concerned with law. They're concerned with tidiness.[84]

Big Boss   Everything will work out, won't it Joe?

Mr Joe   But don't forget: the most difficult problem to overcome is these reports in the foreign press.

Big Boss   They're bastards, you know, Joe. You must pressure the Queen of Astinam into exiling journalists like Carlos.

Mr Joe   It's already been taken care of. Yet we've still got to make sure we don't create any international incidents. This problem of mining copper must be handled as calmly as possible. If necessary we can leave the Naga's village alone. It'll be enough to mine the copper there, but we don't have to process it there also. Sure it'll be more expensive. But this is going to be the future of all mining. Culture will have to change directions because of the pollution problem.

Big Boss   You're just talking like a hippy, Joe!

Mr Joe   That's the best I can do, Boss.

Big Boss   Do you still love your career, Joe?

Mr Joe   I've already worked hard, Boss. What I've just been talking about are ideas that you should consider seriously. I am serious, Boss. This isn't a problem just confined to this country. It's a problem everywhere. You know, Boss, we're not gods. Everything has its limits. I like to work. But there are limits. Leave the Naga alone. UNESCO will start making noises otherwise.

Big Boss   It's clear that I'm not a person who usually retreats. But there is nothing wrong with moving to a new area of enterprise. These days the yoga and religion industries are more profitable than mining. Yes, it looks like I'll have to produce some new prophets.

Mr Joe   That's exactly what I've been thinking of lately.

Big Boss   Hallelujah!

CARLOS GOES HOME

Enter **Carlos**, **Abivara**, **Abisavam**, **Setyawati***, Villagers and* **Dalang***.*

Carlos   My friends, the time has come for us to part. My visa has suddenly been revoked.

Abivara   Carlos, we will not forget you. You have helped our struggle.

Carlos   I hear a voice
The cry of a wounded animal
Someone shoots an arrow at the moon
A small bird has fallen from its nest.

People must be awakened
Witness must be given
So that Life can be guarded.

Abisavam   This is difficult to accept.
We have done no wrong.
We have broken no law.
We have only fought for
Our basic needs.
We know what we need.
No one need dictate to us.

We guard our identity.
We guard the unity of spirit and body.
We are the guardians of nature in this region.
We are duty bound to defend nature from greedy rapists.
But they have forced us
To disregard our spirit and rape nature,
In the name of commerce.

We reject this greed.
Carlos helped us.
(*crying*)

And now
They are exiling Carlos.
We do not accept this.

Setyawati   Carlos, you truly understand our interests. I've been very
moved. The shirt that Abivara asked me to make you isn't finished yet.

Carlos   Don't exaggerate.
My friends of the Naga, thank you for this warmth.
They are expelling me.
I will go.
But our struggle together
Does not finish here.
Overseas I will write even more
About your struggle.

The values that we are fighting for
Will be written in the heavens
Will be written in the earth
Will be printed in the papers
Will be broadcast over radio and television
Will spread from mouth to mouth.

Dalang   The fire of Life still blazes.
The decreed Balance must be defended.
There is no victory
There is no defeat

There is also no disaster
That need be feared.

Courage is in the south
Patience in the north
Hope in the east
And in the west is perseverence.

Abisavam (*facing audience*)

Why must you be afraid?
Of defending the Balance?
Defending Life
Brings serenity.

Yesterday and tomorrow
Are today.
Disaster and good fortune
Are the same.
Horizons beyond us
Horizons within us
Uniting in the soul.

(*The Naga and Carlos march around the stage several times carrying the red and white flag.*)

END OF PLAY

Notes

1   His full name is Willibrordus Surendra Broto Rendra. Biographical
    information on Rendra is from Evan Darwin Winet, 'The Critical Absence
    of Indonesia in W. S. Rendra's Village' in Kiki Gounaridou (ed.), *Staging
    Nationalism: Essays on Theatre and National Identity*, Jefferson, NC:
    McFarland and Company, 2005, pp.141–67; Max Lane, 'Rendra' in *The
    Struggle of the Naga Tribe* by Rendra, trans. Max Lane, New York: St.
    Martin's Press, 1979; Evan Darwin Winet, *Indonesian Postcolonial Theatre:
    Spectral Genealogies and Absent Faces*. London: Palgrave Macmillan,
    2010; and Barbara Hatley, *Javanese Performances on an Indonesian Stage*.
    Honolulu: University of Hawaii Press, 2008.
2   Winet, 'The Critical Absence of Indonesia', p.143.
3   Winet, Evan, 'Modern Indonesian Theatre' in Samuel L. Leiter (ed.),
    Encyclopedia of Asian Theatre, Westport CT: Greenwood, 2007, p.271.
4   Max Lane, 'Translator's Introduction' in *The Struggle of the Naga Tribe* by
    Rendra, trans. Max Lane, New York: St. Martin's Press, 1979, p.xvii.
5   Evan Darwin Winet, 'The Critical Absence of Indonesia in W. S. Rendra's
    Village' in Kiki Gounaridou (ed.), *Staging Nationalism: Essays on Theatre
    and National Identity*, Jefferson, NC: McFarland and Company, 2005, p.146.
6   Lane, 'Translator's Introduction', p.xxxvi.
7   In traditional Javanese shadow plays, or *wayang*, the *dalang* is the puppet
    master. He manipulates the leather puppets that throw their shadows onto
    the screen. He creates the voices for all the characters and memorises
    the whole play. The *wayang dalang* relates aspects of the ancient stories
    to contemporary events and situations. The *dalang* of Rendra's play acts
    primarily in this role of commentator. All the *dalang*'s comments are spoken
    as asides. Only once is there an exception, and that case involves the *dalang*
    being mistaken for somebody else. The *dalang* in the original production was
    played by Sitoresmi Rendra; she portrayed the *dalang* as a humorous, jovial
    and wise person. The *dalang* here has absorbed some of the character of the
    purnakawan, or court clowns, which are the principal figures in the *goro-
    goro* scenes of the *wayang*.
8   Censorship is very stringent in Indonesia. It is necessary to get permission
    from the local security police before a play can be performed. When it is
    suspected that it may contain proscribed matter, permission can only be
    granted by higher authorities. Between 1974 and 1977 Rendra was unable
    to perform in Yogyakarta; none of his recent plays have been published; and
    since the beginning of 1978 the mass media have been forbidden to report his
    activities.
9   *Astina* (without the 'm') is the name of the kingdom in which the Pandawa
    and Kurawa brothers were brought up. After many victories for the Pandawa
    in competitions with their brothers, the Kurawa attacked and exiled them.
    For many years they wandered the forest until they met and gained the
    protection of King Natswapati. In the forest they built the beautiful kingdom
    of Amarta. This in turn was lost to the Kurawa and the Pandawa were exiled

once again. After thirteen years of exile, during which there were attempts to negotiate the return of at least a part of Astina, a Great War (*Bharata Yudha*) broke out. The Pendawa regained Astina, but all their sons had been slain.

10 The word 'society' is a translation of the Indonesian *pergaulan*. The term refers to general social intercourse and not to an organised community.

11 In this one sentence Rendra alludes clearly to two *wayang* terms. Firstly, 'across the sea' or *tanah sabrang* alludes to the *sabrangan* scenes in *wayang* which depict the societies of the ogre kingdoms of overseas lands. The second illusion is to 'the ogres' or *raksasa* who inhabit these overseas lands.

12 The English term 'Big Boss' is well known, as it frequently occurs in the many colourful billboard and newspaper advertisements for B-class American, Hong Kong and Taiwanese gangster films.

13 This Japanese-sounding word is actually a Javanese expression meaning 'yes, well, what else!?'

14 The English word 'magic' used here is one of many words introduced to Indonesia via advertisements of foreign consumer goods.

15 Dalang's response to the Chinese 'Nihao-maa?' (How are you?) is 'bakso', which is the name of a Chinese meat-ball soup popular mainly because of its low cost.

16 The People's Republic of China is the main source of such goods. Coming via Hong Kong, they can be found in retail shops of all sorts, down to village level.

17 Indonesia's national debt at the end of 1977 is estimated at over 15 billion dollars. This is approximately five times the debt incurred by the Sukarno government prior to 1965.

18 These 'Shopping Centres' – the English is often used – are modern-style several storey high buildings containing small stalls and shops. Because of the high cost of renting these stalls frequently the smaller traders of the old markets are unable to obtain a place.

19 The word 'advanced' here is a translation of *dimajukan*. 'Dimajukan' sounds just as awkward in the Indonesian as does 'advanced' in this context.

20 The 'Tonikum' referred to is a brand name of a vitamin tonic. Such tonics and vitamin pills are being vigorously advertised by foreign companies. 'Rice and plant root tonic' refers to *Beras Kencur*, a medicinal preparation using rice and the root of the plant Kamferia Galanga.

21 *Gado-gado* is a salad prepared from soybean cake, cabbage, bean sprouts and sometimes cucumber, potato and egg. It is served with a sauce made of peanuts, sugar, salt, garlic and chillies.

22 Artificial milk-based baby foods are misused by poor mothers for a number of reasons. These include the inability to read instructions (especially when they're in English); the lack of boiling, sterilising and cooling facilities; poverty-level incomes which are insufficient to guarantee a continuing supply of sufficient quantity. In this manner they contribute to child malnutrition and poor health in many areas of Indonesia. Groups supporting breast-feeding have recently begun to organise themselves.

23   Mass-produced ice-cream is being made by several foreign companies, including Australia's Peters' Ice Cream. Peters conducts an especially strong advertising campaign and uses Australian-made powdered milk.

24   Hundreds of Indonesians study in Western countries every year.

25   This statement places the struggle of the Naga tribe against the Astinamese rulers, as it develops later, outside the boundaries of regional or ethnic rebellion. As such it conforms with an important commitment of Indonesia's past political leaders, namely, to Indonesian unity. 'Indonesian Unity' is the third principle of the Panca Sila, a formulation of five basic principles. These principles are Belief in One Divinity, Humanitarianism, Indonesian Unity, People's Representative and Consultative Leadership, and Social Justice for all Indonesians.

26   This refers to the popular cracker called *emping*, made from the fruit of the *mlinjo* tree.

27   Karma here is the concept of deeds always eliciting a response of the same quality; good deeds are responded to by good deeds and bad deeds by bad deeds.

28   As a result of the activities of foreign, especially Japanese, timber corporations, deforestation is becoming a major problem in some parts of Indonesia. The reference to the seas being sold refers to the granting or virtually unpoliceable fishing rights in Indonesian waters to foreign corporations. No one knows how much fish is taken out.

29   During the Sukarno period the land reform issue generated a great deal of controversy and political violence. In the eyes of the present government, support for land reform smacks of Old Order politics, and because of this, people are very hesitant about discussing the problem.

30   This 'slip of the tongue' elicited especially loud and prolonged laughter from the audience. (All comments on audience reaction to the play refer to the first performance in Jakarta in 1975).

31   By defining the Naga's irrigation as technology, Rendra is attacking the widely held conception of technology as being industrial or electronic machinery whose methods can be studied in textbooks.

32   This contrasts the Naga's situation with the reality in Indonesia today. Most tertiary educated youth prefer to remain in the larger cities where both the facilities to use their newly acquired skills and the potential financial benefits are greatest.

33   'Spirit of the One' is a translation of *Rob Yang Widi*. The term *Widi* implies indivisibility. A more literal translation might be 'Indivisible Spirit'.

34   The first two lines of this passage is a well-known Indonesian proverb.

35   'Important person' is a translation of the Indonesian *pembesar* literally meaning someone who is big, a 'big shot'. A *pembesar* is usually both wealthy and powerful, and not disinclined to show it.

36   These are both symbols of Western affluence and modernity. Along with jeans and motor cars they are among the most sought after souvenirs of the Western countries.

37 This remark is undoubtedly aimed at the numerous important political figures and military officials who frequently appear in public wearing sunglasses, no matter how inappropriate the weather or occasion.

38 One result of the rapid expansion of privately owned cars in Indonesia is huge traffic jams, especially in Jakarta. At the same time it has been necessary for seats to be taken out of Jakarta buses in order that they cope with the number of people wishing to use public transport. The increase in traffic has also provided the rationalisation for the banning of the *becak* drivers with the extra miseries of forced night-work, forced migration to other smaller towns, still smaller incomes representing the diminished size of their access to customers as more *becaks* collect in particular areas, or total unemployment and impoverishment.

39 Rendra uses the *wayang* term *jejer* (i.e. scene) in this title.

40 This explicit depiction of Sri Ratu in Indonesian and Central Javanese attire and the latter reference to her accent as being a 'Menteng' accent – Menteng being the suburb in Jakarta where General Suharto lives – cannot but avoid give the impression, intended, or as it were, not intended, that she is a caricature of General Suharto's powerful wife.

41 The cosmetics industry is almost totally dominated by foreign products and advertising.

42 Contrast this statement with the Naga's view of the sun.

43 This exchange between Dalang and Sri Ratu besides its obvious satire of Sri Ratu contains an even more powerful condemnation. The *dalang* in Java is a highly respected occupation, his role reflecting, in a sense, Divinity. As the orderer of the *wayang lakon* or story, he operates as a sort of God. While this similarity should not be taken too literally, it is clear that the failure to recognize a *dalang* in the performance of his work is a sign of primitiveness, and disrespect towards him is profanity.

44 Since the reinstatement of the 1945 Presidential style Constitution in 1959, the President has been concurrently Prime Minister.

45 'Wijaya Kusuma' is also the name of a most exotic and delicate flower that blooms and dies in a single night.

46 The common Indonesian toilet in a bathroom consists of a hole in a concrete floor. People squat over the floor. People squat over the hole. The alternative to toilet paper is water.

47 This comment is aimed at the infamous and luxurious hospitals owned by the National Oil Corporation, Pertamina. The present Community Health Programme receives nowhere the same financing, restricting greatly the effectiveness of village doctors in local health clinics.

48 There is also a Patih (minister) Srenggi in *wayang* repertory who is a particularly villainous personage.

49 This is a telling comparison. Throughout Java, people, if they own houses, will sweep clean their yards as the day's first task. Some take the task extremely seriously and remove from the yard, usually a dirt yard, every loose object, every fallen leaf – pointing to a sort of passion for ultra-tidiness. (On tidiness, see the next scene.)

50   Dissidents and critics in Indonesia are often branded as being people unnecessarily suspicious of the government, and it is said that this lack of trust is an obstacle to development.

51   There are two 'representative' bodies at the national level. The one that meets most frequently is the Council of People's Representatives. This is made up of elected and appointed members who form into factions, according to their political position. There are four important factions: the government-backed majority faction, a Muslim faction (although Muslims are all in factions), and a small nationalist and Christian faction as well as a faction consisting of appointed military officials.

52   Several student activists who were prominent critics of the corruption and bad government of the Sukarno years have since been co-opted into Establishment institutions.

53   The phrase 'the people are still ignorant' (*rakyat masih bodoh*) is a common catch phrase in élite urban culture.

54   This is a comment upon drug-taking among the children of the wealthy, especially in Jakarta. Domestic and other strife among the urban élite, especially that resulting from drug addiction, has been a common theme in popular literature and films.

55   This comment implies that the word *Pembangunan* (Development) has become a 'mantra', which is a word or sound repeated over and over again in a prescribed manner to achieve magical powers.

56   The basic thrust of the prosecutor's case in the trials of the two university students, Hariman Siregar and Aini Chalid, and the lecturer Syahir, all of whom were arrested in the wake of the 1974 student demonstrations, was that they criticised the Broad Lines of Sate Policy which outlined the government's development strategy.

57   'Guidance' here is a translation of the word *pengarahan*, which means 'to direct, point in a direction'.

58   The word translated as 'to note signs' is *mensinyalir* which is mostly used by military intelligence officers.

59   This repeated use of the word *rapi* (tidy) as the essential prerequisite for development parallels the current term used by the Indonesian government, namely *tertib* (ordered). The necessity for 'orderliness' is not a new theme in Indonesian political life. The Dutch colonial rulers used the word *stabile*, and the Javanese princely rulers, the term *tata*.

60   This seems to be a reference to the infamous *ABS* attitude. *ABS* stands for *Asal Bapak Senang* (As Long as the Boss is Happy). It refers to the practice of sending in reports to one's superiors written with the aim of making them feel happy and secure. It is a frequent subject of press comment in Indonesia.

61   This has happened in relation to past food aid given by Australia to Indonesia. Food aid was given with a proviso that part of the aid money be used to buy Australian wheat, which was part of an unsaleable surplus. The wheat was then sold at a higher price than is usual. (See David McLean, 'Australia and the Expansion of Capitalism into Indonesia', *Review of Indonesian and Malayan Studies*, Vol. 6, no. 2, 1972).

62 *Silat* is the traditional martial art found throughout the Malay world. Besides involving the learning of methods of unarmed self-defence, it also requires the study of various meditational disciplines.

63 This scene is a rewritten version of the scene as performed in Jakarta, July, 1975. The major difference is the shortening of the replies by Abivara to Setyawati, making the rewritten scene somewhat faster moving.

64 'Relaxed' is a translation of the word *santai*. *Santai* appears to be a relatively new word in the Indonesian vocabulary. A small controversy occurred in mid-1975 when a cabinet minister made the accusation that too many Indonesians were *santai* and needed to work harder. Since then, the word has acquired a certain infamy.

65 *Paman* or 'Uncle' can be a term of familiar respect used to address someone not related or only distantly related.

66 *Bule*, meaning 'albino', is often used in a slightly derogatory manner to refer to Europeans.

67 The term 'Joint Venture' has already become a part of the Indonesian language with the rapid incursion of foreign companies into Indonesia, usually of the so-called joint venture type.

68 *Proyek Perintah Sri Ratu* or 'Queen's Order Project' is a term sounding very much like *Proyek Instruksi Presiden* or 'Presidential Instruction Project' or INPRES Projects. These are projects for which the President has specifically allocated funds. Signs are erected on the site of such projects, designating them as INPRES and describing the cost and features of the product. The early Javanese kings also used to leave inscriptions at the sites of projects financed by the court, giving the date and the circumstances of the order. This was a part of their efforts to legitimise their rule and increase their status.

69 As there is no indigenous Indonesias equivalent for 'efficient', Rendra uses the term *effisen*.

70 During the late seventies, the Governor of Jakarta, Lt General Ali Sadikin, had from time to time suggested that some of Jakarta's graveyards be made available for further city development. Sadikin had also been criticised for his policy of building casinos and hotels in Jakarta (However he is admired by Rendra in some matters).

71 The *malam tirakatan* or night of meditation has actually been used in protest movements in Indonesia. Student groups held one at the University of Indonesia on 31 December 1973 to protest against foreign investment in Indonesia.

72 It is not uncommon for *Time* and *Newsweek* to disappear from circulation at various times. But it is more usual for offending sections to be blacked out. This applies to all non-Indonesian papers. Local papers are always under threat of closure.

73 'Upgraded' is another English word that has become extremely common in Indonesia: journalists can be 'upgraded', schools can be 'upgraded', traditional puppeteers (*dalang*) can be 'upgraded' and so on.

74 The Indonesian government has declared the official policy of *Pariwisata Budaya* or Cultural Tourism where the local culture is to be made the main tourist attraction.

75 Many traditional Indonesian dances have been shortened drastically and changes in emphasis made so as to cater for the tourist trade.

76 *Partisipasi* according to semi-official doctrine does not require anything more than for people to produce more. Thus peasants should participate in development but at the same time should remain a 'floating mass', not playing any role in politics, other than voting in the six-yearly elections. In the Political Parties Law passed by the Indonesian parliament, political party activity at village level has been severely curtailed and illiterate people have been banned from becoming political party members.

77 In 1975 it was via a report in a French newspaper that most Indonesians heard of the financial problems and unpaid debts of the State oil company Pertamina. 'Upgrading' courses or seminars are frequently held for journalists either by the Government Journalists Association or by the Press Institute.

78 *Kewajaran* (here translated as 'justice') is a frequently recurring word in Rendra's vocabulary. *Wajar* refers to that which is justifiable, or fair or reasonable in the circumstances. Something that is not *wajar* is unjustifiable, unfair and unreasonable.

79 The translations 'you' and 'brother' are really not quite the same as the Indonesian terms Rendra uses here, *kamu* and *saudara*. *Kamu* is the familiar 'you', where *saudara* is the more egalitarian 'you'. Actually in the above context Abivara would be expected to use the term *Bapak* (lit. 'father') as a term of respect to a high-office holder such as the President. Thus the use of *kamu* would be considered highly offensive and even the use of *saudara* would be a slight to the President of Parliament.

80 The inspection tour or *peninjauan* is a basic feature of the political culture of the Indonesian political, especially governmental, elite as it was during the Sukarno period too. It would be familiar to all Indonesians. A government official visits a village or project accompanied by an entourage to more or less give witness to the various advances made, as presented to him by the local officials. At the same time, it seems to act as a part of the expected paraphernalia of the *pembesar* or 'VIP'.

81 The Indonesian term is *dikaryakan*. 'Karyanised' military officers are very common in economic, governmental and political affairs. Although the chairman (or President) of the Parliament at the time of the performance, Idham Chalid, was a civilian and not a 'karyanised' officer.

82 In this play the term 'tidiness for development' is used by those who wish to stifle opposition and dissent. The equivalent phrases in present-day Indonesia would be 'stability for development' or 'order for development'.

83 Accusations that the burnings in Jakarta during the January 1974 riots were the work of *agents provocateur* were made in at least two of the recent three trials of students. In the trial of Hariman Siregar the names mentioned were Liem Bien Kie and Ramadi, a wealthy businessman and a Golkar member of parliament, respectively. In the trial of Moh. Aini Chalid the name Ali Murtopo, a Lt General and political advisor to President Suharto was added. All press and media outlets were forbidden to print the accusation regarding Ali Murtopo as made in the open courtroom.

84 The 'rule of law' issue has been a longstanding one among Indonesian critics
    since Sukarno's time. Both the leading figures of the Human Rights Institute,
    Haji Princen and Yap Thiam Hien, and the leading lawyer of the Legal Aid
    Institute were arrested in the wake of the January 1974 demonstrations.
    Around the time the play was being performed Yap Thiam Hien, who himself
    had been released, was defending a former member of the PKI who was
    being tried for subversion. Two important legal points were raised. First,
    according to Indonesian law, a Court of Justice can only be established by an
    Act of Parliament, whereas the particular Court had been established simply
    by decree. Secondly, Indonesian law provides for witnesses to be questioned
    by the court before the accused instead of after as was occurring. In both
    cases the defence counsels' protests were dismissed almost without any
    justification.

Trương Ba's Soul in the Butcher's Skin

Lưu Quang Vũ
Translated by Kim Nguyen Tran, Tam Van Tran,
Nhung Walsh and Patricia Nguyen
Edited by Patricia Nguyen and Kim Nguyen Tran
Introduced by Patricia Nguyen

Lưu Quang Vũ is one of the most honoured and distinguished modern playwrights and poets of Vietnam, whose work represents the people's sentiments during the era of Đổi Mới ('renovation'). In 1986, the Sixth Party Congress of Vietnam enacted the Đổi Mới policy, which marked the transition of the Vietnamese economy from one that was highly centralised and planned to a socialist-oriented market economy. This period of economic market reform and de-collectivisation came during the post-war era of economic deprivation, which also spurred deep ideological questioning about socialism in Vietnam. Vũ is controversially known for his role as the voice of the people, critiquing the government's economic policies, and honoured as a nationally celebrated figure of renovation in Vietnam.

On 29 August 1988, during a traffic accident crossing Phu Long Birdge from Hai Phong to Hanoi, Vũ, his wife, poet Xuân Quỳnh, and their son Lưu Quang Thơ were pronounced dead. The news of his death shocked the entire country and the Vietnamese artist community. Controversy still remains around Vũ's death as a government conspiracy to silence a dissident voice.[1]

Lưu Quang Vũ was born on 17 April 1948 during the First Indochina War. Influenced by his father, Lưu Quang Thuận, whose plays bolstered propoganda campaigns for the Vietnamese Communist Party during the 1950s and 1960s, Vũ decided to forgo art school to join military service of North Vietnam in 1965. Soon after, Vũ interrogated his political allegiances, from a strong faith in socialist and nationalist ideology to deeply questioning its agenda. During this period from 1970 to 1975, Vũ wrote what is known as 'black poetry', which greatly questioned the Vietnamese system, and remains unpublished to this day. Nevertheless, Vietnam's national discourse reframes Vũ's work as one that represents the personal, moral and sentimental affects of the era rather than any political contestation with the state's role to highlight the personal shifts that occur in periods of transition. In 2000, Vũ, as a national representative of Đổi Mới, posthumously won the Ho Chi Minh Prize for his contribution to renovation.

Trương Ba's Soul in the Butcher's Skin is one of Lưu Quang Vũ's best-known plays and the one for which he is most remembered. The main themes and plot of the play come from a popular Vietnamese folk tale of the same name that has been refashioned in many genres, including television series, films and the traditional opera genres of cải lương and hát bội/tuồng. Vũ has adapted this well-known narrative for the stage, adding details and an undertone that resonate with an audience of the Đổi Mới era. The play 'dramatizes a conflict between the soul and body – a soul that strives towards the highest spiritual fulfillment, trapped within a corrupt and degenerate body'.[2] Through a petty mistake made in the heavens, Trương Ba accidentally has his life taken away and must borrow the butcher's body to house his soul, in order to live on earth. Trương Ba's kind heart and gentle spirit gradually becomes corroded in the body of the butcher. The butcher's body stands in for a critique of how an 'impoverished and corrupted government . . . damages the integrity of individual or citizens living in it'.[3] *Trương Ba's Soul in the Butcher's Skin* embodies Vũ's critique of the Vietnamese government, staging public sentiment during a time of a 'crisis of faith' in socialism as Vietnam transitions towards neoliberal policies of market reforms.

Trương Ba's Soul in the Butcher's Skin

[*Hồn Trương Ba da hang thịt*, 1988]

Các vai- Characters[4]

- Bắc Đầu (Northern Celestial Star Deity)
- Nam Tào (Southern Celestial Star Deity)
- Đế Thích (King of Chess)
- Trương Ba
- Trương Ba's Wife
- Cả, Trương Ba's Son (Anh con trai)
- Trương Ba's Daughter-in-law (Chị con dâu)
- CáiGái, Trương Ba's Granddaughter (Cháu nội Trương Ba)
- Tỵ, Gái's Friend (Cu Tỵ, Bạn cái Gái)
- Trưởng Hoạt (Trương Ba's Neighbor)
- Butcher (Anh hàng thịt)
- Butcher's Wife (Vợ anh hàng thịt)
- Pig Farmer 1 (Lái lợn 1)
- Pig Farmer 2 (Lái lợn 2)
- Lý trưởng (Mayor)
- Trương tuần (Local Police)

ACT 1

Scene: Kingdom of Heaven

The setting takes place in a palace covered in gold. The tiles on the roof are made of jade leaves. The palace is located near a garden of magical peach trees, where the fairies reside. Five clouds rolled up into a shape of a staircase, gorgeously shining beneath the palace. Two heaven deities', Nam Tào and Bắc Đầu, are walking out. Nam Tào holds in his hand a stack of thick books. Bắc Đầu holds a pen and a bottle of ink.

Bắc Đầu (*Shouts*) – Deities, where are you? (*Yells*) – Deities, where are you? (*No answer, so he yells even louder*) – Where are heaven's guardians? Heaven's guardians! (*Shakes his head*) – Nobody is here, where have they all gone?

Nam Tào   The deities must be singing and dancing in the magical peach garden, or they must be at Miss Moon's Palace asking her to make them new clothes. The Heaven guards aren't even doing their job, they've been drinking and gambling all the time lately, forgetting to guard Heaven. Heaven is now just as chaotic as a market, there is absolutely no discipline or order anymore!

Bắc Đầu   At least they could try and pretend to work! Just like you and me, it's hard enough to wake up every morning and show up to work, but we still go and do our job. (*He opens up his book, crosses out a few names, and writes down a few notes on his list. He then puts down his pen on the table and moves his chair. He begins lazily dusting the floor and stairs with a duster, all while shaking his head*) – Even pretending to clean like this would even be acceptable. Why do we, Nam Tào, Bắc Đầu – Heaven's gods, have to work even harder than the help!

Nam Tào   (*Sighs*) – Bắc Đầu, this is awful, Heaven is actually boring! I am fed up with eating magical peaches and listening to heaven's royal music and dance. . . . I'm so claustrophobic here sometimes I think it might be better to go down to Earth working as the Land Protector God, Thổ Địa!

Bắc Đầu   Don't be silly! It's not better on earth! We have gotten used to living this peaceful and luxurious life here. Life will be so harsh down there, everyone has to work so hard. How could we survive living like that? We're already in Heaven, we have everything we need.

Nam Tào   Heaven! People on earth call upon us for miracles when life gets too difficult, or too depressing. They know they can call upon us to alleviate their pains. But who would we call on if we need help?

Bắc Đầu   Hey you'd better keep your voice down!. . . . Can't you keep your mouth shut for a minute!. . . . Forget about it, let's get back to the list.

Nam Tào   Alright, let's review the list! (*Opens the book, yawning*) – It's so early in the morning but I already feel so sleepy . . .

Bắc Đầu   If we do things quickly, we can finish early. There will be a lunch party at the Celestial Emperor's Father's Palace today!

Nam Tào   (*Reviewing the list*) – Let's see . . . (*To* **Bắc Đầu**) – How many people do we have to take away from earth today?

Bắc Đầu   Quite a few! We'll just do whatever, like how we typically work all those other days. Perhaps, we don't even need to review any of them, just cross a few names out to meet the quota?

Nam Tào   Then they will complain that we are not doing our job correctly, and that we cannot distinguish between the lives of those who should live and of those who should die. I know that there are people, who, if we take their lives, it would be such good news for the people on earth. But there are people who still need to live to finish their life's work, so we have to let them live. Nevertheless, there are also people whose work is done, who have been blessed with longevity, so there isn't any reason why they should stay on earth any longer.

Bắc Đẩu   Oh please, if you sit and think everything through like that, you'll be here all day!

Nam Tào   Don't you know that people on earth have changed? They're not like who they were before. They have become very stubborn and disrespectful. If you do something wrong, they will curse at you! It's not easy to force them to die. I go crazy just thinking about them. They're pretty deceitful, they can play tricks, everyday they come up with new types of medicine, helping the sick and dying stay alive. It's so difficult to force those people to die. Heaven's power may not work at all!

Bắc Đẩu   I agree, it's so difficult now! (*Sighs*) – What happened to the good old days, when we could simply order people to live or die and they had to obey immediately? Nowadays, it's not easy being a god! The Thunder God has become less effective, even a little cowardy. His only job is to yell and strike at people, yet his voice has become so weak, and his hands tremble when he strikes someone with thunder.

Nam Tào   (*Looks into the distance*) – Is that Đế Thích? Đế Thích must one of the most relaxed gods here. He just plays chess[5] all day . . .

Bắc Đẩu   I don't know about that. He always looks so sad. And he always seems to play chess alone.

(**Đế Thích** *walks in, holding a chessboard in his hands, while he plays by himself.*)

Bắc Đẩu   Good morning, Đế Thích!

Đế Thích   (*Lifts his head up*) – Good morning!

Nam Tào   Aren't you lucky, wandering around all day. But, why are you always playing alone, don't you have anyone to play with? It must be boring playing all by yourself.

Đế Thích   Yes, it's extremely boring! But to be honest, no one wants to play chess with me. I was proclaimed The King of Chess, which means I am the best chess player. No one will ever be as good as me.

Although that title sounds great and I really enjoyed it at first, ever since I was given the title, no one even dares to play with me. Who could be dumb enough to play chess with The King of Chess? So, I have to play alone. Playing chess by yourself is as boring as racing by yourself. Nothing is interesting anymore! It's so sad!

Bắc Đẩu   (*Nodding*) – Yes, that is really sad! But as The King of Chess, how can you stop playing chess! But if no one challenges you, how do you know you are the best?

Đế Thích   Sometimes, I myself wonder if I am really that great. It has been tens of thousands of years since I last played chess with someone.

Nam Tào   (*Sighs*) – Then it seems none of us are truly happy here; each of us has our own problem!

Đế Thích   I wish someone would play a round of chess with me. (*Addressing* **Nam Tào**) – Or you, would you like to play a game with me? I will give you a head start with two moves.

Nam Tào   No no no, I can't play against you, I don't even know how to play chess . . .

Đế Thích   (*Saddened*) – You see! (*Holds his head in despair*)

Nam Tào   (*Feels bad for* **Đế Thích** *and tries to console him*) – Đế Thích, it is true that in Heaven no one dares to challenge your chess skills. Everyone respects you and your talents. Perhaps, those little people on earth may dare to play against you, they barely know what fear is. They don't even show reverence for the Celestial Emperor. I suppose they probably won't respect Đế Thích either. Down there, maybe there will be someone who wants to challenge you . . .

Đế Thích   Is that right? Are you telling the truth? Wow, why didn't I think of that before? I need to go down there for a trip. . . . This will be great!

Bắc Đẩu   Keep quiet, why you are always so loud! If you want to go, just go quietly. We won't report your disappearance. But in case his majesty the Celestial Emperor finds out, you cannot tell him that we gave you the idea. If you ever blame us, we will deny everything!

Nam Tào   Damn, the laws here in Heaven are so strict. If you blame us for suggesting the idea to you, we will be in deep trouble!

Đế Thích   Who would ever do that! We have been friends for a long time, I am grateful for your idea. I would never do such a thing. . . . Alright, I should leave right now, I am so anxious to finally get to play chess with someone. . . . Goodbye. (*Clears the clouds and flies away*)

Nam Tào He is so strange! He's so different from all the other gods and deities! Even if we helped him out a little, it's still good. He has been so nice to us. The gods would just stab us in the back, but Đế Thích is kindhearted and trustworthy . . .

Bắc Đẩu You're right, maybe Đế Thích is the only good deity left in Heaven. . . . (*Takes a look at the list*) – Anyways, are you done with your work? Have you found enough people whose lives will be taken away tomorrow?

Nam Tào Just a few more left! Now I'm on the page for the Upper town of East Village. . . . The Land Protector God reported that there are two people who need to die: one is a ninety year old man, who has many grandchildren. He has been given the gift of longevity, but it might be time for him to leave earth. The second is an evil person, he is extremely deceitful. He betrays his own friends, plots against them, and takes advantages of others for his own profit. He has caused so much suffering for the people on earth. Even though he is quite healthy, we should kill him!

Bắc Đẩu Hurry up, it's already time to leave for the party at Celestial Emperor's Father's Palace . . .

Nam Tào I'm almost done (*Scanning his finger through the list*) – Here's the name! (*Holds the pen, dips it in the ink, and crosses the name off*) – He will die tomorrow at 11 a.m. . . . Now, where is name of the evil person? (*Searching*) – My vision is so bad lately . . .

Bắc Đẩu (*Impatiently rushes* **Nam Tào**) – We will be late! See, I just heard the sound of the Celestial Emperor's Mother's cloud vehicle pass by! They must be all there by now! (*Begins to fidget impatiently*). I heard it's a big party today!

Nam Tào Don't rush me! Damn, where is that man's name?

Bắc Đẩu Just cross off any name, don't make it such a big deal. Everyone on earth has to die one day anyway!

Nam Tào Fine then, I will just cross off his name next time! I'll cross off another then (*Holds his pen as he reads aloud*) – Trương Ba. . . . Who is this Trương Ba? (*Contemplating*) – Oh well, crossed! (*Crosses his name off the list*) – He will die tomorrow at 7 p.m. (*Closes the book and gives a sigh of relief*) – Alright! (*Stands up*)

Bắc Đẩu   Let's go, I think we can still make it. . . . And you know what, since Đế Thích isn't here, just to help him out, we should discretely remove his portion. So no one will notice his absence, and so . . . (*Elbows lightly to* **Nam Tào** *with a smirk on his face*) – You get his wine, I'll get his food.

Nam Tào   Ha ha, you are so clever!

Blackout – Scene Change

ACT II

Scene: Earth, Truong Ba's Home

Trương Ba *is holding a hoe from his garden. He is a farmer and looks to be about 50 years old with a kind gentle face.* **Trương Ba's wife** *walks towards him from the kitchen with a teapot in her hands.*

Trương Ba   Darling, guess what? The row of custard apple seeds I just planted the other day has sprouted a few baby leaves. And the jackfruit trees are almost as tall as my shoulders.

Trương Ba's Wife   It's so sunny out here, why do you keep toiling in the garden. You're older now, you don't have the kind of energy you used to when you were younger. No one's forcing you to work so hard. And why are you planting jackfruit and custard apples? Can't you plant something else? There's a saying, 'Trẻ trồng na, già trồng chuối'. ('The young plant custard apples, the old plant bananas.') We're both so old and grey now, can we really wait until the jackfruit and custard apple trees bear fruit?

Trương Ba   Well, you can think of it as an investment for our son and his wife, fruits Gái can eat as she grows up.

Trương Ba's Wife   Our son Cả says he doesn't even want to inherit your damn trees. He's not going to slave away in the fields like you! He'll probably sell the fields once we both die!

Trương Ba   Why would he sell our land? There wouldn't even be a Cả if it weren't for these fields. These fields raised him!

Trương Ba's Wife   (*Tsking*) – Even though you are father and son, both of you are different people, with different personalities. Cả complains about how you're so old fashioned and complicated. . . . But he's not the only one, the word around the village seems to be: 'Mr. Trương Ba has gone senile!'

Trương Ba   So, do you believe them?

Trương Ba's Wife   (*Sighs*) – I don't, but . . . but maybe you can be more strategic and perhaps work less in the fields. Farming is not much of a career anymore. It takes so much hard work to tend to the trees and harvest them. Fruits are so cheap in the market now. Prices seem to change so sporadically. . . . I don't even understand the logic . . .

Trương Ba   How could anyone understand! But . . . (*Pauses*) This Cả. . . . Darling, how long have you been in my life?

Trương Ba's Wife   Why are you asking all of a sudden?. . . . Well, it must be more than thirty years already.

Trương Ba   I met you in a singing contest at Tầm port. You were only sixteen, seventeen. I found out you were also an orphan, just like me. You worked hard as a seamstress . . .

Trương Ba's Wife   You really have gone mad. Why are you talking about events that happened so long ago?

Trương Ba   You may have forgotten, but I'll always remember. We got married with nothing in our hands. We worked hard and took care of each other through war, sickness, and poverty. . . . Now your eyes's brightness has dimmed and your forehead has wrinkles, but my love for you is still as strong as it was when I first met you at Tầm port. But you . . . (*Shakes his head*) – You have changed dramatically.

Trương Ba's Wife   I have not changed. But, our daily housework has, I have to take care of everything and worry about so many things. But it looks like you just dropped out of Heaven, never a care in the world, never carefully planning for the future like others. . . . I feel bad for you sometimes!

Trương Ba   You know that I love my fields more than anything else, like the way I love you and love our son and our granddaughter. After that, there are two other things I could never stop: playing chess and drinking green tea.

Trương Ba's Wife   I know that about you, that's why I make sure to have a delicious cup of tea ready for you everyday!

(*Trương Ba's son walks in from another room. He is wearing a bag on his shoulder. His wife – **Trương Ba's daughter-in-law** runs after him.*)

Trương Ba's daughter-in-law   (*Pulls at her husband's shirt*) – You are leaving again?

Cả Yes, if I just sit here, we won't make any money. Tomorrow there is a market in the province. There will be several ships coming from Thanh and Nghệ. Traders will be at the port. If I get there late, they'll buy all the best goods. And then there won't be anything left for me but pig's feed!

Trương Ba's daughter-in-law My dear . . . it'll just be me . . .

Cả I've told you, leave me alone to do my job. The business of buying and selling, how could a country girl like you understand!

Trương Ba Cả, while you go off to the province, you leave the rice fields for your wife to tend, how can she possibly do all that work alone?

Cả If we can't tend to the fields, then we should just do away with them. If anyone wants to buy the fields, we should sell it right away! I can provide for the whole family with my work alone!

Trương Ba Son, you're not really listening to me. Do you really want to become a market trader?

Cả These days, there's no other choice. It's the only way to get rich quick! I make as much money working in the market for one day as I do toiling in the rice fields for a whole year!

Trương Ba Please don't become like your friends. Doing business means you have to work your way around deals, strategizing in ways that breed deceit and immoral mistakes! We have always been hard working people with good ethics, don't know throw it all away!

Cả Father, what age are we living in? Why are you still talking about ethics? People will laugh in your face for even mentioning it! Can ethics put food on the table? And it's not only me, but all the men in this village have gone to do business in the province, can't you see!

Trương Ba Who cares, if they go it's their business, but our family is different . . .

Cả No father, people have changed, you're the only one that thinks in these old ways!

Trương Ba You will get in trouble with the authorities one day for associating yourself with those kind of people!

Cả (*Laughs*) – You clearly have no clue! They work with the authorities. Even mandarins[6] do business! Take for example, Mr Huyện

Tường who lives in our district: while he receives government goods and gifts through the front door, his wife sells them through the back door. As reputable as Lady Huệ is in the capital, she sells her luxurious silk. . . . I'm tired of seeing you and mom work so hard and continue to be so poor. Father, I have been working for only a few months, and the quality of our life is already improving . . . (*Asks his mother*) – Where is that yellow silk shirt I bought for you, why don't you wear it?

Trương Ba's Wife   I can't even wear it, what kind of shirt is this? It's so long and wide . . .

Cả   Oh mom. . . . Women in the province all dress like this! (*Addresses Trương Ba*) I bought a new pack of cigarettes for you and placed it on your bed, have you tried it yet?

Trương Ba   I don't even want them!

Trương Ba's Wife   Your father said those cigarettes smell like burning cow hair!

Cả   Oh come on! Only mandarins can buy this kind of tobacco. You can't even find it in the market!

Trương Ba   (*Adjusts his tone*) – Cả! If you don't want to listen to me, then fine, but you must think of your wife and child.

Trương Ba's daughter-in-law   When you go to the province, you gamble and drink all night, and . . . and . . .

Trương Ba's Wife   Are you still seeing Lý, Mrs Hai Dần's daughter, who sells betel[7] leaves?

Cả   (*His voice wavers*) – It's because. . . . Well, it's because she is my business partner.

Trương Ba's Wife   You know, there is a rumor! Mrs Hạ who sells stork's gallbladder has been telling people: 'Today I went to see a chicken fight at Sòng's temple, and I saw . . .' Don't worry I won't say anything so as to not hurt your wife. But you are sleezy!

Cả   (*Gets angry*) – Go ahead, keep listening to them. . . . Yes, I am bad, I am sleezy! As a man, what's wrong with having five wives and seven lovers?

Trương Ba   (*Pounds his hand on the table*) – Cả!

Cả   I know what you're going to say, you don't have to repeat yourself: 'A father and son have a special connection; A father's love is as steady as Thái Sơn Mountain.' You only conceived me, you and mom just gave me a body. But my soul, it's mine. So whatever I want to do with my life, is my decision! (*Adjusts the bag on his shoulder*) It's late now, I have to go! (*He walks away, his wife tries to stop him.*)

Trương Ba's daughter-in-law   My dear . . .

Cả   (*Yells at her*) – Stop it! (*He pushes her out of the way and walks away without looking at her. His wife holds her face crying.*)

Trương Ba's daughter-in-law   (*Crying and speak to Cả's parents*) – It's my fault. . . . When he started doing business, he brought home so much money and gave me so many beautiful things, I liked it all so much. . . . But now . . . he has become just like his friends, it's all my fault! (*She bursts into tears, running into a room.*)

(**Gai** *has been watching all this time, now runs to* **Trương Ba's** *side as he sits with his head hung low.*)

Gái   Grandpa! My dad yelled at you, he made you sad, didn't he? But I still love you, I will listen to you. We don't need my dad, grandpa, I can still play with you! I just watered your tomatoes for you!

Trương Ba   (*Brushes* **Gái's** *hair*) – Oh, my granddaughter, you are such a good girl . . .

Gái   Grandma said that of everyone in this house, I'm the closest to you, is that true?

Trương Ba   Yes, it is true. (*He hugs* **Gái**) – We get along very well.

Gái   The other day, I told Tý, Aunt Lụa's son, that oranges from your orange trees are this big (*She makes a hand gesture to indicate the size*). . . . He didn't believe me. He said that I am just a boaster! But, I made a bet with him. If I am right, he has to give me his pet bird! Oh look, he's coming! (*She runs to the door*) – Hey Tý, come in!

Tý   (*Stops at the door, reluctant to walk in*) – I am scared of your father. The other day when I came by, he yelled at me, he told me to never come back. He must be afraid that I will steal from him . . .

Gái   Don't worry, my father isn't here! It's my me and my grandpa. He is very kind! Grandpa, this is Tý . . .

Tý   Good afternoon, grandpa!

Gái   Is it ok if I let him in so that he can see your orange trees?

Trương Ba   Come right on in! Pick the most delicious fruits for Tỵ!

Tỵ   (*Folds his arms and bows*) – Thank you so much!

Gái   Let's go to the garden!

(**Trương Ba** *watches the children as they go into the fields.* **Trưởng Hoạt** *walks in.*)

Trương Ba   Good afternoon, Mr Trưởng Hoạt!

Trưởng Hoạt   I saw your wife in the alley. She said you were very upset about your son, Cả. (*Sighs*) – Young people nowadays are all the same! My children too. They don't care about morals or ethics anymore! It makes me so sad just thinking about it! In this village, you're the only one I can really talk to about this . . .

Trương Ba   Why don't you sit down and drink some water, and then we can play a round of chess!

Trưởng Hoạt   When we were young, were we at all like our children now? I don't think we were. . . . Looking back, I followed the Great General to fight against the enemy, defending and protecting our country. I was a soldier for almost ten years! Although we faced several hardships, we were actually very happy! Soldiers and generals took care of each other, it was a brotherhood, we experienced hardships and challenges together. . . . I still remember the time I was surrounded by the enemy at Sắt Forest; I led a group of soldiers following the Great General. In honor of my service, he presented me with a badge for distinguished service and a bottle of wine. I still have the badge and wine on the altar. Everyone knew my name, who didn't know Trưởng Hoạt? But now, kids don't even know who I am and what I did for this country. My wife doesn't even seem to think anything more of me than her pigs or chickens. It must be because we are poor . . .

Trương Ba   Our current conditions force us to dehumanize each other, even though we are all good people inside. Don't take it too personally.

Trưởng Hoạt   Not everyone is as thoughtful as you, you never think ill of anyone . . . (*Sighs*) – For me, all I want to do is play chess to pass the day away . . .

Trương Ba   I don't think of chess as simply a way to get through the day. I really like chess because it is a fair game and places players in an equal position. Whether you are rich or poor, everyone starts with the same number of pieces. Whoever is most clever will win the game.

Playing chess clears the mind, and when we have a clear mind, we have a peaceful heart. Nothing harder to achieve than having a peaceful heart. (*Opens the chessboard. Both sit down to start the game.*)

Trưởng Hoạt   When I was a soldier under the Great General, no one could ever beat me in chess. But I have always admired your clever moves. . . . Be careful there, you might lose your Horse to me. Don't worry, I'll let you make another move!

Trương Ba   Please. Why don't you go ahead!

(*Moments after,* **Trưởng Hoạt** *is stunned and surprised.*)

Trưởng Hoạt   Damn*! (Slaps his thigh)* – Damn! How did I not see that coming? You've had your Chariot there for awhile! How strategic! The Chariot move! I can't seem to find a way out of this. (*Puts his hand on his forehead to think, while sighing*) – There is no other way to get out of this! I surrender! I surrender!

Trương Ba   (*Smiles*) – My Chariot and Cannon are blocking you! Take that. I doubt even Đế Thích could beat this move! (*Laughs arrogantly*) – That's right! Đế Thích would have to surrender to this move! Ha ha! Maybe even ten Đế Thíchs would have to surrender to this move!

(**Đế Thích** *appears by the window. He is dressed as a beggar.*)

Đế Thích   Is that right? (**Trương Ba** *and* **Trưởng Hoạt** *turn around.*)

Trương Ba   What?

Đế Thích   Is it true that even Đế Thích could not beat this move? (*He walks towards the table, focusing on the chessboard.*) – Can I try?

Trương Ba's Wife   (*Walks in from the yard*) – This old man has been sitting outside since you both started playing. (*To* **Đế Thích**) I have already given you our leftovers, including a piece of carmelized fish. We have nothing else, please leave!

Đế Thích   Please let me beat this chess move, then I will leave!

Trưởng Hoạt   Are you crazy? How could you beat this move? Even I, Trưởng Hoạt, the number one chess player in the Great General's army has to surrender, how could you . . .

Trương Ba   Just let him try (*To* **Đế Thích**) – Come on!

(**Đế Thích** *sits on* **Trưởng Hoạt's** *chair while he plays chess with* **Trương Ba**. **Trương Ba's wife** *shakes her head and leaves the room. Moments later . . .*)

Trưởng Hoạt   (*Jumps out of his chair*) – Oh my god, what just happened here?

(*Leaps towards the table and looks closely at the chessboard*) – That's right, you beat it! It's a checkmate! Trương Ba ran out of his pieces!

Trương Ba   (*Surprised, sputtering*) – That can't be! That can't be!

Đế Thích   (*Smiles*) – Look! You don't have any pieces left!

Trưởng Hoạt   Oh my god! Ever since I was born, I have never seen such a move. It must be magic!

Trương Ba   (*Keeps looking up and down at the chessboard and at Đế Thích*) – Tell me the truth: who are you?

Đế Thích   I am . . . a chess player, I am a beggar.

Trương Ba   No, you are not! Only gods or demons can play like that, never an ordinary man.

Trưởng Hoạt   That's right! Tell us the truth, who are you, where are you from? (*Pulls at Đế Thích's collar*) – If you don't tell us, we won't let you leave!

Đế Thích   I. . . . I am Đế Thích.

Trưởng Hoạt   Oh my god! (**Trưởng Hoạt** *kneels down as* **Trương Ba** *quickly stands straight up and bows at* **Đế Thích.**)

Trưởng Hoạt   (*Bows at* **Đế Thích**) – Your honor! We are ordinary men, we didn't realize it was you, we acted disrespectful, please forgive us.

Đế Thích   (*Looks around*) – (*Puts his finger to his mouth*) – Shhh, be quiet, please (*Whispers*) – I sneaked out from Heaven to come down here, please don't talk too loudly, it will be very bad for me!

Trưởng Hoạt   Why would it be bad for you?

Đế Thích   I don't have the luxury of being free like people on earth. The law of Heaven is extremely strict!

Trương Ba   I am so honored! I could never imagine having a chance to play chess with the great Đế Thích. How amazing!

Đế Thích   Amazing? I will ask you a question and you must be honest. Now that you both know I am Đế Thích, would you want to still play chess with me?

Trương Ba   We are ordinary people, but if you let us we would love to continue playing chess with you.

Đế Thích   That's great! Then from now on, I will come down to earth to play chess with you! Allow me to join you! But you have to keep it a secret, do not let anyone know it's me.

Trưởng Hoạt   Yes, of course!

Trương Ba   You can barely keep a secret!

Trưởng Hoạt   No, but with this I can. When I was a soldier working for the Great General, he gave me a top secret document to send. . . . Don't worry I will keep my mouth shut! And even if I tell people, no one will believe me. . . . Wow! Playing chess with Đế Thích! Who could ever believe this!

Đế Thích   See, there you go again . . .

Trưởng Hoạt   No, don't worry, I'll remember to keep it secret!

Đế Thích   (*To Trương Ba*) – I have to return now . . . it's almost 7 o'clock. I have been gone for too long. If the Celestial Emperor finds out (*Frowns*) – They won't let me come back here! It may be a long time before I can visit you two again. (*Pulls* **Trương Ba** *aside to a corner to talk with him in private*) – Trương Ba, you are a very good chess player. Although I won this game, I admire your talent. . . . I must return to Heaven, it's quite boring up there, while here on Earth, there are so many struggles and disasters. I want to give you these incense sticks. They are not the regular kind. When anything bad happens to you, burn one, and I will hear your call for help and find my way down here to help you. If you don't see me coming down, it means they must be guarding me, and I cannot leave. If that happens, please burn three incense sticks. Immediately, you will magically be sent to Heaven to meet me. Can you remember all this? You have to keep this a secret, too! (**Trương Ba** *puts the incense sticks into his shirt and bows to* **Đế Thích**.)

Đế Thích   Farewell to both of you, I'm going home!

(**Trương Ba** *and* **Trưởng Hoạt** *bow to* **Đế Thích**. *Before they raise their heads,* **Đế Thích** *has already disappeared.*)

Trưởng Hoạt   (*Rubs his eyes*) – He's gone! It feels like a dream! (*Looks at the chessboard*) – What a miracle! What a miracle!

(**Trương Ba's wife** *enters.*)

Vợ Trương Ba   What a miracle? It's like you both are living in the clouds! What happened to the beggar?

Trưởng Hoạt   Please be respectful, do you know who that was? He wasn't a beggar, he was . . . oh shit . . . never mind! (*Holds his mouth shut with his hands*)

Trương Ba   You shouldn't judge a person based on what he looks like! Always remember that, alright?

Trưởng Hoạt   (*Looks outside*) – Oh no, it's almost 7 now, I have to go home to chop up the vegetables to feed the pigs, otherwise my wife will yell at me when she comes back. She is very hot-tempered. Everytime she gets angry, it's like your Chariot move, all will be destroyed in her path. Anyways, she wouldn't even care that we just played chess with . . . oh shit . . .! Alright, I am leaving now! (*Walks out in a hurry*).

Trương Ba   (*Puts the incense sticks Đế Thích gave him onto a pillar in the the house and smiles*) – What a miracle! What a miracle! The more I live, the more I see!

Vợ Trương Ba   What are you talking about?

Trương Ba   I said I enjoy living this life! The only thing I regret is not being so young anymore. I wish I could live for another decade. I have so many things I want to do, I want to cultivate these fields to be full of beautiful plants and delicious fruits. (*Pauses*) – It was such a sunny day today and now it's almost dusk. . . . All of a sudden it's so windy. . . . The sky looks like it's expanding. . . . Can you sit here with me, I don't feel well . . . (*His wife sits down next to him.* **Trương Ba** *looks out into the fields*) – The spinach is so green! Oranges are so orange! They look like lanterns. Where is Gái?

Vợ Trương Ba   There, Gái and Tỵ are hanging the birdcage on the wampee tree.[8]

Trương Ba   She is such a good kid! So cute, she looks like you when you were young. . . . Can you get me a glass of water? I feel so short of breath! (*He leans on the frame of the door. His wife hands him a glass of water.*)

Vợ Trương Ba   She plays in the fields all day long . . . (*She looks at him*) Oh no, are you ok? (*Panics*) Are you okay? (*The glass of water suddenly falls to the floor.*) – Oh my god! Are you alright? (*She carefully helps him lay down on the bamboo bed and yells*) – Please! Please! Something is happening to my husband! (*She runs into the yard*) – Gái!

Cả! Mr Trưởng Hoạt! Mr Trưởng Hoạt! (*She runs back in, kneeling down next to her husband*) – Oh my god, why is your face so pale? (**Trưởng Hoạt** *runs toward her*) – Please . . . please help. . . . Maybe he caught a cold?

Trưởng Hoạt (*Hurries in and kneels down next to* **Trương Ba**) – Can you get me some heat or rubbing oil . . . (*He loosens* **Trương Ba's** *shirt and suddenly jumps.*) Oh my God. . . . Mr Trương. . . . (*Addressing* **Trương Ba's wife**) – He's gone, he not breathing anymore!

Vợ Trương Ba What? What? Oh my god! (*She holds her husband*) – Trương! Trương!

Trưởng Hoạt His pupils are dilated! (*Trying to remain calm*) – He was just sitting here with me. . . . What happened? (*He bursts into tears*) – What happened. . . . Trương!

(**Trương Ba's daughter-in-law**, **Gái**, *and* **Tỵ** *run into the house. At the same time,* **Trương Ba's son** – *walks in with several bags in his hands and a few on his shoulders, smiling.*)

Cả (*Shocked*) – What happened?

Trưởng Hoạt Your father . . . your father . . . is gone! (**Trương Ba's son** *drops all of his bags*).

Vợ Trương Ba No, it can't be! No, it can't be! No! No! No!

Blackout – Scene Change

ACT III

Scene: Kingdom of Heaven

Nam Tào Bắc Đẩu - Đế Thích.

Bắc Đẩu (*To* **Đế Thích**) – I already warned you, we can't really help you!

Nam Tào As you sit here, there are guards outside watching you. If you try to sneak away, they will report you right away. Do you see those deities playing by the peach trees? They are actually keeping track of what you are up to!

Đế Thích (*Looks sad*) – It's already been two weeks, since I visited Earth, and these deities haven't left me alone since!

Bắc Đẩu   We promise, we were not the ones who revealed your escape down to Earth! When you left, you left in such hurry that you didn't notice there were a couple of deities who saw you leaving. They were hanging out by the Descending Cloud Gate. After they saw you leave, they started gossiping amongst one another and somehow the message got to the Celestial Emperor that you had left.

Nam Tào   You should have known that those deities like to gossip. They can never keep a secret. Any little piece of information that gets to them will be made public in no time. They also exaggerate everything too.

Bắc Đẩu   Women! They seem to love gossiping about other people's misfortunes!

Nam Tào   They aren't perfect either! There are rumors about them, too! Did you know, recently, there was a scandal about Queen Mẫu Đơn, who sneaked out of Heaven to make a trip to Earth? Something went wrong there because she fell in love with an a man on earth. . . . (*Whispers*) – I heard that it was bad, she got pregnant by the man!

Bắc Đẩu   (*His eyes wide open*) – Wow, that is awful! Interacting with a man on earth, how bad! Are you sure it's true?

Nam Tào   (*Whispering*) – The Thunder God[9] told me. He was ordered to bring a hammer down to punish the man on earth. But then something happened and he must have forgiven the man. I think he must have received bribes in the form of presents . . . Everyone in Heaven is now talking about the scandal between Deity Mẫu Đơn, her lover, and the Thunder God. The Celestial Queen Mother is trying to cover it up.

Bắc Đẩu   Đế Thích's trip to Earth only lasted a few days. When you compare his trip to Deity Mẫu Đơn's, his is nothing. Yet those deities at Celestial Queen Mother's Palace keep making it a big deal, they act as if Heaven is going to collapse because of it! There's a fitting proverb for this: 'Although your own feet are dirty, you burn a torch to find someone else's dirty footprints instead!". ["Chân mình thì lấm bề bề, lại toan cầm đuốc đi rê chân người!'] (*He looks at* **Đế Thích** *with compassion*) – Poor Đế Thích! He looks so miserable! It's so true that one's desire can lead to one's suffering! Now he has to play chess alone again.

Nam Tào   Đế Thích, can I ask you this honestly, people on earth can never play chess at your level. When playing with them, do you find it exciting?

Đế Thích   How can I explain this to you both? People on earth make very different moves when playing chess than the gods and deities do in Heaven. People on Earth, each of them have their own way of making decisions when playing chess. The way they play reflects their own personality and how they think. Their moves are as diverse as their own lives. They are full of joy and sadness, struggle and strength, worry and doubt, and most of all hope. Their chess moves . . . could never be replicated by the gods and deities in Heaven!

Bắc Đẩu   You must have played with many people on earth?

Đế Thích   Many. But the best game I ever had was with a man named Trương Ba.

Nam Tào   Trương Ba? His name sounds familiar. . . . Who is that?

Đế Thích   You'll never guess! He is a farmer, your typical farmer, but his chess moves are phenomenal. He is a very kind and gentle person! I have given him. . . . Nevermind, this may violate the law of Heaven . . .

Nam Tào   Trương Ba. . . . I know I've seen that name somewhere before . . .

Bắc Đẩu   Forget about it! Stop all this chatter! We still have work to do (*Looks at the list*) – Hurry up, and stop thinking so much so we can finish early. My back is killing me, I want to go to the peach garden to ask a few of the deities to massage my back for me.

Nam Tào   I am so sleepy (*Yawns and turns pages of the book*). Alright let's get to work! Who do we need to send off tomorrow?

Bắc Đẩu   (*Listens intently*) – What is that, is someone outside? (*Looks outside the window*) Which deity is walking over there?

Nam Tào   (*Looks out the window too*) – Which deity is she, she looks so unfamiliar: She is wearing a brown shirt, her skirt is rolled up, and she is walking with bare feet. And what is that thing she is holding? Something curvy with a pointy end? (*He addresses* **Đế Thích**) – You have good eyes, can you see what that is?

Đế Thích   Ah, people on earth call it a sickle.[10] Why would a deity need a sickle?

Bắc Đẩu   What kind of deity wears a headscarf like that, and is so tan? I have never met a deity who looks like her. So strange!

Đế Thích   Oh, I think I recognize her!

Nam Tào   She looks angry, she's walking and yelling . . . oh no, it looks like she's is coming towards us! (*Sits down, pretending to work.* **Trương Ba's wife** *walks in*).

Trương Ba's Wife   (*In a loud voice*) – Heaven? Am I really in Heaven? This can't be true! (*To the three gods*) – Good morning, may I ask you all a question? Is this really Heaven?

Bắc Đẩu   Yes, this is Heaven. Who are you?

Đế Thích   (*Shocked*) – That's right, I remember you! You are Trương Ba's wife! (*He runs to her*) – How did you get up here?

Trương Ba's Wife   When I cleaned the house, I saw the incense sticks on the pillar in our home. I lit three sticks and placed them up on my husband's altar. Then, a huge wind suddenly engulfed me and swept me off the ground and all of a sudden I was here. As I looked down below, all I could see were clouds. So, I guess I am in Heaven!

Đế Thích   Hmm, those three incense sticks brought you up here. . . . But what did you say? Why did you put the incense sticks on Trương Ba's altar? Where is he?

Trương Ba's Wife   My dear husband is dead!

Đế Thích   (*Very surprised*) – My god, when did he die? I just played chess with him recently.

Trương Ba's Wife   (*Looks at* **Đế Thích** *trying to think of someone familiar*) – You . . . you are . . .

Đế Thích   I was the beggar. I played chess with your husband, Trương Ba, just two weeks ago.

Trương Ba's Wife   I remember you now! He died that day. Just after you left, he. . . . (*Crying*)

Đế Thích   It can't be! What was the reason for his death? Why didn't he call for me?

Trương Ba's Wife   I have no idea why! He didn't even get a chance to say his last words. He was healthy and happy, and then all of a sudden. . . . But why are you here?

Đế Thích   I live here. I am the King of Chess, Đế Thích, and these two are Nam Tào and Bắc Đẩu, both are gods here.

Trương Ba's Wife   Deities? Gods? Nam Tào? Bắc Đẩu? Then. . . . (*Walks fast to confront* **Nam Tào, Bắc Đẩu**) – Now that I am here, I have to ask you both a question: Why did my husband have to die? Why did you take his life? He was such a good and kind person, how could you. . . . (*She yells at them, hovers the sickle in the air*) – You are so cruel! You are inhumane! (**Nam Tào** *and* **Bắc Đẩu** *scared, move to a corner*) – You have to answer me, why?

Nam Tào (*Sputters*) – Đế Thích, please help us calm her down. . . . We . . . we don't know . . .

Đế Thích (*To* **Nam Tào, Bắc Đẩu**) – You must know. You are the ones who are in charge of the Book of Life and Death. . . . What kind of job are you doing here? Trương Ba was such a good man. He was so kind and generous. And he was very healthy. He must have had at least another twenty years to live . . . you should look at your list again . . .

(**Nam Tào, Bắc Đẩu** *scared of* **Trương Ba's wife's** *sickle, tremble as they open the book quickly.*)

Bắc Đẩu Yes, we are looking at the list! (*They scan the book furiously trying to locate the name*) – Two weeks ago? Here I found it. East Village. . . . Upper town. . . . Trương Ba. . . . Lives for another twenty years . . . but we . . .

Nam Tào Shit, that must be the day . . . the day you hurried me to Celestial Emperor's Father's party. . . . I closed my eyes to cross off a name to meet the quota that day. . . . This is your fault!

Bắc Đẩu Why me? You were the one who crossed off his name!

Nam Tào It was you.

Bắc Đẩu No, it was you.

Nam Tào It was you! It was you!

Đế Thích (*Grumbles*) – This is bad, the way you work kills innocent lives! It was both of your faults! By simply crossing off a name, you killed an innocent person's life!

Trương Ba's Wife You killed my husband even though he didn't commit any crimes, you must bring him back to life, if you don't you'll have to deal with me! (*She jumps on* **Nam Tào.** **Bắc Đẩu** *pulls at* **Nam Tào's** *collar.* **Nam Tào** *tries to run, his shirt is torn.*)

Bắc Đẩu Please, please. . . . It's already done now. Your husband really has died early, but the way I see it, everyone on earth has to die one day anyways . . .

Trương Ba's Wife   Die! Do you know what death is? Have you ever lost a person you love?

Bắc Đẩu   To be honest . . . we are immortal, none of us have to die . . .

Trương Ba's Wife   Then how could you understand death? A person who is living, working, laughing, sharing his joy and sadness, his breath, his labor tending to his land, living happily with his wife and children, taking care of his home, hanging out with his friends . . . has his life suddenly stripped from him. Where he knows nothing, cannot hear a sound, cannot do anything, he is silenced, empty, nothing. His body decays in the cold. . . . Oh my poor husband. . . . If you can kill him, you can make him live again! Return my husband to me!

Nam Tào   We made a mistake. . . . Within three days, we could have asked his soul to come back to his body. . . . But now that he has been dead for two weeks, his body must be decaying. There isn't anything we can do to save him or to revive him back to life. . . . Please understand . . .

Trương Ba's Wife   (*Yells loudly*) – I don't understand! You must revive him! Otherwise I won't leave you alone! Why are the gods in Heaven so cruel! (*She kicks away the chair, takes* **Bắc Đẩu's** *ink bottle and throws it hard on the floor*) – I will destroy your Heaven, I hope you feel shame for what you did!

Nam Tào, Bắc Đẩu   (*Scared*) – Oh my god! (*Runs to hide behind the pillar, unable to speak*) – Help us! Đế Thích!

Đế Thích   (*He tries to calm* **Trương Ba's wife**) – Please calm down, please don't be so angry so that I can think of a solution to save your husband. (*He puts his hand on his forehead thinking*) – It's true what they have said. If it was only three days, it would have been much easier. But now that his body has decayed, even if his soul returns, there is no place for his soul to live anymore . . .

Trương Ba's Wife   My husband's soul? Where did his soul go when he died?

Đế Thích   (*Shakes his head*) – Nowhere. His soul is everywhere, harmonically permeated into the air. It is there but not there, once the soul leaves its home, or the body, it will become nothing, just an illusion! That is the law of Birth and Death!

Trương Ba's Wife   (*Crying*) – My poor husband Trương Ba . . .

Đế Thích (*Suddenly thinks of something*) – That's right! There is only one way. . . . An old deity taught me this before. . . . We might be able to get him back . . . (*To* **Nam Tào, Bắc Đẩu**) – Please look at your list, in East Village, is there any one who died within the last three days?

(**Nam Tào, Bắc Đẩu** *clumsily open the book.*)

Nam Tào   There is . . . there is . . . in Lower town. . . . There is a butcher. I just crossed his name off yesterday.

Đế Thích   Alright! (*To Trương Ba's wife*) – I will bring back Trương Ba by reincarnating his soul into the butcher's body. That is the only way Trương Ba will be revived. His soul, which is untouched, is your husband's soul. But his soul will seek shelter in the butcher's body. We should at least save his soul rather than losing everything. The soul is the most important element in a human being. . . . What do you think about this solution?

Trương Ba's Wife   I don't really understand. But it's up to all of you. All I need is my husband to be alive again.

Đế Thích   You will find it strange at first, but soon you will recognize your husband. Now, you should go back home and find the butcher's house and welcome your husband back . . .

Bắc Đẩu   Trương Ba's soul in the butcher's skin. . . . This is so strange! Đế Thích, this is violation of the laws of Heaven!

Đế Thích   We have to. Please keep this a secret. . . . I'd rather violate the laws of Heaven than kill an innocent person without a real reason. (*To* **Trương Ba's wife**)   Go that way, quickly! Go to the butcher's house! The miracle will become true immediately!

(**Trương Ba's wife** *leaves.* **Đế Thích** *puts his hands together in prayer and starts chanting. The wind and thunder begin to sound as lightening suddenly appears.*)

Blackout – Scene change

ACT IV

Scene: Butcher's House

There is a coffin in the middle of the house. On top of the coffin, there is a candle, incense sticks, and flowers. The **butcher's wife** *wears a white funeral gown with white headband. (footnote about funeral customs?) She sadly holds her head sitting next to the coffin.*

Pig Farmer 1 *and* **Pig Farmer 2** *quietly walk in. They each hold an incense stick with flowers in their hands.*

Pig Farmer 1   We came here to honor your husband, please accept our condolences for your family's loss. We are very sad that . . .

Butcher's Wife   (*Bursts out crying*) – My dear husband, do you see that your two farmer friends are here to visit you, why did you have to go . . .

Pig Farmer 2   This was all so sudden! Just yesterday I drove over a few pigs for him here. He looked very healthy.

Butcher's Wife   Yesterday afternoon he was still working. He used his knife to kill the pigs. He even butchered the meat of two large pigs. I made blood soup, he even ate three or four bowls, drank half the bottle of wine, and then slept. He was snoring loudly . . . until midnight. Then he got a stomachache and said he was cold. I turned on the coal oven to keep him warm. Then I heard him hiccup and he slowly faded away . . .

Pig Farmer 1   (*Shakes his head*) – Life is so strange! You never know when you will die! It is so sad and terrifying!

Pig Farmer 2   (*To Pig Farmer 1*) – Who could have guessed that such a well-built man could get sick so easily and die! I just bought him over two pigs yesterday and he hasn't even paid me yet! (*Lowers his voice*) – Although now is probably not a good time to mention this to his wife, but if I don't let her know, how will I get my money? It's fourty-three *quan*[11], not just a few *quan*. I am afraid he died so suddenly he didn't have a chance to speak his last words. Now if I mention this, his wife may think that I made all of this up! But who would want to tell lies in front of the dead!

Pig Farmer 1   I think you should just let it go. He is dead now. You have worked with him for so long, pay some respect . . .

Pig Farmer 2   I know that. But all the money I invested . . .

Pig Farmer 1   You're always thinking about money. Money isn't everything!

Pig Farmer 2   You're right, but you are not worried. I assume that you may actually feel relief. I can read your mind! You owe the butcher money. A big debt. You must feel good now that he can no longer chase you to ask for his money!

Pig Farmer 1   Aren't you afraid of speaking ill of the dead? That night, you got me drunk, then asked the butcher to gamble with me until he emptied my pockets. . . . And just to let you know, I have already paid off half of the debt . . .

Butcher's Wife Please drink some water and eat some areca nuts and betel leaves[12] . . . (*Pours water*) – Tomorrow when both sides of our families are here, we will bury him . . . (*Wipes away tears from her face*) – How can I live without him? No one will take care of the butcher shop. I have been depending on his health and his labor . . . (*Crying aloud*) – My dear husband, how could you leave me here alone?

(*Suddenly there is a knocking sound from inside the coffin.*)

Pig Farmer 1 What is that sound and where is it coming from?

(*All three look scared but focus on locating the noise.*)

Pig Farmer 2 (*Turns pale, sputters and points to the coffin*) – It's . . . it's coming from in there . . .

(**Pig Farmer 1** *yells. The sound from the coffin is getting louder. The top of the coffin moves. All three gather together. The top falls to the floor. The butcher's body – housing* **Trương Ba's** *soul – (which we will now refer to as* **Trương Ba's Soul**) *– looks around in confusion*).

Hồn Trương Ba It's so hot in here! The air is so thick! Where am I? Who are you? (*Stands up*) – Where is this? (*Raises voice loudly*) My darling wife, where are you?

(*The* **butcher's wife** *in shock stands still.* **Pig Farmer 1** *and* **Pig Farmer 2** *kneel down.*)

Butcher's Wife (*Sputters*) – You . . . you . . . do you have any vengeance . . . to . . .

Pig Farmer 1 (*Keeps bowing in front of* **Trương Ba's Soul**) – Please forgive me, I didn't mean it when I spoke badly about you. Please forgive me, I will pay off my debt and the interest too, please forgive me . . .

Pig Farmer 2 I. . . . I won't even mention that you may still owe me some money. . . . Please rest now, please . . .

Trương Ba's Soul (*Surprised, gets out of the coffin*) What are you talking about? (*To* **Pig Farmer 1**) – You don't owe me anything, why are you kneeling like that, stand up please! (*He intends to help* **Pig Farmer 1** *stand up but* **Pig Farmer 1** *moves quickly back to the wall.* **Trương Ba's Soul**, *stunned, looks around*) – Why am I here? Where is my wife?

Butcher's Wife   I am here, darling, was there something unresolved inside of you that made you sit up? Were there any last words you wanted to say to me before you died?

Hồn Trương Ba   Who are you and why are you saying such things? Why are you talking about death? I'm not dead!

Butcher's Wife   You're really not dead?

Trương Ba's Soul   (*Wavers pushing the* **Butcher's wife** *out of the way*) – What are you doing? Who are you? Why am I here?

Butcher's Wife   Are you not fully awake? (*To both* **Pig Farmers**) – Poor butcher, he is still drowsy! (*To Trương Ba's Soul*) – It's me, you are home, where else would you be!

Trương Ba's Soul   But who are you? I was just talking to my wife! Where is she?

Butcher's Wife   I am here! I am your wife!

Trương Ba's Soul   Don't be crazy! I am not playing a game with you all! (*To the* **Pig Farmers**) – You took me here didn't you? Tell me the truth, where am I?

Pig Farmer 2   This . . . this is a butcher shop . . . your house, you are the butcher . . .

Trương Ba's Soul   Butcher who? Why I am a butcher? I am Trương Ba!

Pig Farmer 2   Trương. . . . Trương Ba! (*Everyone looks at each other*) – He must still be drowsy.

Butcher's Wife   (*Comes to help* **Trương Ba's Soul** *sit down*) – Please sit down to rest. You must still be tired?

Trương Ba's Soul   But I have to go to home*!* (*To himself*) – This is so strange. I was just sitting and suddenly everything turned into darkness. Then I felt really light, as if someone pulled me up into the air. Then everything started moving around me and I couldn't remember anything. Now I wake up here. . . . Or am I still in a dream? (*Pinches his hand*) – No, I am not dreaming! (*Suddenly he looks at his hands again*) – Why do my hands look so different? (*Looks at his body and suddenly realizes he looks different*) – What is this? It's like I am not myself. . . . (*He touches his face*) – Give me a mirror!

(*The* **butcher's wife** *hands* **Trương Ba's Soul** *a mirror.*)

Trương Ba's Soul   (*Looks at the mirror*) – No! This is not me!
(*Looks again carefully and yells*) – No! (*He throws the mirror
away, looking nervous*) – This is not me! (*He is trying to search for
something.*) – Where is my face? Where are my hands and legs? I
am Trương Ba! This person is not me! (*Pauses*) –But. . . . But I am
me. . . . It is clearly me, not somebody else! (*Holds his face*) – Who has
turned me into this?

Butcher's Wife   You . . . what's wrong with you? If you are not you,
who are you then?

(*There are sounds of people's voices outside the gate.*)

Trương Ba's Wife's Voice   This must be the butcher's house!

Trưởng Hoạt's Voice   Where is Trương Ba? (**Trương Ba's wife** *and*
Trưởng Hoạt *walk in.*)

Trương Ba's Wife   Is Trương Ba here?

Trương Ba's Soul   (*Happy*) – My wife! (**Trương Ba's wife** *moves back
one step*) – It's me!

Trương Ba's Wife   No . . . no you are not!

Trương Ba's Soul   (*To Trưởng Hoạt*) – Mr Trưởng Hoạt! Are you both
here to pick me up?

Trưởng Hoạt   (*Shakes his head and moves back*) – No!

Trương Ba's Soul   What is going on here? Why not? Darling, why are
you turning so pale? It's me . . .

Trương Ba's Wife   No! (*Looks around*) – Where is Trương Ba?
Where is my husband? (*Points at* **Trương Ba's Soul**) – Who is this
person?

Butcher's Wife   He is my husband, the butcher. What do you want?

Trương Ba's Soul   No, I am Trương Ba. Please, don't you
recognize me. . . . I was just sitting next to you, I must have had a long
nap . . .

Trương Ba's Wife   You. . . . You are . . . (*She leans on* **Trưởng
Hoạt**) – Trưởng Hoạt, do you think. . . . What did Đế Thích tell me?
Miracle . . . butcher's body. . . . Trương Ba's soul. . . . Oh my god,
perhaps . . . (*She looks at* **Trương Ba's Soul**) – No, he can't be! (*She
covers her eyes, thinking and then asks Trương Ba's Soul*) – Is it true?
Are you Trương Ba?

Trương Ba's Soul   Why are you questioning me like that? You just poured me a cup of tea, you were talking about Gái and how she always plays around my newly planted custard apple trees and jackfruit trees . . .

Trương Ba's Wife   If you are really Trương Ba, let me ask you this: who am I?

Trương Ba's Soul   Do you really need to ask me this? You are my wife!

Trương Ba's Wife   What I mean to ask you is who was I before. How did you meet me? How did we start our lives together? In our home, who do you get along with the most? You have to clearly answer all these questions! Because, my husband Trương Ba would never allow other people to impersonate him!

Trương Ba's Soul   This morning, you told me that I often recall things in the past. You may forget but I remember everything clearly! I could never forget the festival nights at Tầm port in January. I wanted to see your face, but I didn't dare to and so I stood behind your girlfriends instead, covering my face with my hat. . . . Then you and the girls from the fabric district prepared some areca nuts and betel leaves and invited us to come try some. You were so nervous and accidentally cut your pinky finger when chopping the nuts. You still have a scar. . . . You and I were living our lives together. Two times huge storms destroyed our home, five times we survived floods, and four times we ran to find shelter during the war. . . . When you were pregnant with our son Cả, around the time you were supposed to give birth you continued to carry heavy loads of wooden logs every day. And you gave birth to him right next to the forest, because we couldn't make it home in time. . . . Now it has been more than thirty years, after so many years of hardships and struggles. You and I now have a granddaughter, Gái, who you often say gets along the most with me out of all our family members . . .

Trương Ba's Wife   (*Crying*) – Stop, you don't have to say anything else, Trương Ba, it is you! (*She leans on Trương Ba's Soul's shoulder, bursting into tears*) – My husband!

Butcher's Wife   (*Pulls* **Trương Ba's Soul's** *hand*) – Hey, what are you talking about? It's me, I am your wife.

Trương Ba's Wife   No, this is my husband, Trương Ba!

Butcher's Wife   He is not your husband! He is my husband!

(*Both women pull* **Trương Ba's Soul** *from both sides.*)

Pig Farmer 2   I don't understand what's going on! These people are crazy! (*To* **Trưởng Hoạt**) – There is no need to make this such a scene! This is clearly the butcher. Look at him, it's definitely him! Yesterday, I brought over two pigs for him. He owes me fourty-three *quan* and a half.

Trưởng Hoạt   There is something strange going on here! This person . . . although he doesn't look like Trương Ba, talks like Trương Ba! (*To* **Trương Ba's Soul**) – Hey, strange man! Perhaps, Mrs Trương Ba has been missing her husband so much that she has mistaken someone else's husband for her own. But me, I used to be a soldier working under the Great General fighting against the enemy, I can't be fooled as easily, you won't be able to lie to me.

Trương Ba's Soul   Mr Trưởng Hoạt, you don't believe me? You play chess with me every day!

Trưởng Hoạt   Then do you remember the last game we played together?

Trương Ba's Soul   Of course! You moved your Chariot, then used your Horse and attacked me with your Soldiers. You prevented my Horse from crossing the border onto your side. Then you used your Chariot to take all the pieces I had left on the chessboard. I pretended to use my Chariot to attack your Cannon during a strategic moment in the game, but you got stuck there and couldn't move. And then . . . then . . . the beggar . . . he was. . . . No? We both made an oath to keep it secret, to never tell anyone. The beggar was . . . (*Whispers into* **Trưởng Hoạt's** *ear*)

Trưởng Hoạt   Right! That is right! (*Shocked looks at* **Trương Ba's Soul**) – How did you know? Who told you?

Trương Ba's Soul   Who told me? I have never delivered a top secret document for the Great General like you, but I do have integrity! Isn't it true that I am the only one who you told about saving the General's troops when he was surrounded at Sát Forest? When fighting against the enemy you found the way out, you alone moved the entire army forward. You led the enemy to one side of the forest, making them chase only you. Their arrow hit your shoulder. You maneuvered through the mud and the thick grass and the enemy could never catch you. . . . You saved the troops that day, it was you! The injury on your shoulder is from that arrow, whenever the weather changes, it gives you pain. . . . You are a kind man! With a friend like you, I want to live this life forever . . .

Trưởng Hoạt   (*Tears running down his face*) – My friend Trương! Trương! (*He hugs* **Trương Ba's Soul**) – You didn't die. You have come back to us, right?

Trương Ba's Soul   Please take me home! Why do we keep standing here! (*He asks his wife*) – Where is Gái?

Trương Ba's Wife   She is at home waiting for you! She said there is no way you truly died. Let's go home!

(*She holds Trương Ba's Soul's hand, walking out together with* **Trưởng Hoạt.** *The* **butcher's wife** *is still in shock, stands still, unable to stop the three from walking out.*)

Pig Farmer 2   Why are you still standing there? They are taking your husband away! You have to get him back! Where is he going? He has not paid me for the two pigs yet!

Pig Farmer 1   If he wants to go, let him go! He didn't mention anything about the money or debt.

Butcher's Wife   He just came back to life and has already left his wife?

Pig Farmer 2   You have to chase after him! (*Runs out, calling the* **butcher**) Boss! Boss!

Butcher's Wife   (*Runs after him*) – Darling! My dear husband!

Blackout – Scene change

ACT V

Conversation between **Trương Ba's Soul** *and* **Trương Ba's Wife**.

Trương Ba's Soul   So I was almost dead, huh, my dear?

Trương Ba's Wife   Thank goodness for Đế Thích . . .

Trương Ba's Soul   Really! Dead. Not alive anymore. (*Thoughtfully*) Whoever said they aren't scared of death, they're lying. As for me, I'm quite scared! Just the thought that I might have . . . makes me scared. I'm so lucky to be alive. To be able to walk, to labor strenuously, to look at the sun, to eat the fruits of my garden, to smell the fragrant mahogany and jasmine flowers growing on our archway, to drink my favorite sweet tea that you've made. . . . To again be by your side, to look at you. . . . To be alive is such a pleasure!

Trương Ba's Wife   (*Timid, hesitating*) But. . . . But . . . you've . . .

Trương Ba's Soul   I'm very different from how I was before, right? (*Sadly*) You're not yet accustomed to this new appearance of mine?

Trương Ba's Wife   It's been almost a month and I still. . . . I'll gradually get accustomed to it, honey!

Trương Ba's Soul   Why is it then . . . that I can't become accustomed to it myself! Flesh is not like an outfit of clothing that can be easily adjusted to. Maybe outsiders looking in, they could adjust, but my own self here. . . . It's been almost a month. I am myself but it's like I'm also not. . . . Before, this butcher was a stranger to me. . . . (*Examining his own hands*) – my old body, I lived with it for fifty years, but this awkward body . . . (*Shaking his head*)

Trương Ba's Wife   I'll gradually get accustomed. . . . But . . . there are times, I don't understand why, I still think about the features you had before, and miss the person that is resting underground . . .

Trương Ba's Soul   What person? There is only a body underground. And yet you say: It's only the soul that matters! With someone else's body, my soul is still who I am!

Trương Ba's Wife   Let me ask you this: since you've had the butcher's body, how have you been feeling, is it the same as before?

Trương Ba's Soul   Well, my back pain and asthma have gone away. I feel strong and healthy! This butcher was the burliest guy in town!

Trương Ba's Wife   It's true, at every meal now, you eat eight, nine, bowls of rice. Before, you had a weak appetite. And now, you can hold your liquor.

Trương Ba's Soul   (*Bashful*) I don't understand why. Maybe the butcher was an alcoholic. I used to despise those types of activities. I still hate them, but the body I have now is used to its old habits . . .

Trương Ba's Wife   (*Remembering*)You're younger by twenty years now, the butcher was only a bit past thirty. . . . You have your strength, your good eyesight, no more gray hair . . . but me, I'm already old. I'm an elderly lady . . .

Trương Ba's Soul   My dear. . . . I didn't want it to be like this!

Trương Ba's Wife   Yesterday afternoon you visited the butcher's house, didn't you?

Trương Ba's Soul   His wife keeps on coming over here! She understands that I'm not her husband, but that doesn't stop her from crying, insisting, saying that she is lost without anyone to lean on. None of her butcher friends are helping! Her story is so tragic, how can one not pity her. And here I am borrowing her husband's body, the least I could do is give her a hand with some heavy chores. I'm clumsy and don't know how to butcher a pig, but I have to try and give her a hand . . .

Trương Ba's Wife   You've always been one to sympathize with others, but this woman is taking advantage. At first she said she was coming here just to look at you to ease her grief, and then she asks you to do this and that! And I've heard people saying that she's not very trustworthy!

Trương Ba's Soul   Come now, I didn't . . .

Trương Ba's Wife   Her husband has just died, and she tries to convince you to go home with her. If that's not suspicious I don't know what is. It's true, she is attractive and inviting, beating her eyelashes . . .

Trương Ba's Soul   What has that got to do with me? Clearly you're talking nonsense.

Trương Ba's Wife   Sure, I'm ridiculous, old, and senile . . .

Trương Ba's Soul   Honestly . . . (*Upset*) You've never before spoken to me this way! (**Trương Ba's daughter-in-law** *enters*)

Trương Ba's daughter-in-law   (*To Trương Ba's Soul*) I've already weeded around the orange trees and watered all the newly planted trees. And, the plum trees have flowered already, father!

Trương Ba's Soul   (*Happy*) – Is that so? They need to be covered with mud at the roots, and we need to make support frames for the melons. . . . Lots to do. This spring, we have to pay attention to when the young buds come out, in an instant, the whole garden will be full of greenery. When April, May, comes, you and mother can gaze at the fruits to your heart's delight. Did Cái Gái, help her mom do any weeding today?

Trương Ba's daughter-in-law   Yes. She chased away some ants, caught every caterpillar to be found on the leaves, she's very careful and thorough! She said that when grandpa was alive he taught her.. I mean . . . when the other grandpa was here, the old Trương Ba . . .

Trương Ba's Wife   (*To* **Trương Ba's Soul**) How dare she! How many times do we have to tell her: this is your grandpa, this is your Trương Ba. She asks: does that mean there are two Trương Ba's? It doesn't matter how we explain it to her, she doesn't listen and is scared to get near her grandpa. What a shame!

Trương Ba's Soul Don't scold the poor girl. Her young mind can't understand that the outer body and inner being could be different! (*Sadly*) In any case, she is distant now and it makes me sad. Before, us two, we were inseparable. . . . It's my fault. I can't completely live as myself, I have to borrow someone else's body . . .

Trương Ba's daughter-in-law Father, don't be upset. We still love you and respect you just as much as before.

Trương Ba's Soul My daughter, how come my new body doesn't bother or disturb you at all?

Trương Ba's daughter-in-law Before I met Cả, I didn't know who you were. I wasn't yet familiar with your silhouette, your facial features. It was only when I became your daughter-in-law that for the first time, I saw your eyes, your seriousness, and I was fearful at that time. But after a while, living in the same house, you loved and cared for me, you taught me and advised me, and I loved you just like my father at home. You still teach us this: that outside appearances don't matter, it's only the loving heart and open mind of a person that is worth mentioning. When you came from the butcher's house, it only took a few gestures, words, and I recognized you immediately.

Trương Ba's Soul (*Emotional*) Daughter, you are like my own daughter, you may know how to love me more than my own son does.

Cả (*Coming out from another room*) Everyone's talking behind my back again. How could you say I don't love you? Yesterday, you were my father, today you are in a butcher's body, I still treat you just the same. Actually, I think it's even better that you switched bodies! I wish I could do that. Just imagine: all the vendors in the city, all the government officials, they know my face already, it's hard to get anything past them. All of a sudden one day, if I've changed completely from head to toe, I would become an innocent vendor, bringing precious goods from afar. I bet I could hook them all and empty their pockets, even the stingiest person!

Trương Ba's Soul Son! I didn't borrow the butcher's body to do the things you speak of.

Cả Well then why did you?

Trương Ba's Soul Just to live, to survive?

Cả Well, doing what I said is just to survive, too! In order to fight for a place to live that is worthwhile in this world, people will do just about anything! The butcher who you borrowed a body from, he's just like that, too. A clever businessman. Yes. And using his body, now your limbs are stronger, you shouldn't be so wrapped up in this house and garden! Or . . . that's right, you should go to the city with me, and the two of us, we could . . . could . . .

Trương Ba's Soul   So we could cheat the entire populace?

Cả   What does cheat mean, anyways? (*Shaking his head*) Your personality is still exactly the same. . . . I thought that now you would have changed. . . . Listen: even the body you carry isn't yours, you just snuck yourself in there . . . cheating on a few things sold at market is nothing compared to that!

Trương Ba's Soul   But, I didn't want it to be that way, it's not like I enjoy it!

Cả   Whether you wanted it or not, the reality is the same. When you want to survive through any means necessary, then you shouldn't complain about one means being fragrant and one means being fishy!

Trương Ba's Soul   You god-damned . . .! (*Shouting loudly*) Shut your mouth!

Trương Ba's Wife   Please don't shout like that! Your voice isn't as soft and sweet as before, your shout is like thunder, it scares me!

Trương Ba's Soul   (*Angry*) I don't even have the right to speak loudly? Even my voice isn't my own anymore? Is that right? Huh? (*Shouting even louder. Like a dam breaking, reverberating throughout the house. Everyone inside is completely silent.* **Gái** *comes out from a different room, staring at* **Trương Ba's Soul**).

Cả   (*Tsking*) – You just keep on shouting to relieve your anger, but it still won't change anything. It's not just your voice, the entire body that you carry isn't your own. The flesh that is standing there is now something . . . something . . . not honest anymore!

Trương Ba's daughter-in-law   My dear, you can't say that!

Trương Ba's Wife   Son! How dare you say that?

Cả   I'm only speaking the truth. It's strange isn't it, why is everyone scared of the truth?

Trương Ba's Soul   You get out of here right now, and take all of your disgusting practices with you!

Cả   Disgusting? Go ahead, all of you, and judge me. Just ask yourself, who is providing for our family these days that the house is so in order and well-cared for? Even you, father, these days you eat eight, nine, bowls of rice, drink wine, eat meat. . . . The money you make in the fields and garden is just enough to serve your old self, not the butcher's body. Mom was worried sick, but she didn't dare say a word to you. She knew that she could depend only on me, on the money that I brought home from selling in the market. . . . So what are you slapping me around for now? It's come to this and you are still high on your horse!

Trương Ba's Soul   (*Stuttering*) You . . . you . . . (*Violently slaps his son. The son falls to the floor, stumbles back to his feet, holds his cheeks. His mother and wife pull him up.*)

Cả   (*Looking at the blood on his hands*) You've struck me? (*Glaring at Trương Ba's Soul*) – My father never would have struck me like this! Let me tell you something: You are not my father. You are no longer my father!

Trương Ba's Wife   (*Frightened, looking at her husband*) – Good lord, why would you strike him so violently? You've never struck your children before, you always treated everyone you met with such calm gentleness!

(*Gái comes to her father's side, helps him up, resentfully looking at hon* **Trương Ba's Soul**.)

Cả   (*Wiping the blood from his mouth, suddenly laughing, brushes* **Cai Gai** *to the side*) – Very good then! That's the way it should be! That's the way my father should be! Not so timid and shy like before. (*With admiration*) Father, you really are strong! If anyone gives you trouble, you'll know how to smash their face. Good, very good then. (*Laughing loudly, leaves*)

Trương Ba's daughter-in-law   My dear! (*Runs after her husband*)

Gái   You old pig butcher! (*Also runs off*) (**Trương Ba's Soul** *is shocked, looking at his own two hands. The wife of the butcher is peeking out from the door frame.*)

Butcher's Wife   Hey! Mister! (*Waving at* Trương Ba's Soul)

Trương Ba's Wife   (*Coldly*) You're back here again? What do you want?

Butcher's Wife   Mister, my largest pig has broken out of its pen, it's running wild all over the garden, I can't catch him by myself, please come over and give me a hand!

Trương Ba's Wife   Why do you come over here for every little thing? I don't give a damn about your pig!

Butcher's Wife   Before, I never had to lift a finger to handle this kind of work. If I don't come ask him, who can I ask. He is agile and strong . . .

Trương Ba's Wife   My husband isn't a servant who you can order around!

Butcher's Wife   Let me tell you something to set you straight. I've given you a lot of ground for too long! It's true, your husband's soul is there. But his body is still my husband's! If it weren't for my husband, how would your husband do anything, walk, laugh, talk, eat, or drink?

Trương Ba's Wife   Sure, but he doesn't take any pleasure in being in this raw body of your husband's!

Butcher's Wife   That's right, only your husband's soul is worth anything. I don't give a damn about your husband's soul! What I need is a pair of hands and feet, and my husband's strength. He had that strength only because of the years of nurturing and care that I gave to him. I gave him everything he needed. I cooked and served him, I prepared snake wine and tiger bones for him to drink. . . . And even now, you go ahead and ask your husband's soul, every time he comes over when I ask him a favor, I always have delicious food ready to serve him. The other day it was heart, liver, kidney; yesterday it was congee and blood soup. Every time he has complimented me on how delicious the meal was! Is that my husband's body, or your husband's soul, eating? It's only because of my husband's body that your husband is able to satisfy his appetite!

Trương Ba's Wife   Oh please, without my husband's soul, your husband's body would have disintegrated in its grave by now!

Trương Ba's Soul   That's enough! Please! The both of you!

Butcher's Wife   If you don't want your husband to come over to my house, then take his soul back, and give me back my husband's body to bring home!

Trương Ba's Soul   How miserable! (*to Trương Ba's wife*) – I plead with you. (*To the butcher's wife*) – And you, please go home for my sake. Yes, I will go as well . . .

(*The* **butcher's wife** *angrily leaves.*)

Trương Ba's Wife   Now that you're used to the butcher's habits, are you dull-witted because of that blood soup dish, or have you been put under a spell by that immoral woman?

Trương Ba's Soul   Again, with that tone! I'm about to lose my mind!

(*Holding his head and plopping himself down on the bamboo bed.*
Trương Ba's wife *goes outside, irritated.*)

Trương Ba's Soul   (*To himself*) – What a complicated mess this
has become! Taking cover in the body of someone else is not an easy
task. . . . We've lived together for fifty years as husband and wife,
and never have we had suspicions or harsh words for each other like
this . . . (*After a while*) – My wife's anger and blame is not without
reason. . . . But looking at the butcher's wife's situation, it's right to
sympathize with her too . . . (*Pauses*) I still don't understand, when
I'm in this house, next to my beloved plants, I feel that my soul is
uplifted, joyful, elated. But when I'm at the butcher's house, my
heart feels clumsy while my my hands and feet all of sudden are
brisk and active. Especially yesterday, when . . . when I was standing
close to the butcher's wife, my body felt a warmth spreading over
itself. . . . I. . . . But what was I thinking? This is not my flesh, these are
the hands and feet of the butcher! (*Frightened, stands up and paces back
and forth*)

(*Movement and sounds heard outside the door*)

Lý trưởng's Voice   (*Shouting loudly*) – Soldiers, stand guard around
the house, don't let anyone in or out, do you hear? ('*Yes, Sir*' *echoes
in the group.* **Lý trưởng** *and* **Trương tuần** *go into the house, with one
hand holding a cane and the other holding a record book.* **Trương Ba's
wife** *runs outside.*)

Trương Ba's Wife   Greetings, sir Lý!

Lý trưởng   Everyone, come here! (**Trương Ba's daughter-in-law** *and*
Gái *come out,* **Lý trưởng** *points to* **Trương Ba's Soul**) – There he is, it's
this man, right?

Trương Ttuần   Yes, sir Lý, that's the one!

Trương Ba's Wife   What's the problem here, sir Lý?

Lý trưởng   Are you Mrs. Trương Ba?

Trương Ba's Wife   Yes, that's correct, sir.

Lý trưởng   Are you aware, in this village, of who oversees all
activities, keeps track of each and every person? Who?

Trương Ba's Wife   (*Frightened*) Yes, it's you sir, Lý trưởng, sir!

Lý trưởng And yet you still don't know why I've come here? You people really are disgusting, with your disregard for laws and regulations! There has been widespread gossiping in the village, to the point where it's reached the authorities at the district level . . . and they demand answers. . . . This really is a big issue, everyone is talking about this story: how the pig butcher has suddenly left his home, his wife, and is now living with the elderly wife of the Trương Ba . . . (*Turning to* **Trương Ba's wife**) – You've got a lot of guts to steal someone else's husband!

Trương Ba's Wife Listen, sir Lý, the reality is, this actually is my husband, my dear Trương Ba.

Lý trưởng Don't argue with me, old woman! The law is straight forward, no one can deviate from it. There is someone on top to oversee, and down here I, Lý trưởng, am the eyes and ears of the village. Today I've come here in person, with my own eyes, my own hands, to punish the guilty, so I can report back up to the authorities! (*Pointing at* **Trương Ba's Soul**) You! Stand up. If you know what's good for you, you'll tell me again: Who are you? What is your name?

Trương Ba's Soul Respectfully sir, I'm Trương Ba!

Lý trưởng (*With wide eyes*) – Trương Ba? You aren't Hợi, the pig butcher from the Hạ neighborhood?

Trương Ba's Soul No, sir!

Lý trưởng (*To* **Trương tuần**) Alright then, let's check the records! (**Trương tuần** *opens up the record book*) Everything is here: civil status, family registration, ID card, we have records of each and every person in the village, in the records we even have their fingerprints. . . . Here it is (*Reading*) – Tạ Văn Hợi. Occupation: pig butcher at Hạ market, two meters thirteen cm tall. (*To* **Trương tuần**) Measure!

(**Trương tuần** *holds a measuring stick and measures* **Trương Ba's Soul.**)

Trương tuần That's correct!

Lý trưởng (*Continuing to read*) – One small birthmark above the right eyebrow! (*To* **Trương tuần**) – Examine him!

(**Trương tuần** *examines* **Trương Ba's Soul's** *right eyebrow.*)

Trương tuần That's correct!

Lý trưởng (*Continuing to read*) – One scar under the left ear measuring ten cm.

(**Trương tuần** *examines* **Trương Ba's Soul's** *ear.*)

Trương tuần   That's correct, again!

Lý trưởng   Of course it is! Our records are never wrong! Now come closer, let me look at your thumb! (*Taking the finger of* **Trương Ba's Soul**, *examining and comparing it to the fingerprint in the records*) Exactly the same! So it's as clear as day! You can't deny it anymore: You are definitely **Tạ Văn Hợi**, the pig butcher!

Trương Ba's Soul   But. . . . That's not the truth!

Lý trưởng   You are Tạ Văn Hợi! The records have proven this! Don't try to deny it!

Trương Ba's Soul   I don't dare to deny it, this body here is the butcher's, but the soul here is Trương Ba. . . . I am Trương Ba!

Lý trưởng   The law, ordinances, and records don't say anything about souls! What evidence do you have? What shape is your soul, is it square, or round?

Trương Ba's Soul   Well if it is a soul, it doesn't have a shape, it's not square or round, but rather happy, sad, glad, angry, loving, hateful . . .

Lý trưởng   These are all frivolous things! Please, don't make things up in front of me!

Trương Ba's Soul   Why are these frivolous, sir Lý? The soul is the most important part of who a person is . . .

Lý trưởng   I don't give a damn about your soul, I don't know anything about it! All I know is that according to our official records, you are Hợi from Hạ neighborhood! That's all! And to think, a few days ago, someone in your family came to report your unexpected death! The first thing we have to do is invalidate your death certificate. (*Tearing up the death certificate*) – The second thing: you must return to your previous residence, which means your home in Hạ neighborhood. After that, you must continue selling pork at the market. You already accepted our order of pork for the district's soldiers camp for the end of year, surely you will fufill it . . .

Trương Ba's Soul   Sir, my occupation is a gardener, I don't know anything about selling pork . . .

Trương Ba's Wife   My husband isn't going anywhere!

Lý trưởng   Shut your mouth, it's time for the interrogation. (*To Trương Ba's Soul*). – Are you going?

Trương Ba's Soul   No, there's no way I could . . .

Lý trưởng   (*Shouting*) – Where's Tuần? Arrest him! Bring him back to the town hall!

(*We hear 'Yes, sir!' off stage.* **Trương tuần** *comes eagerly forward trying to handcuff* **Trương Ba's Soul**. *His son appears in the door frame.*)

Cả   Hold on a minute, sir Lý, let me discuss this with you first . . .

Lý trưởng   (*Looking upwards*) – Who are you?

Cả   I'm my father's son . . .

Lý trưởng   You. . . . Your face looks a bit familiar . . .

Cả   Sir Lý, you don't recognize who I am? (*Softly, bringing his tone down*) Just a week ago, I just brought you a gift, sir Lý . . . (*Winking*) – about the ship bringing in too many items . . .

Lý trưởng   Oh . . . that's right, I remember now . . .

Cả   There is always a way to settle any issue if we work together and resolve it to everyone's satisfaction. . . . Sir Lý, let's just agree that this is the butcher, we don't know about the soul, but . . . really, if he is or he isn't, what difference does it make to you? Complicated situations arise in life, we don't deny it, but as long as we. . . . I mean – let's just all behave in a reasonable way here, shall we? (*Gives a sign to* **Lý trưởng**, *asking him to step aside.* **Lý trưởng** *crosses his arms and tells* **Trương tuần** *to step back.*)

Lý trưởng   (*To the son*) – What do you want?

Cả   (*Puts a sack of money in front of* **Lý trưởng**) – It's just a small token of appreciation.

Lý trưởng   You've got some nerve, are you bribing me now?

Cả   It's just a token of my good intentions . . . for sir Lý to get some tea . . . (*All of a sudden changing his tone*) – 100 quan! Please sir Lý, let's just brush off this whole situation! Don't make (*Pointing at* **Trương Ba's Soul**) have to return to the butcher's house.

Lý trưởng   How could I! There are orders from above . . .

Cả (*Smiling*) – The authorities are far away. You sir Lý, are near, so it's all up to you!

Lý trưởng (*Pondering*) – It's dangerous. . . . What if someone higher up finds out. . . . Or how about this: during the day, let him just stay here, with this woman (*Pointing at* **Trương Ba's wife**) – and at night, he will go home to the butcher's wife.

Trương Ba's Wife (*In shock*) – No way!

Cả Mom! Let me arrange it, anything can be done! (*To* **Lý Trưởng**) Sir Lý please reconsider . . .

Lý trưởng (*Pondering*) – Or, at least, he needs to stay with the butcher's wife for half the night, waiting until after the night watchmen have finished their rounds of counting people. Then he can return home. That's the only way!

Cả Yes, alright mom. . . . That will have to do!

Lý trưởng (*Shaking the sac of money*) Important matters, changing from one person to another . . . and with just 100 quan, it's not really enough, don't you think?

Cả You don't think it's enough?

Lý trưởng It's not just me here, what about the people at the town hall and their associates, I have to make sure that there isn't any more trouble from the above. It takes a lot, and I'm not kidding around, it's not as simple as avoiding taxes on that one shipment of yours . . .

Cả Don't you worry, sir Lý, I'll take care of the rest, we wouldn't take advantage of you.

Lý trưởng Alright then, let's just consider the matter settled for now. With everyone as witness, starting tonight, he (*Pointing to* **Trương Ba's Soul**) will have to stay at the butcher's house until midnight before going back. And from tomorrow, he will open his pork shop again.

Cả Yes, don't worry sir Lý, he'll open the shop up right away! (*To Trương Ba's Soul*) I'll give you everything you need!

Lý trưởng While at the shop, you must be Hợi the butcher, and at Trương Ba's house, you'll be Trương Ba. So it's settled then?

Cả (*On behalf of his father*) – Yes, everything will be fine!

(*Gái has been standing in the corner silently listening, all of a sudden raises her voice.*)

Gái   No! It's not fine! This person here is not my grandpa!

Lý trưởng   What?

Gái   This person is not Trương Ba!

Lý trưởng   Hmmph!

Gái   My grandpa was skinny, with gray hair and a wrinkled forehead, with bright eyes, a very kind face! But this man, he's bloated and fat, with bushy eyebrows like a broom, he looks so fierce! (*to* **Trương Ba's Soul**) You've deceived the whole house, everyone, but you won't be able to decieve me! You're just pretending to be grandpa, taking over his place in the house. . . . It's not alright!

(**Lý trưởng** *turns to look at the son.*)

Cả   (*Scolding*) – Shut your mouth! What does a child like you know about adult matters! (*to* **Lý trưởng**) Sir Lý, don't mind this mischievous kid! Go away! Go! (*Shoves his daughter out the door, turns back inside, pulls from a cloth bag a string of money and presses it to* **Lý trưởng's** *hands*) Everything will be in place, sir Lý!

Lý trưởng   (*Speaking while putting away the money*) – Everything is getting quite complicated!(*Shouting loudly*) Soldiers! (*The soldiers say 'Yes sir!'*) Retreat! (*To* **Trương Ba's Soul**) Remember what I've told you! (*Leaves*)

Trương Ba's Wife   Thank Heavens! They've left us alone now, son.

Cả   Yes, because I took care of it! Did everyone see that? If it weren't for me, that would have been a complicated mess! My money got something accomplished here! (*to* **Trương Ba's Soul**) With enough money, you can get anything done. Silver will pierce and tear through paper.[13] If you want to keep your soul in the butcher's body, you'll have to be clever to get it done! But don't worry: I'll make it all back from your meat shop! Business is good! I told you before: you being in the butcher's body was a great thing! (*Laughing loudly*)

Scene Change

ACT VI

Scene: The Butcher's House, Evening.

Conversation between **Trương Ba's Soul** *and the* **Butcher's Wife**.

Trương Ba's Soul   (*With sleeves rolled up, a sad face, throwing a few bloody knives into a bucket, saying to the wife of the butcher*) – I've finished with that pig. I've put the feet in this bucket, the butchered meat I've put on the shelf, covered with banana leaves. The heart, liver, and stomach I've put into the basket hanging up there, be careful or else the cat and dog will get to it . . .

Butcher's Wife   (*Hiding her smile*) – That's great, don't you worry. . . . It looks like today, draining the blood and butchering the meat, you've gradually become very skilled at it!

Trương Ba's Soul   (*Bashful*) – It's. . . . I've done alright.

Butcher's Wife   I told you before: it's not really that difficult, right? With your strength (*Holding* **Trương Ba's Soul's** *hand*) These two hands have become so quick and agile!

Trương Ba's Soul   (*Embarrassed, pulling his hand away*) – My work is done, it's late, I have to go home.

Butcher's Wife   Home! Why do you rush like this everyday? Sit down with me for a while. The bowl of blood soup I left for you in the cupboard, did you eat it yet?

Trương Ba's Soul   Yes.

Butcher's Wife   And the cup of wine, did you drink it already?

Trương Ba's Soul   Yes.

Butcher's Wife   And the raw onion? I know how you love raw onion.

Trương Ba's Soul   Yes, I had it, Thank you, ma'am.

Butcher's Wife   Thank you? Why are you so polite? And why are you calling me ma'am?

Trương Ba's Soul   (*Embarrassed*) – Alright. . . . Pardon me, but I have to go . . . it's getting late.

Butcher's Wife   It's raining and cold outside, everything is dark with thick fog. . . . (*Pulls a bottle of wine from under the table and puts in on the table*) Drink a little bit more, this wine is strong but smooth . . . it took me some trouble, I had to go a long distance to buy it (*Pours a glass*) – Drink a glass with me, I'll have some too (*Pours herself a glass*) Come on! (**Trương Ba's Soul** *hesitates, then drinks the glass.*)

Butcher's Wife   (*Drinks*) – It warms the whole body.

Trương Ba's Soul   (*Hurriedly standing up*) – I have to go.

Butcher's Wife   (*Also standing up*) – My dear . . . (*Sadly*) You're going back over there. . . . And I'll be all by myself again, in this empty house. . . . I'm scared . . .

Trương Ba's Soul   (*Compassionately*) – What are you scared of?

Butcher's Wife   I'm scared . . . to be alone. . . . Just stay for a little while longer, just a little while . . .

Trương Ba's Soul   It's getting very late, it's not proper, ma'am!

Butcher's Wife   What does proper mean anyways? You don't even have the right to linger just a little longer? Why do you see yourself as hired help, and leave as soon as you finish your work? This is your home! And I, I'm your . . . why are you so consistently cold with me, abandoning me in such a lonely state . . .

Trương Ba's Soul   I understand that it has been a struggle to be alone, and I don't mind giving you a hand with the butcher's work . . .

Butcher's Wife   I don't need that kind of work. . . . Before I needed it, but now, I don't care about it anymore! I can't live like this forever! I shouldn't be treated so coldly by you. . . . I'm your wife!

Trương Ba's Soul   (*With difficulty*) Ma'am, you know that I'm not your husband, I'm not Hợi. More than anyone, you know that most clearly.

Butcher's Wife   (*After a while of silence*) – I know, I do know! But that's the reason why. . . . I love and value you so much. . . . I married my husband when I was sixteen years old. I lived by his side for ten years, and all through those years, I've never heard him utter sweet and thoughtful words to me. . . . Only vulgar, rude words. . . . Outside of his business and breeding the pigs, he only knew eating, sleeping, and getting drunk. . . . All night long, while close to his wife, he was dead drunk. And the terrible beatings, remembering those beatings makes me terrified . . .

(*The **butcher's wife** closes her eyes, in front of her face appears a flashback: the body of the butcher with **Trương Ba's soul** transforms back into the butcher's body, inebriated and drinking wine, serving himself food and chewing loudly. He gets up clumsily, then violently strikes his wife in the face. Frightened, she backs away slowly. The butcher grabs her hands. She cries out. She opens her eyes, quickly: in front of her is again the butcher with **Trương Ba's soul**, gentle and kind.*)

Butcher's Wife Now, next to me, I still see that strong frame, the same face, but everything else is different. . . . For the first time I know what it's like to hear courteous and gentle words, gestures that are polite and thoughtful. For the first time I feel that I am valued and respected as a person . . .

Trương Ba's Soul But, isn't it true that you had cried, grieving the man who was your husband?

Butcher's Wife Yes! It's not that I hate who my husband was. I was able to bear his ways, I belonged to him, I cried and was miserable when he died. But it was only when you came, or rather when your soul came to my husband's body, that I realized, for a long time I myself wasn't alive. . . . At that time I thought that my life was over. . . . Now I feel as though I've been reborn as a young girl, full of happiness and joy. . . . I thank the heavens for letting your soul join this strong and familiar body! (*holding* **Trương Ba's Soul's** *hands*) I don't want anything more! My perfect husband is here! The person that I've been waiting for all this time! Don't hesitate anymore. . . . I am yours . . . (*embraces* **Trương Ba's Soul**, *passionately*) – Love me, Love me tenderly! These two hands so many times have held me hostage, frightened me, but now everything is different from before! (*Drops her face in* **Trương Ba's Soul's** *chest*)

(*As if being pulled by an overwhelming, strong force.* **Trương Ba's Soul** *also embraces the butcher's wife, caressing her shoulders and strong arms.*)

Butcher's Wife (*Brushing* **Trương Ba's Soul's** *hair*) – I will take care of you, serve you, be devoted to you forever. Please, let's run away, leave everything behind. There won't be Trương Ba's Soul or the butcher's body anymore, just you and me. . . . Let's hide away, to some place where no one knows who we are, a place where there will be no Lý trưởng, no other butchers, even your crafty son won't exist. . . . We'll go right away, tomorrow, across those fields and we'll be in Tằm port, and we'll take the ferry boat from there . . .

Trương Ba's Soul (*As if revived*) – Tằm port, Bến port? (*Bewildered, breaks his embrace with the butcher's wife and stands up quickly*) Tằm port, here? (*Looking at his own hands, frightened*) – No! No! (*Backing away from the butcher's wife*) – What strange entity inside of me lashed out just now? With my weak soul. Please come back to me, Trương Ba! I am Trương Ba. . . . My soul! What have I done? (*Holding his face*) – Oh my wife!

Butcher's Wife My husband! (*Following* **Trương Ba's Soul**, *passionate and pleading*) My husband?

Trương Ba's Soul   (*Shaking his head*) – No! Don't! Let me go! I plead with you! (*As if afraid that he cannot overcome the temptation, backs away slowly out the door*) – No! (*Runs away*)

Butcher's Wife   My husband! (*Stumbles to the floor, sobbing*)

Blackout – Scene Change

ACT VII

Scene: Trương Ba's Home

Trương Ba's Soul *and* **Trưởng Hoạt.** **Trương Ba's Soul's** *face is still sorrowful and in a daze.*

Trưởng Hoạt   (*Quietly looking at* **Trương Ba's Soul**, *shaking his head*) – You always reek of alcohol. You drink too much! I came over today intending to speak to you about this too: you've been ruined by liquor! Everyday bad habits will rot one's soul and mind, sir! Your wife says that during every meal without liquor, your face is pale and stone cold, as if you've lost your soul.

Trương Ba's Soul   Lost my soul? How could I lose my soul!

Trưởng Hoạt   It's not just the wine! If your meal is not exactly what you wanted, you scowl and refuse to eat. You and your wife are always bickering and arguing. As a friend, I'm asking you: Why are you acting so different from your normal disposition?

Trương Ba's Soul   (*Stammering*) I. . . . I myself don't understand it. All of a sudden I crave it. It's this body of mine! Only if you were in my position, would you understand it . . .

Trưởng Hoạt   (*Sighing*) – Who doesn't have a body that is weak. Who doesn't have to struggle against their own body. Take my case, I'm over sixty years old. And I still want to work, I still sometimes want to ride horses as if I were a soldier in the military. But my body won't obey me. My back is hunched, my joints are weak, my hands and feet are exhausted. . . . While you, with the butcher's healthy body, you get to be young again. Meanwhile the rest of us, we're all getting closer to the grave each day.

Trương Ba's Soul   What's the use in living in youth for such a long time, when this body isn't even my own?

Trưởng Hoạt   You keep on saying that! The body you have now is not the butcher's anymore, it's yours. It's your own now, whatever it does, whatever the consequences, you have to accept it. Who else is there to blame? (*Annoyed*) You must want it, why else would you work strenuously at the butcher stand, all day with one hand wielding a sharp knife, and the other hand clutching a sack of money . . .

Trương Ba's Soul   That was all my son's idea and Mr Lý trưởng's orders. . . . That's the only way they'll leave me alone. . . . And, my family's financial situation right now is difficult, everything is expensive so our daily costs are more than before . . . my garden alone isn't enough, I need to depend on the butcher stall . . .

Trưởng Hoạt   You plan and calculate so carefully these days. People were saying that your meat stall buys cheap and sells high, cheating on your measurements before and after, customers have been ripped off enough! Honestly, I don't know what to make of it! But now, I won't talk about that, I won't dwell, otherwise we will argue and annoy each other. How about this, why don't we play a game of chess. At this point, only chess can bring back happiness to the two of us like before. (*Forced laughter*) – Bring the chessboard out here!

(*They bring the chessboard out, and set the pieces.*)

Trưởng Hoạt   (*Frowning, puzzled*) – What are you doing? Your move is . . .

Trương Ba's Soul   What? I wanted to move there. (*Pause*) – Check mate!

Trưởng Hoạt   (*Bewildered*) – Why did you say that?

Trương Ba's Soul   So what if I say that? You still have no way to get out of this!

Trưởng Hoạt   A player with good sportsmanship would never want to win that way . . . (*Giving up*) – Alright, I lose. (*Gets up*) – But Mr Trương, I just can't understand it. Your style of playing is different from before. At first your opening moves seemed in character, but then. . . . There is no more generous, bravery, with the same depth anymore. The way you advance and retreat are like petty gimmicks. And the way you just captured that piece, I'm sorry, that was so low!

Trương Ba's Soul   Well why do you say that? How was that low? Or should we play another round?

Trưởng Hoạt   (*Disheartened*) – No, I don't want to play anymore. I decline. . . . No wonder! You really have changed Mr Trương Ba . . .

Trương Ba's Soul See! Now even you, my best friend, even you . . .

Trưởng Hoạt I wouldn't dare. I'm just an old lowly soldier, barefoot with worn clothes, I wouldn't dare call myself the friend of a butcher. . . . The people close to you are the butcher's wife, the pig farmers, or the higher ups like that Mr Lý. . . . See now, here he is looking for you now. (*Coldly stands in place*) Excuse me, I'm going home. (*Leaves*) (**Lý trưởng** *and the son enter, both of them giggling.* **Lý trưởng** *is tipsy, drunk.*)

Lý trưởng (*To the Son*) – hee hee! The wine at that bar really was delicious! And that girl, the bartender, she was . . . hee hee! Her eyes were coy and her breasts were . . . (*Gesturing*) hee hee!

Cả I told you! If I'm going to take you out, I'm going to really take you out! You know, there are many other places that are even more pleasant. If you're not too busy, once and a while you should make some time to come out with us commoners. . . . (*Winking*) there are other bartending girls out there . . .

Lý trưởng (*With a gaping smile*) – Oh really? Hee hee! To hell with you! Hee hee! But you know, you're right: With all my official responsibilities, sometimes I should enjoy a little break! In order to get some fresh air and keep the blood circulating. . . . Ha ha . . .

Trương Ba's Soul (*Annoyed*) – What's the problem now?

Lý trưởng Oh, my friend, you were sitting here and I didn't even notice! Ha ha. . . . Greetings Mr Trương Ba, or I should say, greetings to the butcher! Us two, we just went out and had a heart-to-heart, it was so much fun! Your son sure knows how to take care of everyone, the higher ups and the lower downs. (*Suddenly remembers, asking the son*) Hey, where is that sack with the wad of money you gave me before, we may have left it at the bar.

Cả (*Laughing*) – How could we forget it, you put it your pocket, right there!

Lý trưởng Ah, here it is, hee hee. . . . So much fun today, really enjoyable! You know: we have to know how to depend on each other, to be reasonable, to compromise, it's really everything! (*To* **Trương Ba's Soul**) – You took cover in one butcher's body, but even if there were ten butchers, I'd be able to take care of you all! That's right! If there were a few more people like Trương Ba here, I would have plenty to drink. Imagine, if the whole village, district, province, were to cloak their souls in other people's bodies? (*Pointing at the son's face*) Who knows, maybe this body of yours isn't really yours? Even myself, it might be the case . . . for all this time, my soul might actually belong to some punk! Hee hee! Wouldn't that be fun!

Trương Ba's Soul (*Rudely*) – Please leave! Just leave me alone in peace!

Lý trưởng (*Still very drunk*) – Listen to me old man, you need to know: You are not only alive thanks to the butcher, but you also depend on me, Mr Lý to survive, too! These days, no one can survive on their own!

Cả Mr Lý is drunk, don't let him make you mad! (*Pulling* **Trương Ba's Soul** *aside*) Don't think that I'm having fun here! He's costing me an arm and a leg! I can't even enjoy the wine when I drink with him. But in this village, he holds all the power, so if we want to get something done, I'd eat his shit if I had to! (*To* **Lý trưởng**) – Alright, it's time for me to take you home.

Lý trưởng Yes, take me back to the town hall, so I can finish my work, I still have to oversee all the village activities . . . (*Stumbles away. The son leads him out*).

Trương Ba's Soul (*Sits, holding his head for a while, then suddenly stands up quickly*) – No, no! I don't want to live like this forever! (*Looking at his own body*) – I'm so tired of being in this place that isn't mine, so tired of this! This cumbersome, bulky body, I'm beginning to be sick of you, I just want to get away, right this minute! If only this soul of mine had a separate form, so it could be away from this body, even if only for a moment!

(*Here begins the scene 'Dialogue between soul and body'. On the stage, Trương Ba's Soul separates from the* **butcher's body** *and appears as a dim shadow of* **Trương Ba**. *The* **butcher's body** *stays sitting on the bamboo bed and is now only a body.*)

Butcher's Body (*Shaking his head*) – Useless, that vague, bland, soul of miserable Trương Ba over there. You can't be separated from me, even if I'm only a body . . .

Trương Ba's Soul Oh, so you can talk, huh? Absurd, there's no way you could be able to talk. You don't have a voice, you're only flesh, a blind body in the darkness.

Butcher's Body Yes I can! A body can speak with its own voice! You already know my voice, you've already been ordered around by that voice. It is precisely because I live in darkness and blindness that I have this powerful strength, that I can sometimes control even that noble, pure, soul of yours!

Trương Ba's Soul   Rubbish! You are only an outer shell, without any purpose or meaning, with no thoughts or feelings!

Butcher's Body   Is that right?

Trương Ba's Soul   Or, if you do, they are only weak and poor ones, that every animal would have: cravings for food, alcohol, meat . . .

Butcher's Body   Of course, of course. Why don't you go on: when you were over at my house. . . . When you were standing next to my wife, your hands and legs trembling, your steamy breath, the knot in your throat. . . . That night, you almost . . .

Trương Ba's Soul   Shut up! That was you, your hands, your breath . . .

Butcher's Body   It's not like I'm jealous! Who would be jealous of their own body? I'm just pointing out that it's such a pity you ran off all of a sudden that night! . . . . Listen, we should be honest with each other for a minute: weren't you a little bit upset? Ha ha, the blood soup, the neck and tail dishes, and all the fragrant spices, didn't they make your soul feel lovely, too? In order to satisfy me, don't you also have to participate a bit in the satisfaction? Now, give me an honest answer!

Trương Ba's Soul   I. . . . I. . . . I already told you to shut up!

Butcher's Body   Clearly you don't dare to answer. You can hide it from other people, but you won't be able to hide it from me! The two of us have merged as one already!

Trương Ba's Soul   No! I still have a separate life: whole, pure, straightforward . . .

Butcher's Body   How amusing! You depend on me for your existence, bend to my needs and desires, and yet you think of yourself as whole, pure, and straightforward!

Trương Ba's Soul   (*Covering his ears*) – I don't want to hear you anymore!

Butcher's Body   (*Shaking his head*) You go ahead and cover your ears! There is no way you can deny my existence! What you ought to do is thank me. I've given you strength. Remember that day when you slapped your son, til his mouth and nose were bleeding? That was your temper plus my strength . . . Ha ha!

Trương Ba's Soul   What do I need your strength for, it's turned me into a cruel person.

Butcher's Body   But I am just the circumstance that you must accept! It's not my fault . . . (*Sadly*) – Why does it seem like you look down on me? I deserve some respect, too! I am the vase that holds your soul. It's because of me that you can till the soil. You can enjoy the sky, trees, your loved ones. . . . It's because of my eyes that you can recognize everything in this world, through my nerves. . . . When someone tries to hurt a soul, it will also hurt the body. . . . Intellectuals like you often believe the soul is more valuable, encouraging people to live for their soul, ignoring their bodies and letting them suffer needlessly. . . . Is it a crime to eat eight or nine bowls of rice, and to crave meat for dinner? The real crime is to not have enough food for the body to be nourished!

Trương Ba's Soul   But. . . . But . . .

Butcher's Body   Let's be fair, Trương Ba! All this time you've been insulting me, but I've been entirely courteous with you (*Under his breath*) I know very much how to yield to your soul . . .

Trương Ba's Soul   Yield?

Butcher's Body   Of course. I sympathize with you, I understand that they have been 'playing games with your soul'. Meaning: during times when you are alone, you go ahead and think you have a virtuous soul, that you are only accepting me in this situation in order to live. After that, you can blame me for any of your questionable actions, so you can feel good about yourself. I know it: you need your pride to be stroked. The soul needs to save face: ha ha, As long as you . . . still do everything needed to satisfy my cravings!

Trương Ba's Soul   Your reasoning is really low, my brother!

Butcher's Body   Hey, so you're calling me brother now? It's not my reasoning, I'm only reminding you of what you've told yourself and others! Like I said, we're not two beings, but one!

Trương Ba's Soul   (*As if hopeless*) – My God!

Butcher's Body   (*Consoling*) – There's no reason to beat yourself up over this! I don't want you to suffer, because I actually need you, too. Let's not argue with each other anymore! There's no other way! We just have to live harmoniously with each other! My poor soul, please come back to me now!

(*Trương Ba's Soul mindlessly goes back into the butcher's body. On the stage, Trương Ba's character disappears. Only the butcher's body with Trương Ba's soul is seated silently on the bamboo bed. . . . Trương Ba's wife enters.*

Trương Ba's Wife   Gái isn't home yet, dear?

Trương Ba's Soul   (*Dazed*) – No.

Trương Ba's Wife   She went over to Ty's house in the morning. Ty is gravely ill.

Trương Ba's Soul   Gravely ill? How come I didn't know?

Trương Ba's Wife   You don't think of anyone else these days. It's a life or death situation for Ty, from last night til now he has been delirious, his mom's eyes are red from constantly crying. Terrible! He's such a good boy. Gái loves her friend, she's shocked. . . . We don't know if the boy will be able to survive, he might . . . (*After a while*) – Why wouldn't the heavens take my body in his place?

Trương Ba's Soul   Why would you say that my dear?

Trương Ba's Wife   (*Thinking*) – I'm telling the truth. . . . Trương Ba, I've thought about this thoroughly: It may be time for me to go . . .

Trương Ba's Soul   Go where?

Trương Ba's Wife   I don't know yet! Become a laborer somewhere, anywhere will do . . . just disappear . . . (*On the verge of tears*) – So that you'll be free . . . to be with the butcher's wife. . . . That would be better than this . . . (*Cries*)

Trương Ba's Soul   My dear! (*After a long while*) – How has it come to this?

Trương Ba's Wife   I know that you love your wife and children with all your heart. . . . It's just that now . . . (*Crying*) You're not you anymore, you're not Trương Ba the gardener of before. Did you know: Your son has decided to sell our garden so that he can open another butcher stall.

Trương Ba's Soul   Really? It can't be!

Trương Ba's Wife   You say it can't be, but I know that in the end it will turn out this way, and you will eventually accept it. . . . It's up to you, I only want you to be happy. I can't help you anymore, I think it'd be best it . . . if. . . . I wasn't here anymore, just like the garden! (*Exits*)

Trương Ba's Soul   My dear! (*Sits down, head in his hands*)

(*When Trương Ba's Soul raises his head, he sees* **Gái** *standing in front of him silently looking at him with scrutiny.*)

Trương Ba's Soul   (*As if begging*) – Gái, my granddaughter . . .

Gái   (*Backing away*) – I am not your granddaughter!

Trương Ba's Soul   (*Patiently*) – Gái, when you're older you'll understand, I am truly your grandfather . . .

Gái   My grandfather is dead. If my grandfather could return, his soul would strangle you to death! How dare you pretend to be my grandfather, dare to touch the plants in my grandfather's garden.

Trương Ba's Soul   In any case . . . granddaughter . . . every morning I till the soil and look after the plants in the garden. Don't you see: only your grandfather would take care of the plants in this way . . .

Gái   Take are of the plants! Hmmph, I had to wait for this moment, when everyone in the house was gone, to tell you this: from now on, don't you dare touch the plants in my grandfather's garden anymore! You say you take care of the plants? Yesterday morning, I was watching when you grafted the orange tree, your clumsy butcher hands crushed the young buds, your huge feet are like shovels, stomping on the precious ginseng saplings! My grandfather would never be so careless and brutal!

Trương Ba's Soul   I didn't think. . . . This is . . . because . . .

Gái   And Tỵ's kite, too. Yesterday afternoon he brought his kite over here to play. You insisted on fixing it, but instead you broke it, ripped the paper, ruining Tỵ's favorite, beautiful, kite! Just a while ago, when he was delirious in his fever, Tỵ asked for his kite to be replaced . . .

Trương Ba's Soul   Really? How terrible . . .

Gái   That's right! It's because of you that Tỵ is suffering even more! Tỵ hates you, too! You're a bad man, evil man! Get out of here! Old butcher, get out of here! (*Sobbing, runs away*)

(**Trương Ba's daughter-in-law** *enters from inside the house, hearing* **Gái's** *last words.*)

Trương Ba's daughter-in-law   (*Calling after her daughter*) – Gái, come back here, Gái! (*Seeing Trương Ba's Soul trembling, immediately comes to his side*) – Father, please don't be angry at the child. . . . She loves her grandfather so much. Every night she cries when missing you. . . . She treasures each little souvenieur that reminds her of you:

the pair of wooden shoes, the bundle of tobacco, especially though, the plants in the garden. . . . It's only because she thinks you aren't her grandfather: No matter how I explain it she won't listen. (*On the verge of tears*) How tormenting this must be for you . . .

Trương Ba's Soul   It's come to this, in the whole house you are the only one who still loves me like before.

Trương Ba's daughter-in-law   Even more than before, father. More than the day you first returned here from the butcher's house. Because I know that now you suffer much more than you did before . . . (*Gently*) And mom suffers more, also. She was planning to go somewhere far away, so that you would be free. It's as if our home is about to fall apart . . .

Trương Ba's Soul   I'm the one who has made your mom suffer. Perhaps on the day your mom buried my body, believed I was dead, she didn't even suffer as much as she does today.

Chị con dầu   Father you have told me: The outside isn't worth mentioning, only the inside counts. But father, I'm scared, because I feel your suffering. . . . Everyday there is a gradual change, a slow disappearing, things don't fit quite right, fade away gradually, to the point where at times, even I don't recognize you anymore. . . . I love you more everyday, but I don't know what to do in order to keep you here, kind and happy the way our father was before. How can it be done, father?

Trương Ba's Soul   (*With a cold face, like a statue*) – And now, even you . . .

Trương Ba's daughter-in-law   Father don't be angry if I've said something wrong.

Trương Ba's Soul   No, I'm not angry. Thank you for telling the truth. For now . . . just go, go so that I can sit here in peace for a while. Go!

(**Trương Ba's daughter-in-law** *slowly exits.*)

Trương Ba's Soul   (*To himself*) – So you've won now haven't you, this body isn't mine anymore, you've found every possible to take over . . . (*After a while*) But how could I give in to defeat, submit to you and lose myself? 'There is no other way!' Oh is that what you say? But is it true that there is no other way? Is it true that there is no other way? I don't need this life that you bring to me! I don't need it!

(*Stands up, clumsily yet assertively goes to the house pillar, takes a stick of incense and lights it.* **Đế Thích** *appears*).

Đế Thích   Trương Ba! (*Sees the pale state of* **Trương Ba's Soul**) Are you ill? This past week they've kept me under tight wraps, I couldn't come down here to play chess with you. But when you lit that incense, I guessed that it was something important, so I risked it and came here. What's the matter?

Trương Ba's Soul   (*After a while*) – Đế Thích, I don't want to continue carrying on in the body of the butcher anymore, I can't do it!

Đế Thích   Why is that? There's nothing wrong!

Trương Ba's Soul   The outside one way, the inside another way. It can't be. I want to be myself, completely.

Đế Thích   So you think everyone gets to be completely themselves? Even I, on the outside, I can't live exactly the way I think on the inside. Even Celestial Emperor, he often has to shape himself to fit his title, Celestial Emperor. On earth and in the heavens, it's the same, including you. Your name was crossed off in Nam Tào's record book. Your real body has disintegrated into mud and dirt, there's nothing left of your form anymore!

Trương Ba's Soul   Depending on others for material things is something that already shouldn't be done. In this case, I must depend on the butcher's own body. You think it's good enough just to live, you don't care how I have to live!

Đế Thích   (*Not understanding*) – But, what do you want?

Trương Ba's Soul   You already told me: If the body of a dead person is still intact, you can make the person's soul return to it. So there, (*Pointing to himself*) the body of the butcher is still exactly intact right here, I will return it to him. Make his soul come back to life in this body.

Đế Thích   How could I trade your precious soul for the mediocre soul of the butcher?

Trương Ba's Soul   It may be mediocre, but it's still his, and it will live harmoniously with his body, they were born to live together. And then there's . . . there's also his wife, too, she really deserves our pity!

Đế Thích   Well then where do you want your soul to live?

Trương Ba's Soul   Anywhere would do, just not here anymore. If you don't help me, I'll. . . . I'll. . . . Jump into the river or stab myself in the throat, that way my soul will be no longer alive, and the butcher's body will be lost too . . .

Đế Thích   How could you plan such a thing! How complicated! I
already broke the heavenly rules once. Up there they are already trying
me for my sins and awaiting judgement. I'm not scared. They threaten,
but what can they really do. If they punish all the gods and deities then
who will the people worship? The difficulty here is finding a place for
your soul to reside in. (*Pacing, thinking, all of a sudden listens carefully*)
Where is that crying coming from? Whose house is that?

Trương Ba's Soul   (*Looking outside*) – It's coming from Lụa's house,
the mother of Tý. That boy Tý is gravely ill. . . . My god, or, has he . . .

(**Gái** *runs into the house, tears overflowing.*)

Gái   (*Calling our hopelessly*) – Mother, Mother! Tý. . . . Tý . . . is dead!
(*Lets out a sob, then runs away.* **Trương Ba's daughter-in-law** *runs
after her.*)

Đế Thích   (*Looking outside*) – That house behind the row of betel
trees there, right? I just saw that boy's soul come flying out through the
rooftop, evaporating like the morning dew. . . . That young Tý, what was
he like?

Trương Ba's Soul   He was the only child of Lụa. He was the best
friend of our Gái. He was very well behaved, smart. I cared about
him very much, and he was very close to me, too. Of course, this was
before. . . . But why did he have to die? Đế Thích – This looks like the
doing of those two, Nam Tào and Bắc Đẩu, hastily crossing off names.
Or it could be Celestial Queen Mother's doing, she doesn't like young
children. No one can go against her orders! (*Worried, pondering*) That's
it, I've got it! Trương Ba! I'll help you one more time! Right away,
you'll return this body of the butcher's, and I'll make your soul go into
the body of Tý. That way the butcher will be able to live, your soul will
have a place to reside, and the body of little Tý won't be lost. What do
you think?

Trương Ba's Soul   Go into the body of Tý? Me?

Đế Thích   Why not? You and the butcher were two strangers, but you
and Tý spent so much time together and were so close, for sure the boy's
body will be accepting . . .

Trương Ba's Soul   Let me think for a little bit. . . . This is all so sudden!
(*Sits down, ponders*) – To live in the body of Tý . . . (*Rambling*) – Me,
an old man, almost sixty years old, while Tý has barely started his life,
at the growing, playful, innocent stage of life. . . . Would this be alright?

(*Closes his eyes*) – Let me try this on for a minute. . . . I would have to explain to Lụa: I'm not your son. She won't cease to love and miss her son. . . . Perhaps I'll have to go live at Lụa's house. . . . And the neighbors, Lý trưởng, Trương tuần. . . . All of those complications. My wife, my children will ponder. How will they take it when their husband, father, is in the body of a boy going on ten? It's not easy being a child! And my Gái, what will she think?

Đế Thích   She would probably enjoy it. She was very close with Tỵ.

Trương Ba's Soul   (*Shaking his head*) – I'm just afraid it will more complicated. Children have to be children, adults have to be adults. If Tỵ all of a sudden became her grandfather, she wouldn't be able to accept that. I've already seen in front of my eyes so many troubles, my dear Đế Thích.

Đế Thích   In the body of a child, you'll have your whole life ahead of you.

Trương Ba's Soul   And then, not long from now, my wife, all my friends like Trưởng Hoạt will one by one lie down. Only I will have to live all those endless years. All by myself in a crowd of youngsters. The things they enjoy, I will hate, and the things I love, they won't care about. I'll be like a guest who has outstayed their welcome, still hanging around when everyone else has gone home. I'll either be lonely and lost, or I'll become a pitiful, hated person, a greedy person who should be dead but goes on living, young and healthy, inconsiderate and inheriting everything life has to offer! It doesn't make any sense! No! I can't steal the tender body of Tỵ (*Looking outside*) – Lụa's crying is so heartbreaking! Losing her child, what is she to do now? (*Suddenly realizing*) Đế Thích, where is Tỵ's soul now?

Đế Thích   I already told you: when a soul leaves its body, there is nothing left of it!

Trương Ba's Soul   Bring Tỵ's soul back into his body, so he can live again!

Đế Thích   Impossible! Tỵ's case. . . . Certainly was an order by Celestial Queen Mother.

Trương Ba's Soul   Please save him! You have to save him! Do you know what a child means to a mother? It means even more than what your Celestial Queen Mother's desires! Đế Thích, for the child, for the child! Please help me this one last time. I'll never cause you any more trouble, I'll never ask you for anything else. (*Takes out the bundle of incense*) – Here! (*Breaks it in half*)

Đế Thích   Trương Ba . . . (*Considers for a very long time, then makes a decision*) Because of my respect for you, I will make Tỵ come back to life, even though I'll be punished heavily for it . . .

But then you . . . in the end, whose body do you want to be in?

Trương Ba's Soul   (*After a long while*) – I've thought about this thoroughly . . . (*Speaking slowly and gently*) I won't live in anyone's form anymore! I'm already dead, I've already been dead!

Đế Thích   Impossible! Your death was only a mistake made up in the Heavens. That mistake was corrected by allowing your soul to live.

Trương Ba's Soul   There are mistakes that can't be corrected. Forcing a solution just makes it more wrong. The only thing to do is not make that mistake ever again. Or repay the debt with some other action. The right thing to do is to make Tỵ come back to life. As for me, just let me die already . . .

Đế Thích   No! You have to live, whatever the price may be . . .

Trương Ba's Soul   I can't live at any price, Đế Thích! There are prices I can't afford, that I cannot pay. . . . It's odd, ever since I had the to courage to make this decision, I've all of a sudden felt like the real Trương Ba, my soul feels crystal clear and pure like before . . .

Đế Thích   Do you understand what you have decided? There will be nothing left of you, you won't be able to participate in anything, happy or sad, anymore! And any regret you may have over the decision won't matter.

Trương Ba's Soul   I understand. Don't you think that I, too, enjoy living? But living like this is more painful than dying. And it's not only I who has to suffer! The people I am closest to have to suffer because of me! That is not the way to convince my son to go back onto an honest path. What good does that life have for anybody? The only people who benefit are old Lý trưởng and Trương tuần's crowd! That's right, only those goddamned people get anything out of it.

Đế Thích   I'm not a goddamned person. . . . I respect you. . . . I'll never be able to play chess with you again? It's because of your playing that everyone in Heaven and Earth knows of my chess skills! Besides you, no one else dares to play chess with me.

Trương Ba's Soul   So to validate your existence I have to continue living untruthfully with myself? No, you need to validate yourself!

Đế Thích   But without playing chess, Đế Thích won't be Đế Thích anymore.

Trương Ba's Soul   People play chess to train and clear their minds, so that they can live better! But you, you only play chess to prove you are a deity! Let me be honest: Even if I'm alive, I won't ever play chess with you anymore! Playing with you is dull! There's nothing more dull than playing chess with a deity!

Đế Thích   (*Thinking*) – People down here on Earth are really strange.

Trương Ba's Soul   Answer me! Are you going to help me or not? If you refuse, then I'll. . . . I'll take care of it myself! You have to help me!

Đế Thích   Return this body to the butcher . . . and then.

Trương Ba's Soul   I'll finally be rid of this bizarre name 'Soul of Trương Ba, Skin of the Butcher'

(**Nam Tào** *and* **Bắc Đẩu** *appear.*)

Bắc Đẩu   Đế Thích, Celestial Emperor ordered us to find you immediately, and bring you two orders. First:

Nam Tào   Celestial Emperor forgives you for your crime of putting Trương Ba's soul into the butcher's body, and will allow Trương Ba to continue living in the body of the butcher. Meaning, from now on that will be considered lawful and no longer breaking any heavenly decrees.

Bắc Đẩu   Order number two:

Nam Tào   Đế Thích you are now forbidden to execute any of your powers on Earth again. After a while, when the sun has set, if you are not present in the heavenly temple, you will be faced with the heaviest punishment anyone in the Heavens has ever had to face:

Bắc Đẩu   You will be exiled to Earth eternally, and you will no longer be immortal as the other deities.

Nam Tào   As your friends we are honestly telling you: you have to quickly return to the heavens, and don't ever get involved in any more of these complicated matters! You've caused such chaos in the heavens and earth, the people down here will start to despise us and not respect us anymore.

Đế Thích   You lost their respect long ago, you just didn't know it.

Bắc Đẩu   Đế Thích, the sun is almost setting! You can't stall anymore!
We're going back first!

Nam Tào   This time, we don't dare to take sides with you and defend
you anymore!

Bắc Đẩu   But we've never defended you anyways. It's more accurate to
say we never had anything to do with you, that's exactly what we'll tell
Celestial Emperor! We can't get in trouble because of you!

(**Nam Tào** *and* **Bắc Đẩu** *disappear*)

Đế Thích   Vile bunch! (*To Trương Ba's Soul*) Well, the Heavens have
allowed you to take the butcher's body then!

Trương Ba's Soul   The Heavens might allow it, but I won't. Đế Thích,
you have to hurry, so that Tỵ will be alive again, and I will be . . .

Đế Thích   (*Choked by tears*) – My dear Trương Ba . . . (*Looking at the
determined face of* **Trương Ba**)   Alright!

Trương Ba's Soul   You should go over to Lụa's house to warn her
before Tỵ comes back to life, so that people won't be frightened.

Đế Thích   (*Looking outside at the sky*) – The sun is almost gone! I have
to go first to Lụa's house to make your soul leave the butcher's body,
and then put the butcher's soul back in his body there, to make sure it all
gets done before the sun sets! I have to go right away! We'll have to part
ways here.

Trương Ba's Soul   I'll be waiting for your powers right here.

Đế Thích   You'll have a minute to gather your thoughts and prepare.

Trương Ba's Soul   There's nothing to gather. On this journey, I've no
luggage to take with me. I'm ready, just go already! Please tell my wife
and children over at Tỵ's house to hurry home so I can speak with them
one last time!

Đế Thích   My dear Trương Ba, you've taught me a lesson that I'd never
learned up in the heavens. Later, it will be the last time I use my powers
as Đế Thích . . . because . . . my dear. . . . I won't return to the heavens
anymore!

Trương Ba's Soul   Why?

Đế Thích   They won't allow me to, and I don't want to, anyways. I'm
so tired of that place. I'll stay here, be a living person, live a life as a
human on earth . . .

Trương Ba's Soul   But you will . . . will . . .

Đế Thích   I won't be immortal? Well that's just like you, like everyone else. Immortality – it's not as great as you think! The only thing is: for all this time as a deity, your Earth seemed strange, unfathomable, I'm afraid I won't be able to stand it. Or. . . . Trương Ba . . . or. . . . I could put your soul into my body, and we could both live?

Trương Ba's Soul   I couldn't live in the body of the butcher, nor a child's, and I won't be able to live in a deity's either. I thank you very much for the offer, but it's not possible! Just live in your own body, with your soul, and you will find a way to live in this strange yet interesting world. Be brave, Đế Thích, I wish you the best (*Goes over to* **Đế Thích**) Farewell to you!

Đế Thích   (*Choking up with tears*) – Farewell to you!

(*They silently look at one another, then Đế Thích hurriedly leaves.*)

Trương Ba's Soul   (*To himself*) – It's only a little while now. . . . I wonder if my son will return in time? (*Looking at his body*) – And soon you won't have to hold my soul anymore, butcher's body! There were times when I hated you and was angry at you, but now that we are almost separated, I don't understand why all of a sudden I feel compassion for you (*Looking at his hands, arms*) – Three months of carrying my soul, your body felt closer and my soul almost collapsed, disintegrated. Now we part ways. You'll return to your wife . . . (*Fighting the sadness*) – That woman, she really is something! Please send her my greetings. . . . You, you won't remember anything about me. . . . But what about her? (*Dazed, longing*) Will she remember me? Could you change your character, for her to suffer less. . . . Now she will demand that you change! Nothing will be like it was before! (*Looking at his leg*) – There is a wound on your calf that is quite deep, from this morning when I accidentally stumbled on a sharp tree root. My wife gave me medicine for it, I've used half of it, there's another half left (*Takes out the bundle of medicine from his coat pocket*) You take it with you, and apply the rest of it tonight so that it will heal faster . . . (*Getting up*) – The sun has almost set (*Pleased*) – There they are, they've come home! (*Calling out loudly*) – My dear wife! My son! (*His wife enters*) – Come here my dear, sit next to me for a bit. I . . . . I . . . . I'm about to go away, very far away, permanently!

Trương Ba's Wife   What are you saying?

Trương Ba's Soul   This time, I've said goodbye to you in time. You've had to suffer through your husband's death two times. But this time. . . . You shouldn't cry, my dear!

Trương Ba's Wife   What are you saying, I don't understand! Who is forcing you to die?

Trương Ba's Soul   Nobody is forcing me. It just has to be that way! You will see that it is the right thing.

(*Trương Ba's* **daughter-in-law** *is now standing next to her mother.*)

Trương Ba's Soul   My daughter-in-law, you've said to me: 'How can we keep your soul pure and whole like you were before'. This is the only way . . .

Trương Ba's daughter-in-law   I understand, father. But father! (*Runs to him and cries in his shoulder*) – I love you . . .

Trương Ba's Soul   My poor daughter, you are so kind! My son has made you suffer greatly!

(*The son – holding many things on his shoulders and arms, messily carrying the bags, from outside comes in, stands in the doorway looking at* **Trương Ba's Soul.**)

Trương Ba's Soul   Son, I'm lucky you've made it, in just a moment, I have to leave!

Cả   Where are you going?

Trương Ba's Soul   Very far away, and forever. Here are my last words for you, my son. Son, put down those things you're carrying, come closer to your father. Because those things won't be able to keep me here.

(*The son drops the items, steps toward his father.*)

There! Just like the day the two of us broke ground on our garden. You should remember one thing: when faced with life and death, everything is meaningless. Only my love for my children, the love you have for each other, is worth remembering. . . . My son, please find the soul of my son from the old days. . . . If not, you'll die! It's also because of this that I'm leaving. . . . Mom and you children, remember to take care of the garden, nurture and teach Gái carefully. I wish her all the pleasures of life that will come. (*To his wife*) Our lives will come to an end, but the day I met you in Tầm port so long ago, will be forever . . .

Trương Ba's Wife   (*Darts forward*) – My dear! My dear!

Trương Ba's Soul   (*All of a sudden feeling dizzy*) – Is it time now?
How quickly that was, Đế Thích? Wait! Wait a minute! Give me just
a little bit more time! I want to see my garden . . . (*Frightened*) –
I didn't get to see Gái, or Trưởng Hoạt! Wait! Let me live! (*Holds
his head*) I won't make it. The sun is setting. . . . Why is everything
so dark? (*Looking for the hands of his wife to hold*) – My dear!
(*Slumps*)

Trương Ba's Wife   Trương Ba! My dear Trương Ba!

Trương Ba's daughter-in-law   Father!

Cả   (*Crying out loudly*) – Father! (*Turning upwards*) – Dear Father!
I've heard your words, I'll be the son that I before, for you. . . . My father
(*The butcher's body now has the soul of the* **butcher** *in it – He slowly
stands up, bewildered, looking around.*)

Butcher   Where am I?

Trương Ba's Wife   Trương Ba!

Butcher   Trương Ba who? Who are you? Where's my wife?
(*Looks around*) Why am I here? Goddamn. I was lying on the bed
with a stomachache, and my wife was getting the hot plate for me!
Where's my wife? And my stomachache has disappeared! God damn
it, this is so bizarre. Or maybe it's like those other drunken times,
when I just collapsed and slept wherever I fell? (*Looking outside*) –
It's almost dark! Damn, the two pigs I just butchered, I left them a
mess at the house, if they've gone bad no one will want to buy it!
(*Hurriedly tries to run away.* **Trương Ba's wife** *struggles to hold
him back.*)

Trương Ba's Wife   Where are you going? And . . . who are you?

Butcher   I'm the pig butcher, who else would I be? But . . . why
do I feel such turmoil inside? (*Shaking his shoulders, hitting his own
forehead*) – What just happened? It's like someone just came and turned
everything upside down! But I can't remember what happened for the
life of me! I'll just have to go home! (*Runs away*)

Trương Ba's Wife   (*Frightened, shocked*) – But what about Trương
Ba? Where is he? My Trương Ba! Where are you? (*Wanders around the
house looking for him*) Where are you?

Blackout – Scene Change

Final Scene

The trees in the garden are quivering in the sunshine. In a corner appears an image of Tý embracing his mom. **Lụa** *is ecstatically embracing and caressing her son . . .* **Trương Ba's** *wife appears in the front of the stage.*

Trương Ba's Wife   Where are you? Where are you my dear?

(*In the midst of the green garden,* **Trương Ba** *appears, flickering.*)

Trương Ba   I'm here my dear. I'm still right here by your side, right at the threshold of our house, in the fire of the stove where you cook, in the bridge over the stream where you wash the rice, in the tray that holds your betel nuts, in the knife you use to cut the grass. . . . I'm not borrowing anyone's body, I'm still here, in our garden, in the goodness of life, in each of the fruits that Gái has nurtured . . .

(*Under a tree, appear* **Tý** *and* **Cái Gái.**)

Gái   (*Holding a custard apple in her hand*) – This custard apple, my grandfather planted! It's large and delicious! Let's share it!

(*She breaks the custard apple in half and gives* **Tý** *one half. The pair eat the fruit deliciously.* **Gái** *pushes the custard apple seeds into the ground.*)

Tý   What are you doing?

Gái   For them to grow another tree. Grandfather told me that. The trees will connect each generation together as they grow up. Forever and ever!. . . .

Blackout

THE END

Notes

1   Nguyen, Khai Thu, 'Moral Dissent: Lưu Quang Vũ and the Melodramatic Performance of Renovation in Post-War Vietnam' in Lara D. Nielsen and Patricia Ybarra (eds), *Neoliberalism and Global Theatres: Performance Permutations*, New York: Palgrave Macmillian, 2012, p.144.
2   Nguyen, Khai Thu, p.155.
3   Ibid.
4   Character names are listed above as they appear in the translation. The names in parenthesis are either the Vietnamese or English translation. We have kept the proper names of main characters and official authority roles.
5   They are playing Chinese Chess, translation of the chess pieces are based off the Chinese version of chess.
6   Mandarins are high-ranking bureaucrats, who are commonly known as noble servicemen who are assistants to the head of the government.
7   Betel Leaves are commonly found in Asia and is typically chewed as a form of relaxation and sociality. It is known for its highly addictive quality as a stimulant and turns a red colour when chewed.
8   Wampee Trees are typically found in Southeast Asia and produce grapefruit-like fruits.
9   The Thunder God is known as the punisher of wrong doings and evil deeds in heaven and on earth. His position is like a military leader who protects and punishes.
10 The sickle is part of the communist symbol of a hammer and sickle, which represents communist unity of the proletariart class. Hammer represents industrial workers and the Sickle represents the agricultural workers.
11 Quan was a currency used during the Chinese colonial era, before French colonisation in Vietnam.
12 Areca nuts and betel leaves are traditionally offered with tea.
13 This is the literal translation of the proverb in the original text. We have added the previous sentence 'with enough money, you can get anything done' to clarify the meaning of the proverb.

SPORTS PICTURES

AGILE RABBIT EDITIONS   DISTRIBUTED BY THE PEPIN PRESS

SPORTS PICTURES

This book contains high-quality images for use as a graphic resource, or inspiration. All the images are stored on the accompanying CD-ROM in professional-quality, high-resolution format and can be used on either Windows or Mac platforms. The images can be used free of charge, up to a maximum of ten images per application. For the use of more than ten images, written permission is required.

The documents can be imported directly from the CD-ROM into a wide range of layout, image-manipulation, illustration, and word-processing programmes; no installation is required. Many programmes allow you to manipulate the images. Please consult your software manual for further instructions.

The names of the files on the CD-ROM correspond with the page numbers in this book. Where applicable, the position on the pages is indicated: T = top, B = bottom, C = centre, L = left, and R = right.

The CD-ROM comes free with this book, but is not for sale separately. The publishers do not accept any responsibility should the CD not be compatible with your system.

Agile Rabbit Editions
P.O. Box 10349
1001 EH Amsterdam
The Netherlands
Fax (+) 31 20 4201152
mail@pepinpress.com

Dieses Buch enthält qualitativ hochwertige Bilder, die für Graphikanwendungen genutzt oder als Anregung herangezogen werden können. Alle Bilder sind in Profi-Qualität und hoher Auflösung auf der beiliegenden CD-ROM gespeichert und lassen sich sowohl auf Windows- als auch auf Macintosh-Systemen bearbeiten. Für jede von Ihnen erstellte Publikation dürfen Sie bis zu zehn Bilder kostenfrei nutzen. Für die Verwertung von mehr als zehn Bildern brauchen Sie eine schriftliche Genehmigung.

Die Dokumente kann man ohne vorherige Installation direkt von der CD-ROM in viele verschiedene DTP-, Bildbearbeitungs-, Illustrations- und Textverarbeitungsprogramme laden. In zahlreichen Programmen ist es möglich, die Bilder weiterzubearbeiten. Genauere Hinweise dazu finden Sie im Handbuch zu Ihrer Software.

Die Namen der Bilddateien auf der CD-ROM entsprechen den Seitenzahlen dieses Buchs. Soweit bei den Bildern die Position auf der jeweiligen Seite angegeben ist, bedeutet T (top) oben, B (bottom) unten, C (centre) Mitte, L (left) links und R (right) rechts.

Die CD-ROM wird kostenlos mit dem Buch geliefert und ist nicht separat verkäuflich. Der Verlag haftet nicht für Inkompatibilität der CD-ROM mit Ihrem System.

Agile Rabbit Editions
PO Box 10349
1001 EH Amsterdam
Niederlande
Fax (+) 31 20 420 11 52
mail@pepinpress.com

Cet ouvrage renferme des images de haute qualité destinées à un usage graphique ou comme source d'inspiration. Toutes ces images de qualité professionnelle sont stockées en haute résolution sur le CD-ROM et sont utilisables sur des plate-formes mac ou windows. Jusqu'à un maximum de dix images par application, l'emploi de ces images est gratuit, au-delà de dix une permission écrite est nécessaire.

Les documents peuvent être directement importés depuis le CD-ROM vers une large variété de programmes: mise en page, manipulation d'images, illustration et traîtement de textes, il n'y a pas d'installation nécessaire. De nombreux programmes permettent la manipulation d'images. Pour de plus amples informations, veuillez consulter la documentation accompagnant vos logiciels.

Les titres des dossiers sur le CD-ROM correspondent aux numéros des pages du livre. Là ou c'est applicable, la position des images sur les pages est indiquée de la façon suivante: T (top) = haut, B (bottom) = bas, C (centre) = centre, L (left) =gauche, et R (right) = droite.

Ce CD-ROM gratuit accompagne le livre et ne peut être vendu séparément. Les éditeurs ne sont pas responsables si le CD-ROM n'est pas compatible avec votre système.

Agile Rabbit Editions
PO Box 10349
1001 EH AMSTERDAM
Pays-Bas
Fax (+) 31 20 4201152
mail@pepinpress.com

Questo libro contiene immagini di alta qualità disponibili per uso grafico o come fonte di ispirazione. Tutte le immagini, di qualità professionale, sono contenute nel CD-ROM in formato "alta risoluzione" e possono essere utilizzate sia in ambiente Windows che Mac. Le immagini sono riproducibili liberamente fino ad un massimo di dieci per applicazione. Per la riproduzione di più di dieci immagini è necessaria l'autorizzazione scritta dell'editore.

I documenti possono essere importati direttamente dal CD-ROM in una vasta gamma di compositori di pagina, di manipolatori di immagini, illustrazioni e programmi di testo. Non è necessaria nessuna installazione. Molti programmi permettono di elaborare le immagini. Per maggiori istruzioni a riguardo vi preghiamo di consultare il manuale del vostro programma.

I nomi dei files contenuti nel CD-ROM corrispondono ai numeri delle pagine del libro. Ove necessario è indicata anche la posizione dell'immagine all'interno della pagina mediante i seguenti codici: T (top) = Alto, B (bottom) = Basso, C (centre) = Centro, L (left) = Sinistra, R (right) = Destra.

Il CD-ROM è un supplemento gratuito al libro e non può essere venduto separatamente. L'editore non è in nessun modo responsabile dell'eventuale incompatibilità del CD-ROM con i programmi utilizzati.

Agile Rabbit Editions
P.O. Box 10349
1001 EH Amsterdam
Paesi Bassi
Fax (+) 31 20 4201152
mail@pepinpress.com

Este libro contiene imágenes de gran calidad que pueden usarse como ilustraciones o como fuente de inspiración. Todas ellas, guardadas en un formato de alta resolución y calidad profesional, están almacenadas en el CD-ROM que se facilita y son compatibles tanto con la plataforma Windows como Mac. Las imágenes pueden utilizarse sin ningún coste adicional, hasta un máximo de diez por aplicación. En el caso de exceder esta cantidad, se precisará un permiso por escrito.

Los documentos pueden importarse del CD-ROM directamente a un amplio abanico de programas de maquetación, manipulación de imágenes, ilustraciones y tratamiento de texto sin necesidad de llevar a cabo instalaciones. Son muchos los programas que permiten manipular las imágenes. Para obtener instrucciones al respecto, consulte el manual de la aplicación.

Los nombres de los archivos contenidos en el CD-ROM se corresponden con el número de páginas del libro. En algunos casos se indica la posición dentro de la página del siguiente modo: T (top) = arriba, B (bottom) = abajo, C (centre) = centro, L (left) = izquierda y R (right) = derecha.

El CD-ROM se adjunta de forma gratuita con el libro y no puede venderse por separado. La editorial no se hace responsable en caso de incompatibilidad del CD con el sistema que utilice.

Agile Rabbit Editions
Apartado de correos 10349
1001 EH Amsterdam
Paises Bajos
Fax (+) 31 20 4201152
mail@pepinpress.com

圖書與雷射碟版權 © 1999 Pepin van Roojen.
版權所有，翻印必究。

本書包含高品質影像，可用於製作圖形或啟發創意。
所有影像均以高分辨率格式儲存在隨附的雷射碟中，品質達到專業
水準，可用於視窗和 MAC 平臺。這些影像可以免費使用，但每項應
用最多不超過十幅影像。如果要超過十幅，需事先獲得書面許可。

文件可以直接從雷射碟輸入應用程式，可配合多種頁面佈局、影像
處理、插圖和文字處理程式，無需裝設。可以使用多種程式，處理
影像。操作步驟，請查閱有關軟體說明書。

雷射碟中檔案名與本書頁號相符，在頁面上的具體位置用下列字母
表示：T = 上端、B = 下端、C = 中央、L = 左、R = 右。

雷射碟隨書奉送，不可單獨出售。如果雷射碟與閣下電腦系統不相
容，出版商概不負責。

Agile Rabbit Editions
P.O. Box 10349
1001 EH Amsterdam
The Netherlands
Fax (+) 31 20 4201152
mail@pepinpress.com

本と CD-ROM　版権　© 1999 Pepin van Roojen.
無断転載を禁ず

本書掲載の画像はグラフィック用やアイデア用の高質画像です。全ての画像は添付の CD-ROM にプロフェッショナルクオリティ、高解像度にて収録されており、ウィンドウズ、マックのどちらでも使用できます。画像は、アプリケーションにつき 10 個まで無料でご使用いただけます。これを超える数については、書面による承諾が必要です。

ファイルは CD-ROM からページレイアウト、イメージ操作、イラスト、ワープロソフトといったいろいろなソフトに直接呼び出すことができます。インストールは不要です。この画像のイメージ操作ができるソフトがたくさんあります。詳しくはご使用のソフトの説明書をお読みください。

CD-ROM 収録ファイルのファイル名は本書のページナンバーに対応しています。ページ上の位置は T = 上、B = 下、C = 中央、L = 左、R = 右で記してあります。

CD-ROM は本書の無料付録であり、別売は不可とします。
CD がご使用のシステムに対応しない場合について、出版社は一切の責任を負いかねますので、ご了承ください。

Agile Rabbit Editions
P.O. Box 10349
1001 EH Amsterdam
The Netherlands
Fax (+) 31 20 4201152
mail@pepinpress.com

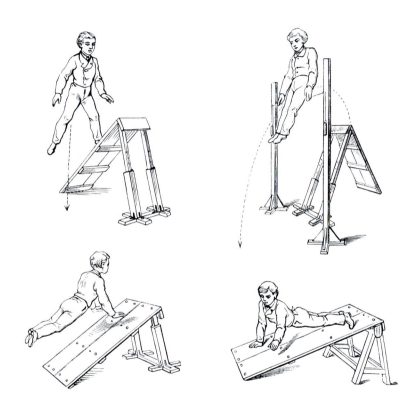

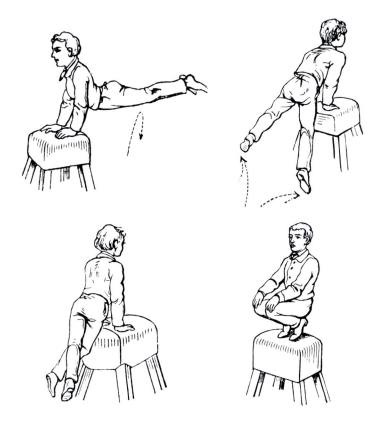

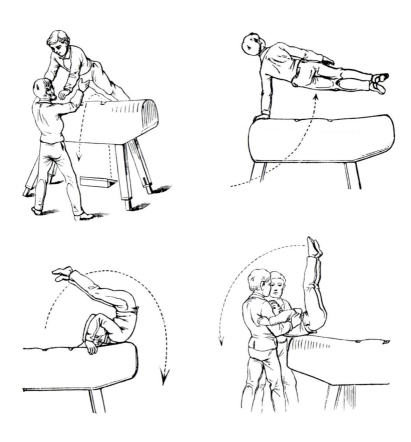

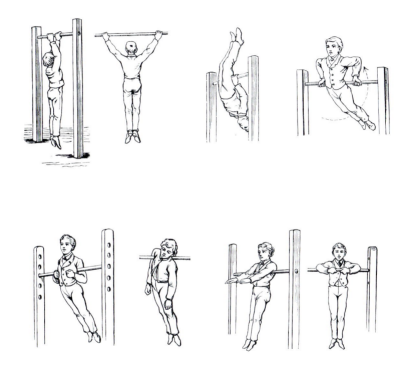

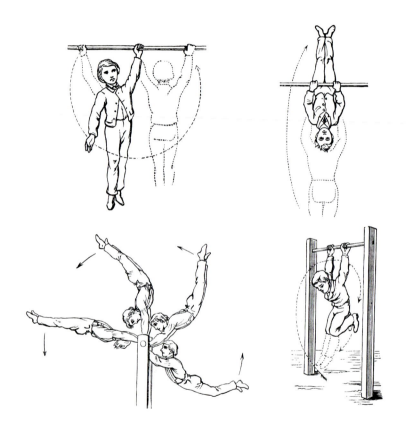

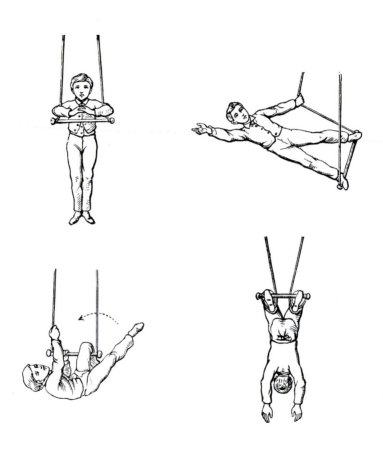

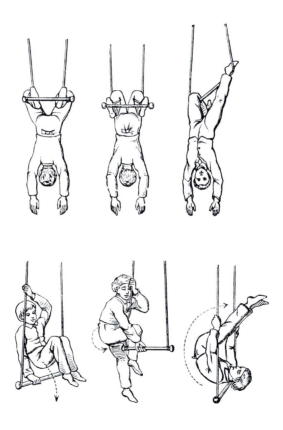

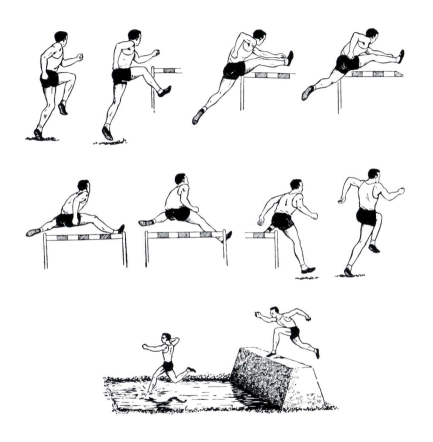

43

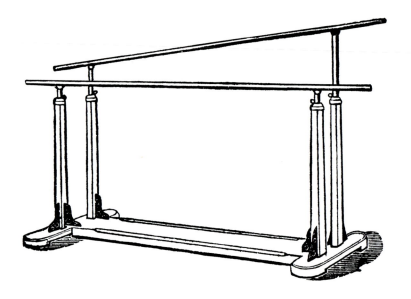

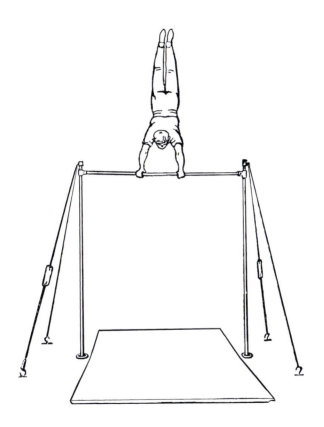

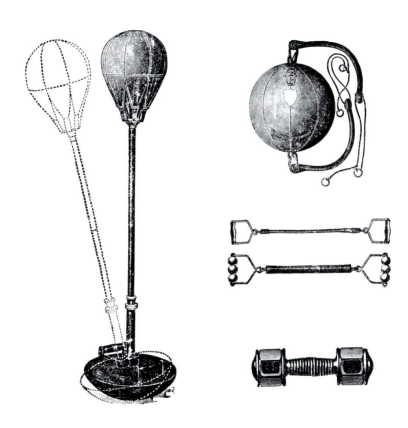

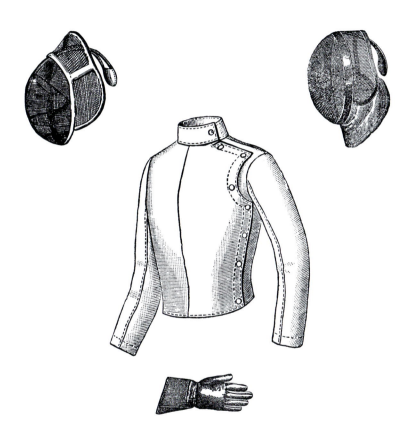

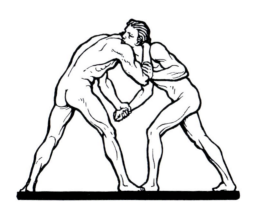

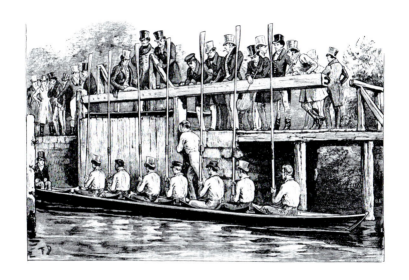

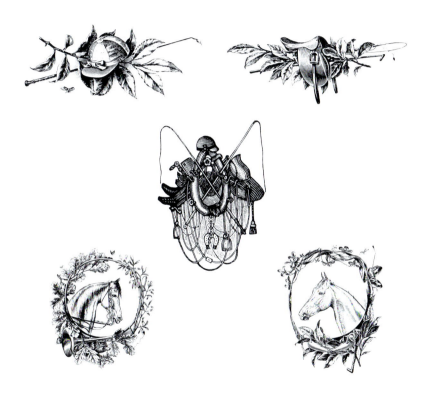

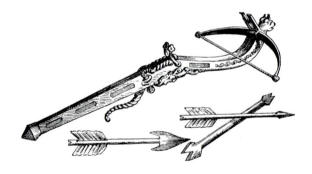

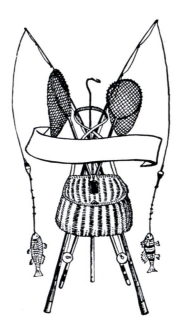

125

140

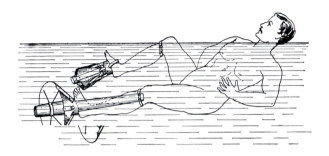

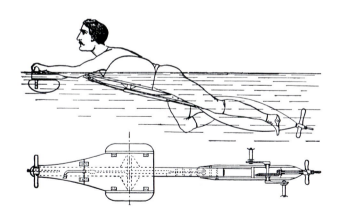

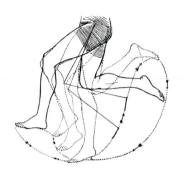

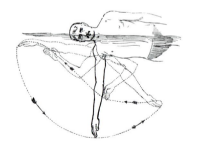

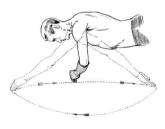

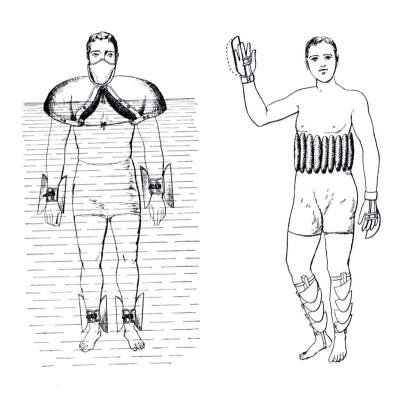

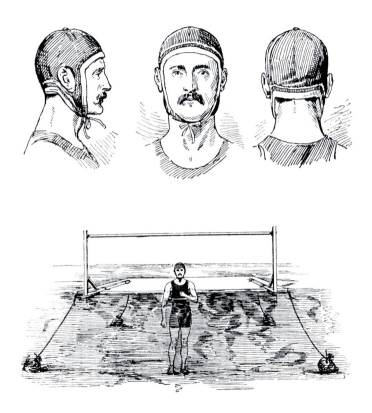

164

174

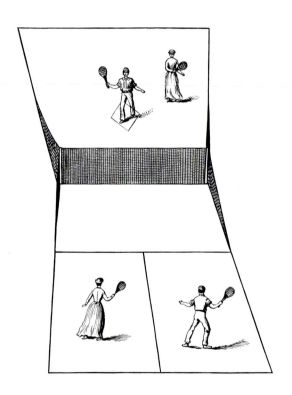

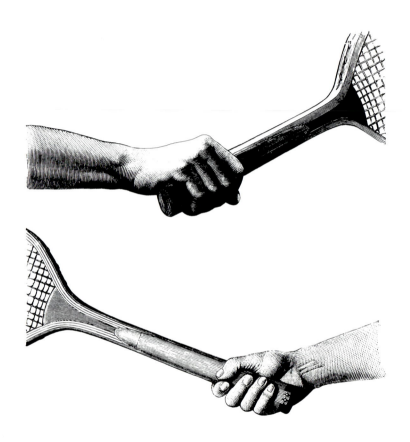

183

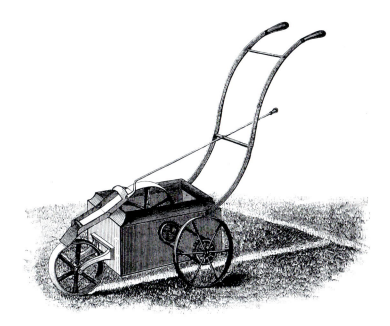

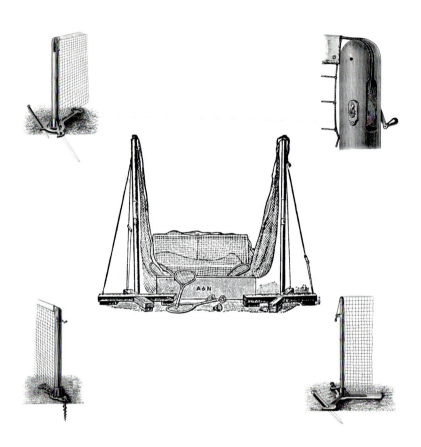

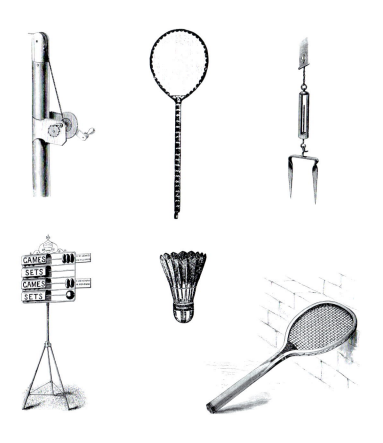

200

203

208

212

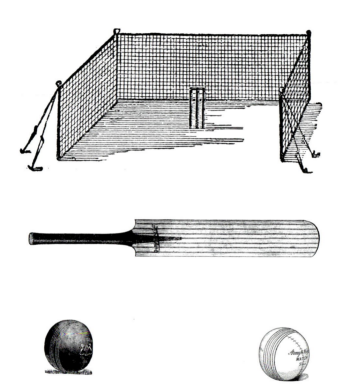

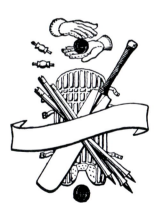

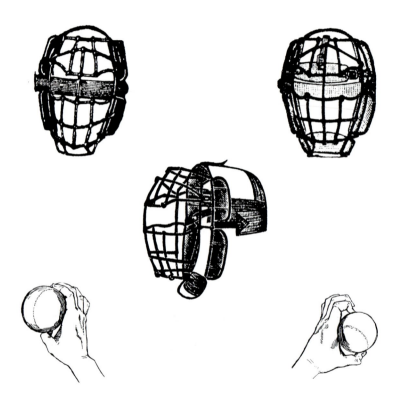

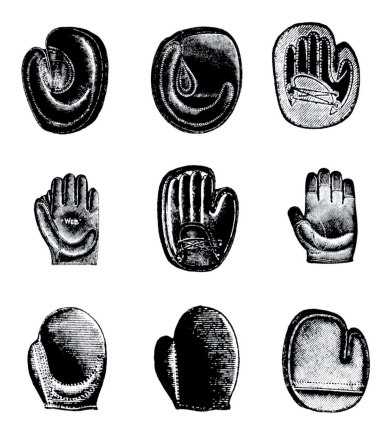

236

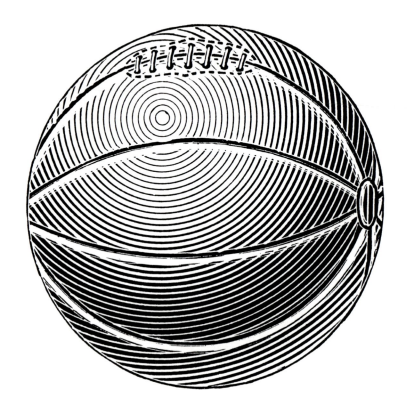

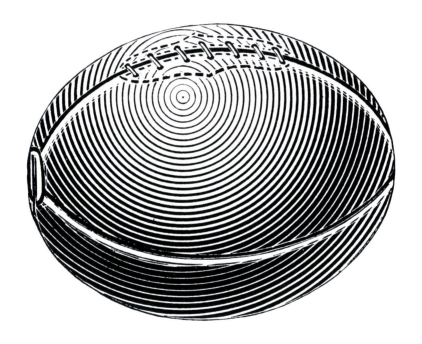

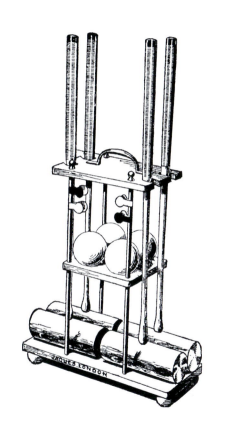

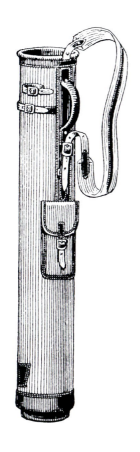
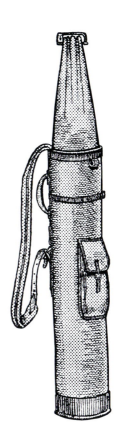

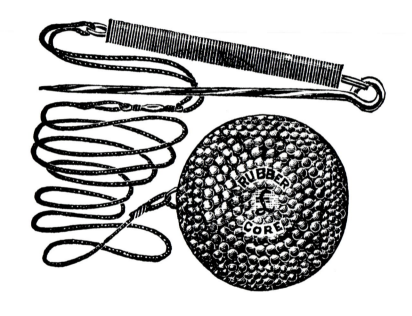

274

275

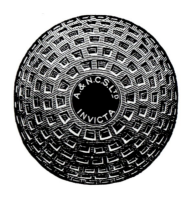

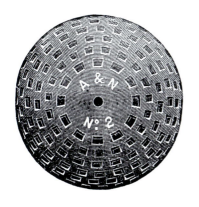

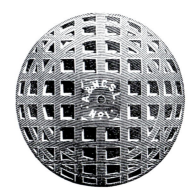

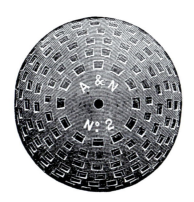

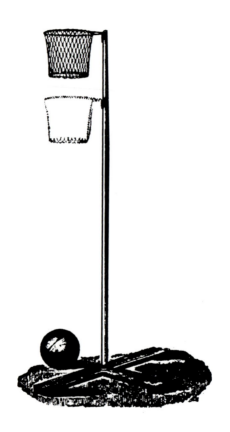

Other books with free CD-ROM by Agile Rabbit Editions:

ISBN 90 5768 004 1   Batik Patterns
ISBN 90 5768 006 8   Chinese Patterns
ISBN 90 5768 001 7   1000 Decorated Initials
ISBN 90 5768 005 x   Floral Patterns
ISBN 90 5768 003 3   Graphic Frames
ISBN 90 5768 007 6   Images of The Human Body
ISBN 90 5768 002 5   Tranport Pictures

Copyright for this edition © 1999 Pepin van Roojen

ISBN 90 5768 008 4

A catalogue record for this book is available from the publishers
and from the Dutch Royal Library, The Hague

This book is edited, designed and produced by Agile Rabbit Editions
Design: Joost Hölscher
Copy-editing introduction: Andrew May
Translations: Sebastian Viebahn (German); LocTeam (Spanish);
Anne Loescher (French); Luciano Borelli (Italian);
Mitaka (Chinese and Japanese)

Printed in Singapore